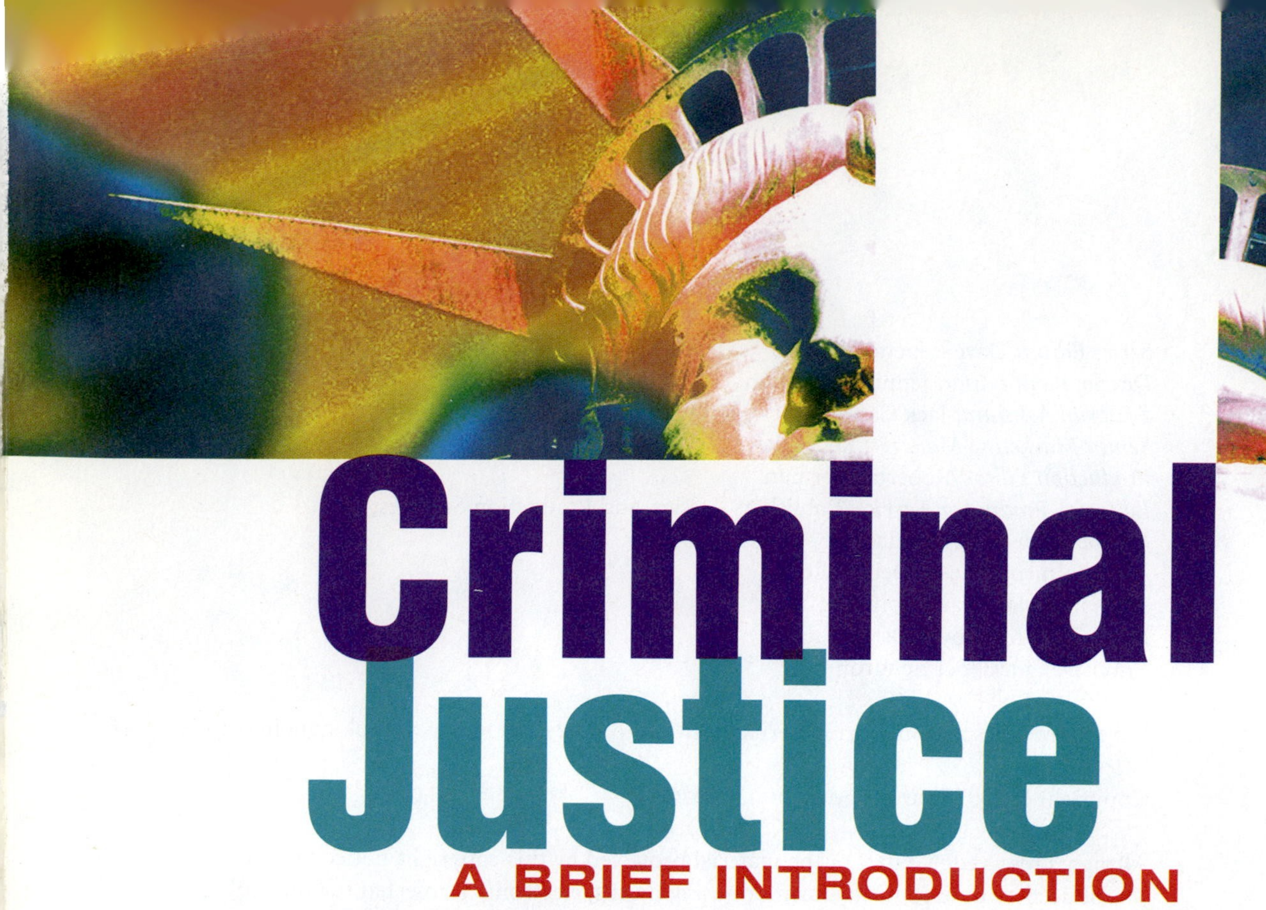

Criminal Justice

A BRIEF INTRODUCTION

James A. Fagin

Lincoln College–Normal

Boston ■ New York ■ San Francisco

Mexico City ■ Montreal ■ Toronto ■ London ■ Madrid ■ Munich ■ Paris

Hong Kong ■ Singapore ■ Tokyo ■ Cape Town ■ Sydney

Series Editor: Dave Repetto
Development Editor: Jennifer Jacobson
Editorial Assistant: Jack Cashman
Senior Marketing Manager: Kelly May
Production Editor: Roberta Sherman
Editorial-Production Service: Publishers' Design and Production Services, Inc.
Composition Buyer: Linda Cox
Manufacturing Buyer: Debbie Rossi
Interior Design: Carol Somberg
Photo Research: Poyee Oster
Cover Designer: Joel Gendron

For related titles and support materials, visit our online catalog at www.ablongman.com.

Library of Congress Cataloging-in-Publication Data

Fagin, James A. (James Arlie)
Criminal justice : a brief introduction / James A. Fagin.
p. cm.
Includes bibliographical references and index.
ISBN 0-205-48907-9
1. Criminal justice, Administration of—United States. I. Title.
HV9950.F346 2006
364.973—dc22
2006050426

ISBN 0-205-48907-9

Printed in the United States of America

10 9 8 7 6 5 4 3 RRD-OH 10

Brief Contents

Contents

chapter 3

chapter 4
Roles and Functions of the Police 138

chapter 5
Police Officers and the Law 190

chapter 8

Courtroom Participants and the Trial 284

chapter 9

Sentencing and Sanctions 320

chapter 10

chapter 11

chapter 12

Tables and Figures

▼Tables

▼Figures

Preface

The challenge of a criminal justice book is to capture the dynamic and ubiquitous nature of the criminal justice system and the academic scholarship on which the academic discipline is based but at the same time connect the text to the real world. The criminal justice system is complex and it can be difficult for students to understand, so it is important that students find the text informative, readable, accurate, and interesting. Both CJ majors and nonmajors will find each chapter interesting and readable. You will find that *Criminal Justice: A Brief Introduction* integrates well with the liberal arts curriculum as it emphasizes how criminal justice is built on the foundation of other disciplines and the interrelationship of CJ to other academic disciplines. You will find it easy to construct lesson plans and lectures that build on the students' global education so that they will see how their lives are touched by the criminal justice system.

Criminal Justice: A Brief Introduction emphasizes that the CJ system is part of a complex, interrelated, and dynamic governance and social system based on checks and balances. I have emphasized how the CJ system is connected to other academic, political, and social systems and values. Also, I think that this approach encourages students to appreciate the academic rigor underlying the CJ system.

The goals of this book are to explain the criminal justice system to undergraduate students, to provide sufficient background knowledge for students to understand important concepts, and to prepare students for success in other criminal justice classes as well as for careers in public service. It introduces the history, influences, and related fields of knowledge that are connected to the criminal justice system. It strives to present a comprehensive, balanced, concrete description of how the criminal justice system works, why it works that way, why it is different from past systems and from systems of other cultures, and how it is influenced by scientific knowledge, social norms, and prevailing beliefs about justice. Thus, the book enlightens students on the reasons behind the development and evolution of contemporary situations in the criminal justice system. For instance, it explains why the United States has a decentralized law enforcement model, why local police have difficulty responding to terrorism and international drug trafficking, why jurisdictional conflicts exist among criminal justice agencies, and why prisons are overcrowded.

The text stimulates the student to read about criminal justice, it encourages the student to do further research, and it emphasizes that the student should understand that one of the most important and powerful relationships between citizens and government is defined by the criminal justice system.

Criminal Justice: A Brief Introduction strives to cover the important aspects of the CJ system for introductory students. It emphasizes the criminal justice system as part of a complex, interrelated, and dynamic social system based on checks and balances. Also, I recognize that many topics—such as criminology, criminal law, juvenile justice, and corrections—are separate courses in the criminal justice curriculum.

Also, I believe that both the text and the instructor are essential to effective learning. Thus, I assume that you will adapt the chapter contents to your teaching style, your geographical area, and the students in your class. You will skip some material and you may supplement other topics to arrive at the balance that is appropriate for your class, city, and state.

Criminal Justice: A Brief Introduction examines how the events of September 11, 2001, have changed the criminal justice system and sorts out how new values continue to affect the CJ system. In this manner, the text emphasizes the dynamic, value-driven nature of the criminal justice system.

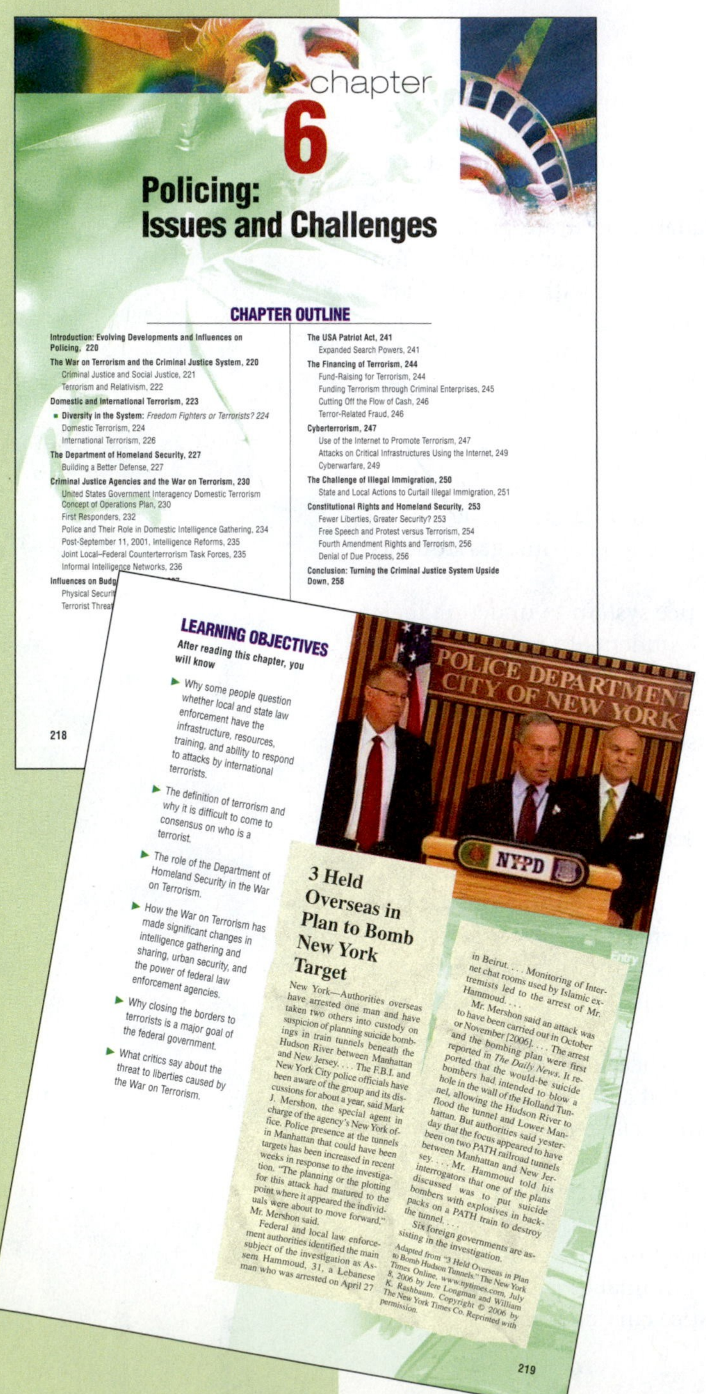

chapter 6

Policing: Issues and Challenges

CHAPTER OUTLINE

218

LEARNING OBJECTIVES

After reading this chapter, you will know

- Why some people question whether local and state law enforcement have the infrastructure, resources, training, and ability to respond to attacks by international terrorists.
- The definition of terrorism and why it is difficult to come to consensus on who is a terrorist.
- The role of the Department of Homeland Security in the War on Terrorism.
- How the War on Terrorism has made significant changes in intelligence gathering and sharing, urban security, and the power of federal law enforcement agencies.
- Why closing the borders to terrorists is a major goal of the federal government.
- What critics say about the threat to liberties caused by the War on Terrorism.

3 Held Overseas in Plan to Bomb New York Target

New York—Authorities overseas have arrested one man and have taken two others into custody on suspicion of planning suicide bombings in train tunnels beneath the Hudson River between Manhattan and New Jersey. . . . The F.B.I. and New York City police officials have been aware of the group and its discussions for about a year, said Mark J. Mershon, the special agent in charge of the agency's New York office. Police presence at the tunnels in Manhattan that could have been targets has been increased in recent weeks in response to the investigation. "The planning or the plotting for this attack had matured to the point where it appeared the individuals were about to move forward," Mr. Mershon said.

Federal and local law enforcement authorities identified the main subject of the investigation as Assem Hammoud, 31, a Lebanese man who was arrested on April 27 in Beirut. . . . Monitoring of Internet chat rooms used by Islamic extremists led to the arrest of Mr. Hammoud. . . .

Mr. Mershon said an attack was to have been carried out in October or November [2006]. . . . The arrest and the bombing plan were first reported in *The Daily News*. It reported that the would-be suicide bombers had intended to blow a hole in the wall of the Holland Tunnel, allowing the Hudson River to flood the tunnel and Lower Manhattan. But authorities said yesterday that the focus appeared to have been on two PATH railroad tunnels between Manhattan and New Jersey. . . . Mr. Hammoud told his interrogators that one of the plans discussed was to put suicide bombers with explosives in backpacks on a PATH train to destroy the tunnel. . . .

Six foreign governments are assisting in the investigation.

Adapted from "3 Held Overseas in Plan to Bomb Hudson Tunnels." The New York Times Online, www.nytimes.com, July 8, 2006 by Jere Longman and William K. Rashbaum. Copyright © 2006 by The New York Times Co. Reprinted with permission.

219

Organization

Criminal Justice: A Brief Introduction is organized into 12 manageable chapters that can be covered in their entirety in a single term, while still allowing instructors to incorporate additional topics of their choosing. The text begins with three foundational chapters on the criminal justice system and the criminal justice process. Next, three policing chapters are followed by three chapters on the courts. After two substantive chapters covering corrections, the text concludes with a look ahead into the future of criminal justice.

Instructors are provided with two distinct options for the introductory criminal justice course. *Criminal Justice: A Brief Introduction* is derived from Fagin, *Criminal Justice*, Second Edition, also available from Allyn & Bacon. *Criminal Justice*, Second Edition, is more comprehensive with 17 chapters, including separate chapters on the following topics: victimology, homeland security, and the juvenile justice system—topics that are covered in *Criminal Justice: A Brief Edition* but not as extensively. *Criminal Justice,* Second Edition, also features individual chapters on probation and parole and community corrections, topics that are combined into a single chapter in *Criminal Justice: A Brief Introduction*. In addition, *Criminal Justice*, Second Edition, offers chapter coverage of criminological theory and more expansive coverage of the historical development of American policing and international criminal justice.

Pedagogy

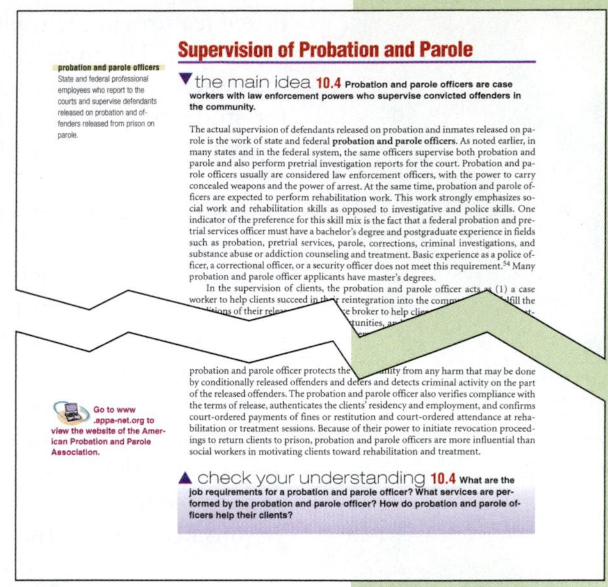

Supervision of Probation and Parole

probation and parole officers State and federal professional employees who report to the courts and supervise defendants released on probation and offenders released from prison on parole.

▼ the main idea **10.4** **Probation and parole officers are case workers with law enforcement powers who supervise convicted offenders in the community.**

The actual supervision of defendants released on probation and inmates released on parole is the work of state and federal **probation and parole officers.** As noted earlier, in many states and in the federal system, the same officers supervise both probation and parole and also perform pretrial investigation reports for the court. Probation and parole officers usually are considered law enforcement officers, with the power to carry concealed weapons and the power of arrest. At the same time, probation and parole officers are expected to perform rehabilitation work. This work strongly emphasizes social work and rehabilitation skills as opposed to investigative and police skills. One indicator of the preference for this skill mix is the fact that a federal probation and pretrial services officer must have a bachelor's degree and postgraduate experience in fields such as probation, pretrial services, parole, corrections, criminal investigations, and substance abuse or addiction counseling and treatment. Basic experience as a police officer, a correctional officer, or a security officer does not meet this requirement.[54] Many probation and parole officer applicants have master's degrees.

In the supervision of clients, the probation and parole officer acts … (1) a case worker to help clients succeed in … reintegration into the comm… …fill the …

… probation and parole officer protects the … from any harm that may be done by conditionally released offenders and deters and detects criminal activity on the part of the released offenders. The probation and parole officer also verifies compliance with the terms of release, authenticates the clients' residency and employment, and confirms court-ordered payments of fines or restitution and court-ordered attendance at rehabilitation or treatment sessions. Because of their power to initiate revocation proceedings to return clients to prison, probation and parole officers are more influential than social workers in motivating clients toward rehabilitation and treatment.

Go to www.appa-net.org to view the website of the American Probation and Parole Association.

▲ check your understanding **10.4** **What are the job requirements for a probation and parole officer? What services are performed by the probation and parole officer? How do probation and parole officers help their clients?**

Criminal Justice: A Brief Introduction has numerous student-friendly features to enhance the students' interest and retention. Each chapter provides students with learning objectives, a summary of the chapter, a systematic check of reading comprehension, vocabulary review, and end-of-chapter questions that provoke thought and encourage students to examine aspects of the chapter in greater detail. Students will be able to maximize their performance in your course.

Each chapter opens with a **Chapter Outline,** a list of **Learning Objectives,** and a **Chapter-Opening Vignette** that provides a relevant real-life example from today's headlines of an event in the criminal justice system. Some of the illustrated chapter-opening stories are humorous, others are serious, but all are real. For example, it is true that a Texas legislator wanted to ban "suggestive high school cheerleading" because he thought it led to sexual immorality, and a long-time priest justified stealing $100 a week from the collection plate because he considered it his retirement plan. Although there is a certain humor to these situations, there are underlying serious questions concerning the role and purpose of the criminal justice system.

Chapters systematically give students the opportunity to check their retention and comprehension of the material. At the beginning of each main section of text, **The Main Idea** briefly summarizes what is important to remember about that section. Then, at the end of each main section of text, **Check Your Understanding** asks students to answer review questions about the section of text they just read. Key terms are bolded in the chapter narrative and defined in the margins in the **page-by-page Glossary.** Also in the margins are **web links** that contain useful, stable URLs that students can access for more practical or in-depth information about the criminal justice system. These websites put students in contact with local, state, federal, and international criminal justice agencies and reference materials.

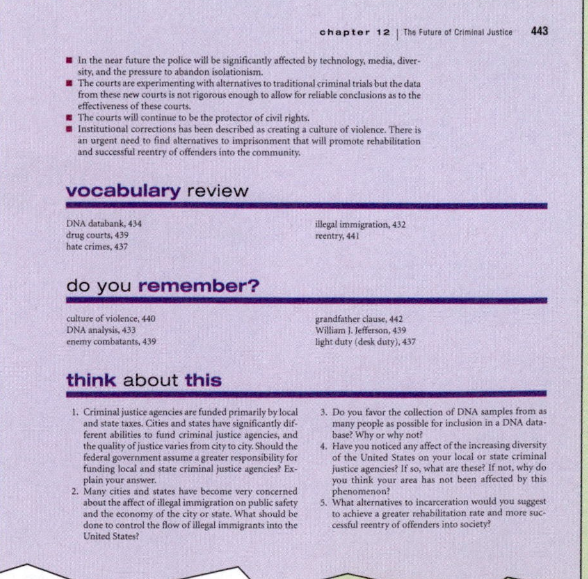

chapter 12 | The Future of Criminal Justice 443

- In the near future the police will be significantly affected by technology, media, diversity, and the pressure to abandon isolationism.
- The courts are experimenting with alternatives to traditional criminal trials but the data from these new courts is not rigorous enough to allow for reliable conclusions as to the effectiveness of these courts.
- The courts will continue to be the protector of civil rights.
- Institutional corrections has been described as creating a culture of violence. There is an urgent need to find alternatives to imprisonment that will promote rehabilitation and successful reentry of offenders into the community.

vocabulary review

DNA databank, 434
drug courts, 439
hate crimes, 437
illegal immigration, 432
reentry, 441

do you remember?

culture of violence, 440
DNA analysis, 433
enemy combatants, 439
grandfather clause, 442
William J. Jefferson, 439
light duty (desk duty), 437

think about this

1. Criminal justice agencies are funded primarily by local and state taxes. Cities and states have significantly different abilities to fund criminal justice agencies, and the quality of justice varies from city to city. Should the federal government assume a greater responsibility for funding local and state criminal justice agencies? Explain your answer.
2. Many cities and states have become very concerned about the affect of illegal immigration on public safety and the economy of the city or state. What should be done to control the flow of illegal immigrants into the United States?
3. Do you favor the collection of DNA samples from as many people as possible for inclusion in a DNA database? Why or why not?
4. Have you noticed any affect of the increasing diversity of the United States on your local or state criminal justice agencies? If so, what are these? If not, why do you think your area has not been affected by this phenomenon?
5. What alternatives to incarceration would you suggest to achieve a greater rehabilitation rate and more successful reentry of offenders into society?

Chapters close with a **Chapter Summary, Vocabulary Review, Do You Remember?** (a list of key names and events with page references), and **Think about This** questions. **Think about This** presents provocative questions designed to stimulate critical thinking about the application of chapter concepts to real-world situations. These questions do not have "right" and "wrong" answers but are designed to generate discussion and debate about the practical outcomes or implications of important concepts in the chapter.

Features

Boxed features in each chapter provide an examination of an aspect of the criminal justice system. The three types of features are Criminal Justice in the Media, Diversity in the System, and Careers in the System. Each box closes with critical thinking questions for students to answer and link to chapter content. **Criminal Justice in the Media** examines the influence of the mass media and entertainment media on crime, public responses to crime, and people's assumptions about the criminal justice system. **Diversity in the System** highlights how the criminal justice system both reflects and responds to American diversity in race, ethnicity, age, gender, and social class, and how sometimes the criminal justice system itself becomes a source of injustice. These features also illustrate how the criminal justice system changes in response to changing values and laws and how the criminal justice system is used as a tool to bring about equality. **Careers in the System** gives students an inside look at what people who work in the system do and how they feel about it, as well as practical information and advice about salaries, academic requirements, and career strategies. For example, students need to know that the FBI does not hire people without experience, that deputy sheriffs may be required to work in the jail before they can get other assignments, and that jails and prisons need many other professionals besides correctional officers.

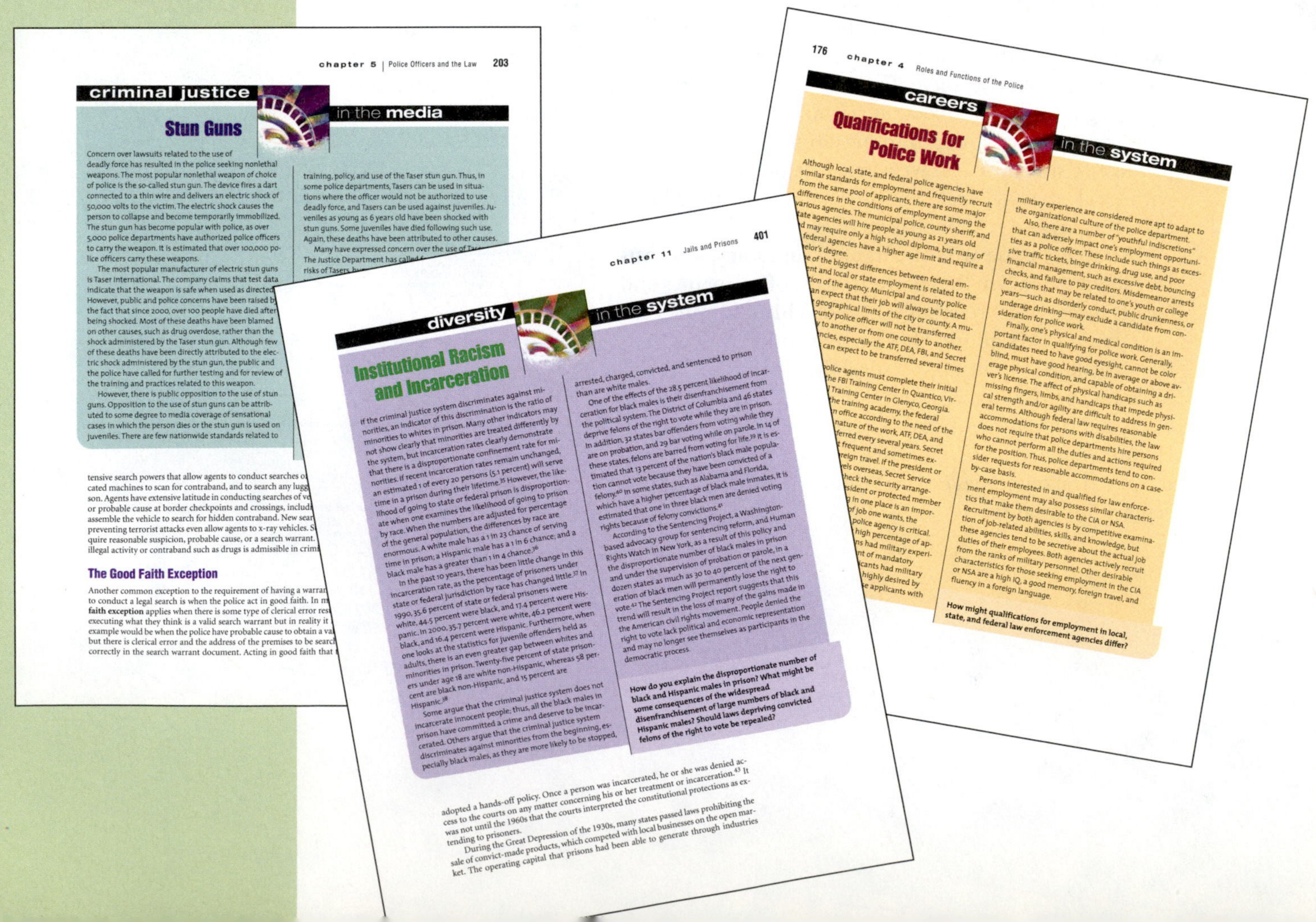

Supplements

We carefully designed a supplement package that supports the aims of *Criminal Justice: A Brief Introduction* in order to provide both students and instructors with a wealth of support materials to ensure success in teaching and in learning. Most supplements are available at no cost when packaged with the textbook so students can benefit from them without incurring additional expense.

Instructor Resources

Instructor's Manual and Test Bank Each chapter in the Instructor's Manual contains Chapter-at-a-Glance, Learning Objectives, Vocabulary Review, Chapter Summary, Discussion Questions, Teaching Tips and Suggestions, Class Activities, and Web Links. Each chapter in the Test Bank consists of 40 Multiple Choice Questions, 15 True/False Questions, 20 Fill-in-the-Blank Questions, and 6 to 8 Essay Questions.

TestGen EQ Computerized Testing Program This computerized version of the Test Bank is available with Tamarack's easy-to-use TestGen software, which lets you prepare tests for printing as well as for network and online testing. It provides full editing capability for Windows and Macintosh.

Blackboard and WebCT Test Item Files Both of these popular online learning platforms are available for use with Fagin, *Criminal Justice: A Brief Introduction*.

PowerPoint Lecture Presentations This complete set of chapter-by-chapter PowerPoint lecture presentations contains approximately 20 slides per chapter specific to Fagin, *Criminal Justice*. The slides reinforce the main ideas of each chapter.

Videos Qualified adopters receive one or more videos. Contact your publisher's representative for more information.

The Blockbuster Approach: *Teaching Criminal Justice and Criminology with Video,* Second Edition This supplement effectively guides the instructor on how to successfully integrate feature films into the introductory course and offers hundreds of film suggestions for the general topics covered in the course.

Custom Publishing Opportunities Create your own customized reader with content and organization that matches your course syllabus. Select from hundreds of readings available through *Boundaries,* the Pearson Custom Publishing database in deviance, crime, and criminal justice. The anthology includes readings on a variety of topics, such as terrorism and white-collar crime, and includes news articles from the latest headlines and a wealth of state-specific information. You may also include your own writing, course-related information, or readings from outside sources. Contact your publisher's representative for more information on how easy and inexpensive it is to go Custom.

Student Resources

MyCrimeLab This interactive and instructive multimedia resource can be used as a supplement to a traditional lecture course, or to completely administer an online course. MyCrimeLab features a text-specific e-book, with multimedia and assessment icons in the margins. These icons launch to exciting resources such as animations, video clips, audio explanations, activities, and more. MyCrimeLab also features a unique assessment program, including pre- and posttests, along with an Individualized Study Plan that helps students achieve success. Geared to meet the teaching and learning needs of every instructor and every student, MyCrimeLab is a valuable tool for any classroom setting. www.mycrimelab.com.

***Careers in Criminal Justice,* Second Edition** This set of biographies of criminal justice professionals helps students and professors answer the often-asked question, "What can I do with a degree in criminal justice?" The text provides meaningful answers to a specific, targeted audience—typical students who are taking their first criminal justice course. The biographies are organized by various subfields and include discussions of what can be done with a B.A., M.A., Ph.D., or a combination of degrees. It is available at no cost when packaged with the text.

State Supplements Allyn and Bacon currently offers 11 state supplements, each a 48-page booklet with state-specific information on each state's criminal justice system. The following states are currently available: CA, FL, IL, KY, MI, NC, NY, OH, PA, TX, and WV.

To the Student

The criminal justice system is one of the most dynamic, powerful, and ubiquitous powers of government, touching the lives of everyone in society, not just criminals and not just those who work in the system. The criminal justice system is a complex set of relationships between citizens and government. The nation's founding principles of democracy, justice, and equality are played out in the everyday interactions of citizens and police, in the Supreme Court's power to declare certain laws and behaviors unconstitutional, and in society's responses to crime and problems such as illegal drug use, juvenile murderers, and overcrowded prisons. The criminal justice system is complex and can be difficult to understand, but it is also exciting, changing, and very important to you. Every individual will have some contact with the criminal justice system during his or her lifetime.

Criminal Justice: A Brief Introduction describes the responsibilities of the agencies, the roles of the personnel, and the interrelationships of criminal justice to political agencies and social values and other factors that influence the criminal justice system. It also focuses on change. Since the terrorist attacks on the World Trade Center and the Pentagon on September 11, 2001, there have been many changes in the criminal justice system and heightened interest in how and why the criminal justice system works. There is renewed interest in how the criminal justice system fits into the big picture of security and justice.

This text is informative, accurate, and contemporary. It contains examples of horrific crimes, outrageous behaviors, new technologies, new criminal justice programs, and shocking examples of innocent people caught up in the criminal justice system. However, today's news story will soon be replaced by tomorrow's news story. Often the criminal justice system is confronted with new situations, such as the War on Terrorism, that require innovation and change. As a result of new policing strategies, new correctional philosophies, new drug rehabilitation programs, and new threats from domestic and international terrorism, the criminal justice system has and will continue to undergo tremendous change in your lifetime. It is important that you understand these changes, because they will affect you. They will make a difference in the civil liberties you have, in your legal rights and responsibilities, in your quality of life, and in your feelings of safety and security.

Criminal Justice: A Brief Introduction provides a balanced viewpoint that is both critical and admiring of the American criminal justice system, its roots, and its transformations. It presents an honest look at the criminal justice system, warts and all, as opposed to superficial or uncritical presentations that gloss over the deficiencies, weaknesses, and injustices of the system. This book is intended to provoke critical thinking and debate. It does not shy away from talking about a criminal justice system that at times seems to ignore common sense and appears to act opposite to its goal of providing "justice." You are encouraged to question the effectiveness of a system that on one hand upholds law, and on the other hand is capable of abusing constitutional rights, ignoring scientific knowledge, and imprisoning the innocent. I encourage you to dig deeper into the workings of the criminal justice system, to examine your beliefs about justice, and to assess the efficiency and effectiveness of the criminal justice system.

Acknowledgments

It is said that it takes a village to raise a child, and without a doubt it takes a team to bring a book like this to publication. Dozens of people have worked to make this book possible. Allyn and Bacon, a Pearson Education Company, has provided a number of very talented and dedicated people to help me. Editor Dave Repetto was amazing in managing the development and timeline of this book. He coordinated the work of numerous people and without his support and talent it would not have been possible to meet the deadlines for this text. Also, Dave provided an excellent support team to work on this edition including Ohlinger Publishing, which helped in the difficult task of redacting material from *Criminal Justice,* Second Edition; Roberta Sherman, production editor, who artfully managed the manuscript through the various stages of production, including photo research and design; and Poyee Oster, photo researcher. An important partner in producing this text was Lynda Griffiths. This is the second book with which Lynda has assisted me and I find her talent amazing. Her skillful editing helped me say what I mean and mean what I say. Her review of the manuscript and questions helped me to communicate what was often a complex idea in a manner that could be clearly understood. Her assistance in maintaining the unity and focus of *Criminal Justice: A Brief Introduction* was invaluable. I thank her for the numerous consultations at all hours and times that she provided in the writing of this book. I extend thanks to editorial assistant, Jack Cashman, and associate editor, Deb Hanlon, who coordinated the supplement package.

Market research targeting introductory criminal justice instructors who prefer brief texts yielded hundreds of responses which directly impacted how we built *Criminal Justice: A Brief Introduction*. We are grateful to all these survey respondents. In addition, we would like to thank the following reviewers: Pearl Jacobs, Sacred Heart University; Christine S. Janis, Northern Illinois University; Michael Kaune, St. Francis College; Elizabeth L. Lewis, North Georgia College and State University; Emmanuel Onyeozili, University of Maryland Eastern Shore; and Amy Thistlethwaite, Northern Kentucky University.

I would also like to thank the reviewers of *Criminal Justice,* Second Edition, for their insightful comments that were useful in the development of the brief version: Charles A. Brawner, III, Heartland Community College; Matthew DeLisi, Iowa State University; Lior Gideon, John Jay College of Criminal Justice; Sgt. Michael Goodwin, Solano Community College; Michael L. Jordan, Lamar University; Kimora, John Jay College of Criminal Justice; Jeffrey D. Lane, Georgia State University; Kim M. Lersch, University of South Florida; John Riley, University of Alaska, Anchorage; Lawrence M. Salinger, Arkansas State University; Gregory B. Talley, Broome Community College; and Tracy F. Tolbert, California State University, Long Beach.

The foundation for this text was the comprehensive edition of *Criminal Justice*. That book would not have been possible without the support of Jennifer Jacobson, and I extend my gratitude to her for her assistance, support, and encouragement. Also, I would like to thank Tom Jefferies and Janice Wiggins-Clarke for their roles in bringing the first edition of this book to print and Mary Ellen Lepionka who was the Senior Development Editor. I am especially thankful to Janice for her work and guidance in getting this project started.

Many reviewers took the time to make invaluable suggestions that contributed to *Criminal Justice,* Second Edition. They are Laura Bedard, Florida State University; Charles Chastain, University of Arkansas, Little Rock; Tere Chipman, Fayetteville Technical Community College; J. Allan Cobb, Adjunct Faculty, University of Louisville and Boston University; Joel Powell Dahlquist, Moorhead University; L. Edward Day, Pennsylvania State University, Altoona; Richard H. De Lung, Wayland Baptist University; C. Randall Eastep,

Brevard Community College; Richard Finn, Western Nevada Community College; Robert M. Freeman, Shippensburg University; Pamela Hart, Iowa Western Community College; G. G. Hunt, Wharton County Junior College; Michael Kane, Coastal Bend College; Charles S. Kocher, Cumberland Community College; Robert L. Marsh, Boise State University; Donna Massey, University of Tennessee, Martin; William J. Mathias, University of South Carolina; Kenneth Mentor, New Mexico State University; Bernie Meyer, University of Pittsburgh, Bradford; Robert P. Morin, California State University, Chico; Angela M. Nickoli, Ball State University; Victor Ortloff, Troy State University; Steve Owen, Radford University; Scott R. Senjo, Weber State University; Jeanette M. Sereno, California State University, Stanislaus; Gregory B. Talley, Broome Community College; Ronald Walker, Trinity Valley Community College; and, David Wedlick, Westchester Community College.

I extend my heartfelt thanks to the numerous colleagues who have assisted me in the preparation of this textbook. I would like to give special thanks to my mentor, Dr. Dae H. Chang, a fine scholar, gentleman, and friend. I also thank the thousands of students who for more than two decades enrolled in the criminal justice classes that I taught. Their probing questions, requests for additional explanations, and interest in understanding the complexities of the criminal justice system have helped me hone my skills in explaining the criminal justice system in this textbook. My students' enthusiasm for understanding the criminal justice system is at the heart of my effort in developing this textbook. I hope it will be of fundamental value to future students as they pursue their careers in criminal justice or related fields.

Finally, I extend my deepest thanks and gratitude to my wife, Gretchen, and my children, James-Jason, Elizabeth, and Émilie, to whom I have turned often for support and assistance. Their sacrifices during the many evenings that I was working on this book were remarkable, and I dedicate this book to them.

About the Author

James Fagin's diverse background lends itself beautifully to introductory textbook authorship.

Experience

Hands-on background and experience in law enforcement

Jim Fagin's experience includes both extensive academic experience and experience as a commissioned law enforcement officer and consultant to numerous criminal justice agencies. He was special assistant to the Carbondale Police Department (Illinois); commissioned police reserve officer for the Kansas City Police Department (Kansas); commissioned academy training officer for the Wyandotte County Sheriff's Department (Kansas); and training academy lecturer for the Wichita Police Department, Leavenworth Police Department (Kansas), the Honolulu Police Department, and the State of Hawaii Sheriff's Department. In addition, he has been a consultant to numerous major local, state, and federal criminal justice agencies, including the Federal Bureau of Investigation and the United States Secret Service. Dr. Fagin was a member of the first victim's rights commission for the state of Kansas. He also served as a consultant for Leavenworth Federal Penitentiary to help them address security problems in Federal Prisons Industries. He was an instructor for the Law Enforcement Assistance Administration agency and provided numerous seminars to senior law enforcement executives on management and supervision throughout the United States. As a member of the Hawaii Chapter of the John Howard Association, Dr. Fagin was an advocate for reentry services for convicted offenders reentering the community. His direct real-life experience in law enforcement gives *Criminal Justice* a special relevance, authenticity, and passion.

Expertise

An expert in areas of criminal justice of greatest contemporary concern

Jim Fagin is an expert and consultant on terrorism, computer crime and computer technologies in criminal justice, management, and executive decision making. His other special areas of expertise include community policing, police recruitment, and police performance, including stress management, prison security, and victims' rights. He has published and conducted seminars internationally in these areas. In its currency, examples, comparative insights, and practical applications, *Criminal Justice* reflects these areas of expertise.

Educator

A recognized educator in the administration of justice

Jim Fagin received his B.A. degree from the University of Nevada, Las Vegas, and his M.S. and Ph.D. from Southern Illinois University. He has taught criminal justice courses for almost 30 years and has been involved in ground-breaking nontraditional and in-service criminal justice education programs for Wichita State University and Chaminade University of Honolulu. The American Society of Public Administration named him "Outstanding Educator" in 1996. His interest in higher education in criminal justice began when he became interested in training police to respond to domestic disturbances. From this beginning, he served as a curriculum developer for the U.S. Department of Justice Law Enforcement Assistance Administration, an organization with whom Dr. Fagin also worked to upgrade the knowledge and skills of criminal justice managers and to train police officers in management and organization. He was a pioneer in computer crime and has provided training to numerous police and correctional agencies in hostage negotiations. Today, Dr. Fagin remains active in the criminal justice field. His commitment to teaching is reflected in his *Criminal Justice: A Brief Introduction* and in the second edition of *Criminal Justice,* both of which feature an applied and practical, student-centered framework, and in the recently published *When Terrorism Strikes Home: Defending the United States* © 2006 Allyn & Bacon.

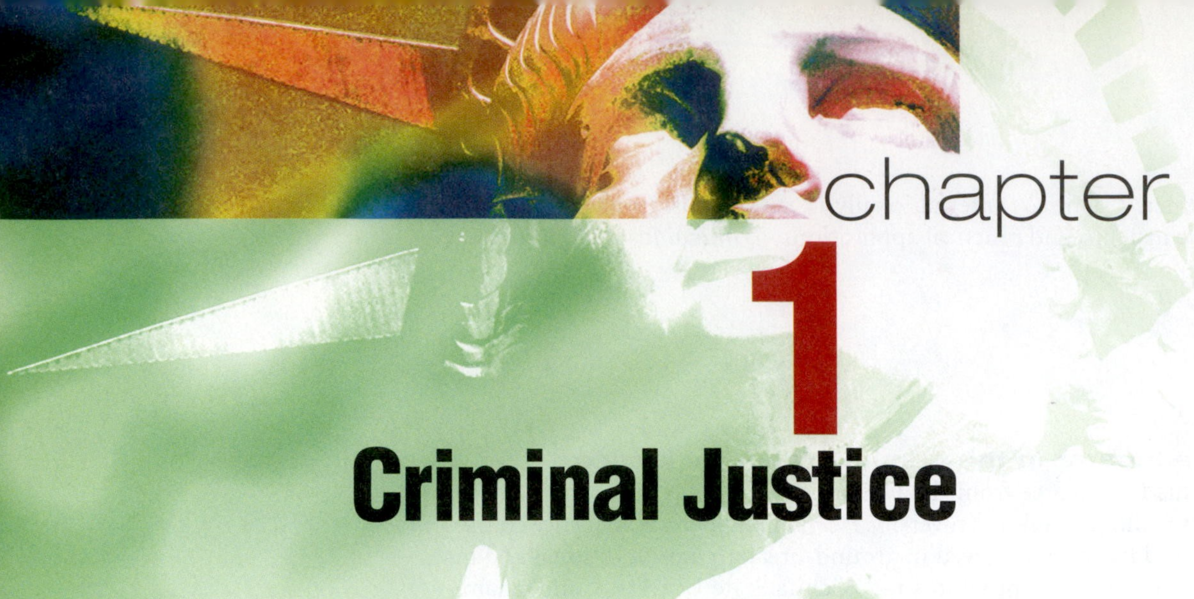

chapter 1
Criminal Justice

CHAPTER OUTLINE

LEARNING OBJECTIVES

After reading this chapter, you will know

- The four phenomena that stirred interest and led to changes in the criminal justice system.
- The key issues surrounding the need to balance the maintenance of order and individual rights.
- The process and flow of the criminal justice system.
- The due process model of criminal justice.

Protest against Ohio Neo-Nazi March Turns Violent

TOLEDO, OHIO (AP)—A crowd that gathered to protest a white supremacists' march Saturday turned violent, throwing baseball-sized rocks at police, vandalizing vehicles and stores, and setting fire to a neighborhood bar, authorities said.

At least two dozen members of the National Socialist Movement, which calls itself "America's Nazi Party," had gathered at a city park to march under police protection. Organizers said they were demonstrating against black gangs they said were harassing white residents. Violence broke out about one-quarter of a mile away along the planned march route shortly before it was to begin.

For several hours, about 150 police officers chased bands of young men through the area. Officers wearing gas masks fired tear gas canisters and flash-bang devices designed to stun suspects, only to see the groups reform and resume throwing rocks and bottles. Finally, police marched shoulder-to-shoulder down the street shouting to people to stay inside, and the crowd of several hundred dispersed. At least two dozen people were arrested on charges including assault, vandalism, failure to obey police and failure to disperse. "We frankly could have made a couple hundred arrests easily," [a police officer] said.

The mayor had appealed to residents the night before to ignore the march. He said the city wouldn't give the Nazi group a permit to march in the streets but couldn't stop them from walking on the sidewalks like other citizens. When the rioting broke out, Ford tried to negotiate with those involved, but "they weren't interested in that." He said they were mostly "gang members who had real or imagined grievances and took it as an opportunity to speak in their own way."

From Associated Press, "Protest against Ohio Neo-Nazi March Turns Violent," *The New York Times*, October 15, 2005.

introduction:

People and Processes in Criminal Justice

Citizens of the United States have the right to free assembly and free speech but rights guaranteed by the U.S. Constitution may be restricted when those actions harm others. The members of the National Socialist Movement have the right to public assembly and the citizens of Toledo, Ohio, have the right to express their disapproval of what the National Socialist Movement stands for. However, when citizen actions become violent, authorities have a duty to stop the violence and to protect the community. When the mayor of Toledo was unable to negotiate with those opposed to the march to achieve a peaceable rebuke of the march, it was necessary to use force and to arrest those who committed the violence. Regardless of their motivation for violence, those arrested will be processed by the criminal justice system and if found guilty will be punished for their actions.

The criminal justice system plays an important role in a democratic society. In a large, diverse, and complex society the maintenance of law and order requires authorities who are empowered to restrict the liberties of citizens to use force to compel obedience of the law and to sanction those who disobey society's laws. Yet, at the same time, citizens must be free to exercise the liberties guaranteed by the Constitution. Thus, the law must allow the reasonable exercise of freedoms when those actions do not cause harm to others. Balancing the exercise of civil liberties against the need for law and order is a difficult and complex mission. For example, the march in Toledo by approximately two dozen neo-Nazis resulted in rioting and violence; on the same weekend, however, a gathering on the Washington Mall of approximately 100,000, known as the Millions More Movement, concluded with no arrests and no violence.[1]

The criminal justice system is more complex and more important than most people understand. Often an individual's understanding of the criminal justice system focuses on some personal aspect he or she has encountered, such as traffic enforcement. Some people get most or

The Constitution provides citizens the right of freedom of assembly and speech. Over 100,000 gathered for the Millions More Movement on October 15, 2005, to listen to emotionally charged speeches by such controversial persons as Malik Shabazz of the New Black Panther Party accuse the government of extreme actions against blacks. Despite the large crowd and fiery rhetoric there were no problems that threatened public order or safety. Officials in the criminal justice system often must decide who has the right to hold public protests, when they can protest, and where they can protest. Making such judgment calls is difficult as the size of the crowd or the emotion of the rhetoric does not necessarily predict which protests will be violent and threaten public safety. Can you suggest guidelines that officials should follow in making decisions that restrict the right to assembly and speech?

all of their information about the criminal justice system from the media. However, information obtained from the news media is often incomplete and the entertainment media usually provide an inaccurate and unrealistic portrayal of the criminal justice system.

If the police arrest you for a crime, what happens next? How do you prove your innocence? How does a person end up in prison? What are the safeguards that prevent the conviction—and perhaps wrongful execution—of an innocent person? The American criminal justice process is a complex interaction of numerous agencies. The process from arrest to trial to incarceration can take years. This chapter examines the American criminal justice process, the agencies that make up this system, and the decisions that are made as the accused is processed through the system.

As you will see, the criminal justice system can be viewed as an input–process–output model. Basically, the criminal justice system detects and selects people to be processed by the system, processes them through the system, and then provides a means for their exit from the system. The agencies, people, and resources used by the criminal justice system are all focused on moving people through the system from arrest to an exit portal.

The purpose of this text is to provide an overview and understanding of a very complex system composed of thousands of agencies and millions of people. Such a task requires a certain degree of generalization. Thus, the criminal justice system described may not reflect exactly the local or state criminal justice system where you live. It is necessary to understand the larger purposes and goals of the criminal justice system and to know about its history to comprehend this explanation. This chapter (1) examines significant events in the last half-century that have been extremely influential in the development of today's criminal justice system, (2) discusses the role of the criminal justice system in balancing individual rights versus the power of government, and (3) discusses the people and agencies that comprise the criminal justice system. The criminal justice system is commonly divided into three subcomponents: police, courts, and corrections. Each of these subcomponents is discussed in detail.

A Brief History of the Criminal Justice System

the main idea 1.1 Public awareness of safety issues in the 1960s made crime a government priority and led to legislation to improve the criminal justice system.

Rioting and the Fear of Crime

The mid-1940s is a good starting point for the study of the modern criminal justice system. Prior to World War II, the criminal justice system was dominated by political influences, there was little national attention focused on the criminal justice system, the federal agencies and federal government were not significant players, the crime rate was generally low, and for the most part any problems with the criminal justice system were perceived as problems concerning local administration, concerns, and reforms.

Even immediately after World War II, the criminal justice system did not rise to national prominence. A decade of prosperity followed the end of World War II, and crime and the criminal justice system were of little concern to the average citizen. For the most part, there were no academic departments of criminal justice at colleges and universities, because there was little interest or reward in studying the subject. Four phenomena stirred interest in the criminal justice system and led to its prominence as one of the most examined and criticized aspects of the government: (1) the civil rights movement, (2) the Vietnam War, (3) the rising crime rate and the public's increased awareness, and (4) the terrorism attacks of September 11, 2001. In many respects, these four influences were interrelated and cumulative in their effect on the criminal justice system.

Civil Rights and War Protests

For information on the Vietnam War, see http://historyplace.com/unitedstates/vietnam/.

Protests against institutional racism and U.S. involvement in the Vietnam War posed major challenges to the criminal justice system. Prior to the Civil Rights Act of 1964, businesses, hotels, restaurants, and public transportation could and did refuse service with impunity to citizens of color. For example, in 1956, the University of Alabama expelled its first black student, Autherine Lucy, on the grounds that her presence was a threat to public order. In the South, blacks were frequently the victims of lynching, violence, and denial of public and private services.

When citizens, both black and white, protested racial discrimination, they were often opposed by violence—even death. In 1961, when civil rights workers attempted to

Rosa Parks in an act of civil disobedience challenged local laws that denied blacks equal rights in the use of public transportation. Her arrest initiated a boycott of public transportation resulting in integration of public transportation. At times the criminal justice system does not distinguish between criminal justice and social justice resulting in both civil disobedience and violence. Does social injustice justify civil disobedience? Is violence an appropriate response to social injustice? Should the criminal justice system take into account the motives of offenders protesting social injustice in arrest and punishment related to civil disobedience or violence? Dr. Martin Luther King Jr. said that civil disobedience in response to social injustice shows the highest respect for the law. Do you agree?

desegregate the bus stations and waiting rooms, the bus in which they were traveling was fire-bombed and the demonstrators were beaten. NAACP leader Medgar Evers was murdered, and, due to the complicity of the police in the crime, it took decades to bring his killer to justice. Civil rights protesters often feared not only the violence of the mob but also that of local law enforcement.

To visit the website of the National Civil Rights Museum located in Memphis, TN, see www.civilrightsmuseum.org. The museum's exhibits document the historical struggle for equality and social justice in the United States.

Civil rights leader Martin Luther King Jr. promoted the tactic of civil disobedience, which also challenged the criminal justice system. One of the most well-known examples of civil disobedience occurred in 1955 when **Rosa Parks** refused to move to the rear of the bus, as required by the law, and was arrested. Although King advocated nonviolence, there were many who rioted. Rioting during the 1960s caused millions of dollars in property damage, the injury of thousands of people, and the deaths of dozens.

Political protests against U.S. involvement in the Vietnam War also generated acrimonious conflict in which the police often were captured on film engaged in brutality against the protesters. For example, on the Kent State University campus in 1970, National Guard troops opened fire on unarmed student demonstrators, killing four and injuring many more.

During this period, the crime rate continued to climb, to the point that, according to a 1965 Gallup poll, Americans viewed crime as the most serious problem in the country.[2] In 1968, 31 percent of Gallup survey respondents said they were afraid to walk in their own neighborhoods at night, and by the end of 1972, the number had risen to 42 percent. Many citizens thought the police were part of the cause, not the solution, to the rising crime rate. The **President's Commission on Law Enforcement and Administration of Justice** concluded that most people had lost confidence in the ability of the police to maintain law and order.[3]

The War on Crime

The criminal justice system appeared to be failing. To counter the attack of crime and social disorder, on July 25, 1965, President Lyndon Johnson declared a **War on Crime.** He authorized a series of federal presidential commissions to study crime and justice in the United States and to recommend suggested reforms to restore public confidence. A study of the criminal justice system, with an eye on reform, was a great challenge, and many people thought the task impossible. The American Bar Association declared that the criminal justice system in America was, in reality, a "nonsystem."[4]

See www.ojp.usdoj.gov/reports/98Guides/blf.txt for a discussion of the impact of the President's Crime Commission.

The findings of the President's Crime Commission concluded that fear of crime had eroded the basic quality of life for many Americans. It also recognized the importance of crime prevention, as opposed to crime fighting, and the necessity of eliminating injustices in the criminal justice system. To win the war on crime, the commission called for the development of a broad range of services in response to the crime problem, strategies to attract better-quality personnel at all levels of the criminal justice system, research into the problems of crime and criminal administration, greater resources at all levels of the system, and much greater community and civil involvement.[5]

Omnibus Crime Control and Safe Streets Act of 1968

In response to recommendations of the President's Crime Commission and demands from the public, substantial resources were added to the criminal justice system. For example, to attract better-qualified personnel, the police had to increase salaries; as a result, policing costs skyrocketed in major cities.[6] To help defray these costs, local and state governments sought assistance from the federal government, whose response was to pass the Omnibus Crime Control and Safe Streets Act of 1968. This act is a watershed in criminal justice history in the United States, as it is the point of origin from which major changes in the criminal justice system were derived.

The **Omnibus Crime Control and Safe Streets Act of 1968** created the **Law Enforcement Assistance Administration (LEAA)** and the Law Enforcement Educational Program (LEEP). The LEAA acted as a conduit for transfer of federal funds to state and local law enforcement agencies. However, these funds were not without "strings."

The LEAA appointed the **National Commission on Criminal Justice Standards and Goals,** which had the purpose of formulating specific standards and goals for police, courts, corrections, juvenile justice, and crime prevention. To receive the generous funds available from the federal government that were dispersed by the LEAA, local and state agencies had to show that they had implemented the commission's standards and goals. Many of the advances made within law enforcement agencies were a result of compliance with standards and goals necessary to qualify for federal funds.

See www.Petersons.com to visit the website of the Thomson Peterson's guide to colleges. You can search the web for colleges and universities that offer degrees in criminal justice and related fields.

The **Law Enforcement Educational Program (LEEP)** was a branch of the LEAA. The goal of LEEP was to promote education among criminal justice personnel. The program was directly responsible for the drastic increase in education for police officers. The LEEP grants and loans paid the tuitions of criminal justice personnel (other than attorneys) and students who promised to enter criminal justice after graduation (other than as an attorney). The impact of this funding was significant. In 1966, there were 184 programs offering criminology or criminal justice courses. By 1978, that figure rose to over 1,000 colleges and universities offering degrees ranging from associate to doctorate levels.[7] At its peak in 1975, LEEP funded the education of 100,000 students and spent $40 million on criminal justice education.[8]

After massive amounts of federal assistance, numerous reform efforts, and the adoption of innovative strategies by the police, courts, and corrections, public confidence in the criminal justice system was restored and the crime rate dropped. People felt safe to go out in public again. Residents of large cities reported that they felt safe using public transportation. Violent crime rates for nearly all categories dropped. Local and state governments found equilibrium in funding the criminal justice system and the other needs of government. Things were looking up for public confidence in the criminal justice system until **September 11, 2001** (or **WTC 9/11,** as the event came to be known).

See www.cia.gov/terrorism/ for the Central Intelligence Agency War on Terrorism website.

Domestic strife caused the crisis of confidence in the 1960s and 1970s, but the crisis in the twenty-first century was caused by a foreign attack on the United States. Just as President Johnson declared a war on crime, President Bush declared **War on Terrorism.**

President Bush appointed a new Cabinet position—Office of Homeland Security—to coordinate the antiterrorism activities among federal law enforcement and intelligence agencies. The attack on the WTC led to a call for greater police powers, including expanded authorization for wiretaps, expanded powers of search and seizure, and expanded powers to detain foreign nationals. Billions of dollars were added to the budgets of criminal justice agencies in the effort to restore public confidence, including confidence in the ability of the government to protect its citizens.

Legitimate government depends on the effective operation of the criminal justice system. Citizens have granted the criminal justice system great powers, including the power of life and death. Thus, criminal justice is a much more complex endeavor than simply enforcing the law or waging a war on crime, drugs, or terrorism. When challenged with a choice between safety and liberty, people often choose safety over liberty. The War on Terrorism poses one of the most serious threats since the 1960s to the balance between safety and liberty.

▲ check your understanding **1.1** **How does loss of public confidence in public safety affect the criminal justice system? What four phenomena impacted the public's confidence in public safety?**

Law and Order versus Individual Rights

the main idea 1.2 The rights of individuals in the United States are limited by the need to maintain social order, while the powers of government are limited by the principles stated in the U.S. Constitution.

Democratic governments promote the value of freedom but must place limits on individual freedoms. Actions that would cause alarm or harm are prohibited for the common good. Thus, one has freedom of speech, but the Supreme Court has ruled that this does not give one the freedom to shout "Fire" in a crowded theater, where such a false alarm could result in the harm of others.

This concept of limiting freedom for the common good is very old. For example, the Greek philosopher Aristotle argued that it was necessary that people be governed by law due to their inability to govern themselves (1) because of a tendency to react to fear and emotion rather than reason[9] and (2) because people are subject to corruption.[10]

In the United States, it is argued that individual freedom is limited (1) to ensure order within society, (2) to protect citizens from one another, and (3) to promote the common welfare. Society uses several means to achieve these goals, including informal and formal sanctions. **Informal sanctions** include social norms that are enforced through the social forces of the family, school, government, and religion. These social institutions teach people what is expected for normative behavior. In addition to teaching normative behavior, these primary social institutions also provide punishment when people violate **social norms.** In the informal system, parents punish children for disobedience, bosses reprimand employees, teachers discipline students, and religious groups call on offenders to repent for their sins.

Social order and the common welfare also are promoted through use of **formal sanctions** (such as laws) found within the criminal justice system. Frequently, the informal and formal systems of order maintenance overlap. For example, it is immoral, according to some people, to be naked in public. Also, in most places, it is *illegal* to be naked in public. It is considered wrong to steal or to hurt other people, and it is also *illegal* to do these things.

For the most part, people conform to the rules of society, including both formal and informal rules. However, when someone breaks the rules of society, the system responds. Formal sanctions are carried out by the criminal justice system. In the United States, the **criminal justice system** is based on the enforcement of obedience to laws by the police, the courts, and correctional institutions. When group and society norms are codified into law, government has the power to compel obedience to the rule on pain of punishment, including death.

The more homogeneous and stable the people and their belief systems, the fewer the violations of social norms. In a homogeneous, stable society with a common belief system, there is less need for reliance on a formal **system of social control** to maintain order and regulate interactions. Social control systems operate most effectively and efficiently where there is constant and unified, overt and covert, cultural and social support from all control agencies.[11] When this support is consistently reflected in all social control agencies and value systems of a society, people tend to conform, and they regulate their interactions rather than depend on external force and threats of punishment to abide by the social contract. However, contemporary U.S. society is not characterized by a homogeneous and stable group of people with a common belief system. Rather, the United States is characterized by great diversity in race, religion, ethnicity, and values.

The criminal justice system has assumed an important central role in **order maintenance.** For the most part, people would prefer to go about their everyday business without giving much thought to the criminal justice system. Citizens seem to prefer an

informal sanctions Social norms that are enforced through the social forces of the family, school, government, and religion.

social norms The expected normative behavior in a society.

formal sanctions Social norms enforced through the laws of the criminal justice system.

criminal justice system The enforcement, by the police, the courts, and correctional institutions, of obedience to laws.

system of social control A social system designed to maintain order and regulate interactions.

order maintenance A system of maintaining the day-to-day life of ordinary citizens, a primary goal of the criminal justice system.

invisible criminal justice system—a system that does not intrude into day-to-day life but devotes its time to chasing "bad guys" and leaves "ordinary" citizens alone. Nevertheless, the criminal justice system is an important part of conflict resolution, crime prevention, order maintenance, and the preservation of individual liberties.

The Balance between Individual Rights and the Power of Government

See http://plato.stanford.edu/entries/locke/ for more information on John Locke and *Two Treaties of Government*.

In *Two Treaties of Government* (1690), philosopher **John Locke** argued that all human beings are endowed with what he called "natural rights." These rights are given to people by a power higher than government, and people cannot be deprived of them. Governments exist, according to Locke, to serve individuals. People surrender certain rights with the understanding that they will receive as much, or more, in other benefits, such as safety, order, and preservation of property rights. Locke said that the purpose of government is to regulate and preserve property and to employ the force of the community in the execution of laws and in the defense of the commonwealth from foreign injury—and all of this only for the public good.[12] Locke conceded that the government must have the power of physical force to protect people and their property from the physical violations of others.[13] However, this power was to be balanced against the need to preserve individual liberty.

John Locke's philosophies had a great influence on Thomas Jefferson when he drafted the Declaration of Independence.[14] This document declares that people have unalienable rights given to them by their Creator. These rights include life, liberty, and the pursuit of happiness. It states that government derives its power from the consent of the governed and that "whenever any form of government becomes destructive of these ends, it is the right of the people to alter or to abolish it, and to institute a new government, laying its foundation on such principles, and organizing its powers in such form, as to them shall seem most likely to effect their safety and happiness."

One of the principles on which the United States was founded — as expressed by John Locke, Thomas Jefferson, and John Stuart Mill and the Bill of Rights — was that citizens have certain inalienable rights or rights that cannot be taken away even if citizens consent to losing these rights. One of the most basic of these rights is the right of freedom of speech guaranteed by the First Amendment. However, the Supreme Court has ruled that this right can be restricted when the exercise of this right causes harm to others. A wave of patriotism following the September 11, 2001, attacks has resulted in several bills to amend the Constitution to prohibit flag burning. Why do you favor or oppose this prohibition?

figure 1.1

The Bill of Rights

Amendment I

Congress shall make no law respecting an establishment of religion, or prohibiting the free exercise thereof; or abridging the freedom of speech, or of the press; or the right of the people peaceably to assemble, and to petition the Government for a redress of grievances.

Amendment II

A well regulated Militia, being necessary to the security of a free State, the right of the people to keep and bear Arms, shall not be infringed.

Amendment III

No soldier shall, in time of peace be quartered in any house, without the consent of the Owner, nor in time of war, but in a manner to be prescribed by law.

Amendment IV

The right of the people to be secure in their persons, houses, papers, and effects, against unreasonable searches and seizures, shall not be violated, and no warrants shall issue, but upon probable cause, supported by Oath or affirmation, and particularly describing the place to be searched, and the persons or things to be seized.

Amendment V

No person shall be held to answer for a capital, or otherwise infamous crime, unless on a presentment or indictment of a Grand Jury, except in cases arising in the land or naval forces, or in the Militia, when in actual service in time of War or public danger; nor shall any person be subject for the same offence to be twice put in jeopardy of life or limb; nor shall be compelled in any criminal case to be a witness against himself, nor be deprived of life, liberty, or property, without due process of law; nor shall private property be taken for public use, without just compensation.

Amendment VI

In all criminal prosecutions, the accused shall enjoy the right to a speedy and public trial, by an impartial jury of the State and district wherein the crime shall have been committed, which district shall have been previously ascertained by law, and to be informed of the nature and cause of the accusation; to be confronted with the witnesses against him; to have compulsory process for obtaining witnesses in his favor, and to have the assistance of counsel for his defence.

Amendment VII

In Suits at common law, where the value in controversy shall exceed twenty dollars, the right of trial by jury shall be preserved, and no fact tried by a jury, shall be otherwise re-examined in any Court of the United States, than according to the rules of the common law.

Amendment VIII

Excessive bail shall not be required, nor excessive fines imposed, nor cruel and unusual punishments inflicted.

Amendment IX

The enumeration in the Constitution, of certain rights, shall not be construed to deny or disparage others retained by the people.

Amendment X

The powers not delegated to the United States by the Constitution, nor prohibited by it to the States, are reserved to the States respectively, or to the people.

The first ten amendments were passed by Congress on September 25, 1789, and were ratified on December 15, 1791.

The Constitution of the United States of America reflected a distrust of a strong centralized government. The new government defined in the Constitution consisted of three independent branches: the executive, the legislative, and the judicial. The Constitution divided power among these three branches of government and provided checks and balances. It set up a federal court system and gave power to the states to set up court systems as they deemed appropriate. The original ten amendments, called the Bill of Rights, were added to the Constitution in 1791. The **Bill of Rights** delineated certain guaranteed freedoms of citizens, such as trial by jury, freedom of speech, and the right to be secure in one's home from unreasonable search and seizure (see Figure 1.1). Originally, the Bill of

See www.archives.gov/national-archives-experience/charters/charters.html to visit the website of the National Archives. You can view and download high-resolution images of the Declaration of Independence, the Constitution, and the Bill of Rights. In addition, the website has articles and media presentations about these documents.

Rights applied only to actions of the federal government. However, the U.S. Supreme Court has used the due process clause of the Fourteenth Amendment to extend many of the rights to protect individuals against action by the states.[15]

Compared with today's government, the state and federal government of the late 1700s intruded only minimally into the day-to-day life of its citizens. There were no full-time municipal police, no federal or state income taxes, only two federal law enforcement agencies (U.S. Marshall's Office and Office of Postal Inspector), and few federal and state crimes defined by law. By comparison, today's government has grown in complexity and intrusiveness into the day-to-day affairs of its citizens.

▲ check your understanding **1.2** **Why and in what ways is individual freedom limited in the United States? How do formal and informal sanctions help maintain order? What is the role of the criminal justice system in order maintenance? What rights were provided in the Constitution and in the Bill of Rights?**

The Search to Define the Criminal Justice System

▼ the main idea **1.3** **The criminal justice system is a dynamic model of interrelated, independent agencies that operate under numerous checks and balances. These agencies process criminal offenders through a complex system of decision points.**

See www.abacon.com/sociology/soclinks/cj.html for links to law enforcement, corrections, courts, and many other criminal justice websites.

When examining the criminal justice system, there are two perspectives: (1) the agencies and people involved in the criminal justice system and (2) the processes and flow of the criminal justice system. This book discusses various agencies and the people who work in them, but the criminal justice system is much more than the sum of its components. To understand the criminal justice system, it is necessary to examine the interactions, checks and balances, and decisions that are made. Each person and agency in the criminal justice system has a certain amount of autonomy, but each is also controlled by the criminal justice system. By exploring the balance between autonomy and control, you can appreciate the ever-changing, flexible, and responsive nature of the criminal justice system. Thus, the criminal justice system is not a static model, but a dynamic model that is constantly evolving, changing, and redefining itself. This dynamic nature has always been a characteristic of the U.S. criminal justice system, and the description of it in this book is only a portrait of one place and time. Also, the criminal justice system differs from state to state.

Agencies and People

The criminal justice system is divided into three categories of agencies: police, courts, and corrections. Each of the agencies in the criminal justice system is independent. There is no single agency that has oversight control of all of the criminal justice agencies. This decentralization and autonomy is an intentional characteristic of the American criminal justice system. One of the values of the early founders of the United States was a mistrust of a strong, centralized government and as a result, the U.S. government was created with numerous checks and balances. This philosophy is mirrored in the criminal justice system.

diversity in the system

Criminal Justice versus Social Justice

The Declaration of Independence declares that "all men are created equal." The Fourteenth Amendment to the Constitution guarantees that the law will be applied equally to all citizens. It says, "No State shall make or enforce any law which shall abridge the privileges or immunities of citizens of the United States; nor shall any State deprive any person of life, liberty, or property, without due process of law; nor deny to any person within its jurisdiction the equal protection of the laws." Despite these guarantees, equality and social justice are not always practiced by government and society.

One of the most serious offenses against equality and social justice in the United States was the practice of vigilante justice known as *lynching*. Although lynching was common as early as the colonial period, its early use was mostly a form of extra-legal execution generally used against accused criminals. The term *lynching* was named for Colonel Charles Lynch, who used the practice during the American Revolutionary War to deal with Tories and criminal elements.[16] After the American Civil War the victims of lynchings were primarily, but not exclusively, black. Black victims were lynched for various reasons, including "registering to vote, arguing with a white man, disrespect to a white woman, shoplifting, drunkenness, elopement, insults and refusing to give evidence, . . . being obnoxious, disorderly conduct, indolence, suing white man [sic], vagrancy and unpopularity."[17] It is difficult to estimate the number of lynchings but one estimate is that there were 10,000 lynchings between 1878 and 1898.[18]

Lynching involved far more than simply hanging the victim. Victims were often humiliated, tortured, burned, dismembered, castrated, beaten, whipped, and shot. It was not uncommon for the victim to be shot hundreds of times prior to being lynched.[19] Lynchings were most often public events. Photographs were taken of the event and sold afterwards. Sometimes the victim's fingers and toes were cut off, his teeth pulled out by pliers, and he was castrated before the audience. Often these "souvenirs" would be sold.[20] Victims would be lynched in public places and left hanging for people to see. Postcards were often made from the photographs of the lynching.

During the late nineteenth century and early twentieth century lynchings were carried out without fear of prosecution. The first recorded prosecution of a white man for punishment for a lynching was not until 1909 (*U.S.* v. *Shipp*, 214 U.S. 386,1909).[21] In June 2005, the United States Senate issued a formal apology to victims of lynchings for its repeated failure, despite the requests of seven presidents, to enact a federal law to make lynching a crime. Those who participated in lynching did not fear the law or prosecution. Lynchings were often performed in front of crowds of thousands of people, yet no one was ever prosecuted. Often, the mob was led by local police or local police aided and abetted.

Press coverage of lynchings was typically unsympathetic to the victim. The tone of most articles implied support or at least passive acceptance of the vigilante justice.[22] Lynchings have been described as "the most powerful machine of racism, violence and murder our nation has ever seen before or since."[23]

There were voices protesting the abridgement of human and constitutional rights. The National Association for the Advancement of Colored People (NAACP) was launched as an antilynching campaign, the *New York Times*, the *Atlanta Constitution*, and other newspapers denounced the practice of lynching in 1922.[24] However, the law did not come to the aid of those subject to this terrorism. In the 1930s, legislation was proposed to make it a federal crime for any law enforcement officer to fail to exercise his responsibilities during a lynching incident. The legislation failed to gain enough votes to pass.[25] As a result, blacks suffered grievously as local, state, and federal law enforcement turned a blind eye toward lynchings. Jim Crow laws and the ability of whites to inflict brutality and death on blacks without fear of punishment seemed to condone this racial violence.

Ideally, criminal justice and social justice reflect the same just principles and laws. In the perfect world what is legal would also be just. However, the criminal justice system has numerous examples where during certain periods of time the criminal justice system has failed various groups of people.

Think of a contemporary example where there is a gap between criminal justice and social justice. When the criminal justice system systematically fails to provide social justice to a class of people, what is the affect on society?

The most significant agencies in the criminal justice system are (1) the police, (2) the courts, (3) the probation and parole agencies, and (4) the jails, prisons, and other correctional agencies. These agencies exist in the local, state, and federal levels of government. Each jurisdiction has its own distinctive criminal justice agencies that provide services to the local, state, or federal government. For example, there are local police, state police, and federal police. Likewise, there are local, state, and federal courts and correctional institutions.

One of the difficulties of capturing the dynamics of this multilevel system is understanding that the local, state, and federal political agencies, although independent, are at the same time united and interdependent. For example, a defendant arrested by the municipal police for loitering can end up pleading his or her case before the U.S. Supreme Court. While the criminal justice system has been described as an input–output model, it is also appropriate to describe the courts as the hub of the criminal justice system. In a sense, the activities of the criminal justice system are arranged around the mission of the courts.

Over 2 million people are employed by the criminal justice system.[26] However, each of the thousands of criminal justice agencies hires its own employees. There is no central employment agency for the criminal justice system. Each agency sets standards of employment, defines job responsibilities and duties, and pays its employees independently of central control. As a result, there is great diversity in the educational achievement, skills, knowledge, and abilities of the people who work in the criminal justice system. One community may require police officers to have only a high school diploma, whereas another community may require a bachelor's degree. One city may have no requirements of legal training for its municipal judges, whereas another city may require that municipal judges meet strict standards for education and other qualifications.

One may be tempted to think of the criminal justice system as a wedding cake with three layers: local, state, and federal. However, the analogy of a wedding cake implies that each political entity is separate and that there is a hierarchy with local political entities at the bottom and the federal government at the top. This is not accurate; a better analogy is to think of the criminal justice system as a picket fence. In the **picket fence model**, the horizontal boards in the fence represent the local, state, and federal governments, and the vertical boards represent the various functions within the criminal justice system, such as law enforcement, courts, and corrections (see Figure 1.2). For example, local municipal courts have their own mission, personnel, and resources. However, a case can be appealed from a local municipal court to a state court, and from a state court to a federal court. Thus, each court system is separate, but each is linked by a vertical picket.

Process and Flow

The process and flow of the criminal justice system refers to the means by which people accused of a crime enter the criminal justice system, are found guilty or not guilty, and are punished or exit the system. This process, from being accused of a crime to final disposition or exit from the criminal justice system, can take years or even decades to complete. There is no standard time limit for processing a case through the system. Different defendants with similar charges and circumstances can take significantly different amounts of time for their cases to go through the system.

picket fence model Model of the criminal justice system, with the local, state, and federal criminal justice systems depicted as three horizontal levels connected vertically by the roles, functions, and activities of the agencies that comprise them.

The flow of a person through the criminal justice system is not a one-way process. People can enter the system, be processed up to a certain point, and exit the system, only to be brought back into the system at a later time. A good example of this is the case of the four Los Angeles police officers accused of using excessive force in the traffic stop of motorist Rodney King. These officers were arrested, tried in state court, found not guilty of the charges against them, and freed. However, they were brought back into the system at the federal level. Federal charges of civil rights violations were filed

figure 1.2

The Picket Fence Model of the Criminal Justice System

Local, state, and federal governments are separate but are linked by common activities, goals, and interests. In this model, the horizontal "boards" represent the various levels of government. Each is separate, but vertical "pickets" join them. (Note that the horizontal boards are not equal in size; local government performs the majority of criminal justice activities.) Examples of the links joining levels of government include federal funding, which may link local and state programs to the federal government; combined efforts to combat terrorism or other special tasks; the system of appeals by which a municipal court case could be appealed all the way to the U.S. Supreme Court; and projects such as prison reform, community policing, delinquency and gang outreach, and drugs and organized crime.

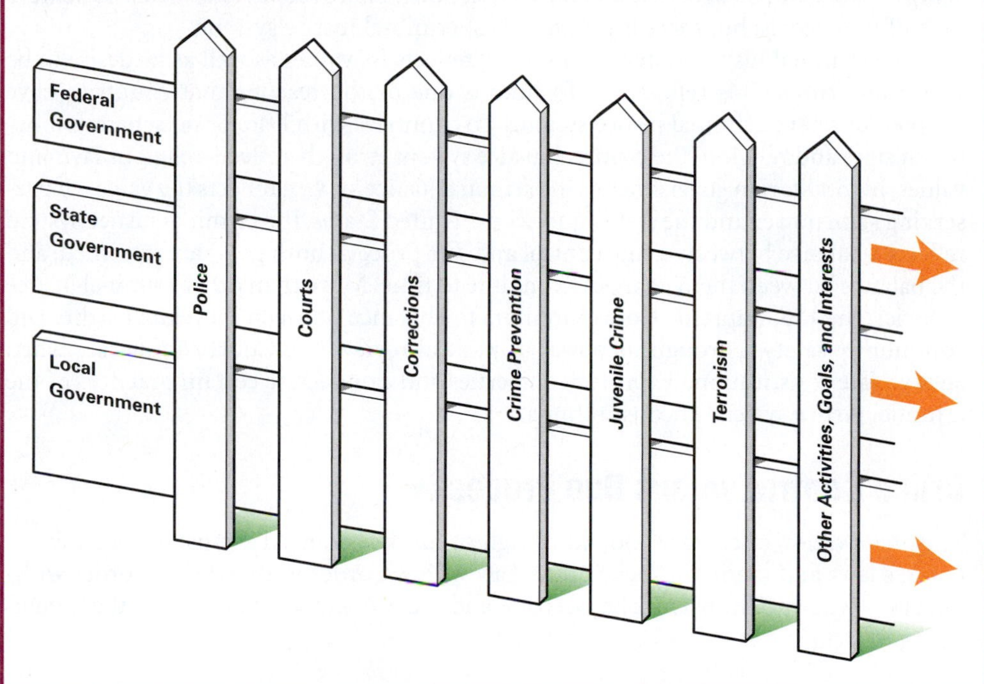

against these officers, and they were arrested, tried, and convicted of these federal charges.

No agency or person oversees the status of an offender's process through the criminal justice system. Rather, each agency processes people through their part of the system independently, which often results in bottlenecks. Aggressive police strategies resulting in a significant increase in arrests for drunk driving can overwhelm the court's ability to process the increased number of cases. A get-tough sentencing philosophy can result in many more inmates than the prisons can house. There is no "traffic cop" to direct the flow and process of people through the criminal justice system.

check your understanding 1.3 **Why is the model of the criminal justice system more like a picket fence than a wedding cake? What agencies and processes do the vertical and horizontal boards in the picket fence model represent?**

Criminal Justice Models

the main idea 1.4 The criminal justice system has the goals of both crime control and due process. These goals sometimes conflict with each other.

The criminal justice system has more than one purpose. One of the primary purposes is to provide for the orderly interaction of citizens in a complex society. The criminal justice system also has the goal of promoting socially approved behaviors, morals, and values. Another goal is to provide an environment that promotes commerce by encouraging honesty and trust in commercial transactions. There are various means to achieve each of these goals, but there is no single best criminal justice system.

The criminal justice system of a society reflects its values as well as its desire to be safe from crime. This reflection of values is one of the reasons that countries have adopted different criminal justice systems. In countries with little or no separation between state and religion, the criminal justice system strongly reflects religious laws and values. In totalitarian governments, the criminal justice system reflects the values of preserving state power and the status quo. In the United States, the criminal justice system reflects a balance between crime control and due process; both goals are esteemed, and the balance between them changes from time to time. More than other criminal justice agencies, the U.S. Supreme Court monitors the balance between individual rights and community safety. Through its power of judicial review, the Court can declare when laws violate constitutionally protected liberties and can declare certain practices of the criminal justice system unconstitutional.

Crime Control versus Due Process

The preservation of citizens' individual rights must be balanced against the necessity to enforce laws and maintain social order. Law without order is anarchy, but order without law is tyranny. The balance between law and order resembles a pendulum that swings

During the years that Earl Warren was chief justice of the U.S. Supreme Court, there was a great emphasis on due process, even at the expense of crime control. During this era, court decisions such as *Mapp* v. *Ohio, Gideon* v. *Wainwright,* and *Miranda* v. *Arizona* ushered in a new era of due process rights. Similar decisions extended this protection of individual rights to juveniles, prisoners, probationers, and parolees. How do the crime control and due process models of criminal justice differ?

back and forth between the two values. For example, in the western frontier in the late 1800s, there was minimum concern for due process: Justice was quick, simple, and often violent. At times, justice was carried out by the courts, but at other times citizens took justice into their own hands. Concern for due process swung to its most liberal extent in the 1960s and then back to the right again with the "law and order" platform on which Richard Nixon based his campaign for the presidency. In that period of social unrest, many people were receptive to the promise of crime control, community safety, and swift—preferably harsh—justice for the offender. This emphasis on efficient and effective justice is known as the **crime control model.**

The United States is a representative form of democracy and as such, the values of individual liberty and pursuit of happiness are considered as important as crime control. Crime control cannot be achieved at the expense of constitutionally protected liberties. The emphasis on ensuring that individuals are protected from arbitrary and excessive abuse of power by the government is known as **due process**. Due process means that in the quest for crime control, the government is bound to follow certain rules and procedures. Even if a person is guilty, if the government does not follow the rules and procedures in obtaining a conviction, the courts can void the conviction.

The basic source of due process rights is the U.S. Constitution and the Bill of Rights, both of which guarantee protections against unreasonable searches, forced and self-incriminating testimony, excessive bail and fines, and cruel or unusual punishment, as well as rights to a speedy public trial by jury. Other due process rights have been crafted by court rulings and rules of evidence, including the right to an attorney to represent a defendant in a serious criminal case, the right to be treated equally before the court, and the right to be informed of one's rights.

The combined emphasis on crime control and due process results in a criminal justice process that is slow, contradictory, and oriented toward protecting the rights of the accused as opposed to securing justice for the victim. This orientation guards against abuse of power by police, prosecutors, courts, and corrections at the expense of swift and sure justice for the victim. This decision is a deliberate choice, not an accidental characteristic of the criminal justice system. By insisting that the government operate within certain limitations in securing the conviction of the accused, citizens are protected against the misuse of the enormous power of the government, which could be brought to bear in prosecuting the individual. Thus, justice may be delayed—or even denied—in favor of protecting the due process rights of the accused. It is better that a guilty person should escape the punishment of justice than an innocent person should be wrongfully punished. As mentioned earlier, this value stems from the mistrust of a strong, centralized government held by early leaders of this country.

The central premise of the criminal justice due process model is the **presumption of innocence.** Regardless of overwhelming evidence against the accused, the court proceeds on the presumption that until the guilt of the accused is proven beyond a reasonable doubt in a court of law, the defendant will be treated as if he or she were not guilty of the charges. The crime control model, on the other hand, has the opposite presumption: If common sense and evidence clearly indicate guilt, the accused awaiting trial should be treated as such for the protection of the community. In the crime control perspective, community safety and quality of life are threatened by pretending that a career burglar, serial rapist, or pedophile is not guilty until proven guilty when the evidence clearly suggests otherwise.

Because the criminal justice system is subject to political influence, it is not surprising that political party labels have been applied to these two models. The due process model is frequently associated with liberals, and the crime control model is identified with conservatives. Attitudes toward crime can take on political significance, especially during election campaigns. In addition, as in the nation's two-party system, the criminal justice system shifts back and forth between the two models. Factors such as prosperity, low crime rates, and the absence of media coverage of horrific and frightening crimes promote more concern over due process issues such as equality, justice,

crime control model Model of the criminal justice system in which emphasis is placed on fighting crime and protecting potential victims.

due process Rules and procedures for protecting individuals accused of crimes from arbitrary and excessive abuse of power by the government.

presumption of innocence Most important principle of the due process model, requiring that all accused persons are treated as innocent until proven guilty in a court of law.

The U.S. Supreme Court has ruled that regardless of the public's fear of street beggars, their actions are protected by the First Amendment. Despite this ruling, some police departments continue to enforce prohibitions against begging that may be unconstitutional. Beggars can be regulated but they cannot be completely banned from public places. However, it is difficult to legislate when, where, and how begging can be conducted. What actions by street beggars should be prohibited? What public places should they be prohibited from begging?

and human dignity. However, rising crime rates, an economic downturn, or sensational media coverage of a ghastly crime can cause the public to demand quicker police response, tougher sentencing, and less concern for the rights of the accused.

Adult versus Juvenile Criminal Justice Process

The criminal justice system has separated the processing of adults and juveniles. At the beginning of the twentieth century, the American criminal justice system crafted a separate and unique system for juvenile justice. Although utilizing many of the same criminal justice agencies and concepts as the adult criminal justice system, the juvenile justice system is significantly different.

Under most circumstances juveniles who are less than 18 years old are processed by the juvenile criminal justice system. Juveniles who commit particularly appalling violent crimes or whose repetitive involvement in serious crime suggests that they and community safety are no longer served by the juvenile justice system can be waived to the adult criminal justice system.

The mission of the juvenile justice system emphasizes rehabilitation and restorative justice rather than punishment and retribution. The juvenile justice system avoids the use of terms such as *arrest, trial, guilt,* and *sentencing.* Juveniles are not arrested but are processed into the system by "intake" officers. Juveniles have hearings without juries. Juvenile hearings are closed to the public and the media. Until recently, juveniles were not even permitted to be represented by an attorney. Juveniles are not found guilty by a jury; their cases are **adjudicated** (i.e., their cases are decided by a judge). Juveniles do not serve time for offenses they commit; they are remanded to the custody of the state for rehabilitation. The operating premise of the juvenile justice system is that the juvenile can be rehabilitated and reintegrated into society.

adjudicated A court case is decided without determination of guilt, especially in juvenile court, when a judge places a juvenile in the custody of the state for treatment or confinement.

The juvenile justice system has its own court system and criminal justice agencies dedicated to processing juveniles through the justice system. There is no separate police for juveniles, but many police departments have identified police officers who specialize in juvenile crime and offenders and work closely with the juvenile courts. Juveniles are not

careers in the system

Juvenile Probation Officers

Juvenile probation officers are the backbone of the juvenile criminal justice system. The job responsibilities of the juvenile probation officer are diverse, including "police-like" supervision of court-imposed probation terms; traditional probation services similar to those provided by adult probation officers; counseling; investigation; social work; and securing community resources for clients, including referrals to social service agencies, family counseling, substance abuse counseling, and mental health counseling.

Juvenile probation officers work with juveniles as well as adults because often the juvenile probation officer must work with the juveniles' parents or guardians. Juvenile probation officers often must interact with potentially violent youths who could pose harm to themselves or others and must conduct home visits in neighborhoods that may pose a risk of injury to the officer. The ability of juvenile probation officers to carry weapons is quite diverse. Some jurisdictions do not permit them to carry any type of weapon; others allow them to carry intermediate weapons such as mace or batons; and other jurisdictions allow juvenile probation officers to carry firearms.

The juvenile probation officer's employer may be the county, the judicial district (e.g., they work for the district court), or a central state office. As a result of the various possibility of employers, the salary, conditions of work, and opportunities for advancement vary greatly from employer to employer. Generally, juvenile probation officers will make from $30,000 to $50,000. Salaries tend to be higher in large urban court districts and state juvenile service offices. Federal juvenile probation officers tend to make higher salaries than most county juvenile probation officers, but there are few federal probation officer positions open and they tend to be filled by persons with previous experience.

Advancement opportunities will be determined to a large degree by the size of the juvenile probation office. In small offices with a limited number of employees, there may be virtually no advancement opportunities beyond immediate supervisor of the juvenile probation officers in the office. Most juvenile probation positions require a bachelor's degree. Often, the degree can be from a variety of disciplines, including counseling, criminal justice, criminology, psychology, social work, or related degrees in the social sciences. It is not uncommon for juvenile probation officers to have a master's degree, which may be required for advancement.

Prior experience in casework, counseling, community or group work in a social service, corrections, or juvenile agency may be required. Usually there is no pre-employment physical fitness testing or examination to pass to be eligible for the position. The position nearly always requires a valid driver's license because travel is a frequent job requirement.

Unlike police officers, agencies hire juvenile probation officers on an individual basis, not in cohorts. The physical requirements for the job usually require good health but are far less rigorous than those required for law enforcement. Often, probation officers are provided only with a few days or few weeks of training prior to employment. However, there may be a longer period of on-the-job training once hired.

The caseload of a juvenile probation officer will vary significantly depending on the employer. Typical caseloads are 30 to 50 juveniles but can be as high as 100 to 200. Burnout is a common occupational hazard for the new juvenile probation officer. He or she must work with an at-risk population often with inadequate resources and with little support from the child's family or school.

The juvenile's background may include physical, psychological, and sexual abuse. Juveniles may be trapped in gangs or abusive homes or suffer from substance dependency. Children may have been substance dependent since they were 11 years old. Most serious offenders have poor academic skills and are unlikely to graduate from high school or obtain skills that will allow them to compete in the job market for well-paying jobs. Some of the children are suicidal.

Under these conditions, many juvenile probation officers find that they cannot handle the stresses of the job and move to other employment. Others are spurred on by the challenge to rehabilitate the child and secure the resources necessary to "save" the child and work harder to achieve their goals. Generally, juvenile probation officers are more counselors than they are law enforcement agents. Persons interested in becoming a juvenile probation officer should have the aptitude and skills that would allow them to succeed as counselor and social worker.

How do the duties of juvenile probation officers differ from that of adult probation officers and police officers? What college courses would be of benefit to a juvenile probation officer?

permitted to be incarcerated with adult offenders at any time during the criminal justice process. Thus, there are separate correctional and rehabilitation agencies for juveniles.

Toward the end of the nineteenth century, the concept of ***parens patriae***, or "state as parent and guardian," began to become the predominant theme in structuring state agencies responsible for juveniles. For example, the adoption of legal reforms that granted the state the inherent right to assume custody of children and a codified assemblage of children's laws culminated in the creation of a separate children's court system in 1892.[27] Cook County (Chicago), Illinois, is recognized as the site of the first juvenile court. Established in 1899, the distinguishing characteristic of the Illinois juvenile court was the concept of **original jurisdiction**. Unlike other states that had separate courts for young offenders that were part of the criminal justice system, the Chicago juvenile court had exclusive jurisdiction over juveniles. That is to say, the juvenile court was the only court that had authority over juveniles. Juveniles could not be tried, for any offense, by the criminal court unless the juvenile court granted its permission for the accused juvenile to be moved from the authority of the juvenile court. This process was referred to as "waiving" the juvenile to the criminal court.

Furthermore, only the juvenile judge—not the prosecutor, the police, or the criminal court judge—had the authority to waive the juvenile to criminal court. The juvenile court was "self-contained," or "independent," in that it had its own intake process; in other words, it did not depend on the prosecutor to bring cases before the court. Also, it had its own probation and parole system and its own correctional system. The juvenile court did share the services of the police in that the court did not have its own law enforcement agents responsible for the detection and apprehension of juvenile offenders.

In addition to processing youthful offenders for criminal offenses, the Cook County juvenile court assumed total and in a sense "absolute" control over the juvenile. In exercising the right of *parens patriae,* the juvenile court assumed superior authority over the authority of the "natural" parents or guardian. The juvenile court was established not as a criminal court but as a government agency to provide youthful offenders and their victims with a comprehensive and balanced approach to justice.[28] The court operated on the principle of "the best interests of the child."[29] As a result, the court had original exclusive jurisdiction not only of children who had committed crimes but of any child whose welfare and well-being was in question. The philosophy underlying this authority was that "the delinquent child was also seen as in need of the court's benevolent intervention."[30]

Juveniles are classified as status offenders or delinquents. **Status offenders** are children who have committed an act or failed to fulfill a responsibility that if they were adults the court would not have any authority over them. Common status offenses are failure to attend school, running away from parents or guardians, and engaging in behaviors while legal for adults is considered harmful for children.

Delinquents, on the other hand, are accused of committing an act that is criminal for both adults and juveniles. The criminal justice system divides crimes into felonies and misdemeanors, but there is no similar division in the juvenile court. Since the focus of the court is on the welfare of the child, there is less concern about serious versus minor offenses, as such concern focuses on the punishment for the offense and not on the welfare of the offender. Further, the authority of the juvenile court is time limited. Felonies have sentences of 5, 10, 20 years or even life without parole. The juvenile court has custodial authority of the offender only during his or her youth. This limit has been defined differently by the various states. In some states, the custodial authority of the juvenile court extends until the offender is 18 years old; in other states, the juvenile court may retain custodial authority until the offender is 23 years old. With such limited custodial authority it would not be possible for the court to impose lengthy sentences as punishment. Thus, the distinction between misdemeanor crimes and felony crimes is not as pivotal in juvenile court as in the criminal justice system. Hence, a juvenile delinquent is a person under the authority of the juvenile court who has committed an offense that if

parens patriae Legal assumption that the state has primary responsibility for the safety and custody of children.

original jurisdiction When the juvenile court is the only court that has authority over juveniles. Juveniles cannot be tried, for any offense, by the criminal court unless the juvenile court grants its permission for the accused juvenile to be waived to criminal court.

status offenders Children who have committed an act or failed to fulfill a responsibility that if they were adults the court would not have any authority over them.

delinquents Juveniles accused of committing an act that is criminal for both adults and juveniles.

he or she were an adult would be considered criminal. Therefore, the term *juvenile delinquent* can fail to clearly identify the nature of the offender's crime. Juvenile delinquents include offenders who have committed petty crimes such as theft, vandalism, and simple assault (or fighting); the classification also includes offenders who have committed robbery, rape, and murder. However, in 2000, the Office of Juvenile Justice Delinquency and Prevention sought to identify juveniles who had committed more serious crimes. They used the term *juvenile superpredators* to identify juvenile delinquents who engage in serious violent crime.

Each state has established its own juvenile court system. Thus, there is great variety in the names of the agencies as well as the mission and the operational philosophy of each state **juvenile court.** Despite these differences among the states, a clear distinction emerges between a state's juvenile court and its criminal court. Table 1.1 summarizes the comparison of the two systems. There are eight points of comparison. The first of these points of comparisons is the *operating assumptions* of each of the systems. The juvenile justice system is founded on a mission statement that emphasizes rehabilitation as the primary goal, whereas rehabilitation is not the primary mission statement of the criminal justice system. The criminal justice system is based on the assumption that sanctions and punishment may result in rehabilitation. The second point of comparison is the emphasis on *prevention.* The juvenile justice system strives to stop the offender from committing future delinquent or criminal acts. Ideally, if the juvenile court achieves its mission, the offender would never end up in criminal court, as his or her criminal behavior would be extinguished. The criminal justice system has no such comparable mission but it does recognize the importance of education and prevention as a strategy for crime reduction. Third, although both the juvenile system and the criminal court system use *law enforcement* as the primary means of detecting and bringing offenders to the court, there is a significant difference in how the police perform their tasks for each of the systems. Numerous restrictions are placed on the police in their dealing with juvenile offenders. For example, the police are restricted in the information they can release about juvenile offenders and must provide prescribed standards of care in the apprehension of juveniles. Fourth, the juvenile court decides what cases to file, whereas the prosecutor plays a key role in bringing cases before the court in the criminal court. In Table 1.1 this is referred to as *intake and prosecution.* Fifth, although both systems desire to protect the public from dangerous offenders prior to trial, the pretrial *detention* of juveniles has standards different from the criminal justice system. Sixth is *adjudication and conviction.* Both systems provide for an examination of the facts of a case by a judge, but the juvenile event is significantly different from the criminal trial. Juveniles do not have the right of trial by jury and the juvenile court proceedings are "quasi-civil," not criminal. Further, juvenile court proceedings are not public proceedings. Seventh, perhaps one of the most obvious differences between the two systems is in the *disposition* of juveniles and the *sentencing* of criminal offenders. The mission of the court is to rehabilitate—not punish—the juvenile offender. As a result, a wide range of dispositional alternatives are available for the juvenile judge. Finally, although both systems provide for various forms of probation and parole, *aftercare* is a key component of the juvenile justice system. The reintegration of the juvenile into society, family, school, and work is a primary mission of the juvenile justice system.

The Office of Juvenile Justice and Delinquency Prevention provides many resources on juvenile justice. To view OJJDP's homepage, go to www.ojjdp.ncjrs.org.

In the beginning, the juvenile court operated without much review by the courts. Unlike the criminal justice system, both state supreme courts and the United States Supreme Court did not provide significant review and oversight of the juvenile justice court. The Supreme Court essentially adopted a **"hands-off" policy** similar to its view of prisoner rights for adults prior to the Warren Court. Juvenile jurisdiction extended well beyond the jurisdiction exercised over adults by the criminal courts. As such, juveniles were effectively denied the rights afforded under the equal protection clause of the Fourteenth Amendment. The justification for this exclusion was that the juvenile received less due process but the court demonstrated a greater concern for the interests of the juvenile. Essentially the view underlying the position of the Court was that operating

juvenile court A court that handles juvenile welfare cases and cases involving status offenders and delinquents. Some juvenile courts may handle additional matters related to the family.

table 1.1

Comparison of State Juvenile Courts and Criminal Courts

Although the juvenile and criminal justice systems are more alike in some jurisdictions than in others, generalizations can be made about the distinctions between the two systems and about their common ground

Juvenile Justice System	Common Ground	Criminal Justice System
Operating Assumptions		
• Youth behavior is malleable. • Rehabilitation is usually a viable goal. • Youth are in families and not independent.	• Community protection is a primary goal. • Law violators must be held accountable. • Constitutional rights apply.	• Sanctions should be proportional to the offense. • General deterrence works. • Rehabilitation is not a primary goal.
Prevention		
• Many specific delinquency prevention activities (e.g., school, church, recreation) are used. • Prevention is intended to change individual behavior and is often focused on reducing risk factors and increasing protective factors in the individual, family, and community.	• Educational approaches are taken to specific behaviors (drunk driving, drug use).	• Prevention activities are generalized and are aimed at deterrence (e.g., Crime Watch).
Law Enforcement		
• Specialized "juvenile" units are used. • Some additional behaviors are prohibited (truancy, running away, curlew violations). • Some limitations are placed on public access to information. • A significant number of youth are diverted away from the juvenile justice system, often into alternative programs.	• Jurisdiction involves the full range of criminal behavior. • Constitutional and procedural safeguards exist. • Both reactive and proactive approaches (targeted at offense types, neighborhoods, etc.) are used. • Community policing strategies are employed.	• Open public access to all information is required. • Law enforcement exercises discretion to divert offenders out of the criminal justice system.
Intake—Prosecution		
• In many instances, juvenile court intake, not the prosecutor, decides what cases to file. • The decision to file a petition for court action is based on both social and legal factors. • A significant portion of cases are diverted from formal case processing. • Intake or the prosecutor diverts cases from formal processing to services operated by the juvenile court, prosecutor's office, or outside agencies.	• Probable cause must be established. • The prosecutor acts on behalf of the State.	• Plea bargaining is common. • The prosecution decision is based largely on legal facts. • Prosecution is valuable in building history for subsequent offenses. • Prosecution exercises discretion to withhold charges or divert offenders out of the criminal justice system.
Detention—Jail/lockup		
• Juveniles may be detained for their own protection or the community's protection. • Juveniles may not be confined with adults unless there is "sight and sound separation."	• Accused offenders may be held in custody to ensure their appearance in court. • Detention alternatives of home or electronic detention are used.	• Accused individuals have the right to apply for bond/bail release.

table 1.1

(Continued)

Juvenile Justice System	Common Ground	Criminal Justice System
Adjudication—Conviction		
• Juvenile court proceedings are "quasi-civil" (not criminal) and may be confidential. • If guilt is established, the youth is adjudicated delinquent regardless of offense. • Right to jury trial is not afforded in all States.	• Standard of "proof beyond a reasonable doubt" is required. • Rights to be represented by an attorney, to confront witnesses, and to remain silent are afforded. • Appeals to a higher court are allowed. • Experimentation with specialized courts (i.e., drug courts, gun courts) is under way.	• Defendants have a constitutional right to a jury trial. • Guilt must be established on individual offenses charged for conviction. • All proceedings are open.
Disposition—Sentencing		
• Disposition decisions are based on individual and social factors, offense severity, and youth's offense history. • Dispositional philosophy includes a significant rehabilitation component. • Many dispositional alternatives are operated by the juvenile court. • Dispositions cover a wide range of community-based and residential services. • Disposition orders may be directed to people other than the offender (e.g., parents). • Disposition may be indeterminate, based on progress demonstrated by the youth.	• Decisions are influenced by current offense, offending history, and social factors. • Decisions hold offenders accountable. • Decisions may give consideration in victims (e.g., restitution and "no contact" orders). • Decisions may not be cruel or unusual.	• Sentencing decisions are bound primarily by the severity of the current offense and by the offender's criminal history. • Sentencing philosophy is based largely on proportionality and punishment. • Sentence is often determinate, based on offense.
Aftercare—Parole		
• Function combines surveillance and reintegration activities (e.g., family, school, work).	• The behavior of individuals released from correctional settings is monitored. • Violation of conditions can result in reincarceration.	• Function is primarily surveillance and reporting to monitor illicit behavior.

Source: Howard N. Snyder and Melissa Sickmund, *Juvenile Offenders and Victims: 1999 National Report* (Washington, DC: Office of Juvenile Justice and Delinquency Prevention, NJC Document No. 178257, 1999), pp. 10–12.

under the doctrine of *parens patriae* the purpose of the court was not to punish the juvenile but to provide "solicitous care and regenerative treatment."[31]

During the 1960s, the Supreme Court abandoned its "hands-off" doctrine and began to examine the need for due process rights for juveniles. In a series of decisions the Supreme Court radically redefined the due process rights of juveniles. Figure 1.3 presents an overview of juvenile due process decisions.

The adult criminal justice system has been shaped and influenced by extensive Supreme Court rulings, legislation, and oversight by the public and media. As a result, it is possible to provide a general overview of the adult criminal justice system that fairly accurately reflects the processing of adult offenders among the various states. However, the juvenile justice system is much more diverse. Although Supreme Court decisions have provided more commonality in the due process rights of juveniles, the actual processing, the agencies, and the personnel involved in moving a juvenile from intake to rehabilitation

figure 1.3

Overview of Juvenile Due Process Supreme Court Decisions

A series of U.S. Supreme Court decisions made juvenile courts more like criminal courts but maintained some important differences.

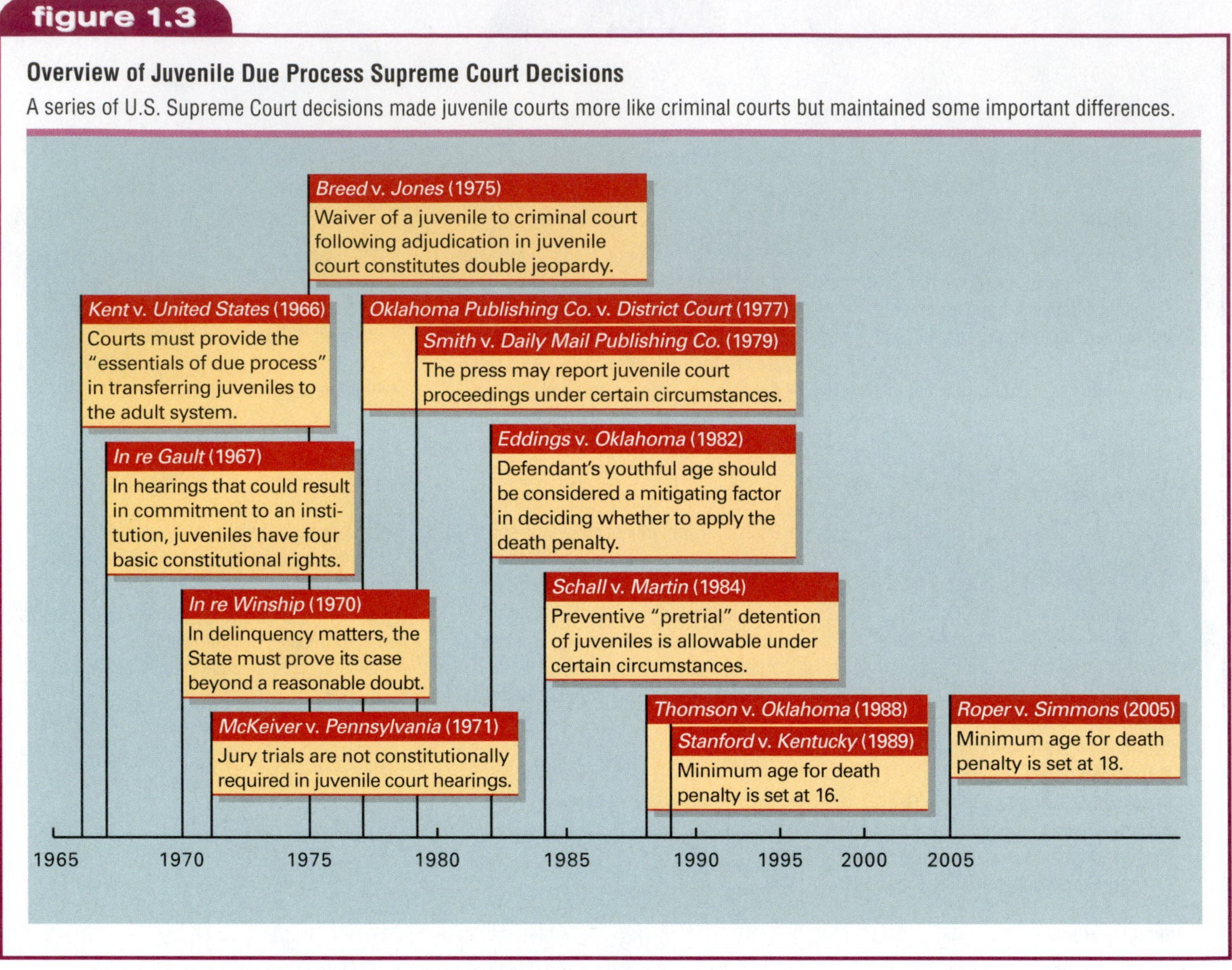

Source: Adapted from *Juvenile Offenders and Victims: 1999 National Report* (Washington, DC: Office of Juvenile Justice and Delinquency Prevention, 1999).

differs from state to state. In a sense, there is no one juvenile justice system but a collection of juvenile justice systems. Each state has a unique procedure for processing juveniles. How juveniles are processed through the system depends a great deal on which state and sometimes which geographical region of the state the juvenile court is located.

The unique nature of the juvenile system of each state provides some difficulty in generalizing the case flow through the juvenile justice system. The case flow for each state differs and the names of the various agencies, courts, detention facilities, and aftercare services are not consistent from state to state. Figure 1.4, which shows a general diagram of the processing of a case through the juvenile justice system, may not be a good representation of the case flow in each state. However, it does provide a general overview of the processing of juveniles from intake to disposition.

Juveniles were not always separated from adults in the criminal justice system. In fact, the separation of juveniles and adults is a relatively new practice, dating back only to 1899. The purpose of the juvenile court is to protect the young offender from the criminal justice system's tendency to impose sanctions rather than rehabilitation and is based on the premise that the young offender does not have the same criminal intent as the adult offender. Also, the juvenile justice system is based on the premise that the young offender can be rehabilitated and that society would be better served by rehabilitating children rather than punishing them.

Recent events have caused some to give considerable thought to the functioning of the juvenile justice system. School shootings, gang violence, depraved killings, rape, and even accusations of juvenile suicide bombers have caused some to call for the examination of the principles on which the juvenile justice system is founded, the criminological theories that focus on the young offender, and the ability of the juvenile justice system to rehabilitate the offender and protect society from juvenile violence and mayhem.

Despite statistics that show otherwise, there is a public perception of a widespread violent juvenile crime wave that has had substantial influence on the juvenile justice system. Juvenile offenders are seen as a threat to be punished and incarcerated. Those who believe juvenile crime is "out of control" also believe that the juvenile justice system is perceived as an "easy out that gives a meaningless slap on the wrist to violent youth."[32] Thus, there are forces at work that continue to transform the juvenile justice system.

The concept of *double jeopardy* is designed to protect an individual from being subjected to the hazards of a trial and possible conviction more than once for an alleged offense. The concept is rooted in the early English courts and the history of its evolution and application in the United States is quite complex. See http://caselaw.lp.findlaw.com/data/constitution/amendment05/02.html for a discussion of the history of double jeopardy.

State versus Federal Criminal Justice Systems

There are two distinct criminal justice systems in the United States: the federal system and the state system. Each state has the autonomy to design its own criminal justice system. From state to state there are differences in each of the criminal justice systems. These differences are discussed in more detail in later chapters that focus on the various criminal justice agencies. The federal government has its own separate criminal justice system that

figure 1.4

The Juvenile Criminal Justice System

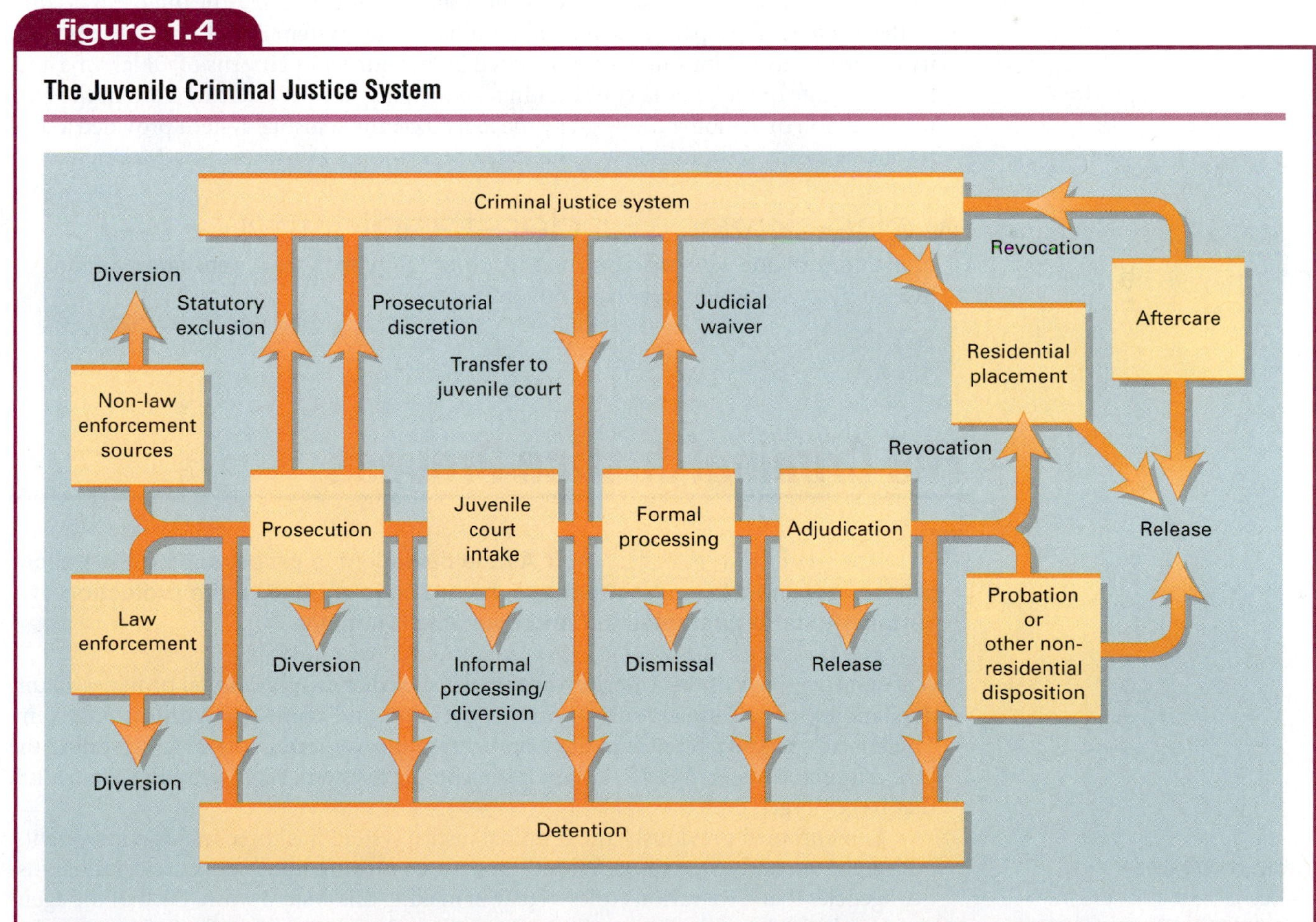

This chart gives a simplified view of caseflow through the juvenile justice system. Procedures vary among jurisdictions.

Source: Juvenile Offenders and Victims: 1999 National Report (Washington, DC: Office of Juvenile Justice and Delinquency Prevention, 1999).

is distinct from the state system. Thus, there is a system of federal police, courts, and correctional agencies that operates separately from state agencies. Both criminal justice systems are subject to the overview of the U.S. Supreme Court and resemble each other in the processes and agencies that define the system. However, it is important to note that the two systems are not interchangeable.

A defendant is processed into one or the other of these systems, depending on certain criteria regarding the offense committed, where it was committed, and by whom it was committed. For example, if a husband and a wife were to get into a domestic dispute and harm one another, normally this would be a matter for the local police and the state criminal justice system. However, if this event were to occur in a national park or on a federal reservation, federal police and federal courts would handle it. Military personnel and aircraft passengers who commit offenses are subject to federal jurisdiction. Native Americans living on reservation lands are subject to the jurisdiction of the Tribal Indian Police or the federal government. The criminal justice process for the federal and the state criminal justice systems is similar in terms of the processing of the offender through the particular system. The significant difference is that each system has its own personnel, process, and agencies for processing defendants through the system.

There are some offenses in which the defendant may be processed by both the federal and the state criminal justice systems. Some offenses are both federal and state offenses, and each system retains the right to prosecute the accused. In such cases, it is possible that the accused can be charged and processed through both systems. For example, Timothy McVeigh's offense against his victims in the bombing of the Oklahoma City federal building was both a federal and a state offense. Because the offense was committed on federal property, the federal criminal justice system could claim responsibility for prosecuting him. His actions resulted in the murder of citizens of Oklahoma and, thus, the state of Oklahoma could claim responsibility for prosecuting him. In the end, the execution of Timothy McVeigh by the federal criminal justice system provided a final resolve as to any responsibility of the state of Oklahoma in prosecuting McVeigh.

▲ check your understanding **1.4** **How do the crime control and due process models differ? Why is there a separate criminal justice system for adults and juveniles?**

The Criminal Justice Process

▼ the main idea **1.5** **As the defendant is processed by the police, prosecution, courts, and corrections, he or she is entitled to the protection of certain rights to guarantee fair and equitable treatment.**

A general overview of the American criminal justice **due process model** provides an understanding of the interaction—both cooperation and conflict—within the system. There is no specific reference in the Constitution nor is there a federal law defining the U.S. criminal justice process. Rather, it is a complex system, represented in Figure 1.5, that has emerged over time.

due process model
Model of the criminal justice system in which emphasis is placed on protecting the rights of the accused.

As mentioned previously, the criminal justice system has three major components: police, courts, and corrections. Within these three major components are criminal justice agencies that have various roles to play in making this system work. Each of the agencies is independent, but they must work together. Each has a limited role in processing the defendant, and the system has a built-in process for moving offenders from the police to the courts to corrections. Six major processes in the criminal justice system are (1)

figure 1.5

The Criminal Justice System

This is a model of the sequence of events in the criminal justice system produced by various Commissions charged with studying the criminal justice system. It is a model of the *typical* sequence of events and does not accurately reflect the actual process in each state. The actual criminal justice process may differ from this model in that in some states the bail hearing is the first hearing or the Grand Jury process is different from what is shown in this model.

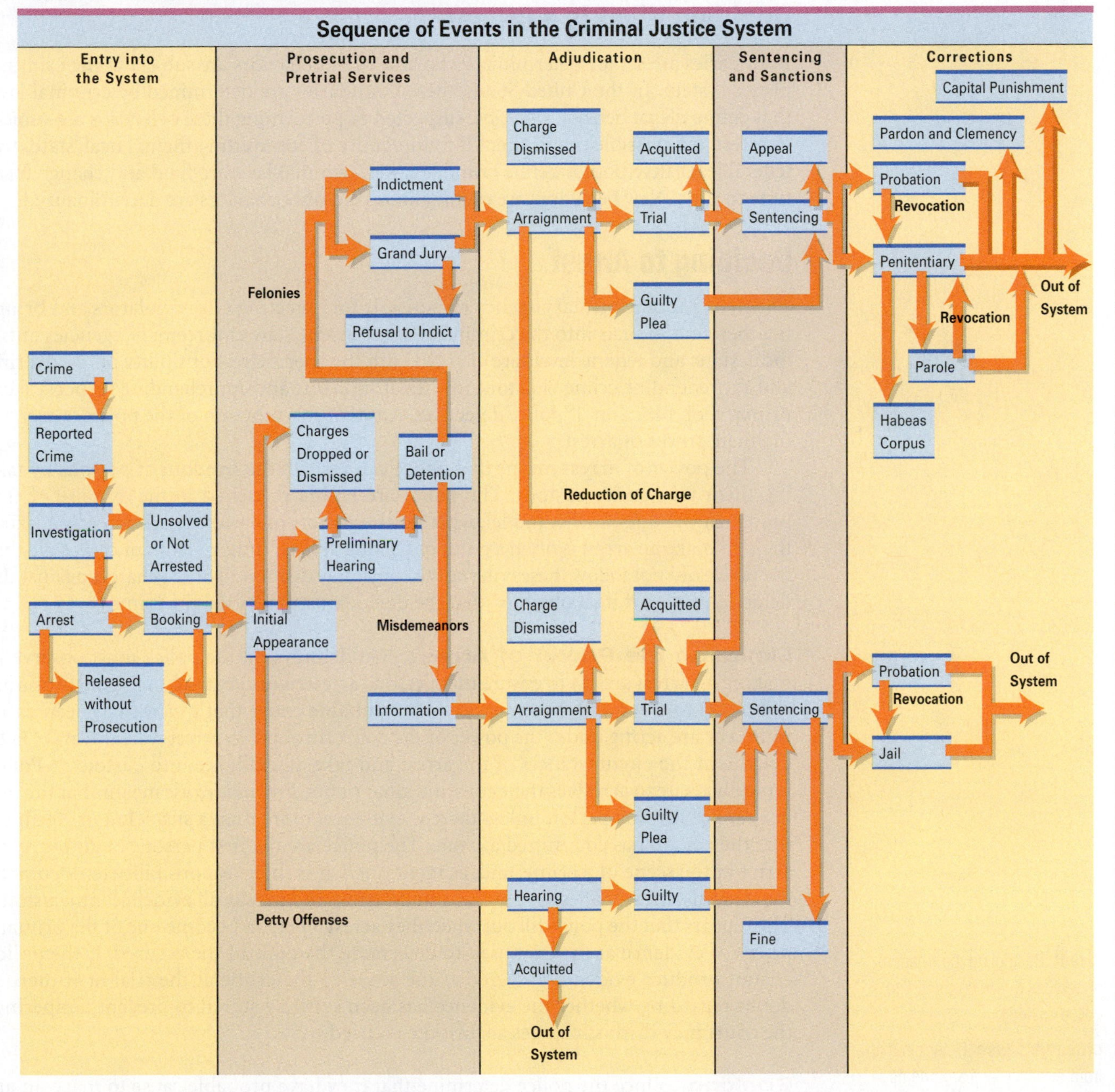

deciding what is a crime, (2) detecting a crime and arresting a suspect, (3) determining whether the accused is to go to trial, (4) determining guilt, (5) deciding on a punishment for the convicted, and (6) administering the prescribed punishment (carrying out the sentence). Remember, the description of the process of the criminal justice system differs significantly from state to state (and between state and federal). The process described in this text will not accurately reflect the criminal justice process in all states.

Deciding What Is a Crime

Boundaries are set for determining who and what behaviors are subject to the criminal justice system. In the United States, these boundaries are determined by criminal laws that define illegal behaviors. People suspected of performing these behaviors are subject to arrest and possible punishment if found guilty of committing them. Local, state, and federal legislative bodies define criminal laws. Criminal laws are fluid and change from time to time. New behaviors are criminalized, and old behaviors are decriminalized.

Deciding to Arrest

The police are the primary agency responsible for detecting crime violators and bringing these individuals into the criminal justice system. Law enforcement agencies at the local, state, and federal levels are charged with the specific responsibility of discovering and apprehending crime violators. Investigating crime and apprehending suspects is the primary job function of police detectives. Another job function of the police is exercising their power of arrest.

The power of **arrest** means that police can restrict the freedom of persons by taking them into police custody. The police are highly regulated in the exercise of this power. In the due process model, whether the police followed the criteria authorizing them to make an arrest is often a point of serious debate. If the defendant can prove that the police did not follow these criteria, the court may dismiss all of the charges against the defendant, even if it is "obvious" that the defendant committed the crime.[33]

Limits on the Power of Arrest Guidelines that the police must observe in making an arrest are (1) to ensure that persons arrested understand their constitutional rights, (2) to arrest only when police have **probable cause** that a crime has been committed or are acting under the power of the court through an arrest warrant, and (3) to document the circumstances of the arrest and take all evidence into custody.[34] Police typically recite to arrestees their constitutional rights. *Probable cause* means that the police cannot arrest a person unless there is evidence, more than a suspicion or "feeling," that the person has committed a crime. The police are the first persons of authority to arrive at the scene of a crime, and, as mentioned, it is their responsibility to document the circumstances that existed at the time of arrest and to take all evidence into custody. The reports that the police fill out when they arrest a person become one of the primary pieces of evidence at the trial used to determine the guilt of the accused. If the police cannot produce evidence gathered at the scene of the crime at the trial or if there is doubt regarding whether the evidence has been securely stored to prevent tampering, the court may dismiss charges against the accused.

Booking Once the police determine that they have probable cause to make an arrest or arrest a person through the power of an arrest warrant, they must process that person so that he or she may be forwarded on to the next step in the criminal justice system—determining if the accused will stand trial. The way they do this is to complete formal paperwork that (1) establishes the identity of the person and (2) charges the person with a specific violation of the criminal law. **Booking** is the procedure that acts as the transition point for moving the arrested person from the police department into the jurisdiction of the court.

arrest Restricting the freedom of persons by taking them into police custody.

probable cause Determination from evidence and arguments that there are valid reasons for believing that the accused has committed a crime.

booking Police activity that establishes the identification of an arrested person and formally charges that person with a crime.

If the identity of arrestees cannot reliably be established, the police are empowered to hold them in booking until their identities can be established. People who refuse to identify themselves are booked as "John Doe" or "Jane Doe," and the police attempt to establish their identities by fingerprint match. Identification is a critical factor in law enforcement. Fingerprint databases frequently match persons booked for minor offenses with outstanding warrants on more serious charges, and they often match persons booked in one state with crimes committed in other states. What are the other steps in bringing a suspect to trial?

Police transport the arrested person to a booking facility, where the arrestee may be detained for up to two days. At the booking facility, the police establish positive identification of the person arrested, cross-checking social security number, driver's license number, and date of birth with the physical appearance of the person to determine that the arrestee is properly identified. Photographs and fingerprints are taken of the arrested person, and these fingerprints may be checked against those stored in law enforcement databases. Once identity is established, other local, state, federal, and international law enforcement agencies are contacted to check to see if there are any outstanding warrants for the arrest of the person booked.

While the booking facility is establishing the identity of the arrestee, the arresting officer consults with supervisors, detectives, and perhaps the prosecuting attorney regarding the charges to be filed against the person. In making an arrest report, it is common for the police to charge the person with multiple offenses, beginning with the most serious offense. An example of an arrest report is presented in Figure 1.6.

After the allowed 48 hours of detention have elapsed, police must formally charge the person with a crime or release him or her. If the police release the person without filing charges, they may rearrest that person at a later time for the same offense when they feel they have more substantial evidence. If police formally charge a suspect with a crime, the person is moved to the next step in the criminal justice process.

Deciding to Prosecute

In this next step of the due process model, the prosecuting attorney reviews the charges filed by the police and the supporting evidence collected. If the prosecutor does not believe there is sufficient evidence to justify the charges, he or she can refuse to accept the case from the police, in which case the police may be liable for a civil lawsuit for false arrest. If the prosecutor accepts the case, the defendant is processed further in a preliminary hearing and arraignment, beginning with the first appearance.

figure 1.6

COMMONWEALTH OF PENNSYLVANIA
COUNTY OF: ______________________

POLICE CRIMINAL COMPLAINT

Magisterial District Number:
District Justice Name:
Address:

Telephone:

COMMONWEALTH OF PENNSYLVANIA
VS.

DEFENDANT: NAME and ADDRESS

Docket No.:
Date Filed:
OTN:

Defendant's Race Ethnicity ☐ White ☐ Asian ☐ Black ☐ Hispanic ☐ Native American ☐ Unknown	Defendant's Sex ☐ Female ☐ Male	Defendant's D.O.B.	Defendant's Social Security Number	Defendant's SIO (State Identification Number)

Defendant's A.K.A. (Also known as)	Defendant's Vehicle Information Plate Number State	Registration Sticker (MM/YY)	Defendant's Driver's License Number State

Complaint/Incident Number	Complaint/Incident Number if other Participants	UCR/NIBRS Code

District Attorney's Office ☐ Approved ☐ Disapproved because: ______________________

(The district attorney may require that the complaint, arrest warrant affidavit, or both be approved by the attorney for the Commonwealth prior to filing Pa.R.Cr.P. 107.)

(Name of Attorney for Commonwealth - Please Print or Type) (Signature of Attorney for Commonwealth) (Date)

I, ______________________
(Name of Affiant - Please Print or Type) (Officer Badge Number / I.D.)

of ______________________
(Identify Department or Agency Represented and Political Subdivision) (Police Agency ORI Number) (Orginating Agency Case Number (OCA))

do hereby state: (check appropriate box)

1. ☐ I accuse the above named defendant, who lives at the address set forth above
   ☐ I accuse the defendant whose name is unknown to me but who is described as ______________________

   ☐ I accuse the defendant whose name and popular designation or nickname is unknown to me and whom I have therefore designated as John Doe

   with violating the penal laws of the Commonwealth of Pennsylvania at ______________________
   (Place-Political Subdivision)

   in ______________________ County on or about ______________________

   Participants were: (if there were participants, place their names here, repeating the name of above defendant)

2. The acts committed by the accused were:
   (Set forth a summary of the facts sufficient to advise the defendant of the nature of the offense charged. A citation to the statute allegedly violated, without more, is not sufficient. In a summary case, you must cite the specific section and subsection of the statute or ordinance allegedly violated.

(continued)

Police Arrest Report

Each police agency has its own type of arrest report, but all such forms are similar in that on the arrest report, the police officer must clearly identify the defendant and accuse him or her of a specific crime. In the arrest report, the officer must explain what the defendant did that caused the arrest. The district attorney's office will review the arrest report and either approve or deny it. The district attorney's office may choose to dismiss all charges, to accept some of the charges, or to charge the defendant with other crimes. The police officer must have knowledge of the law to properly identify the various elements of the crime.

(Continuation of No. 2)

POLICE CRIMINAL COMPLAINT

Defendant's Name:
Docket Number:

all of which were against the peace and dignity of the Commonwealth of Pennsylvania and contrary to the Act of Assembly, or in violation of

1. ________ (Section) ________ (Subsection) of the ________ (PA Statute) ________ (counts)
2. ________ (Section) ________ (Subsection) of the ________ (PA Statute) ________ (counts)
3. ________ (Section) ________ (Subsection) of the ________ (PA Statute) ________ (counts)
4. ________ (Section) ________ (Subsection) of the ________ (PA Statute) ________ (counts)

3. I ask that a warrant of arrest or a summons be issued and that the defendant be required to answer the charges I have made. **(In order for a warrant of arrest to issue, the attached affidavit of probable cause must be completed and sworn to before the issuing authority.)**

4. I verify that the facts set forth in this complaint are true and correct to the best of my knowledge or information and belief. This verification is made subject to the penalties of Section 4904 of the Crimes Code (18 PA. C.S. § 4904) relating to unsworn falsification to authorities.

________________________, ____ ________________________ (Signature of Affiant)

AND NOW, on this date ________________________, ____, I certify that the complaint has been properly completed and verified. An affidavit of probable cause must be completed in order for a warrant to issue.

(Continued)

figure 1.6

Police Arrest Report *(Continued)*

POLICE CRIMINAL COMPLAINT

Defendant's Name:
Docket Number:

AFFIDAVIT of PROBABLE CAUSE

I, ____, BEING DULY SWORN ACCORDING TO LAW, DEPOSE AND SAY THAT THE FACTS SET FORTH IN THE FOREGOING AFFIDAVIT ARE TRUE AND CORRECT TO THE BEST OF MY KNOWLEDGE, INFORMATION, AND BELIEF.

____
(Signature of Affiant)

Sworn to me and subscribed before me this _________ day of ____________________, _____.

____________ Date ____, District Justice

Source: Commonwealth of Pennsylvania Police Criminal Complaint.

first appearance Judicial hearing before a magistrate, following booking. The magistrate judge reviews the charges, advises defendants of their rights, and sets bail.

First Appearance After the paperwork is forwarded to the prosecuting attorney, the accused is brought before a magistrate judge for a **first appearance.** Magistrate judges are judicial officers with authority to evaluate charges filed by police against the accused and determine if the charges are legitimate according to state statutes and federal laws. Magistrates also advise the accused of his or her legal rights and determine if the person has legal representation. When charges are filed that may result in a prison sentence of six months or more, the magistrate determines if the person has sufficient funds to obtain legal counsel. If it is determined that the accused cannot afford a lawyer, the court appoints an attorney to represent him or her at no charge.

Bail Finally, the magistrate decides if the person should be released on bail or held in a correctional facility until a later time. **Bail** is a promise, sometimes backed by a monetary guarantee, that the accused will return for further proceedings in the criminal justice system. Bail cannot be set before the first appearance because until that point, the actual charges against the person are not known. For minor charges, the amount of bail may be set by a schedule of established fees. Fees are usually based on the fine that typically is levied against the person if found guilty. The higher the fine for guilt, the greater the bail set by the magistrate. At the first appearance, the accused is not asked how he or she intends to plead (e.g., guilty or not guilty). Guilt is not yet an issue. The first appearance is concerned with due process and securing the rights of the accused, and it may take only a few minutes to complete the entire process.

Preliminary Hearing After charges are filed against the person in the first appearance, he or she moves to the next step in the criminal justice system. The **preliminary hearing** is sometimes referred to as a "probable cause" hearing, reflecting its purpose. At the preliminary hearing, the judge takes an active role in asking questions of the prosecution and the defendant.

In this hearing, it is the responsibility of the prosecution to convince the judge that there is probable cause to believe that (1) an offense as defined by the criminal laws of the jurisdiction has been committed within that jurisdiction and (2) the defendant accused of the offense committed it. The charges against the defendant may be changed from those charged at the first appearance. New charges can be added, and old charges can be dropped. The prosecution must specify the offense, the law it violated, and the date the offense was committed.

Defense counsel can challenge the evidence of the prosecution. If the prosecution cannot convince the judge that the evidence presented would cause a reasonable person to believe that the defendant committed the specific crime alleged, the judge has the authority to dismiss the charges against the defendant. If charges are dismissed, the prosecution may gather additional evidence and/or modify the charges and bring the defendant before the court again. If, on the other hand, the judge is convinced that a reasonable person would believe that the defendant committed the offense, the defendant proceeds to the next step in the criminal justice system: the arraignment. The issue of bail for the defendant can be raised again at the preliminary hearing. Bail can be raised, lowered, or revoked.

Information or Indictment An alternative method of bringing a person to trial is the grand jury system, the only secret judicial process in the criminal justice system. A **grand jury,** as the name implies, is a panel of citizens who are selected to hear evidence against an accused person. In many ways, a grand jury proceeding has the characteristics of a trial. It is held in a courtroom; a judge presides over the proceedings, and the prosecutor presents witnesses and evidence to convince the members of the grand jury that the defendant has committed an offense. The major difference is that defendants are not present at the sitting of the grand jury, cannot have an attorney represent them at the grand jury proceedings, and may not even be informed that they are the subjects of the grand jury's attention. Although some states have decided to allow defendants to be present, in many states defendants in a grand jury session do not know what charges have been filed against them and are not given a chance to rebut the evidence or deny the charges. After the grand jury session is over, the members of the grand jury are not allowed to discuss in public the cases and evidence they heard. The grand jury does not determine guilt. Rather, it fulfills the same purpose as the preliminary hearing: to determine if there is probable cause that the defendant committed the crime that the prosecution alleges.

If, after hearing the evidence of the prosecution, the grand jury believes there is probable cause that the defendant committed the crime, it returns an indictment against the defendant. An **indictment** is a formal, written legal document forwarded to the court,

bail Release of a defendant from custody on the promise, often secured with a monetary bond, that the defendant will return to court at the necessary times to address the charges.

preliminary hearing Hearing before a magistrate judge in which the prosecution presents evidence to convince the judge that there is probable cause to bring the defendant to trial.

grand jury Panel of citizens similar to a trial jury that decides whether there is probable cause to indict a defendant on the charges alleged.

indictment The formal verdict of the grand jury that there is sufficient evidence to bring a person to trial.

asserting that there is probable cause that the defendant committed an offense. This indictment authorizes the court to issue an arrest warrant for the defendant. The court delivers the arrest warrant to the prosecution, which delivers it to the police. Armed with this arrest warrant, the police have the authority to arrest the defendant. If the grand jury does not find probable cause that the defendant committed the crime, the prosecution cannot process the defendant into the criminal justice system. If the prosecution cannot obtain an indictment through the grand jury, it can use the preliminary hearing to bring the defendant to trial.

A grand jury indictment offers certain advantages because it can be sealed. If sealed, the decision of the grand jury remains secret and is not disclosed to the public or to the defendant. The arrest warrant that the court authorizes does not have to be served immediately. In cases in which there are multiple defendants, such as in drug trafficking or organized crime cases, the grand jury allows the prosecution and police to obtain indictments and arrest warrants against all of the defendants without tipping them off that they have been targeted for arrest and prosecution.

Arraignment An indictment by a grand jury does not establish the guilt of the defendant. It only provides the prosecution with the authority to process the defendant to the next step in the criminal justice system: the arraignment. The **arraignment** is the last step in determining if the defendant will go to trial. At the arraignment, the defendant appears before the court with his or her attorney to hear the formal charges that the prosecution alleges. These charges may differ substantially from the charges initially filed by the police. A charge of first-degree murder may be reduced to homicide. Burglary may be reduced to trespassing. Multiple counts and multiple charges against the defendant may be reduced to a single charge. A defendant accused of a dozen burglaries may be charged with only one. A defendant accused of killing four people may be charged with the murder of only one.

The reason for reducing charges to the one for which there is the best evidence is to reduce the likelihood of having to change charges later in the process. After arraignment, the prosecution cannot change the charges before the trial. If the prosecution wants to change the charges at that point, the current charges must be dropped and the whole process must begin again with a probable cause hearing or new indictment. Thus, once charges are filed, the prosecution is committed to proving those charges. Even if new evidence emerges, changing the charges is not undertaken lightly. This procedure ensures that the defendant will have a fair opportunity to prepare his or her defense. If the charges against the defendant could be changed after the arraignment and before the trial, the defense would not know what evidence to prepare for the trial or what evidence it should prepare to refute the new charges.

arraignment Short hearing before a judge in which the charges against the defendant are announced and the defendant is asked if he or she is guilty or not guilty.

plea Defendant's statement that he or she is guilty, not guilty, or offers "no contest."

motion Formal request by the prosecution or defense for the court to rule on any relevant matter in a case, such as the competency of the defendant to stand trial, the location of the trial, the jurisdiction of the court, or objections to evidence gathered by police.

Motions and Pleas At the arraignment, after charges are read, the judge asks the defendant for a **plea.** The defendant or the defendant's attorney is expected to answer in one of three ways: (1) not guilty, (2) guilty, or (3) no contest (*nolo contendere*). If the defendant does not respond to the question of guilt, the judge enters a plea of not guilty for the defendant and sets a trial date.

A number of pretrial motions may be made at the arraignment. A **motion** is a formal request of the court by the prosecution or the defense for a ruling on a particular matter. Motions about pleas may concern such matters as the competency of the defendant to stand trial, the location of the trial, the jurisdiction of the court, and objections to evidence gathered by the police. Additional motions may be made later.

Setting a Trial or Sentencing Date As mentioned earlier, the arraignment process may take only a few minutes. If the defendant pleads not guilty or "stands mute before the court" (refuses to enter a plea), a trial date is set. If the defendant pleads guilty or no contest, there is no need for a trial. In this case, the judge sets a sentencing date. No evidence is presented, no witnesses are called, and the defendant does not have the opportunity to deny guilt. When the defendant is returned to the court, it will be to hear the sentence for the offense. Because of the serious consequences of a guilty plea, a judge is not obligated to accept the defendant's guilty plea at the arraignment. The judge may enter a not guilty plea on behalf of the defendant if the judge believes the defendant is not competent to plead guilty or does not understand the charges. If the judge does this, a trial date is set for the defendant.

See www.courttv.com, the website of Court TV, for a wealth of information on the courts, as well as specific information on dozens of trials, current and past.

Determining Guilt

The trial is the judicial process that determines whether the defendant is guilty. Only the trial court can make this determination. The judge or the jury makes the actual decision as to whether the defendant committed the crime. Some states allow defendants to waive their right to a jury trial and leave the decision as to guilt to the judge. This type of trial is called a bench trial. In a **bench trial,** the judge acts as both referee and jury. In a **jury trial,** the judge has the authority to determine the sentence if the defendant is found guilty, but the jury, not the judge, determines guilt.

The Trial In a jury trial, after hearing the evidence, the jury is asked if the defendant is guilty or not guilty as charged. The jury is instructed to use only the evidence presented at the trial to make this decision. If the jury cannot come to a unanimous verdict as to the guilt of the defendant, the judge may request that the jury go back and achieve a verdict. If the jury still cannot decide on a verdict, the judge will declare a mistrial due to a deadlocked jury, or hung jury. In the case of a mistrial, the prosecution has the option of requesting a new trial. A new trial as a result of a mistrial does not violate the defendant's protection against being tried twice for the same crime. If, however, the jury returns a verdict of not guilty, the defendant is acquitted and set free.

Plea Bargaining Trials are expensive, involve considerable criminal justice personnel, require public civil service (i.e., jury duty), and are unpredictable. Both prosecutors and defense attorneys have legitimate reasons for wanting to avoid a trial. In fact, most cases do not go to trial. In more than 80 percent of the criminal cases filed against defendants, the defendant pleads guilty.[35] This high percentage of guilty pleas is attributable to plea bargaining. Sometime during the criminal justice process, even after the trial has started, the defendant may contact the prosecution and request that a deal be made. The prosecutor also may initiate the request for a plea bargain. In **plea bargaining,** the defendant agrees to plead guilty if the prosecution will change the charge to a crime carrying a lighter sentence, to one with fewer counts, or in return for a promise of reduced sentence. Prosecutors do not have the resources to take every good case to court, so they depend on plea bargaining to deliver justice efficiently. Another means of settling a case while avoiding a trial is **diversion.**

Deciding on a Punishment

After the trial, the defendant is released if found not guilty. If the defendant is found guilty, a punishment must be imposed. It is the responsibility of the judge to determine the punishment. However, the judge does not administer the punishment. He or she only decides what punishment is legal and appropriate. Each offense has a specified punishment, but often the range of punishment is broad; for example, the punishment for homicide may range from 1 to 20 years in prison. In addition to imprisonment, the judge may impose a fine, sentence the defendant to community service, require the defendant to seek drug or mental health counseling, or suspend the sentence.

Sentencing To determine which **sentence,** or punishment, the defendant is to receive, the judge is guided by the law and input received from the presentence investigation report. The law provides such guidelines as the minimum and maximum length of imprisonment and the maximum fine that can be assessed against the defendant. The

bench trial Judicial process to determine the guilt or innocence of a defendant in which the determination is made by a judge, not a jury.

jury trial Judicial process to determine the guilt of a defendant in which the determination is made by a jury, not a judge.

plea bargaining Negotiations between the prosecution and the defense for a plea of guilty in exchange for reduced charges or a lighter sentence.

diversion Sentencing option in which the defendant is diverted from the correctional system through alternatives such as community service.

sentence Disposition of a case by determining the punishment for a defendant convicted of a crime.

Defendants have a constitutional guarantee of a fair public trial by a jury of their peers for all serious offenses. An offense is serious if a defendant with a guilty verdict could receive a sentence of six months or more in jail or prison. A *fair trial* means that no substantial mistakes were made that could have affected the fairness of the court's decision as to the guilt of the defendant. A *public trial* means that the press, media, and public cannot be barred from attending the trial. However, the court does not need to accommodate everyone who wants to attend, and some states do not allow the media to air broadcasts of trials to the public.

law may restrict sentencing options or give judges great latitude in sentencing. Federal criminal codes tend to be more restrictive in specifying the term of imprisonment than are state criminal codes.

Both federal and state judges depend on information provided in a **presentence investigation report,** an investigation by a probation and parole officer or presentence investigator. This report includes evidence other than that presented during the trial. During the trial, the evidence that can be considered by the jury to determine guilt is restricted to only that which relates to the specific offense of which the defendant is accused. Other information not permitted as evidence includes, for example, previous crimes the defendant committed and the defendant's employment status. The presentence investigation, however, gathers information about the defendant's employment record, family relationships, financial responsibilities, contributions to the community, and prior convictions. Prior convictions and any lack of cooperation on the part of the defendant can result in a harsher sentence. This information, the defendant's entire life, can help a judge determine an appropriate sentence. Once sentenced, the defendant is convicted and there is no longer a presumption of innocence. At this point, the convicted defendant is considered guilty and loses many of the due process rights that were guaranteed before conviction.

During the time that the presentence investigation is being conducted, the convicted defendant is held in a correctional institution or is released on bail until the sentencing report is complete. Those convicted of state crimes are held in a state or county correctional institution, and those convicted of federal crimes are held in a federal correctional institution or may temporarily be held in a state facility until sentencing. Convicted defendants released on bail are required to appear before the court at their sentencing hearing.

presentence investigation report Report on the background of the convicted defendant and any other information relevant for determining the most appropriate sentence.

sentencing hearing A gathering before a judge who hears appeals, in which the prosecution and the defense argue the accuracy of the presentence report and the appropriateness of the sentence.

Appeal Sentences may be appealed. The prosecution can protest that the sentence is too lenient and does not protect the community. The defendant can argue that the sentence is beyond that required for rehabilitation and community protection, is cruel and unusual, or does not confirm to sentencing guidelines. At a **sentencing hearing,** the judge listens to the arguments of the two sides and determines the final sentence to be imposed.

The defendant retains the right to appeal to a higher court both the sentence and the conviction. A defendant convicted in a state court can appeal to the state supreme court and then to the U.S. Supreme Court. A federal defendant can appeal to the U.S.

criminal justice in the media

Diversion Options

Judges have been given great latitude in the sentences they can impose on offenders and have used this authority to craft creative and innovative ones. In both the juvenile and adult criminal justice systems, judges, guided by the philosophy that overburdened and often brutal prisons do not promote rehabilitation and, in fact, may promote the criminality of the defendant, have sought to avoid processing the defendant further into the system.

Juveniles are the prime targets for diversion sentencing. Juveniles who commit "minor" crimes, such as shoplifting, are often offered the opportunity to avoid entering the juvenile justice system if they will attend classes designed to extinguish the unlawful behavior. Men who have been arrested for domestic violence may be offered the opportunity to avoid prison if they attend anger-management classes. Drug addicts can have the charges against them dropped if they seek treatment. First offenders who are employed and have a family to support may be offered the chance to avoid prison if they agree to abide by such conditions as alcohol or drug counseling, regular payment of child support, and no further negative contact with the police.

Some jurisdictions may offer offenders a "deferred agreement of guilty" plea, or DAG. With a DAG, the judge sets the sentencing aside for a period of time, usually one year. If during that period of time defendants comply with the orders of the court to receive appropriate assistance from alcohol treatment, drug treatment, or anger-management agencies and do not have any negative contact with the police, the charges against them will be dismissed. In a sense, their records will be wiped clean, as the official record will show they were found not guilty and they will not suffer any of the consequences of a guilty verdict on their records. A DAG plea is often used in domestic violence cases. Abusive spouses who get help and are able to maintain healthy relationships with their mates can have the charges dismissed.

Diversion sentencing is done with good intentions, but, as mentioned, it is also in response to an overburdened correctional system. There are simply not enough beds in prisons to accommodate the increasing number of inmates.[35]

What are the advantages and disadvantages of diversion for the correctional system? For communities? For offenders? For alcohol or drug abusers? For juveniles? How can "deferred agreement of guilty" pleas be criticized as unfair?

Supreme Court. Appeals courts can choose to hear or reject the appeal. An appeal must be made on a claim that the defendant was denied a fair trial. The defendant cannot appeal on the grounds that he or she is innocent; the philosophy of the court is that the decision regarding guilt has been settled. The purpose of the appeal is to correct judicial errors that might have occurred.

Carrying Out the Sentence

Once the court determines the appropriate punishment for the defendant, he or she is transferred to the custody of a correctional agency. Three main categories of agencies in corrections are (1) institutional corrections, (2) probation and parole, and (3) community corrections. Institutional corrections include jails, state prisons, and federal penitentiaries. Probation is a sentence served outside of a correctional institution, and parole is a form of early release from prison. Community corrections are intermediate sanctions administered in a community setting.

Corrections Once transferred to a correctional institution, the convicted defendant is referred to as an inmate. The presumption of innocence and many of the due process

figure 1.7

The Criminal Justice Funnel

The actual number of cases varies from year to year, but the percentage of cases that are disposed of at the various stages of the criminal justice system remains fairly constant.

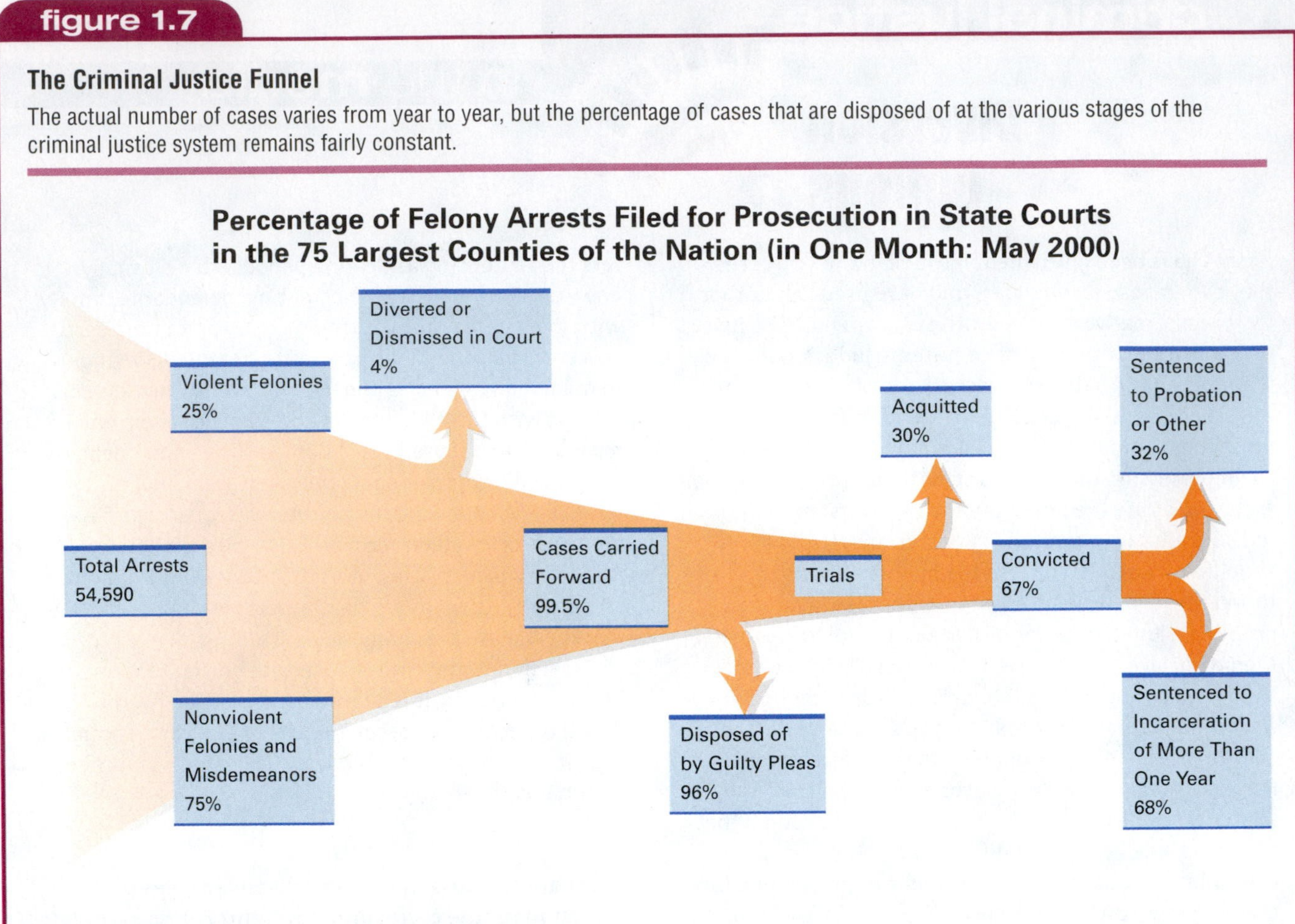

rights to which the defendant was entitled up to this point are gone. The criminal justice system now focuses on the role of punishment and rehabilitation. One of the most acrimonious debates in corrections is the purpose of confinement in a correctional institution. Is the purpose to punish inmates while in prison by the use of harsh conditions and physical discomfort, or is the purpose to rehabilitate inmates so that, when released, they will be able to integrate into society as productive citizens?

Probation and Parole Most sentences do not require that the defendant serve time in a prison or penitentiary.[36] When the defendant is sentenced to serve time in a prison or penitentiary, however, he or she may not serve the full term of the sentence. The court may impose a sentence and suspend it if the convicted defendant abides by certain conditions, or the sentence may be cut short due to the good behavior of the inmate while in prison.

The Office of Federal Probation and Parole supervises defendants convicted of federal crimes. Each state has its own probation and parole agency that supervises those convicted of state crimes. Probation and parole are distinctly different but are often handled by the same agency and personnel. **Probation** provides the convicted defendant the opportunity to avoid serving time in prison by fulfilling certain conditions imposed by the court. **Parole** allows the defendant to serve less than the maximum sentence imposed by the court, based on his or her behavior and progress toward rehabilitation while in prison. Community corrections include various intermediate sanctions, such as house arrest, community service, drug rehabilitation, and restitution.

probation Disposition in which a convicted defendant is offered an opportunity to avoid serving any time in prison by agreeing to fulfill conditions set forth by the court.

parole Early release from prison before the maximum sentence is served, based on evidence of rehabilitation and the good behavior of the inmate.

▲ check your understanding 1.5 What is required before police can arrest a suspect? Before the prosecution can bring the defendant to trial for a crime? Before a defendant can be convicted of a crime? How is a punishment determined and carried out? Do convicted criminals lose their due process rights?

conclusion:

Goals of Due Process

As you can see, the criminal justice system operates like a funnel that channels cases through various agencies in ever-narrowing outlets (Figure 1.7). In this funneling operation, due process is the driving force.

Due process does not protect the rights of the innocent or the victim. It protects the rights of the accused, without regard to guilt. Therefore, at times when the guilty appear to be advantaged by due process rights, some persons protest the ineffectiveness of the criminal justice system. The criminal justice system is ineffective, but it is ineffective on purpose. The American criminal justice system has its origins in a revolt against tyranny and a strong, centralized government that usurped the rights of its citizens. A decentralized system with many checks and balances on the various semiautonomous agencies and their personnel ensures maximum preservation of constitutionally guaranteed liberties and rights. It takes a long time and great resources to process a person through the criminal justice system from arrest to conviction, but this is the way it is supposed to be. The criminal justice system is not designed for efficiency. A popular saying is that "the wheels of justice grind exceeding slow but fine." There may be argument as to whether it grinds fine, but it is assuredly true that it grinds slowly.

chapter **summary**

- The criminal justice system consists of (1) people and agencies and (2) process and flow and is undergoing constant change. The system is divided into three categories of agencies: police, courts (the hub of the criminal justice system), and corrections (including probation and parole agencies and jails and prisons).
- There is no single agency or office that acts as "traffic cop" to direct people through the criminal justice system, which is driven by due process procedures and decision points and is not a one-way process. The decentralization of the criminal justice system, as in the picket fence model, is designed to safeguard the individual rights defined in the U.S. Constitution.
- The criminal justice system reflects the values of society. The values reflected in the American criminal justice system are a balance between crime control and due process. The central premise of the due process model is the presumption of innocence. Due process protects the rights of the accused.
- The criminal justice system has separate processes for dealing with adults and juveniles. The mission of the juvenile justice system is rehabilitation and restorative justice. There also are separate state, federal, and international criminal justice systems.

- Six major processes in the criminal justice system are (1) deciding what is a crime, (2) detecting crime violation and making an arrest, (3) determining if the accused is to go to trial, (4) deciding guilt in the trial, (5) determining punishment, and (6) administering the punishment. Overall, these processes act like a funnel for moving people through the criminal justice system.
- The police are responsible for investigation, arrest, and booking, which establishes the identity of the person and charges the person with a specific violation of criminal law. A magistrate judge reviews the charges to determine if they are legitimate, advises the person of his or her legal rights, and determines bail.
- A case moves from the police to the prosecutor via the preliminary hearing, in which probable cause is established for believing that the defendant has committed the charged offense. In some cases, prosecutors use the grand jury system to obtain a secret indictment and arrest warrant for a suspect.
- At the arraignment, the defendant pleads not guilty, guilty, or no contest to the charges. Guilt is determined by the judge in a bench trial or by the jury in a jury trial. Most cases do not go to trial but are settled by plea bargaining or by diversion.
- The judge determines the appropriate sentence for a convicted defendant, based in part on data in a presentence investigation report. Convicted defendants lose many due process rights, starting with the right to a presumption of innocence. The sentence is announced at a sentencing hearing, at which time the prosecution and defense can debate the sentence. Appeals of a verdict are based on alleged judicial errors, not innocence.
- The convicted defendant may become an inmate in a correctional facility, but most sentences do not require the serving of time in a prison. Probation calls for fulfilling certain conditions imposed by the court to avoid incarceration. Parole permits, under certain conditions, early release from a correctional facility.

vocabulary review

adjudicated, 18
arraignment, 34
arrest, 28
bail, 33
bench trial, 35
booking, 28
crime control model, 17
criminal justice system, 9
delinquent, 20
diversion, 35
due process, 17
due process model, 26
first appearance, 32
formal sanctions, 9
grand jury, 33
"hands-off" policy, 21
indictment, 33
informal sanctions, 9
jury trial, 35
juvenile court, 21
motion, 34
order maintenance, 9
original jurisdiction, 20
parens patriae, 20
parole, 38
picket fence model, 14
plea, 34
plea bargaining, 35
preliminary hearing, 33
presentence investigation report, 36
presumption of innocence, 17
probable cause, 28
probation, 38
sentence, 35
sentencing hearing, 36
social norms, 9
status offenders, 20
system of social control, 9

do you remember?

Bill of Rights, 11
Law Enforcement Assistance Administration (LEAA), 8
Law Enforcement Educational Program (LEEP), 8
John Locke, 10
National Commission on Criminal Justice Standards and Goals, 8
Omnibus Crime Control and Safe Streets Act of 1968, 8
Rosa Parks, 7
President's Commission on Law Enforcement and Administration of Justice, 7
September 11, 2001 (WTC 9/11), 8
War on Crime, 7
War on Terrorism, 8

think about this

1. Both the due process model and the crime control model focus on the offender and not the victim or the crime. Should more concern be given to the victim and the crime? If so, how should this be done?
2. Each state has its own criminal justice process, agencies, and personnel. What would be the advantages and disadvantages of requiring the states to adopt a common standard for its criminal justice system? What are some arguments for and against this idea?
3. The police are the primary agency with the responsibility of deciding if someone should be arrested, and the prosecutor (also called district attorney in some states) is the primary agency with the responsibility of deciding if an arrested person should go to trial. What would be the potential for abuse in arrest and prosecution if such powers resided primarily in one criminal justice agency?
4. Is the juvenile jutice system too soft on juvenile offenders?

research navigator

Visit the Research Navigator website (www.researchnavigator.com), login and select the criminal justice data base in ContentSelect. Type in the key words "Risk and Reluctance." This search will bring up the article "Risk and Reluctance in Criticizing Minorities" by Phillip Pertimutter. Society has enacted speech codes and hate crime laws to protect minorities. This article looks at the risk and reluctance in legitimate criticism of minorities and questioning the cause of continued problems in minority communities. Sample the article and answer the following questions:

1. Pertimutter says that while well intended "white guilt" can adversely affect the relationship between whites and minorities. According to Pertimutter what are some of the ways "white guilt" contributes to the problems of minorities rather than helping minorities?
2. What are some of the examples Pertimutter cites of double standards based upon race being that are applied to juries and judges?
3. According to Pertimutter why is there a lack of research on the cause of minority problems related to quality of life, economic advancement, social disorder, and crime?
4. According to Pertimutter how does "white guilt" affect attitudes, laws, and policies concerning illegal immigration?

chapter 2

Understanding and Measuring Crime

CHAPTER OUTLINE

LEARNING OBJECTIVES

After reading this chapter, you will be able to

- Explain the difference between nonscientific and scientific explanations of crime.
- Describe the influence of classical and neoclassical criminological theories on modern criminology and the criminal justice system.
- Compare and contrast the biological, psychological, and sociological theories of crime causation.
- Give examples of how the biological, psychological, and sociological theories of crime causation have affected the criminal justice system.
- Explain the importance of accurate crime statistics and the affects of crime statistics on the criminal justice system.
- Compare and contrast the data obtained from the Uniform Crime Report, the National Crime Victimization Survey, and other sources.
- Describe how certain crimes such as illegal drug trafficking, transnational crime, cybercrimes and identity theft, corporate and white-collar crime, crimes against the elderly, crimes against women, organized crime, and gun crime pose special problems for the criminal justice system.

Priest Admits That He Stole $50,000 from Collections

GARDEN CITY, N.Y., FEBRUARY 17–A priest accused of illegal gun possession and making harassing phone calls admitted that he stole $50,000 from collection plates of a Bethpage church over five years to finance his retirement, prosecutors said. Rev. John F. Johnston, 64, pleaded guilty to grand larceny, a felony. Father Johnston, who told investigators he skimmed $100 per week as his "401(k) plan," agreed to return $50,000 to the church.

Father Johnston, who has been a priest for 40 years, was arrested in October after the police received complaints he had been making obscene phone calls to a high school. When investigators went to Father Johnston's apartment they found an unlicensed gun, the bag full of stolen cash, Nazi memorabilia and pornography, investigators have said.

After Father Johnston's arrest, priests, students and others who knew him described him as a precise and supportive literature teacher, an aloof colleague and a haughty neighbor. He was ordained in 1964, served as an associate pastor in three parishes and taught at schools in the New York region for more than 20 years.

Adapted from "Priest Admits That He Stole $50,000 from Collections," *The New York Times,* February 18, 2004 by Patrick Healy. Copyright © 2004 by The New York Times Co. Reprinted with permission.

Introduction:

Why Would He Do It?

We frequently think of criminals as "evil" people who harm others without regard for the injury and suffering they cause. We are tempted to believe that we can recognize criminals by their looks. We are willing to believe that certain people are good. And we want to think that the causes of criminality—such as poverty, drug use, abuse, gang membership, and lack of economic opportunity—can be identified and could be changed if only we had the collective commitment to focus on eliminating these conditions. However, Father Johnston illustrates that stereotypes of criminals are nearly always false and the belief that the causes of criminality can be easily identified is unfounded. Why would a priest steal from the church were he had said Mass on Sundays for 30 years? How could he justify stealing from the collection plate as his retirement plan? Why would he make obscene phone calls to a high school, have Nazi memorabilia, pornography, and an unregistered gun? Although these are difficult questions to answer, there are theories of crime causation that would assert that such behavior can be explained by social, psychological, or biological factors.

People have had opinions regarding the cause of crime since the beginning of civilization. Early nonscientific theories emphasized moral weakness and evil spirits as the cause of criminality. At such time in history a crime like Father Johnston's would have simply been explained as sin or moral weakness. It would have been said that "the devil made it him do it."

Starting with early nonscientific theories and progressing to modern theories, this chapter examines the history and theories related to the study of crime from the viewpoint of scholars from various academic and professional disciplines. This chapter shows how the scientific explanations of criminality have evolved from simple theories with few variables to complex theories built on extensive data and research. It then discusses how crime is measured and examines some high-profile crimes in more detail.

Moral Perspectives

the main idea 2.1 Theories about the causes of criminal behavior began with nonscientific beliefs about good and evil and the moral order.

The study of human behavior can be approached from two major perspectives: the scientific method and the nonscientific method. Early explanations of deviant and criminal behavior were derived primarily from nonscientific methodologies. Most of these nonscientific investigations searched for principles underlying human conduct and thought based on logic or beliefs assumed to be true. These principles often were based on social and religious morals instead of empirical observations and facts. It was believed that people are, or can be, inherently evil.

Later theories explaining criminal behavior are based on scientific inquiry, which involves observation and isolation of variables relating to cause and effect. The study of the causes of crime is called *criminology.*

Good versus Evil

A common starting point in examining human behavior from the nonscientific viewpoint is the debate over the underlying nature of humans: Are humans predisposed to good or bad behavior? The question as to whether humans are naturally bad or good has been debated in virtually every society. On the one hand, it is argued that humans are naturally selfish, evil, and violent. For example, the medieval political philosopher Niccolo Machiavelli (1469–1527) argued that humans, if left to their own nature, would naturally tend toward bad behaviors. He believed that humans must be controlled by rules and by threat of punishment and that behavior is determined by one's social status.

On the other hand, there are those who argue that humans are naturally good. Thus, external control of people through law and authority is not necessary or is only minimally required. The fewer laws, the better. Laws are only necessary as a guide, for it is believed that, for the most part, if left to their own instincts, humans would coexist in peace.

Basic assumptions about human nature underlie the various contemporary theories that explain criminal behavior. In Western civilization, the foundation for the explanation of criminal behavior is rooted in the religious beliefs of the European Middle Ages and the Renaissance. During this time, the Catholic Church and, later, the Protestant church were influential in defining morality and ethics in society.[1] As a result of the strong influence of religious values on society, there was little differentiation between sin and crime. The Catholic Church was the major source of criminal law during Europe's Middle Ages, and the Church was an active agent in determining the guilt of individuals accused of breaking the law.

The common belief of people from the Middle Ages to the Age of Enlightenment was that bad behavior and thoughts were caused by sin. If asked why someone was bad, the most common answer given by people at that time would be that the person was morally weak or had succumbed to temptations of the world, such as greed or lust, or temptations of Satan.

In the American colonies, the infamous **Salem witch trials** of 1692 are a testament to the extent that people believed in evil spirits, supernatural explanations, and a cosmic battle of good against evil. During this time, any unusual event in one of the colonies was attributed to mystical powers, including coincidences, unusual diseases,

In the Salem witch trials, villagers were put to death for acts performed when allegedly possessed by the devil. What is a general name for the ancient view of crime causation based on concepts of spirit possession and inherent evil or sinfulness?

and misfortunes.[2] In their sermons, prominent preachers regularly warned parishioners of the dangers of witchcraft, satanic possession, and the devil. In an effort to rid colonial Massachusetts of the devil's presence, citizens used the judicial process as a protection against satanic influences, and this led to the witchcraft trials. Between 1672 and 1692, there were 40 cases filed involving the devil in the Massachusetts Bay Colony. During the height of the witchcraft trials in 1692, over 150 people were arrested, 19 people were hung for practicing witchcraft, 1 was pressed to death, and 4 died while in prison awaiting trial.[3]

Evolutionary Theories

A significant landmark in criminological theories was the publication of naturalist Charles Darwin's (1809–1882) theory of evolution. Darwin's theory of natural selection shifted the focus from nonscientific explanations to scientific explanations of human behavior. And efforts to explain criminal behavior scientifically moved criminological theories outside the Church. At the same time, however, people in Darwin's day ascribed moral values to evolutionary stages. Good and evil still applied but in the form of adaptive behavior versus maladaptive behavior.

Darwin's theory, which specifically addressed evolution and adaptation in lower order plants and animals, was quickly applied to humans. Darwin's premise was that species evolve through survival of the fittest, and that not all organisms evolve equally. This idea revolutionized criminological thought, because the argument was advanced that people who committed criminal acts did so because they had failed to evolve properly or at all. Thus, criminals were not only different, they were subhuman, and the fact that they were either misfit or not fully human was the reason for their bad behavior.[4] Modern theories have abandoned this belief.

▲ check your understanding **2.1 What were some reasons given for criminal behavior historically? How did Darwin influence the concept of criminal behavior? What perspective replaced the moral and social evolution explanations?**

Explaining Criminal Behavior

▼ the main idea **2.2 Criminology is the scientific study of criminal behavior, which is related to the concept of deviance. Theories in criminology contribute to explaining, predicting, and preventing crime.**

The twentieth century ushered in a new era of scientific inquiry. Many of the scientific fields that emerged at the turn of the twentieth century, such as sociology, psychology, and psychiatry, offered innovative theories to explain human behavior. Scholars quickly adopted this new knowledge to explain criminal behavior, and, often, the validity of these new explanations was tested through the criminal justice system.

The goal of the criminologist is to discover verifiable principles, concepts, and theories "regarding the process of law, crime, and treatment or prevention."[5] Modern criminologists have abandoned the concept that crime is caused by evil or the devil. Instead, they seek to find relationships between criminal behavior and the principal determinants or causes of that behavior. As determinants and causes, criminologists study the role of variables such as the environment, genetics, social relationships, poverty, unemployment, education, population, intelligence, parenting, and personality. What specific variables cause or contribute to which criminal acts? Because of ethical standards—for instance, the ability to conduct scientific experiments with humans is very limited—criminologists often must use indirect or secondary evidence to test their theories. Much of the data gathered by criminologists are in the form of observations and surveys expressed as statistical frequencies and correlations.

Role of Theories in Criminology

In his or her studies, the criminologist studies both the formal systems for the control of behavior, such as the legal system, and the informal systems of control, such as the family, school, social group, and religious affiliation. The criminologist is interested in observing what happens when there are conflicts among these various control systems. Which factors are most influential in determining behavior? Do all people react the same in similar circumstances, or is one's behavior also influenced by other qualities, such as self-control and personality? By studying such behaviors and gathering reliable data about individuals and their social environment, the criminologist seeks to construct theories that can be used to predict behavior.

The purpose of a theory is not to predict what a specific individual will do in a specific case. **Theories** attempt to define general principles that will apply in a number of similar cases, but not necessarily all cases. Thus, if 95 of 100 people would act a certain way under certain conditions, the claim could be made confidently that the variables correlate significantly with the behavior, despite the fact that for 5 people, the variables did not cause them to commit a crime.

▲ check your understanding **2.2 What is the goal of criminology? What is the purpose of theories?**

Explanations of Criminal Behavior

▼ the main idea **2.3 Theories of the causes and consequences of criminal behavior can be grouped into four perspectives, based on their assumptions about what determines criminal behavior.**

As you can imagine, numerous theories have been put forth to explain criminal behavior. This chapter does not attempt to review all the criminological theories, because such a review is beyond the scope of this book. Instead, this chapter focuses on theories that have had significant impact on the criminal justice system.

There are hundreds of theories that attempt to explain crime, and these are grouped together in terms of their common elements. These groups of theories are called *schools of thought.* A common element used to define schools of thought is the body of assumptions on which the theories are based. These assumptions state what is most important in explaining criminal behavior.

Using this methodology to group theories produces four main perspectives or paradigms for the determinants of criminal behavior: (1) the classical perspective, (2) the biological perspective, (3) the psychological perspective, and (4) the perspective of social determinism. This chapter examines major theories in each of these four schools of thought. Keep in mind, however, that in reality, theories influence one another, share common elements, undergo changes, are discarded, and often are reinvented.

theories Statements of relationship or of cause and effect that attempt to explain or predict behavior or events; theories are macro, middle range, or micro depending on the number of cases and level of generalization.

careers in the system

Criminologist

A number of people earn their living studying crime and criminals. Many people whose jobs are the study of crime and criminals are employed as teachers or researchers in colleges and universities, in government agencies, or in firms devoted to social science research. Most criminologists have a background in sociology, and criminology also is an avenue to careers in criminal justice and law. Criminology was a field of academic study long before criminal justice departments emerged in colleges and universities in the 1960s. Employment as a criminology or criminal justice professor or researcher at a college or university usually requires a terminal graduate degree, such as a doctoral degree or a law degree. Two-year colleges often prefer to hire teachers who have experience in the criminal justice field and have at least a master's degree. Criminologists also work in public safety, corrections, government, law, health and human services, and business.

People with training in criminology may be involved in analyzing data collected by the FBI and other agencies and may also work in crime mapping or crime profiling. Criminologists who do psychological profiling of criminals often have a graduate degree in psychology or psychiatry rather than sociology, and also have extensive experience working in the mental health profession.

Profiling is a specialized field and does not employ many people. Psychological profilers typically have full-time mental health positions and do psychological profiling of criminals on an as-needed basis. There simply is not enough demand for psychological profiling to create a large job market. The FBI has a unit devoted to psychological profiling. However, only senior agents with extensive experience and mental health professionals are appointed to this unit. Unlike some portrayals in the entertainment media, newly appointed FBI agents are not assigned to the special detective units that do psychological profiling.

The future of criminology looks promising, especially in the study of crimes of the twenty-first century and their victims and perpetrators. These studies are focusing, for example, on violent crimes, crimes involving domestic and international terrorism, high-tech fraud and computer crimes, drug crime, and trafficking in humans.

What might be some advantages of having an advanced degree in criminology? If you decided to become a criminologist, what type of crime or criminal do you think you would like to study and try to explain or predict?

In classical and neoclassical theories, the explanation for crime is based on the assumption that criminal behavior is a matter of choice. The individual has free will to choose to commit or refrain from criminal behavior. The individual's choice of behavior is influenced by a rational analysis of the gain to be achieved from committing the criminal act versus the punishment or penalty that could be suffered if sanctioned by society for the criminal behavior. Theories that share this assumption of free will and rational choice are commonly called **classical school** theories or **neoclassical school** theories.

classical school Theories of crime causation based on Cesare Beccaria's assumption that criminal behavior is a matter of free-will choice.

neoclassical school A later version of classical theory in which children under the age of 7 and offenders suffering mental disease should be exempt from criminal liability because their conditions interfere with the exercise of free will.

Two theorists representing the classical and neoclassical theories are Cesare Beccaria (1738–1794) and Jeremy Bentham (1748–1832), considered the founders of classical and neoclassical criminology, respectively. Their theories were a radical departure from the contemporary thought of their time. When published, these theories were not labeled "classical" but were the cutting edge of criminological thought. It is only in historical hindsight that they are called classical.

Classical and Neoclassical Theory

Cesare Beccaria, known as the founder of classical criminology, is extremely important in criminological theory because his theories on crime marked the beginning of a new approach to criminological thought. Beccaria's ideas actually preceded the development of criminology as an academic discipline. Beccaria was an Italian nobleman and jurist who was dissatisfied with the justice system of his time and attempted to bring about change. During the 1700s, the Italian criminal justice system was a barbaric system that leaned toward extreme punishments and questionable justice. Laws were unwritten, arbitrary, and unfairly applied. The situation was made worse by unschooled judges whose decisions were often arbitrary and based to a large degree on the social class of the accused. The punishments handed out by the court consisted of corporal and capital punishments that were considered a source of public entertainment. Defendants had no rights, there was no due process, and torture was regarded as an effective interrogation method.

The ideas of Cesare Beccaria had a major influence on the development of criminology. According to Beccaria, what are the causes of criminal behavior, and how can it be prevented? What school of thought did Beccaria promote? How did his views differ from those of Jeremy Bentham?

On Crimes and Punishment Beccaria composed only a single volume addressing his concerns about the criminal justice system of Italy, *Dei delitti e Delle Pene,* published in 1764 and translated into English in 1768 under the title *Of Crimes and Punishments.*[6] Beccaria probably had no idea that his short text would become the single work responsible for a revolution in the philosophy of criminal justice. Even today, Beccaria's ideas seem completely contemporary and can be clearly identified as the foundation underlying the contemporary American criminal justice system.

Beccaria was not the first person or the only person during his time to advocate the principles found in *Of Crimes and Punishments.* However, his essay clearly summarized the concept of the criminal justice system as a social contract based on logic, goal orientation, and humanistic principles. The concepts in his books—innocent until proven guilty, trial by a jury of one's peers, the right of appeal, the classification of crimes, equal treatment of all people before the court, and so on—reflect the principles of American jurisprudence.

The Pain-Pleasure Principle Beccaria was influenced by the Age of Enlightenment. His ideas on the cause of criminal behavior were based on the philosophical axiom that people are rational. He reasoned that people seek to do that which brings them pleasure and to avoid that which causes pain. Beccaria further assumed that members of society are responsible for their actions. He advocated certain, swift punishment of appropriate intensity and duration for the offense committed, for the purpose of deterring people from committing crimes.

Neoclassical Theory The English philosopher and scholar **Jeremy Bentham** is credited with the formation of the neoclassical school of criminology,[7] which is similar to the classical school in that the basic foundation is the concept that criminal behavior is a free-will choice and the choice to commit criminal behavior can be deterred by pain and punishment. The major difference between Beccaria's classical criminology and Bentham's neoclassical school is that Bentham believed that Beccaria's unwavering accountability of all offenders was too harsh. Bentham believed in mitigating circumstances. Whereas Beccaria would hold a child of age 5 or 6 just as responsible for a law violation as an adult, Bentham argued that children under the age of 7 and offenders suffering mental disease should be exempt from criminal liability. His most significant contribution to criminological thought was his work *An Introduction to the Principles of Morals and Legislation,* written in 1780 and published in 1789.

Like Beccaria, Bentham reasoned that people are human calculators who logically evaluate the pleasure to be gained by the commission of an act versus the punishment to be suffered for it. When the pain of punishments outweighs the pleasure to be derived, individuals refrain from criminal behavior. Thus, the goal of the criminal justice system was to craft laws and punishments such that the pleasure from engaging in criminal behavior was less than the pains of punishment. Harsher prohibitions and punishments were both unnecessary and inefficient. If one were deterred from theft by the threat

In a cabinet in the foyer of University College, London, sits the preserved body of Jeremy Bentham on view to the public and linked to the Internet via video cameras. Bentham's philosophy of utilitarianism emphasized education, democratic reform, and rational decision making. He assumed that criminals were rational persons who did not differ substantially from noncriminals, an uncommon view in his time. More popular was Lombroso's theory that criminality was a defect in human evolution.

of 3 strokes of the cane, then a threat of 20 strokes or of hanging made the judicial system seem ignorant and inappropriate.

Bentham's theorems regarding the balancing of pain and pleasure as a means to discourage criminal behavior is known as the ***felicitic calculus***—the pain versus pleasure principle. Bentham's philosophy is called "utilitarianism," and states that a rational system of jurisprudence provides for the greatest happiness for the greatest number of people. Based on the principles that people act rationally and that the punishment should fit the crime, Bentham's neoclassical philosophy became the foundation of the English jurisprudence system, and hence the American jurisprudence system. His concepts are easily recognized in principles set forth in the Declaration of Independence and the Bill of Rights. Bentham's influence on the English criminal justice system was enormous, starting with the philosophy that youthful offenders and mentally defective offenders are not fully responsible for their behavior.

The other three schools of thought—the biological, psychological, and sociological theories of criminal behavior—differ from the classical and neoclassical models in that they reject the concept that crime is a matter of free choice. According to these theories, criminal behavior is caused by various social, psychological, biological, economic, and environmental factors—a position referred to as *positivism.* Positivists emphasize the importance of the scientific method to determine the factors that cause or contribute to criminal behavior.

The Positive School

The scientific method emphasizes that knowledge about criminal behavior should be gathered using tools such as observation, surveys, case studies, statistics, and experimentation. The **positive school** includes most modern theories of criminology. Sociology and psychology are the two academic disciplines that have made significant contributions to the understanding of crime causation. Biology, chemistry, and medical science (including genetics) have also made important contributions to the scientific understanding of crime and criminals.

The explanation that crime is a matter of free-will choice was the predominant criminological theory from about the mid-1700s to the mid-1800s. The scientific revolution of the late 1800s challenged free-will theories, however. Scholars and scientists suggested that, contrary to the free-will premise, perhaps people commit crimes because of uncontrollable internal or external factors that can be observed and measured. Some of the factors thought to predetermine behavior were heredity, physical appearance, physiological factors, poverty, and even the shape of the bumps on one's head! These positivist scholars and scientists were also known as *determinists.*

▲ check your understanding **2.3** **What are the four basic perspectives on the determinants of criminal behavior? On what assumptions are classical, neoclassical, and positivist theories based? How did these theories influence the American criminal justice system?**

felicitic calculus In classical and neoclassical theory, such as Jeremy Bentham's, the pain–pleasure principle by which people decide whether or not to commit a crime.

positive school School of thought that emphasizes the importance of the scientific method to determine the factors that contribute to criminal behavior.

Biological Explanations

▼ the main idea **2.4** **Biological explanations focus on inherited predispositions toward criminal behavior.**

Darwin's *Origin of Species* (1859) provided an important portal for the development of new criminological theories. One of the dilemmas in the advancement of criminological theories was the belief commonly held in Christian theologies that humankind was created by God in God's image and therefore is inherently good. This foundational belief, while consistent with the free-will school of thought, posed great difficulties for any theory asserting that some people are not created good but are bad from birth. To say that one was born bad seems to place the fault with God or to deny the goodness of God's creation. If people are good from birth, on the other hand, then it becomes necessary to explain how one becomes bad. The theory of evolution and adaptation of the species provided an answer to this question.

Darwin proposed what was then a radical and, according to some people, heretical view—that evolved to the argument "humans are fundamentally animals, developed from a common biological ancestry along with all animals and other living things."[8] Darwin proposed that animals are controlled by certain factors of heredity and environment that are beyond the realm of self-control or free will. Animals adapt to their environment through deterministic biochemical and physical forces. Species are influenced by their past heredity because they are in a constant state of evolution, though some, like birds, appear to diversify greatly and others, like sharks, hardly at all.

Crime as an Inherited Characteristic

Two studies attempting to apply a heredity model to the analysis of criminal behavior were the **Richard Dugdale** (1841–1883) study of the Jukes family and the study of Martin Kallikak's family tree by Henry Goddard (1866–1957). These studies, although flawed in their conclusion, suggested that criminality is an inherited trait. Needless to say, these studies were not scientific. For one thing, they failed to identify and account for all the variables that might be involved in the outcomes. Despite this and other defects in scholarship, studies like these set the stage for developments in the positive school of criminology. Cesare Lombroso's theory of the "criminal man" was the first important theory to emerge.

Lombroso and Criminality

See http://sociology.about.com; enter "Lombroso" in the search window for more information on Lombroso and the positive school of criminology.

Cesare Lombroso (1835–1909) was an Italian medical doctor who took an interest in the causes of criminal behavior. He was particularly influenced by previous scholars whose writings suggested that criminality was inherited. He was influenced by Darwin's theory of adaptation and nonadaptation, Gall's theory of phrenology, and other applications of evolutionary theory. For example, it was believed that criminal types are throwbacks to an earlier stage of evolution.

For his theory explaining criminal behavior, Lombroso collected extensive data from Italian prisoners and Italian military personnel. Lombroso believed that criminal behavior was a characteristic of humans who had failed to fully develop from their primitive origins, such that criminals are closer to apes than to contemporary humans. He described criminals as a retarded species and as "individual mutations or natural accidents living among civilized humans." Criminals could be differentiated clearly from noncriminals on the basis of distinctive physical features, such as protruding jaws, sloping foreheads, left-handedness, and red hair. Lombroso concluded that criminals were a case of "atavism"—a throwback to primitive times.[9]

Criminals were born inferior, prehuman, according to Lombroso. Thus, little could be done to prevent such persons from becoming criminals or to rehabilitate them. Criminality was not a result of choice or rational thought but a result of flawed human development—or lack of development. Lombroso made extensive physical measurements to define what he called the "criminal man."[10] The study of the physical traits of criminals was called **atavistic stigmata.**

atavistic stigmata Physical characteristics, representing earlier or prehuman stages of evolution, that were believed to distinguish criminals from others.

Lombroso's theories were further developed by **Raffaele Garofalo** (1852–1934) and Enrico Ferri (1856–1929). Although the theories of Garofalo and Ferri contained significant deviations from those of Lombroso, the central theme was that criminals should not be held morally responsible for crimes because they did not choose to commit crimes. The positive school of criminology, led by Lombroso, Garofalo, and Ferri, argued that the concept of free will is a fiction. Lombroso suggested that preventive actions would have little or no impact on the prevention of criminal behavior. Ferri was more hopeful that preventive measures could overcome congenital tendencies. He favored obliging criminals to work, believing that a strong work ethic could help a criminal overcome defects of character. Garofalo focused more on psychic anomalies and the reform of the judicial system of Italy. For example, he argued that juries were ill equipped to make judgments regarding the fate of criminals because criminality was more a medical condition than a moral defect. This "medicalization of crime" had an enduring impact on the criminal justice system and is commonly associated today with drug-related crimes.

During the late 1800s, Lombroso and his contemporaries' theories on criminality were immensely popular both in Europe and America. Lombroso's influence was so pervasive that he is referred to as the "father of modern criminology." Although his theories have all been rejected as scientifically invalid, he is honored for the way he attempted to formulate them. Rather than rely on logic or philosophy or morality, he emphasized the role of empirical observations and careful collection of data to test one's theory.

Influence of Biological Determinism Despite the fact that Lombroso's theory was later invalidated, it was and continues to be influential in the study of criminology. For example, his theory influenced the way convicted persons were treated in prison. Emphasis on corporal punishment and moral correction through religious instruction was replaced by an emphasis on identification, isolation, and extermination.

Body-Type Theories

An idea that has persisted is Lombroso's premise that criminal behavior can be identified by physical appearance. Various theories continue to be based on the assumption that body physique is a reliable indicator of personality and, hence, criminality. Methods for detecting a relationship between some physical attribute and personality include Chinese face reading, handwriting analysis, and palm reading. In the mid-twentieth century, criminologists were influenced by the research of **Ernest Kretschmer** (1888–1964), **William Sheldon** (1889–1977), and **Sheldon** and **Eleanor Glueck.** The writings of these criminologists formed the basic tenets of the **somatotype school** of criminology. The somatotype, or body-build, theory is based on the assumption that there is a link between the mind and the body and that this link is expressed in the body type of the person.

Sheldon was influenced by the theories of Darwin and built on the work of German psychiatrist Ernest Kretschmer. Kretschmer concluded that there are three types of physiques: asthenic (lean), athletic (muscular), and pyknic (round). Sheldon linked personality to body type by an extensive study of 40,000 male subjects in which he correlated body types with the results of personality tests. Similar to Kretschmer, he concluded that there are three body types: ectomorph (lean), mesomorph (athletic), and endomorph (round). Sheldon claimed to have found a positive correlation between criminality and the mesomorphic (athletic) body type. Somatotype theories have largely been replaced by modern biological explanations.

somatotype school Theories of crime causation based on the assumption that there is a link between the mind and the body and that this link is expressed in body types, and based on Cesare Lombroso's theory that a criminal can be identified by physical appearance.

Modern Biological Explanations

Lombroso proposed his theory of criminality without benefit of the knowledge provided by modern genetic science. As the contribution of genetics to various human conditions

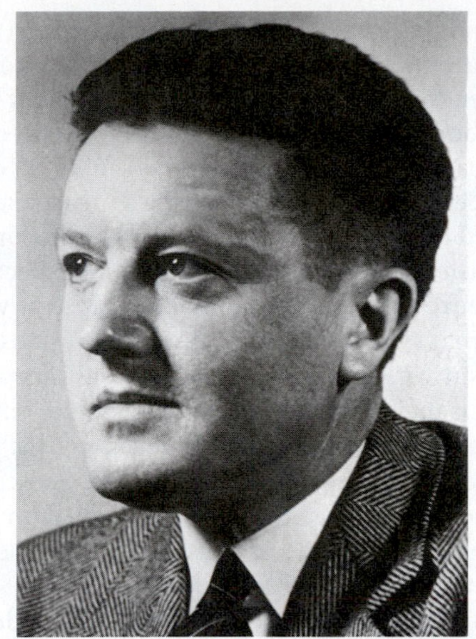

How did Cesare Lombroso, William Sheldon, and Sigmund Freud (see page 76) contribute to biological and psychological explanations of criminal behavior? What are some other theories that suggested biological or psychological causes of crime rather than cases based on morality and free will?

was recognized, several studies revisited Lombroso's basic axiom that criminality is inherited. Studies of identical twins performed by Karl O. Christiansen[11] and others all concluded that, for identical twins, if one twin engaged in criminal behavior, the probability that his or her identical twin would be a criminal was statistically significantly higher. Another study indicated that in the case of adopted children, the criminality of the biological parent appears to have greater influence on the adopted child than the criminality of the adoptive parents.

Proponents of the biological perspective on criminal behavior argue that some people are born with a biological predisposition to be antisocial—to behave in ways that run counter to social values and norms. Unlike early biological determinists, modern biocriminologists concede that environmental factors can inhibit or stimulate hereditary predispositions for criminality. **Biocriminology** focuses on research into the roles played by genetic and neurophysiological variables in criminal behavior, how important they are, and what can be done to modify them.

Modern biology-based theories identify a diverse number of variables suspected of contributing to criminal behavior. Often these theories have emerged after scientific discoveries have revealed new knowledge about how the brain works and the contribution of genetics to behavior. For example, as the role of chromosomes became clear in influencing certain human characteristics, the XYY chromosome theory of violent behavior emerged. The **XYY chromosome theory** stems from genetic research on the characteristics of DNA chromosomes.[12] The normal male has an X and a Y chromosome in the cells that determine the sex of a person. It was discovered that some males have an extra Y chromosome, and studies of prisoners convicted of violent crimes have found a high correlation between conviction for a violent crime (as opposed to a property crime) and the presence of an extra Y chromosome in the male. Multiple sex chromosomes in both males and females contribute to various abnormalities.

biocriminology A new field in criminology encompassing modern biological approaches (such as neurochemistry and neuroendocrinology) to explain criminal behavior.

XYY chromosome theory Biological theory of crime causation that an extra Y chromosome may lead to criminal behavior in males.

Theories of Aggression In modern biological theories, ideas about causes of crime are expressed in research about causes of human aggression. In an application of neuroendocrinology, for instance, a glandular theory of crime argues that an imbalance of the body's chemicals is the cause of violent behavior. **Katherine Dalton**'s study of female crimes concluded that 49 percent of all crimes of 156 female subjects were committed either just before or during a menstrual period. Her argument is that hormones released during those times are responsible for aggressive behavior. However, this finding (basically 50-50) is what one would expect, given the law of averages![13]

Neurochemistry posits that the cause of violent behavior is the effect of nutrition on humans. This theory is based on the observation that chemicals, food additives, preservatives, and certain foods can stimulate aggressive behavior. A popular related theory is that refined sugar causes hyperactivity and aggression in children.[14] The effect of sugar actually was used as a defense in the murder trial of Dan White. White killed San Francisco mayor George Moscone and city supervisor Harvey Milk, but claimed that the murders occurred after he binged on Twinkies and soda pop as a result of depression. The defense was billed in the news media as the **Twinkie defense.** Interestingly, White received a reduced sentence.

Some aggression theorists attribute gender differences in aggression to biological programming related to survival of the species. Nearly all violent crimes are committed by males, and males account for approximately 90 percent of all convicted criminals. These data suggest that sex-linked aggression that helped ensure the survival of the species in prehistoric times may be a contributing factor in modern criminality.

Another example is the link aggression theorists see between population density and violence. The hypothesis that overcrowding causes crime is consistent with data showing that violent crime is predominately an urban phenomenon. Generally there is more violent crime per unit of population in larger cities than in smaller cities or rural areas. However, data from comparative international studies of crime fail to support this hypothesis. If overcrowding and population density is a prime cause of violence behavior, then Tokyo and Singapore should have much more violence than major U.S. cities, but they do not.

Criminality and the Brain Other biological theories of crime causation come from studies of **minimal brain dysfunction (MBD)**, autonomic nervous system studies, and brain pathology. Minimum brain dysfunction studies show that violent behavior is caused by small disruptions of normal brain functioning, detectable only through electroencephalogram (EEG) measurements of electrical impulses emitted by the brain. This theory suggests that MBD may be responsible for a variety of behavioral problems including attention deficit hyperactivity disorder. Studies have found that the autonomic nervous system (ANS) is the primary control center for the fear response. Children with a quick ANS response learn to react to stimuli with fear, and generally that fear inhibits any desire to engage in criminal activities. Individuals with a slow ANS response are not so inhibited. A number of research studies indicate that people who exhibit criminal behavior tend to have slower ANS responses. Autonomic nervous system studies may offer insight in efforts to understand sociopathic or psychopathic behavior. Finally, brain pathology studies have focused on the impact of disease, trauma, and central nervous system disorders on the brain as causes of violent behavior.

minimal brain dysfunction (MBD) A biological explanation of crime, suggesting that small disruptions of normal brain functioning are responsible for violent behavior.

▲ check your understanding **2.4** **What are the contributions of Lombroso and his followers to criminology? How did the biological explanations of the positivists and determinists influence the criminal justice system? How do studies of twins, human aggression, and the brain contribute to our understanding of criminal behavior?**

Psychological Explanations

See www.freud.org.uk for further information on Freud and psychoanalysis.

the main idea 2.5 The psychoanalytical theory that criminal behavior is driven by unconscious forces and personality theory have received limited acceptance in the criminal justice system.

Freud and Psychoanalysis

At the end of the 1800s, **Sigmund Freud** introduced the new **psychoanalytic theory**. In the twentieth century, the science of psychoanalysis became universally accepted as a way of understanding previously unexplainable human behavior.[15] Freud based his theory on the underlying assumption that behavior is not a free-will choice but is controlled by subconscious desires. Furthermore, not all behavior is rational. Some behaviors are not only irrational but also destructive. Yet, despite the self-destructive nature of some behaviors, Freud said that frequently people are unable to control them. At the root of Freud's theory is the concept of the id, the ego, and the superego. Freud hypothesized that human thoughts and actions are controlled by these three components of the mind. The ego can be considered the logical, thinking part of one's consciousness. The superego controls moral and value choices. It is what allows a person to distinguish right from wrong. The id is the subconscious impulses and chaos that, if allowed to influence behavior and thought, result in dysfunctional and harmful behaviors. The id, ego, and superego are not physical structures found in the brain but psychological forces. Although these psychological forces are not biological in nature, they exert powerful control over human behavior and actions.

Freud did not focus on the study of criminal behavior. However, his theory of psychoanalysis has been extensively applied to the study of criminals. Freud's theory provides a completely different perspective on criminal behavior. To simplify a fairly complex theory, it could be said that in Freudian theory, crime is a symptom of unresolved psychological conflict.[16] This conflict is caused by free-floating feelings of guilt and anxiety. *Free-floating* means there is no specific cause that the person can identify for the guilt. He or she just feels guilty but does not know why. Freudian theory attributes this guilt to traumatic psychological events that happened in childhood. These events have been repressed and the person is not aware of their influence on his or her emotions and behaviors.

To alleviate the feelings of guilt, the person commits a crime so that he or she will be punished. The punishment brings temporary relief. However, because the punishment is not truly related to the source of the feelings of guilt, the guilt returns and it is necessary for the person to commit another crime so that he or she will once again receive the relief of punishment. This dysfunctional cycle of guilt and criminal behavior continues because, in reality, the punishment received cannot alleviate the feeling of guilt.

The perspective that crime is rooted in dysfunctional, psychologically induced behaviors has received limited acceptance by the criminal justice system. This explanation of criminal behavior does not lend itself to crime prevention and rehabilitation programs, which may require extensive treatment by mental health professionals over an extended period. The criminal justice system recognizes the need for defendants to be mentally competent to stand trial, for offenders to have access to the defense of insanity, for youths to have drug counseling, and for prison inmates to have psychological counseling, but there are no large-scale government programs whose purpose is to improve the mental health of a large number of potential delinquents or offenders. Psychological examination of the mental health of the offender has not been a significant perspective of crime prevention programs.

psychoanalytic theory
Sigmund Freud's theory that behavior is not a free-will choice but is controlled by subconscious desires.

criminal justice in the media

Crime and Fame

Murders, especially mass murders and serial murders, and crimes committed by celebrities fascinate the public. Murder is the least committed crime and mass murder and serial murder are even rarer. (Mass murderers kill more than one victim at a single time, whereas serial murderers kill more than one victim at a time over a period of time.) Despite this fact, perhaps because of it, murder—especially mass murder and serial murder—receives tremendous media attention. Murder trials—particularly when they combine both murder and famous persons—often capture the attention of the entire nation. For example, the O. J. Simpson murder trial was one of the most watched television programs in the history of network Nielsen ratings.

People are fascinated by individuals who are capable of committing monstrous crimes. The extent of public interest in such crimes was evident by the competition among tourism officials in the San Francisco Bay Area to have the trial of Scott Peterson for the murder of his wife, Laci, and their unborn son, located in their city. Tourism officials and various city convention and visitors' bureaus lobbied aggressively to have the mega-media event in their city, knowing that the trial would bring millions of dollars to the "winning" city.[17] When it was decided to hold the trial in San Mateo, city officials estimated the trial would inject at least $8 million into the county's economy.[18]

Often, the media and public are amazed that serial and mass murderers "appear so normal" and that in the case of serial murderers their crimes may span over years or decades. For example, serial nurse killer Charles Cullen admitted to murdering 29 patients to make him the worst serial killer in the states of New Jersey and Pennsylvania. He told officials that he may have killed as many as 40 people, which, if true, would make him one of the nation's most prolific serial murderers.[19] During his numerous public interviews he never appeared remorseful or concerned over his crimes. He described his crimes in accurate detail with almost no emotion.

Coral Eugene Watts claims to have killed 22 people in Texas, Michigan, and Windsor, Ontario, during a killing spree that spanned over 20 years. He was caught when, in 1982, Houston police received a tip of a burglary and homicide he planned. Dennis Rader, known as the Wichita, Kansas, BTK (bind, torture, kill) serial killer, killed 10 victims over a 30-year period. Rader was a former Boy Scout leader, church president, and city employee. He demonstrated no symptoms of insanity or psychological delusions, and was described by many neighbors as a "neighborly type."[20] At his trial Rader spent an hour describing in minute detail how he tortured and killed victims. His confession was characterized as emotionless, like "someone reading out of a phonebook."[21]

Furthermore, the victims of these killings often are innocent persons who have minimal or no direct interaction with the killer. Sometimes the victims are family members. For example, in 2001, Andrea Yates drowned her five children one by one in a bathtub. In March 2005, Marcus Wesson killed nine victims—a 24-year-old woman and eight of his children ranging in age from 1 to 17. The deaths were the largest mass killing in the history of Fresno, California, a city of 440,000.[22] Also, in 2005, Terry Ratzmann, upset about something in the sermon, walked out of a meeting of the Living Church of God and returned later in the week to a church meeting and opened fire on members in the meeting. He fired 22 bullets in less than a minute and killed seven church members.

All of the publicity and study of mass and serial killers has contributed little theory and knowledge to the field of criminal justice compared to the more mundane studies that focus on crime causation and the various social and psychological variables affecting delinquency. No pattern or common trait has emerged that explains serial and mass murders.

Media coverage and public interest in mass and serial murder may be exceeded only by interest in crimes—almost any crime—committed by a sports figure or celebrity. Whether it is radio commentator Rush Limbaugh charged with drug abuse, allegations of sexual assault against comedian Bill Cosby, actor Robert Blake accused of murder, or rapper Kimberly Jones (known as Lil' Kim) being convicted for perjury, when a well-known celebrity is accused of a crime, there is disproportional media coverage and public interest in the crime. The bigger the celebrity, the more disproportional the media coverage. For example, the trial of Michael Jackson was an international media circus.

It is front-page news when famous sports figures are accused of crime. For example, television and newspaper

Celebrities receive extensive media coverage when they are accused of a crime. The Michael Jackson trial attracted international media coverage and fans from around the world. Celebrities may spend millions of dollars on their defense team. Do you think that there is a different standard of justice for wealthy celebrities?

media were relentless in attempting to find out any details they could when basketball star Kobe Bryant was accused of rape. The news media even aired shows touring the hotel room in which Bryant allegedly assaulted his victim.

Sports superstars do not have to commit murder or rape to get front-page headlines, however. Sports stars charged with drug crimes also merit front-page news. For example, it was news when Ravens running back Jamal Lewis was charged with drug trafficking and when Giants receiver David Tyree was charged with drug possession. When five team members of the Indiana Pacers were charged for brawling with fans at a game, the news media even conducted public opinion polls asking respondents what they thought about the penalty the players received. Never would a public opinion poll be conducted asking respondents what they thought of the penalty for assault given to a nonfamous person.

Even crimes committed by school sports players can be front-page news. For example, allegations of sexual assaults by lacrosse players at Duke University and football players at the University of Colorado at Boulder were given national media coverage.

Such high-profile media coverage can present unique challenges for the criminal justice system. Trials of celebrities can result in media coverage that can threaten to eclipse the purpose of the justice system. When media organizations from around the world converge on a trial, even everyday mundane procedures of the criminal justice system become the talk of news and entertainment shows. Such media coverage can make it difficult to assure defendants a fair and impartial trial. Celebrity trials attract high-powered lawyers, often result in prolonged and expensive trials, cause courtroom security problems, and can make it nearly impossible to find jurors who are impartial. It may be necessary to interview hundreds of potential jurors before a jury can be selected. Furthermore, it is difficult to ignore the impact of the celebrity's fame on the criminal justice process. It may be difficult for jurors to see superstars as just "regular" defendants. For some superstar defendants this can work in their favor. For others, such as boxer Mike Tyson, it may work against them. Although some argue that celebrities receive favorable attention, celebrities are not immune from conviction. For example, Winona Ryder was convicted of shoplifting and Martha Stewart went to prison. Finally, it is impossible to overlook the impact that the wealth of a celebrity can have on the quality of justice.

Why do you think the media and the public are so interested in sensational crimes and crimes by famous persons? Are there any harms that result from disproportional media coverage of sensational crimes? If so, what are they? Do you believe that superstars receive more favorable treatment by the criminal justice system? Explain your answer.

Personality Theories and Psychopathic Behavior

One of the psychology-based theories that has gained some acceptance and use in the criminal justice system is Samenow and Yochelson's theory of the **criminal personality**.[23] Their theory hypothesizes that criminals have a different way of thinking than noncriminals. The criminal sees and responds to the world differently, and Yochelson and Samenow identified as many as 52 patterns of thinking common to the criminals they studied in their research. Criminals, they said, are angry people who feel a sense of superiority, have a highly inflated self-image, and do not expect to be held accountable for their acts. Other personality researchers described criminals as lacking self-control, responsibility, and respect for others. However, criminologists have remained skeptical of the relationship of personality to criminality. Nevertheless, it is clear that some criminals exhibit psychopathic behavior and that possible relationships between mental illness and criminality cannot be denied.

▲ check your understanding **2.5** **On what assumptions are psychological theories based? How was Freud's psychoanalytical theory applied to criminal behavior? Why has this theory been rejected in the criminal justice system? Are there links between personality and criminality?**

See www.courttv.com to go to the Court TV website to view media coverage of trials.

See www.crimelibrary.com/serial_killers for information on famous serial killers.

Sociological Explanations

▼ the main idea **2.6** **Sociological theories of criminal behavior consider environment, social class, social disorganization, social learning, social interaction, cultural deviance, and social conflict.**

In the twentieth century, the belief that criminal behavior is strongly influenced by the environment, social processes, and social structure gained in popularity until it became the predominately accepted explanation for criminal behavior. These sociological theories of crime causation reflected the changing American environment, scientific knowledge, social norms, and values of the time. From 1900 to approximately 1950, U.S. society underwent tremendous social, environmental, scientific, and cultural change. The United States became a world industrial leader, relatively lax immigration laws admitted waves of immigrants from Europe, and the introduction of numerous new inventions, such as the telephone, automobile, and television, caused profound change. Not surprisingly, many social scientists concluded that these variables had great impact on social behavior, especially criminal behavior.

Social Determinism

Theories based on the idea that society—social forces and social groups and institutions—is the cause of crime reflect a philosophy of **social determinism**. Society—not free will, biology, or psychology—determines criminal behavior. The earliest sociological theories to emerge focused on the poverty and dysfunctional social environments of communities with higher than normal crime rates. Later theories postulated that criminal behavior is influenced by social relations and social interactions.

criminal personality Theories from psychology that identify personality traits and habits of mind believed to be associated with criminality.

social determinism The assumption that criminal behavior is caused by social factors and social forces rather than by moral, environmental, psychological, or biological causes.

Social Disorganization as the Cause of Crime

Early sociologists found crime and the criminal convenient and interesting subjects for study. The University of Chicago had one of the earliest sociology departments in the

United States. **Robert Ezra Park** (1864–1944) was one of the founders of this department, and he focused on explaining and understanding social disorder. Park believed that human behavior is influenced by the environment and that an overcrowded and disordered environment leading to social isolation contributes to deviant and criminal behavior.[24] Gathering data from the surrounding Chicago area, Park and his students engaged in a comprehensive study of the relationship between urbanization and social isolation, based on **Emile Durkheim**'s theory of anomie. **Anomie** is a feeling of "normlessness" and lack of belonging that people feel when they become socially isolated. According to Durkheim, people with anomie lack the ties to society that would inhibit them from committing crimes against society.

See www.csiss.org/classics/content/26 for graphics illustrating Park and Burgess's theory of 5 Natural Urban Areas of Chicago.

Social Disorganization Theory In the early 1900s, Chicago grew rapidly due to industrialization and immigration. Park's research demonstrated that criminal behavior was independent of individual characteristics and much more dependent on disruptive social forces. This is called **social disorganization theory**.[25] Subsequent studies by Clifford Shaw and others demonstrated that Chicago was divided into territorial patterns with distinct populations.[26] Each population had a distinct ecological niche and a life of its own that was more or less conducive to crime. This environment-based theory of criminal behavior became known as zone theory.

Zone Theory According to **zone theory**, developed by Park and Burgess, social environments based on status differences—poverty, illiteracy, lack of schooling, unemployment, and illegitimacy—are powerful forces that influence human interaction. For example, large groups of immigrants who entered Chicago as part of the urbanization and industrialization process tended to concentrate near the industrial section of the city. Because of their limited financial resources, limited language abilities, differences in cultural values, and the general poverty of their social environment, these groups of immigrants tended to become socially isolated and their youth had higher rates of juvenile delinquency. Studies by Shaw and McKay showed that from 1900 to 1933 the highest rates of delinquency persisted in the same neighborhoods of Chicago, even though the ethnic composition changed.[27] Thus, the basic cause of delinquency was not the ethnicity of the juveniles, but the social structures, institutions, and environmental variables in that zone. As one moved away from the industrial heart of the city, the rates of delinquency dropped.

Since the 1930s, social disorganization theory and especially zone theory have had a strong influence on crime prevention efforts. Based on the assumption that social conditions such as unemployment, poor schools, and substandard housing are significant factors contributing to delinquency and crime, many government-sponsored programs have attempted to fight crime by improving employment opportunities, social services, schools, and housing. **Crime prevention through environmental design (CPTED)** was founded on the theory that crime prevention is related to environmental design, particularly housing design. Using CPTED principles, many housing projects have been planned in hopes that attention to environmental details such as public space, lighting, and population density will reduce the higher than normal crime rate associated with public housing projects.[28] Another crime prevention program rooted in social disorganization theory is the "broken window theory." This crime prevention program is based on the idea that signs of neighborhood neglect, community deterioration, and tolerance of petty crime all contribute to more crime and crime-inducing environments.[29]

anomie Emile Durkheim's concept of normlessness and social isolation as symptoms of a dysfunctional society and causes of deviant behavior.

social disorganization theory Theories of crime causation based on the assumption that social conditions such as poverty, unemployment, poor schools, and substandard housing are significant factors contributing to delinquency and crime.

zone theory Environmental theory of crime causation based on the belief that structural elements of society such as poverty, illiteracy, lack of schooling, unemployment, and illegitimacy are powerful forces that influence human interaction.

crime prevention through environmental design (CPTED) Theory that crime can be prevented through environmental design, particularly urban housing design.

Differential Association Theory

Other theories of causes of criminal behavior focused on the actors rather than on their environment. Implicit in these theories is the idea that behavior is learned and socialized through observation and interaction in groups. Learning theory and the concept of socialization, concepts shared by both sociology and psychology, were the basis for

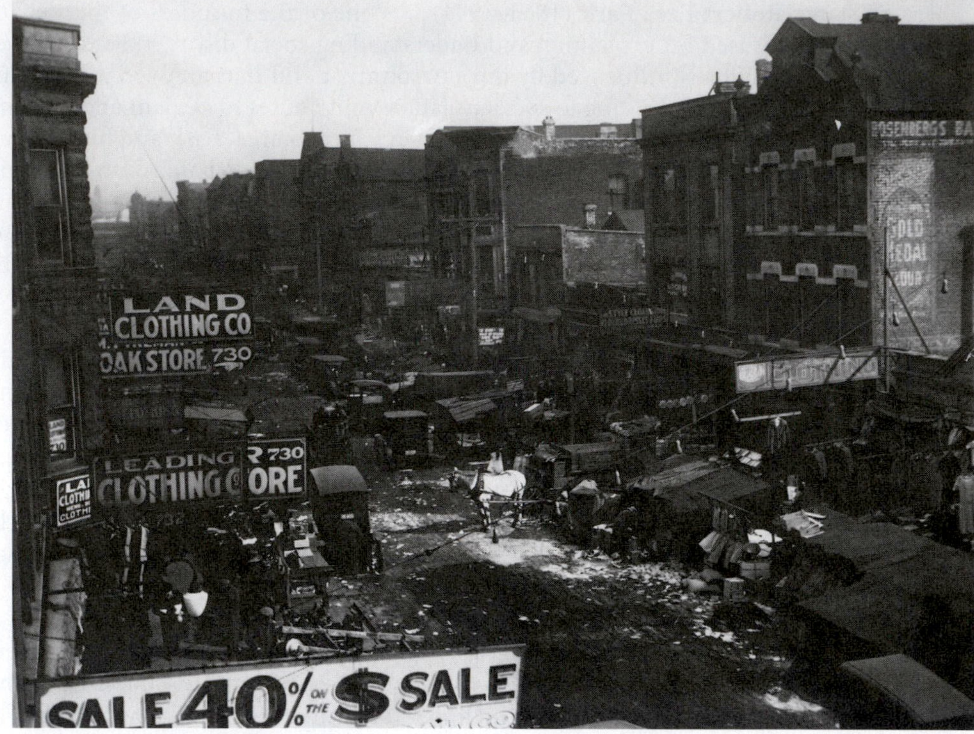

In the 1920s, vast urban slums developed around Maxwell Street and other commercial areas in Chicago. What developments in early twentieth-century criminology were responses to conditions in urban environments such as those seen in this photograph? What sociological explanations of crime emerged from studies of social forces such as urbanization?

Sutherland's **differential association theory,** which proposes that criminal behavior is learned entirely through group interaction. This theory, proposed by **Edwin Sutherland** (1883–1950), argues that criminal behavior is learned in intimate peer groups that reward or reinforce antisocial or delinquent behaviors.[30] Thus, a life of crime is culturally transmitted through peer groups. The more a youth associates with deviant peers than with others, the more "socialized" the youth becomes to a life of crime. One reason that this theory is popular is because it offers an explanation of delinquency that does not depend on other sociological factors that may be involved in crime causation, such as social disorganization.

Sutherland's explanation did not refer to environmental or class factors or to economic motivation, poverty, or opportunity. Criminal behavior was not explained as an expression of economic needs or moral–cultural values, and criminals were not necessarily mentally defective, morally bankrupt, or economically deprived. Rather, Sutherland emphasized that criminal or deviant behavior is simply learned behavior. He believed that criminal behavior does not originate in the social status of the person, poverty, inadequate housing, or substandard schools. Rather, criminality is learned in the same manner as other learned behaviors in the normal course of socialization.

Because of its basis in learning theory, differential association theory can explain white-collar crime and crime by upper-class adolescents. Differential association theory emphasizes that if a "good kid" from a middle- or upper-class family has criminal friends whom he or she esteems, then during the normal course of social interaction with them the "good kid" will learn criminal behavior.

differential association theory Edwin Sutherland's theory that criminal behavior is learned through association with a peer group that engages in criminal behavior.

Extensions of Sutherland's theory have identified other agents of socialization, especially the mass media, that may contribute to the learning of delinquent behavior and aggressive behavior. Other theories focus on the mechanisms by which learned criminal behavior persists.[31] Whether a behavior persists depends on behavioral principles such as reinforcement; that is, behavior persists when it is rewarded or reinforced in some way, whereas behavior that is punished or ignored may be extinguished. A teenager may learn how to shoplift from his or her peers, for instance, but getting caught stealing a candy bar may be so unpleasant that the teen never again engages in that behavior.

Although learning theories continue to dominate criminological thought and social programming, they have several significant shortcomings. They do not adequately explain how and why a person chooses to learn criminal behavior. Why is it that one police officer spends a lifetime career in close association with criminals without esteeming their criminal values, while another police officer begins to accept those values and engages in criminal behavior soon after employment? Learning theory does not explain why a person who has two friends, one law abiding and one criminal, chooses to emulate and learn from one and not the other.

Social Control Theories

Theories of crime causation that emphasized the role of social disorganization gave rise to others, such as social control theories, strain theories, and cultural deviance theories. These theories start with the assumption that because the majority of people, including members of the lower classes, are not criminal, there must be some social factors that operate against deviant and criminal behavior.[32]

Social control theory emphasizes that social and cultural values exert control over individuals' behavior and that social institutions enforce those values. Social institutions that contribute to the formation of social values are the family, school, neighborhood, religion, and government. These institutions exert control both informally (e.g., parental disapproval or social rejection) and formally (e.g., school suspension or arrest). The influence of informal and formal systems of social control makes people basically law abiding to the extent that they identify with and conform to social expectations.[33]

Data from comparative criminology studies support the premise of social control theory. International surveys of crime indicate that countries with very strong informal social control systems have the lowest crime rates. Social control theories posit that when social institutions are intact and have strong influence, deviant behavior is minimized, and when social institutions begin to deteriorate, crime increases.[34]

Containment Theory **Walter Reckless's** (1899–1988) **containment theory,** for example, proposes that there is a dual defense system against deviant behavior. He believed that there are "outer containments" and "inner containments" that suppress criminal behavior.[35] Outer containments are variables such as positive role models, opportunity for individual achievement, cohesion among members of a group, sense of belongingness, and identification with the group. However, if outer containments fail to prevent deviant behavior, a second defense is the influence of inner containment. Inner containment variables include a good self-concept, self-control, a strong ego, and a well-developed conscience.

Reckless proposed that in addition to the forces that keep one from criminal behavior, there are forces that tend to push one toward criminal behavior. Acting against inner and outer containment are internal pushes, such as the need for immediate gratification, restlessness, and hostility, as well as external pressures, such as poverty, unemployment, and blocked opportunities. Reckless believed that the dynamic interaction of these factors determines the outcomes of one's behavior. The most conducive situation for criminal behavior is one in which there is weak inner and outer containment and strong internal pushes and external pressures. Under such conditions, the likelihood of criminality is high.

Neutralization Theory **Gresham Sykes** and **David Matza's neutralization theory** is based on the assumption that one cannot completely resist criminal behavior and that most people have committed some criminal or deviant act at one time or another. These researchers focused on variables similar to those of Reckless's inner containment. They have argued that deviant and criminal behavior produces a sense of guilt and that

social control theory Theories of crime causation based on the assumptions that people's belief in and identification with the values of their society and culture influence their behavior.

containment theory Walter Reckless's theory that people are deterred from deviant behavior because of the influence on individuals of both internal and external social control factors.

neutralization theory Gresham Sykes and David Matza's theory that criminals learn techniques that allow them to rationalize their behavior, deny responsibility for harm, and avoid being guilt ridden.

Sociological explanations of crime focus on criminal acts as learned behavior. Dysfunctional societies, disordered neighborhoods, law-breaking street gangs, and abusive families create criminals. What are the names and principal ideas of these theories based on social determinism?

the pains of conscience are sufficient to keep most people from engaging in extended and extensive criminality. How, then, do people overcome their guilt so as to be able to carry on a continued career of crime? Sykes and Matza's explanation is that criminals learn neutralization techniques—for example, rationalizing their behavior and denying responsibility for harm they cause—that allows them to avoid being guilt ridden.[36]

The shortcoming of neutralization theory is that it does not explain the prime motivation. Why would some people learn neutralization techniques to continue to engage in criminal behavior, while others are detoured and cease criminal activity? Because neutralization techniques appear to be basic psychological defenses, such as rationalization, denial, and appeal to higher loyalties, anyone could employ these techniques to avoid guilt, but only a few choose to do so.

Bond Theory A third offshoot of social control theory is **Travis Hirschi's social bond theory**, which explains behavior as an interaction of four variables: attachment, commitment, involvement, and belief.[37] According to social bond theory, these variables lead to strong social and emotional ties to social values and norms and to the community, which have the effect of lessening deviant behavior. Proponents of the social bond theory focus on evidence that the bonds that help prevent delinquency appear to be weakening in contemporary society. They point to breakdowns in school discipline and oversight, widespread erosion of the authority of teachers, and less effective parenting as evidence that the bond of attachment is weakening. They see evidence of less commitment, involvement, and belief in declining civic participation and civility in general, further weakening the social bonds that inhibit criminal behavior.

A criticism of social control theories is that important variables, such as attachment, are abstract concepts that are difficult to operationalize, measure, and test scientifically. This also makes it difficult to compare the levels or strengths of the different variables as determinants of criminal behavior.

Labeling Theory Explanations emphasizing society's control over individual behavior through symbolic interaction include labeling theory. **Labeling theory** focuses on crime from the perspective of society's reactions to and expectations of delinquents and criminal offenders. **Frank Tannenbaum**[38] and **Howard Becker**[39] contributed significantly to the development of labeling theory. Labeling theory does not focus on the person or the crime or even the circumstances of the crime but on people's social reactions to behavior. Becker's perspective is that deviance is created by society, because society defines norms and norm violations. Everyone violates some criminal laws in his or her lifetime. A youth may engage in illegal behavior, but it is society that makes the juvenile a delinquent, not the behavior itself.[40] The belief in labeling theory underlies the practice of withholding from the public the names of juveniles alleged to have committed criminal acts. According to labeling theory, the public would treat the youths as delinquents, possibly trapping them into a lifetime of deviant behavior. Essentially, the label that society attaches to them becomes true, like a self-fulfilling prophecy.

social bond theory Travis Hirschi's theory that strong social and emotional ties to social values and norms lessen the likelihood of deviant behavior.

labeling theory Frank Tannenbaum and Howard Becker's theory that people are strongly influenced by society's expectations of them, such that juveniles labeled as criminals are more likely to become criminals.

strain theory Robert Merton's theory that people are naturally law-abiding but resort to crime when frustrated in finding legitimate means to economic success.

Strain Theory

Some sociologists focus on impacts of class differences on behavior. Strain theories, for example, have as their starting point the belief that all members of society subscribe to a set of cultural values defined by the middle class. The most important value, economic success, was assumed to be universal in society, especially in the early twentieth century before government safety nets existed to help citizens in need. Sociologist **Robert Merton** formulated a popular **strain theory** based on the assumption that people are law-abiding but will resort to crime when they are frustrated in finding legitimate means to economic success.[41] His theory assumed that people are motivated to achieve the comforts and security of a middle-class lifestyle, but that some people find they cannot achieve this goal through traditional, socially acceptable means. Unable to adapt, these individuals might then resort to illegal means.

Merton believed that social conditions, especially poverty and ethnicity, are powerful factors in determining the adaptations individuals make to socially prescribed goals and the lifestyles that develop as a result. It was predicted that the greatest proportion of crime would be found in the lower classes because, Merton believed, lower-class people have the least opportunity to reach middle-class goals legitimately. However, in its emphasis on crime as a product of economic frustration, Merton's theory has limited value in explaining crimes of passion and white-collar crimes by members of the middle and upper classes. Also, in such a diverse society as the United States, it may be presumptuous to assume that everyone shares the same value system and common goals. Nevertheless, strain theory has had a major impact on the government's response to crime. Programs such as Head Start, Job Corps, and others aimed at providing economic opportunities to the poor and disadvantaged are justified by the belief that economic opportunity deters crime.

See http://faculty.ncwc.edu/toconnor/criminology.htm, the Criminology Mega-Site, for information on all the perspectives on causes of crime, including radical criminology.

Cultural Deviance Theories

Whereas strain theories are based on the core values of the wider society, **cultural deviance theories** are based on the idea that the values of subcultural groups within the society have even more power over individual behavior. Subcultures have different, sometimes conflicting, values.[42] Organized crime families, juvenile gangs, and hate groups can be described as deviant subcultures, for example. Within these groups, behaviors defined as deviant by outsiders actually are expected among insiders and are seen as normal.[43] Cultural deviance theorists focus on differences in values and norms between mainstream society and subcultural groups, including immigrant groups who entered the United States during the first half of the twentieth century.

Cultural deviance theories begin with the assumption that subgroups or subcultures within a society have different value systems. **Albert Cohen** defines distinct subcultures in terms of variables such as parental aspirations, child-rearing practices, and classroom standards. Cohen uses the term **reaction formation** to describe how lower-class youths reject middle-class values, which they perceive they cannot achieve, embrace new countervalues that are the opposite of middle-class values, and create unique countercultures.[44] Members see the new values as obtainable and accept them as a measuring rod of normative behavior, and the counterculture reinforces these values.

For example, **Walter Miller** pointed out that whereas middle-class values include patience, sharing, honesty, and politeness in adolescents, delinquents reject these values and substitute values such as toughness, risk taking, group loyalty, spontaneity, intensity, danger and excitement, smartness, luck, and group autonomy. According to Miller, members of delinquent subcultures are not impressed by and do not attempt to achieve middle-class benchmarks of success, such as succeeding in school and getting a good job. Striking out against society, delinquents embrace antisocial values, often including random acts of violence against property or persons.[45]

cultural deviance theories Theories of crime causation based on the assumption that criminal behavior is learned through participation in deviant subcultures or countercultures within a society.

reaction formation Albert Cohen's term for his cultural deviance theory in which lower-class youths reject middle-class values that they cannot attain and instead join countercultures that express the opposite values.

Conflict Theories

Another perspective on crime causation emphasizes that crime has less to do with deviant behavior than with competition and conflict between social classes and institutional discrimination. Conflict theorists do not focus on individual motivation or learning or on group interaction. Rather, they focus on how a society's system of social stratification (division of society into social classes) and social inequality influence behavior.[46] **Conflict theories** are based on the assumption that powerful ruling political and social elites—persons, groups, or institutions—exploit the less powerful and use the criminal justice system to their own advantage to maintain their power and privilege.[47] In this view, criminology is the study of crime in relation to society's haves and have-nots.

Theories of crime based on social inequality have their roots in the social criticisms of Karl Marx and Friedrich Engels in nineteenth-century Europe. Marxism assumes a division between the poor (workers) and the rich (property owners, capitalists) in which the rich control the various social, political, and economic institutions of society. The rich use their power and position to control the poor.[48] The criminological theories associated with Marxism, referred to as "radical criminology" or "new criminology," however, do not advocate Marx's solution, which was the violent overthrow of the ruling class. Instead, present-day conflict theorists suggest that reducing social inequality is the only or best way to reduce criminal behavior.[49]

Richard Quinney argued, for example, that the criminal justice system is a state-initiated and state-supported effort to rationalize mechanisms of social control, which are based on class structure. The state is organized to serve the interests of the dominant economic class. Criminal law was seen as an instrument that the state and the ruling class use to maintain and perpetuate the social and economic order.[50]

Feminist criminology, which is based on the conflict model, focuses on gender inequality as well as class inequality as a basis of crime. **Feminist criminology** assumes that the underlying cause of criminal behavior by females is the inequality of power between men and women. Advocates such as **Freda Adler,**[51] **Meda Chesney-Lind** and Kathleen Daly,[52] and Rita J. Simon[53] argue that inequality of political, economic, and social power and wealth is the root cause of female criminal behavior.

Conflict theorists have strongly criticized mainstream criminology and the criminal justice system. Radical criminologists such as **William Chambliss** saw the law and the system as a means of institutional discrimination rather than as a means of providing fairness in justice.[54] Although efforts have been made to address these criticisms of the criminal justice system, conflict-based theories of crime causation have not had a role in crime prevention or rehabilitation programs. For one thing, conflict theorists have depended more on philosophical and political arguments than on data from quantitative studies, necessary for an objective examination of the hypotheses regarding crime causation.

Conflict theories do not explain why the ruling elite is so prejudiced against the poor or why it is impossible for the poor to benefit under capitalism in a democratic society. Nevertheless, it would be a mistake to dismiss them as entirely without merit. Conflict theorists point out that the primary focus of mainstream criminology and the criminal justice system is property crimes and crimes against persons. Disproportionate attention to these crimes often obscures the greater social harm done by white-collar crimes, corruption, political crimes, and other abuses of power. Conflict theorists also point to flaws in the criminal justice system that appear to be based on class distinctions, although critics argue that the system often is self-correcting.

As you can see, there is no single theory that explains crime. Various theories, summarized in Table 2.1, have appeared in an attempt to explain crime throughout history based on the scientific knowledge and social values of the era in which they were developed.

conflict theories Theories of crime causation based on Marxian theory or the assumption that the sources of criminal behavior are class conflict and social inequality.

feminist criminology Field based on the assumption that gender inequality lies at the heart of crimes in which women are the victims or the perpetrators.

▲ check your understanding **2.6** **On what assumptions are sociological explanations of criminal behavior based? What are the original sociological theories of criminality? How do theories based on social disorganization, association, social control, strain, cultural deviance, and social conflict compare?**

table 2.1

Explanations of Criminal Behavior

Type of Explanation	School of Thought	Theory	Proponent	Cause of Crime	Solution to Crime
Moralism				Evil; sin Spirit possession	Elimination of offenders from society
Free Will	Classical	Pain–pleasure principle	Cesare Beccaria	Rational free choice	Deterrence through pain of punishment over pleasure of crime
	Neoclassical	Utilitarianism	Jeremy Bentham	Rational free will except for the young and insane	Deterrence through laws fitting the punishment to the crime
Biological Determinism	Evolutionary	Darwinism; concept of atavism	Cesare Lombroso Richard Dugdale (Ada Jukes)	Heredity; no free will and thus no moral accountability	Prevention impossible; give medical treatment (and castrate or sterilize criminals)
		Somatotype	William Sheldon	Inherited predispositions revealed through body type	Prevention through identification
	Biocriminology	XYY chromosome hormones; nutrition; MBD (minimal brain dysfunction)		Physiological disorders or chemically induced aggression	Medical treatment and control
Psychological Determinism		Psychoanalytical theory	Sigmund Freud	Psychopathology; irrational, unresolved, unconscious conflict from guilt/anxiety from childhood trauma	Counseling and rehabilitation
		Criminal personality		Antisocial attitudes and lack of self-control	Early childhood intervention
Social Determinism	Environmentalism	Zone theory	Robert Ezra Park	Society; dysfunctional social environments	Reduce anomie through environmental design and urban renewal; reduce poverty
	Interactionism	Differential association theory	Edwin Sutherland	Socialization in delinquent peer groups	Diversion and reeducation
		Cultural deviance	Albert Cohen	Socialization in deviant subculture or counterculture	Distinguish cultural diversity and dissent from deviance

(continued)

table 2.1

Explanations of Criminal Behavior *(Continued)*

Type of Explanation	School of Thought	Theory	Proponent	Cause of Crime	Solution to Crime
Social Determinism *(Cont.)*	Social control			Breakdown of social institutions; lack of conformity	Enforcement of social values and norms; strengthening of institutions, such as the family; strengthening of social and emotional bonds to others and to society
		Containment theory	Walter Reckless	Loss of self-control and social control	
		Neutralization theory	Gresham Sykes/ David Matza	Rationalization of antisocial acts	
		Social bond theory	Travis Hirschi	Loss of sense of attachment	
		Labeling theory	Howard Becker	Society's reactions to deviance	
	Structuralism			Social structure; structure of opportunity	Level the playing field; provide equal opportunity
		Strain theory	Robert Merton	Frustration in achieving middle-class goals legitimately because of poverty or ethnicity	Eliminate frustrations and disadvantages or help people overcome them
		Differential opportunity	Richard Cloward and Lloyd Ohlin	Blocked opportunities to reach goals	
		Conflict theory		Social inequality; class conflict; institutional discrimination	Social and political equality; redistribution of wealth and power in society
			Richard Quinney	Criminal justice system as a weapon of the ruling class; racial discrimination	Equal rights; equal protection
			Freda Adler	Gender inequality	Equal rights; equal protection

Counting Crime

the main idea 2.7 Statistics on crime and research on the operation of police, the courts, and corrections drive public policy and underlie development and change in the agencies that make up the criminal justice system.

The understanding of the causes of crime is important to many aspects related to the criminal justice system. Just as important is the ability to measure the number and types of crimes committed and to know the reliability and validity of these measures. The number of crimes committed affects the criminal justice system in many ways. However, counting crime can be an inexact science. Josiah Stamp, an early American critic of government statistics, said, "The government is very keen at amassing statistics. They collect them, add them, refer them to the *n*th power, take the cube root, to prepare wonderful diagrams. But you must never forget that every one of these figures comes in the first instance from the [village watchman], who just puts down what he damn pleases."[55]

Visit the Bureau of Justice Statistics at www.ojp.usdoj.gov/bjs/ and follow links to explore statistics on crime, victims and perpetrators of crimes, and the criminal justice system. The Uniform Crime Report can be viewed at FBI.gov.

Crime statistics and measures of the criminal justice system are subject to error, and the further one goes back, the more prominent the error appears. Today, various official agencies, such as the Federal Bureau of Investigation, the **Bureau of Justice Statistics,** and the National Criminal Justice Reference Service, gather and disseminate data about nearly every aspect of the criminal justice system. The gathering of criminal justice statistics is a recent phenomenon. Quantitative data older than the 1970s is untrustworthy. For instance, the New York City coroner's office recorded 323 homicides in 1913, but the police filed only 261 homicides. Likewise, in 1915, the San Francisco Police Department reported only 50 homicides, but the coroner reported 71.[56]

As you read in Chapter 1, public fears about crime control and order maintenance arose during social upheavals dating to the 1950s, but the roots of those fears began in the 1920s, when crime was perceived mainly as a big-city problem. After World War I, more people migrated to the cities. As urban populations swelled, the public became more concerned with crime. In the 1920s, Cleveland, Ohio, and Chicago, Illinois, were among the first major cities to perform crime surveys.[57,58] These surveys were motivated by the desire to correct what were perceived as major deficiencies in the criminal justice system. The basic premise was that the absence of crime is the best measure of police effectiveness. If reforms to the criminal justice system were effective, it was believed that the results would be reflected in decreasing crime rates.[59]

The public perception that the Great Depression of the 1930s brought a crime wave heightened interest in counting crime. The news media exaggerated the crime wave with colorful stories of organized crime figures and infamous public enemies such as John Dillinger, Charles "Pretty Boy" Floyd, George "Baby Face" Nelson, and Bonnie Parker and Clyde Barrow. Stories of bank robberies were front-page news. The public was entertained with stories of shoot-outs with the police.

Passage of the Eighteenth Amendment, which prohibited the manufacture, sale, and possession of alcoholic beverages, added fuel to the fire. The Prohibition Amendment, or the Volstead Act, as it was called, increased rather than decreased crime as gangs warred for control of the lucrative illegal sale of alcoholic beverages. Crime bosses such as Al Capone appeared to be immune to arrest because of pervasive corruption within the criminal justice system. The average citizen was left with the impression that crime was everywhere and no one could do much about it. Without a way to determine objectively whether crime was increasing or decreasing, the public had no idea which side—the criminal justice system or the criminals—was winning. Without crime statistics, it was not possible to determine the impact of money spent, resources invested, reform efforts, and new laws on the problem of crime.

The Uniform Crime Report

The problem with determining crime rates was that there existed no single standard for collecting and counting crime data. Based on the efforts of the International Association of Chiefs of Police Committee on Uniform Crime Reports, on June 11, 1930, Congress passed the first federal legislation mandating the collecting of crime data. The Federal Bureau of Investigation (FBI) was charged with the responsibility of collecting crime data from police departments and disseminating the data to the nation. While these efforts served a public purpose, law enforcement officials also saw crime data as a way to exploit the fear of crime to justify their requests for additional personnel and increased resources.[60] As a result, crime data were collected and used in a manner that tended to emphasize the pervasiveness and seriousness of crime.

The Crime Clock One of the data presentation strategies used by the FBI during this period, and still in use today, is the **Crime Clock,** which reported how often a crime occurred (see Figure 2.1). The Crime Clock was used to emphasize that crime occurred nearly all of the time. For example, according to the Crime Clock, larceny–theft occurred every 4.5 seconds, burglary was committed every 15.4 seconds, and aggravated assault every 34.6 seconds. It was easy for citizens to conclude that they could hardly walk outside without becoming a crime statistic. These data are terribly distorted, however. Although it may be accurate to say that a murder occurs every 33.9 minutes, it does not mean that every 33.9 minutes, a murder occurs in every community. It means that every 33.9 minutes, a murder occurs somewhere in the United States. Furthermore, murders

figure 2.1

Crime Clock

The Crime Clock should be viewed with care. The most aggregate representation of UCR data, it conveys the annual reported crime experience by showing a relative frequency of occurrence of index offenses. It should not be taken to imply a regularity in the commission of crime. The Crime Clock represents the annual ratio of crime to fixed-time intervals.

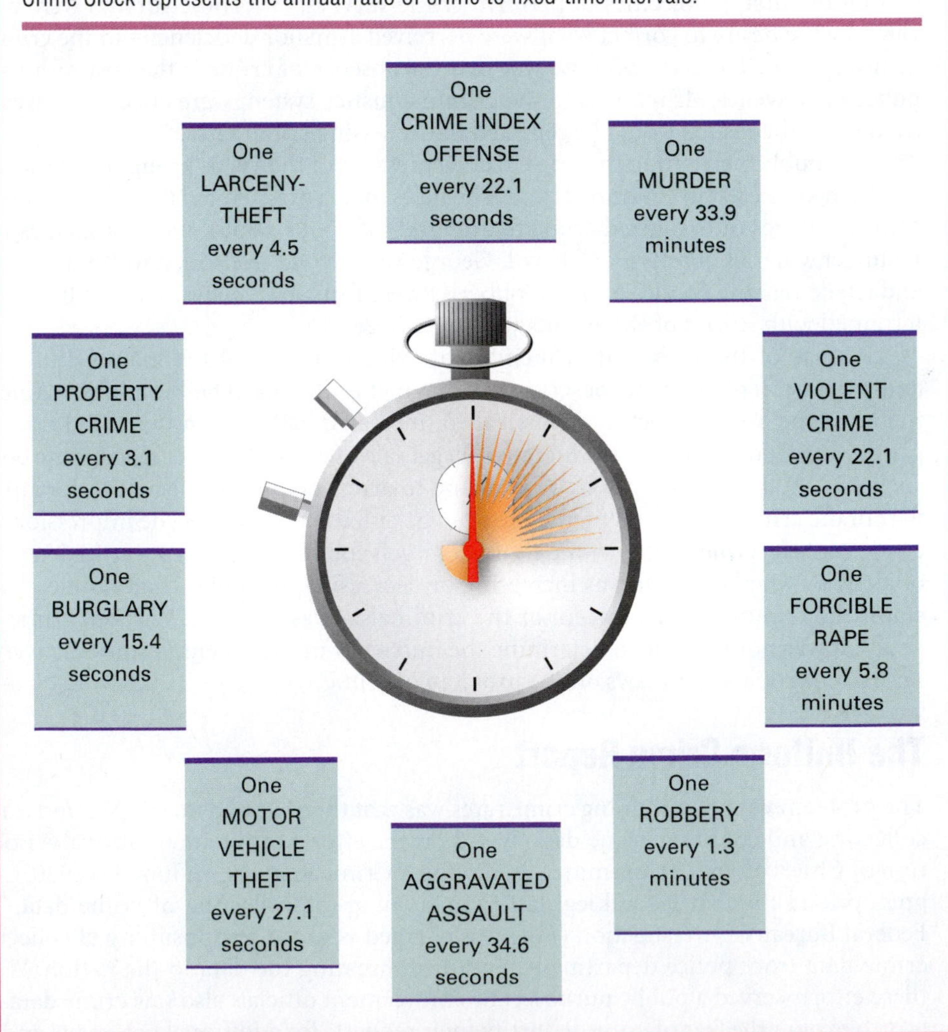

Source: Federal Bureau of Investigation, *Uniform Crime Report, 2002.*

Crime Clock Data presentation strategy used by the FBI to report crime rates in terms of how often a crime occurs.

are not randomly distributed among cities but tend to be concentrated in urban areas. Rural communities may go years or even decades without a murder. Even in large cities such as New York, Los Angeles, Chicago, and Atlanta, murder does not happen every 33.9 minutes. If that were the case, there would be about 2 homicides every hour and 48 murders in a single day! Despite the inflationary statistics the Crime Clock generates, it continues to be used as a method of presenting crime data.

Uses of UCR Data Over the years, crime data collected by the FBI and published under the title ***Uniform Crime Report*** **(UCR)** have become useful as databases for examining crime trends. These data are used for numerous purposes: a measure of crime rates, a factor in indexes calculating quality of life in U.S. cities, and a factor in policy decisions. Based on UCR trend data, municipalities may decide to add more police officers to their force. Grants aimed at crime prevention and curbing drug crime use UCR data to measure effectiveness. The release of new UCR data is often anxiously awaited by many agencies, because they want to know if recent changes such as community policing, neighborhood watches, or "get-tough" sentencing policies have had an impact on the crime rate.

UCR Data Collection The UCR had its origins at a time when there were no computers, no computerized databases, and no statistics and graphics software. Crime data were collected, stored, and transmitted manually. Collecting and reporting crime data was a labor-intensive process. Most police departments kept file cabinets filled with cards detailing each crime. The cards were arranged by case number and offense and were filed under the various crime categories (murder, rape, burglary, etc.). Anyone wanting to know the number of burglaries committed during a particular period had to go to the file cabinet, pull the cards for burglary, and count the number of cards one by one. Under the circumstances, the FBI had to adopt rules for counting crime that were consistent with the limitations imposed by the system.

The Hierarchy Rule Each crime card contained the information for one case or incident based only on the most serious charge. In a single incident, several crimes might have been committed. A person might have been both robbed and assaulted, and both crimes would be noted in one police report, recorded on one card, and filed under "robbery." This method of counting only the most serious crime in incidents involving multiple crimes is called the **hierarchy rule.** Also, if more than one victim were involved in the incident (e.g., a group of people was robbed), the UCR reported only the most serious offense for the incident as a whole and not for individual victims. As you can imagine, use of the hierarchy rule results in an undercounting of crime.

In addition, the UCR does not report data for all crimes. Only a few crimes have been selected for inclusion in the UCR database. Again, the decision to limit the number of crimes tracked was based initially on the limitation that all crime data were paper-based and manually counted. It was simply not feasible to count all crimes. In all, the UCR provides data for 27 criminal violations, which are divided into two categories: serious crimes and less serious crimes.[61] The serious crimes are reported in Part I of the UCR, and the less serious crimes are reported in Part II. The 8 crimes in Part I, called **Index Crimes**, are murder, forcible rape, robbery, aggravated assault, burglary, larceny, motor vehicle theft, and arson. All of these crimes except arson are sometimes called "high-fear" crimes or "street" crimes. Data for the remaining crimes are reported in Part II of the UCR (see Table 2.2).

At the time the FBI started gathering UCR data, arson was not included in Part I crimes. The intention of Part I crimes was to gather data about those crimes that appeared to have the greatest impact on quality of life and of which people had the greatest fear of victimization. Arson was not added to the Part I UCR until 1979. Arson is a crime against habitation and buildings, whereas the other Part I crimes are those against people.

hierarchy rule Practice in data collection for the FBI's *Uniform Crime Reports* of counting only the most serious crime in incidents involving multiple crimes or with multiple victims of the same crime.

Index Crimes The eight crimes in Part I of the *Uniform Crime Reports:* murder, forcible rape, robbery, aggravated assault, burglary, larceny, motor vehicle theft, and arson.

table 2.2

FBI's *Uniform Crime Report* Part I and Part II Offenses

Part I Offenses (Crime Index)	Part II Offenses *(Continued)*
Criminal Homicide Murder, nonnegligent manslaughter, and nonjustifiable homicide. Manslaughter by negligence is a Part I crime but is not included in the Crime Index.	**Stolen Property** Buying, selling, receiving
	Weapons Carrying, possessing
Forcible Rape "Carnal knowledge"; includes sexual assault; does not include statutory offenses	**Prostitution and Commercialized Vice**
	Sex Offenses Statutory rape and offenses against morality
Robbery "Taking" or attempting to take anything of value from a person by force, threat, or fear	**Drug Abuse Violations** State or local laws against unlawful possession, sale, use, growing, or manufacturing of opium, cocaine, morphine, heroin, codeine, marijuana, and other narcotic and dangerous nonnarcotic drugs
Aggravated Assault Attack on a person for the purpose of inflicting bodily harm, usually through use of a weapon	
	Gambling
Burglary Breaking or entering a structure to commit a felony or theft, including attempt	**Offenses against Family and Children** Nonsupport, neglect, desertion, abuse
Larceny Includes theft of property that does not involve force, violence, or fraud	**Driving under the Influence** Of alcohol or drugs
Motor Vehicle Theft Does not include motorboats, construction equipment, airplanes, or farming equipment	**Liquor Laws** State or local laws
	Drunkenness
Arson Willful or malicious burning or attempt to burn any property for any reason	**Disorderly Conduct**
	Vagrancy
Part II Offenses	**All Other Violations** Of state or local laws
Simple Assault No weapon or serious injury	**Suspicion** Suspect released without charge
Forgery and Counterfeiting	**Curfew and Loitering Laws** Persons under age 18
Fraud	**Runaways** Persons under age 18 in protective custody
Embezzlement	

Clearance Rates The UCR reports the number of crimes and statistics on the clearance rate of crimes. **Clearance rate** refers to the percentage of crimes solved versus those that are unsolved. *Solved* means that the police believe they know the perpetrator of the crime. *Solved* does not mean that the perpetrator has been arrested, prosecuted, convicted, or incarcerated. It merely means that the police are reasonably certain they know who committed the crime. In most cases, a crime is "cleared" by the arrest of the suspect, but police consider the crime cleared if they *believe* the suspect committed the crime, regardless of whether there is a conviction. Other cases in which a crime is cleared even though the suspect is not charged or tried include the suspect's death, immunity from arrest, or flight beyond the reach of U.S. law enforcement.

Why UCR Data Are Inadequate There are several major shortcomings of UCR data that encourage the collection of crime data by other means. One shortcoming is that UCR data represent only crimes that are *known* to the police; unreported crimes are not included. The lack of this type of information is particularly significant: People often do not report crimes because they have lost confidence in the police, which includes both confidence in the ability of the police to do something about the crime and confidence that the police are not corrupt and that no harm will come to innocent people if they report a crime.

clearance rate Percentage of reported crimes determined to be solved.

In addition, the UCR (1) includes data only about local and state crimes, not federal offenses; and (2) depends on the voluntary cooperation of local and state police agencies for data collection. When the UCR began, federal law enforcement agencies did not play as prominent a role in crime fighting as they do today. Today, nearly all local and state police agencies report crime data to the FBI, but this was not always the case. In the early years, many local police departments did not report crime data because they lacked adequate record keeping or personnel to gather the facts or because they feared embarrassment or simply did not want to report the data. To this day, there is no official sanction of local and state police for failing to report crime data to the FBI.

Finally, UCR data are about local and state crimes, and definitions of crimes are not the same from place to place. In one jurisdiction, a felony theft may require the taking of property valued at $100, whereas in another jurisdiction, the limit for felony theft may be $1,000. One of the most bothersome problems is the definition of *rape.* The UCR uses a definition that is not as inclusive as that used by states that have adopted progressive sexual assault criminal codes. The UCR defines *forcible rape* as "the carnal knowledge of a female forcibly and against her will." This definition excludes many offenses that are counted as sexual assault by many states.

The National Incident-Based Report System

The FBI recognized the shortcomings of the old UCR crime data survey methods and instituted a plan to address many of these problems. Taking advantage of the computer technology that is now possible in crime reporting, the new system, called the **National Incident-Based Reporting System (NIBRS),** is now more than a simple frequency count of crime. Under NIBRS, additional data about crimes will be reported, including information on place of occurrence, weapon used, type and value of property damaged or stolen, personal characteristics of the offender and the victim and the nature of any relationship between the two, the disposition of the complaint, and so on. The new NIBRS data will provide much more insight into the crime picture, and researchers will have greater success in correlating crime data with other factors suspected of contributing to the incidence of crime and effective crime prevention.

Other Sources of Crime Data

National Crime Victimization Survey

Another major data collection effort to address the shortcomings of the UCR data is the **National Crime Victim Survey (NCVS).** The NCVS dates back to 1972, when it was recognized that a significant number of crimes go unreported to the police. Some of the reasons that crime victims do not report crime to the police is that they believe the police will or can do nothing about it, they fear retaliation and further victimization, they fear that they will be arrested because of their immigration status, and they might believe that the police are part of the problem. Unreported crime was called the "dark figure" of crime, and many authorities believed that knowledge about unreported crime could significantly change the conclusions, theories, and responses of the criminal justice system that were being based only on UCR data. Table 2.3 provides a summary of the comparison of the UCR and the NCVS crime data.

Find interesting data from diverse sources at the Criminal Justice Sourcebook, www.albany.edu/sourcebook.

The NCVS collects victimization information from a representative sample of U.S. households.[62] Each household in the sample is interviewed twice a year, and a household is part of the national sample for 3½ years. The NCVS was authorized in 1972 and the first survey was in 1973. The goals of the victimization survey were:

- To develop detailed information abut the victims of crime
- To initiate a data-collection effort detailing the consequences of crime
- To provide systematic information on the dark figure of crime by estimating the number of crimes not reported to police and estimating the types of crimes not reported to police

table 2.3

Comparison of UCR and NCVS Crime Data

	UCR	NCVS
Date and reason for origin	Authorized by Congress in 1930 in response to public fear of "crime wave"	Began in 1972 to discover "dark figures" of crime (i.e., unreported crime)
Data gathered by	FBI	Bureau of Justice Statistics and U.S. Census Bureau
How data are gathered	Crime reported to the police, who in turn report it to the FBI	Random biannual survey of 42,000 households; excludes crime victims less than 12 years of age
Level of analysis	Reports individual crimes	Surveys all members in a household
Publications	*Uniform Crime Report:* Crime in the United States (quarterly and annual reports)	*Crime and the Nation's Households* *Criminal Victimization* *Annual Report on Criminal Victimization in the United States*
Crimes included in report	Part I—murder, rape, robbery, aggravated assault, burglary, larceny-theft, motor vehicle theft, and arson Part II—simple assault, forgery and counterfeiting, fraud, embezzlement, stolen property, vandalism, weapons, prostitution, sex offenses, drug law violations, gambling, offenses against the family, DUI, liquor law violations, public drunkenness, disorderly conduct, vagrancy, curfew/loitering, and runaways	Rape, robbery, assault, burglary, personal and household larceny, and motor vehicle theft; does not collect crime data concerning murder, kidnapping, victimless crimes, commercial robbery, and burglary of businesses
Major weaknesses	Underreports crime because crimes not reported to the police are not counted; simple frequency count of crime	Crime data error due to false or exaggerated crime reports not known; does not have crime data beyond 1972
Major strengths	Historical data back to 1930; official data of crime reported to police	Captures data on crime not reported to the police; captures data on completed and attempted offenses; provides victimization data about the relationship of victim-offender, location of crime, and other data related to the crime
Major contribution to criminology	Provides standardized data on crime, crime rates, and comparative data for states and cities. The Crime Index is used in many measures of quality of life and effect of crime prevention and drug-use prevention programs.	Revealed a significantly higher rate of crime than that reported by the UCR. Data about crime victimization allows criminologists to build explanations as to the causes of crime.
Improvements being made	Inclusion of sexual assault crimes rather than just rape, data about crime victimization, hierarchy rule modified, more comprehensive data on dollar loss, persons involved, and weapons data	Better methods to ensure accurate reporting of data, more comprehensive data on domestic violence, data regarding alcohol and drug use by offenders, data on gang-related crime

- To provide uniform measures of selected types of crime, and
- To permit comparisons over time and types of areas.[63]

The NCVS gathers data about crime incidents such as the relationship between victim and offender, the use of drugs or alcohol, bystander behavior, suspected offender gang involvement, and self-protection measures taken by the victims. The survey gathers data from crime victims; it does not gather data about homicide. The following list shows the kinds of data included in the NCVS.

Type of criminal victimization	Crime reporting to police
Month victimization occurred	Reasons for nonreporting
Time victimization occurred	Offender characteristics
Location of victimization	Drug and/or alcohol use
Victim–offender relationship	Victim characteristics
Self-protective actions taken	Psychological consequences (victim)
Self-protection outcomes	Financial consequences (victim)
Type of property loss	

The National Crime Victimization Survey provides important data not gathered by the Uniform Crime Report, but it also has deficiencies. The NCVS depends on self-reported data by the victim, which may be inaccurate. The survey is sent to households, so it does not reliably pinpoint the geographical location where the crime occurred, as do the UCR data. Also, household members who have previously withheld information about victimization from family members are not likely to report their victimization in the NCVS.

The early surveys were called the National Crime Survey (NCS). After about two decades of data gathering, shortcomings of the NCS data were revealed. As a result of demands for better data on violence against women, the NCS was revised in 1993 to provide more information on the extent of victimizations that occurred within the family. Also, methodological adjustments were made in the NCS to help people recall victimization incidents more accurately and reliably. As a result of these changes, there are some cautions that should be observed when comparing trend data prior to 1993 to trend data after 1993 (see Figure 2.2).

Comparisons between UCR data and NCVS data have consistently confirmed the belief that there was, indeed, a vast difference between reported crime data and victimization data. A comparison of the reported incidents of sexual assault by the NCVS and

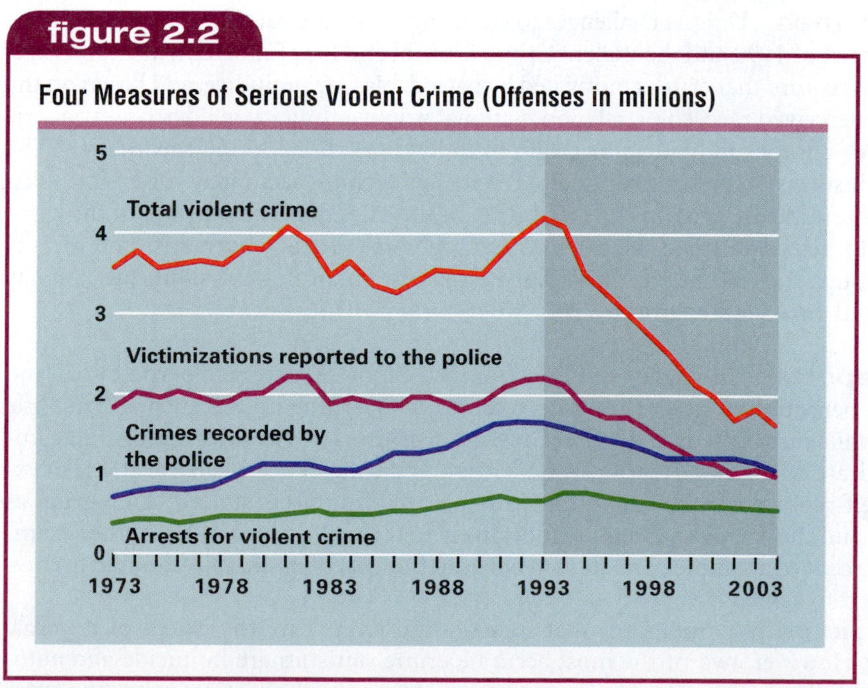

Note: The serious violent crimes included are rape, robbery, aggravated assault, and homicide. The National Crime Victimization Survey redesign was implemented in 1993; the area with the lighter shading is before the redesign and the darker area after the redesign. The data before 1993 are adjusted to make them comparable with data collected since the redesign.

the UCR indicates that the UCR significantly underreports sex crimes. In 2002, the UCR reported 95,136 forcible rapes, whereas the NCVS reported 322,060 rapes. Robbery, aggravated assault, burglary, and larceny were all reported by the NCVS at rates two or three times greater than rates given in the UCR data.

With data from two databases, researchers can compare trend data of reported crime to estimated total crime. Often, these data are revealing, as reported crime in the UCR may increase not because of an actual increase in the crime rate but because of the increase in reported crime.

State-Sponsored Research State-sponsored research includes surveys of crime similar to the UCR, conducted by the individual states, and surveys of crime in public schools, including colleges and universities. These crime surveys are useful in that the crimes reported match the criminal codes used by a state. Statistics on crimes such as sexual assault and larceny are much more likely to be accurate. Schools and colleges and universities are not required to report their crime data to the FBI for inclusion in the UCR data, however. If a crime occurs on school property or a college or university campus, unless that crime is also reported to the police, it is not included in the UCR data, although public disclosure is required.

Campus Crimes As of 1992, the **Crime Awareness and Campus Security Act** has required colleges and universities to report crime data. Every institution must make a public disclosure of the crimes occurring on its campus whether or not these crimes were reported to the police. Some school districts have begun to report crimes that occur on school property. For example, in the past at a K–12 school when a student's lunch money was taken by force, such incidents often were unreported or were handled by the school administration outside of the criminal justice system. Now these incidents are being reported as robberies, which has caused an apparent increase in crime. As a result of this act, students and parents can obtain specific crime data about any college or university campus of their choice.

Hate Crimes Unique challenges to counting crime are raised by the **Hate Crime Statistics Act** of 1990 and the Violent Crime Control and Law Enforcement Act of 1994. These acts require that crimes motivated by hatred, bias, or prejudice, and based on the actual or perceived race, color, religion, national origin, ethnicity, gender, or sexual orientation of another individual or group of individuals, be reported separately.[64] The criminal justice system has struggled to report such crimes accurately. Often it is difficult to determine or agree on the motivation of the offender. The purpose of the legislation is to help determine the extent of crimes committed by extremist and racially biased groups such as the Ku Klux Klan, neo-Nazis, tax protesters, skinheads, antigay groups, and anti-Semitic groups.

Self-Reports Crime data gathered from self-reports (surveys of perpetrators' and potential perpetrators' reports of their offenses) concerning crimes such as drug use, driving while intoxicated (DUI), and consensual crimes such as prostitution and gambling indicate that the UCR seriously underreports the incidence of such crimes. For example, self-reported crime data indicate that many drug users started using drugs as juveniles and that heroin addicts are most likely to commit crimes.[65] As another example, 60 percent of a sample of adult men between the ages of 20 and 30 admitted to driving while intoxicated.[66]

The picture that emerges is that statistics fail to capture the extent of criminal behavior. However, two of the most accurate crime statistics are homicide and automobile theft. Homicide rates are accurate because there is a body. Data regarding automobile theft is consistent from survey to survey because most people report the theft of their automobile to the police as a requirement to collect insurance on loss of the vehicle. Other than for these two crimes, it is difficult to get an accurate picture of just how much crime is committed and who commits it.

One final note regarding counting crime is the warning that crime statistics are only a snapshot of the past. Crime statistics indicate what crime has occurred, not what crime will occur. There is a delay between the gathering and reporting of crime statistics, and it is possible that an alarming report of rising crime rates is inaccurate. Crime rates might already have dropped by the time a report is issued and might continue dropping, making drastic action unnecessary. Thus, looking at crime statistics is like looking into the rearview mirror of an automobile, which shows you where you have been but not where you are going. Crime trends may take some time to establish with any certainty.

▲ check your understanding **2.7 How is crime counted in federal and state data collection? What are the problems with the UCR, NCVS, and other methods of reporting as sources of data on crime? Why are accurate data on crime so important, yet so difficult to achieve?**

Special Categories of Crime

▼ the main idea **2.8 Drug trafficking, transnational crimes, cybercrimes, corporate crime, crimes against the elderly, crimes against women, organized crime, and gun crimes pose special problems for the criminal justice system.**

Sir Robert Peel declared that the absence of crime is the measure of the effectiveness of the police. More than the measure of the effectiveness of the police, it is the measure of the effectiveness of the criminal justice system. The main purpose of the criminal justice system is to fight crime and it is to this end that all of the various agencies and personnel contribute to that goal.

There are some crimes that a single law enforcement agency, no matter how hard it works and how much resources it has to devote to the investigation of the crime, simply cannot defeat. Some problems go beyond the criminal justice system. For example, although illegal drug trafficking and abuse is a law enforcement problem, it cannot be defeated by more aggressive enforcement, more arrests, and longer prison sentences alone. The drug crime problem is also a health problem, a family problem, an economic problem, an international problem, and a societal problem.

This discussion will focus on several crime problems to examine in more detail. These crimes have been selected because they have a significant ongoing impact on the criminal justice system and society and they are crime problems that can be solved only with extensive cooperation and better partnerships with other agencies and with the community. The crime problems selected for examination are (1) illegal drug trafficking and use, (2) transnational crime, (3) cybercrimes and identity theft, (4) corporate and white-collar crime, (5) crimes against the elderly, (6) crimes against women, (7) organized crime, and (8) gun crime.

Drug Crimes

In 2002, over 15 percent of all arrests were attributed to drug abuse.[67] Figure 2.3 shows that since 1992, the number of inmates incarcerated for drug-related offenses has risen

figure 2.3

Inmates Incarcerated for Drug-Related Offenses, 1992–2002 (In thousands)

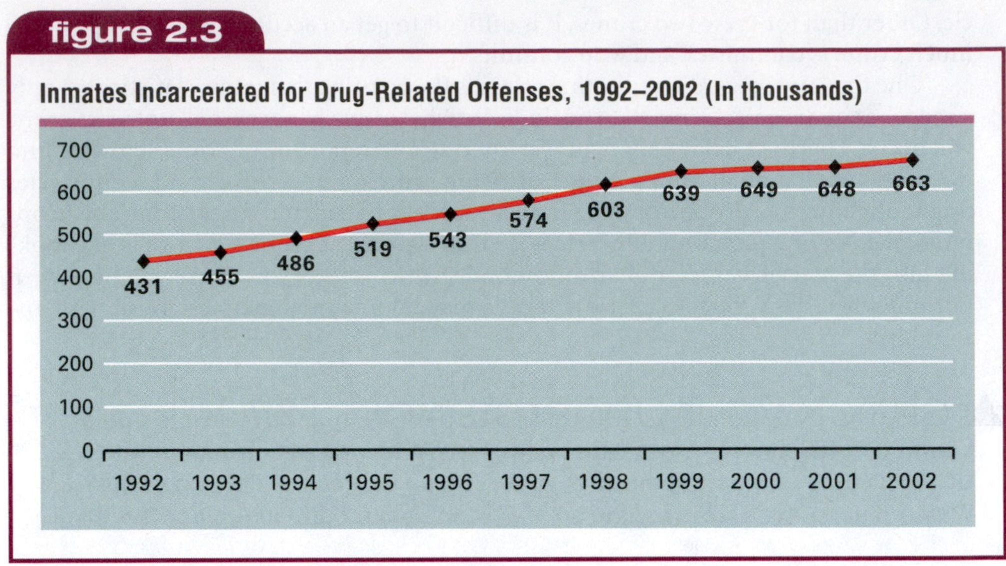

Source: "Storming the Fortress" reprinted from the February 21, 2000 issue of *Business Week,* by special permission, copyright © 2000 by the McGraw-Hill Companies, Inc.

from approximately 430,000 to over 660,000. In 2004, approximately 25 percent of inmates were incarcerated for a drug-related offense. In addition to being a serious criminal justice problem, drug abuse is a societal and health problem. It is among the top five health problems in terms of economic impacts. The economic impact of drug abuse as a health problem is exceeded only by the economic impact associated with alcohol abuse (which could be considered in the same category as drug abuse) and heart disease.[68]

To combat what is seen as one of the country's most serious criminal and societal problems, the federal government and states have focused significant attention to reducing drug trafficking and abuse. As with the former War on Crime and the contemporary War on Terrorism, the federal government has declared a War on Drugs. Officials describe the problem of drug trafficking and abuse as having a global and fatal impact on individuals and society.

Approximately 2.8 million Americans are "dependent" on illegal drugs, and an additional 15 million fall in the less severe "abuser" category.[69] Illegal drug use is a problem in all communities. The response of society and the criminal justice system to the challenge of illegal drug use generates great debate. Some accuse the criminal justice system of creating a "prison-industrial complex" that crowds jails and prisons with nonviolent drug offenders at the expense of cheaper and more effective treatment. Some point to the mockery of legalized alcohol and tobacco when marijuana is classified as a Schedule I narcotic on a par with heroin. Five times more deaths are attributed to alcohol and over 20 times more deaths are attributed to tobacco products than are caused by drug abuse.[70] The War on Drugs also is criticized for institutional racism. Human Rights Watch reports that 482 of every 100,000 black men are in prison for a drug crime, compared with just 36 of every 100,000 white men. Blacks make up 62 percent of the nation's imprisoned drug offenders, despite accounting for just 13 percent of the population.[71] Antidiscrimination activists have even accused the Central Intelligence Agency of introducing crack cocaine to Los Angeles.[72]

The American **War on Drugs** developed during the Nixon and Reagan eras. The ambitious goal of the Anti-Drug Abuse Act of 1988 was to create a drug-free America by 1995. In pursuit of that goal, the criminal justice system adopted extensive and harsh criminal penalties against drug users and drug trafficking. Critics have pointed to the failure of the War on Drugs to reduce drug use, while at the same time inflicting much "collateral damage" on society. Government spends about two-thirds of its $19.2 billion drug budget on law enforcement and interdiction. The National Institute on Drug Abuse argues that drug abuse is a disease rather than a moral weakness, and users should receive medical treatment instead of imprisonment. Polls show that two-thirds of Americans favor treatment over jails.[73]

The extensive laws in the United States against the use, possession, and trafficking in illegal drugs are relatively recent criminal justice strategies. The first major federal law regulating drug use was the **Harrison Narcotics Act** of 1914. Until that legislation, opium, morphine, heroin, and cocaine were sold legally in the United States without prescription or prohibition. Many over-the-counter medicines contained these drugs. At one time, even beverages such as Coca-Cola contained cocaine. The Harrison Narcotics Act required that these drugs be dispensed only by prescription, and heroin continued to be legally available by prescription until 1920.[74] Marijuana was virtually unregulated until the **Marijuana Tax Act** of 1937, which levied a $100 per ounce tax on cannabis. It was not until the **Boggs Act** in 1951 that the use, possession, and sale of marijuana was made illegal and heroin was removed from the list of medically useful substances. The major piece of legislation that defines the criminal justice strategy in the War on Drugs is the **Comprehensive Drug Abuse Prevention and Control Act** of 1970. Title II of this act is known as the Controlled Substance Act. It created five schedules of psychoactive drugs, classified by their abuse potential and degree of psychoactivity, and established penalties.

Additional legislation has strengthened the ability of the law enforcement agencies to take punitive measures against drug users and trafficking. The **Anti-Drug Abuse Act** of 1988 created the first cabinet-level post of drug czar and the **Office of National Drug Control Policy (ONDCP)**. It created new civil punishments for convicted drug offenders, such as denial of federal benefits. It also focused more attention on curbing recreational drug use. The Crime Control Act of 1990 created enhanced penalties for drug use or trafficking in "drug-free school zones," allowed federal agents to seize property associated with drug crime, and established federal funds for drug education programs at schools. The Violent Crime Control and Law Enforcement Act of 1994 budgeted federal money for treatment and drug courts, but endorsed the death penalty for drug trafficking and drug-related murders and established the "three strikes" law, allowing a life sentence for violent felony or drug offenders. However, despite this increasingly tougher stance against illegal drugs, the criminal justice system has not found an effective strategy to win the War on Drugs.

Drugs and Crime Some critics argue that the criminal justice system is losing the War on Drugs and should abandon its present course of action. They call for decriminalizing some drug offenses. Politicians and even former chiefs of police argue that the "holy war against drugs is having an insidious effect on law enforcement."[75] The Governor of

To protect children from drugs, laws have been adopted that increase the penalties for drug trafficking in and near schools. Do you think such laws are effective in reducing drug trafficking?

According to the National Institute of Drug Abuse (NIDA), failure to understand addiction as an illness may explain in part why historic strategies focusing solely on the social or criminal justice aspects of drug use and addiction have been unsuccessful. This viewpoint argues that zero-tolerance policies and incarceration of nonviolent drug users through tough sentencing are contrary to the growing body of scientific literature. What is the solution to drug use and drug-related crime?

New Mexico, Gary Johnson, called for the legalization of drugs, from marijuana to heroin, with the idea that the best strategy is "Control it. Regulate it. Tax it. Educate people truthfully about its dangers. If we legalize it, we just might have a better society."[76]

Opponents to legalization point to statistics on the social harms as well as crimes associated with drug abuse. Annually, about 20,000 deaths are attributable to drug abuse, more than double the number from 1990.[77] About 110,000 individuals are estimated to have contracted HIV through intravenous drug use.[78] The economic cost of drug abuse is projected to continue to rise almost 6 percent annually. Americans spent approximately $64 billion for illegal drugs in 2000—more than eight times the total federal outlay for research on HIV/AIDS, cancer, and heart disease.[79]

Drugs and drug-using behavior are linked to crime in several ways. Effects of drug use include criminal behavior—such as robberies, prostitution, or thefts to get money to buy drugs—and violence as a result of drug wars among rival traffickers. About 35 percent of all state and federal prison inmates and 15 percent of local jail inmates are incarcerated for drug-related crimes.[80] One alarming fact regarding the relationship between drugs and crime is that in 2000, between 52 and 80 percent of the adult males booked tested positive for drug use.[81] The crime-related costs of drug abuse exceed $100 billion annually. Property damage for victims of drug-related crime exceeds $180 million annually. Nearly $5.5 billion is spent in legal adjudication.[82]

As cities are mounting antidrug strategies with some impact, small towns are facing an upsurge in drug dealing and drug crime. Many drug dealers are fleeing the cities and moving to the affluent suburbs. Relocation brings new law enforcement problems as small-town police officers clash with big-time drug dealers and cope with unfamiliar experiences with homicides, drive-by shootings, methamphetamine laboratories, increasing rates of drug abuse, and gangs. Small-town police often are ill-equipped and poorly trained to combat the rising drug problems they are now facing.[83] Local law enforcement agents have difficulty conducting undercover operations with limited resources.

Drug Abuse: Medical Model versus Criminal Justice Model One of the most acrimonious debates regarding drug abuse is whether drug users are criminals who deserve to be punished by the criminal justice system or victims suffering from a treatable medical condition. The present model strongly suggests that drug users are criminals and incarceration in jails and prison is the appropriate punishment for their behavior. However, new research strongly suggests otherwise. The **National Institute on Drug Abuse** (**NIDA**) has concluded,

> Dramatic advances over the past two decades in both the neurosciences and the behavioral sciences have revolutionized our understanding of drug abuse and addiction. Scientists have identified neural circuits that are involved in the actions of every known drug of abuse, and they have specified common pathways that are affected by almost all such drugs. Research also has begun to reveal major differences between the brains of addicted and nonaddicted individuals and to indicate some common elements of addiction, regardless of the substance.[84]

The National Institute on Drug Abuse recognizes a gap between scientific knowledge concerning addiction and the response of the criminal justice system and the public. It claims that the lack of appreciation of drug abuse as a public health problem is one of the major reasons why there has been "a significant delay in gaining control over the drug abuse problem."[85] Thus, NIDA criticizes conventional thinking about drug abuse as outdated from both clinical and policy perspectives.[86]

Synthetic Drugs — Made in the United States The Bush Administration has made marijuana the focus of its antidrug efforts because it is the most abused drug in the United States and it is considered a "gateway" drug that leads to the use of harder substances. However, many criminal justice experts are critical of making marijuana the priority focus of the antidrug program, claiming that **methamphetamine,** or "meth," is America's most dangerous drug. Methamphetamine is the most widely used and clandestinely produced synthetic drug in the United States.[87] It can be easily and cheaply produced virtually anywhere in the United States. It requires little technical skills to "cook" meth and the materials to make it are readily and legally available.

Methamphetamine is an epidemic across the United States. Federal estimates are that more than 12 million Americans have tried methamphetamine and that 1.5 million are regular users. Despite its widespread use and claims by law enforcement officials that methamphetamine is the number-one drug problem, many people never saw the methamphetamine epidemic coming.[88] Methamphetamine has emerged as a drug epidemic only recently but its spread has been extremely rapid. For example, New York state law enforcement officials did not find their first methamphetamine laboratory until 1999 but by 2003, there were 73 methamphetamine laboratories discovered.[89] In a 2003 survey, many states reported that methamphetamine laboratories and abuse were the "single most serious law enforcement issue [the state] is facing, and has ever faced."[90]

Methamphetamine was first synthesized by a Japanese chemist in 1919, and was used by both Axis and Allied troops in World War II to keep them alert and motivated.[91] In the 1950s, it was commonly prescribed as a diet aid and to fight depression.[92] It was criminalized in 1970 but many states had relatively light sanctions against the manufacture or use of the drug.

The illegal manufacture and abuse of methamphetamine first started in the West and spread to the East. At first, it was manufactured and sold by motorcycle gangs, but later Mexican trafficking organizations and organized crime became involved in "cooking" and distributing the drug. Its early association with motorcycle gangs is noted by one of the nicknames for the drug—"crank," as motorcycle gangs would hide the drug in their motorcycle crankcases. Today, methamphetamine is produced in all 50 states and by a wide variety of persons. Many meth labs are referred to as "mom and pop" labs or "homemade" labs, as they are literally labs that a couple operates out of their home.

Methamphetamine is the major reason for the rise of drug abuse arrests in rural cities.[93] One theory for the rise of methamphetamine laboratories in rural areas is that an essential requirement is a place to set up a laboratory that will not be detected by law enforcement officials. Methamphetamine laboratories give off a distinctive odor from the anhydrous ammonia associated with the manufacture of the drug, so isolation is important in avoiding detection. In rural counties where there may be hundreds of square miles and less than a dozen law enforcement officers to patrol the county, small rural cities are ideal locations for methamphetamine laboratories.

There is relatively little research on why methamphetamine has become the drug of choice. It is assumed that some reasons are that it is cheaper than cocaine, has a high that lasts 8 to 16 hours, compared to a couple of hours for cocaine, and can be easily manufactured. Since it can be easily manufactured virtually anywhere, there is no long international distribution network; any city can become a major methamphetamine distribution center overnight. Most methamphetamine users are white, female, less affluent, and living in rural areas and west of the Mississippi.[94]

Methamphetamine as a Health Hazard Methamphetamine laboratories are dangerous not only for those who manufacture the drug but for those in the vicinity of a methamphetamine lab. In the manufacture of methamphetamine, extremely hazardous toxics are produced as a by-product. For each pound of methamphetamine, approximately five pounds of toxic waste are left behind. Also, deadly and flammable fumes are given off during the process, resulting in both a danger to health and an extreme fire hazard. This threat is so great that one out of every five labs is discovered because of fire or explosion.[95] The meth labs are also potentially hazardous to first responders such as police and firefighters. When firefighters arrive at the scene of a

methamphetamine Better known by its street names, *ice, crack*, and *crank*, methamphetamine is a synthetic drug that is inexpensive to make and can be made almost anywhere and by anyone. It is highly addictive and harmful. Meth abuse is spreading rapidly throughout the United States.

Meth labs pose serious dangers for law enforcement personnel. They produce dangerous fumes, toxic by-products, and serious fire hazards. Many meth labs are discovered because of explosion or fire. What could be done to reduce the demand for meth and thereby reduce the number of meth labs?

methamphetamine laboratory fire or explosion, they can be seriously injured by the toxic gases or explosion. During a raid on a meth lab police officers may be exposed to deadly toxic chemicals. Thus, when police or firefighters know they are confronting a raid of a meth lab or a fire or explosion caused by the manufacture of methamphetamine, they employ decontamination suits and special procedures for responding to hazardous materials.

Refer to www.justthinktwice.com, a teen-oriented website run by the DEA featuring graphic photographs of the affect of meth use on one's looks.

Reducing Methamphetamine Manufacture and Use Because methamphetamine can be manufactured in the United States, international interdiction efforts used by law enforcement to reduce the supply of marijuana, cocaine, and heroin do not work with methamphetamine. As a result, new strategies must be developed and used in fighting methamphetamine abuse. The three most common efforts to fight the methamphetamine epidemic are traditional law enforcement drug raids and enforcement, education and public relations campaigns, and efforts to make it more difficult to obtain the ingredients to manufacture the drug. In an effort to reduce the manufacture of methamphetamine, states have attempted to restrict what are called the precursor ingredients necessary for the manufacture of methamphetamine.

Most states have focused their efforts on restricting the sale of pseudoephedrine. Initially, methamphetamine was manufactured using ephedrine, a chemical found in over-the-counter cold medicines. When laws were passed to restrict the sale of ephedrine, the cooks simply switched to a related compound, pseudoephedrine.[96] Pseudoephedrine, commonly called "pseudo," was also a common ingredient in over-the-counter cold medicines such as Sudafed.

When laws restricted bulk sales of pseudoephedrine, cooks turned to a practice called **smurfing,** the buying or stealing of large quantities of cold medicines from stores. To stop smurfing, states passed laws requiring stores to remove products with pseudoephedrine from the open shelves. Also, laws were passed limiting the number of products that could be bought.

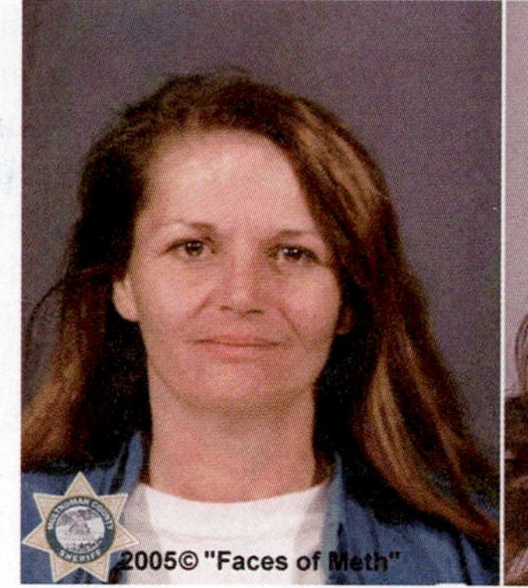

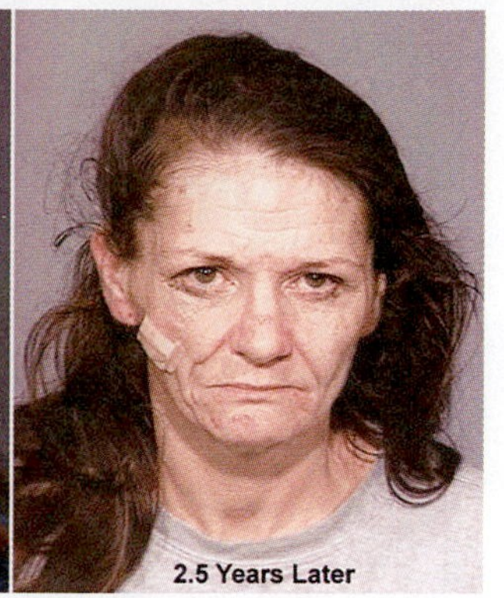

Antidrug campaigns try to find advertising campaigns that will keep young people from trying drugs. One campaign to discourage meth use emphasizes the effects of meth use on one's physical appearance. In this campaign, pictures are shown of meth users before they started using meth and several years after meth use. Do you think antidrug public ads and educational campaigns are effective in discouraging young people from using drugs?

Transnational Crime

Each country has its own criminal justice system, but it is obvious that there must be some means by which countries may collaborate in the prosecuting of offenders. Certain offenses and offenders threaten more than community safety within their country. Also, in today's highly mobile environment, the offender may commit offenses in several countries or may commit an offense in one country and escape to another. Such offenses are called *transnational crime*. There is no international criminal justice system, but there are two primary cooperative efforts among nations to deal with the problem of transnational crime: the United Nations (UN) and the International Police Association (INTERPOL).

The UN is involved in numerous international missions, including criminal justice, but does not have legitimate authority within the borders of a nation without the invitation and cooperation of the host nation. The criminal justice mission of the UN involves four primary goals. The first goal of the UN is to conduct surveys to gather data about international and comparative crime. The United Nations World Crime Surveys gather data from member states for the purpose of providing a snapshot of comparative criminal activity. The second goal of the UN is to provide peacekeeping efforts in countries in which the domestic police are no longer able to perform their duties or in which domestic police do not exist.

The third mission is to promote crime prevention. The UN encourages member nations to focus on the problems of crime, links governments for innovative and cooperative solutions, and promotes regional and international agreements to strengthen international cooperation in crime prevention. The UN plays an important role in preventing crimes involving transnational terrorism and drug trafficking.

Finally, the UN seeks to promote a common standard of justice and fair treatment of defendants and convicted persons. Through resolutions such as the **International Bill of Human Rights** and the Standard Minimum Rules for the Treatment of Prisoners, the UN has worked to secure fair and just treatment of the accused by the criminal justice systems of the world.

The **International Police Association (INTERPOL)** depends on the cooperative effort of participating nations. First formed in 1914, INTERPOL had no significant presence in international criminal justice until after World War II, when it became a clearinghouse for information on offenses and suspects believed to operate across national boundaries, especially in cases of international terrorism and drug trafficking.

In the United States, the contact point for INTERPOL is the U.S. Department of Justice. Under the authority of the Justice Department, a cooperative unit called the National Central Bureau draws on personnel from a dozen federal law enforcement agencies. INTERPOL–U.S. National Central Bureau does not have original jurisdiction but performs crime scene investigations and initiates investigations of criminal activity. Its focus is centered more on identifying and apprehending criminal offenders who have fled the jurisdiction of the countries in which they committed their crimes.

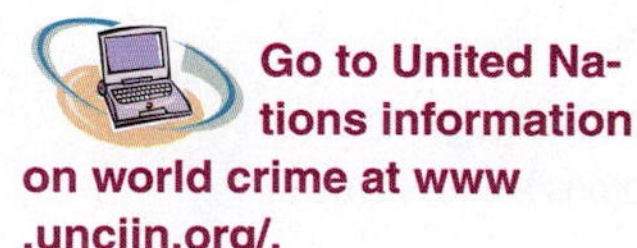

Go to United Nations information on world crime at www.uncjin.org/.

smurfing Buying or stealing of large quantities of cold medicines from stores.

Americans traveling abroad sometimes become victims of crime or suspects or perpetrators of crimes and thus become involved in the criminal justice systems of other countries. Other countries' systems can be quite different, and Americans often find themselves challenged to cope with them. For instance, many countries do not have laws guaranteeing civil rights or due process, or even human rights. Concepts of justice and appropriate punishment for crimes vary widely. For example, Yektan Turkyilmax, a Turkish citizen who is a Ph.D. candidate in cultural anthropology at Duke University, was arrested on June 17, 2005, as he tried to leave Armenia for Turkey with about 90 secondhand books he had purchased legally at bookstalls in the open-air market in Yerevan, the Armenian capital. The books were related to his dissertation research that focused on Turkish and Armenian nationalism from 1908 to 1938.[97] Unbeknownst to Turkyilmax, Armenia law prohibits the export of books older than 50 years without government permission. At his trial all of the booksellers who testified said they were either unaware of the law themselves or had not told Yektan about it. Despite this testimony and Turkyilmax's disclaimer that he was also ignorant of the law and had no criminal intent, he was convicted and could have received eight years in prison. He was given a two-year suspended sentence and allowed to leave Armenia. Not all encounters with foreign criminal justice systems are so dramatic, however, but many more Americans are more likely to have to deal with the criminal justice system of another country.

International cooperation in law enforcement is needed for public safety as well as for crime control. For example, pirates are still a major threat in many parts of the world, with hundreds of attacks on ships and crew members each year. Today, ships that are worth millions of dollars have small unarmed crews that are easy targets for pirates.[98]

Drug Trafficking One of the most serious transnational crimes, other than terrorism, is drug trafficking. The challenge of combating drug abuse is that many drugs are imported illegally into the United States and may even be bought and sold by nations to finance political movements and wars. The drug trade is a vast international market. Moving drugs from nation to nation and then to the street level involves colossal management challenges. Problems include the cultivation of hundreds of thousands of acres of drug crops, **trafficking** hundreds of tons of illegal drugs across continents and through intermediaries and a maze of specialized border smuggling organizations, establishing a network of mid-level distributors, and selling the drugs to the users.[99] In addition, there is the problem of money. The drug trade relies on the international banking system to launder billions of dollars each year. As a result of **money laundering**, the drug trade often must resort to reverse smuggling, as it is necessary to smuggle out of the country enormous quantities of cash, which often weigh two to three times more than the drugs that were smuggled in.[100] To accomplish this task, the drug trade has had to organize into complex and vast international networks and alliances. In some countries, drug organizations are able to buy politicians, police, and judges to the point that they virtually operate without fear of apprehension by law enforcement. Sometimes, these so-called drug lords exercise such political and economic influence in countries that they constitute a shadow government, exercising great control over the legitimate government of the country. **Narco-terrorism**, ruling by fear and corruption, describes the practices of these drug lords.

The federal government has recognized the important role that international drug markets play in drug abuse in the United States and has undertaken new strategies for intercepting drugs at the borders and dismantling the drug networks that transport and distribute both the drugs and the illicit proceeds from their sale. The U.S. attorney general has directed the **Organized Crime Drug Enforcement Task Force (OCDETF)** to ensure that law enforcement efforts target the most significant drug-trafficking organizations.[101]

The primary law enforcement agencies involved in drug law enforcement have been the federal **Drug Enforcement Agency (DEA)** and state and local police. The OCDETF program, created in 1982, hopes to make a significant impact on reducing the supply of

trafficking Movement of illegal drugs across borders.

money laundering Concealment of the source of money.

narco-terrorism The redefinement of drug trafficking as terrorism, used to emphasize its significance.

drugs in the United States. The OCDEFT program works collaboratively with other federal drug programs, such as the High Intensity Drug Trafficking Areas program and the Treasury Department's Financial Crimes Enforcement Network, to have an impact on the most sophisticated trafficking organizations. One of the lessons learned in drug law enforcement is that cooperation among the decentralized law enforcement agencies is effective in disrupting drug trafficking.

The law enforcement battle with drug traffickers was profoundly affected by the September 11, 2001, terrorist attacks on the World Trade Center and the Pentagon. As a result of these attacks, border and airport security was increased significantly. Initially, security efforts linked to counterterrorism reduced drug trafficking between borders, but subsequently, seizures of illegal drugs have been on the rise. Nationally, seizure of illegal drugs at airports, seaports, and border checkpoints increased by 17.1 percent in the last three months of 2001, compared with the same period the year before.[102]

The War on Drugs: An International Problem The War on Drugs is far more than a law enforcement or criminal justice problem. Fighting international drug trafficking has become integrally associated with homeland security, the War on Terrorism, and international relations. For example, the U.S. invasion of and occupation of Afghanistan has thrust the United States into the role of coordinating, equipping, and financing the antidrug efforts of that country. Afghanistan is the world's leading source of heroin and opium. In 2004, Afghanistan supplied 87 percent of the world's illicit opium production. There is wide consensus in the government and the military and among humanitarian organizations that the drug trade now threatens all of America's goals in Afghanistan.[103] The irony is that as the United States attempts to help Afghanistan build a new democratic-based government, money from the sale of illegal drugs is a major source of financing terrorist groups opposed to the U.S. presence in Afghanistan.

In the past, the U.S. military has tried to provide assistance to the Afghanistan government rather than lead the fight against the production and sale of poppies, opium, and heroin, but this strategy has not been effective. In 2005, the U.S. government committed $257 million to the counternarcotics campaign and authorized the U.S. military to significantly increase its role in halting the production and sale of poppies, opium, and heroin.[104] The U.S. State Department, the Drug Enforcement Agency, and the U.S. military are operating in Afghanistan with a mandate to suppress the drug-trafficking problem.

United States–Mexican Relations Transnational drug crime has affected the U.S. relationship with both Mexico and Canada. The U.S.–Mexican border has always been porous and plagued by the inability to control illegal immigration. Prior to September 11, 2001, this problem was considered primarily as an immigration and crime problem. After 9/11, the Department of Homeland Security views the inability to secure the U.S.–Mexican border as a homeland security problem. In March 2005, Porter J. Goss, the director of the Central Intelligence Agency, told the Senate Armed Services Committee that the United States was vulnerable to terrorists entering the country from Mexico.[105] Fear of uncontrolled illegal immigration and terrorists entering the United States from Mexico has promoted the construction of a security fence between some parts of the United States and Mexico, and some have called for a security fence along the entire southern border. For example, in December 2005, the House of Representatives passed a bill to build an additional 700 miles of tall double fences along the border to stop illegal immigrants.

The illegal drug trade between Mexico and the United States has reached the point where the violence associated with the illegal drug trade is spilling over and affecting U.S. tourists and business persons who visit border towns. As drug cartels assume more control and influence of border towns, not only is there an increase in drug trafficking-related violence but there is also an increase of other violent crimes such as kidnapping for ransom, murder, and sexual assault.[106] A Federal Bureau of Investigation agent assigned to Laredo, Texas, said he believed that at least one person is killed in the Mexican border town of Nuevo Laredo each day and at least two people are kidnapped every month.[107]

Drug trafficking and drug-related violence has risen to the level of international diplomatic concern, as recent allegations claim that some of the drug trafficking and violence is carried out by Mexican law enforcement and military officials. For example, in January 2006, Hudspeth County sheriff officers (near El Paso, Texas) reported an armed confrontation with drug-smuggling suspects dressed in Mexican military-style uniforms using a Mexican military-issued Humvee and weapons.[108] It is reported that Mexican military units have entered the United States 216 times since 1996.[109] Such charges have drawn critical denials from the Mexican government. However, despite these denials, the Mexican government continues to be accused of promoting illegal immigration and turning a blind eye toward drug smuggling and law enforcement and military officials who participate in drug trafficking. The accusations have caused a strain in U.S.–Mexican relations.

Cybercrime and Identity Theft

Computer and Internet technology is causing drastic changes in and to the criminal justice system. It has provided new tools to investigate crime, to manage information, to communicate, and to enforce the laws. However, at the same time, computer and Internet technology have created new ways to commit crimes and even new crimes.

Responding to the challenge of computer-related crime and **cybercrime**—crimes against computers and the use of computers to commit crimes—is changing the way the criminal justice system operates. For example, Internet crime is increasing so rapidly that the criminal justice system cannot keep up with it. Many law enforcement problems in computer-related crime and cybercrime are a result of (1) a chronic lack of talented people qualified to investigate and prosecute cybercrimes and (2) legislation that has not kept up with the various criminal acts that are possible using the computer and the Internet.

Trained law enforcement experts are needed because traditional investigative techniques often are ineffective in investigating cybercrime. Few forensic agents have been trained to find and understand incriminating data on hard drives, and the complexity of evidence gathering makes computer crimes complicated to prosecute.[110] Computers are routinely seized in cases involving crimes such as fraud, embezzlement, child pornography, cybertheft, and malicious hacking, but there are not enough forensics experts qualified to examine the hard drives of these computers for the evidence that will allow the police to prosecute offenders. In some departments, the backlog of hard drives that need to be examined is so great that police are running out of room to store seized computers.[111] This backlog can be detrimental to innocent owners of seized computers, which police can retain as evidence until the statute of limitations runs out on the crime. One Texas business owner took a federal agency to court and won a $300,000 damage suit for the business losses he suffered after his computers were seized and not returned in a timely manner.[112]

The prosecution of computer and cybercrimes is hampered by the lack of legislation defining them. For example, *piggybacking, page jacking*, and *denial of service* are new technocrimes that are not clearly understood and defined in the criminal justice system. **Piggybacking** is a form of cybertrespass. However, the definition of *cybertrespassing* is not clear because there are search engines that routinely search computer sites, and computer sites that legitimately search and compile information from other websites.[113] In **page jacking**, a program captures a user's computer and directs the computer to a website that the user did not want to go to and cannot exit from except by turning off the computer. Often, page jackers direct the user to pornographic websites, and the concern of the public is that juveniles could be unwillingly exposed to obscene material as

cybercrime Crimes against computers, or the use of computers to commit crimes.

piggybacking A form of cybertrespassing.

page jacking A program that captures a user's computer and directs the computer to a website that the user did not want to go to and cannot exit from except by turning off the computer.

they use the Internet. The page jacker's motivation is financial gain through sales of website advertising to pornography companies. By forcing Internet users to the sites, they increase their profit margins from both advertising and possible sales to new consumers of porn.[114] **Denial of service** is considered a prank by hackers and is becoming one of the most common problems on the Internet. In a denial of service attack, the hacker attempts to crash or clog the targeted Internet site by overloading the website with too many requests for information for the website to respond.[115] A glossary of the language of cybercrime is presented in Figure 2.4. Other new cyberproblems include everything from illegal kidney auctions on eBay to computer waste poisoning people in developing countries.

Computers also are used by criminals in the course of committing traditional crimes better and faster. For example, nearly 50 percent of all counterfeit money is printed using personal computers.[116] The Internet also has provided a new and better way to commit many frauds. One cybercriminal used Internet chat rooms and fraudulent "news web pages" to drive up the price of the stock he held.[117] Fraud on the Internet is so common and serious that the Department of Justice and the Federal Bureau of Investigation have a website to address fraud committed over the Internet: the **Internet Fraud Complaint Center (IFCC)**.

Go to the Internet Fraud Complaint Center at www.ifccfbi.gov to examine the scope and nature of Internet fraud or to report suspected terrorist activity.

Cybercrimes can be committed by juveniles as well as by adults. In fact, many juveniles are attracted to various cybercrimes, such as hacking, software fraud, and other forms of Internet mischief. Children have access to computers and frequently feel that trading copyrighted material such as movies, video games, and music is not a crime. Others engage in hacking and fraud. The extent of juvenile Internet crime is shocking. Juveniles who get caught often get light sentences or only civil fines. One U.S. Department of Justice official suggested that the extent of juvenile Internet crime is so pervasive that it is beyond law enforcement. He lamented that juvenile cybercriminals have no sense of ethics that what they are doing is wrong.[118]

Identity Theft **Identity theft** is a new crime and is the leading consumer fraud complaint. Identity theft was first recognized as a serious problem in the late 1990s. Today, the Federal Trade Commission (FTC) states that 15 million persons reported that they had been victims of identity theft within a year.[119] Identity theft accounts for nearly 50 percent of all consumer fraud complaints received by the FTC. The costs of identity theft are enormous. For example, the financial losses to consumers and businesses were estimated to exceed $50 billion in 2003 and the cost to law enforcement to investigate identity theft ranges from $15,000 to $25,000 each case.[120]

Identify theft is defined as knowingly transferring or using, without lawful authority, any name or number that may be used, alone or in conjunction with any other information to identify a specific individual with the intent to commit, or to aid or abet, any unlawful activity. Identity theft is usually associated with other frauds. For example, offenders may use victims' personal information to open new credit card accounts and bank accounts, collect on insurance policies, secure loans or mortgages, submit fraudulent tax returns to collect the refunds, and submit applications for fraudulent social security payments. One of the unique characteristics of identity theft is that offenders are repeatedly victimized. An individual offender can be victimized for years.

Identity theft became a federal crime in 1998, with the passage of the **Identity Theft Assumption and Deterrence Act**. In 2004, the **Identity Theft Penalty Enhancement Act** enhanced sentences for offenders, recognized the use of identity theft by terrorists, created the crime of aggravated identity theft, and eliminated the possibility of probation for aggravated identity theft. The U.S. Postal Inspection Service, the FBI, the Secret Service, and the Federal Trade Commission all have various responsibilities in responding to the crime of identity theft.

It is not necessary to use a computer or the Internet to commit identity theft, but the crime is greatly enhanced when they are used.

denial of service An attack in which the hacker attempts to crash or clog the targeted Internet site by overloading the website with too many requests for information for the website to respond.

identity theft Using a name, unique identifying number, or personal information to commit another crime such as fraud or concealment of an offender's true identity.

figure 2.4

The Language of Cybercrime

The Weapons

Back doors	Unauthorized, hidden way to gain access to a program. Usually placed in the software by the person who wrote the program or had access to it. Difficult to detect if written by the software engineer and embedded in the original program. These allow the person unauthorized access to the program virtually at will.
Buffer overflow	A technique for crashing or gaining control of a computer by sending too much data to the buffer in a computer's memory. Usually, this attack does not cause permanent damage but can cause the computer network to go down.
Denial of service (DOS)	One of the most common attacks on a computer network, primarily because it is so easy to execute. The attacker sends more requests for information to a network than the network can handle. This causes the computer system to overload and slow down or crash. In more sophisticated attacks, the hacker gains unauthorized control of many other computers and uses these computers to send bogus requests for information. No harm is done to the computer database, but the system cannot process requests from legitimate users. DOS can be used to cover up another more serious attack.
Dumpster diving	Sifting through a company's garbage to find information to help break into their computers. Sometimes, the information is used to make a stab at social engineering more credible. (See section on social engineering later in table.)
Logic bombs	An instruction in a computer program that triggers a malicious act. Logic bombs can be programmed to activate on certain dates, such as Christmas or Friday the 13th, and are named after this characteristic.
Malicious applets	Tiny programs, sometimes written in the popular Java computer language, that misuse your computer's resources, modify files on the hard disk, send fake e-mail, or steal passwords. The damage can be very destructive, as it destroys or corrupts files. Because malicious applets can use the host computer's e-mail to attack other computers, which in turn can attack other computers, the damage can be extensive.
Password crackers	Software that can guess passwords by repeatedly trying different passwords until the correct one is found. The software is basically a dictionary that simply tries every word in the dictionary. Nonsense words, uncommon foreign words, or passwords with a combination of letters and numbers make it more difficult for this software to discover the correct password.
Scans	Widespread probes of the Internet to determine types of computers, services, and connections. In this way, the bad guys can take advantage of weaknesses in a particular make of computer or software program.
Sniffers	Programs that covertly search individual packets of data as they pass through the Internet, capturing passwords or the entire contents. Often, the user is unaware of the action of the sniffer, as the purpose is to gain data that can be used later as opposed to the data that the sniffer examines.
Social engineering	A tactic used to gain access to computer systems by talking unsuspecting company employees out of valuable information, such as passwords. Because many users use passwords based on family members' names, birthdays, and anniversary dates, even seemingly innocent information such as the names of the children in the user's family, may allow the hacker to guess the password.
Spoofing	Faking an e-mail address or web page to trick users into passing along critical information like passwords or credit card numbers.
Trojan horse	A program that, unknown to the user, contains instructions that exploit a known vulnerability in some software. The program is hidden in another "innocent" program so the user is unaware of the threat.
Virus	A virus is a malicious program used by hackers that spreads by attaching itself to another program. When the user runs that program, the virus attaches itself to more programs. The virus program itself remains hidden, so the user will not be aware of the actions of the virus. If any programs are transferred from the infected computer to a "healthy" computer, the healthy computer may become infected.
Worm	A worm is a piece of software that takes over the resources of a computer and uses them for its own purposes. A worm is self-contained in that it does not infect other programs. A common worm program is one that duplicates itself every time it is run. As the size of the worm program grows, all room on the disk for other programs is taken over by the worm. And as the worm program grows, other programs run slower, and eventually the user's hard disk is full.

figure 2.4

(Continued)

The Weapons	
War dialing	Programs that automatically dial thousands of telephone numbers in search of a way through a modem connection. A common attack is to use war dialing to obtain access to the long-distance telephone lines of a company's computer and then place unauthorized long-distance telephone calls.
The Players	
White-hat hackers	Good guys often employed by companies to find the weaknesses of a system or software. White-hat hackers can also be freelancers who attempt to find the vulnerabilities of the Internet, network, or software but are not hired by a company to do so. Law enforcement often is critical of these freelance white-hat hackers, because finding the weakness of a computer system or the Internet requires the hacker to attempt unauthorized access.
Black-hat hackers	The bad guys. They crash systems, steal passwords, look at confidential data, and send malicious e-mail. Often, their only motive is the thrill of being able to beat the system. Black-hat hackers can be juveniles as well as adults.
Crackers	The really bad guys. Hackers for hire, who break into computer systems to steal valuable information for their own financial gain, not for the kicks of it. These are the professional criminals who have found that they can make more money in cybercrime than old-fashioned robbery.
Script bunnies	Wannabe bad guys. Hackers with little technical expertise or ability who download "point and click" programs—scripts—that automate the job of breaking into computers. Often, these programs are downloaded from chat rooms on the Internet. They require little knowledge to operate, and there are many computer systems that lack even the most elementary protection against such novice attacks. Script bunnies can be pre-teen hackers who simply "want to be cool."
Insiders	"The Benedict Arnolds" of cybercrime. Bad guys with a grudge. Employees, disgruntled or otherwise, working solo or in concert with outsiders to compromise corporate systems. The damage done by these cybercriminals can be extensive, due to their inside knowledge of the system. Some attacks by insiders have gone undetected for years.

Source: "Storming the Fortress" reprinted from the February 21, 2000 issue of *Business Week*, by special permission, copyright © 2000 by the McGraw-Hill Companies, Inc.

One of the more common Internet-based identity theft scams is called **phishing**. Phishing got its name in the 1990s when America Online charged users by the hour for Internet service. Teenagers sent e-mails and instant messages pretending to be AOL customer service agents to AOL account holders in an effort to obtain account identification and passwords they could use to log-in without having to pay for AOL's service. These messages claimed there was a problem with the AOL account and asked the users for account identification and passwords. This practice was called *fishing*, or phishing. Today, phishers send fraudulent e-mails purporting to be from nationally known banks, credit card companies, and Internet services such as eBay and PayPal.

The phishers may be opportunistic individuals but many are members of organized criminal groups in Russia, East European countries, and Asia.[121] These phishers advise the receiver that there is some problem with his or her account or that there is suspect activity related to the account (see Figure 2.5). The receiver is told if he or she does not respond to the e-mail, the account will be closed. Receivers are given a hyperlink to click to respond that looks very similar to the legitimate link and logo of the purported company. However, if the victims click on the link, they are taken to a clandestine website where they are asked to submit their account numbers and personal information—all for the purposes of supposedly resolving the problem or the greater irony of confirming that their accounts are secure.

phishing Sending fraudulent e-mails in an attempt to commit identity theft.

figure 2.5A

Example 1 of Phishing E-Mail

From: Monster Network Customer Support [support@monster.com]
Sent: Tuesday, August 08, 2006 4:34 AM
To: James A. Fagin
Subject: Monster.com information

Dear Monster Customer,
We were unable to process the recent messagers on your account. To ensure that your account is not suspended, please check your information by clicking here.
Monster Network Customer Service

figure 2.5B

Example 2 of Phishing E-Mail

From: Bank Of The West Customer Support <support@bankofthewest.com>
Subject: Bank Of The West Security Message
Message: Dear Bank Of The West customer,

We have noticed unusual activity on your account. You need to verify and approve the charges before we allow any additional activity.
Please follow the link below:

Bank Of The West Online Banking
Bank Of The West Customer Support

Phishing is ubiquitous. One estimate is that 4 percent of e-mails are identity theft attacks.[122] Despite the fact that phishing is so widespread, many Internet users are unaware of the dangers of phishing. A 2005 study by the Pew Internet and American Life Project reported that 70 percent of Internet users had not heard of phishing or were not aware of e-mail scams used to obtain personal information that could be used to commit identity theft and related crimes.

See www.nsopr.gov for the National Sex Offender Public Registry website. See www.pameganslaw.state.pa.us/ for an example of a state sex offender registry. Google provides the ability to map where sex offenders live in your neighborhood. Go to www.mapsexoffenders.com and type in your address and up pops a map of your neighborhood with red flags marking the residences of registered sex offenders.

Concerns about the Use of the Internet by Predators The Internet has become the tool of choice for child pornographers and child sex offenders and predators. Child sex offenders can use the Internet to lure young victims into meetings.[123] Often, young adolescents in a sense contribute to their own risk by engaging in potentially dangerous Internet communications with adult strangers and sometimes even by posting personal information and provocative photographs on Internet services such as MySpace.com, where child predators can simply search for a victim. In addition to public education campaigns about safe Internet practices aimed at both parents and children, the criminal justice system has become more aggressive in fighting child predators using the Internet. Some states have passed new laws making it a felony to use the Internet to stalk, lure, or entice a minor for abduction or sexual assault. For example, a 2004 South Carolina law mandates a 10-year sentence for each online offense in which a sexual offender uses the Internet in an attempt to victimize a child.

White-Collar and Corporate Crime

Until Edwin Sutherland (1883–1950) advocated in his theory of differential association that crime was a learned behavior, most theories of crime causation implied or asserted that those who committed crimes were of the lower socioeconomic class or were morally defective. Sutherland, in a 1939 speech to the American Sociological Society, introduced the concept of *white-collar crime* to define someone of high social status who committed crime. Because Sutherland's theory did not depend on the satisfaction of base needs, poverty, maladapted family relations, criminal peer pressure, or environment as a precursor of criminal behavior, his theory of white-collar crime was unique. He posited that persons of respectable status and even great wealth could and did commit criminal behavior. Sutherland was not so much concerned that such persons committed crimes such as murder, rape, robbery, and assault; rather, his focus was that some people of high

careers in the system

Computer Security and Cyberpolice

If you want to chase computer hackers, bring online child pedophiles to justice, and defend the nation's computers against attacks by foreign countries and terrorists, which criminal justice agency do you apply for and what will they teach you in the police academy? Do you apply for Net Force, headed by Alex Michaels, and join the elite group of government law enforcement agencies that use sophisticated virtual reality supercomputers to chase bad guys across the Internet? No! Net Force is like Hawaii Five-O. It is a fictional law enforcement agency that has no counterpart in reality. There is no criminal justice agency in the real world like Net Force, a fictional law enforcement agency created by author Tom Clancy.[124]

There are very few full-time law enforcement agents whose job is to surf the Web to catch cybercriminals. Local police do not recruit or hire people as police officers who are dedicated to fighting cybercrime. The FBI is the federal criminal justice agency that has official responsibility for responding to Internet crime, but there are only about 200 agents assigned to National Infrastructure Protection Center squads nationwide.[125] Local police departments do not recruit for officers with computer skills or have the ability to train officers in this area. Furthermore, departments cannot pay the competitive salaries demanded by civilian computer experts. Thus, the departments often have to rely on officers who have educated themselves in computer skills, perhaps working with computers as a hobby or personal interest. These officers, sometimes known as *byteheads,* are assigned to white-collar crime details and computer crime because no one else in the department is qualified for the assignment. Most police officers are unaccustomed to using digital evidence and cyberevidence and find it difficult to investigate such crimes.[126] An additional challenge to the bytehead is getting others in the criminal justice system to understand the complexity of digital evidence, especially at trials. Jurors and judges often have difficulty comprehending evidence presented in computer and cybercrime cases.[127]

Police academies offer no training in digital evidence or how to fight cybercrime. Students interested in careers in fighting cybercrime will have to obtain a college degree in computer security. Most computer security degrees are at the master's level. The student must first complete an undergraduate degree in computer science and then specialize in computer security, much the same as a medical doctor first obtains his or her medical degree and then goes for additional schooling to become a surgeon, heart specialist, psychiatrist, or other medical specialist. One of the few, and the first, undergraduate degrees in computer security in the United States is offered by East Stroudsburg University of Pennsylvania.

Why might the need for people with degrees in computer security continue to grow? Who might employ people with such a degree? How do you think state and local law enforcement agencies should address problems of investigating cybercrime and gathering and analyzing digital evidence? Do you think you might ever be interested in becoming a bytehead?

status and wealth actually used their social economic position to illegally obtain more wealth and power. The Federal Bureau of Investigation defines white-collar crime as "those illegal acts which are characterized by deceit, concealment, or violation of trust and which are not dependent upon the application or threat of physical force or violence."[128] The most common forms of white-collar crime are related to fraud, illegal use of one's office for financial gain, and illegal stock trading and other commercial financial transactions.

The criminal justice system for the most part has ignored white-collar crime. Such crimes are not included in Part I crimes reported in the Uniform Crime Reports and data regarding the socioeconomic status of offenders are not collected. Police and prosecutors have committed few resources to discovering and prosecuting white-collar criminals. Furthermore, when white-collar criminals are convicted they often receive relatively light sentences, even when their crimes resulted in millions of dollars of illegal gain for the offender.

It is only in recent times that white-collar crime has become a concern of criminal justice agencies and the public. Financial losses from such offenses such as antitrust violations, computer and Internet fraud, credit card fraud, phone and telemarketing fraud, health care fraud, environmental law violations, tax evasion, securities fraud, insider trading, bribery, kickbacks, public corruption, and money laundering have impinged on the American public to the extent of over $300 billion annually.

Those who commit white-collar crimes include the most respectable and wealthiest of persons in society, including mayors, governors, vice presidents, and presidents. In 2006, Mayor Ron Gonzales of San Jose was indicted on public corruption charges, and Lynwood, California, mayor Paul Richards was found guilty of multiple counts of fraud, money laundering, extortion, making false statements to investigators, and depriving the public of honest services. Former Illinois governor and one-time Nobel Prize nominee George Ryan was found guilty of 18 charges of racketeering, mail fraud, making false statements to FBI agents, and income tax violations in 2006. Vice President Spiro Agnew was convicted of bribery while in the White House, and President William Clinton and Hillary Clinton were extensively investigated for alleged white-collar crimes but were not indicted.

See www.nw3c.org to visit the homepage of the National White Collar Crime Center. The National White Collar Crime Center is a congressionally-funded, non-profit corporation and their mission is to support law enforcement in the prosecution of economic and high-tech crimes.

Often, perpetrators of white-collar crime succeed in their criminal enterprises because they are able to induce criminal justice personnel to assist them. For example, in 2006, Ronald Matthews, the former police chief of East Saint Louis, was sentenced to federal prison for attempting to shield a politically connected businessman, Ayoub Qattoum, from a criminal probe alleging violation of federal gun laws. Also, white-collar criminals are opportunitists, as demonstrated by the widespread fraud committed by perpetrators who claimed to be 9/11 victims or victims of Hurricane Katrina. Fraudulent claims by these offenders resulted in millions of dollars of false aid claims.

When corporations or officers of corporations commit financially motivated, nonviolent crimes using their corporate status and resources, it is called *corporate crime,* as opposed to white-collar crime. In recent years there have been a number of high-profile prosecutions for corporate crime. The most publicized of these were the prosecution of CEO Martha Stewart; Ken Lay, CEO of Enron; and lobbyist Jack Abramoff. All three of these persons were extremely wealthy but chose to use their position and power to gain additional wealth by illegal means. Enron is one of the largest cases of corporate fraud, and the prosecution and conviction of Enron officers and the Arthur Anderson accounting agency resulted in the collapse of the companies. Many thousands of employees lost their jobs as well as their retirement savings, and states suffered financial losses through the collapse of Enron stock. At the same time, Enron executives continued to make millions of dollars, even as the company headed for destruction.

Although lobbyist Jack Abramoff did not employ the number of employees that Enron did, the illegal activities of Abramoff had great impact because the scandal involved prominent politicians. In January 2006, Abramoff pleaded guilty to fraud, tax evasion, and conspiracy to bribe public officials. The investigation revealed that Abramoff coordinated illegal payments to politicians and congressional staffers in return for favorable votes on bills.

One of the lessons learned from these high-profile prosecutions is that effective interagency cooperation is necessary to properly regulate and prosecute corporate giants.

Crimes against the Elderly

Criminal victimization is not equally distributed across the age spectrum and neither is fear of criminal victimization. In fact, there is an inverse relationship. Older persons are much less likely to suffer criminal victimization, including both violent crime and property crime.[129] Figure 2.6 shows the relative risk of victimization by age groups. This data analysis by the Bureau of Justice Statistics indicates that the elderly experienced nonfa-

figure 2.6

Comparative Risk of Victimization by Age Groups, 1993–2002

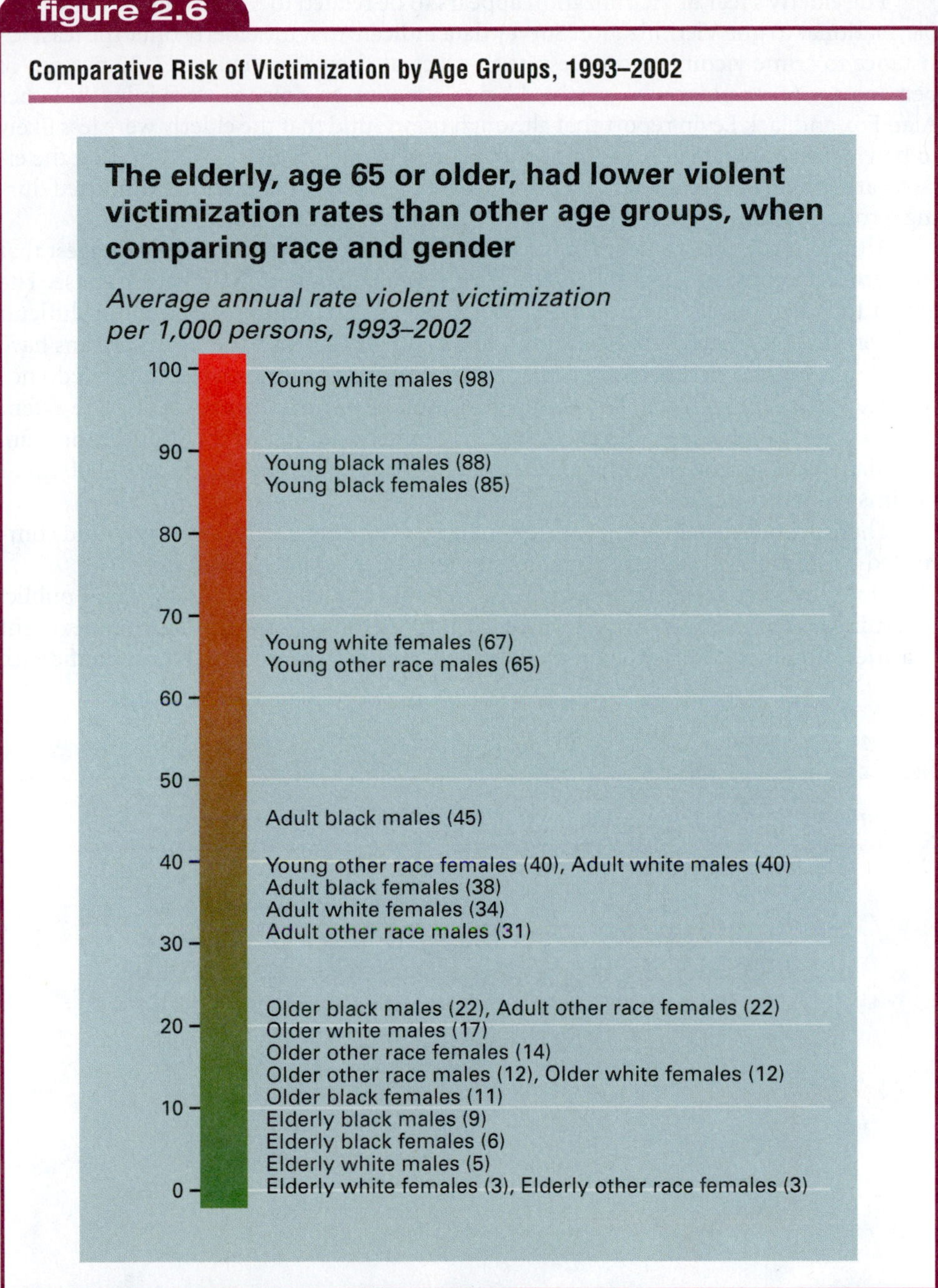

Source: Patsy Klaus, *Crimes against Persons Age 65 or Older, 1993–2002* (Washington, DC: U.S. Department of Justice, 2005), p. 1.

tal violent crime at a rate one-twentieth that of young persons (4 per 1,000 age 65 or older versus 82 victimizations per 1,000 persons age 12 to 24).[130] Households headed by persons age 65 or older experienced property crimes at a rate of about one-fourth of that for households headed by persons under age 25.[131] The Bureau of Justice Statistics reports that the only crime for which the elderly were victimized at about the same rates as most other age groups was purse snatching and pocket picking or personal larceny. The age group most likely to suffer criminal victimization is persons under 24 years old but they have the least fear of victimization. The group least likely to suffer criminal victimization is persons over the age of 50 but they have the highest fear of being victimized.

The elderly's fear of victimization appears to be related to fear of injury. For example, National Crime Victimization Survey data indicate that the elderly offer the least resistance to crime victimization. Despite this fact, as shown in Figure 2.7, 22 percent of persons age 65 or older who reported being a victim of violence were injured. James Alan Fox and Jack Levin report that although they found that the elderly were less likely to be victimized, when they examined the data in greater detail they found that the elderly are actually at greater risk than younger age groups for homicide committed during a robbery.[132]

Although the elderly are not at great risk of violent victimization data suggest that they are frequently targeted for financial crimes and exploitation and elder abuse. The extent to which the elderly are victims of financial crimes and exploitation is difficult to determine. Estimates show that between 20 and 60 percent of adult Americans have reported being the victim, or attempted victim, of financial crimes but the data do not separate prevalence estimates across age.[133] Another problem in estimating the extent of the crime is that elder fraud is dramatically underreported. As mentioned, there are no reliable data for the elderly as a subset but it is estimated that only 1 in 10,000 fraud victims reports the crime to the authorities.[134]

There are two general categories of financial crimes against the elderly: fraud committed by strangers and financial exploitation by relatives and caregivers.[135]

Fraud by strangers generally involves the same scams used on the general public. These include such scams as prize and sweepstakes frauds, solicitation to nonexistent charities, home and automobile repairs fraud, travel fraud schemes, and confidence

figure 2.7

Injuries Suffered by Elderly Victims of Violent Crime

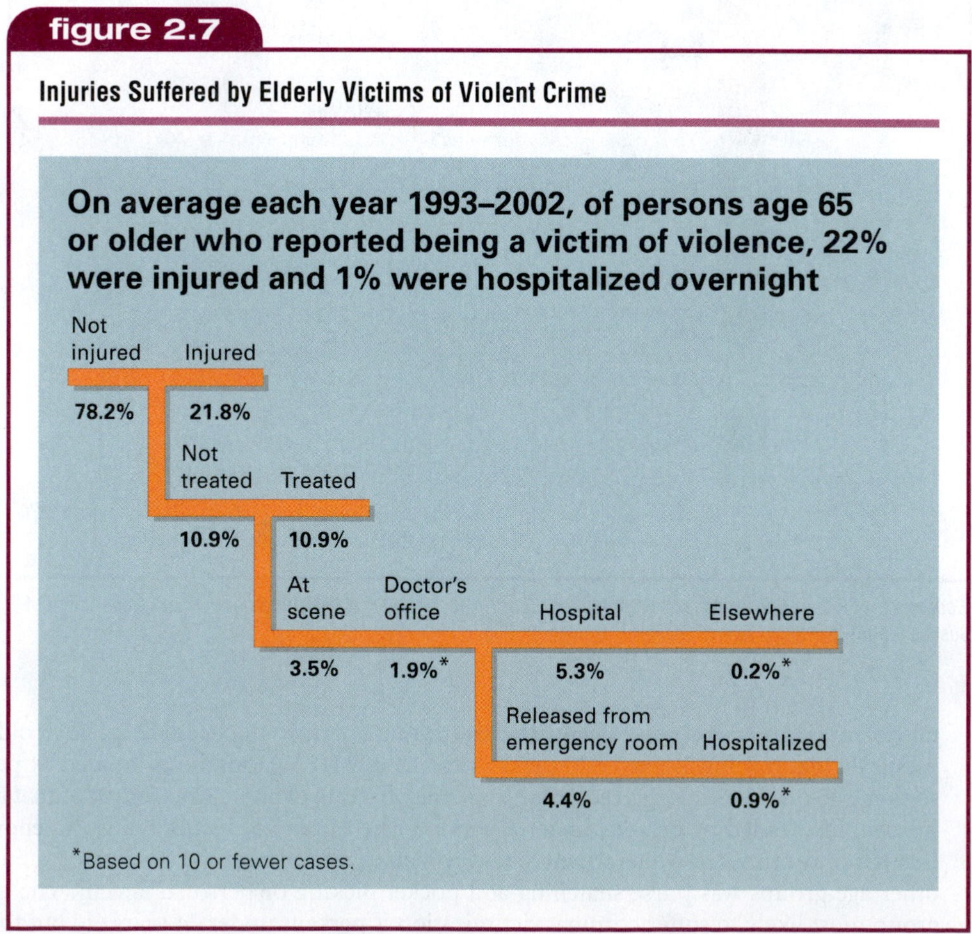

Source: Patsy Klaus, *Crimes against Persons Age 65 or Older, 1993–2002* (Washington, DC: U.S. Department of Justice, 2005), p. 3.

games, including "Nigerian scams" in which the victim is promised large sums of money if he or she will assist in a financial transaction that the offender claims not to be able to do or claims the victim has won a lottery (which he or she did not enter) but needs to pay taxes on the winnings or to make a "deposit" to secure the winnings. In addition, the elderly are especially suspect to an assortment of fraud schemes related to health, such as bogus or overpriced health, funeral, and life insurance, and various scams promising health remedies and miracle cures. These scams may be executed by telemarketing, mail, or even face-to-face contact.

Most elderly victims do not report when they have been defrauded. Some reasons for this lack of reporting are that they may feel ashamed or they may fear others will think they cannot care for themselves, which may trigger placement in a nursing home or long-term care facility.[136] Furthermore, if they do report the crime, there are certain characteristics of the elderly that may impair the investigation. If the victim is cognitively impaired, he or she may not remember the details that would allow for a successful investigation. If the offender is caught, the elderly victim may make a poor witness in court or be intimidated by the court proceedings and refuse to testify, or the victim's health may make it difficult for him or her to cooperate in the prosecution of the offender.

The second general category of financial fraud and exploitation is committed by relatives and caregivers. In this case, financial fraud may be accompanied with physical abuse or negligent health care. Common forms of financial exploitation include establishing joint bank accounts under the guise of helping the elder with his or her financial affairs, having the victim sign over deed or title transfer documents, or obtaining power of attorney and durable power of attorney and then misusing this authority to enrich the relative or caregiver.[137]

It is as difficult, or even more so, for law enforcement to respond to victimization of the elderly by relatives and caregivers as it is for them to respond to crimes committed by strangers. The relationship between the victim and offender may be such that it is almost impossible to discover the offense. Even the victim may not know that the trusted person is victimizing him or her. Sometimes elderly victims' only awareness of their victimization is when they find that they are out of funds or that their property has been "legally" transferred to another.

Crimes against Women

The laws concerning crimes against women are illustrative of how dominant cultural values are reflected in the criminal justice system. Until recently, both civil and criminal law reflected a view of the rights of women as distinct from the rights of men. For example, women did not get the right to vote until the passage of the Nineteenth Amendment in 1920. Other indicators of the status of women were evident in the many states women could not purchase or own property in their name, women were not given equal access to education, and women were not given equal pay in the workforce. This status was reflected in the criminal justice system by the fact that until after World War II many law schools denied admission to women based on their gender, and until the late twentieth century women could be excluded from jury duty. The laws regarding violence against women reflected this cultural bias. Until the eighteenth century a woman was considered the property of her father or her husband and any violent crime against the woman was considered an offense not against the victim but against the husband or father.

Women experience less victimization than men except for domestic violence and rape or sexual assault. Also, women experience a lower rate of murder per 1,000, but their assailants are almost always men and frequently known to her, such as spouse or boyfriend. The same trend applies to violent crime other than murder, as 64 percent of women were assaulted by nonstrangers compared to 48 percent for men.

Some of the most controversial issues regarding crimes against women have to do with rape and sexual assault. For example, until the mid-twentieth century many states required that for a conviction of rape the woman had to "resist with her utmost effort" throughout the entire assault. If at any time she failed to resist, it was presumed that she consented to the sex. Also prior to 1970, in most states the law defining rape excluded the woman's husband. It is only in the last decades that modern statutes have redefined the laws of rape. Most states have adopted statutes of sexual assault rather than rape as a way of emphasizing the violent nature of the crime. Also, most courts have adopted rules of evidence known as "rape shield" laws that restrict what questions the defense counsel can ask the victim regarding her sexual history and activity not related to the crime.

Although significant reforms have been made in the United States regarding equality of rights for women who have been victimized, there are many countries in the world where crimes against women still reflect a culture of dominant male superiority.

For example, in Kyrgyzstan, approximately half of the married women today were snatched from the street by their husbands in a custom dating back to the twelfth century known as *ala kachuu.* Rather than declining, the custom is growing and about one-third of Kyrgyzstan's brides are taken against their will.[138] The practice has been illegal since 1994 but the law is rarely enforced. Russell Kleinbach, a sociology professor at American University in Bishkek, said, "Most people don't know it's illegal."

If a woman is kidnapped by a man and kept in his home overnight, her virginity becomes suspect, her name is disgraced, and she will find it difficult to attract any other husband. Her only choice is to consent to become the bride of the man who kidnapped her. Most modern women object to the practice and live in fear of being abducted.[139] However, the behavior is the cultural norm and eventually most of the women abducted must consent to the marriage. Suicide and homicide often are the alternatives for those who refuse to accept the custom.

Mukhtar Mai of Pakistan was sentenced to be gang-raped by tribal authorities for an alleged improper relationship by her teenage brother with the sister of one of the men accused of raping her. Mai filed charges against the men but Pakistani law requires four witnesses to a sexual assault, so although the men were initially convicted, the court reversed their convictions.[140] International Human Rights groups took up Mai's cause and pressured the Pakistan government for justice. The hostility against Mai for reporting the rape became so great that she was forced to seek 24-hour police protection. Most women in Pakistan who are raped commit suicide or leave their village or Pakistan.[141]

When Mai continued to speak about her injustice she was placed under house arrest. When she was invited to the United States to speak about her ordeal she was denied permission to leave the country. In an interview with the *Washington Post,* Pakistani President Pervgez Musharraf suggested that Pakistani women were making false or exaggerated claims of rape as a way of procuring financial support and visas from foreigners. He said, "You must understand the environment in Pakistan. This has become a money making concern. A lot of people say, 'If you want to go abroad and get a visa for Canada or citizenship and be a millionaire, get yourself raped."'[142] Worldwide public outrage against the actions of the Pakistani government resulted in the Pakistani Embassy in Washington, DC, issuing a statement saying that Mai was "not under detention and has no bar on traveling abroad."[143]

However, perhaps one of the most serious examples of denial of women's rights is the practice of *honor killings.* In a number of countries—such as Afghanistan, Jordan, India, and Pakistan—under sharia law, the law of Islam, certain behaviors by women are so strongly thought to bring dishonor and shame on the family that it is the practice of family members to kill those women who commit violations of cultural norms.

Usually honor killings are spurred by allegation of adultery, sexual misconduct, or even accidentally touching a man's hand. Honor killings can result from such behaviors as conversing with men, working with men in farm fields, or speaking fondly of a man over the telephone.[144] One 16-year-old Pakistani girl was killed by her family because a young man at a wedding reception caught hold of her hand during a dance.

Despite the fact that honor killings are illegal in Pakistan, it is estimated that more than 1,200 women a year were killed in 2004 in the name of "family honor."[145] The United Nations reports that at least 5,000 women worldwide are killed each year to restore family honor.[146] In Pakistan, more than 80 percent of defendants accused of honor killings were acquitted. In Jordan, it is reported that women who survive an attempt on their life in the name of family honor are put in prison supposedly for their own protection.[147]

As a result of the migration movement and recent upheaval in the Middle East there are growing minority communities throughout the world where honor killings are the conduct norm. Honor killings are becoming a problem for European nations such as Sweden, the Netherlands, Germany, France, and Great Britain. Britain reported that as many as 100 deaths of Middle Eastern female immigrants may be the result of honor killings.[148]

In North Dakota, immigrants who practice the Romani culture believe that girls should and must be married as young as 14 years old. State law requires girls to be a minimum of 16 years old before they can be legally married. Despite the conflict with the law, the tradition for some families is so important that they break the law rather change their ways. One immigrant father from Kosovo said, "It doesn't matter where I am. I will follow my tradition. I don't want to be ashamed."[149]

Often the controversy regarding sexual assaults against women is brought to the public's attention by alleged crimes that receive nationwide publicity. For example, the alleged 2004 sexual assault by basketball star Kobe Bryant quickly resulted in allegations over the alleged victim's sexual history and whether she consented. Despite rape shield laws, the alleged victim's name quickly surfaced to the public, resulting in death threats against her. In 2006, allegations of sexual assault by three Duke University lacrosse players against a woman hired to dance for a party ignited nationwide debate that reflected the long-standing controversies regarding sexual assault as the woman's character and history were attacked. The controversy was heightened by racial implications that the woman was black and the alleged offenders were White, upper-class young men.

Organized Crime

The *Organized Crime Control Act* defines organized crime as "the unlawful activities of . . . a highly organized, disciplined association." The history of organized crime can be traced back to 1282 in Palermo, Sicily, and the birth of the Sicilian Mafia, but U.S. law enforcement interest in organized crime has never become a priority. Organized crime was not included as a Part I Index crime. In fact, until the 1950s and the Kefauver Committee Report, federal law enforcement appeared to ignore organized crime.

The challenge of organized crime to law enforcement is that traditional models of crime fighting, crime prevention, and law-enforcement resources and response are not effective in detecting or deterring organized crime. Members of organized crime often operate parallel legitimate businesses to provide a cover for their illegal activities and the ability to engage in money laundering, which is the transfer of illegally obtained money into what are claimed as legal profits from the legitimate businesses.

Organized crime groups are called *crime syndicates* or *crime families*. These groups are characterized by a secret hierarchical organization of leadership and an infrastructure that enables the organization to engage in illegal activities usually for the purpose of financial gain. To operate effectively, organized crime groups need a degree of support from the public and a criminal justice system that can be induced to provide illegal assistance. Public support is usually prompted by the organized crime group providing a service, although illegal, that is desired by a segment of the public. Common services include loan sharking, bookmaking, gambling, prostitution, pornography, drug trafficking, and illegal alcoholic beverages. The support of key criminal justice personnel and politicians is usually obtained by bribery, blackmail, and intimidation.

The history of organized crime is associated with closely knit immigrant groups but is clearly not limited to such groups. Organized crime groups can include motorcycle gangs, hate groups, gangs, terrorists, and corporations that engage in environmental crimes, price fixing, or insider trading. Organized criminal groups are not limited to certain ethnic groups popularized in the media. Organized criminal groups are in every country. In Colombia, it is the Medellin Cartel; in Canada, it is the Bandidos; in China, it is the Triads; in Italy, it is the Mafia or Cosa Nostra; in Japan, it is the Yakuza; and in Russia, it is the Russian Mafia. In each country the basic mission, operation, and infrastructure are similar.

In the United States, organized crime received a significant boost with the passage of the Volstead Act, which outlawed the manufacture, distribution, and possession of alcoholic beverages. Organized crime groups quickly stepped in to provide the public with illegal alcoholic beverages, and the profits from this enterprise enabled organized crime groups to expand into other criminal and legitimate enterprises. Today, organized crime has encroached into legitimate businesses such as licensed gambling, building construction, trash hauling, and dock loading enterprises.

Organized crime groups can be international, regional, or local in their operation and influence. International criminal activities may include drug trafficking, arms dealing, people smuggling, and trafficking in human beings. These criminal organizations move goods, services, and money across international boundaries and have extensive resources to support their criminal activities. Regional criminal organizations may engage in such crimes as car theft (chop shops), smuggling or manufacturing untaxed alcohol or cigarettes, bid-rigging, extortion, and gambling. Local organized criminal groups do not have the sophistication and resources of the other two groups and are sometimes categorized as "semi-organized" crime. For example, local outlaw motorcycle gangs operating in a limited geographical area as small as a county or city may engage in prostitution, gambling, drug trafficking, and illegal and after-hours alcoholic beverage sales.

It is a challenge for local and state law enforcement to fight organized crime because of the national or international capacity of organized crime groups and the enormous resources they command. As a result, the Federal Bureau of Investigation (aided by other federal agencies such as the Internal Revenue Service and the Drug Enforcement Administration and supplemented with local enforcement personnel) has assumed the primary responsibility for fighting organized crime.

Despite the harm done by organized crime, it is a poplular theme for the media. Television series such as *The Sopranos* and movies such as *The Godfather* provide an image of organized crime that is often appealing to the public. Do popular media images of organized crime make it more difficult for law enforement to combat organized crime?

Criminal activity engaged in by organized crime groups is referred to as *racketeering*. One of the tools that has been useful in the prosecution of organized crime figures is the **Racketeer Influenced and Corrupt Organizations Act,** commonly referred to as RICO. The RICO laws were passed as part of the Organized Crime Control Act of 1970. The RICO law provides that a person or a group that commits any 2 of 35 crimes—27 federal crimes and 8 state crimes—within a 10-year period and, in the opinion of the U.S. Attorney bringing the case, has committed those crimes with similar purpose and results can be charged with racketeering (Chapter 96 of Title 18 of the United States Code). One of the more effective tools of RICO prosecutions is that if convicted, the racketeer must forfeit all property and money gained directly or indirectly from the racketeering. Thus, if the money gained from illegal activity is funneled into a legitimate business, both assets are subject to forfeiture. This clause can result in the federal government seizing millions of dollars of assets in addition to criminal penalties, civil penalties, and prison time.

Organized criminal groups are opportunistic and flexible. They have quickly moved into Internet crime, including identity theft, pornography, fencing stolen goods, online extortion, and use of the Internet as a secure means of worldwide communication. Internet services such as eBay have provided organized criminal groups with the ability to move stolen goods worldwide with minimum risk.

Gun Crime

It is estimated that there are over 200 million guns in private hands in the United States. Although most of these firearms are used legally and responsibly, about 10 percent of violent victimizations involve a firearm and 70 percent of homicides are committed with a firearm.[150] Also, approximately 25 percent of armed robberies involve the use of a firearm.[151] Programs, policies, and laws aimed at reducing the use of firearms in crimes have been controversial. Much of the controversy is because the focus of these programs, policies, and laws has primarily been on restricting gun ownership and possession.

These tactics have been controversial because a significant number of people are opposed to restricting gun ownership, claiming that such policies are unconstitutional, do not achieve the goal of reducing gun crime, and increase the risk of criminalization for the unarmed citizen. The claim that restricting gun ownership is unconstitutional is based on the Second Amendment to the United States Constitution, which states, "A well regulated militia being necessary to the security of a free State, the right of the People to keep and bear arms shall not be infringed." Advocates of gun ownership argue that the Second Amendment is a guarantee that citizens have virtually unlimited rights to gun ownership, free from restrictions on the types and number of guns that can be owned and the registration of guns owned.

Although the Second Amendment is short and appears rather straightforward in its language, it has generated significant controversy and opposing interpretations before the U.S. Supreme Court. The Supreme Court has not agreed that the Second Amendment has given citizens broad rights to gun ownership, unfettered by legal restrictions, prohibition, and registration.

During the nineteenth century gun crime and gun control were not significant issues. There were few laws restricting gun ownership and gun crime was not a high-fear crime. This situation was due in part to the rural nature of U.S. society and the relatively unsophisticated firearms in use compared to modern firearms. However, the twentieth century ushered in a new era of urbanization and advancements in the firepower and deadliness of firearms. It is not surprising that New York City was the first to adopt a gun control law that significantly restricted the rights of its citizens to own firearms. In 1911, New York City enacted the Sullivan Act, one of the oldest gun control acts in the United States, which requires citizens to obtain a license to carry a concealed weapon. Today, gun ownership and registration is governed by numerous local, state and federal

Racketeer Influenced and Corrupt Organizations Act (RICO)
Provides federal prosecutors with the ability to charge a person with racketeering activity, which carries a greater penalty, rather than just the specific crimes committed.

laws. However, federal legislation has had the most significant influence in restricting gun ownership.

Major federal gun control legislation in the United States has been spurred by key gun crimes that have rallied politicians and citizens to enact new laws. The earliest federal gun control legislation was the 1934 **National Firearms Act**. This act did not ban firearms but required the registration and paying of a tax for "silencers," all fully automatic and burst-fire firearms, all rifles with a barrel length less than 16 inches and shotguns with a barrel length less than 18 inches, and certain other weapons classified as destructive devices. The act required a background check and a $200 tax per weapon. In 1934 (during the Depression), a $200 tax was about five months' salary. Thus, this tax was a significant disincentive for the average person to own such weapons. It is believed that the initiative for this legislation was the widespread public sale and use of the Thompson submachine gun by mob members trafficking in illegal alcohol during the Prohibition Era. The 1934 act was supplemented in 1938 with the Federal Firearms Act, which required anyone involved in the selling of firearms to obtain a Federal Firearms License from the Secretary of Commerce. The cost of the license was only $1 annually, as the purpose of the act was to require a record of the names and addresses of those who purchased firearms in an effort to prohibit the selling of firearms to certain people restricted from gun ownership, such as felons.

The next major federal gun control legislation was the **Gun Control Act** of 1968. The act was initiated by the assassination of President John F. Kennedy, who was killed by a mail-order gun, the assassination of Martin Luther King Jr., and the assassination of presidential candidate Robert Kennedy. The Gun Control Act adopted new restrictions on firearms sales, including the banning of mail-order sales of firearms and prohibiting the sale of firearms to convicted felons, the mentally incompetent, drug users, and certain other persons. The Gun Control Act required that all firearms bear a serial number. One of the more controversial provisions of the act was the "sporting purposes" standard, which required that firearms must "be generally recognized as particularly suitable for or readily adaptable to sporting purposes," excluding surplus military firearms. In 1972, enforcement of the Gun Control Act was given to the Department of the Treasury's Alcohol and Tobacco Tax Division of the Internal Revenue Service, and the agency was renamed the Bureau of Alcohol, Tobacco and Firearms (ATF). (The ATF was reorganized by the Homeland Security Act of 2002.)

See www.psn.gov to view the Project Safe Neighborhoods webpage.

Other important federal legislation includes the 1986 Firearms Owner's Protection Act, the 1990 Crime Control Act, the 1994 Brady Handgun Violence Prevention Act, and the 1994 Violent Crime Control and Law Enforcement Act. The Firearms Owner's Protection Act provided both benefits and restrictions to gun owners. It provided gun owners the right to transport firearms across state lines for lawful activities and forbade the U.S. government or any agency for it from keeping a registry directly linking non-National Firearms Act firearms to their owners. The act further restricted the sale of machine guns, regulated ATF inspections of firearms dealers, and augmented, modified, and clarified who could possess a firearm. The Violent Crime Control and Law Enforcement Act of 1994 is best known for its ban on assault-type weapons. (The ban sunset on March 2, 2004.) The Brady Act is best known for its requirement that gun purchasers must wait five days and must pass a background check to purchase a firearm. (The waiting period for the act expired in 1998 and was replaced by the National Instacheck System managed by the FBI.)

National Firearms Act
Early national legislation that restricted ownership of certain weapons, such as machine guns, by requiring owners to register and pay a tax.

Gun Control Act
Legislation that banned the mail-order sale of firearms and placed other restrictions on firearms sale.

Many cities and states continue to propose and adopt new gun control legislation, including nearly complete bans on gun ownership. Current federal legislation is aimed at reducing *straw purchases*. Straw purchases are when a person purchases a gun for someone who cannot legally own a gun.

Many programs that strive to reduce gun crime have begun to refocus their efforts. Statistical data show that crime involving the use of a firearm is significantly higher for 15- to 24-year-olds and significantly higher for Blacks and Hispanics.[152] Furthermore, crimes involving guns are more likely to occur in certain geographical areas rather than

figure 2.8

Nonfatal Firearm-Related Violent Crimes, 1993–2004

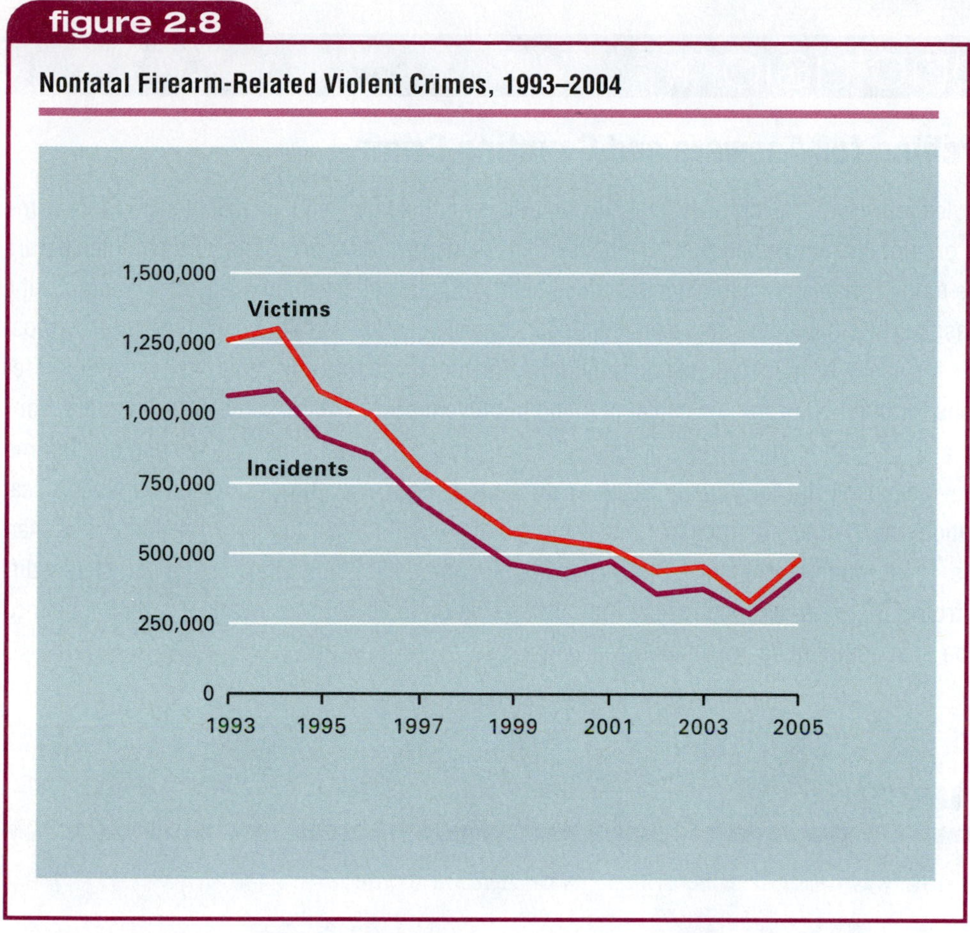

Note: The violent crimes included are rape and sexual assault, robbery, and aggravated assault.
Source: **National Crime Victimization Survey** (NCVS).

being randomly distributed. One federal program that has aggressively strived to reduce gun crime using this focused approach is the Project Safe Neighborhoods (PSA) initiated in 2001. This program is committed to developing partnerships with federal, state, and local agencies to target specific communities for PSA campaigns aimed at reducing gun crime. Campaigns frequently focus on reducing gang-related violence. Gun crime is higher in large cities, therefore many major cities have undertaken similar efforts to target resources for the reduction of gun violence, including Boston's Gun Project's Operation Ceasefire (2001), Indianapolis's Police Department's Directed Patrol Project (2002), St. Louis's Consent-to-Search Program (2004), and Los Angeles's Operation Ceasefire in Los Angeles (2005). The effect of recent campaigns and laws appears to be positive. Overall, the use of firearms in the commission of a nonfatal crime has declined significantly since 1993. In 1993, firearms were used in approximately 11 percent of violent crimes (excluding murder), and this number dropped to 6 percent in 2003 (see Figure 2.8).

▲ check your understanding **2.8** **What do drug trafficking, transnational crimes, cybercrimes, corporate crime, crimes against the elderly, crimes against women, organized crime, and gun crimes have in common? Why do these crimes pose special problems for the criminal justice system?**

conclusion:

Searching for Answers and Counting Crime

No single theory explains crime. Often, advances in scientific knowledge reveal the flaws in a crime theory or suggest a new theory. It is not easy to explain crime because of its very complex nature and the many variables that influence criminal behavior and modern theory reflect that complexity.

Despite their flaws and shortcomings, sociological theories of crime causation are the most popular for use by criminologists and the criminal justice system. Sociological explanations offer solutions for building programs and attempting to prevent crime. At the same time, it is unreasonable to expect a single theory to emerge in the near future that will explain the cause of all crime and provide a blueprint for the rehabilitation of all criminals. Yet, without an underlying theoretical foundation, the various attempts to reduce crime and to rehabilitate offenders is nothing more than a guess. Most modern criminologists have abandoned the belief that criminals are completely different from other citizens. The focus of criminology is on isolating those variables that appear to have the greatest influence on human behavior.

chapter summary

- Prior to Beccaria, the cause of crime was thought to be evil spirits or yielding to the temptations of sin.
- Criminology is the scientific study of verifiable principles, concepts, and theories regarding the process of law, crime, and treatment or prevention.
- Criminology uses theories to develop hypotheses about the causes of crime. All good theories have explanatory power that can be generalized to the population under study.
- The major perspectives concerning crime causation are the classical perspective, the biological perspective, the psychological perspective, and the sociological perspective.
- Classical and neoclassical theories of crime, such as Beccaria's and Bentham's, assume that crime is a rational free-will choice based on the pleasure–pain principle.
- Biological theories of crime, such as Lombroso's, assume that crime is an inherent or innate predisposition, not an act of free will. Biology-based theories have focused on body types, twin studies, body chemistry, and genetics.
- Psychology-based theories such as Freud's assume that criminal behavior is the expression of repressed feelings, personality maladjustment, or mental illness.
- Sociological theories assume that crime is caused not by body, mind, or individual motivation, but by society. Social groups and institutions create the conditions that lead to criminal behavior. The belief that society is at the root of crime is called social determinism.
- The belief that crime is caused by social disorganization—poverty, unemployment, inadequate housing, breakdown in family values, violence in the media, failure of the schools—is the theoretical basis for many crime prevention and treatment programs. Social disorganization theory and zone theory are based on the role of environment in causing crime.
- The theory that is most accepted in the criminal justice system is Sutherland's theory of differential association and other learning theories. These theories say that crime is a learned behavior. Thus, crime can be unlearned.
- Theories based on the dynamics of social control and the role of interpersonal interaction say that behavior, including conformity and deviance, is shaped by individuals' re-

sponses to others' expectations. Examples are containment theory, neutralization theory, social bond theory, and labeling theory.

- Merton's strain theory identifies strain between societal goals and the means for achieving these goals as a source of criminal behavior. Individuals who cannot achieve the goals legitimately tend to reject or substitute for the goals or turn to illegitimate means.
- Cohen's theory of deviant subcultures identifies reaction formation as a cause of delinquency and criminal behavior in youth gangs.
- Conflict theories are based on the assumption that social inequality is the cause of crime through imbalances of power in the system. Some conflict theorists believe that the rich and powerful use the criminal justice system to oppress the poor and maintain their own positions. Feminist theories focus on the role of gender inequality in criminal behavior.
- No single theory explains crime, but theory is important in developing crime prevention and treatment programs.
- Accurate crime data are important to the criminal justice system for many reasons.
- The two most commonly used measures of crime data are the Uniform Crime Report and the National Crime Victimization Survey. Each has its own strengths and weaknesses.
- Other sources of crime data include state-sponsored research, campus crime data, hate crime data, and self-report crime data.
- Drug trafficking and abuse is one of most serious crimes threatening society.
- Transnational crimes can only be dealt with by a coordinated response of various criminal justice agencies, including criminal justice agencies of other nations.
- Cybercrimes and identity theft pose new challenges to the criminal justice system, as fighting these crimes requires new skills and resources.
- White-collar and corporate crimes have received more attention as recent high-profile cases have made the public more aware of these crimes.
- As a larger percent of the population is aging, one of the fears of the elderly is being victimized.
- Crimes against women reflect social values. Internationally there is a wide range of social values reflected in the criminal justice system of nations.
- Nearly ignored until the 1950s, the criminal justice system now recognizes the importance of fighting organized crime .
- Efforts to combat gun crime are controversial because of the opposition of some to restricting gun ownership. However, new tactics have reduced gun crime significantly since 1993.

vocabulary review

anomie, 59
atavistic stigmata, 51
biocriminology, 53
classical school, 48
clearance rate, 70
conflict theories, 64
containment theory, 61
Crime Clock, 68
crime prevention through environmental design (CPTED), 59
criminal personality, 58
cultural deviance theories, 63
cybercrime, 84
denial of service, 85
differential association theory, 60
felicitic calculus, 50
feminist criminology, 64
Gun Control Act of 1968, 98
hierarchy rule, 69
identity theft, 85
Index Crimes, 69
labeling theory, 62
methamphetomine, 79
minimal brain dysfunction (MBD), 54
money laundering, 82
narco-terrorism, 82
National Firearms Act, 98
neoclassical school, 48
neutralization theory, 61
page jacking, 84
phishing, 87
piggybacking, 84
positive school, 50
psychoanalytic theory, 55
Racketeer Influenced and Corrupt Organizations Act (RICO), 97
reaction formation, 63
smurfing, 81
social bond theory, 62
social control theory, 61
social determinism, 58
social disorganization theory, 59
somatotype school, 52
strain theory, 62
theories, 47
trafficking, 82
XYY chromosome theory, 53
zone theory, 59

do you **remember?**

Freda Adler, 64
Anti-Drug Abuse Act, 77
Cesare Beccaria, 48
Howard Becker, 62
Jeremy Bentham, 49
Boggs Act, 77
Bureau of Justice Statistics, 67
William Chambliss, 64
Meda Chesney-Lind, 64
Albert Cohen, 63
Comprehensive Drug Abuse Prevention and Control Act, 77
Crime Awareness and Campus Security Act, 74
Katherine Dalton, 54
Drug Enforcement Agency (DEA), 82
Richard Dugdale, 51
Emile Durkheim, 59
Sigmund Freud, 55
Raffaele Garofalo, 51
Eleanor Glueck, 52
Sheldon Glueck, 52
Harrison Narcotics Act, 77
Hate Crime Statistics Act, 74
Travis Hirschi, 62
Identity Theft Assumption and Deterrence Act, 85
Identity Theft Penalty Enhancement Act, 85
International Bill of Human Rights, 81
International Police Association (INTERPOL), 81
Internet Fraud Complaint Center (IFCC), 85
Ernest Kretschmer, 52
Cesare Lombroso, 51
Marijuana Tax Act, 77
Robert Merton, 62
Walter Miller, 63
National Crime Victim Survey (NCVS), 71
National Incident-Based Reporting (NIBRS), 71
National Institute of Drug Abuse (NIDA), 78
Office of National Drug Control Policy (ONDCP), 77
Organized Crime Drug Enforcement Task Force (OCDETF), 82
Robert Ezra Park, 59
Richard Quinney, 64
Walter Reckless, 61
Salem witch trials, 45
William Sheldon, 52
Edwin Sutherland, 60
Gresham Sykes and David Matza, 61
Frank Tannenbaum, 62
Twinkie defense, 54
Uniform Crime Report (UCR), 69
War on Drugs, 76

think about this

1. Although there are numerous theories and much debate on crime causation, often the criminal justice system must adopt basic principles on which to base prevention programs. Why? How do theories relate to practice? Consider a crime prevention or rehabilitation program such as DARE, Crime Watch, Project Exile (a get tough on crime program involving firearms), or community policing. On what theoretical perspectives are these programs based? How successful are they in addressing the primary factors associated with criminal behavior?
2. One of the most important concepts in crime causation is whether one believes that crime is a matter of free-will choice, biology-based programming, or psychologically motivated behavior, or is caused by social interaction and variables in the environment. For example, if crime is an inherent predisposition over which the offender has minimal control, then incarceration and prison time would not be a deterrent to crime. What do you believe is the primary cause of criminal behavior? What are the implications of your belief for the treatment of criminals?
3. Most people who study crime and criminals accept that violent crimes against persons and property—murder, rape, robbery, burglary—are the most serious crimes. However, others who study crime and criminals believe that white-collar crime, corruption, and environmental crime are more harmful to society. Do you agree? Why or why not? Do you think the government and the criminal justice system use violent crimes to distract people from possible threats to their freedom from government, big business, and the ruling class? Explain your answer.

research navigator

Visit the Research Navigator website (www.researchnavigator.com), login and select the criminal justice data base in ContentSelect. Type in the key words “Revisiting Prediction Models.” This search will bring up the article “Revisiting Prediction Models in Policing: Identifying High-Risk Offenders” by Wesley Jennings. While this article includes a technical discussion of the statistical hypotheses tested by the author, you only need to focus only on the article’s findings in your review of the article. Sample the article and answer the following questions:

1. The article focuses on the use of knowledge gained from criminology to assist practitioners in the criminal justice field. How would the application of predictive research in the field of criminology benefit the criminal justice system?
2. How has corrections (including probation and parole) used predictive risk assessment techniques?
3. What are some of the influences which encourage law enforcement to develop and adopt the use of predictive risk assessment techniques?
4. How could law enforcement use knowledge gained from reliable and effective predictive risk assessment techniques? What would be the advantage to the police in the use of this knowledge?

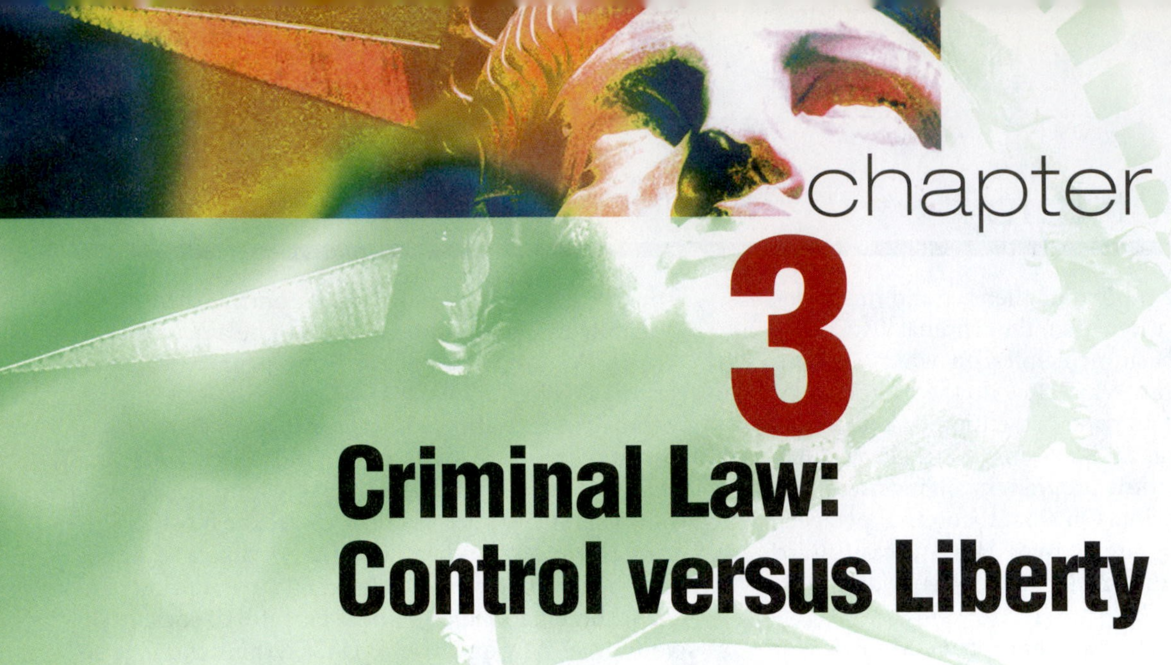

chapter

3 Criminal Law: Control versus Liberty

CHAPTER OUTLINE

LEARNING OBJECTIVES

After reading this chapter, you will know

- How federal, state, and local criminal laws are created and changed.
- Why limits are imposed on criminal laws and how those limits are defined.
- The major elements of a crime that must be present to prosecute offenders for their actions.
- The major defenses against charges of criminal conduct and how those defenses are defined.
- How crimes are categorized and defined according to the Model Penal Code.
- How criminal liability for crimes and the seriousness of crimes are determined.

Texas Legislation Adds a Bah! to Sis and Boom

HOUSTON, MAY 5—Texas, the home of the Dallas Cowboys Cheerleaders and the National Cheerleaders Association, may have put modern cheerleading on the map, but the Texas House of Representatives, concerned that high school cheerleading is becoming too raunchy, has approved a bill that would allow state education officials to prohibit "overtly sexually suggestive" cheering and drill team routines.

The legislation, sponsored by Representative Al Edwards, a Houston Democrat and ordained minister who once proposed a measure to amputate the fingers of drug dealers, now goes to the Senate, where it lacks a sponsor. It also lacks some of its original teeth; a provision that would have allowed a cut in state financing to schools that permit racy routines was removed. Edwards argued bawdy performances are a distraction for students resulting in pregnancies, dropouts and the spread of sexually transmitted diseases.

Eric Howze, the owner and director of the Southwest Cheer Academy, said the measure was "completely ridiculous. What's defined as lewd by one person is skill, talent and hard work to another."

Supporters of the bill, however, argued that something had to be done to prevent student cheerleaders from mimicking the provocative dances seen on MTV, the routines of some professional sports teams' cheering squads and suggestive performances in cheerleading movies.

Just what would be defined as too suggestive under the bill remains vague, though. The measure leaves that to the Texas Education Agency. The Agency would be empowered to write a letter to a school district to request a review on whether a routine was unacceptably racy.

The American Civil Liberties Union said the measure was unnecessary because state law already prohibits public lewdness by students on or near a school campus.

—Adapted from Associated Press, "Texas House Bans 'Suggestive' Cheerleading," The New York Times Online, www.nytimes.com, May 4, 2005 and "Texas Legislation Adds a Bah! to Sis and Boom," The New York Times Online, www.nytimes.com, May 5, 2005 by Simon Romero.

introduction:

There Ought to Be a Law

Texas lawmakers are not alone in their quest to add new laws to regulate and prohibit that which is considered harmful to society. In February 2005, Virginia legislator Algie T. Howell Jr. visited a juvenile and domestic relations court and was shocked to see juveniles wearing pants that ride so low on the hips as to expose a strip of boxers or briefs. Concerned about the morality of such dress, he introduced a bill that would fine anyone who "wears and displays his below-waist undergarments in a lewd or indecent manner" 50 dollars. Also, in March 2004, County Commissioners in rural, conservative Rhea County in Tennessee (the county where John Scopes was convicted for teaching evolution in what was known as the "Scopes Monkey Trial") passed a resolution banning gay people from the county. After two days and a firestorm of attacks, the commissioners reversed the ban.

There are numerous new laws at every level of government proposed all the time. Some become the law of the land, whereas others are defeated. Some new laws concern major social and economic issues such as stem cell research, mandatory sentencing, assisted suicides, and medical use of marijuana. Other laws address smaller issues such as Germantown's (Tennessee) debate about whether to pass an ordinance regulating when garage doors can be opened or Madison's (Wisconsin) consideration of legislation that would legalize cat hunting. Germantown wanted to regulate garage doors to promote a sense of community decorum by requiring citizens to keep garage doors closed except for brief times when necessary. Madison, concerned about the decimation of songbirds by free-roaming cats, debated whether to make such cats—including any domestic cat not under the owner's direct control or any cat without a collar—an unprotected species. If listed as an unprotected species, hunters could obtain a small-game license and legally hunt these cats.

Laws are central to the regulation of behaviors. Laws determine what behaviors are legal and what punishment one can receive when one breaks the law. Although legislators and the public desire to have laws that reflect community values and promote orderly conduct and the safety of the community, not all proposed laws are permissible. For example, if Rhea County Commissioners had not revoked the county's ban on gays, most likely the courts would have declared the ban unconstitutional. Some laws, although offensive to certain people, are permissible. For example, laws legalizing cat hunting may offend many people, but the courts have upheld such laws.

This chapter will examine how laws are made and the principles that laws must conform to or risk being declared unconstitutional by the courts. It discusses the elements of a crime—that is to say, what is required to prove in court that someone violated the law. The chapter will also present some of the major defenses against charges of criminal conduct. Finally, it will discuss some of most common crimes defined by law, the history and development of these laws, and important elements necessary in obtaining convictions for these crimes.

The Rule of Law

the main idea 3.1 Federal, state, and local government bodies can enact criminal laws.

In 1198, Pope Innocent III wrote to the Emperor of France that the pope was like the sun and the emperor was like the moon. The sun was greater than the moon, and the moon derived its light from the sun. In other words, the pope was greater and more powerful than the emperor. For the next three centuries, the royal rulers of England and France engaged in a continuous power struggle as to who was the supreme authority. King Henry VIII appeared to tip the balance of power to royalty when in 1534 he proclaimed himself the head of the Church of England and the king of the land.[1] He claimed to be both the moon and the sun.

After breaking away from England, the American colonies rejected the authority of both the Church and the king as the supreme authority and declared that the United States is founded on the superiority of the rule of law. The **rule of law** declares that the standards of behavior and privilege are established not by kings or religious leaders but by rules and procedures that define and prohibit certain behaviors as illegal or criminal and prescribe punishments for those behaviors. All people, regardless of rank, title, position, status, or wealth, are accorded the same rights and privileges under the law. Three major categories of law are civil law, administrative law, and criminal law. This chapter focuses on an examination of criminal law.

check your understanding 3.1 What is the rule of law? Name the three major categories of law.

The Making of Law

the main idea 3.2 Local, state, and federal governments create laws for a number of reasons. Each has a distinctive process for making laws.

Why do governments—local, state, and federal—create criminal laws? The **American Law Institute,** a private, voluntary association of distinguished judges, lawyers, and law teachers, gives five reasons for laws[2]:

1. To forbid and prevent conduct that unjustifiably and inexcusably inflicts or threatens substantial harm to individual or public interests
2. To subject to public control persons whose conduct indicates that they are disposed to commit crimes
3. To safeguard conduct that is without fault from condemnation as criminal
4. To give fair warning of the nature of the conduct declared to constitute an offense
5. To differentiate on reasonable grounds between serious and minor offenses

Specific laws may be passed because it is thought that they prohibit actions that are harmful to society. For example, prohibitions against murder, rape, robbery, and arson are seen as serving all people in society. Such conduct is prohibited because it is considered harmful in itself, or ***mala in se.*** Other laws may be passed because it is felt by some that there is a need to regulate certain actions—for example, parking regulations, minimum drinking-age limits, and various licensing regulations. This conduct is ***mala prohibita***—prohibited only because of the law and not because it is necessarily harmful or inherently evil.

At www.ali.org/, the official website of the American Law Institute, learn more about the institute and its programs.

rule of law Principle that standards of behavior and privilege are established by laws and not by monarchs or religious leaders.

mala in se Acts that are crimes because they are inherently evil or harmful to society.

mala prohibita Acts that are prohibited because they are defined as crimes by law.

Much debate is generated about what laws should be passed and what purposes the law actually serves. Some laws are based on the morals and values of the community. Laws against abortion, obscenity, same-sex marriages, and drug use often are based on moral and ethical beliefs not shared by all members of society. Some laws are passed based on public fear. Kidnapping was made a federal crime after the kidnapping and murder of Charles Lindbergh's child, for example. And Megan's Law, which requires the registration of sexual offenders, was passed after a sexual offender unknown to the community abducted and murdered a small child.

Ideally, laws serve the public good (the consensus model), but sometimes laws benefit a small group or special interests (the conflict model). The actual laws of the land are derived from (1) federal criminal laws, (2) state criminal laws, and (3) local criminal laws. Each level of government has the authority to enact laws within its jurisdiction.

Federal Criminal Laws

Federal criminal laws are found in (1) the U.S. Constitution, (2) *U.S. Criminal Codes*, (3) judicial decisions interpreting codes, and (4) executive orders. The only crimes defined in the U.S. Constitution are treason and sedition, but the Constitution provides for the establishment of the court system and the process by which laws may be enacted. The Constitution also provides the reference for judging the validity of laws. Laws that are contrary to the freedoms and rights provided by the Constitution and its amendments may be declared null and void by the U.S. Supreme Court.

The ***U.S. Criminal Codes*** is the publication that contains all of the federal laws. Federal criminal laws must originate in the House of Representatives or the U.S. Senate. A senator or representative introduces a proposal (known as a bill) to create a new law or modify an existing law. The merits of the bill are debated in the House or Senate and a vote is taken. If the bill receives a majority vote, it is passed on to the other house of Congress where it is again debated and put to a vote. If any changes are made, the amended bill must be returned to the house of Congress where it originated and voted on again. This process continues until the House and Senate agree on a single version of the bill. The bill is then forwarded to the president, who can sign the bill into law, veto it, or take no action, in which case the bill may die when Congress adjourns. If the president vetoes a bill, Congress can pass the law over the president's veto by a two-thirds vote of both Houses. A bill becomes law when it is published in the *U.S. Criminal Codes.*

Federal criminal laws can be modified or influenced by judicial decisions. Federal judges cannot make law, but their influence can be so great that the end result is nearly the same.[3] Rules governing the use of evidence in a trial, for instance, come from the courts rather than the legislative bodies, but the impact is the same as if they were laws. Finally, although not in a strict sense a criminal law, the president can issue executive orders that have the weight of law in prohibiting and regulating certain conduct.

State Criminal Laws

The sources of state criminal laws are the state constitution, state criminal codes, common law, and judicial decisions interpreting codes and the common law. Each state has the right to enact criminal laws seen as appropriate for its citizens. This autonomy leads to great variety in laws, but most states have similar criminal laws because (1) all state criminals laws must preserve the rights guaranteed in the U.S. Constitution, (2) many states (approximately 22) have adopted portions of their criminal codes from the Model Penal Code by the American Law Institute in 1962, (3) state criminal laws had as their common origin early English common law, and (4) if one accepts the consensus model, then laws will serve similar public benefit in each of the states.

State constitutions cannot negate any right guaranteed in the U.S. Constitution, but a state's constitution can add to rights not covered by the U.S. Constitution. For example, Alaska and Hawaii have added the right of privacy as a guaranteed freedom for the citizens of their states, whereas privacy is only an implied right in the U.S. Constitution. Most state criminal codes are passed by state governments in a similar manner as the federal criminal codes. A bill must originate in one of the state legislative bodies, be passed by both bodies, and then be endorsed by the governor of the state. Like the president, state governors have veto power and the power to create rules and regulations through executive orders.

In their particulars, state criminal codes differ significantly among states. For example, some states prohibit consensual sex among persons of the same sex, whereas other states permit such conduct. Some states allow citizens to carry concealed weapons, whereas other states have strict prohibitions against this practice. Any person within a state is under the jurisdiction of the laws of that state regardless of the person's state of residence or citizenship. Thus, a person from a state that permits carrying a concealed weapon who travels to a state that prohibits such behavior must conform to the laws of the state he or she is in. Likewise, a state's criminal laws are not applicable outside that state's boundaries. Thus, Utah prohibits gambling, but its bordering state, Nevada, has legalized gambling. If a Utah resident travels to Nevada, Utah's prohibition against gambling does not prevent the Utah resident from gambling while in Nevada.

One of the distinctions between federal criminal laws and state criminal laws is the area of law known as **common law,** or unwritten law. Criminal law in the United States was greatly influenced by early English common law. English criminal law was based on the assumption that the vast majority of citizens were illiterate and thus would not understand written law. Written laws were stated simply, leaving it to judges to interpret and apply laws to specific situations. For example, as written, the law simply declared that murder is prohibited or that it is against the law to disturb the peace. The law offered no guidance as to what behaviors constituted disturbing the peace or the grounds for determining that a person had committed murder. This judge-mediated common law became the basis for criminal law in the American colonies.

This pattern of law can be seen in today's small claims courts and traffic courts. Also, the power of the judge to interpret law is illustrated on television shows on which a "judge" resolves a dispute by applying general principles from contract law and arbitration to decide the case. As in common law, the judge interprets from the law which principles should be used to judge the conduct of the parties. Federal courts and federal judges are specifically prohibited from operating under the rules of common law.

common law Unwritten, simply stated laws from the English common laws, based on traditions and common understandings in a time when most people were illiterate.

Local Criminal Laws

The sources of local criminal laws are city or county charters, municipal or county ordinances or violations, common law, and judicial decisions of municipal judges interpreting codes and common law. Nearly all local criminal laws are misdemeanors or violations.

This person is paying the fine for a traffic violation. What kind of a law has been violated? Is it a federal, state, or local law? What are the differences between laws that originate at the local, state, or federal levels? What are the sources of laws in the United States, and how are laws made?

diversity in the system

Blue Laws

There are laws on the books, some of which are enforced, that prohibit certain behaviors on moral grounds, based on standards of morality from colonial times. For example, some states have laws prohibiting certain types of commercial transactions, the operation of entertainment establishments, or the selling of tobacco or alcohol on Sunday. These laws restricting Sunday sales and entertainment have their roots in colonial government. In 1732, a colony of Puritan settlers in New Haven, Connecticut, adopted a set of laws for the governance of their settlement. These laws reflected the deeply held religious beliefs of the people and had harsh punishments for offenses such as Sabbath breaking, drunkenness, and immodest dress.

The privilege of voting and holding official office was contingent on good standing in a church of the colony and loyalty to religious values. For example, in Protestant New Haven, the law provided that a Catholic priest found within the colony could be seized by anyone and without a warrant. The punishment for the first offense of trespass by a priest was banishment, and the second offense was punishable by death. It was also forbidden to give food or lodging to a Quaker, Adamite, or other "heretic." Persons who converted to the Quaker religion were banished from the colony and could be put to death if they returned.

New Haven's laws also forbade the wearing of "clothes trimmed with gold, silver, or bone lace, above two shillings by the yard." Adultery was punishable by death. Persons found to engage in fornication were required to be married or punished "as the court may think proper." Married persons were required to live together upon punishment of imprisonment for failure to do so. The punishment for theft, which included picking an ear of corn growing in a neighbor's garden, was death. Celebrations and festive entertainment on Christmas or saints' days were prohibited.

These laws based on colonial codes of morality are called **blue laws,** but the origin of the name is obscure. The term first appeared in 1791 in the writings of Reverend Samuel Peters' book *General History of Connecticut.* Peters said the laws were written on blue paper and were so named for the color of the paper, but whether this is the exact origin of the term cannot be determined.

Other settlements in the American colonies adopted similar blue laws requiring obedience to the religious values of their communities. Today, the influence of these old laws still can be seen in state statutes. These blue laws are most evident in bans on certain behaviors, sexual morality, and what are known as Sunday closing laws. For example, hunting on Sunday is banned or restricted in 15 states and 32 states restrict alcohol sales. Other laws prohibit sodomy, cohabitation of unmarried couples, and fornication. Some state laws limit business hours on "the Sabbath," presumably to allow employees time to attend worship service, or restrict the sale of nonessential items.

These blue laws are anachronistic but they also are potentially harmful, and some restrictions, particularly those regarding sexual conduct and morality, have been declared unconstitutional by the courts. Often it is only when these laws are challenged and declared unconstitutional that they are removed from the legal codes. For example, in May 2005, the American Civil Liberties Union filed a lawsuit to challenge the constitutionality of a 1805 North Carolina law prohibiting unmarried couples from living together. North Carolina is one of seven states that have laws prohibiting cohabitation of unmarried couples. Pender County Sheriff's Department dismissed a dispatcher because it was found out that contrary to the 1805 law she was cohabitating with her boyfriend. When she refused to move out or to get married she was fired. The lawsuit challenges the firing of the Pender County sheriff's dispatcher, arguing that the law is unconstitutional and cannot be used as grounds for dismissal. If the court rules the 1805 law is indeed unconstitutional, then it will be removed from the legal codes.

Some states have repealed their blue laws on their own. However, often it takes years of effort by citizen groups to get blue laws repealed. For example, in May 2005, Boston repealed a 1675 law that still was on the books that forbid American Indians from entering the city unless escorted in the city by "musketeers." It took Native American interest groups and other activists about eight years to get the law repealed. Even though blue laws may not be enforced, there is opposition by some who are opposed to the repeal of the blue laws. Thus, when Massachusetts state senator Cynthia Stone Creem introduced legislation to repeal blue law bans on blasphemy and adultery, there was significant opposition to the legislation. Those opposed to the repeal argued that although not enforced, the laws made a statement about morality and "something would be lost" if the laws were repealed.

The federal courts have upheld the constitutionality of some state and local blue laws because they do not violate federal laws. However, commercial competition has forced many communities to abandon their prohibitions against Sunday commerce and entertainment. In a competitive free market where beliefs about morality are no longer universal, shoppers flock to neighboring communities without blue laws. Some businesses will not locate in communities that restrict Sunday sales. When Orlando, Florida, repealed its law against Sunday sales of alcoholic beverages in 1999, sales for beer and wine jumped 10 to 15 percent and new businesses moved into the city.[4]

On what were the blue laws based? Do you think laws should be continually updated to reflect changes in morality? Why have blue laws persisted, and in what circumstances should they be changed? Is repeal of blue laws on economic grounds in the common interest of all citizens of a community?

Serious criminal conduct is called a **felony,** and less serious criminal conduct is called a **misdemeanor.** The difference between a felony and a misdemeanor is usually defined by the amount of time in prison or jail one can receive as punishment for violation of the statute. Felonies commonly are crimes for which one can receive a punishment of one year or more in a state prison, whereas misdemeanors are crimes for which one can receive a punishment of one year or less in a state prison or county jail.

Violations, a relatively new classification of prohibited behaviors, commonly regulate traffic offenses.[5] A **violation** is less than a misdemeanor and may carry the punishment of only a fine or suspension of privilege, such as losing one's driver's license temporarily. Many states have redefined traffic offenses as violations that used to be classified as misdemeanors. The advantage is that violations free up the resources of the criminal courts for more serious cases and allow for speedier processing of cases through the system.

Local criminal codes are the product of city councils and county governments. Similar to the president and governors, chief executive officers of the city and county have the power to prohibit or regulate behavior through executive orders. Otherwise, there is great diversity in the way municipalities and counties draft and pass local criminal codes. Local criminal codes have limited jurisdiction and are enforceable only within the city or county limits. Local criminal codes cannot deny rights guaranteed by the state constitution or the U.S. Constitution.

▲ check your understanding **3.2 What are the five reasons given to justify the making of laws? How are federal, state, and local criminal laws similar and dissimilar?**

The Limits of the Law

▼ the main idea **3.3 Criminal law is founded on the principle of rule of law and is based on principles of rationality and justice.**

felony Serious criminal conduct punishable by incarceration for more than one year.

misdemeanor Less serious criminal conduct punishable by incarceration for less than a year.

violation An illegal action that is less serious than a misdemeanor and may carry the punishment of only a fine or suspension of privilege.

The founding of criminal law on the principle of rule of law means that the power of government is limited. Unlike royalty in the Middle Ages, which had limitless absolute power, governments are limited in the behaviors that can be declared criminal and in the punishments that can be applied for violations of criminal laws. Seven benchmarks are used to assess the legality of criminal laws:

1. Principle of legality
2. Ex post facto laws

figure 3.1

Limits of the Law

Rule of Law			
Rationality		**Justice**	
Legality	Laws must be made public before they can be enforced.	**Due Process**	Government must treat people equally and fairly before the law.
Ex post facto	Actions prior to enactment of laws cannot be punished after the fact.	**Right to Privacy**	Laws must not violate reasonable personal privacy of citizens.
Void for Vagueness	Laws must take care to define crimes clearly.	**Cruel and Unusual Punishment**	Laws must state the punishment for crimes, which must be proportional to the seriousness of the crime.
Void for Overbreadth	Laws must not prohibit behaviors that are legally protected.		

3. Due process
4. Void for vagueness
5. Right to privacy
6. Void for overbreadth
7. Cruel and unusual punishment

These principles apply to local, state, and federal laws. Figure 3.1 briefly summarizes the limits of criminal law.

Principle of Legality

Government cannot punish citizens for specific conduct if no specific laws exist forewarning them that the conduct is prohibited or required. This **principle of legality**, which has its roots in the Roman Empire, requires that laws must be made public before they can be enforced. When a law is passed, it must be published in an official government publication to become valid. Until the law is published, even though it is passed, it is not binding on behavior. Thus, it is possible that there will be a gap between the time that a behavior is prohibited and the time that the prohibition can be enforced by the police. Regardless, the principle of legality also declares that any behavior that has no law against it is legal. Thus, prostitution is legal in some counties of Nevada, not because there is a law allowing it but because there is no law prohibiting it.

principle of legality The belief that specific laws defining crimes and penalties for crimes must exist and be made public before the government can punish citizens for violating them.

Ex Post Facto Laws

Ex post facto ("not after the fact") laws are related to the principle of legality. This **ex post facto law** principle declares that persons cannot be punished for actions committed before the law prohibiting the behavior was passed.[6] For example, Timothy Leary, a university psychology professor, experimented with and advocated the use of LSD prior to the time that laws were passed making possession or use of LSD illegal. Despite public

ex post facto law A law related to the principle that persons cannot be punished for actions committed before the law prohibiting the behavior was passed.

knowledge and his acknowledgment that he used LSD prior to the passing of laws prohibiting its use, charges could not be brought against him. When he continued to use LSD after the law was passed, however, he was arrested, although the charges against him had to be limited to offenses he committed after the drug law was published.

The principle of ex post facto law also prohibits government from increasing the punishment for a specific crime after the crime was committed. Assume, for instance, that a person is convicted of mass murder in a state that does not have the death penalty. The public, upset by the brutality of the crime, may support a successful campaign to change the law and adopt a death penalty for mass murder. Even with the new law, however, the convicted person's sentence cannot then be changed from life in prison to death.

The government also cannot reduce the amount of evidence or alter the kind of evidence required for conviction when the offense was committed. If a person committed a crime on January 1, was arrested for the crime on January 30, and was scheduled for trial on July 1, a change in the law any time after January 1 regarding the kind of evidence required for conviction when an offense is committed could not be applied in court to the detriment of the defendant (although a change could be applied to the defendant's benefit).[7] Generally, the defendant has to be tried under the rules of evidence and laws that were in effect at the time the alleged crime was committed.

Due Process

The principles of due process are extrapolated from the U.S. Constitution and Bill of Rights. The principle of due process states simply that government must treat people fairly and equally before the law. There are two types of due process rights: substantive and procedural. **Substantive due process** limits the power of governments to create crimes unless there is compelling, substantial, public interest in regulating or prohibiting the conduct. The government, in a sense, is limited in what can be declared illegal. Conduct deemed illegal for which there is no rational justification for the law violates the principle of due process. Governments, in other words, cannot make arbitrary and capricious criminal laws.

Recent examination of the law for gender bias has resulted in a number of laws being declared unconstitutional because of violation of due process. Laws that apply to only one sex are violations of due process. Thus, a New York law that prohibited females from sunbathing on public beaches topless was struck down as unconstitutional because it applied only to females. The court ruled that the law had to apply equally to both sexes.

Procedural due process requires the government to follow established procedures and to treat defendants equally. Procedural laws regulate the conduct of the police and the courts and the criminal justice system in general. These laws, called "rules of evidence," define, for example, what is fair treatment, what order of events must be followed, what types of evidence can be admitted at a trial, and the rights of defendants.

Because of procedural due process, case law precedents play a big role in adjudication in the U.S. system of justice. Attorneys can argue that the court must allow similar evidence or testimony as was admitted in the past in similar cases. This case law system, called ***stare decisis,*** is not common to all criminal justice systems, however. For example, France uses the Continental system, in which each case is compared with the elements of the written law rather than with past cases.

In the United States, although *stare decisis* guides their actions, the courts can interpret cases and decide to what extent a case is like or unlike any previous cases. To change the basis on which precedents are judged, a court must explain why it is changing its interpretation and what the new criteria for judgment are. A case in which such a change of opinion is declared by the court is called a "landmark case." Since the 1960s, for example, the U.S. Supreme Court has issued numerous landmark decisions affecting

substantive due process Limits on the power of governments to create crimes unless there is compelling, substantial public interest in regulating or prohibiting the conduct.

procedural due process The requirement that the government must follow established procedures and treat defendants equally.

stare decisis The U.S. system of developing and applying case law on the basis of precedents established in previous cases.

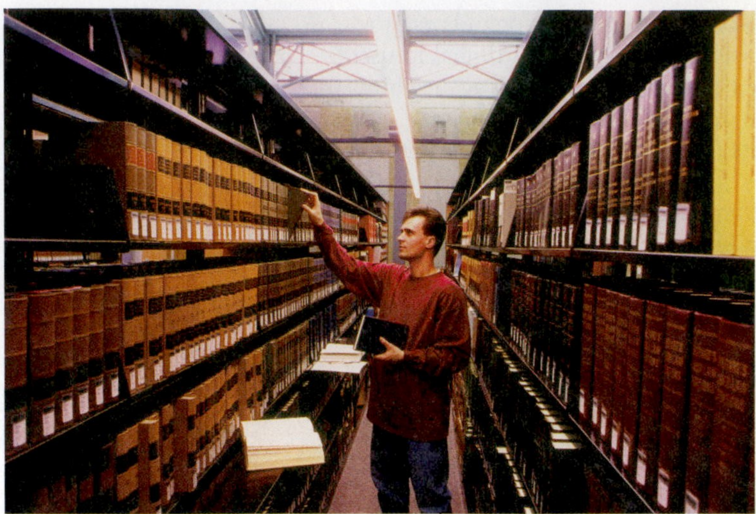

What does it mean to live in a social system with rule by law? What are the alternatives? What does it mean that the legality and limits of laws in the United States are decided on the basis of a system of *stare decisis?* Generally what document is the ultimate authority on the legality of laws?

the criminal justice system in matters such as search and seizure, confessions, cruel and unusual punishment, and prisoner rights. Because of the practice and importance of *stare decisis,* criminal attorneys must have excellent research abilities and access to records of previous court cases.

Void for Vagueness

The law must say what it means and mean what it says. Laws that do not provide reasonable guidelines that define the specific prohibited behaviors are **void for vagueness.** For instance, a New Jersey statute that made it a crime to be a member of a gang was struck down because the court declared that the word *gang* was too vague.[8] In another example, in the municipal court of Lincoln, Nebraska, a man was convicted of violating Section 9.52.100 of the Lincoln Municipal Code declaring, "It shall be unlawful for any person within the City of Lincoln . . . to commit any indecent, immodest or filthy act in the presence of any person, or in such a situation that persons passing might ordinarily see the same." On appeal, the Supreme Court of Nebraska reversed the conviction on the grounds that "the dividing line between what is lawful and what is unlawful in terms of 'indecent,' 'immodest,' or 'filthy' is simply too broad to satisfy the constitutional requirements of due process."[9]

Laws must use wording that clearly specifies what behavior or act is unlawful. Vague wording subject to different interpretations, such as "immoral," "indecent," "too close," or "interfere with," does not provide the average person with sufficient information to determine if their behavior is in violation of the law. If a law is so vague that members of a Boy Scout troop may be considered to be in violation of a prohibition against belonging to a "gang," the law is vague.

Right to Privacy

Laws that violate reasonable personal privacy may be declared void. The right to privacy is not clearly delineated in the U.S. Constitution but is a constructed right, inferred from the provisions of the First, Third, Fourth, and Ninth Amendments. Some state constitutions, such as those of Alaska, Florida, and Hawaii, have explicit rights to privacy that can be far-reaching. For example, under the protection of Alaska's right to privacy, the possession of small amounts of marijuana in the privacy of one's home is insufficient grounds for an arrest warrant or search.[10]

Right-to-privacy claims have resulted in several well-known U.S. Supreme Court decisions. The Court has struck down laws that made it a crime for married couples to use contraceptives[11] or for a person to possess pornography within the privacy of one's home.[12] However, the Court has upheld state statutes making it a crime to possess child pornography or to commit sodomy in the privacy of one's home.[13] Thus, privacy is not an overarching right that permits otherwise harmful or prohibited behaviors merely because they are performed in one's home.

void for vagueness Laws that are illegal because they do not provide clear and reasonable definitions of the specific behaviors that are prohibited.

void for overbreadth Laws that are illegal because they are stated so broadly as to prohibit legal activities as well as illegal activities.

Void for Overbreadth

Laws that have been declared **void for overbreadth** are laws that go too far; that is, in an attempt to prevent a specific conduct, the law not only makes that conduct illegal but it also prohibits other behaviors that are legally protected. Void-for-overbreadth laws frequently are connected with free speech and expressive conduct. Cases challenged for overbreadth that have made their way to the U.S. Supreme Court involve laws prohibit-

Criminal laws must specify the punishment for a crime, and the punishment must meet the principle of proportionality; that is, it must be appropriate to the seriousness of the offense. The United States Constitution makes it illegal to exact "cruel and unusual" punishment, which in an earlier age could be used on any offender for any kind of offense. What are the six other benchmarks used to assess the legality of a criminal law?

ing activities such as public protest, nude dancing, panhandling, erotic art, and flag burning.[14]

A law that is void for overbreadth is not vague in what it prohibits (like a law that is void for vagueness); rather, it simply prohibits legal activities as well as illegal activities. For example, in an attempt to provide a better quality of life, the city of New York prohibited panhandling or begging in the New York subways because panhandlers and beggars frightened passengers. The law was not vague in what it prohibited, but it could also be applied to prohibit free speech activities, which are protected under the U.S. Constitution.[15] Not all activities can be justified under the claim of free speech, however. The court upheld an Indiana statute banning nude dancing in public, for instance, on the grounds that the statute did not prohibit dancers from expressing themselves but only from expressing themselves while nude.[16]

Cruel and Unusual Punishment

To be valid, a law must specify the punishment to be applied for violation of the law. If that punishment is in violation of the Eighth Amendment prohibiting **cruel and unusual punishment**, it may be declared unconstitutional. This legal philosophy appears to be based on the premise of classical criminology that punishment should be appropriate to the crime. Although the argument of cruel and unusual punishment has frequently been applied to cases involving the death sentence, the focus of the prohibition is on applying the **principle of proportionality** for the appropriate punishment for a crime.[17] This focus involves much more than just appeals about the merits of the death penalty. The roots of this principle extend all the way back to the Magna Carta, which prohibited excessive fines.

To read a thought-provoking essay that discusses issues in Canada on cruel and unusual punishment, follow links at www.nacdl.org/.

Numerous cases have been appealed on the claim that the punishment was cruel and unusual. ***Weems* v. *United States*** (1910) has been used as a criterion for judging the limits of proportionality. Weems was convicted of falsifying a public document, was sentenced to 15 years of hard labor in chains, and was permanently deprived of his civil rights. The U.S. Supreme Court overturned the conviction on the grounds that the punishment was not proportional to the harm done by the crime.[18] However, the Court has not overturned a death penalty sentence on the grounds that the death penalty is cruel and unusual. The Court has ruled only that the death penalty must be fairly and equally applied.[19]

cruel and unusual punishment Punishment that violates the principle of proportionality and is considered too harsh for the crime committed; prohibited by the Eighth Amendment.

principle of proportionality The belief that less serious harms should carry lesser punishments than more serious harms.

The U.S. Supreme Court also has decided that sentencing a seriously ill person to prison does not constitute cruel and unusual punishment if adequate medical treatment for the condition is available.[20] Sentencing a person to prison for drug addiction is cruel and unusual, as drug addiction is deemed an illness rather than a criminal behavior. However, sentencing a person for possessing or using drugs is not cruel and unusual.[21] The Court has ruled that the use of corporal punishment in prison is cruel and unusual punishment and has prohibited such punishment.

▲ check your understanding **3.3** **How does a bill become a law? What are the seven benchmarks used to assess the legality of a criminal law, and in what circumstances is each benchmark applied?**

Elements of a Crime

▼ the main idea **3.4** **The actions and intent of the criminal, as well as the seriousness of the crime, all carry weight in determining punishment.**

Punishments specified by law are based on the principle of proportionality. Less serious harms, such as misdemeanors, carry lesser punishment than more serious harms, which are classified as felonies. However, even within felonies there are various degrees of punishment. Even the same act, such as the killing of a human being, may be punished by a sentence ranging from one year in prison to the death penalty. Determining what punishment should be attached to a crime depends on the conduct and the intention of the actor or perpetrator. The actions and intentions of the person who commits a crime are called the **elements of a crime**. Each crime is defined by these elements. Two important elements are *actus reus* and *mens rea*.

The actions of the person are referred to as the ***actus reus*** of the crime. The intent of the person is referred to as the ***mens rea***. In assessing whether a crime has been committed and the seriousness of the crime, the law examines what the person did, the person's state of mind or intentions, whether the person's actions were the cause of the outcome, and the specific harm that resulted from the actions.

Actus Reus

American law is firmly rooted in the classical criminological principle that crime is a voluntary action; that is, a person chooses to commit a crime. As a result, one of the first elements necessary to assert that a crime has been committed is that the actions of the person must be voluntary. An old British case of ***King* v. *Cogdon*** is cited as the benchmark for determining the voluntariness of an action. In that case, Mrs. Cogdon, who suffered from delusions, was found not guilty of the axe murder of her daughter. During her sleep, Mrs. Cogdon had a delusion and while "sleep walking" struck and killed her daughter. The British Court ruled the act was involuntary. Involuntary actions do not extend to conduct that is foreseeable, however. For example, a person who has an epileptic seizure while driving a car and as a result causes someone's death can be held accountable for the death. For a person with epilepsy, losing control of a motor vehicle is a foreseeable possibility.[22]

People have an obligation to conduct themselves in such a manner so as not to create harm to others. Thus, "accidental" injuries may be deemed voluntary even if the people deny that they intended to inflict harm. For example, a person whose thumb slips while holding back the hammer of a pistol, causing the wounding or death of another, is considered to have voluntarily committed the act even though the defendant denies the intention to fire the weapon.[23] The *actus reus* of some crimes does not require a bodily

elements of a crime The illegal actions (*actus reus*) and criminal intentions (*mens rea*) of the actor along with the circumstances that link the two, especially causation.

actus reus The actions of the person committing a crime as defined by law, one of the key elements of a crime.

mens rea The state of mind and intent of the person committing the *actus reus*, one of the key elements of a crime.

or physical action and can consist of verbal actions. Crimes such as conspiracy, solicitation, terroristic threats, and inciting to riot are examples of crimes whose *actus reus* consists of verbal acts.

Failure to Act There are some crimes in which the *actus reus* is the failure to act or a lack of action. These are called **crimes of omission**. The criminal intent of a crime may be the failure to act when there is a legal duty to act. A lifeguard employed by the government is under a legal obligation and may be considered guilty of a crime if while on duty he or she fails to act to save a swimmer in distress. However, if that same lifeguard, while on vacation in another state, observes a swimmer in distress and fails to act to offer assistance, he or she may be criticized for failing a moral duty but has committed no crime.

In crimes of omission, hospitals, caregivers, and even bystanders can come under the requirement of a legal duty to help another. For example, if you help someone when you are under no duty to do so but fail to exercise reasonable care for the safety and security of the person you are attempting to help, then you may be regarded as having criminal liability.[24] It is fear of criminal (or civil) liability that causes some people to refuse to act when they could render life-saving care to a victim. As a result, a number of states have passed "Good Samaritan" laws that extend legal protection against civil or criminal action against a person who renders aid to someone in distress. Some states even require that motorists stop and render reasonable aid for persons they observe who appear to be in distress. For example, Alaska requires that motorists render assistance to stranded motorists, and failure to do so is considered criminal. Given Alaska's climate and vast stretches of wilderness, failure to render aid to a stranded motorist could result in the death of the person.

Parents are considered to have a legal duty to aid and assist their children. Failure to fulfill this duty can be criminal. The court has ruled that even if the danger is from another parent, as in the case of child abuse, the parent has a legal duty to assist the children when under attack or at risk of physical danger.[25] This means that the spouse of an abusive parent could be charged with a crime even though the spouse did not cause harm to the child. The failure to prevent harm is criminal. Thus, a parent who fails to seek medical attention for his or her child could be held criminally liable in the event of the child's death. The same legal duty does not extend to the marital relationship, however. If a spouse fails to seek medical attention for his or her partner, who dies as a result of the lack of care, there may be no legal duty to make this action criminal.[26]

Possession as *Actus Reus* Possession of an illegal or prohibited item can constitute the *actus reus* of a crime. In a case in which a person has an illegal firearm in the trunk of his or her automobile, possession of the weapon is considered the *actus reus* of the crime. Three types of **possession** are recognized by the Model Penal Code: constructive possession, knowing possession, and mere possession.[27]

It is deemed *constructive possession* when a person does not have physical or actual possession of the illegal item but the defendant exercised, either singularly or jointly, care, custody, control, and management over the contraband, and the defendant knew that what he or she possessed was contraband. A drug dealer who mails a package of drugs or gives it to another to deliver is considered to have constructive possession of the drugs even though he or she does not have actual possession.

It is deemed *knowing possession* when a person has actual possession and knows that what he or she possesses is contraband, whereas it is considered *mere possession* when a person has actual possession of an item but does not know that it is contraband. However, mere possession may not be sufficient *actus reus* to constitute a crime. Assume that a person rents a car from a reputable rental agency and is stopped by the police for an equipment defect. During the course of the stop, the police discover that cocaine has been concealed in a secret compartment in the trunk of the vehicle. If the person who rented the vehicle had no knowledge of the contraband, this is mere possession and may not be criminal. Also, if the person has possession of the contraband but is unaware of

crimes of omission Crimes resulting from the failure to act or the lack of action rather than the commission of illegal acts.

possession Knowingly having, holding, carrying, or knowing the location of an illegal or prohibited item; can constitute the *mens rea* of a crime.

the nature of the item, this is mere possession and may not be criminal. Thus, a delivery driver who, in the course of normal business, transports illegal contraband from point A to point B has mere possession of the contraband, and that is insufficient *actus reus* to constitute a crime.[28]

Mens Rea

The second critical element in determining the criminality and seriousness of an act is the *mens rea,* or criminal intent, of the actor, sometimes referred to as "guilty mind." A person who extends his or her arm and hand in the gesture of a yawn and stretch might strike and harm a person nearby. The blow may cause great physical pain but was not struck with the intent to cause harm. In such a case, in which the action is voluntary but the harm is unintentional, the person is said to lack *mens rea,* and no crime has been committed. (The injured party may seek damages under civil suit wherein *mens rea* is not a requirement.) The general principle of law is that an act is not bad without a guilty mind.

Intent The only direct evidence of *mens rea* is the defendant's confession. Otherwise, in criminal law *mens rea* is determined primarily by circumstantial or indirect evidence. In examining the criminal **intent** of a person, there are four different states of guilty mind that can be applied to an action: (1) general intent, (2) specific intent, (3) transferred intent, and (4) constructive intent.[29]

General intent refers to the logical outcomes associated with a criminal act—the *actus reus.* A person who intentionally strikes someone on the head with a heavy instrument is assumed to have intended to harm the person. *Specific intent* refers to the legal requirement of the elements of a crime. For example, burglary requires the commission of a trespass with the intent to commit a crime, and larceny requires the taking of property with the intent to carry it away and permanently deprive the owner of the property. Without the specific intent to commit a crime, trespass cannot be elevated to burglary, and without the specific intent of permanently depriving the owner of the property, the taking of property may be nothing more than "borrowing."

Transferred intent covers incidences in which a person injures another but did not intend to harm the party. An interesting application of this *mens rea* is the principle of felony murder. This principle says that if, during a bank robbery, a police officer responding to the bank alarm shoots at the robber but misses and hits an innocent bystander, the bank robber may be charged with the bystander's murder. The police officer had no criminal intent to harm the bystander, and the robber did not intend for the officer to shoot the bystander. However, under the principle of transferred intent, the criminal intent of the bank robber is applied to the *actus reus* of the death of the bystander. A more common application of the principle of transferred intent is when two persons are arguing and one commits an act intended to harm the other but instead harms an innocent third party. The criminal intent to harm the other person in the argument is transferred to the harm suffered by the third party.

It is considered **constructive intent** when an actor did not intend to harm anyone but should have known that his or her behavior created a high risk of injury. A common situation for the application of constructive intent is injury or death caused by a person who fires a gun into the air in an act of celebration, such as on New Year's Eve. The person who fired the gun had no intent to harm anyone, but constructive intent assigns *mens rea* on the principle that the person should have known that this behavior created a high risk of injury.

In assigning *mens rea* to a crime, the Model Penal Code distinguishes four types of intent: purposely, knowingly, recklessly, and negligently.[30] Each has a lesser degree of criminal intent, and as a result, the punishment assigned to each differs according to the degree of criminal intent. A person who causes the death of another purposely is guilty of murder and can be punished by death or extended imprisonment, whereas a person who causes the death of another recklessly is guilty of manslaughter and will receive a lesser punishment.

intent Criminal intentions or the state of "guilty mind" in *mens rea,* including general, specific, transferred, and constructive intent.

constructive intent When an actor did not intend to harm anyone but should have known that his or her behavior created a high risk of injury.

figure 3.2

Elements of a Crime

	1. *Actus reus*	2. *Mens rea*	3. Concurrence
Necessary and Sufficient Characteristics	• Voluntary behavior • A physical or verbal act or failure to act • Possession of an illegal item	• Confession of criminal intent • Assumption of general intent • Evidence of specific intent • Transferred intent in a felony crime • Presence of constructive intent • Strict liability crime	• Completeness of the crime • Direct connection between *actus reus* and *mens rea* • Evidence of crime causation from the union of *actus reus* and *mens rea* • Inchoate offenses
Examples	• Breaking into a car • Taking disks from work for personal use • Failing to perform a legal duty • Making terrorist threats	• Acting purposefully to cause injury • Knowing that an act or failure to act will cause injury • Causing injury by recklessness or negligence	• Acting on intent to deprive a car owner of his/her CD player • Carrying out a plan to murder a spouse • Soliciting, conspiring to commit, or attempting crimes

The relationship between *actus reus* and *mens rea* is illustrated in Figure 3.2. The figure shows how actions and intent must produce or intend to produce harm for there to be a crime. Harm caused by actions without criminal intent are accidents or negligence. Criminal intent without any actions is not a crime.

Strict Liability Some actions are considered criminal without the necessity of any criminal intent, and these actions are called **strict liability crimes**. Parking violations are an example of a strict liability law. The registered owner of the illegally parked vehicle is held liable for the fine regardless of whether he or she parked the car, was operating the car, or even had knowledge of the parking violation. Consider the case of a son who borrows the family car and receives a parking violation but throws the citation away and does not inform anyone. The son who committed the act is not held liable for the parking violation. However, the parent, the registered owner of the vehicle, is held accountable even though he or she had no knowledge of the citation.

Most strict liability laws cover minor actions, such as illegal parking, but some concern felony crimes. For some states, escape from prison is a strict liability crime. In ***State v. Marks,*** a prisoner fell out of a truck returning from a work detail, and fellow prisoner, Marks, jumped out, he claimed, to assist the inmate who fell. When the driver noticed the missing prisoners, he returned and found the two waiting beside the road. Marks was charged with the crime of escape.[31] The conviction was upheld on appeal on the grounds that the statute did not spell out a requirement for any specific intent to be formed by the prisoner to commit the crime of escape. In some states, statutory rape or sexual relations with a person under the age of consent is a strict liability crime. The state considers the welfare of children an important issue and places an affirmative burden on the defendant to positively establish the age of the sexual partner even in cases in which the sex is claimed to be consensual.[32]

strict liability crimes Actions that do not require criminal intent to be defined as crimes, such as parking violations.

As an example, see a list of Texas criminal laws regarding inchoate offenses at www.bakers-legal-pages.com/pc/pct04.htm.

Incomplete Crimes or Inchoate Offenses

Concurrence is the legal requirement that there is a union of *actus reus* and *mens rea;* that is, a perpetrator had criminal intent at the time the perpetrator's act caused harm. **Causation** means that the resulting harm is the direct outcome of this union of *actus reus* and *mens rea.* Consider the case of an employee who harbors ill will toward a supervisor. Assume that the employee is in danger of losing his or her job and a performance review is imminent. The employee strikes the supervisor in the parking lot with his or her automobile and causes harm. Is the action a crime or an accident? If the employee had no criminal intent at the time he or she hit the supervisor, then it is an accident. The principle of concurrence requires that criminal intent is present at the time of the act, such that having criminal intent prior to or following the act does not satisfy the requirement. The requirement of concurrence raises questions about **incomplete crimes**, in which the *actus reus* and *mens rea* do not coincide but would have if the person had completed all he or she planned or if circumstances had been different.

One cannot be convicted of a crime for thinking about murder, rape, robbery, larceny, burglary, or any other crime. The law punishes people only for what they do, not what they think. Crimes that go beyond mere thought but do not result in completed crimes are called incomplete crimes or inchoate offenses. The three common **inchoate offenses** are (1) solicitation, (2) conspiracy, and (3) attempt. Attempt, conspiracy, and solicitation stand on a continuum, with attempt closest to and solicitation farthest from actual commission of the crime.

Solicitation **Solicitation** is the urging, requesting, or commanding of another to commit a crime. The other person does not have to have *mens rea* or any intent whatsoever of complying with the solicitation to commit the crime. Thus, a person who solicits an undercover police officer to commit murder, to engage in illegal sexual behavior, or to commit any crime may be charged with solicitation.[33] Solicitation is a criminal charge against the person making the offer, command, or encouragement, not against the person to whom the offer is made. The crime of solicitation requires specific criminal intent. A person who makes a remark such as, "Wouldn't it be neat to steal that car and take it for a ride," to a general group of people has not satisfied the specific intent required for solicitation.

Conspiracy Conspiracy requires no *actus reus* other than communication. A plot to commit a bank robbery is not conspiracy if it is not shared or if no steps are taken in preparation for the planned robbery. **Conspiracy** by definition requires two or more people to plan a crime. Actions that require two people, such as fornication, bigamy, bribery, and gambling, are not considered examples of conspiracy. Thus, if a correctional officer accepts money to help an inmate escape, the two could not be charged with conspiracy. The appropriate criminal charge would be bribery, which requires at least two persons—one to make the offer and the other to accept the offer.

Conspiracy requires that two or more people take steps in preparation for the commission of a crime. Any step or steps taken may constitute conspiracy. In the case of a bank robbery that is anticipated to take months to plan and hundreds of steps to execute, the first meeting of the parties involved to discuss how to proceed constitutes a conspiracy. Furthermore, the parties to a conspiracy do not have to meet face to face. They may satisfy the requirements of conspiracy by any form of collaboration, including verbal, written, or electronic. As another example, if two or more persons plan to commit forgery and take steps to obtain a certain type of paper required to commit forgery, this is sufficient *actus reus* to constitute conspiracy. The supplier of the items needed for the commission of a crime is not guilty of conspiracy unless the supplier is aware of the illegal use planned for the materials.[34]

Attempt What happens when things do not go as the criminal planned and he or she is not able to complete the intended criminal activity? Has a crime been committed?

concurrence The legal requirement for a crime that there is a union of *actus reus* and *mens rea.*

causation The legal requirement for a crime that the harm is the result of the union of *actus reus* and *mens rea.*

incomplete crimes Crimes that go beyond thought, but the *actus reus* and *mens rea* do not coincide because the plans were not carried out for any reason.

inchoate offenses Incomplete crimes such as solicitation, conspiracy, and attempt.

solicitation The incomplete crime of urging, requesting, or commanding another person to commit a crime.

conspiracy Criminal act requiring no *actus rea* other than communication.

Yes, he or she has committed the crime of **attempt**. For most crimes that can be committed there is a corresponding crime of attempt—that is, attempted murder, attempted kidnapping, attempted rape, attempted burglary, and so forth. Attempt is the closest act to the completion of the crime and therefore carries a greater punishment than conspiracy or solicitation but a lesser punishment than if the crime had been completed.

Consider the case of ***State* v. *Wagner*** in which Wagner approached a woman in a laundromat from behind.[35] He had a gun and forced her into the laundromat's bathroom and demanded that she remove her clothes. The victim was able to escape before Wagner could commit any further crime. Wagner was convicted of attempted kidnapping and sentenced to 72 years in prison despite the fact that he was unable to complete the full intent of his criminal activity or restrain his victim.

Renunciation of Criminal Intent It is possible that a person may have criminal intent and may take steps toward completing a crime but then change his or her mind before the crime is fully executed. Does renunciation of criminal intent absolve one of punishment? No, it does not.[36] If a person approaches a bank with a mask, a gun, and a demand note for the teller and then changes his or her mind and goes home, the person nevertheless has satisfied the criminal intent requirement to be charged with attempted bank robbery. If a person intends to commit burglary but is frightened away by a noise after committing trespass, the person has satisfied the criminal intent requirement to be charged with attempted burglary. A person who demands sex under threat of force but is "talked out of it" by the victim has satisfied the criminal intent requirement to be charged with attempted rape.[37] The law does not take the view that a stroke of luck or a retreat from criminal activity based on fear of getting caught makes one immune from criminal prosecution.

▲ check your understanding **3.4 What are the elements of a crime? How are offenses differentiated between minor and serious crimes? Is a person who commits the *actus reus* of a crime liable for the offense under all circumstances? If not, what determines criminal liability? What are some examples of liability for incomplete crimes?**

Criminal Defenses

▼ the main idea **3.5 Several defenses, defined by law, can be used in court to excuse an accused offender or to lessen his or her criminal liability.**

The fact that a person has committed the act required by law to constitute a crime does not mean that the person will be held criminally liable for that crime in a court of law. There are numerous defenses that a person can offer at trial as defense. Two types of **defenses** to criminal charges are a perfect defense, in which the person is excused from all criminal liability and punishment, and an imperfect defense, in which the person's liability or punishment is reduced. The most common defenses are:

- Alibi
- Consent or condoning by the victim
- Entrapment, frame-up, and outrageous government conduct
- Immunity, privilege, or acting under the authority of another
- Involuntary actions
- Mistake or ignorance of fact or law
- Necessity

attempt An incomplete criminal act; the closest act to the completion of the crime.

defenses Justifications or excuses defined by law by which a defendant may be released from prosecution or punishment for a crime.

- Self-defense
- Youth
- Insanity

Alibi

The use of an **alibi** as a defense requires that the defendant present witnesses who will give testimony in court or other evidence establishing the fact that he or she could not have committed the offense. The most common alibi strategy is for defendants to claim that they could not have been at the scene of the crime at the time the crime was committed and to offer witnesses who will testify to that fact. The jury is the ultimate judge of an alibi. The jury may choose to believe or to not believe the testimony of alibi witnesses or the evidence presented.

Consent or Condoning by the Victim

Boxing, wrestling, hockey, and other sports can often result in injury or even death. If the injury occurs during the normal course of the rules of engagement, the player causing the injury can offer **consent** as a defense. However, if the injury is outside the accepted standards of conduct for the sport, the defense of consent is not valid. For sports like boxing, in which the object of the sport is to inflict injury on the other contestant, consent can be a defense even if the opponent dies. For other sports, like basketball, in which fighting among the players is prohibited by the rules of the game, the defense of consent cannot be used in cases of deliberate physical assault on another player.

The defense that the victim said it was okay—condoned the act—is not a valid defense for criminal actions.[38] For example, consent is not a valid defense in mercy killing or assisted suicide. Dr. Jack Kevorkian constructed a "suicide machine" to help terminal patients end their life. Despite the "victims'" consent—even plea—for his assistance to commit suicide, the Michigan Court did not recognize the defense of consent. Likewise, consent is not a defense in murder–suicide pacts, and in those cases, any surviving member can be charged with murder.

Entrapment, Frame-Up, and Outrageous Government Conduct

Entrapment and outrageous government conduct are related to the principle that the defendant's criminal actions must be voluntary. If the defendant did not have the *mens rea* or the means necessary to commit a crime, he or she would not have acted. However, if agents of the government provided both the *mens rea* and the means to commit the crime, the courts have ruled that the defendant may be defended on the grounds of **entrapment** or outrageous government conduct. Entrapment is an *affirmative defense,* which means that the defendant must admit that he or she committed the crime as alleged. The person is not innocent but claims that if it had not been for the actions of the government agents, he or she would not have committed the crime.

Entrapment is different from *encouragement,* in which law enforcement officers may pretend they are victims or co-conspirators in crime, for example, or may promise the suspect benefits from committing the crime, or may offer to supply materials or help the suspect obtain contraband. Encouragement becomes entrapment when the government agents actually provide the motivation and the means to commit the crime.[39] The concern of the court is that otherwise innocent persons should not be induced to commit crime by the government. This concern also affects undercover sting operations.[40] For example, in sting operations involving prostitution or drugs, the police must be aware of the street price of sex and drugs, because if the undercover agent offers illegal goods or services at too low a price, the defendant may claim entrapment.

alibi A witness or evidence in court establishing that the defendant could not have committed the crime.

consent A defense in criminal law in which the defendant claims the action that caused the injury or death occurred during normal, acceptable standards of conduct.

entrapment A legal defense that agents of the government provided both the *mens rea* and the means necessary to commit the crime.

Immunity or Privilege

In the defense of **immunity**, the accused has special protection against being prosecuted. Four forms of this defense are diplomatic immunity, legislative immunity, witness immunity, and privilege. The U.S. government extends diplomatic immunity to certain government officials of foreign countries while they are in the United States. *Diplomatic immunity* grants the foreign diplomat complete immunity from any criminal prosecution, including murder and traffic violations. There are disadvantages to diplomatic immunity, especially in an age of international terrorism. However, there has been no serious movement to remove this protection. In return for extending immunity to foreign diplomats, U.S. diplomats in foreign countries receive the same protection. If a foreign diplomat commits a serious felony crime in the United States, the only recourse is to ask for the diplomat's recall to his or her country or to request that the country voluntarily waive the diplomat's immunity.

See www.ediplomat.com/main/immunity.htm for a discussion of diplomatic immunity.

A lesser form of immunity extended to lawmakers in the United States is *legislative immunity*. Based on abuse by government agents, dating back to the English rule of the American colonies, most representatives and senators receive limited immunity from arrest while the legislature is in session. Unlike diplomatic immunity, legislative immunity only postpones the time that the legislator can be arrested until after the legislative session is adjourned. Also, legislative immunity does not protect the legislator from arrest for felonies and treason.

An interesting affirmative defense, normally afforded only to the guilty, is *witness immunity*. The defendant admits to the criminal acts as charged but in exchange for his or her cooperation with a government investigation is granted immunity from further prosecution based on the offered testimony. Essentially, in hopes of catching more culpable criminals, the government promises the defendant that any information he or she gives that could incriminate other criminals will not be used against the defendant in a court of law. Witness immunity is commonly used in organized crime, drug trafficking, and corporate crime cases.

Immunity is not a defense in cases in which defendants claim they were acting only under the orders or advice of a superior authority—unless that authority is authorized by law to interpret the law. Relying on illegal advice or acting on the advice of someone who does not have the legal authority to give such advice does not negate criminal liability. For example, in the 1980s, John Ehrlichman, one of the Watergate break-in defendants, claimed that he was acting under the authority of Richard Nixon, then president of the United States. The Court refused to grant immunity from prosecution, however, because even the president does not have the power to authorize burglary. In another famous case, Lieutenant William Calley, tried for committing atrocities against civilians during the Vietnam War, offered as a defense that he was only following the orders of his superiors.[41] Even if such orders had been given—even in wartime—they would have constituted illegal advice, and Calley's criminal liability would not have been reduced.

The defense of *privilege* is the claim that the defendant committed a violation of the law but was immune from punishment because of his or her official office or duty. For example, the courts have recognized as a privilege the right of operators of emergency vehicles to violate traffic regulations when responding to a call. As another example, a correctional officer who shoots an escaping prisoner may not be liable for murder. Even if the escaping prisoner is unarmed and no immediate threat to the correctional officer, the officer's actions may be justified if he or she is acting within the scope of duty.

immunity A legal defense that the accused is exempt from prosecution because of diplomatic immunity, legislative immunity, witness immunity, or professional privilege.

Involuntary Actions

The American criminal justice system is based on the assumption that the actions of the defendant were voluntary. If defendants can establish that their actions were not of their own free will but were the result of a third person or involuntary condition, this can be a defense against criminal liability. A simple example of this defense is when a bank teller gives the bank's money to an armed robber. It could be argued that the bank teller does not have the authority to give away the bank's money, but the teller has not committed a crime because the actions are not voluntary. The teller is operating under **duress**.

In this defense, the cause of the acts, as well as the acts that constitute the crime, must be involuntary. A person who voluntarily consumes alcohol, achieves a drunken stupor, and commits a crime while in that state cannot claim a defense of involuntary action, even with no memory of ever having acted. Getting drunk is voluntary behavior, and a similar test is held for crimes committed during drug conditions.[42] If a person is unknowingly drugged by someone and then engages in criminal behavior, the defense of involuntary actions may be valid. However, a person who chooses to take a hallucinogenic drug and commits a crime while under its influence cannot use the defense of involuntary actions during a drug condition.

Case law has established that under certain conditions defendants must accept responsibility for knowing when they are consuming drugs or alcohol. In one case, the defendant claimed involuntary action as his defense to the charge of driving while intoxicated. He claimed that he attended a party and drank "punch" that he was told falsely did not contain alcohol. The defendant consumed enough punch to be legally drunk and was arrested for DUI as he drove home from the party. The court ruled that the defendant should have been able to recognize the signs of intoxication as he continued to consume the beverage. Thus, despite the misinformation he received, he should have been able to determine his condition and remained liable for his offense.

Duress cannot be used as a defense against the charge of murder, however. If a person murders another but claims that he or she did so only because of coercion or duress through threats made against family members or personal friends, this is not a defense. The court has ruled that even in such a dire situation, with awful potential consequences, a person does not have the right to take the life of another.

Mistake or Ignorance of Fact or Law

The presumption of the law can be contrary to common sense. In Charles Dickens's novel *Oliver Twist,* Bumble and his wife are arrested for the manner in which they operated the orphanage in their charge. Bumble appeals to the authorities that it was his wife's scheme and that he is an innocent party. He is told that the law presumes the husband to be the head of the wife and therefore his defense falls on deaf ears. Bumble replies if the law presumes the man to be in command of his wife, "then the law is an ass." In this case, his **mistake or ignorance of fact or law** did not constitute a legal defense.

The U.S. criminal justice system places an affirmative burden on citizens to be aware of the laws of the land and proceeds as if this is the case. As mentioned previously, laws are published as a matter of public record, partly so offenders cannot claim ignorance of the law as an excuse for their behavior. The assumption that people know the law imposes a twofold burden. First, the government must make the law known, and, second, citizens must be held accountable, however complex the law and whatever the difficulty in knowing it. Most citizens know very little of the many volumes of law that govern their lives, but the law usually does not recognize *ignorance of the law* as a valid defense. Ignorance of the law may be considered a defense if the law in question is so unusual or obscure that the court finds that a reasonable person would not have knowledge of it. However, simple ignorance of the law is not a defense against prosecution or punishment for crimes.

Mistake or ignorance of fact, on the other hand, is a valid defense. If at the end of class you pick up a backpack that you think is yours and walk out of the class, have you stolen the backpack if it in fact belongs to another student? What if the backpack contains a large amount of money or valuable property? Does that change the situation? *Mistake or ignorance of fact* is a defense that claims to negate the requirement of *mens*

duress A legal defense in which the accused acted involuntarily under threat of immediate and serious harm by another person.

mistake or ignorance of fact or law An affirmative legal defense claiming that the defendant made a mistake or acted out of ignorance and therefore did not meet the requirement for *mens rea.*

rea, or criminal intent. Thus, there is a great difference between the standard used to distinguish ignorance of the law and mistake of fact.

If a person has a reasonable belief that the action he or she is doing is legal, mistake of fact may be a valid defense. If your backpack resembled the backpack that you mistakenly picked up and if you do not take steps to permanently deprive the owner of his or her property, whatever its value, then you have not committed theft, and mistake of fact is a reasonable defense. However, a restaurant patron who walks away with another customer's leather coat instead of his or her cloth coat would have difficulty convincing the court that he or she had made a mistake of fact.

Necessity

The defense of necessity is sometimes known as the defense of the "lesser of two evils." **Necessity** is an affirmative defense in which the defendant must admit that he or she committed the act but claim that it was done because of necessity or need and not because of *mens rea.* This defense is commonly used against charges of property crime, such as trespass, theft, or burglary.[43] In the classic case in which this defense is successful, defendants are faced with life-threatening situations and choose to commit illegal acts to save their lives. For example, a cross-country skier caught in an unexpected blizzard may break into a mountain home, start a fire, and consume food found there. Under normal circumstances, these actions constitute the crime of burglary, but because of the threat of death from exposure to the elements, the court may recognize the defense of necessity as a perfect defense. However, there are limits to the defense of necessity. For example, if a hiker is lost in the woods and sets a fire with the hope that search and rescue will see the smoke from the fire but the fire gets out of control and becomes a forest fire that does extensive damage, the court will refuse to allow the defense of necessity for liability for the forest fire. The court has ruled that the person must take reasonable precautions that his or her actions do not endanger others.

Can necessity be used as a defense against murder? This is a grim question that has come before the court. If a group of people is stranded without food, can they kill and eat one of their numbers to preserve their lives? The British court has refused to recognize this defense, but the U.S. court has allowed it as a perfect or an imperfect defense.[44] To be an acceptable defense, the necessity must be immediate and specific and the person must be chosen by lot. All members of the party must have an equal opportunity of being killed and eaten.

Self-Defense

The claim of **self-defense** is a complex defense usually associated with murder and physical assault. Again, this is an affirmative defense: The defendant admits to the murder or assault but claims he or she lacked criminal intent. The lack of criminal intent is based on the claim that the defendant was protecting himself or herself from deadly attack or serious bodily injury.[45] The courts have also recognized self-defense when applied to (1) protecting another from deadly attack or serious bodily injury and (2) defending one's home from invasion. The self-defense used by the defendant must be appropriate and proportional to the force used by the attacker. Before deadly force is justified as self-defense, the attacker must create a situation in which the defendant fears death or great bodily harm. Timing is a controversial issue in capital cases involving the claim of self-defense. Is a routinely abused spouse or child justified in killing an attacker when not under immediate threat of deadly attack or serious bodily injury?[46] The courts have decided differently on different occasions, leading to stronger legislation designed to prevent or combat domestic violence. Generally, however, the standard courts use to judge whether the force the defendant used in self-defense was justifiable is whether a reasonable person would feel he or she was in immediate danger of death or great bodily injury.[47]

necessity An affirmative legal defense claiming the defendant committed the act as a result of forces of nature and therefore did not meet the requirement for *mens rea.*

self-defense An affirmative legal defense in which a defendant claims he or she committed the crime in defense of self and lacked criminal intent.

The use of self-defense in protecting one's home against invasion also varies significantly in different states. Some states require that, when reasonable, the occupant of the house must first attempt to flee from the home to escape attack. Other states do not have such a requirement but follow the "castle doctrine," which means that occupants have the unqualified right to protect their home against trespass.[48] Most states do not permit the claim of self-defense in resisting arrest—whether lawful or unlawful—by a police officer.[49]

Youth

A 14-year-old boy steals a car, refuses to stop when pursued by the police, and ends up destroying the vehicle in a high-speed crash. Is he just a kid and therefore held to a different standard of culpability than an adult? Since 1899, the answer for the U.S. criminal justice system has been "yes." Prior to 1899, age was a defense based on the British principle that children under 7 years of age, and possibly even under 14 years of age, could not form *mens rea.* Children over age 14 were considered capable of forming *mens rea,* but youths could be offered as an affirmative defense if the defendant could demonstrate lack of *mens rea.* Operating under the British standard, defendants as young as ages 11 and 12 were hung for the crime of murder in the American colonies.

In 1899, Cook County (Chicago) adopted the use of the juvenile court. This separate court system operated under significantly different rules and standards of proof to adjudicate the crimes of youthful offenders under the age of 18 separately from adult offenders. The use of the juvenile court quickly caught on and is now practiced in all 50 states.[50]

The states and the federal government have set the age of *mens rea* at 18. Each state has provisions allowing younger offenders to be held accountable for their actions in adult court under certain circumstances. Controversy over the accountability of juvenile offenders occurs most often in cases of murder. Juveniles as young as age 14 have been stripped of the protection offered by the juvenile court and had their trial transferred to adult court.

Insanity

The **insanity** defense has an interesting connection to Sir Robert Peel, father of modern policing. In 1843, Daniel M'Naghten suffered the paranoid delusion that Sir Robert Peel, then prime minister of England, intended to kill him. Based on this belief, M'Naghten undertook to kill Peel first in what he perceived as a form of self-defense. M'Naghten obtained a pistol and lay in wait for Peel to pass by. Fortunately for Peel but unfortunately for his secretary, Edward Drummond, M'Naghten shot, missed Peel, and struck and killed Drummond.[51]

M'Naghten was tried for murder but was acquitted based on his successful insanity defense.[52] M'Naghten's acquittal was the fifth acquittal based on the insanity plea of a commoner who had attacked a person of nobility. The Queen expressed alarm over the frequent successful use of the insanity defense and called for a commission to develop legal guidelines for the use of the insanity defense. The House of Lords, England's highest court, formulated a new—and much more stringent—standard for the insanity defense. Under the new standard, a defendant was not to be considered insane unless he or she met two conditions: (1) He or she must suffer from a disease or defect of the mind and (2) the disease or defect must cause the defendant either not to know the nature and quality of the criminal act or not to know that the act was wrong. This standard for insanity was commonly called the M'Naghten standard, rule, or test, and became the primary standard for the insanity defense in Great Britain and the United States for over a century.

insanity A legal claim by a defendant that he or she did not understand the difference between right and wrong or was suffering from a disease or mental defect that made the defendant unable to appreciate the criminality of his or her action.

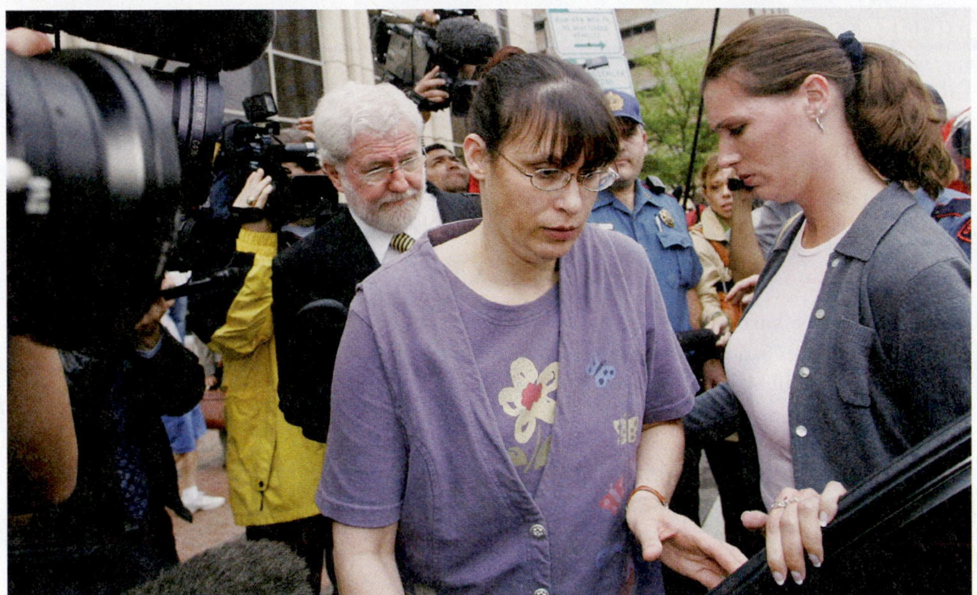

Andrea Yates pleaded not guilty by reason of insanity for the drowning deaths of her children. The jury had to decide if she knew the difference between right and wrong. Expert witnesses were called by both prosecution and defense. The jury had to determine what Yates's state of mind was when she drowned her children. Do you think jurors have the knowledge and ability to make such decisions?

The M'Naghten rule requires that the defendant does not understand that his or her actions are illegal, wrong, or punishable. A defendant who flees after committing a crime, who attempts to conceal his or her crime, or denies his or her guilt may not meet the standard for the M'Naghten rule for judging insanity based on these actions, which indicate that he or she knew the crime was wrong. The M'Naghten rule requires that the defendant be like a very young child who is unable to form a concept of right and wrong and therefore does not fear punishment because he or she does not appreciate the criminality of the action. Because of this requirement, the M'Naghten standard is also known as the Right-Wrong test of insanity. Interestingly, if M'Naghten had been tried using this standard, he would not have been successful in avoiding conviction.

Other Criminal Defenses

Defendants have claimed that it was their victims' fault that they committed a crime, that they were motivated by patriotism, or that there was no personal gain for them. These defenses have not received serious recognition by the court as legitimate defenses against criminal prosecution. Rapists have argued that provocative clothes worn by their victims contributed to their *mens rea.* Lieutenant Colonel Oliver North argued that any crime he committed in the Iran-Contra scandal was motivated by his desire to protect democracy and the United States. Defendants who have stolen from large business only to give the profits of their crime to the poor have used the "Robin Hood" defense to claim that they did not personally gain from the fruits of their crime. These defenses have not been readily accepted by the court.

Figure 3.3 summarizes the various defenses to a crime. Defenses to a crime can be divided into two major categories, alibi defense and affirmative defense. In *alibi defense,* the defendant denies that he or she committed the crime and offers proof that he or she could not have done so. Usually this proof involves an alibi—that is, evidence that at the time of the crime the defendant was not at or near the scene of the crime. *Affirmative defenses* can be divided into justifications, excuses, and exemptions. In each, the defendant admits to some of the elements of the crime but denies that all of the elements were present. Usually in these defenses the defendant admits to the *actus reus* but denies criminal intent.

figure 3.3

Criminal Defenses

Alibi Defense
Burden of proof is on the defense, which must present evidence that the defendant was not at or near the scene of the crime at the time the crime was committed.

Affirmative Defense
Burden of proof is on the defense, which must present additional evidence that the defendant, though he or she committed the crime, should not be found guilty because of extenuating circumstances.

Justifications	Excuses	Exemptions
• Involuntary actions • Duress • Self-defense • Necessity • Entrapment	• Youth • Insanity or diminished capacity • Mistake or ignorance of law or fact	• Consent • Immunity or privilege

▲ check your understanding **3.5** **What are 10 common defenses by which defendants accused of crimes can seek to escape prosecution or punishment? What conditions are necessary for each defense to succeed in court? How is homicide divided into serious and less serious offenses? What are some examples of defenses that are likely to fail?**

Crimes by Law

▼ the main idea **3.6** **The Model Penal Code classifies crimes into categories by victims as well as defines specific offenses of crimes.**

Crimes are defined by laws, and the laws governing society are numerous, complex, and diverse. The federal, state, and local governments have specific, different, and overlapping criminal codes. It would be impossible to discuss here the criminal laws of each of the 50 states, the federal government, and the thousands of county and municipal governments, and it would be a useless exercise to select a single state and use it as an example. What could be true of larceny in Louisiana may not be true of larceny in California. To simplify the teaching of the law and propose guidelines for effective legislation, in 1962 the American Law Institute published a code of criminal laws. These guidelines, called the **Model Penal Code,** have been adopted by law schools as the bases for their curriculum and are used by most textbooks on criminal law.

The Model Penal Code classifies crime according to the victim of the crime. Crimes are classified in the following ways:

- Crimes against the state
- Crimes against persons
- Crimes against habitation
- Crimes against property
- Crimes against public order
- Crimes against public morals

A discussion of the numerous laws governing all of these criminal behaviors is beyond the scope of this chapter, which presents a brief summary of only the more serious offenses, using the definitions and principles of the Model Penal Code. The criminal laws proposed by the Model Penal Code are based on logic and reflect the history of criminal law. Each crime has a definition that includes a description of the actions that constitute criminal behavior and the criminal intent that must accompany the actions. The Model Penal Code is based on the principle that laws should reflect the continuum of harm that is possible. Generally, the more harm to a person or society done or intended, the more serious the crime.

Crimes against Persons

In the Model Penal Code, crimes against persons include homicide, rape, sexual assault, kidnapping, robbery, and assault and battery. These specific offenses are discussed to illustrate important points about criminal law: the elements required for an offense, the grading of the offense, and how the offense and the punishment reflect social values.

Homicide The defining of **homicide**—the killing of one human being by another—takes into account the harm done to the victim and the different degrees of criminal intent. Based on the degree of harm intended, homicides are divided into murder and manslaughter. **Murder** is divided into *first-degree murder*—the premeditated and deliberate killing of another—and second-degree murder. *Second-degree murder* includes the killing of another without premeditation, with the intent to inflict serious bodily injury but not death, as the result of extreme recklessness, and during the commission of a felony in which there was no intent to kill or injure another. **Manslaughter** is the killing of another without malice—that is, without the specific intent to kill. The Model Penal Code divides manslaughter into three categories: voluntary, involuntary, and vehicular.

Rape or Sexual Assault The crime of **rape,** or the more contemporary term *sexual assault,* shows how criminal codes reflect changing social values. Rape is also one of the few behaviors in which criminal liability is determined by the intent rather than the act, because consensual sex, unlike nonconsensual sex, is not a crime. The lack of consent makes rape a crime.

Historically, rape was rooted in the concept of carnal knowledge, sexual intercourse by a man with a woman not his wife, forcibly and without her consent.[53] In the Middle Ages, rape was a crime against property. The "victim" was the husband or the father of the woman, as she was considered the property of her husband or, if unmarried, her father. From the 1600s to the early 1970s, the crime of rape focused on the element of consent. Women had to show by physical resistance that they did not consent. The law required that women must use all the power at their command to resist the attack. If at any time they did not resist, the sex was considered consensual. Even consent obtained by fraud did not constitute rape.[54] Sexual intercourse with women incapacitated by intoxication or mental deficiency and with minors was regarded as rape whether the victim was forced or gave consent.

Model Penal Code Guidelines for U.S. criminal codes published in 1962 by the American Law Institute that define and classify crimes into categories according to victim, including crimes against the state, persons, habitations, property, public order, and public morals.

homicide Murder and manslaughter.

murder All intentional killings and deaths that occur in the course of aggravated felonies.

manslaughter The killing of another without malice, without the specific intent to kill.

rape (sexual assault) Nonconsensual sexual relations.

This woman, a victim of sexual assault, is giving a statement about the crime and her assailant. How is sexual assault defined by law? What is statutory rape, and what role does consent play? This victim was beaten, and she did not resist her attacker out of fear of graver harm. Does her lack of resistance lessen his criminal liability or the seriousness of his offense? How does the Model Penal Code help to answer these questions?

New Standards for Determining Consent Starting in the 1950s, many state courts adopted a new standard for determining consent, called "measured resistance." In Virginia, for example, the law according to the new standard does not require a woman to resist to the utmost of her physical strength if she reasonably believes that resistance would be useless or would result in serious bodily injury.[55] Since the 1950s, states that required proof that the victim resisted the assault have dropped this element of proof.

Starting in the 1970s, numerous other changes have been made to the elements necessary to prove rape. Many states have changed the classification from rape to sexual assault to more clearly identify the crime as an assault as opposed to a sexual act. *Sexual assault* has been defined to include all sexual penetration with the penis or any other object. States also have enacted statutes recognizing that men also can be raped, by women or by men. The marital rape exception has been eliminated in many states. Finally, some states have enacted rape shield laws that prohibit the defense from questioning the victim about past sexual experiences.[56]

Kidnapping The elements of the crime of kidnapping are rather complex. The crime originated in the mid-seventeenth century and originally referred to the taking of children for use as servants or laborers in the American colonies. The word originated from combining *kid,* a term that referred to children, and *napper,* a slang term for thief, to form the concept of *child theft.* The taking of a woman was the crime of abduction. As for men, in early English common law it was not kidnapping unless the man was taken out of the country. Eventually, the term *kidnapping* was used to describe the taking away of a person against the person's will.

Kidnapping requires the taking away by force of a person against his or her will and holding that person in false imprisonment. In defining kidnapping, the taking of a person against his or her will is commonly called *asportation.* Thus, one of the elements of kidnapping is that it must be proved that the defendant moved the victim against his or her will from one place to another. The question of how far a victim has to be moved to qualify as asportation can differ significantly from jurisdiction to jurisdiction. As mentioned, in early English common law, the asportation element required that a male victim had to be moved outside England. Eventually, modern statutes have adopted definitions in which even forced movement of a small distance qualifies as meeting the definition of asportation. For example, if a person is taken from a sidewalk and forced into the perpetrator's vehicle only a few feet away, this movement may be sufficient to satisfy the element of asportation. If a perpetrator does not move his or her victim, the lesser crime of false imprisonment or unlawful restraint may be applicable.

Log on to www.kidnapnews.com to obtain information about foreign abductions.

Robbery In common speech, robbery is frequently confused with burglary. **Robbery** is the taking and carrying away of property from a person by force or threat of immediate use of force. A couple might declare that while they were out for the evening someone broke into their house and robbed them. This is burglary. Houses are burgled, but only people can be robbed. The mistake is understandable because robbery actually involves the elements of two crimes: theft from crimes against property, and assault from crimes against persons.

robbery The taking and carrying away of property from a person by force or threat of immediate use of force.

assault The crime of willfully inflicting injury on another.

Assault and Battery **Assault** is defined as inflicting injury on another, whereas *battery* is the unlawful striking of another. The actual state codes governing assault and battery vary significantly. Some states use the terms interchangeably or have defined the crime as "assault and battery" instead of one crime called "assault" and another crime called "battery." The elements of the crime that have to be proven do not require great physical harm or injury. In *United States* v. *Masel,* for example, spitting was considered sufficient injury to satisfy the element of inflicting harm for the crime of assault. *Mayhem* is an offense similar to battery, but the elements of mayhem require unlawfully and violently depriving the victim of full use of any part of body, such as a hand, foot, or eye.

If a firearm or other dangerous weapon is used in the crime, it becomes the more serious offense of aggravated assault/battery. Simple assault is considered a less serious crime, but aggravated assault/battery is considered a more serious crime and is reported by the Federal Bureau of Investigation as a Part I crime.

Crimes against Habitation

Burglary and arson are crimes committed against places where people live. Both offenses require specific criminal intent. **Burglary** requires the person to commit the crime of trespass with the specific criminal intent to commit a crime thereafter. **Arson** requires the specific criminal intent to commit a malicious burning. Both offenses have a long history dating back to English common law, which reflects the values placed on the importance of securing a safe place for persons to live.

Burglary Burglary has its roots in the English common law of breaking and entering. Originally, burglary was an offense that applied only to invasion of the home at night. *Breaking and entering,* as it was known then, meant the actor committed an illegal trespass during the night against a place where people lived, with the intent to commit another crime once the trespass was accomplished. The purpose of English common law was to protect the people in their home while the occupants were present and in a relatively defenseless state (i.e., sleeping). Thus, a person who committed the same act of breaking and entering during the day committed theft or *trespass,* a lesser crime, not burglary.

In a time when modern police patrol of neighborhoods was unknown, society primarily relied on civil behavior and the threat of severe sanctions for violations that threatened the safety of the community. Burglary was a capital offense. Furthermore, the burglar, if caught, was at the mercy of the homeowner, because the law allowed the homeowner to use any force necessary to defeat the burglar. Today, most jurisdictions do not allow the victim to use deadly force against a burglar unless there is threat of death or serious bodily harm.

Modern Burglary Statutes The modern offense of burglary combines two less serious crimes—trespass and intent to commit a crime—into a serious felony crime. The Model Penal Code and most state codes define several degrees of burglary, do not limit burglary to a nighttime offense, and expand burglary to include property other than homes, such as cars, campers, airplanes, tents, and vacation cabins. Burglary does not require breaking and entering or the intent to steal.[57] A person who remains in a habitation when not authorized to do so satisfies the criminal intent in burglary. For example, someone who enters a public building during authorized hours and hides until after-hours is considered to have committed the specific intent of trespass required in burglary. The modern offense of burglary does not require the burglar to actually "break" anything, and entering a marked, restricted space is burglary even if there is no door, lock, or obstacle to open or cross.

It is common to think of burglary as a crime involving the intent to steal something. Modern burglary statutes require only that once the person commits the trespass, he or she intends to commit another crime, whether a felony such as theft or a misdemeanor such as vandalism. A person who commits only trespass with no specific intent to commit another crime has not satisfied the specific criminal intent required for the crime of burglary. Modern burglary statutes also cover a multitude of structures where people live and sleep, in addition to abandoned homes and partly constructed houses. Again, the offense requires the offender to commit a trespass. Thus, a person who pulls up the stakes

burglary A combination of trespass and the intent to perform a crime.

arson The malicious buming of a structure.

criminal justice in the media

The Effect of Media on the Law

Two opposing philosophies of law are (1) laws reflect the consensus of all those governed by the law, and the prohibited acts are considered harmful, which is *mala in se;* and (2) laws reflect the values of only certain groups, and the prohibited behaviors are illegal simply because it is against the law, or *mal prohibita.*

One of the most controversial debates as to what conduct norms should be reflected in the law is the legality of same-sex marriage. The same-sex marriage controversy is promoted in large part due to the media attention given to this issue. Celebrity same-sex marriages, threats of arrest of mayors and pastors who issue marriage licenses or perform same-sex marriages, and media events profiling various "first" same-sex marriages keep this issue before the public. Also, politicians and various individuals and groups campaigning for and against same-sex marriages create high-profile and often inflammatory media coverage of the controvesy.

Until recently, same-sex marriages were rejected as legal unions sanctioned by law in all the states. The battle to change state marriage laws to legalize same-sex marriages has embroiled the entire nation to the extent that both sides are calling for constitutional amendments to support their moral position on this volatile issue. Cities and states that have changed their marriage laws to permit same-sex marriages have become lightning rods in a national debate.[58] Opponents of same-sex marriage argue that the harm of legalized same-sex marriages "could

In a multicultural society often there are gaps between legal behavior and the values of subgroups in the society. The controversy concerning same-sex marriages has resulted in numerous legal challenges and appeals to the U.S. Supreme Court. To what degree should the law accommodate the values of different subgroups in a multicultural society?

be the downfall of Western civilization."[59] Opponents of same-sex marriage base their opposition on strongly held moral beliefs justified by religious values and doctrine.[60]

The criminal justice system has issued a confusing message on same-sex marriages. Some city officials have declared such marriages legal and some state courts have declared legal prohibitions against such marriages as unconstitutional. Same-sex marriage licenses have been issued by officials in San Francisco, California; Portland, Oregon; Asbury Park, New Jersey; New Paltz, New York; and Madrid County, New Mexico, only to be declared illegal by state officials or state courts. Officials issuing marriage licenses to same-sex partners were threatened with criminal prosecution. For example, the mayor of New Paltz, New York, was charged with 19 criminal counts for marrying gay couples.

The public opposition to same-sex marriages has been significant. Many groups have proposed "defense of marriage" amendments to their state constitutions that would prohibit legalization of same-sex marriage. Same-sex marriage bans have been passed by several states and legislation to allow same-sex marriages has been defeated in other states. At the federal level, opponents of same-sex marriage have proposed both constitutional amendments and federal legislation to strip the state and federal courts of jurisdiction over same-sex marriage cases.[61] Proponents of same-sex marriage compare their battle to legalize such marriages to the discrimination reflected in the law up unto the 1970s that prohibited interracial marriages.[62]

Massachusetts is at the front of the debate regarding the legality of same-sex marriages. On April 11, 2001, seven same-sex couples who were denied marriage licenses in Massachusetts sued Suffolk Superior Court in Boston to challenge the state's ban on gay marriages. On May 8, 2002, the Suffolk Superior Court ruled against granting marriage licenses to same-sex couples. Later that year, there was an initiative to amend the commonwealth's constitution to ban gay marriages but it failed. The couples appealed their case to the Massachusetts Supreme Judicial Court. In 2003, the Supreme Judicial Court ruled that it is unconstitutional to bar gay couples from marriage. In May 2004, Massachusetts started issuing same-sex marriage licenses and almost immediately hundreds of same-sex couples applied for marriage licenses.

However, the Supreme Judicial Court's ruling did not please everyone. Twelve of the state's 1,200 justices of the peace resigned rather than perform same-sex marriages. Numerous public protests took place against the court's ruling. Governor Mitt Romney invoked a 1913 law prohibiting marriage licenses to anyone who does not intend to live in Massachusetts in an effort to prevent same-sex out-of-state couples from coming to Massachusetts to get married. However, many town officials indicated that they intended to ignore the prohibition and issue licenses to out-of-state couples.[63] Conservative groups across the United States have poured millions of dollars into campaigns opposed to same-sex marriages.

Legal same-sex marriages have opened a Pandora's Box of new legal issues. Can a same-sex couple file state and federal tax returns as "married"? Do employers have to provide same-sex partners with the same insurance benefits received by heterosexual couples? Will other states have to recognize the legal status of same-sex couples who are married in Massachusetts even if same-sex marriages are illegal in those states? If Massachusetts amends its constitution to prohibit same-sex marriages or if federal legislation or a constitutional amendment is passed prohibiting same-sex marriages, what will be status of those couples who have already legally married?

To what degree do media coverage and high-profile endorsements and condemnations of same-sex marriage influence the law? How does one decide which arguments in the media are valid in considering a constitutional amendment or state law that would define same-sex marriages as legal or illegal?

of a camper's tent and drags off the tent and all its contents has committed theft. But a person who enters the tent and takes property from it has committed burglary.

Arson English common law did not consider it a crime for a person to burn or destroy his or her own property. The intentional or accidental burning of one's home or even the property of another was not arson. Arson was a crime only if the burning was malicious. The Modern Penal Code reflects changes in community concerns regarding safety and defines as arson the willful and malicious burning or attempted burning of any structure, including one's own. Because of the many motivations a person may have for burning a structure and the serious harm that can come to innocent parties, nearly all malicious burnings constitute arson.[64]

Modern arson codes also include destroying a structure by the use of explosives. Arson includes the burning of homes, factories, personal property, and vehicles. If the structure is occupied, even if the arsonist is unaware of this fact, the crime is more serious. A person who destroys property by malicious burning for the purposes of defrauding an insurance company commits arson even if there is no danger or harm to others.

Crimes against Property

Numerous statutes define offenses against property, including theft, larceny, embezzlement, receiving stolen property, false pretenses, forgery, and uttering. These various modern offenses originated in the ancient felony of larceny, which covered only the wrongful taking of the property of others. Originally, having property taken through fraud, dishonesty, or false statements was not considered an offense.[65] Early English common law considered it the responsibility of the property owners to see to it that they were not cheated or defrauded. If someone were foolish enough to fall victim to lies or con games, the law would not assist the owner in attempting to recover the property or punish the taker. Changing social values, increasing complexity in the business world, and disregard for the old principle of *caveat emptor* ("let the buyer beware") have resulted in numerous new crimes. Modern criminal codes concerning crimes against property make it illegal to take stocks, bonds, checks, negotiable paper, services and labor, minerals, crops, utilities, and even trees. Virtually all property falls within the scope of modern larceny statutes.

Larceny Larceny is the most commonly committed crime in the United States. The Modern Penal Code defines **larceny** as the wrongfully taking and carrying away of another's property with the intent to permanently deprive the property's owner of its possession. The temporary taking of property, even if unlawful, is not larceny. The theft of motor vehicles is defined by separate criminal codes, but the same criteria apply. Thus, taking a car to use it temporarily is not theft; it is defined as the crime of joy-riding.

Summary of Classifications of Crimes

Figure 3.4 provides an overview of the classification of crimes in the Model Penal Code. This figure illustrates how the Model Penal Code classifies crimes by the victim. A victim need not be a person; there are crimes against the state, against habitation (dwellings or places where people live), property (as in vandalism), public order, and public morals. Generally, this classification grades the punishment for crimes according to the victims. That is to say, crimes against the state and person are punished more severely than crimes against property, public order, or public morals. Also, within each classifi-

larceny Wrongfully taking and carrying away of another's property with the intent to permanently deprive the property's owner of its possession.

figure 3.4

Classification of Crimes in the Model Penal Code

The State	Persons	Habitation	Property	Public Order	Public Morals
• Treason • Sedition	• Murder • Rape • Sexual assault • Kidnapping • Robbery • Assault	• Burglary • Arson	• Theft • Larceny • Embezzlement • Fraud • Receiving stolen property • Forgery	• Disturbing the peace • Inciting to riot	• Prostitution • Gambling

cation crimes are graded according to seriousness. Thus, the punishment for murder is more severe than the punishment for assault.

▲ check your understanding **3.6** **How are the crimes of homicide, rape, robbery, assault, burglary, arson, and larceny defined and evaluated in terms of acts, seriousness, and intent? How have laws against persons, habitations, and property changed to reflect societal changes? Why is it difficult to write laws prohibiting the illegal taking of property?**

conclusion:

Criminal Law Is a Pillar of Social Order

Thousands of offenses are defined by local, state, and federal criminal codes. Precision is required in establishing criminal intent for crimes such as murder, robbery, and rape, and there is general agreement that these offenses should, indeed, be classified as crimes. For other offenses, there is not only debate as to the criminal intent necessary to prove an offense but there is also disagreement as to whether any intent is sufficient to make the offense a crime. Citizens and the courts disagree sharply, for example, on the criminal intent necessary to prove offenses such as profanity, obscenity, unlawful assembly, and restricted speech. Many citizens claim that the Second Amendment gives them the right to possess and use firearms; others argue that no such right exists in the Constitution.

Often the debate as to what is a crime and what is legal behavior defines the limits of personal freedom. Many argue that laws prohibiting fornication, same-sex marriages, prostitution, homosexuality, and sodomy are rooted in religious values and should not be crimes. Laws that give the police the right to restrict public protest gatherings or to limit political messages are criticized as infringements on First Amendment freedoms. Others argue that greater harm would be done without the ability to regulate possible conflict among groups, to provide order for public meetings, and to prevent interference with the normal work of others.

As new values are embraced by society, new laws are created. Concern over harm to members of minority groups has resulted in the demand for hate-crime legislation. Concern over gun deaths has increased the demand for prohibitions against the ownership and use of firearms. And concern about the separation of religion and the state is at the root of many debates about the law. The criminal law code is constantly changing. For example, fearful that drivers who use cell phones may be a danger to others as well as to themselves, New York, New Jersey, and Washington, DC, have passed laws prohibiting drivers from using cell phones while operating a vehicle. Other states have partial bans or bills pending. Some states are considering legislation that would ban newly licensed teenage drivers from using cell phones while operating a vehicle. At times a law is in conflict with other social values. For example, many charities have turned to Texas Hold'em Poker tournaments and other games of chance, such as Bingo and Casino Night, as fundraisers only to find that they may run afoul of the state's gambling laws.

It can be difficult to define the *actus reus* and criminal intent that constitute the dividing line between criminal behavior and protected personal rights. Frequent violation of laws by citizens causes general disrespect for the law and for all aspects of the criminal justice system. Likewise, laws that give police too much discretion or do not clearly identify the harm to society erode citizens' respect for the law. Laws that reflect the religious values of only some of the citizens of society or that treat the poor with fear and suspicion do not strengthen the bonds of civilized behavior. A critical question in assessing the constitutionality of laws is the balance between the need for conformity and public safety versus privacy rights and individualism. The principle of the law is the most important part of the criminal code. Even laws with minor punishments may be appealed all the way to the U.S. Supreme Court, based on the principle of the law alone.

chapter **summary**

- The U.S. criminal justice system is founded on the rule of law.
- Separate criminal codes define offenses for local, state, and federal governments.
- Laws must meet certain standards to be considered constitutional: principle of legality, ex post facto laws, due process, void for vagueness, right to privacy, void for overbreadth, and cruel and unusual punishment.
- An offense is defined as an act (*actus reus*) committed with criminal intent (*mens rea*) and a resulting harm (concurrence).
- The punishment for an offense must be specified in the law or the law is void.
- Sometimes the *actus reus* of a crime may be words, the failure to act, or the possession of contraband.
- There are two types of criminal intent: general and specific. Some crimes require proof of specific intent. Strict liability laws do not require the proof of criminal intent.
- Actions that do not result in completed crimes are punishable as conspiracy, solicitation, or attempt.
- Common defenses to the charges of criminal conduct include alibi, consent, entrapment, immunity, involuntary actions (such as duress), mistake or ignorance, necessity, self-defense, youth, and insanity.
- Most law schools and law textbooks use the Model Penal Code to teach law. State criminal codes may be similar, but there may be significant differences.
- The Model Penal Code classifies crimes according to the categories of crimes against the state, crimes against persons, crimes against habitation, crimes against property, crimes against public order, and crimes against public morals.
- Punishments for crimes are graded by the harm and criminal intent of the actor.
- Often a crime is a complex matter of determining the intent of the actor. Homicide can be classified along a continuum from first-degree murder to negligent homicide, depending on the *mens rea*.
- Crimes reflect social values. The offense of rape has been significantly redefined over the years as society has redefined the role and rights of women. Laws against breaking and entering originally protected homes from trespass and theft at night, but modern burglary laws protect many types of property and under numerous circumstances, not only at night. Larceny, the most common crime committed, is difficult to legislate against because of the numerous ways things can be taken, the difficulty of defining intentional versus unintentional taking, and the various ways in which property changes hands in the normal course of business and social interaction.

vocabulary review

actus reus, 116
alibi, 122
arson, 131
assault, 130
attempt, 121
burglary, 131
causation, 120
common law, 109
concurrence, 120
consent, 122
conspiracy, 120
constructive intent, 118

crimes of omission, 117
cruel and unusual punishment, 115
defenses, 121
duress, 124
elements of a crime, 116
entrapment, 122
ex post facto law, 112
felony, 111
homicide, 129
immunity, 123
inchoate offenses, 120
incomplete crimes, 120
insanity, 126
intent, 118
larceny, 134
mala in se, 107
mala prohibita, 107
manslaughter, 129
mens rea, 116
misdemeanor, 111
mistake or ignorance of fact or law, 124
Model Penal Code, 129
murder, 129
necessity, 125
possession, 117
principle of legality, 112
principle of proportionality, 115
procedural due process, 113
rape (sexual assault), 129
robbery, 130
rule of law, 107
self-defense, 125
solicitation, 120
stare decisis, 113
strict liability crimes, 119
substantive due process, 113
violation, 111
void for overbreadth, 114
void for vagueness, 114

do you remember?

American Law Institute, 107
blue laws, 110
King v. *Cogdon,* 116
State v. *Marks,* 119
State v. *Wagner,* 121
U.S. Criminal Codes, 108
Weems v. *United States,* 115

think about this

1. What are the advantages of a system that operates by the rule of law? Whom do the laws protect? In the United States, as a result of the rule of law, people who commit a crime may go unpunished if the criminal justice system fails to protect the rights of the criminal. Does the rule of law harm society through excessive safeguards on the rights of the accused?
2. The laws of the criminal justice system are based on the principles of classical criminology. What are these principles? Are they compatible with modern psychological, scientific, and medical knowledge? Is there a need to seriously examine the underlying principles of the criminal codes? How might those principles be changed and to what end?
3. The United States has a complex system of numerous local, state, and federal criminal codes. Some argue that there are too many laws and not enough law enforcement. One single criminal code for all states would greatly reduce the complexity—even the conflict—of the criminal codes. What would be the advantages and disadvantages of a single criminal code for the United States?

research navigator

Visit the Research Navigator website (www.researchnavigator.com), login and select the criminal justice data base in ContentSelect. Type in the key words "The Assault on Democracy." This search will bring up the article "The Assault on Democracy" by Matthew Rothschild. In this article Rothschild is critical of the affect of the Military Commissions Act on the rights of citizens. Sample the article and answer the following questions:

1. What does the Military Commissions Act authorize the President of the United States to do?
2. Rothschild's criticism is one-sided in that he does not address the role of the Military Commissions Act in reducing potential harm or terrorist acts that "alien unlawful enemy combatants" could perform. He implies that the current criminal justice system is sufficient to respond to the threat of foreign "terrorists." Do you think that the current criminal justice system is sufficient to prevent another major terrorist attack?
3. If one accepts that the Military Commissions Act is effective in preventing another major terrorist attack on the United States, why would one, such as Rothschild, oppose legislation that would make society safer?
4. When dealing with balancing individual liberties and rights with the need to provide social order and public safety, should the rights of persons who are considered extreme threats be curtailed or eliminated? Explain your answer?

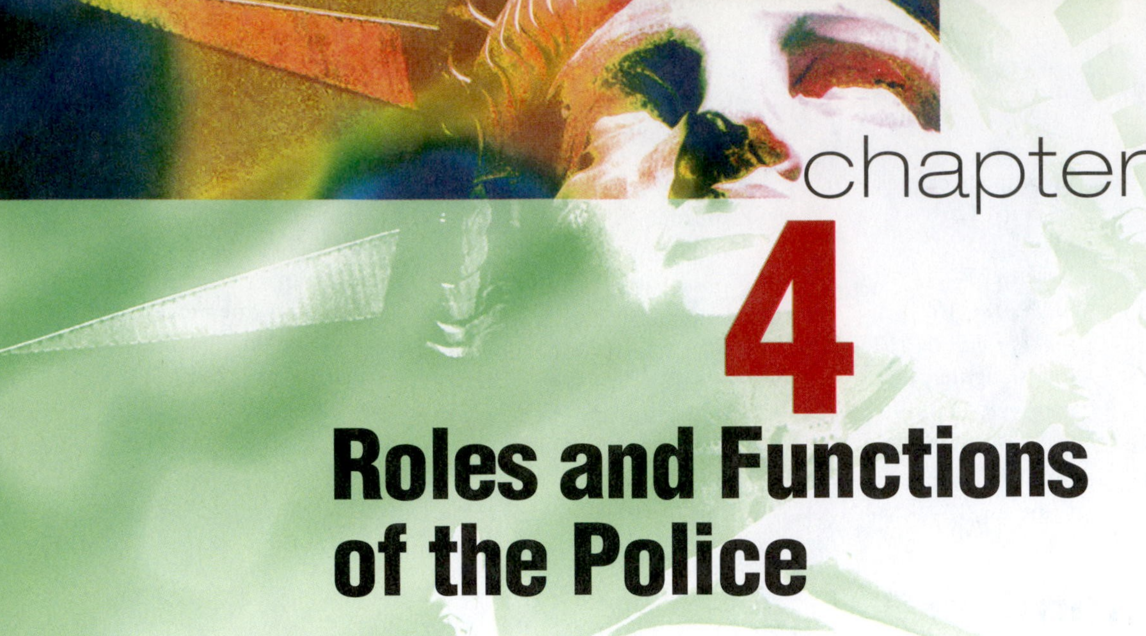

chapter 4
Roles and Functions of the Police

CHAPTER OUTLINE

LEARNING OBJECTIVES

After reading this chapter, you will understand

- How American policing developed and its connection to the London Metropolitan Police of 1828.
- How social values and other factors influence policing.
- How local, state, and federal police agencies are organized and what their major responsibilities are.
- How community–police relations affect policing strategies.

Police and Owners Begin to Challenge Looters

NEW ORLEANS—Across New Orleans, the rule of law, like the city's levees, could not hold out after Hurricane Katrina. The desperate and the opportunistic took advantage of an overwhelmed police force and helped themselves to anything that could be carried, wheeled or floated away.

Many people with property brought out their own shotguns and sidearms. Some frightened homeowners took security into their own hands. John Carolan was sitting on his porch in the thick, humid darkness just before midnight Tuesday when three or four young men, one with a knife and another with a machete, stopped in front of his fence and pointed to the generator humming in the front yard, he said. One said, "We want that generator," he recalled. "I fired a couple of rounds over their heads with a .357 Magnum," Mr. Carolan recounted. "They scattered." He smiled and added, "You've heard of law west of the Pecos. This is law west of Canal Street."

introduction:

Life without the Police

When confronted with violent behavior and lawlessness, citizens are comforted to some degree by the fact that they can call 9-1-1 to summon the services of professionals trained to deal with crime. People call the police because they believe that the police are trained and equipped to handle these kinds of problems and that the police have the authority and ability to do something.

If there were no police, what would people do? When the police were unable to provide law and order to the city after Hurricane Katrina, the people had to take their own actions to protect their lives and property. Overwhelmed by the crisis, preoccupied with search and rescue, and seriously shorthanded and lacking resources and equipment, New Orleans law enforcement officers could not respond to calls for assistance. Without the police, citizens were helpless against looters and resorted to protecting their property by standing guard with loaded weapons.

Hurricane Katrina brought a temporary breakdown in law and order that was quickly restored. What if there were no local police, no state police, no federal police? Although the police are the most visible representatives of the government in U.S. society and the police are the most prominent institution responsible for maintaining law and order, they are a relatively new social institution. The creation of the police was an inevitable product of the modern industrial state.[1] The employment of full-time, paid, uniformed personnel by cities to fight crime and perform public services is a relatively new social experiment in pubic order and justice. This chapter examines the emergence of the police in the United States and the historical roots of the police. It then discusses the administrative organization of the contemporary police and the role and function of county law enforcement agencies, local police, state police, and federal law enforcement.

For documents, photos, and on-line activities on the history of policing, go to www.ablongman.com/criminaljustice.

The Development of Policing in America

▼ the main idea **4.1 American methods of maintaining social order and dealing with crime have roots in England. However, unique factors gave rise to new policing strategies.**

The origins of modern policing can be traced to September 29, 1829, when Sir Robert Peel's London Metropolitan Police became the first documented, full-time, uniformed, paid police department in the world. With the onset of the Industrial Revolution and the growth of the cities, crime in England's cities became a major problem. Previous systems depending on citizen volunteers and individual responsibility proved ineffective and inefficient as mechanisms for maintaining order in the growing urban population centers. In 1653, Oliver Cromwell tried a military solution to the problem of maintaining law and order in the cities. He divided England into 12 districts and placed a military general, who exercised discretionary police powers, in charge of each district. This strategy of policing by the military proved effective in lowering the crime rate, but it also reduced personal freedoms and was in sharp contrast to rising expectations of democratic values. The citizens of England found this solution worse than the problem. They expressed their dissatisfaction through public protests and rioting, resulting in the rescinding of Cromwell's scheme of military rule of the country.

In 1745, Parliament appointed a committee to study crime. The committee found that crime was a problem in the cities and predicted that it would get worse. The city of Westminster took more positive steps, enacting the **Westminster Watch Act of 1774** to deal directly with the problem of public law enforcement. Focusing on working-class leisure activities, the act was intended to control sex, swearing, drinking, and brawling.[2]

Using a system of night watchmen, bailiffs, and gate guards, Westminster attempted to make its streets safer. Despite various reform efforts, street crime in London continued to grow worse. When city merchants demanded that street crime had to be reduced for the sake of commerce, the government responded by creating a special agency of "theft-catchers," the **Bow Street Runners.** In 1748, Brothers Henry and John Fielding were appointed as administrators or chief magistrate of a uniformed, full-time police force to provide policing on foot in the inner city, on horse patrol in the suburbs, and a special unit to catch thieves and criminals.[3]

In 1828, **Sir Robert Peel** was appointed to the office of Home Secretary of England. As home secretary, he needed to deal with the growing problem of street crime in London. Peel lobbied for an act of Parliament that would allow him to do something for the city of London similar to what he accomplished in Ireland. He wanted to create a system of full-time paid constables to be used to fight crime. In 1829, Parliament passed "An Act for Improving the Police in and Near the Metropolis," better known as the **London Metropolitan Police Act.** Under the leadership of Sir Robert Peel, a full-time, paid, uniformed police agency was established to promote public safety, enforce the criminal codes, and bring criminals to justice.[4]

Within 10 years, Peel's police agents were accepted by the average citizen as an essential element in public order.[5] Peel's strong association with the formation of the London police is evident in that the street name for the new officers was "bobbies," named after Robert (or Bob) Peel.[6] Peel's police force brought social order to the cities of England and was to become the model for policing in most nations in western Europe and the United States.

Read about Sir Robert Peel and the history of the London Metropolitan Police at www.met.police.uk/history/.

▲ check your understanding 4.1 What led English cities to adopt London-style policing in the 1800s?

Law and Order in the Colonies

▼ the main idea 4.2 Unique regional politics and economics gave precedence to local law enforcement in the United States.

The eastern coast of the United States was settled primarily by the British, and it is not surprising that policing prior to 1776 was modeled after British-style policing. In the Colonies, kings were replaced by local authorities such as governors. However, without the feudal system of England, which tied the serf to the manor, and with vast expanses of unexplored and unclaimed lands in the New World, social order took a unique turn. The tithing system, which depended on close kin relationships and a strong tie to the land, was useless.

Because most of the early settlements in the New World encountered a harsh and sometimes violent environment, social order was based on the "good of the community." For example, in the Jamestown colony in Virginia, founded in 1608, adherence to Dale's Law—the law of the colony—was strictly enforced for the survival of the community.[7] Those who would not conform to the laws of the community would be ostracized, which could have the same effect as a death sentence in the hostile environment. Likewise, the settlers of the Plymouth colony signed the Plymouth Compact, in which they pledged to conform their behavior to activities that promoted the good of the community.[8]

As the settlements in the New World gradually evolved into ports, farms, towns, and cities, the system of maintaining public order more and more resembled the British system of sheriffs, constables, and magistrates. Towns

Sir Robert Peel and the London Metropolitan Police Act of 1829 transformed law enforcement in England and America. What principles of law enforcement did Peel promote? How were these English "bobbies" chosen as police officers? How were they equipped to do their job? How were U.S. police modeled after the "bobbies" but equipped differently? Why were Peel's bobbies referred to as "blue devils"? Negative initial public reaction reflected two ongoing challenges in policing: balancing individual liberties with the public good and applying laws equally regardless of social class.

Find out about the history and goals of the International Police Association at www.ipa-usa.org/.

and cities adopted the British system of the night watch staffed by volunteers and convicted offenders.

Policing in the United States, 1776–1850

There is no definite date at which one can say that cities in the United States adopted London-style policing. However, by the 1890s, the London-style policing system had become the general practice in large U.S. cities. Gradually, the various municipalities abandoned the use of part-time personnel and volunteers and adopted London-style policing in an effort to provide for public safety. For example, Philadelphia created night-watch and day-watch police forces in 1830, funded largely by a donation from Stephen Girard, a wealthy manufacturer who felt a London-style police department would be beneficial. New York City combined its day and night watch into a single police department in 1844.[9] Boston established a single police department in 1855.[10] By the 1880s, some 50 years after Peel had introduced the concept of a full-time, paid police force to London, London-style policing had become widespread in U.S. cities.

With independence from Britain, the new United States of America pursued its own ideas of policing. Wary of strong central government, the United States adopted a system of shared and fragmented power that favored local control of policing. Local, state, and federal governments shared power in a complex system of checks and balances.

The **Tenth Amendment** of the U.S. Constitution states that any power not enumerated in the Constitution as a federal government power is a state government power. Policing was not mentioned in the Constitution as a federal power, so policing was considered a local matter. Thus, the new federal government had limited police powers. For example, when the federal government was first formed, the only federal law enforcement agencies were the U.S. Postal Inspectors and the U.S. Marshals. The U.S. Marshals Office performed few law enforcement duties, and the U.S. Postal Inspectors focused on promoting the safety and reliability of the delivery of the mail.

At the local level, the sheriff's office was the only police agency, and the sheriff departments occupied most of their time with jail operations, courtroom security, and the serving of court papers. Furthermore, the powers of the sheriff were limited in several ways. The office became an elected rather than an appointed position. In fact, today the sheriff is still the only law enforcement administrator to gain office by election.

Policing in the United States, 1850–1900

In the United States, as in England, urbanization was the primary influence on the development of a new policing system. In the mid-1800s, rapid social change occurred through changes caused by the Civil War and dramatic population growth due to immigration. The population of New York City, for example, increased from 250,000 in 1845 to 620,000 in 1855. By the beginning of the Civil War in 1861, the city's population was near 800,000 and nearly half were foreign-born.[11] These immigrants often were seen as a "dangerous" class of people, the source of crime.[12] Several criminological theories of this era were based on the assumption that crime is class-specific, a characteristic of the poor, who typically were minorities.[13] Often the mix of minorities and newly arrived immigrants created social and economic conflict, resulting in violence and riots.

As in England, public safety—or the lack of it—in urban centers was the impetus for the development of new concepts in policing. However, there were significant differences between the London-style metropolitan police and the U.S. police. The major difference was the lack of centralized government control, professionalism, and focus on crime prevention. The source of these differences was the power of home rule.

Tenth Amendment Amendment of the United States Constitution that proscribes that all powers not explicitly granted to the federal government are reserved as state powers.

Under the principle of home rule, the state can delegate to the municipalities the power to establish a municipal government, tax its citizens, establish its own laws, raise a police force, and establish courts and correctional facilities. Thus, each city, separate and autonomous from other cities, from the state, and from the federal government, can establish a criminal justice system and a police force of its own design. Also, each municipal department is under the absolute power of the municipal government. Police departments during this period were seen as merely the enforcement branch of the political machines that ran the city. Also, because of the perception and use of the police for politically partisan purposes, there was little emphasis on selecting and training qualified officers. Selection was based largely on political loyalties and favors.[14] Thus, American-style policing mimicked London-style policing more in form than in function.

Vigilantes and Posses in the Wild West

A unique chapter in the history of policing is the development of policing in the American West during the late 1800s. While New Yorkers lived under relatively civilized conditions in the second half of the nineteenth century, conditions were quite different for people living in the comparatively uninhabited "Wild West." A philosophy of national expansion, the discovery of gold, an uncommonly strong sense of self-importance, and a reckless disregard for the rights of people who differed from those of European background resulted in numerous injustices and frequent violence toward Native Americans and others. The tales of the gold, American Indians, violence, lawlessness, and opportunity for unrestrained individual freedom lured the farmers, miners, ranchers, fortune seekers, immigrants, and an assorted lot of adventurers westward.

Use searches to read first-person accounts by Edward Riley and Elizabeth Roe about their experiences with western frontier justice in the 1870s at this Library of Congress site: http://memory.loc.gov/ammem/.

The development of policing in America varied regionally. Cities of the East followed English models early, with a trend toward full-time, paid, uniformed police forces. Uniquely American conditions delayed this development in other regions, however, such as in the "Wild West." When under threat, citizens of the West banded together temporarily to protect property and secure public order. They joined mounted posses to pursue outlaws and often made quick, harsh judgments about the guilt or innocence of alleged offenders and the punishment they should receive. With few official law enforcement officers, judges, law courts, and correctional facilities, vigilante justice was almost always violent or deadly. How was the development of American local law enforcement affected by the unique situation of slavery in the South?

The West was a place where none of the historical models of policing applied. Often, a small number of white settlers, gold miners, or trappers migrated westward in hopes of better fortune and settled in remote cities such as Kansas City, Dodge City, and Denver, and territories such as Nebraska, Oregon, Texas, and California. Not until the end of the 1800s, when the train and the telegraph helped connect these places and reduce their remoteness, did cities in these areas begin to resemble their eastern counterparts. Public safety was maintained primarily by personal defense, **vigilantism**, town marshals, U.S. marshals, and the U.S. Army. In this environment, justice was often quick, brutal, or nonexistent. Without convenient access to the court system, farmers, ranchers, and gold miners frequently made their own justice, and the use of firearms and lynch mobs became the trademark of justice in the West. Outlaws were much more likely to be shot or lynched by posses than tried in a court of law and imprisoned.[15]

In settlements near a military post or fort, the U.S. Army was the official provider of law and order. Because most of the West was territorial land and not states, settlements did not have the power of home rule and thus could not legally form their own local police agencies. The U.S. Marshals Office assumed responsibility for civilian law enforcement but often lacked enough manpower to cover the vast geographical area.

Beginnings of Private Policing

The lack of competent local police during the nineteenth century created business opportunities for some. Merchants, railroads, banks, and even the federal government were in need of professional security and investigative services. With no public agency to fulfill these needs, they turned to private agencies. During the mid-1800s, private security agencies such as Brinks, Pinkerton, and Wells Fargo provided investigative services and protection of private property. These private agencies filled the void created by the widespread corruption found in local police and the geographical jurisdiction limitations of local police in the absence of state or federal police.

Today, private policing is a multibillion-dollar business. There are five or six times more private police agents than there are public police agents.[16] Brinks, Pinkerton, and Wells Fargo continue to be world leaders in private security. Merchants and citizens still hire private police for about the same reasons they did in the mid-1800s: to protect private property, to secure the services of professional guards, and to investigate matters that, although important to the client, may be of lesser importance to the public police.

Policing in the Southern States

The need for a night fire watch, the growth of the cities, and the resulting fear of street crime have been cited as the roots of the police force. In the southern states, policing also had its roots in "slave patrols."[17] **Slave patrols** were established as early as the 1740s in the colonial southern states. Southern states passed laws giving any white freeman the right to stop, search, and apprehend any black person—slave or free. In fact, the law of most southern states presumed all blacks to be slaves.[18] Free blacks were required to carry proof of their liberty with them at all times. The membership of the slave patrols was loosely defined. In Georgia, "all urban white males aged 16 to 60, with the exception of ministers of religion" were considered members of the slave patrol, and it was their duty "to search and examine all Negro-Houses for offensive weapons and ammunition."[19] In addition to the powers of search and seizure, the slave patrols had the power to "inflict corporal punishment on any slave found to have left his owner's property without permission."[20]

The pre–Civil War slave patrols brutally oppressed blacks. Many southern whites feared that a violent insurrection by the slaves was an imminent possibility. To prevent

vigilantism The system by which citizens assume the role and responsibility of official law enforcement agencies and act independently, often without observation of due process and rights, to take justice into their own hands.

slave patrols Civilian groups in the southern states whose primary role was to protect against rioting and revolts by slaves.

diversity in the system

The First Black Police Officers

Hubert Williams and Patrick V. Murphy gathered data documenting the first appointments of black men as police officers.[24] According to their research, the first black police officers appeared after the Civil War as a result of Reconstruction in the southern states. The first appointments were in Selma, Alabama, in 1867; Houston, Texas, in 1870; and Jackson, Mississippi, in 1871. New Orleans, which had a police board composed of three black members out of five, appointed a police force that included 177 blacks by 1870. The first black police officer in the North was in the city of Chicago in 1872. By 1894, there were 23 black police officers in Chicago. Washington, DC, appointed its first black officer in 1874; Indianapolis in 1876; Cleveland in 1881; and Boston in 1885.

According to Williams and Murphy, these early appointments of black males to the police department were not well received by other officers and the white population of the cities. For example, when black males were appointed to the Philadelphia Police Department, several white officers quit the force in protest. When black males were appointed in July 1868 to the Raleigh, North Carolina, police department, the local newspaper, the *Daily Sentinel*, ran a headline that read "The Mongrel Regime!! Negro Police!!" The article concluded that the appointment of the four black police officers was "the beginning of the end."

The black officers did not receive equal treatment, pay, or responsibilities. Whereas most white officers were recruited from the ranks of the laboring class, black police officers frequently were overqualified in both education and previous experience. Despite the above-average qualifications of the black police, they were frequently restricted to working only in black communities. Because black police officers were generally poorly received by the white citizens of the community, they had limited authority and were not permitted to stop, search, or arrest whites. Race riots occurred in Jackson and Meridian, Mississippi, when black police officers attempted to exercise authority over whites. Chicago required that black police officers work in plain clothes to avoid drawing public attention to them.

Where, when, and in what historical context were African Americans first hired as police officers? How did race affect their role and function as officers of the law?

insurrection, many southern cities with large slave populations organized "foot and mounted patrols to prevent slaves from congregating and to repress any attacks upon the racial and social status quo."[21]

Black Codes After the Civil War, the southern states circumvented the emancipation of the slaves by adopting **Black Codes.** Virtually all of the former Confederate states adopted laws aimed specifically at nullifying the rights granted to the recently freed slaves.[22] Black Codes in South Carolina, for example, restricted former slaves from any occupation other than farmer or servant unless they paid an annual tax, ranging from $10 to $100, which was considered an enormous amount of money at the time.[23] Blacks were prohibited from renting land in urban areas. They could be punished by fine or involuntary plantation labor for such criminalized behaviors as using "insulting" gestures or language, doing "malicious mischief," and preaching the Gospel without a license.[25] Interracial marriage was prohibited by state law.[26] The belief and practice of both society and the legal system was that blacks had fewer civil rights than whites, and the emphasis was on maintaining this inequality.[27]

Southern police departments defined their mission as protecting the white population from the threat of violence at the hands of the slaves and later, freed slaves. So intense was this fear that laws often were enacted to protect the white citizens from even the most remote threat posed by blacks. For example, in the early 1800s, Charleston,

Black Codes Laws passed by southern states after the Civil War to disenfranchise freed slaves.

Use searches to read more about the Black Codes, *Plessy* v. *Ferguson,* and Jim Crow laws at http://afroamhistory.about.com.

South Carolina, passed the Negro Seaman's Act, requiring free black seamen to remain on board their vessels while in Carolina harbors or to be imprisoned at night.[28] If the seamen came ashore, they were subject to arrest and could be sold into slavery. Similar statutes were enforced by other coastal slave states. (The jail that was built in Charleston to house "free Negro seamen," including Jamaicans, still stands and is now a tourist site.)

Plessy v. Ferguson The different treatment of blacks under law came to the attention of the Supreme Court in the landmark decision of ***Plessy* v. *Ferguson*** (1896).[29] The Supreme Court found state laws that required segregation of the races in public accommodations to be constitutional. This court case established the doctrine of "separate but equal" treatment of minorities, specifically African Americans. The result of this official recognition of the constitutionality of segregation was immediately seen in police departments. The employment of black police officers, both in the South and in northern cities, was suspended. Even the New Orleans Police Department, which employed 177 black officers in 1870, employed no black officers by 1910.[30] The lack of employment of black police officers remained the norm until strong civil rights legislation was passed in 1967. The "separate but equal" doctrine was not declared unconstitutional until the landmark case *Brown* v. *Board of Education* (1954).

▲ check your understanding **4.1 What developments in law enforcement were uniquely American? How did Amendment X of the U.S. Constitution and *Plessy* v. *Ferguson* affect the development of policing? What was the impact of *Brown* v. *Board of Education?***

Foundations of Modern American Policing, 1900–1930

▼ the main idea **4.3 Urban growth and professional practices introduced by August Vollmer changed the American policing system.**

The emergence of the United States as a world-class industrial leader after World War I brought significant changes to all aspects of U.S. society and government. Increased population density in New York, Boston, Philadelphia, Detroit, and Chicago increased ethnic diversity and strained social service agencies, including schools, public health, and housing. This strain was reflected in social disorder. After World War I, most people considered the primary threats to public order to be street violence, gangs, and vices such as gambling, drinking, and prostitution.[31] The widespread adoption of the electric light allowed citizens to continue their activities—including their criminal activities—all night long, both indoors and out. The automobile, the airplane, and the telephone changed opportunities for crime, and advances in weapons, including automatic weapons and semiautomatic pistols, increased the firepower of both criminals and police. Figure 4.1 provides a timeline of the historical development of U.S. policing prior to World War II.

Labor Conflicts and Local Police

Plessy* v. *Ferguson (1896) U.S. Supreme Court landmark case that established the "separate but equal" doctrine that allowed racial segregation.

Many blamed the problems of social disorder on immigrants, the poor, and the lower class. New York Police administrator Raymond Fosdick in 1914, for example, declared that crime was caused by the unrestrained lower class. Also, labor strife between companies and the newly emerging unions was a significant source of public disorder.[32]

figure 4.1

Historical Development of American Policing Prior to World War II

1000–1700

The tithing system, Office of Sheriff, and principles of due process and home rule develop in Europe during the Middle Ages.

1116 Henry I issues the *Legis Henrici* (Law of Henry)
1215 John I signs the Magna Carta
1608 Dales Law in England's American colony of Virginia
1653 Oliver Cromwell establishes military districts

1700–1800

The Industrial Revolution and gin influence the development of policing in England. The American Revolution sets the United States on a different course.

1737 George II levies taxes for a night watch
1748 Bow Street Runners in London
1774 Westminster Watch Act establishes public law enforcement in England
1787 U.S. Constitution ratified by the states
1787 U.S. Postal Investigation Service established
1789 U.S. Marshals Service established in the United States by Judiciary Act
1791 First ten amendments to the Constitution (Bill of Rights) ratified

1800–1850

Paid, uniformed, full-time police become the norm in European and American cities.

1800 Thames River Police established
1828 Sir Robert Peel appointed as Home Secretary for England
1829 London Metropolitan Police established by an act of Parliament
1830 Philadelphia establishes a night watch and a day watch
1835 Municipal Corporations Act standardizes metropolitan police forces in England
1844 New York City combines day and night watches into London-style police department

1850–1900

The Wild West, slavery, and the American Civil War uniquely affect the development of policing in America.

1865 U.S. Secret Service established
1867 First black police officers appointed in Alabama
1878 *Posse Comitatus* Act grants U.S. marshals the power to deputize
1896 *Plessy* v. *Ferguson* institutes racial segregation

1900–1930

World War I, urbanization, and labor conflicts influence the development of American policing.

1905–1932 Contributions of August Vollmer, chief of police of Berkeley, California, led to the modernization and professionalization of American police departments.

Early police forces were often used by those with political and economic power for their own advantage. During the late 1800s and early 1900s, the police were used against the emerging labor unions as *strike breakers.* Police would break up strikes, pickets, and protests. Often, the actions of the police were violent and resulted in injuries and deaths. Would you say that today the police are used by those with economic and political power for their advantage?

Labor conflicts and strikes were frequent and often violent, even deadly. There were 57,000 labor strikes between 1899 and 1915.[33] Citizens and governments turned to the local police officer as the front-line defense against public disorder.

The local police officer of the early 1900s was far different from his contemporary counterpart. For example, a veteran Boston police officer of 1913 was recruited from the working class and made $1,400 per year after 6 years of service. A cop on the day shift worked 75 hours a week, and one on the night shift worked 87 hours a week. He received 1 day off in 15. He received little or no training prior to being hired, or afterward. He was hired on the basis of his obedience to authority, physical strength, and size.[34] Many departments had a 6-foot minimum height requirement. Officers worked without the benefit of radio communications and patrolled their beats on foot or horseback.

During these early years of policing, an important debate occurred. The police, for the most part, were being used to maintain social order through enforcement of the laws and a forceful, sometimes brutal response to law breakers. Local police departments were seen primarily as extensions of the political parties that ran the cities. As Americans universally began to adopt local policing systems to combat crime and public disorder, debate arose regarding the role and function of the police. The presence of an armed police force empowered with the rights of search and seizure raised the question of how to balance individual rights and public safety. The use of police departments by corrupt politicians and powerful private business owners called into question the difference between criminal justice and social justice. One of the key persons who was influential in shaping U.S. policing was August Vollmer.

August Vollmer and the Professionalizing of Policing

August Vollmer was the chief of police of Berkeley, California, from 1905 to 1932. Vollmer's vision of policing was quite different from that of most of his contemporaries. He believed the police should be a "dedicated body of educated persons comprising a distinctive corporate entity with a prescribed code of behavior."[35] He was critical of his contemporaries and they of him. San Francisco police administrator, Charley Dullea, who later became president of the International Association of Chiefs of Police, refused to drive through Berkeley in protest against Vollmer.[36] Fellow California police chiefs may have felt their opposition to Vollmer was justified, given his vocal and strong criticism of other California police departments. For example, Vollmer publicly referred to San Francisco police as "morons," and in an interview with a newspaper reporter, he called Los Angeles police "low grade mental defectives."[37]

Because of his emphasis on education, professionalism, and administrative reform, Vollmer often is seen as the counterpart of London's Sir Robert Peel and is sometimes called the father of modern American policing. Vollmer was decades ahead of his contemporaries, but he was not able to achieve significant change in policing during his lifetime. It remained for Vollmer's students to implement change. For example, O. W. Wilson, who became chief of police of Chicago, promoted college education for police officers and wrote a book on police administration that reflected many of Vollmer's philosophies.[38] It was adopted widely by police executives and used as a college textbook well into the 1960s.

Vollmer is credited with a number of innovations. He was an early adopter of the automobile for patrol and the use of radios in police cars. He recruited college-educated police officers. He developed and implemented a three-year training curriculum for police officers, including classes in physics, chemistry, biology, physiology, anatomy, psychology, psychiatry, anthropology, and criminology. He developed a system of signal boxes for hailing police officers. He adopted the use of typewriters to fill out police reports and records, and officers received training in typing. He surveyed other police departments to gather information about their practices.[39] Many of his initiatives have become common practice within contemporary police departments.

Vollmer's contributions included the use of scientific crime detection practices, training for police officers, selection of police officers based on performance testing, and a vision of an expanded role of the police officer in the community beyond that of "thief catcher." His innovations brought him national recognition. Although Vollmer was not successful in changing the course of policing during his lifetime, he was important in signaling the direction it should and eventually did go.

▲ check your understanding **4.3** **How did immigration and urbanization influence policing in the United States? How did August Vollmer contribute to the development of professional American police forces?**

Contemporary Policing

▼ the main idea **4.4** **One of the most distinctive characteristics of U.S. policing is that there are thousands of police agencies, each with their own jurisdiction. Generally, the jurisdiction of policing can be divided into local police, state police, and federal police.**

Who Are the Police?

The police have evolved into the most visible representative of the government in U.S. society. Despite their high visibility, however, most people's knowledge about the police comes from the media, either in the form of entertainment shows or news coverage. Although the media can give the viewer insight into the world of policing, the media can also be the source of some ill-conceived notions about the police. For example, televison's long-running police show *Hawaii Five-O* prompted many tourists to visit the famed police agency while vacationing in Hawaii. Not only is there no such police agency, Hawaii is one of the few states without a state police agency. One needs to look beyond the media to examine the police and what they do. Many people do not know what the police actually do, how they are organized, or the source and limits of their authority.

For more information on the roles and functions of the police, go to www.ablongman.com/criminaljustice.

One of the most distinctive characteristics of policing in the U.S. criminal justice system is that it is performed by over 17,000 fragmented, semi-autonomous law enforcement agencies.[40] Most of these agencies (over 12,000) are under the control of a city government. Over 3,000 law enforcement agencies are sheriff's departments. There are approximately 1,700 special police and 49 state police agencies.[41] There are fewer than 100 federal law enforcement agencies and of this number, only about 6 are well known to the public.[42] Each police agency is autonomous; it has its own chief administrator, headquarters, rules and regulations, jurisdiction, training standards and facilities, retirement plan, salary scale, and uniform. The uniforms worn by the officers of the various police may appear identical to the casual observer, but each department has its own unique uniform, badge, and identification card.

Furthermore, no single agency has oversight responsibility for all of these different police agencies. There is no central authority, person, or agency to coordinate police activities, to enforce compliance with rules, to investigate charges of police abuse of power, or just to see to it that the police are doing a good job. Given the great number of police agencies and the lack of centralized control, it is not surprising that there are frequently overlapping jurisdictions and responsibilities and even duplication of services.

In trying to understand the country's system of policing, a good starting point is to examine the **jurisdiction** of the various agencies. Each law enforcement agency's powers, responsibilities, and accountability are determined by its jurisdiction. Jurisdiction refers to the geographical limits such as the municipality, county, or state in which officers of the agency are empowered to perform their duties. Jurisdiction also refers to the legitimate duties that the department can perform. Some agencies have a relatively small geographical jurisdiction but a large number of legitimate duties. Other agencies have an expansive geographical jurisdiction but limited legitimate duties. For example, the geographical jurisdiction of the municipal police officer ends at the city limits, but Federal Bureau of Investigation (FBI) agencies have geographical jurisdiction in all 50 states, the District of Columbia, U.S. territories, and certain federal reservations. However, the legal jurisdiction of the FBI is limited to federal laws mandated by the Congress. Federal law enforcement agencies and courts do not have the common law jurisdiction of municipal police. FBI agents do not enforce traffic laws, do not make arrests for disorderly conduct, do not patrol the streets of the city, and do not respond to 9-1-1 calls. Furthermore, FBI agencies can investigate a crime only if it meets certain conditions, such as occurring on federal property or violating a federal law. Using jurisdiction as a criterion, the thousands of police agencies can be divided into five different types depending on their jurisdiction: county, municipal (town or city), state, special, and federal law enforcement.

jurisdiction Geographical area of responsibility and legitimate duties of an agency, court, or law enforcement officer.

▲ check your understanding **4.4** **What is jurisdiction? How do the jurisdictions of law enforcement agencies differ?**

Federal Law Enforcement

the main idea 4.5 Three types of federal law enforcement agencies are the military, civilian, and Indian Tribal police. Civilian law enforcement agencies, particularly the FBI, have been reorganized to respond to terrorist threats.

The history of policing prior to 1900 focuses primarily on the development of local (municipal and county) policing. Prior to 1900, federal law enforcement agencies played a very limited role in law enforcement. When the United States gained its independence, the new government established only two federal law enforcement agencies in 1789: the U.S. Marshals Office and the U.S. Postal Investigation Service. Another federal law enforcement agency was not needed until the U.S. Secret Service was founded in 1865. Federal law enforcement agencies such as the Federal Bureau of Investigation (FBI), the Bureau of Alcohol, Tobacco, and Firearms (AFT), and the Drug Enforcement Agency (DEA) that are well known today originated after 1900 in response to emerging needs that could not be filled by local or existing law enforcement agencies.

Federal law enforcement agencies are similar to local and state law enforcement agencies in that they are decentralized and specialized. Federal law enforcement agencies, each with a different jurisdiction and administrative leadership, have been developed to handle the enforcement of federal laws. These agencies are under the administrative control of the executive branch of the federal government. The president, with the approval of the Senate, appoints the chief executive officers of the various federal law enforcement agencies. The title for the chief executive officer of most heads of federal law enforcement agencies is "director." Federal law enforcement agencies do not use the military-style titles common to local police. Federal law enforcement personnel are generally called "agents." However, the head of the U.S. Marshals Office is called the U.S. Marshal and law enforcement personnel are called "deputy U.S. Marshals." Some federal law enforcement officials wear police-type uniforms; others wear "plain clothes" (i.e., business suits). Chief executive officers of federal law enforcement agencies are appointed by the president with the consent of the Congress. Most directors "serve at the pleasure of the President." Although the president needs the approval of the Senate to appoint a director, he or she does not need the approval of the Senate to remove a director. This relationship creates an atmosphere in which directors of the various agencies have to work to maintain the appearance of neutrality and fairness, yet must not make decisions contrary to the goals and mission of the president. If the director were to fall into disfavor with the president, he or she could be dismissed.

Federal Jurisdiction and Police Powers

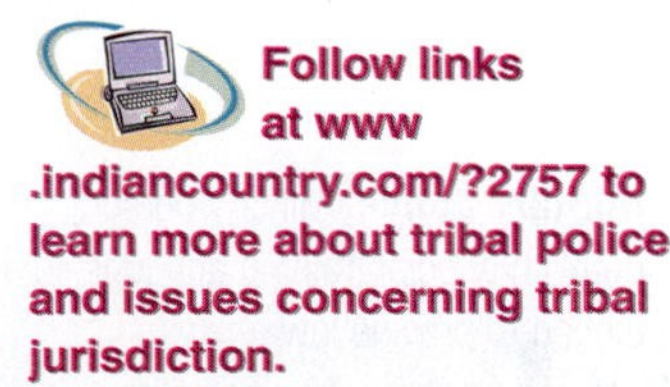

Follow links at www.indiancountry.com/?2757 to learn more about tribal police and issues concerning tribal jurisdiction.

Unlike the limited geographical jurisdiction of local and state police, most federal agencies have jurisdiction in all 50 states, the District of Columbia, and U.S. territories. The legal jurisdiction of federal law enforcement agencies is fragmented and overlapping. The legal jurisdiction of each agency is determined by legislation and executive orders. Also, federal agencies are often charged with the same responsibilities as state and local law enforcement agencies. For example, both the FBI and state and local law enforcement agencies have jurisdiction over bank robberies, kidnappings, and drug crimes. There is no hierarchy of authority, as local, state, and federal law enforcement agencies are independent of each other. In contrast, many foreign governments have chosen to centralize the law enforcement function within their country. Countries such as Canada, France, Great Britain, Japan, Mexico, and Sweden have much more centralized control of their law enforcement agencies.

federal law enforcement Law enforcement agency under the control of the executive branch of the federal government.

Federal agencies with police powers can be divided into three types: military, Indian Tribal police, and civilian agencies. There is some overlap in this classification, as some federal civilian agencies also have jurisdiction on Indian and military reservations.[43] There is a difference between military and civilian police agencies, because federal legislation prohibits the military from performing civilian law enforcement duties. This prohibition against the use of military troops to perform civilian law enforcement was established by the Posse Comitatus Act passed in 1878. Recently, exceptions have been made to allow various military agencies to assist in law enforcement efforts against international drug trafficking and terrorism. However, for the most part, military personnel are still prohibited from exercising civilian law enforcement duties.

Military Police and Tribal Police

Local and state police agencies do not have jurisdiction to enforce federal laws on military and Native American reservations. To maintain order, to provide criminal and noncriminal investigative services, and to provide police services to service personnel and on military bases and installations throughout the world, the various branches of the U.S. military service use military personnel who have the power to make arrests and carry firearms. For example, the **U.S. Army Criminal Investigation Command** provides services similar to those provided by detectives in civilian police departments. The U.S. Army Military Police duties are very similar to those provided by municipal police. The **military police** are responsible for preventive patrol, responding to reports of illegal or disruptive activities, arresting law violators, traffic control, crowd control, handling of emergencies, or other law enforcement responsibilities as would be handled by their civilian counterparts in a municipal police department. The U.S. Navy has taken a different approach to investigating serious crimes. Unlike the Army, the Navy employs civilians to provide investigative services. The **Naval Criminal Investigative Service** employees are not military personnel but civilians hired by the Navy to provide services on Navy bases and installations similar to duties performed by civilian police detectives.

American Indian reservations are considered sovereign territories, where local and state police have no jurisdiction. Federal police and the military have limited jurisdiction on these reservations. Each Native American reservation has the legal authority to establish its own **tribal police** to provide police services. In addition to tribal police departments, police services on tribal lands are provided by the FBI and the Bureau of Indian Affairs. The jurisdiction of each agency is not easily defined and in the past has been the subject of conflict, particularly between the tribal police and the FBI.[44]

Research suggests that public safety on American Indian reservations has been neglected by the U.S. criminal justice system, resulting in a public safety crisis on the reservations.[45] The rate for violent victimizations per 1,000 Native Americans age 12 or older for 1992–1996 (124 violent crimes per 1,000 Native Americans) was more than twice the rate for the nation (50 per 1,000 persons).[46]

The issues of policing Native American tribal lands is complicated by questions concerning the legal jurisdiction of tribal police. Although tribal police have jurisdiction over Native Americans living on tribal lands, their jurisdiction over nontribal residents is restricted.[47] Another issue is that the tribal police are not held to the same state or federal training requirements as other police officers.

The federal government has recognized this problem, and since 1999 federal grants totaling $89 million have been awarded to reservation police departments nationwide to increase the ranks of uniformed officers, enhance community policing efforts, and sustain trial courts.[48] Additional revenues are being requested. In 1995, the attorney general established the **Office of Tribal Justice** to coordinate tribal issues for the Department of Justice. Intended to increase the responsiveness of the Department of Justice to Native American tribes and citizens, the purpose of the Office of Tribal Justice is to ensure better communication by serving as a permanent point of contact between the Department and federally recognized tribes.[49] A 1997 report by the Department of Justice concluded, "In sharp contrast to national trends serious and violent crime is rising significantly in Indian country and law enforcement in Indian country, as it presently

military police Military personnel with special training and jurisdiction to provide law enforcement services on military installations.

tribal police Police agency that provides police services on Native American reservations. Tribal police operate independently of local, state, and federal police due to a special relationship between the United States and Native Americans living on reservations.

exists, often fails to meet basic public safety needs."[50] The report also concluded that tribal governments do not consider the FBI to be an appropriate provider of police services on tribal lands. Due to the isolation and sovereignty of Native American tribes, the problems of policing on tribal lands do not readily parallel those of local or state police agencies.

Civilian Federal Law Enforcement

The United States does not have a national police agency. Instead, the nation has adopted a system of approximately 50 semi-autonomous agencies under the command of various departments in the federal government. Rather than an agency with general police powers similar to the local police, each federal agency has a specialized function, and its jurisdiction is limited by legislative authority or statutory law. Federal police agencies do not enjoy the freedom and expansive jurisdiction provided by common law, as their legal jurisdiction is established by legislation. The legal jurisdiction of the various federal law enforcement and investigative agencies is limited to the enforcement of federal laws.

Federal agencies categorize their personnel with arrest and firearms authority into one of six categories according to their primary area of duty: criminal investigation, corrections, police response and patrol, noncriminal investigation, court operations, and security and protection (see Figure 4.2). Some agencies can have multiple duties. For example, the U.S. Marshals Service has responsibility for court operations and criminal investigations. Likewise, the U.S. Secret Service is responsible for protecting the president and investigating counterfeiting. The diversity of duties of the various agencies is widespread. For instance, some federal law enforcement agencies have duties limited to security of the White House, national parks, or federal museums, whereas other federal law enforcement agencies have worldwide responsibilities. Also, they differ significantly in size and budget, as some of the agencies employ hundreds of officers and others employ thousands of agents. We will provide a brief discussion of the most well known federal agencies: the U.S. Marshals Service; the U.S. Postal Investigation Service; the U.S. Secret Service; the Federal Bureau of Investigation; the Bureau of Alcohol, Tobacco, and Firearms; and the Drug Enforcement Agency. The formation of the Department of

figure 4.2

Responsibilities of Civilian Federal Law Enforcement Agencies

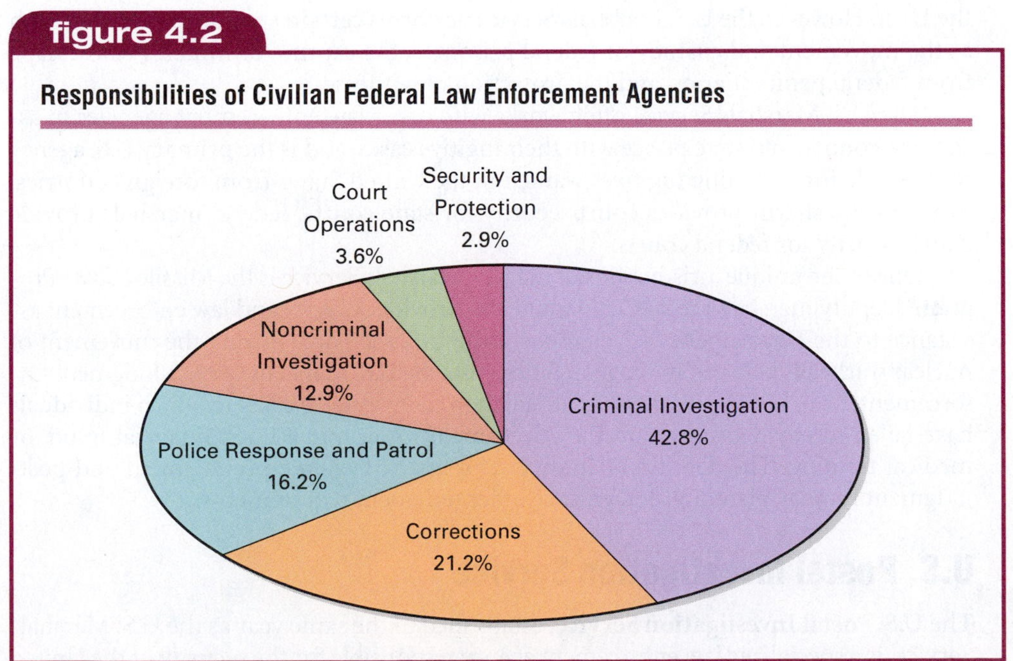

Homeland Security had a major influence on the organizational structure and responsibilities of many federal law enforcement agencies. In an effort to provide coordination and unity of command for the various semi-autonomous federal agencies, the Department of Homeland Security assumed operational or oversight responsibilities for many of the federal law enforcement agencies.

U.S. Marshals Service

See the U.S. Marshals Service at www.usdoj.gov/marshals/.

The **U.S. Marshals Service,** whose roots were in the English system, was one of the first two federal law enforcement agencies established by the Judiciary Act of 1789. The federal Marshals Service was the first federal agency with general law enforcement powers. The U.S. Marshals Service was responsible for providing security for federal courts, serving the papers of the federal courts, and enforcing federal laws.

During the late 1800s, federal marshals were responsible for maintaining law and order in the western territories, but they often lacked the necessary manpower and resources to carry out such responsibilities. To supplement their manpower, federal marshals were authorized to enlist the service of civilians and the military to help them perform their duties. This power to "deputize" civilians and military troops for law enforcement purposes is known as *posse comitatus* and is a practice that has its roots in early English law enforcement practices in Great Britain. When federal marshals deputized private citizens, the federal government had to pay these citizens for their services. Therefore, federal marshals frequently used military troops.

From 1854 to 1878, it was quite common for federal marshals to command the assistance of military troops to help perform civilian law enforcement duties. However, the cost of enforcing civilian law with military troops quickly became too expensive for the federal government, and the power of *posse comitatus* was revoked in 1878. Although initiated primarily for economic reasons, this prohibition against using federal troops for civilian law enforcement has continued to be a guiding principle in U.S. law enforcement. When territories became states, the responsibility for law enforcement was transferred to the state and local government and eventually the law enforcement powers of federal marshals became more specialized.

Today, the law enforcement jurisdiction of the U.S. Marshals Service still includes federal court security and serving the papers of the federal courts, but its law enforcement duties tend to be limited, compared to other federal agencies such as the FBI and the DEA. However, the U.S. Marshals Service performs certain specialized services such as the movement and custody of federal prisoners, the capture of inmates who escape from federal penitentiaries, and the protection of witnesses.

The U.S. Marshals Service often works with other law enforcement agencies to assist city, county, and state police with their fugitive cases, and is the primary U.S. agency responsible for returning fugitives wanted in the United States from foreign countries. Whereas the sheriff provides court security for state courts, federal marshals provide court security for federal courts.

One of the unique jurisdictions of the U.S. Marshals Service is the Missile Escort Program. Deputy marshals are specially trained to provide security and law enforcement assistance to the Department of Defense and the U.S. Air Force during the movement of nuclear warheads between military facilities. Also, the U.S. Marshals Service Judgment Enforcement Team (JET) program has jurisdiction to investigate cases in which individuals have failed to pay debts owed to the government for criminal fines, financial fraud, or medical training. The deputies identify debtor assets, facilitate prejudgment and post-judgment remedy planning, and enforce other judgment requirements.

U.S. Postal Investigation Service

The **U.S. Postal Investigation Service,** established in the same year as the U.S. Marshals Service, is a specialized law enforcement agency responsible for the security of the United

States mail, mail carriers, and investigation of mail fraud. Its law enforcement agents are called postal inspectors and are employed by the United States Postal Service. The Postal Investigation Service has both armed and unarmed investigators. Postal investigation agents have the power of arrest, search and seizure, and the power to carry firearms. Their geographical jurisdiction extends to wherever there is U.S. mail service; however, their primary law enforcement responsibilities are limited to crime related to protecting the integrity of mail services. The Postal Investigation Service has always had a low-key profile despite the fact that it is one of the larger-staffed federal law enforcement agencies and has an impressive record of effectiveness. Often the ranks of postal inspectors are filled from the ranks of mail carriers.

See the United States Postal Investigation Service at www.usps.gov/websites/depart/inspect/.

U.S. Secret Service

Another early federal law enforcement agency was the **U.S. Secret Service,** founded in 1865. Initially, this agency was under the control of the Department of the Treasury, as its primary duties related to investigating the widespread counterfeiting and currency violations that followed the Civil War. Immediately following the Civil War, there were numerous legal currencies in circulation. Counterfeiting was widespread in part because it was legal for large companies, banks, and states to print and mint legal tender, or money. Also, the technology for printing money used by the federal government was relatively primitive, and the forgery of acceptable quality counterfeit money was not difficult. Some estimates place the percentage of counterfeit money in circulation immediately after the Civil War as high as 50 percent. The Secret Service was effective in fighting counterfeiting and bringing counterfeiters to justice. In addition to the efforts of the Secret Service, the federal government restricted the printing of legal tender to the federal government and advances in the printing of money made it more difficult to counterfeit. Thus, soon the newly formed law enforcement agency was lacking something to do.

Starting in 1894, the Secret Service provided informal part-time protection of President Cleveland. However, no agency was charged specifically with the full-time responsibility and resources for protecting the president from assassination or harm. The president, like any other citizen, went about his duties and life without the protection of federal bodyguards. Motivated by the assassination of President William McKinley at Buffalo, New York, in 1901, the duties of the Secret Service were expanded to include the protection of the president.

Over time, the protective duties of the Secret Service were expanded. Today, the Secret Service protects the president's family, the vice president and designated members of his family, former presidents and their minor children, and widows of former presidents. With the assassination of presidential candidate Robert Kennedy (1968), Congress again expanded the protection responsibilities of the Secret Service to include major presidential and vice presidential candidates. The U.S. Secret Service also protects visiting heads of foreign governments. In addition, the Secret Service has been responsible for protecting national treasures such as the Declaration of Independence, the Constitution of the United States, the United Nations Charter, and other valuable documents and works of art, including the Magna Carta when it was brought to the United States for exhibit. Eventually the protection responsibilities became the primary focus of the U.S. Secret Service.

In 1984, Congress enacted legislation making the fraudulent use of credit and debit cards a federal violation and authorized the Secret Service to conduct investigations. Other criminal investigative responsibilities of the Secret Service include federal-interest computer fraud, identity theft and fraudulent identification documents, and civil or criminal investigations related to federally insured financial institutions and telemarketing fraud.

Following the creation of the Department of Homeland Security, the administrative responsibility for the U.S. Secret Service was transferred from the Treasury Department to the Department of Homeland Security in 2003. Also, the Patriot Act increased the Secret Service's role in investigating fraud and related activity in connection with computers and the Internet and computer-based attacks on the nation's financial, banking, and telecommunications infrastructure.

Federal Bureau of Investigation

For information on the Federal Bureau of Investigation, go to www.fbi.gov/.

The **Federal Bureau of Investigation (FBI)** was not created until the twentieth century; however, it is perhaps the most famous of the federal police agencies. The forerunner of the FBI, the Bureau of Investigation, whose agents were unarmed, was created by executive order in 1908 by President Theodore Roosevelt. The primary purpose of the bureau was to provide detective services to the executive branch of the government. The Bureau of Investigation at first focused on finding Communist agents in the United States. Following the overthrow of the Russian czar at the beginning of the twentieth century, Americans feared that the newly formed Communist government would export its violence to the United States.[51] Following the bombing of several federal officials by radical Communists, the United States used the services of the newly created Bureau of Investigation in an operation called the Palmer Raids to bring those responsible to justice and to round up and deport "dangerous" Communists who were in the United States.

The FBI became a prominent federal police agency during the 1930s under the leadership of J. Edgar Hoover. During this time, agents of the FBI waged a war on crime that resulted in the FBI killing John Dillinger, Pretty Boy Floyd, Baby Face Nelson, Ma Barker, Alvin "Creepy" Karpis, and other gangsters. Unlike the negative publicity and critical review that results today when police agents use deadly force, the social context of the time was such that the killing of gangsters by the FBI was widely accepted as a great contribution to public safety.[52]

Responsibilities of the FBI Since 1930, the responsibilities of the Federal Bureau of Investigation have grown steadily. In 1930, the FBI was designated the national clearinghouse for the newly legislated *Uniform Crime Reports.* In 1935, the FBI established the National Police Academy. In 1939, in response to the needs caused by World War I, the FBI was charged by President Franklin D. Roosevelt with the responsibility for domestic intelligence matters relating to espionage, sabotage, and subversive activities.[53]

The investigative and enforcement authority of the FBI, like all federal police agencies, is strictly limited to federal laws and specifically delegated federal authority. Through legislation such as the Mann Act in 1910, the Lindbergh Law in 1932, the Fugitive Felon Act in 1934, and the National Firearms Act in 1934, the FBI has been able to assume additional criminal responsibilities. However, the FBI is not a national police force. It does not have control or jurisdiction over state and local police agencies.

Official duties of the FBI include investigations into organized crime, white-collar crime, public corruption, financial crime, fraud against the government, bribery, copyright infringement, civil rights violations, bank robbery, extortion, kidnapping, air piracy, terrorism, foreign counterintelligence, interstate criminal activity (including crime using the Internet), fugitive and drug-trafficking matters, and other violations of federal statutes. Recent federal legislation has expanded the jurisdiction of the FBI to include antigang authority and a greater role in terrorism, Internet, and computer crime.[54]

In addition to criminal investigation and domestic intelligence responsibilities, the FBI also maintains and operates a sophisticated crime lab and makes the technical expertise of the crime lab available on request to other police agencies free of charge. The FBI crime lab provides invaluable expertise to police departments (e.g., fingerprint identification). Unlike its British counterpart, Scotland Yard, which selectively collects fingerprints, the FBI has attempted to amass a universal personal identification system. As early as 1935, J. Edgar Hoover proposed to the public that every person in the United States, including children, should have his or her fingerprints on file with the FBI Civil

Each law enforcement agency has its own distinctive uniform, organizational structure, jurisdiction, and mission. Federal (*top left*), state (*top right*), county (*bottom left*), and municipal (*bottom right*) agencies have unique uniforms to identify the officers of that agency. There are no universal regulations that specify how law enforcement officers are to dress. Do you think most people are aware of the distinctive uniforms for the various law enforcement agencies?

Index Division. The idea of a universal fingerprint system has never been accepted, but the FBI has collected millions of them.

The FBI also maintains the National Crime Information Center (NCIC), the nation's largest databank of computerized criminal information on wanted felons, convicted (paroled) felons, and stolen items such as automobiles, boats, guns, and securities. Nearly every police agency participates in the NCIC, and it has been an invaluable tool in law enforcement in this highly mobile, contemporary society.

Reorganization of the FBI Following September 11 Prior to the September 11, 2001, terrorist attacks on the United States, responding to terrorism was only one of the many missions of the FBI, and it was not the top priority. FBI agents were restricted from using the Internet as a tool for gathering information, and administrative guidelines prohibited "FBI field agents from taking the initiative to detect and prevent future terrorist attacks, or act unless the bureau learns of possible criminal activity from external sources."[55] Following the September 11 attacks, however, public and congressional scrutiny resulted in a significant reorganization of the FBI.

To combat future terrorism, FBI Director Robert Mueller asked for hundreds of new agents, better computer resources, and a redirected mission and priorities that will force the FBI to change its organizational culture and shed its traditional case-oriented focus on criminal activity.[56] Mueller hopes to build "a Federal Bureau of Prevention whose central mission is to collect, analyze and act on information that will help prevent attacks."[57] Mueller told Congress, "The FBI must become better at shaping its workforce, collaborating with its partners, applying technology to support investigations, operations and analyses, protecting our information and developing core competencies."[58] The new FBI priorities are[59]

- Protect the United States from terrorist attack.
- Protect the United States against foreign intelligence operations and espionage.
- Protect the United States against cyber-based attacks and high-technology crimes.
- Combat public corruption at all levels.
- Protect civil rights.
- Combat transnational and national criminal organizations and enterprises.
- Combat major white-collar crime.
- Combat significant violent crime.
- Support federal, state, local, and international partners.
- Upgrade technology to successfully perform the FBI's mission.

The FBI also reorganized its Counterterrorism Division, established the Office of Intelligence, and placed more emphasis on coordinating with other agencies and using intelligence information more effectively. As a result of all the changes, the FBI is focusing its recruitment on candidates who possess skills beyond those associated with traditional criminal investigation. The critical skills that the FBI is now seeking in new agents include computer science, other information technology specialties, engineering, physical sciences (physics, chemistry, biology), foreign language proficiency (Arabic, Farsi, Pashtu, Urdu, Chinese, Japanese, Korean, Russian, Spanish, and Vietnamese), foreign counterintelligence, counterterrorism, military intelligence experience, and fixed-wing pilots.[60]

Bureau of Alcohol, Tobacco, and Firearms

For information on the Bureau of Alcohol, Tobacco, and Firearms, go to www.atf.treas.gov.

The origins of the **Bureau of Alcohol, Tobacco, and Firearms** (**ATF**) were related to the need to enforce tax laws. Initially, the agency's activities were focused on tax evaders. Early in U.S. history, the taxing of alcoholic beverages became a significant source of income for the federal government and there was the need to collect taxes from those who evaded the taxes. In 1862, Congress created the Office of Internal Revenue within the

Treasury Department and authorized the agency to investigate criminal evasion of taxes. The Office of Internal Revenue was to eventually become the ATF.

The prohibition against the manufacture, sale, and distribution of alcoholic beverages in 1919, known as the Eighteenth Amendment or the Volstead Act, had significant impact on the enforcement duties of the Treasury Department. Even after the Twenty-First Amendment repealed prohibition, the Treasury Department retained important enforcement duties related to the taxation and regulation of the legitimate alcohol industry. The agency was popularized in the media for its campaign against the legendary and infamous "rum runners" and "moonshiners" during the Prohibition era.

New duties were added to the Treasury Department with the passage of the National Firearms Act in 1934, as the department was charged with the duty of collecting federal taxes on certain types of firearms. In 1952, the Internal Revenue division of the Treasury Department was reorganized and the Alcohol and Tobacco Tax Division was created. In 1968, the Gun Control Act was passed. In addition to regulatory responsibilities for firearms, the department also assumed responsibility for explosives. To fulfill these responsibilities, the Treasury Department created the Alcohol, Tobacco, and Firearms Division. In 1970, the Organized Crime Control Act increased the ATF responsibilities for explosives. In 1972, the functions, powers, and duties related to alcohol, tobacco, firearms, and explosives were transferred from the Internal Revenue Service to ATF. In 1982, the Anti-Arson Act made arson a federal crime and gave ATF responsibility for investigating commercial arson nationwide.

In 2003, the Bureau of Alcohol, Tobacco, and Firearms was transferred under the Homeland Security bill to the Department of Justice. The law enforcement functions of ATF under the Department of Treasury were transferred to the Department of Justice. The tax and trade functions of ATF remained with the Treasury Department with the new Alcohol and Tobacco Tax and Trade Bureau. The agency's name was changed to the Bureau of Alcohol, Tobacco, Firearms, and Explosives to reflect its new mission. However, the initials ATF used to identify the agency continue in common use.

Drug Enforcement Agency

Another high-profile federal law enforcement agency is the **Drug Enforcement Administration (DEA).** The DEA, founded in 1973, is one of the newest federal law enforcement agencies. The mission of the Drug Enforcement Administration is

> to enforce controlled substances laws and regulations of the United States and bring to criminal and civil justice systems of the United States, or any other competent jurisdiction, those organizations and principal members of organizations involved in the growing, manufacture, or distribution of controlled substances appearing in or destined for illicit traffic in the United Sates; and to recommend and support non-enforcement programs aimed at reducing the availability of illicit controlled substances on the domestic and international market.[61]

This mission gives the DEA virtually worldwide jurisdiction but at the same time makes it one of the most focused of the federal law enforcement agencies. Despite its worldwide jurisdiction, unlike other federal law enforcement agencies, its mission focuses primarily on violations and education related to controlled substances.

The growth of the DEA has been fairly impressive: The origins of the DEA were in the Bureau of Narcotics and Dangerous Drugs (1968–1973), which had responsibilities primarily for regulation and inventory oversight of controlled substances. The War on Drugs and the new emphasis on the perceived dangers of criminal drug marketing and use has made the DEA a major law enforcement agency. There are nearly 5,000 DEA agents and the DEA is the lead agency in countering the use of illicit drugs in the United States.

The worldwide jurisdiction of the DEA is attributed in part to the rise of the international drug cartels in the 1980s, particularly the Medillin cartel. Worldwide drug cartels have created the phenomena of "narcoterrorism" whereby drug lords in some countries operate virtually undisturbed by law enforcement. Also, the linkage of international drug trafficking as a fund-raising activity for terrorism has emphasized the role and importance of drug enforcement.

Other Federal Agencies with Police Powers

Other federal agencies with law enforcement powers include such agencies as the Internal Revenue Service (IRS), the National Park Service, the National Forest Service, the U.S. Fish and Wildlife Service, the U.S. Air Marshals, and a number of small agencies with limited legal jurisdictions. Although these agencies perform important functions, they do not tend to rise to nationwide focus under normal circumstances. However, it must be remembered that each of these agencies operates independently from each other and there is no single federal law enforcement agency that provides coordination and oversight over all federal law enforcement agencies.

Two agencies not included in the discussion of federal law enforcement agencies, but sometimes confused with such agencies because of their portrayal in the media, are the **Central Intelligence Agency (CIA)** and the **National Security Agency (NSA).** Both of these large government agencies have responsibilities related to national security, but their focus is threats posed by foreign governments and powers. In fact, the CIA is prohibited by law from conducting any operations on American soil other than those that are administrative. Law enforcement operations related to domestic national security are handled by the FBI.

▲ check your understanding **4.5 What are the types and responsibilities of federal law enforcement agencies?**

The State Police

▼ the main idea **4.6 State police agencies enforce traffic laws and investigate criminal activities.**

The geographical jurisdiction of the state police is limited by the state boundaries, and their legal jurisdiction is determined by legislation. **State law enforcement** agencies can be divided into three major types: traffic enforcement, general criminal investigation, and special investigation. Some states, such as Kentucky, have a single state police agency that is responsible for both general criminal investigation and traffic enforcement. Other states have created distinct agencies for each function. The state of Kansas, for example, has two separate agencies: the Kansas Bureau of Investigation, which is responsible for general criminal investigations, and the Kansas Highway Patrol, which is responsible for statewide traffic enforcement. Some states, such as Missouri, do not have a state police agency empowered with general criminal investigation authority. The state of Hawaii has neither a state highway patrol nor a statewide general criminal investigation agency. The state legislature of each state has the authority and discretion to establish the state police agencies that they think most appropriate for the needs of their state.

state law enforcement Law enforcement agencies under the command of the executive branch of the state government, such as the highway patrol and state police.

Highway Patrol

State police agencies that focus on traffic enforcement are commonly called "highway patrol." The legal jurisdictions for these agencies are limited to enforcing the traffic laws

careers in the system

Police Ranks and Promotions

Ranks and specialties usually are identified by uniform insignia. For example, in many departments, advancement is indicated by stripes on the sleeve of the officer's uniform or the "collar brass" that the officer wears. In some departments, the badge an officer carries is another distinction. When promoted from patrol officer to sergeant, an officer might trade in his or her silver-colored or "tin" badge for a gold badge, indicating the supervisory powers of a sergeant. Rank also may be distinguished by the color of the uniform or of the braid on the hats officers wear.

In the United States, until recently all police officers had to start at the bottom of the pyramid as a patrol officer. It was not possible to start as a sergeant, detective, or lieutenant without working one's way up the pyramid. Even higher-ranking officers with previous experience usually are started at an entry-level rank if they move to another department, although progressive departments permit officers to retain the same rank. A college degree, highly desired among recruits, mainly allows an officer to shorten the length of time before he or she can take the sergeant's exam.

Advances in rank bring additional power, prestige, and administrative responsibilities, as well as increases in salary. A sergeant is a "field supervisor" or "line supervisor," and a patrol sergeant may supervise as many as 30 patrol officers. Lieutenants usually have responsibility for a complete unit, such as "day watch" or "detectives." Larger departments have a greater number of higher-ranking positions and thus greater opportunity for promotion. Although young officers might be attracted to a small city, advancement in a small police department is limited because advancement is possible only when a higher position is vacated.

Many departments have minimum qualifications for officers seeking to be detectives. Commonly, patrol officers are expected to serve 1 to 5 years before becoming eligible to be a detective, and some departments require a minimum rank of sergeant. After successfully passing the sergeant's examination, the officer's name is placed on a promotion list. Officers who make the highest scores are placed at the top of the list and are promoted to administrative patrol duty or detective until open positions are filled. Patrol sergeants and sergeant detectives hold the same rank and receive similar base pay.

Lateral, or horizontal, career moves are available in addition to steps for upward mobility. In a lateral transfer—as often as every two or three years—an officer remains at the same rank but assumes new duties. A patrol officer could request transfer to the police academy and work as an instructor. A detective could work his or her way up to burglary, sex crimes, or homicide investigator. An officer could ask to be transferred to personnel, research and development, the crime lab, or to diverse special assignments, such as SWAT team member or school officer.

As a municipal police officer, how would you most likely begin your career? What career choices would you have along the way, and how would those choices affect your mobility in the system?

and promoting safety on the interstate highways and primary and secondary roads of the state. Generally, state traffic enforcement officers do not provide general preventive patrol services to neighborhoods, as do municipal police, or engage in the investigation of crimes. Using automobiles, motorcycles, airplanes, and helicopters, state highway patrol officers enforce the various traffic laws of the state, render assistance to motorists, and promote highway safety. Highway patrol officers have the powers of arrest and search and seizure, and are allowed to carry firearms.

To compare and contrast local, state, and federal law enforcement agencies and opportunities, use links at www.policeemployment.com/.

The chief executive officer of the state's highway patrol agency is normally called a "director," and he or she is appointed by the governor of the state. Candidates for the highway patrol are selected through the use of competitive civil service procedures. Highway patrol officers are state employees and may be transferred throughout the state. Whereas municipal police officers are commonly called "cops," state highway patrol officers are commonly called "troopers." Because of the distinctive wide-brimmed hat worn by some state police highway patrol, which is similar to that worn by "Smokey the Bear" (from the advertising campaign to prevent forest fires), highway patrol officers are also often called "Smokey the Bear," "Smokies," or just "the Bear."

Criminal Investigation

State police agencies may have law enforcement powers similar to the municipal police in that they are authorized to conduct criminal investigations, perform routine patrol, and provide police services. So as not to duplicate the law enforcement services provided by municipal and county police, state police focus on the investigation of statewide crimes, such as those involving drugs and narcotics, or crimes that occur in more than one jurisdiction, such as a mobile crime ring, organized crime, or serial murder. In counties in which the sheriff's department cannot provide police services to unincorporated areas in the county, the state police may provide services to these areas. Sometimes, small towns or villages will contract with the state police to provide police services for a fee rather than attempt to have their own police department.

State police can also have jurisdiction for investigation of crimes where the municipal or county police may appear to be biased. In cases in which there are charges of political corruption of local officers, voter fraud, or bribery of state officials, it may make sense to give jurisdiction for these investigations to the state police.

▲ check your understanding **4.6 What are the various types of state law enforcement agencies and their responsibilities?**

Special Police

▼ the main idea **4.7 Special police agencies have limited jurisdictions, responsibilities, and powers.**

Special police agencies include both state and local agencies that have limited geographical jurisdictions, such as airport police, park police, transit police, public school police, college and university police, public housing police, game wardens, alcoholic beverage control agencies, and special investigative units. The largest single employer of special police is the New York City Transit Police, with over 4,000 full-time officers, nearly one-third of all special police officers in the United States. Most special police departments are small; about two-thirds of the special police departments have fewer than 10 full-time employees.

Special police have limited jurisdiction both in geography and police powers. They are hired, trained, and equipped separately from municipal police officers, sheriff's deputies, and state officers. Special police officers seldom receive much attention from the public, and because of the nature of their work, they may often be mistaken for security guards. They are not security guards, because they are government employees with police powers. For example, state colleges and universities have to provide security for the campus. Many of the state colleges and universities have a police department rather than a security department.[62] The employees of these campus police have general police powers on the state campus, have the right to make arrests and conduct searches, and have the authority to carry and use firearms. They are a police department, but they provide services only for the campus. They do not provide routine patrol services other than on the college campus nor do they provide other police services to the

special police Police with limited jurisdiction. Special police have very narrowly defined duties and sometimes extremely limited geographical jurisdiction.

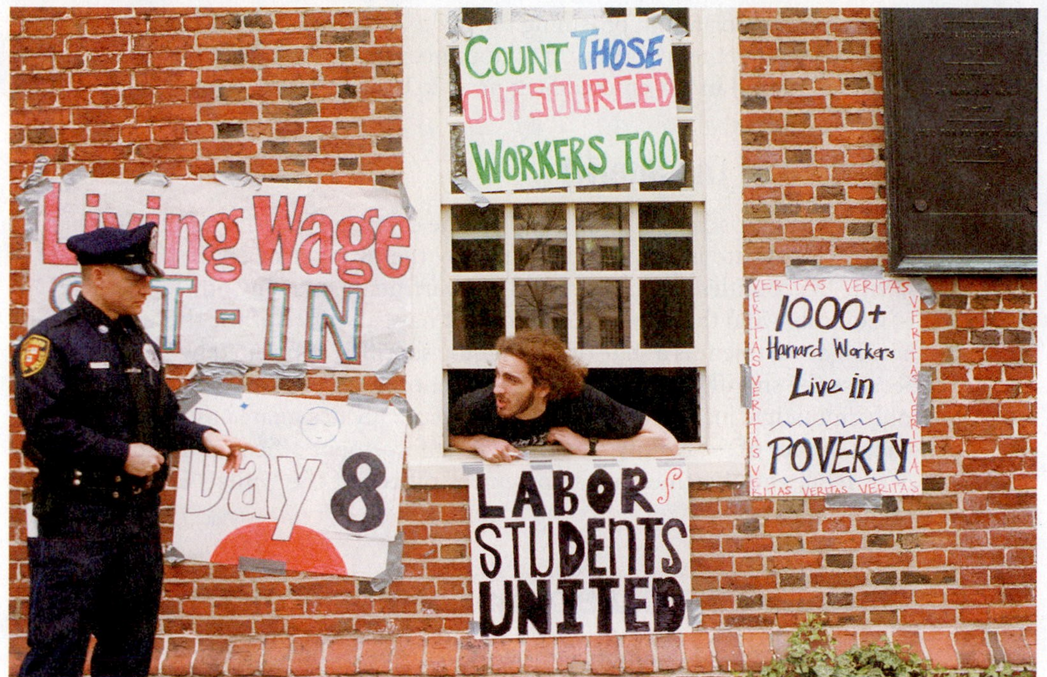

There are two types of campus security officers: noncommissioned security officers and commissioned police officers. What are the arguments for one over the other? What additional powers do commissioned police have? Which do you think would be more expensive?

general community. Although the special police agencies perform essential services, are the source of a substantial number of jobs, and contribute significantly to the public safety of citizens, they have had little impact or influence on the development of the criminal justice system.[63]

▲ check your understanding 4.7 Who are the special police? How are special police different from municipal and state police?

County Law Enforcement Agencies

▼ the main idea 4.8 County law enforcement is performed primarily by the elected office of sheriff.

The sheriff's office is the oldest local policing authority in the United States. When the United States was founded, the Office of the Sheriff was the primary **local law enforcement** agency, as police agencies under the jurisdiction of the city did not become common until the late 1800s. The Office of the Sheriff came from England, but in the U.S. system, rather than being appointed by the Crown, the *sheriff* is elected by popular vote of county residents. In contrast, police chiefs and directors of state and federal law enforcement agencies obtain their positions through political appointment.

For information on the Office of the Sheriff, see www.pasheriffs.org/pasheriffhistory.htm.

local law enforcement
Municipal or county law enforcement; also includes certain special police agencies with limited jurisdiction, such as campus police.

The normal term of office for the sheriff in the 1800s was two years, but most modern sheriffs are elected to four-year terms. In many county elections, sheriffs are expected to affiliate with a political party and to raise funds to campaign for the position. Qualifications to run for sheriff are minimal. The most common requirements are a minimum age and no felony convictions. Campaign, political affiliation, and public appeal are more important in obtaining the office of sheriff than job experience, education, or law enforcement abilities. It is not uncommon for some sheriffs to have no previous background in law enforcement prior to being elected.

Jurisdiction of the Sheriff

The geographical jurisdiction of the sheriff is the county. Thus, the number of sheriff's departments in a state is largely determined by the number of counties. The state of Texas, with 255 counties, has more sheriff's departments than any other state. The District of Columbia and the state of Alaska do not have an office of the sheriff. In Hawaii, the sheriff's department is a state office, and the sheriff is appointed by the governor.[64]

Because the sheriff has countywide jurisdiction, whereas local police departments have only municipal jurisdiction, the sheriff is generally designated as the **chief law enforcement officer** of the county. The chief law enforcement officer of the state is the attorney general, and the chief law enforcement officer of the United States is the U.S. attorney general.

See the International Association of Chiefs of Police at www.theiacp.org/.

Administrative Structure of the Sheriff's Department

The sheriff is empowered to appoint officers to help him or her carry out the duties of the office. These officers are called **deputy sheriff** officers. The second in command of the sheriff's office sometimes retains the old English title of undersheriff.[65] Deputy sheriffs wear different uniforms than local police within their county to distinguish the two departments. The star-shaped badge worn by the deputy sheriff is a carryover from the old English office of the sheriff, whereas officers in most police departments wear shields.

During most of the nineteenth and twentieth centuries, deputy sheriffs were selected for their jobs based on political patronage. The sheriff could personally select any one he or she wanted for the job without regard for qualifications for the position or competitive examination. The deputy sheriffs selected to help carry out the duties of the office were chosen because of their personal loyalty to the sheriff. Deputy sheriffs did not have job security or protection against casual dismissal. They retained their job "at the pleasure of the sheriff" and could be dismissed even without cause.

This system of selecting deputy sheriffs was based on the belief that an elected sheriff should be able to appoint employees on the basis of loyalty. Deputy sheriffs were expected to assist in the sheriff's reelection campaign, and this support was more important than job knowledge, ability, or skills. Until the mid-twentieth century, deputy sheriffs were even expected to contribute financially to the sheriff's campaign. If a sheriff failed to win reelection, the incoming sheriff had the authority to dismiss the deputy sheriffs and award the jobs as political patronage to those who helped him or her win office. Thus, new deputy sheriffs could assume their jobs immediately without the benefit of training.

Today, there are state-mandated minimum training requirements for law enforcement officers. As a result of court rulings prohibiting the dismissal of deputy sheriffs for failing to campaign for the sheriff (or in some cases campaigning for the sheriff's opponent), most sheriff's departments use a civil service selection process for the appointment of sworn officers. Deputy sheriffs are selected based on competitive examinations that test job knowledge, skills, and abilities and can be dismissed from their jobs only for legitimate reasons.

chief law enforcement officer Title applied to the sheriff of the county because his or her jurisdiction is greater than that of the local police agencies within the county.

deputy sheriffs Law enforcement officers working for the Office of the Sheriff. All law enforcement officers in the sheriff's office, regardless of rank, are deputy sheriffs.

officer of the court Law enforcement officer that is used by the court to serve papers, provide courtroom security, and transport defendants.

Law Enforcement Duties of the Sheriff

The sheriff's department can have three major responsibilities: law enforcement duties, serving as **officers of the court**, and operating the county jail. The Office of the Sheriff was the first and only local law enforcement agency in the late eighteenth and early nine-

careers in the system

Working in the Sheriff's Office

Most sheriff's departments have few employees, despite the large geographical responsibility and multipurpose nature of the sheriff's departments. Of the 3,000 sheriff's departments in the United States, only 12 have more than 1,000 sworn personnel and fewer than 100 have more than 250 sworn personnel. Most sheriff's departments (43 percent) employ fewer than 10 full-time officers. In some cases, the department can be very small, as about 50 departments employ just 1 or no full-time officers other than the sheriff.[66]

Overall, the salaries for entry-level deputy sheriffs tend to be slightly lower than those of entry-level municipal police officers (see Table 4.1). Also, the salary of the sheriff tends to be lower than that of the chief administrative officer of a municipal police department.[67]

The functions and organizational structure of the sheriff's department are major considerations in making career choices. The sheriff's department traditionally had three major areas of responsibility: law enforcement, court security and officers of the court, and jail operations. Court security and the serving of court orders is the duty most commonly performed by sheriff's departments today.

To meet the need for people in each of these areas of responsibility, some sheriff's departments have a dual-entry system and others have a single-entry system. In the dual-entry system, a person applies specifically to be either a deputy sheriff in patrol or a correctional officer in county jail operations. Correctional officers receive different training, have different duties, and receive different pay. Individuals who enter as correctional officers usually are not "sworn" officers with the power of arrest and the right to carry a firearm. Jail personnel go through a shorter academy and often receive lower pay; in fact, some sheriff's departments have been known to transfer a deputy sheriff from road patrol to jail operations as punishment for errant behavior.

At the same time, in some county jails, personnel are supervised by sergeants, lieutenants, and captains who are in the deputy sheriff track. In those cases, deputy sheriffs eligible for promotion may find that they have to choose between transferring to a position in jail operations or declining the promotion and staying in road patrol at their present rank.

In a single-career track, all personnel in the sheriff's department enter as jail personnel. After serving a period of time, usually one year, as a correctional officer, a person can apply for promotion to deputy sheriff and undertake police training at the academy. This system is used by small- and medium-sized sheriff's departments that have difficulty getting qualified applicants to work in the jails. The deputy sheriff also may have to work in court security or prisoner transport.

If you worked in a sheriff's department, what would you do? How would your career progress if you were in a dual-entry system? How would your job compare with that of a municipal law enforcement officer?

table 4.1

Comparison of Entry Salaries of Sheriff's Departments and Local Police

	Sheriff		Local Police	
Population Group	***Minimum Salary***	***Maximum Salary***	***Minimum Salary***	***Maximum Salary***
Large, over 1,000,000	\$32,900	\$46,100	\$33,960	\$51,300
Medium, 50,000 to 99,000	\$24,900	\$30,600	\$34,100	\$43,300
Small, less than 2,500	\$21,700	\$23,100	\$20,900	\$22,900

Source: Ann L. Pastore and Kathleen Maguire, eds., *Sourcebook of Criminal Justice Statistics* (Washington, DC: Bureau of Justice Statistics, USGPO, 2005), p. 50.

The Office of the Sheriff provides law enforcement at the county level. Unlike other policing authorities in the United States, the sheriff is elected by popular vote. Campaigning, political affiliation, and public appeal are some of the characteristics important in an election. What is the origin of this practice? What are the minimum legal requirements to become a candidate? How long is the term that a sheriff serves? How is the Office of the Sheriff different from municipal, state, or federal organizations?

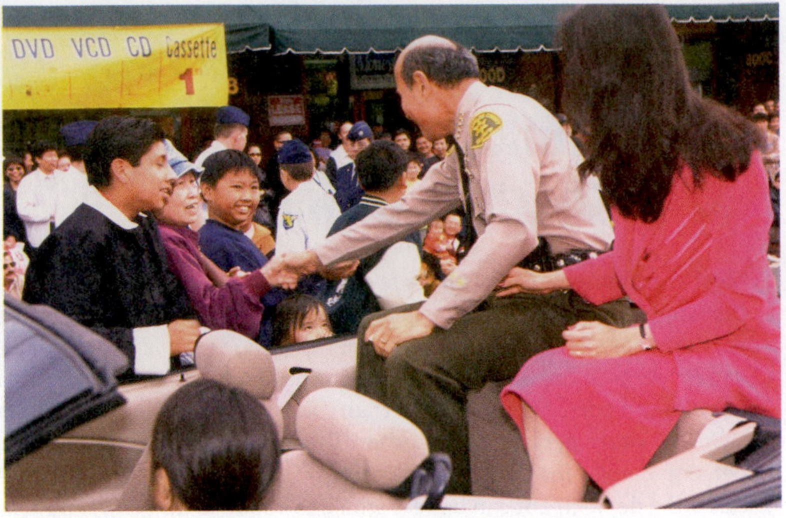

teenth centuries. The sheriff and his deputies were empowered to enforce the laws of the county and state, to make arrests, to engage in preventive patrol, and to carry firearms. The law enforcement jurisdiction of the sheriff exceeded that of the municipal chief of police. As municipalities grew, both geographically and in population, many city limits extended to the limits of the counties in which they were located. With the rise of municipal policing in the latter half of the twentieth century, the role of the sheriff in providing law enforcement services has diminished. Today, in practice it is often the municipal police who assume major responsibility for law enforcement and the sheriff's department that provides police services for citizens who live in unincorporated or rural areas of the county. However, in some major metropolitan areas very little of the county is unincorporated, and the law enforcement services of the sheriff overlap those of municipal police. In some cases, the sheriff's department provides few or no law enforcement services. In other cases, duplication of functions and overlapping jurisdictions lead to cooperation or conflict between departments.

Serving the Court and Operating the County Jail

The sheriff's department is the law enforcement agency used by the state court system to serve warrants, summons, and papers of the court; to provide court security; and to transport prisoners to and from the courtroom. For this reason, deputy sheriff officers are known as "servants of the court." Initially, the serving of court papers was a major source of income for the sheriff. Most sheriffs received little pay for their position and were allowed to keep for their personal use some or all of the fees charged to serve the papers of the court. This practice has not completely disappeared, and in many counties the sheriff's department still gets to keep part of the fees paid to serve court papers. The historical reason for this practice is that the concept of financing government operations from personal income taxes was not instituted until the passage of the Seventeenth Amendment, which made the collecting of personal income taxes constitutional. Throughout the nineteenth century, all government agencies and services were financed by a system of fees, tariffs, or property taxes. Modern practices allow for the budgeting of law enforcement from public funds.

The third responsibility of the sheriff's department is the operation of the county jail, also originally a source of income for the sheriff. The sheriff would be given a budget by the county to take care of the prisoners in the county jail, but could keep unspent funds for his personal use. The sheriff could also charge other agencies such as cities, the state, or the federal government to temporarily house prisoners in the county jail. In the late 1800s and early 1900s, the sheriff's office and the jail were frequently housed in the county courthouse. In some of the rural counties, the sheriff's personal living quarters were also attached to the county jail, as the sheriff was the primary security for the jail at night. Today, many counties have transferred the responsibility of jail operations to special correctional agencies.

▲ check your understanding 4.8 By what titles are chief executive officers of law enforcement agencies known, and how do they obtain their positions? What are the three traditional duties of the sheriff's office?

The City Police: "The Cops"

▼ the main idea 4.9 The municipal police force is the most local and visible representation of government in the community.

When most people refer to "the police" they mean the municipal police—not the sheriff, state police, or federal police. Many town and city residents appear not to appreciate or notice the difference among deputy sheriffs, state police, and municipal police officers. Commonly referred to simply as "the cops," municipal police officers far outnumber all other types of law enforcement officers combined. (The origin of the term *cops* is lost in history. Many believe it is the English slang "coppers," referring to badges made of copper metal that early night watchmen wore around their necks, or an acronym for "constable on patrol.")

Each incorporated town or city in the United States has the power to establish its own police department and laws. Thus, there are over 12,000 municipal police departments. Typically, the size of the municipal police department increases as the population of the city increases, and the largest police departments are found in the largest cities, as shown in Table 4.2.

table 4.2

Ten Largest U.S. Police Departments, 2000

State	Agency	Number Sworn Personnel
New York	New York Police Department	40,435
Illinois	Chicago Police	13,466
California	Los Angeles Police	9,341
Pennsylvania	Philadelphia Police	7,024
Texas	Houston Police	5,343
Michigan	Detroit Police	4,154
District of Columbia	Washington Metropolitan Police	3,612
Maryland	Baltimore Police	3,034
Texas	Dallas Police	2,862
Arizona	Phoenix Police	2,626

Source: Ann L. Pastore and Kathleen Maguire, eds., *Sourcebook of Criminal Justice Statistics* (Washington, DC: Bureau of Justice Statistics, USGPO, 2005), p. 54.

Go to www.communitypolicing.org/ for more information on community policing.

Large cities may employ thousands of police officers, but most municipal departments are much smaller. Over 90 percent of the municipal police departments employ fewer than 50 officers and serve populations of less than 25,000.[68] The police department is one of the major expenses of the city. The budget for a small police department will average about $1.7 million per year, and large departments may have budgets that exceed $300 million.[69] New responsibilities related to the War on Terrorism have strained the budgets of many police departments.

Jurisdiction of Local Police

The geographical jurisdiction of the municipal police officer is limited to the city limits. Once outside his or her municipal jurisdiction, a local police officer's powers to arrest, search, or even carry a firearm may not be recognized. For example, if a Los Angeles police officer were to take a vacation to Hawaii, he or she would have no police powers in Hawaii and would be prohibited from carrying a concealed firearm.

Although the geographical jurisdiction of municipal police officers is limited compared to county, state, and federal agents, their legal jurisdiction is the most comprehensive of all of the police agencies. Municipal police officers have the authority to enforce both city and state laws, and often their authority is based on common law rather than statutory law. Common law authority gives the officers broad discretion in determining which behaviors are illegal.

As cities have merged into large metropolitan areas, police departments have responded by expanding the geographical jurisdiction of the municipal police officer through intercity agreements. In large metropolitan areas such as Dade County (Florida), Los Angeles, and Las Vegas, intercity and county agreements have established the **metro police**. These agreements provide for greater geographical jurisdiction to avoid the problems that would develop if the police did not have any powers outside of their city limits.

Administrative Structure of the Municipal Police

The chief administrative officer of the police department is usually called the **chief of police**. The chief obtains his or her position by appointment. In smaller cities, the chief may be directly appointed by the mayor or city council. In larger cities, the chief may be appointed by a police commission appointed by the city council. Unlike the sheriff, who is elected for a specified number of years, the chief may have no guarantee of the term of his or her appointment. For this reason, chiefs are said to "serve at the pleasure of the mayor or the city council." This political relationship between the chief and city administrators has influenced local policing.

The second-in-command of the police department is usually called the **deputy chief** or assistant chief. This person is selected by the chief from among the higher-ranking police administrators. Promotions among other ranks and the hiring of new police officers for the department are usually accomplished through competitive civil service exams based on job-related skills, abilities, and knowledge. These officers are called "sworn" personnel because they must take an oath to uphold the laws of the city, state, and county and to execute faithfully the responsibilities of their office.

"Nonsworn" personnel of the police department, such as secretaries, office workers, and technicians, are referred to as "civilian" employees. Civilian employees do not have the powers granted to sworn police personnel of arrest, search and seizure, and the right to carry a firearm. Sworn personnel normally enjoy what is referred to as "civil service protection," which means that after completing their probation period of employment, they cannot be dismissed from their jobs without cause and due process.[70]

Police departments have a system of military-style ranks in a hierarchical pyramid, with a chain of command from officer to chief.[71] This is termed a *command-and-control structure*, as in the organizational chart in Figure 4.3. Although also organized in terms

metro police Local police agency that spans several geographical jurisdictions, such as cities or city and county.

chief of police Title of the chief administrative officer of a municipal police agency. The chief obtains his or her position by appointment from the mayor, city council, or other designated city agency, such as the police commission.

deputy chief Title of the second in command of a municipal police agency. This is a position appointed by the chief of police.

figure 4.3

Command-and-Control Structures (Honolulu Police Administration)

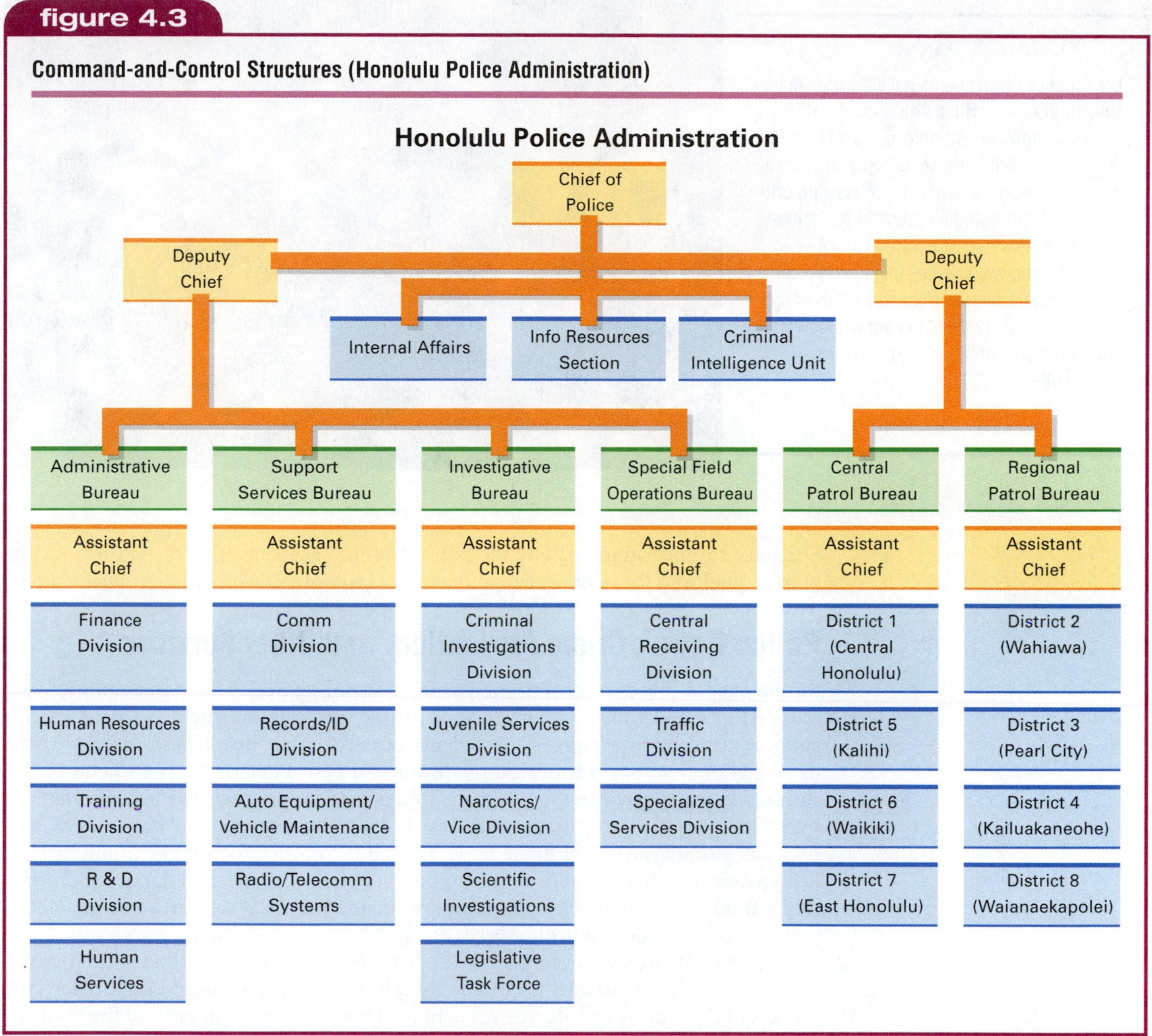

Source: Reprinted by permission of the Police Department of the City and County of Honolulu, Hawaii.

of a command-and-control structure, federal law enforcement agencies do not use military titles; instead, they use titles such as field agent, supervisor, agent-in-charge, and director.

The police organizational chart differentiates among the various functions that the department performs. The most common divisions are patrol, detective services, and support services. The patrol division is the largest organizational unit. Detective services include the investigation of crimes such as fraud, burglary, arson, and homicide. Larger departments allow for specialization among detectives, including juvenile officers, vice squad (gambling and prostitution), and other divisions based on types of crime. Support services might include special units for community crime prevention, drug education in schools, juvenile delinquency, child abuse, missing children, drunk drivers, gangs, domestic violence, repeat offenders, hate crimes, victims' services, and more.[72]

Local police departments have a paramilitary system of ranks, with a police chief as the chief law enforcement officer. What is the order of ranks in the hierarchy? How are ranks indicated? How are ranks filled? How do officers move through the system in the course of their careers? What might be some strengths and weaknesses of a hierarchical organizational structure with a pattern of linear advancement? What are some benefits and drawbacks of lateral career moves in law enforcement?

Specialty support units include the police training academy, the air patrol unit, the bomb squad, and the reserve or auxiliary police (volunteers who assist in police duties).

Police Patrol, Crime Prevention, and Other Services

Municipal police are responsible for a wide variety of services. The most commonly demanded services of the municipal police include traffic enforcement, accident investigation, patrol and first response to incidents, property crime investigation, violent crime investigation, and death investigation. Municipal police departments also end up assuming de facto responsibility for many things that are not their job, because they are one of the very few government agencies available 24 hours a day, 7 days a week, and they will dispatch an officer to the scene. Thus, it is common to find that municipal police agencies also have responsibilities for animal control, search and rescue, emergency medical services, civil defense, communication and technical support services, jail operations, **order maintenance**, and even fire fighting in some cities.

In an effort to save money, some smaller cities have combined the police department and the fire department. Commonly called the Department of Public Safety, the officers of these departments receive training in both law enforcement and fire fighting. A small number of full-time fire-fighting personnel are employed by the city to staff the fire station and drive the fire engine, but most of the fire fighters are police officers. These officers perform routine patrol but carry fire-fighting equipment and uniforms in the trunk of their patrol cars. If there is a fire, they respond to the scene of the fire and perform fire-fighting duties.

Contrary to the image promoted in the media of the police officer as primarily engaged in crime fighting, the reality of police work is that most police officers spend only a small portion of their time in crime-fighting activities[73] (see Table 4.3). Unlike the police officers in television series who receive misdemeanor and felony calls each episode, most real police officers are more likely to receive numerous calls for service and order maintenance. It is not uncommon for officers to complete a shift without making any arrests for criminal behavior.

order maintenance Noncrime-fighting services performed by the police, such as mediation, providing for the welfare of vulnerable persons, and crowd control.

Serving Shifts and Districts

The organizational structure of the police department is also based on geography. Departments divide the geographical area for which they are responsible into small units called districts, beats, or precincts. Each geographical unit is given a name or number relating to its location, its natural boundaries, or its place in the local economy, such as business district, warehouse district, waterfront, or downtown. The size of a unit, and the number of officers assigned to it, is based on population density and demand for police services in the area.[74]

Finally, the organizational structure of the police department is shaped by time. Unlike many businesses, the police must provide services all day, every day, 365 days a year. To provide this coverage, it is necessary to have "shifts" or "watches," each with its own administrators and support personnel. Days typically are divided into three 8-hour shifts, and rookies typically are assigned "new officer watch," the 11 P.M. to 7 A.M. shift. It is common practice to rotate personnel among shifts, but more popular and innovative schemes include shifts of 4 days a week at 10 hours a day with 3 days off every week.

table 4.3

How Police Officers Spend Their Time

Type of Activity	Percentage of Time
Preventative patrol	29.45
Crime-related activity	26.34
Administrative activity	12.3
Traffic-related activity	11.32
Order-maintenance activity	8.73
Unavailable for assignment	5.13
Medical-related activity	2.26

Source: "What Police Do" by Jack R. Greene and Carl B. Klockers in *Thinking about Police,* 2/e edited by Carl B. Klockers and Stephen D. Mastroiski, pp. 273–284, 279. Reprinted by permission of The McGraw-Hill Companies, Inc.

▲ check your understanding **4.9** **What is the jurisdiction of the local police? How are police departments organized, and what are their job functions in the community?**

Selection of Police Officers

▼the main idea **4.10** **Major influences on police professionalism are the quality of applicants hired and the training they receive.**

Every police department is faced with the challenge of recruiting and retaining highly qualified men and women to fill the ranks of the police department. Large cities, such as New York and Chicago, have to recruit thousands of police officers each year. Most smaller cities recruit only one or two per year. However, regardless of the number of police officers that must be recruited annually, the process of becoming a police officer is a highly demanding and complicated process and many of those who apply will be denied employment with the police. The process of becoming a police officer weeds out many applications and many drop out on the way. For example, only about 30 percent of those who sign up for the initial police officer examination for New York City's police department ever show up for the test and only one in ten of those who pass the written examination ends up getting hired as a police officer.

Check out the Office of the Police Corps and Law Enforcement Education at www.ojp.usdoj.gov/opclee/.

The process of becoming a police officer is unlike applying for an entry-level position in private industry. The hiring process takes months to complete and the initial training can take up to six months. During this time applicants will be screened, examined, tested, observed, stressed, and evaluated in many different ways. They will be tested for their physical, psychological, and intellectual fitness as police officers. The object of this extensive screening and training process is to produce police officers who can perform their duties to the high professional standards demanded by the department, the community, and the law. Furthermore, the selection of police recruits is important because police departments tend to promote from within the ranks of existing officers.

diversity in the system

The Civil Rights Act of 1972

An example of the impact of legislation on police professionalism is seen in the passage of legislation regulating the hiring of police officers. Minorities and women were effectively barred from police work until the **Civil Rights Act of 1964** was amended in 1972. The Civil Rights Act of 1964 exempted governmental agencies from the provisions of equal employment opportunity. The 1972 amendment subjected governmental agencies to the same standards of equal employment requirements as private businesses. Until this legislation was passed in 1972, law enforcement agencies could and did refuse to hire women and minorities with impunity. As a result, prior to 1972, police departments were predominately staffed by white men. If a woman or person of color submitted an application to be a "policeman" (the most commonly used title for the position prior to 1972), she or he could be told that the application was refused simply because of gender or race. It was not illegal for police departments to discriminate in hiring. The argument advanced by the police departments and accepted by many in society was that policing was "man's" work and that women would not be able to perform police duties effectively. Men of color were refused employment primarily because of beliefs related to racial prejudice.

The 1972 amendment of the Civil Rights Act of 1964 prohibited discrimination in hiring based on gender, race, and religious affiliation. As a result, hiring standards that resulted in a bias toward the selection of white men came under scrutiny. When it could be demonstrated in court that the hiring standards used by a department resulted in a bias in the choosing of officers based on gender, race, or religious affiliation, the court issued binding rules that prohibited the practice.

For example, one the greatest obstacles for female applicants was the physical fitness test required by police departments. The physical fitness test of many departments prior to 1972 emphasized upper body fitness as measured by the ability to do push-ups, pull-ups, rope climbs, and wall climbs. Women failed these tests at a much greater rate than did male applicants. When women challenged these entrance tests, police departments were unable to defend them; they were not relevant to job-related skills and abilities. It is recognized that a police officer should have a certain level of fitness, but police departments could not justify that applicants who could perform 50 push-ups would make better police officers than those who could perform only 35 or 20. Some departments required that applicants be able to climb a 10-foot wall with the use of a rope. When challenged in court, however, departments were not able to show how in the course of an officer's daily duty he or she would have to climb a 10-foot wall. Today, police departments must demonstrate that all job requirements for the position of police officer are related to job knowledge, skills, and abilities.

Although it can be said that minorities and women are still underrepresented in local policing, their representation is increasing. Many departments have undertaken very aggressive recruiting campaigns to increase the number of female and minority officers in their departments. Demographic and employment trends strongly suggest that employment by police departments will increasingly reflect American racial and ethnic diversity and trends toward gender equity.[75] Although progress is being made in increasing the diversity of the police, few departments reflect the diversity of the community they serve. Most police departments are about 90 percent male and about 77 percent white. As the size of the department decreases, so does the diversity of police officers.

An interesting observation regarding women in policing is that male police recruits generally tend to be in their early 20s, but female recruits tend to be older. Many females appear to apply for police work after working in unrelated occupations. One theory is that females find that police work pays better and has better benefits, greater opportunity for advancement, and better job security than most occupations that are traditionally dominated by females.

How did the Civil Rights Act of 1972 change the way police departments are staffed and the way officers are recruited?

In the early twentieth century, police officers were white men hired on the basis of their size, strength, and loyalty to their superiors. Today, police departments want their officers to reflect the diversity within the community and be motivated to continue their education. Police officers are trained to high standards of ethical behavior, and their loyalty tends to be to one another and to the communities they serve. What are the requirements for becoming a law enforcement officer today?

Thus, sergeants are selected from the patrol officers of the department, lieutenants are selected from the sergeants of the department, and captains are selected from the lieutenants of the department. Thus, when the police department hires a new recruit, he or she must be considered a potential future leader of the department.

Today, employment as a local law enforcement officer is open to many more people than it was 50 years ago, and as a result there is a significant difference in today's police officer compared with the typical officer then. Fifty years ago, police officers were recruited to a large degree based on size, strength, and the ability to follow orders, and nearly all officers were white men. This picture has changed substantially for the better.

Historically, police departments hired minimally qualified applicants, and often the new police officer received no training. As late as the mid-1960s, it was not uncommon for police and sheriff departments to hire new officers and put them to work without any training. Today, the selection and training of police officers is highly sophisticated and the standards for hiring and training are among the highest for an entry-level position.

There is no universal hiring process that must be used by local police agencies. Each city and county department sets its own entrance requirements, salary levels, testing procedures, and timetable. Although there are no universally required criteria and procedures, over the years—due to state regulations, public expectations, Supreme Court decisions, and civil and criminal liability cases—police agencies have adopted a set of hiring procedures. These procedures are fairly uniform from department to department, despite the autonomy each department enjoys. The discussion of the hiring process and requirements tends to focus on local police departments. However, the hiring process and requirements for state and federal law enforcement positions are very similar to that discussed for local police agencies.

Supreme Court decisions have required that hiring standards must reflect job-related requirements, cannot be arbitrary, and cannot discriminate on bases of race, national origin, religion, or sex.[76] The major impact of these decisions has been to eliminate minimum height requirements, which were once as high as 6 feet for some police departments; to eliminate nonjob-related physical tests such as climbing 10-foot walls; and to eliminate discrimination based on race, color, and gender.

The hiring process for police officers is normally regulated by municipal, county, or state civil service rules. Civil service rules mandate that positions in law enforcement be filled by competitive evaluation of candidates based on job-related criteria. The usual process for hiring includes a written test, an oral interview, a physical examination, fitness testing, psychological testing, a background check, a drug-screening test, and, in some departments, a polygraph examination.[77]

See the Federal Law Enforcement Education Training Center at www.fletc.gov/.

As mentioned earlier, the requirements for employment used by local police departments are much more rigorous than those used by private businesses for entry-level jobs. Local police departments use an extensive screening-out procedure, leading to a lengthy employment process. It is not uncommon for the application process to take months for a candidate to complete. Some departments have recognized the hardship that a long application process may impose on a candidate and have taken steps to shorten it, but, as Figure 4.4 suggests, the hiring process is still lengthier than that used by private industry.

A prominent change in minimum job qualifications for police officers has been an increased emphasis on recruiting from a more educated pool of applicants.[78] The requirement of a minimum of a high school education was not universal in the 1960s. College-educated officers were rare. Even college-educated police executives were rare, as it is estimated that less than 1 percent of local police chiefs had a bachelor's degree in the 1960s. Today, nearly all local police departments require a minimum of a high school diploma or general equivalency degree (GED) to apply for employment.[79,80]

A 1967 presidential commission recommended that a four-year college degree should be the minimum requirement for employment as a local police officer.[81] Although this standard has not been adopted universally, a number of police departments require some college or a four-year college degree to apply for the position of police officer.[82]

A major factor that promoted the emphasis on college-educated police officers was the federal **Law Enforcement Assistance Administration (LEAA)** program. From the late 1960s to the early 1980s, the federal government administered an educational loan and grant program under the LEAA, called the **Law Enforcement Educational Program (LEEP),** to encourage criminal justice personnel and applicants to attend college. Under LEEP, college students who indicated their desire to join a police department after graduation, as well as employed police officers, could obtain student loans to attend the colleges of their choice. In return for remaining in the criminal justice system after graduation from college, their educational loans were forgiven. Nearly 100,000 students took advantage of this government program.[83] The impact was so great that hundreds of community-college and four-year college programs started offering criminal justice majors to meet the demand.

The LEEP program was discontinued in the early 1980s, but the number of college-educated police officers has continued to grow. Other factors, such as the adoption of new communication and computer technologies by the police, continue to increase the demand for college-educated police officers. For example, computer literacy is becoming a common job requirement for police officers, as all police departments serving more than 50,000 people use computers, and nearly 25 percent of larger departments (100,000–1,000,000) use laptop computers.[84]

figure 4.4

Police Hiring Process

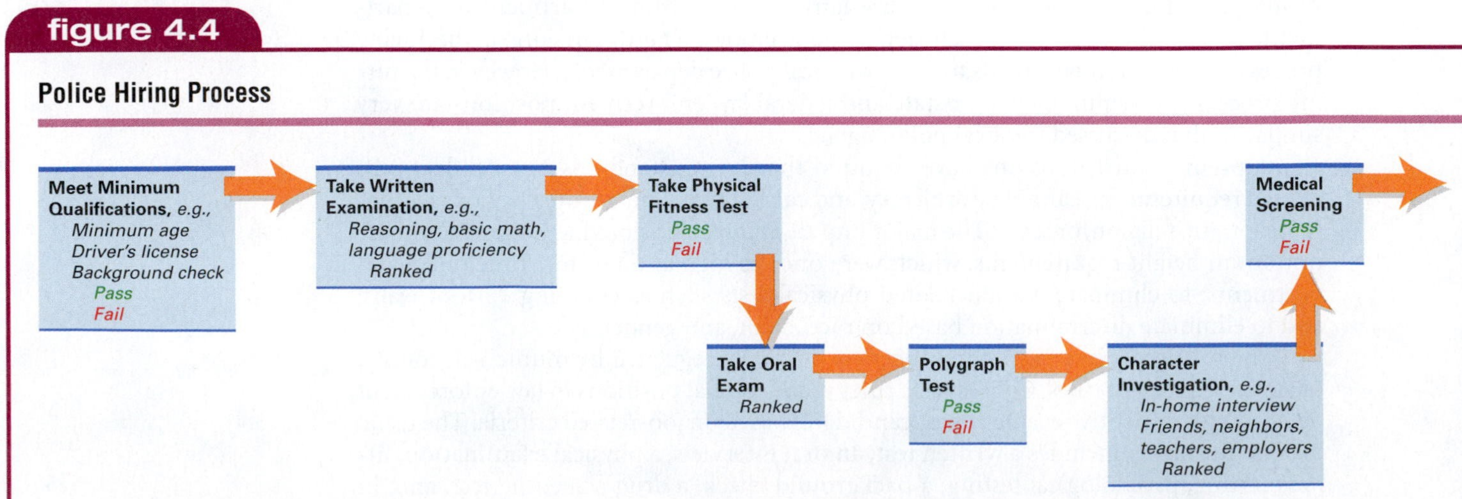

Minimum educational standards must be met before someone is allowed to apply for the position of police officer, but the hiring process is competitive, and it is often the candidates with greater-than-minimum qualifications who are selected. For example, in one midwestern sheriff's department, although the minimum educational level was a high school diploma or GED, 14 percent of the deputy sheriffs had an associate degree, 9 percent had a bachelor's degree, and one deputy sheriff had a master's degree.

Because of better working conditions, increased pay, and the adoption of competitive written examinations, departments find that they can recruit candidates with above-minimum qualifications. In addition, as more police departments adopt competitive written examinations for recruiting and promotion, college-educated candidates frequently find that they have an advantage over those without a college education.

Some police departments attempt to recruit college-educated candidates by offering additional pay for employees who have college degrees. For example, 64 percent of local police departments with 100 or more sworn officers offer educational incentive pay and reward officers for educational achievement beyond the high school diploma.[85] Despite arguments by some that college-educated officers are overqualified for the job because of the routine nature of the work,[86] the trend continues toward recruiting from a pool of college-educated applicants.[87]

State laws have had a great impact on the training that police departments must provide to new officers and on minimum standards for yearly training.[88] Starting in the late 1960s, the states have passed laws requiring higher and higher minimum training standards. Today, most new police officers must receive between 400 and 1,100 hours of training before they are allowed to exercise their powers as a police officer.[89] In addition, many states have required that every police officer must complete a minimum number of hours of training each year to retain their police powers. As a result of such laws, the job knowledge of new police officers today is far more extensive than in the past.

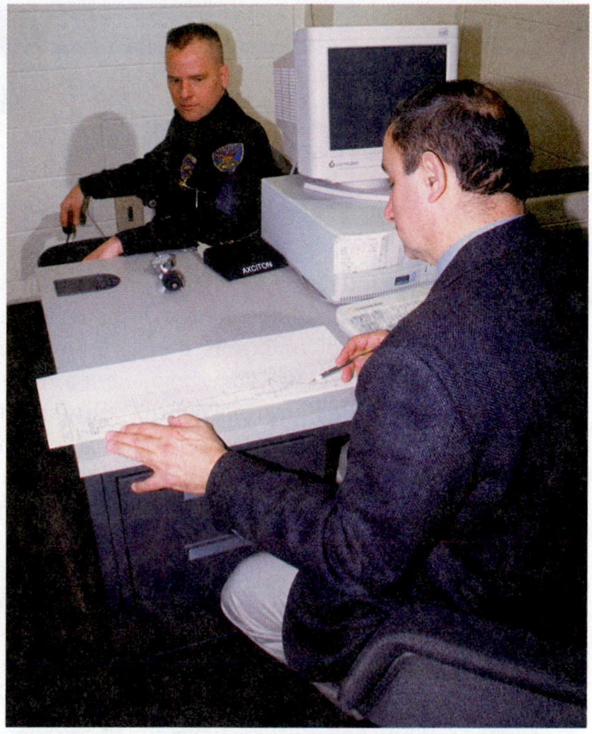

The polygraph measures responses to stress, such as blood pressure, breathing rate, and galvanic skin response. To the extent that a subject finds lying stressful, a polygraph examiner can determine whether he or she is being deceptive in answering the questions. Although the polygraph is not permitted as evidence in a criminal court, scientific research has indicated that it is 85 to 90 percent reliable in detecting deception. The most common behaviors about which subjects lie are drug use, immoral or illegal sex, homosexuality, concealed medical problems, concealed debts (e.g., gambling debts), and other vices that would disqualify the candidate. Why is deception an undesirable trait in law enforcement?

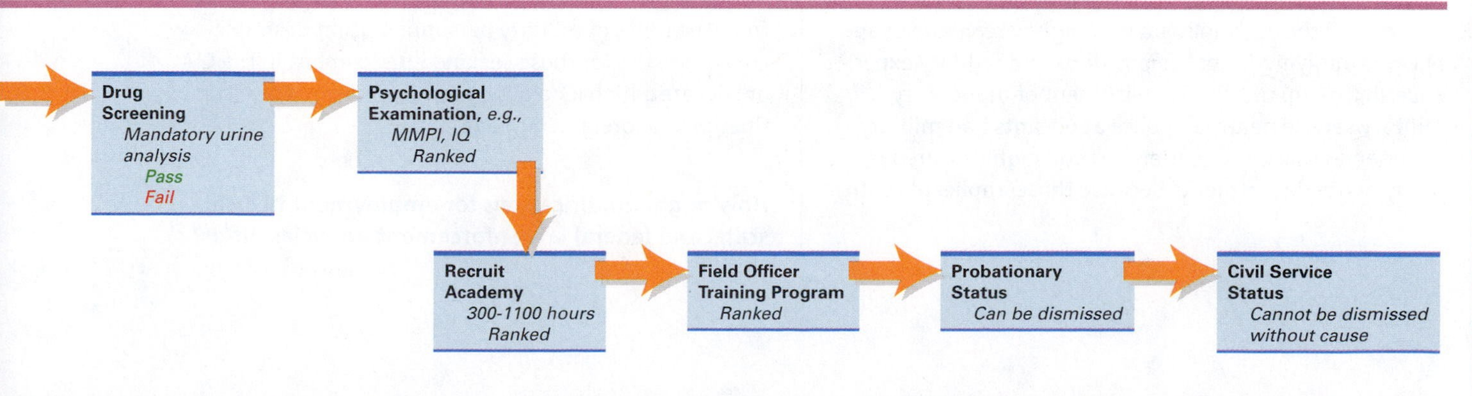

careers in the system

Qualifications for Police Work

Although local, state, and federal police agencies have similar standards for employment and frequently recruit from the same pool of applicants, there are some major differences in the conditions of employment among the various agencies. The municipal police, county sheriff, and state agencies will hire people as young as 21 years old and may require only a high school diploma, but many of the federal agencies have a higher age limit and require a bachelor's degree.

One of the biggest differences between federal employment and local or state employment is related to the jurisdiction of the agency. Municipal and county police officers can expect that their job will always be located within the geographical limits of the city or county. A municipal or county police officer will not be transferred from one city to another or from one county to another. In federal agencies, especially the ATF, DEA, FBI, and Secret Service, agents can expect to be transferred several times in their careers.

Most federal police agents must complete their initial training either at the FBI Training Center in Quantico, Virginia, or the Federal Training Center in Glenyco, Georgia. After completion of the training academy, the federal agent is assigned to an office according to the need of the agency. Because of the nature of the work, ATF, DEA, and FBI agents may be transferred every several years. Secret Service agents can expect frequent and sometimes extended travel, including foreign travel. If the president or other protected person travels overseas, Secret Service agents travel in advance to check the security arrangements and travel with the president or protected member during the entire trip. If staying in one place is an important consideration for the type of job one wants, the choice between a federal or local police agency is critical.

Up until the early 1980s, a very high percentage of applicants applying for police positions had military experience. In fact, up until the abolishment of mandatory military service nearly all police applicants had military experience. Military experience is still highly desired by many police departments because those applicants with military experience are considered more apt to adapt to the organizational culture of the police department.

Also, there are a number of "youthful indiscretions" that can adversely impact one's employment opportunities as a police officer. These include such things as excessive traffic tickets, binge drinking, drug use, and poor financial management, such as excessive debt, bouncing checks, and failure to pay creditors. Misdemeanor arrests for actions that may be related to one's youth or college years—such as disorderly conduct, public drunkenness, or underage drinking—may exclude a candidate from consideration for police work.

Finally, one's physical and medical condition is an important factor in qualifying for police work. Generally, candidates need to have good eyesight, cannot be color blind, must have good hearing, be in average or above average physical condition, and capable of obtaining a driver's license. The affect of physical handicaps such as missing fingers, limbs, and handicaps that impede physical strength and/or agility are difficult to address in general terms. Although federal law requires reasonable accommodations for persons with disabilities, the law does not require that police departments hire persons who cannot perform all the duties and actions required for the position. Thus, police departments tend to consider requests for reasonable accommodations on a case-by-case basis.

Persons interested in and qualified for law enforcement employment may also possess similar characteristics that make them desirable to the CIA or NSA. Recruitment by both agencies is by competitive examination of job-related abilities, skills, and knowledge, but these agencies tend to be secretive about the actual job duties of their employees. Both agencies actively recruit from the ranks of military personnel. Other desirable characteristics for those seeking employment in the CIA or NSA are a high IQ, a good memory, foreign travel, and fluency in a foreign language.

How might qualifications for employment in local, state, and federal law enforcement agencies differ?

This applicant for police officer will be interviewed by a hiring panel. Because police officers frequently work with minimum supervision, they must make decisions very quickly—often with life-and-death consequences—without consulting anyone. The oral interview attempts to evaluate the candidate's ability to perform in this type of environment. The panel typically asks, "Why do you want to become a police officer?" If the candidate tells the panel that she wants to join the police department to "help people" or "fight crime," she might receive a low score. Why?

After candidates are interviewed, tested, and screened, a number of selected candidates are given notices to report to a **police academy** and undertake up to 1,100 hours of training. Larger departments have a permanent staff, physical facilities, and resources for the academy, but smaller departments may have to send officers to regional academies, where officers from several different departments are trained.The academy emphasizes academic learning, physical fitness, and development of the recruits' aptitude for police work. In the academy, the recruit learns the specific laws of the state, county, and/or city of his or her jurisdiction.[90]

Most departments use some form of in-service training or **field-training program** to further evaluate the suitability of the candidate for police work after graduation from the training academy.[91] During this period of time, the academy graduate works directly under the supervision of an experienced officer. The experienced officer evaluates the "street-sense" and attitude of the new officer and assesses his or her ability to be a good cop.[92]

The field-training program may last only several weeks, but most departments keep the newly hired officer on a probationary status for up to a year. During this time, the department reserves the right to dismiss the officer without having to show cause. For example, during the probationary period, an officer could be dismissed for unprofessional behavior, which, if committed after the probation period, would result only in a reprimand or temporary suspension.

▲ check your understanding **4.10** **How are police officers selected? What training standards and benchmarks must police recruits meet?**

Policing Strategies

▼ the main idea **4.11** **Styles of policing reflect community values and police–community relations.**

One of the more powerful influences on police professionalism and community satisfaction with police services is how the police go about their job of providing services and

police academy Facility or programs for the education and training of police recruits.

field-training program Probationary period during which police academy graduates train in the community under the direct supervision of experienced officers.

Read an article on the impact of women in law enforcement on policing styles at www.csmonitor.com/atcsmonitor/specials/women/work/work011200.html.

Read "Ethics, Integrity and Police Culture" at www.interpol.int/Public/Publications/ICPR/ICPR483_1.asp.

what services the police think are most important to provide.[93] Police scholar James Q. Wilson proposed that rather than viewing police behavior as random and independent of community values, the style of policing and hence the behavior of the police officer should be viewed as closely related to the type of city government and community expectations. Wilson assumed that even neighboring police departments could have different styles of policing reflecting the differences of each in city government and community expectations.[94]

An important point to emerge from the studies of Wilson is the premise that there is a link between police behavior and community values. The police do not act randomly, nor do they develop values in a vacuum. Police strategies reflect a department's values, which reflect community values. This view suggests that community values influence everything the police do. Community values influence attitudes, behaviors, and policies.

Changing Police–Community Relations

Over the last 100 years, the relationship between the police and the community has changed. Ideas about competent, professional police behavior ultimately come from broader social forces. One of the major characteristics of the police–community relationship during the 1950s through 1970s, for example, was the schism between the police and the community.[95]

Community Policing

During the 1960s and 1970s, the crime rate began to climb. Cities burned. Drugs, gangs, and crime became pandemic. The image of police omnipresence proved to be a myth as cities were consumed with disorder and riots that the police could neither prevent nor control. Fear of crime, increasing violence, mistrust of the police, and serious doubts about the professionalism of the police resulted in widespread dissatisfaction with police services—especially with the municipal police.[96] It is not surprising that since the late 1980s new policing strategies have been adopted by many police departments as a reflection of the public's dissatisfaction with traditional policing. One of these new policing strategies came to be known as "community policing."[97]

Community policing developed during the 1960s and 1970s as citizen disenchantment with police services and criticisms of police professionalism led to experimentation with different policing strategies.[98] One of the early strategies used during this period was team policing.[99] **Team policing** attempted to establish small units of police personnel who would assume responsibility for public order and crime control within a geographical area. It was thought that this decentralization would encourage more police–community involvement. Unfortunately, because of the incompatibility of the decentralized decision-making strategy of team policing and the highly centralized command-and-control administrative model of policing, team policing was strategically incompatible. Team policing enjoyed only brief and limited popularity. Most citizens and police saw little organizational change in policing under team policing. It was more of an add-on rather than a radical new strategy.[100] Community policing is enjoying far more success than team policing.[101]

team policing Decentralizing development during the 1960s and 1970s in which small units of police personnel took responsibility for a particular geographical area.

community policing Decentralized policing programs that focus on crime prevention, quality of life in the community, public order, and alternatives to arrest.

What Is Community Policing? Despite its popularity and widespread use, there is no universally accepted definition of **community policing**. As a result, many police departments have declared that they have adopted community policing; however, each community policing program is different.[102] The common characteristics of community police are these:

criminal justice in the media

What Is the Truth about Police Work?

How accurately does the media portray the truth of police work? The public image of the police is strongly influenced by broadcast media, especially television, and this image has changed over time. For example, Chief **William H. Parker** (1950–1966) was credited with improving the image of professionalism and honesty of the Los Angeles Police Department through a collaboration with network television. Parker consulted with Jack Webb on the then-popular TV show, *Dragnet*. In *Dragnet*, the TV personae of Detective Sergeants Joe Friday ("Just the facts, ma'am") and Bill Gannon became the image of police professionalism, for which, as a result, the LAPD received a worldwide reputation. In the 1990s, that reputation was shattered by the Ramparts corruption scandal, and, again, the media—in the form of investigative journalism—played a prominent role in public perceptions of the police.

Police series on television and police movies, both action dramas and comedies, are among the most popular genres in the United States, and these media emphasize the violence, danger, and excitement of police work. Live-action television, referred to as "reality TV," features series such as *COPS* and depicts car chases, bank robberies, hostage events, and shoot-outs. Even real cops watch TV shows and movies about the police, and, for better or worse, the job expectations of candidates for positions of police officer are influenced by what these potential recruits see in the media.

The police portrayed in the media often act contrary to the professional standards and legal requirements governing police officers. The purpose of the media is to entertain the viewer, thus, often the police are portrayed in highly unrealistic behaviors. For example, police officers engage in violence against criminals that would result in lawsuits or criminal charges in real life; they perform searches without probable cause or search warrants, which would result in the dismissal of the evidence; or they act as a "one-man" crusade against crime in the city completely ignoring the organizational limitations placed on individual police officers. In some media portrayals, police officers may shoot a person, or in some cases a number of persons, without the realism that results when a police officers shoots someone in the line of duty. In real life, a shooting results in an immediate investigation by Internal Affairs, the administrative suspension of the police officer until the investigation is completed and it is determined whether the officer was justified in the shooting, and perhaps a mandatory psychological examination to determine the officer's fitness to return to duty. Often, it is difficult to distinguish between "real" police work and "media images," as often the media portray "realistic"—even "documentary-style"—shows that blur the line between "real" and "entertainment."

What image of the police and police professionalism is popularized today, compared with Chief Parker's day? Overall, are portrayals of the police in the media positive or negative? To what extent do you think the portrayals are "real"?

- Focus on decentralized strategies that promote crime prevention rather than rapid response, crime investigation, and apprehension of the criminal[103]
- Focus on promoting the quality of life of the community and public order rather than law enforcement[104]
- Use of alternatives other than arrest and force to solve the cause of the problem rather than responding to the symptoms of the problem[105]

See the Community-Oriented Policing Services site at www.usdoj.gov/cops/.

The common elements of community policing are proactive police services that emphasize decentralized crime prevention, preventing the recurrence of crime, and promoting the quality of life in the community.

Crime and the criminal justice system are very popular in the entertainment media. Some of television's most popular shows are crime programs such as *CSI, Law and Order,* and *COPS.* Often, the media's depiction of the criminal justice system does not accurately reflect reality. However, there are complaints that crime shows such as *CSI* provide criminals with tips on how to avoid getting caught. How do television and movies influence the public's attitude toward criminal justice?

Broken Windows and Zero Tolerance Although each police department has approached community policing differently, an underlying theme of community policing is a partnership between the police and the community. In this partnership, the police become problem identifiers, dispute resolvers, and managers of relations rather than crime fighters, law enforcers, and the "thin blue line."[106]

Underlying this strategy of public order is the philosophy of the "broken window."[107] In an interesting experiment, an automobile was parked in a neighborhood and left. It was discovered that the automobile was more quickly vandalized if a window on the parked automobile was broken than if the automobile was left undamaged. The message sent by the broken window was, "Nobody cares—other acts of vandalism are okay."

Community policing involves citizens in quality-of-life issues in their neighborhoods that, if addressed, may reduce delinquency and crime. How does community policing differ from traditional policing models? According to this chapter, what are some drawbacks of community policing? What have been some unexpected negative and positive outcomes of community policing efforts?

When applied to a neighborhood, the **broken window theory** means that if vacant buildings are left untended, if graffiti is tolerated, and if public order violations such as public drinking, disruptive behavior by youths, and vandalism are permitted, these will be signals to people that nobody cares about the community, leading to more serious disorder and crime.[108]

One of the strategies associated with the broken window philosophy is strict enforcement for minor violations of the law, such as public drinking, after-hours use of parks, loitering, and even jaywalking. This strict enforcement is called the **zero-tolerance** strategy, and the assumption behind this strategy is that it will send the message to more serious lawbreakers that if even such minor offenses are noticed by the police, then more serious offenses also will bring prompt police action. According to the broken window theory, tolerance by the police and the community for people breaking "small laws" demonstrates the community's apathy and leads to more serious crime.

Police Partnership and Public Order Studies conducted in the 1970s indicated that much police work actually involved order maintenance as opposed to crime fighting.[109] In fact, in only about 5 percent of all dispatched calls in most cities does the officer have a chance to intervene or make an arrest. Despite the emphasis of the police on rapid response time, these studies suggested that rapid response time was, in general, an ineffective crime-fighting strategy. The philosophy of community policing holds that order maintenance, not law enforcement, is the root of crime fighting. If a community has a high degree of public order, more serious crime is less likely to develop.[110]

Frequently, when police seek to enter into a partnership with the residents of a neighborhood to promote public order and to fight crime, both sides must learn to trust each other and to communicate. Both the police and the community are not accustomed to working with each other. The old division between "us and them" or "police and civilians" had worked effectively to separate the community and the police. In working in partnership with the community, sometimes community expectations were quite surprising to the police. In one attempt to establish community policing in a public housing project, police officers thought that initially the residents would want to see the police direct their resources toward fighting drug dealing, violence, or youth gangs. To their surprise, the major complaint of the residents was illegally parked cars and abandoned vehicles.

In meetings with the residents of the housing project, community police officers learned that despite a long history of trying to get some response to their numerous complaints about abandoned vehicles, they had had no success. The residents had repeatedly called 9-1-1 but had been advised that abandoned vehicles were handled by another city department. Calls to this department failed to produce any results. Taking up the challenge, community police officers assigned to the housing project coordinated efforts between the police and the city department that handled abandoned vehicles and, in one weekend, removed dozens of abandoned vehicles from the parking lot and streets surrounding the housing project. Once the police proved their ability to get a "small" thing done, such as removing abandoned vehicles, the housing residents developed more trust in the police and began to supply them with information about drug dealing and criminal activities in the housing project. As one resident summarized the situation, "If the police can't do anything about an abandoned car, what can they do about drug dealing?"

Problem-Oriented Policing Community policing emphasizes attacking the root problem that causes crime instead of responding to the symptoms of the problem by arresting offenders and taking victimization reports. This approach to crime fighting is sometimes called "problem-solving policing" or "problem-oriented policing." **Problem-oriented policing** emphasizes three main themes:[111]

- Increased effectiveness by attacking underlying problems that give rise to incidents that consume patrol and detective time

broken window theory Belief that ignoring public order violations and disruptive behavior leads to community neglect, which fosters further disorder and crime.

zero tolerance Strict enforcement of the laws, even for minor violations.

problem-oriented policing Proactive type of community policing that focuses on solving the underlying problems of delinquency and crime.

- Reliance on the expertise and creativity of line officers to study problems carefully and develop innovative solutions
- Closer involvement with the public to make sure that the police are addressing the needs of citizens

Rather than being reactive, problem-solving policing emphasizes the role of the police as proactive—acting before the crime is committed. Traditionally, police are reactive. They respond to a crime or call for service. Once they respond, they take steps to solve the crime or catch the criminal or resolve the conflict. Seldom, or never, are they expected to take steps to find out what was the cause of the crime or conflict and what would prevent it from recurring.[112]

If calls for police services were randomly distributed throughout the city and each call were unique, there would be little reason for the officer to attempt to find the cause of the crime or conflict and initiate strategies to address the cause rather than the symptom. Efforts to find and address the cause of a problem take considerably more time and resources than traditional policing. However, studies indicate that the demand for most police services comes from a relatively small portion of the city's residences and that police frequently respond repeatedly to the same problem or crime. Whether it is a domestic disturbance call, a burglary call, or a call reporting public drinking and disorderly behavior in a park, the police frequently find themselves returning to the same location to deal with the same problem. Problem-oriented policing focuses on resolution of the problem.

Scanning, Analysis, Response, and Assessment (SARA) One commonly used technique in problem-solving policing is **scanning, analysis, response, and assessment (SARA).**[113] *Scanning* is the process of gathering data about the incident that would allow the officer to place it in a broader frame of reference. It allows the officer to define the problem. *Analysis* is the search for information that would let the officer understand the underlying nature of the problem and its causes and consider a variety of options for its resolution. *Response* requires the officer to work with citizens, businesses, and public and private agencies to implement a solution that would impact the cause of the problem. Instead of making an arrest, the goal of the officer is to prevent the crime from happening again. The final stage, *assessment,* requires the officer to follow up on the initiative taken to see if it has had the desired effect. If it has not, the problem requires reexamination for new solutions. The SARA technique is based on the premise that if the police solve the problem that caused the crime, the extra resources used to solve the problem will be recovered by the time saved in repeat calls (see Figure 4.5).

When the Newport News (Virginia) Police Department used this problem-solving approach on real-world problems, the results were impressive. Working on the crime problems of household burglaries, personal robberies, and larcenies from automobiles, the Newport News Police Department was able to reduce household burglaries by 35 percent, personal robberies in the downtown area by 39 percent, and larcenies from automobiles in the downtown area by 53 percent.[114] However, to accomplish this result, the officers had to do more than rapidly respond to 9-1-1 calls. Officers had to think through the cause of a problem, assess the community resources for solving the problem, and implement a solution. This strategy is significantly different from traditional policing, which emphasizes rapid response to calls, high-speed cars, high-tech weapons, and impressive arrest statistics.[115] For example, to reduce the burglary rate, the Newport News Police Department found that it was necessary to get involved in enforcing building codes, tracking down "slum landlords," and educating residents about crime prevention.[116] Other cities have found that these strategies also apply to the problems of gangs and prostitution.

figure 4.5

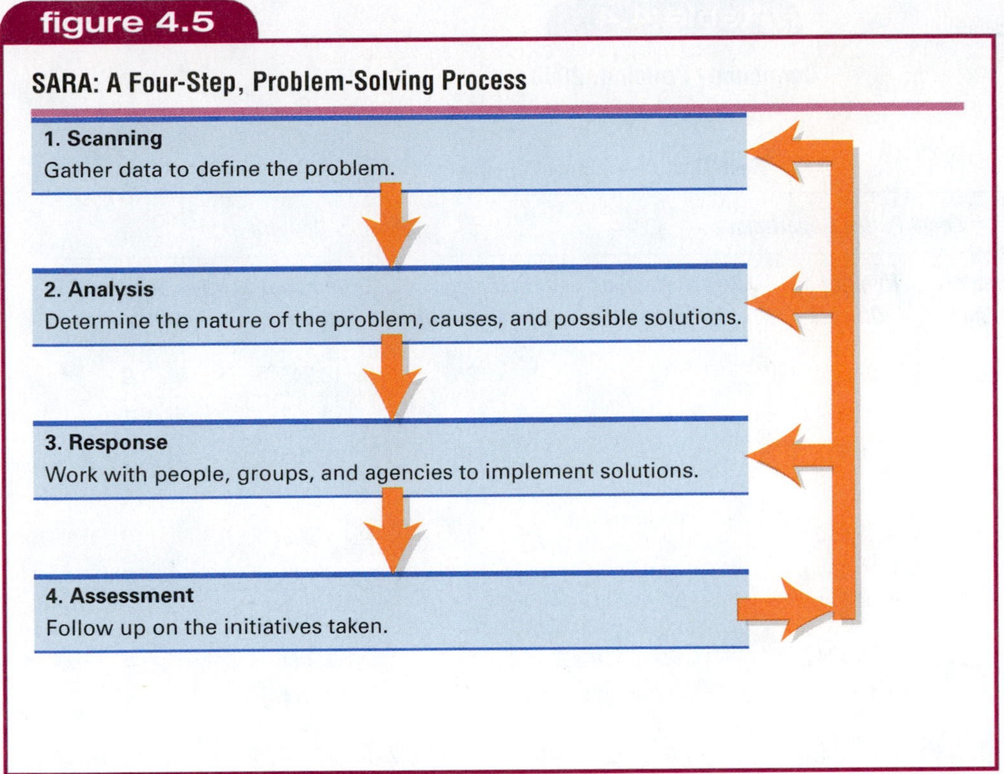

SARA: A Four-Step, Problem-Solving Process
1. Scanning
Gather data to define the problem.
2. Analysis
Determine the nature of the problem, causes, and possible solutions.
3. Response
Work with people, groups, and agencies to implement solutions.
4. Assessment
Follow up on the initiatives taken.

Source: William Spelman and John E. Eck, *Problem-Oriented Policing* (Washington, DC: National Institute of Justice, January 1987), p. 4.

Challenges of Community Policing If community policing is so great, why isn't everyone doing it? Community policing is not without its critics, who believe that community policing, like team policing before it, will soon be a historical footnote in policing strategies. Critics argue that community policing will not last because, like team policing, it requires that decision making be decentralized in the police administrative structure. Problems are solved through decisions made by the lowest-ranking persons in the organization. Unless there is the need to involve greater organizational resources, such as a concern with a citywide problem, problems are addressed at the bottom of the organizational pyramid rather than the top.[117] Table 4.4 shows that despite the lack of a common definition and criticisms of community policing, many local police departments and sheriff's departments report utilizing community policing.

Decentralization of Decision Making The decentralization of decision making runs counter to the traditional paramilitary command-and-control organizational culture of the police. Community policing strategies require the "shifting of people and authority out of headquarters and specialists units back to field commands."[118] Despite the criticisms of traditional police command-and-control structures, after over 100 years of use, many police officers, especially the command-and-control officers, have grown accustomed to it and even prefer it over the newer community policing strategies. Some opponents argue that "despite scholarly opinions, the street cops tend to prefer the quasi-military style."[119] This argument is based on the assumption that the traditional law enforcement strategy gives the police officer a better sense of control, structure, and direction in an otherwise chaotic environment.

table 4.4

Community Policing, 2000

Population Served	Full-Time Community Policing Officers					
	Local Police Departments			*Sheriff's Departments*		
	Percentage of Agencies Using	*Number of Officers*	*Average Number of Officers*[a]	*Percentage of Agencies Using*	*Number of Officers*	*Average Number of Officers*[a]
All sizes	66%	102,598	12	62%	16,545	9
1,000,000 or more	100	33,214	2,208	65	3,502	161
500,000 to 999,999	85	8,617	297	73	1,156	23
250,000 to 499,999	95	6,866	180	73	2,225	26
150,000 to 249,999	94	8,580	53	72	2,025	10
50,000 to 149,999	93	7,167	20	68	1,747	7
25,000 to 49,999	83	7,854	12	59	2,087	6
10,000 to 24,999	72	9,184	7	54	2,190	5
2,500 to 9,999	63	12,745	5	63	1,614	4
Less than 2,500	60	8,370	3			

Sources: U.S. Department of Justice, Bureau of Justice Statistics, *Local Police Departments 2000,* NCJ 196002 (Washington, DC: U.S. Department of Justice, February 2003), p. 15, Table 32; U.S. Department of Justice, Bureau of Justice Statistics, *Sheriffs' Offices 2000,* NCJ 196534 (Washington, DC: U.S. Department of Justice, 2003), p. 15, Table 32.

Note: Community policing promotes organizational strategies to address the causes and reduce the fear of crime and social disorder through problem-solving tactics and community partnerships. A fundamental shift from traditional reactive policing, community policing stresses the prevention of crime before it occurs. The implementation of a community policing plan supports and empowers front-line officers, decentralizes command, and encourages innovative problem solving. In some jurisdictions these officers may be known as community relations officers, community resource officers, or named for the community policing approach they employ.

[a]Excludes agencies that did not employ any full-time community policing officers.

The Lakewood (Colorado) Police Department's experiment in nontraditional police uniforms and ranks seems to support this observation that police officers prefer traditional structures. Under Chief Charles Johnson, Lakewood Police Department officers switched from traditional police uniforms to blazers and gray trousers. They also discarded the use of military ranks such as sergeant and lieutenant. After three years, however, the department found that the nontraditional structure and uniforms created more problems than they solved and abandoned their use. For example, personnel from other departments were confused when interacting with Lakewood's officers because they were unable to identify their rank and authority. Lakewood police officers found the new uniforms less practical for everyday police work and more expensive.[120]

Need for Retraining The change in the police role when community policing strategies are adopted has caused many police officials and scholars to feel that a shift to community policing would require extensive retraining efforts, and they believe that officers would resist adopting the characteristics required in their new role.[121] Community policing requires a more educated officer and an officer with creative problem-solving abilities.[122] Police officers must view members of the public as a potential resource in crime fighting rather than as potential criminals. It has been suggested that this shift in viewpoint may be difficult for many police officers.[123] Whereas all citizens are supposed to be treated fairly and in a professional manner, some police officers have developed critical attitudes that make it difficult for them to apply this standard. It is possible that many officers would not want to become more sensitive and open to their environment or more involved in the day-to-day lives of the people in the community.[124] The police officer's separation or isolation from the community makes it possible for him or her to engage in grisly interactions such as assaults, accident victims, and shootings, day after day as duty demands, without becoming impaired by emotional overload. According to Hernandez, "For the cop, a certain amount of insensitivity may be synonymous with survival."[125]

If some officers resist the change to a community policing style, it can cause an increased burden on other officers, resulting in burnout. One of the findings in surveys of departments that adopt community policing strategies is that not all officers "get with the program." As a result, other officers must make up for their work. For example, in the Minneapolis "Cop-of-the-Block" program, officers were supposed to make personal contacts with residents of the community. A survey found that one officer alone accounted for about half of all recorded personal contacts.

Crime Displacement versus Elimination Other concerns about community policing strategies refer to the displacement of crime to noncommunity-policing areas.[126] Although community policing and problem-solving strategies may reduce robberies, burglaries, prostitution, or car thefts in one neighborhood, they may not eliminate the crimes but merely drive them to another part of the community or to another community, where they become someone else's problem. For example, when Wichita, Kansas, responded to the community demand to clean up prostitution, extensive police and community efforts were effective not in eliminating the street prostitutes but only in moving them to another part of the community that was less vocal about the problem. Several years later, the same pattern repeated when the police initiated a campaign to clean up drug activity. A crackdown on drug dealing in one part of town merely resulted in the problem moving to another part of the community. Many believe that the dislocation of crime is a major problem with community policing.

Minority Communities Some people have expressed serious concern over the ability of community policing strategies to work in minority neighborhoods.[127] They cite the fact that "empirical studies have shown that community-oriented approaches that are effective in most neighborhoods work less well, or not at all, in areas inhabited by low-income blacks and other minority groups."[128] Supporters of community policing dispute this claim, and it is not clear what effect the minority race or ethnicity of an officer has on community policing efforts in minority neighborhoods.

Tyranny of Neighborhoods A final concern over community policing strategies is the "potential tyranny of neighborhoods" that would suppress "persons who for one reason or another are considered objectionable."[129] Most community residents would support the efforts of neighborhood watch groups and police to reduce public intoxication in parks, drug dealing in housing projects, and gang violence near schools, but what happens when the police and community turn their attention to other goals? For example, some community groups have been active in opposing the release of paroled offenders back into their communities. Such community opposition has attracted the attention of the American Civil Liberties Union, which has expressed concern over potential violations of constitutional and privacy rights.

In an effort to promote quality of life and to fight crime, neighborhoods may mistake diversity and tolerance for crime and disorder. Neighborhoods can be places of congeniality, sociability, and safety, but they can also be places of smallness, meanness, and tyranny. The minority youth walking in a white neighborhood may find that he becomes a target of the police and the community because he is different, not because he is criminal.

The Future of Community Policing The jury is still out on the benefits of community policing strategies, although they are popular with the public. It is too early to tell if community policing strategies will be universally adopted. As more police departments document their efforts at community policing strategies, data will accumulate. It may be that community policing strategies might have little impact on crime rates, but a much greater impact on the community's fear of crime.

Traditional police strategies have emphasized crime fighting and investigation and have paid little if any attention to citizens' fear of crime. Police have assumed that fear is caused by criminal victimization. They reasoned that if criminal victimization is reduced, fear of crime would naturally diminish. However, research has shown that the causes of fear of crime do not stem so much from criminal victimization as other interactions and environmental cues.[130] The level of fear of crime does not necessarily go down as the crime rate drops. Community policing may be an effective strategy for reducing citizens' fear of crime, because one of the positive effects of the adoption of community policing strategies seems to be that it promotes the belief by citizens that the community has been empowered. Citizens feel less helpless in the face of rising crime rates. Even in communities where crime rates do not decrease with the adoption of community policing strategies, the self-confidence of the community seems to improve and the fear of crime decreases.

It still remains to be seen how flexible police administrations are willing to be in restructuring police departments, because the classical organizational structure of policing has endured since Robert Peel's first police department. One of the important tests will be whether the organizational structure and culture will reward the individual officer who participates in community policing. If officers who participate in community policing are seen by the police culture as not doing "real police work" and are passed over for choice assignments and promotions, officers will soon abandon their commitment to community policing despite encouraging crime statistics or community accolades.

▲ check your understanding **4.11** **What are some specific community policing strategies that have been tried, and on what factors does their success depend?**

conclusion:

The Police and the Public

During the 1960s, police departments were frequently described as "closed societies." Phrases such as "the blue curtain" described the isolation of police from the public and the solidarity of the police against public scrutiny. Although the blue curtain did not disappear, it definitely parted. The public and police administrators have taken steps to make the operation of the police more open to the public. The police have responded to social values and modified their behaviors. There is still the need for oversight, as there will always be those police officers who abuse their power or honest differences of opinion between the police and the public regarding what constitutes professional and acceptable law enforcement practices.

One of the problems concerning police oversight and professionalism is the concern of the police with efficiency in fighting crime and maintaining social order and the concern of the public with preserving constitutionally protected rights. Often the two concerns are antagonistic. Practices that promote efficiency in law enforcement could undermine the rights of citizens.

Recruitment, screening, education, training, administration, and leadership all contribute to the development of police professionalism and accountability to the community. However, achieving acceptable standards of police professionalism must remain an ongoing goal. The standards that define acceptable professional behavior and practices today may be condemned tomorrow by the public, the courts, the media, or even progressive police administrators as unacceptable.

chapter summary

- A modern police force as we know it first emerged in 1829 in London. The fear of crime was one of the major factors that caused the development of the police. It was not until the end of the nineteenth century that London-style policing became widespread in the United States.
- Policing is a state power under the Constitution. As a result, the United States has a fragmented system of thousands of semi-independent local, county, state, and federal police. A strong federal policing presence did not emerge until after the 1900s.
- August Vollmer is the father of American policing. However, he was largely unsuccessful during his lifetime in getting other police departments to adopt his progressive philosophy.
- Federal law enforcement agencies developed in response to the need to combat new challenges in crime fighting and to enforce new federal laws. The oldest federal agencies are the U.S. Marshals Service, the U.S. Postal Investigation Service, and the U.S. Secret Service. Most other federal law enforcement agencies emerged after 1900.
- The sheriff is the chief law enforcement officer of the county and has the traditional responsibilities of the sheriff, including law enforcement, court service and protection, and jail operations. The sheriff is the only elected chief executive officer of a law enforcement agency. Officers are called deputy sheriffs and usually wear a star-shaped badge.
- The municipal police are the most visible and numerous of the police agencies. Although having limited geographical jurisdiction, municipal police have the broadest legal jurisdiction. Many cities have signed intercity agreements that allow metro police to expand the geographical jurisdiction of the city police. The chief of police is appointed by the mayor, city council, or police commission and does not have civil service job protection.
- Each state has a different structure for their state police. The common responsibility of the state police is traffic enforcement (highway patrol) or general criminal investigation, or both. The chief executive officer is the director and obtains his or her position by appointment, usually by the governor.
- There are many small, specialized law enforcement agencies with limited jurisdiction, such as the airport police, transit police, and public housing police. The New York City Transit Police is the largest of these types of agencies.
- There are several types of federal law enforcement agencies: military, American Indian tribal police, and civilian law enforcement agencies.
- Police professionalism is achieved through extensive testing of applicants who apply for the position of police officer, including written, oral, physical, medical, moral character, psychological, and polygraph examinations.
- Personnel selected for the position of police officer attend a police academy, followed by a period of field training and probation.

- Policing is influenced by community values.
- Community policing attempts to develop a partnership between the police and the community and emphasizes crime prevention and quality-of-life issues rather than crime fighting.
- Criticisms of community police strategies include the decentralization of authority, lack of training, displacement of crime, ineffectiveness in minority communities, and the potential tyranny of neighborhoods over personal liberty and community diversity.

vocabulary review

Black Codes, 145
broken window theory, 181
chief law enforcement officer, 164
chief of police, 168
community policing, 178
deputy chief, 168
deputy sheriffs, 164
federal law enforcement, 151
field-training program, 177
jurisdiction, 150
local law enforcement, 163
metro police, 168
military police, 152
officer of the court, 164
order maintenance, 170
Plessy v. *Ferguson*, 146
police academy, 177
problem-oriented policing, 181
slave patrols, 144
special police, 162
state law enforcement, 160
team policing, 178
Tenth Amendment, 142
tribal police, 152
vigilantism, 144
zero tolerance, 181

do you remember?

Bow Street Runners, 141
Bureau of Alcohol, Tobacco, and Firearms (ATF), 158
Central Intelligence Agency (CIA), 160
Civil Rights Act of 1964, 172
Drug Enforcement Administration (DEA), 159
Federal Bureau of Investigation (FBI), 156
London Metropolitan Police Act, 141
National Security Agency (NSA), 160
Naval Criminal Investigative Service, 152
Office of Tribal Justice, 152
William H. Parker, 179
Sir Robert Peel, 141
Scanning, analysis, response, and assessment (SARA), 182
U.S. Army Criminal Investigation Command, 152
U.S. Marshals Service, 154
U.S. Postal Investigation Service, 154
U.S. Secret Service, 155
August Vollmer, 149
Westminster Watch Act of 1774, 141

think about this

1. If you had the power to determine the minimum qualifications for police officers, what qualifications would you require, and why?
2. The U.S. military services have programs allowing people to enter the various branches of the service as commissioned officers without having to serve any time in the enlisted ranks. Should the police department allow college graduates to enter the police department directly as detectives or lieutenants? Do you think that college graduates should be required to attend the same training academy as noncollege graduates, or should they be allowed to attend an accelerated course?
3. Civil rights legislation has required equal employment opportunities for women and minorities. However, women still make up only about 6 to 11 percent of the average police department. Even in police departments that are aggressive in recruiting female officers, the percentage of female officers is relatively low. Why?
4. Can community police strategies that require a trust relationship between the police and citizens work in minority neighborhoods where, historically, the police and the community have been at odds with each other? In neighborhoods with high gang activity? In neighborhoods with a history of rioting and antipolice demonstrations?

research navigator

Visit the Research Navigator website (www.researchnavigator.com), login and select the criminal justice data base in ContentSelect. Type in the key words "The loss of Talent." Select the article "The Loss of Talent: Why Local and State Law Enforcement Officers Resign to Become FBI Agents and what Agencies Can Do About It" by Mark D. Bowman, *et al.* The recruitment of highly qualified officers by local and state police departments is a challenging and expensive process. Some officers will leave their agencies because they will find that they prefer other work; however, often the best officers leave local and state agencies to join the Federal Bureau of Investigation. Sample the article and answer the following questions:

1. Why is it important for local and state police officers to retain the officers in their department?
2. What are some of the reasons that local and state officers leave their departments for employment with the Federal Bureau of Investigation?
3. What can local and state agencies do to retain officers who may consider resignation in favor of employment with federal law enforcement agencies?
4. What are the harms to the community when highly qualified local and state officers resign to seek employment with federal law enforcement agencies?

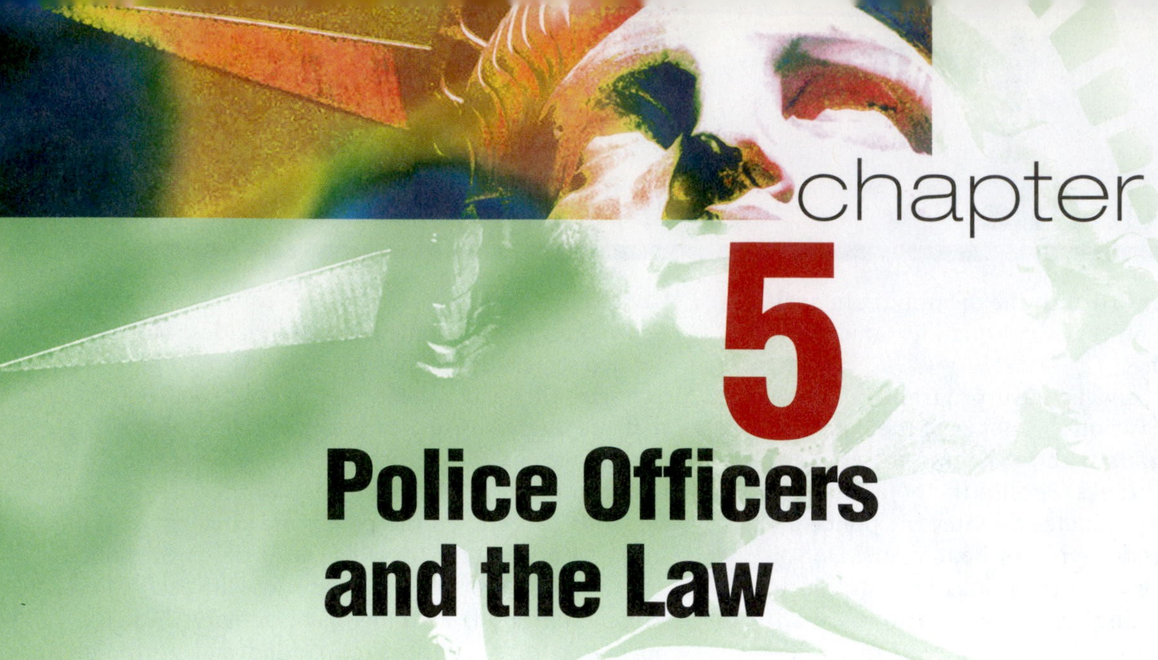

chapter 5

Police Officers and the Law

CHAPTER OUTLINE

LEARNING OBJECTIVES

After reading this chapter you will be able to

- Define due process and identify procedural laws that guarantee due process.
- Explain how the rules of evidence influence police behavior.
- Describe how police procedure reflects case law relating to the Fourth and Fifth Amendments.
- List exceptions to the exclusionary rule regarding search and seizure.
- Identify situations that can make evidence from interrogations, confessions, and arrests inadmissible in court.

Police Blunder Ends Case Against Poker Players

BALTIMORE (AP)—Charges against 80 poker players arrested in a major gambling raid will be dropped, prosecutors say, because the police quoted the wrong statute when the players were charged.

The police raided the Owl's Nest club, arresting 95 people and seizing more than $25,600 in cash, thousands of poker chips, decks of cards, liquor and beer. They called it the biggest gambling raid in the city since Prohibition.

The players were charged under a law that says people may not "keep, rent, or occupy" a building for the purpose of gambling, but prosecutors said that another section of the law prohibiting a "bet, wager or gamble" should have been used. An assistant state's attorney said that if the players had been charged appropriately, "we might have taken a different route."

From Associated Press, "Police Blunder Ends Case Against Poker Players," *The New York Times*, November 11, 2005.

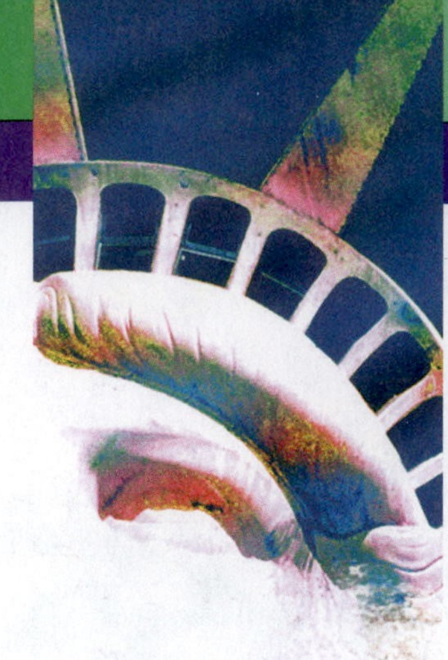

introduction:

Procedural Law and Oversight of the Police

The criminal justice system is governed by **procedural law**—a body of laws for how things should be done at each stage of the criminal justice process. This includes court procedures, such as rules of evidence, and police procedures, such as search and seizure, arrest, and interrogation.

The rules and procedures governing criminal law can be very precise. When these rules are not followed, those accused of violating a criminal law often cannot be prosecuted, as in the case of the poker players arrested in the raid by Baltimore police officers. Failure to charge those arrested with the proper violation of the criminal law resulted in charges being dismissed against them. Even in serious felonies such as murder, rape, and child sex offenses, failure to provide the accused the rights guaranteed to them or to follow the procedures required by procedural law can result in their release from the criminal justice system. The police are responsible for the detection of crimes, the investigation of crimes, and the arrest of the alleged offender. However, as they perform these responsibilities they are required to do so without violating the rights provided to the accused.

Procedural laws are developed through legislative and judicial oversight. Police practices are affected by city and county councils, state legislatures, and the federal Congress. These legislative bodies can pass laws that limit or expand police jurisdiction, create standards, and provide remedies for police practices not acceptable to the community. For example, some states, such as the Commonwealth of Pennsylvania, have in recent years passed legislation restricting the use of radar speed traps by municipal police in response to allegations of abuse.[1]

Police conduct also is influenced by the judiciary, especially the U.S. Supreme Court, as in the well-known ruling that a suspect being placed under arrest must be informed of his or her rights prior to questioning. The tremendous influence that the Supreme Court exerts is indirect, however, and may take years, sometimes decades, to correct police malpractice. Because of the separation of powers and checks and balances in U.S. government, the Supreme Court cannot issue a direct order to a police department or state or federal law enforcement agency dictating how they should act. Similarly, according to the separation of powers, police officers have the power to arrest people, but not the power to prosecute people for the charges on which they have been arrested. The power to file a criminal complaint against a defendant—even to decide who will be brought to court to face charges and who will not—rests with the judicial branch of government in the hands of the district attorney or attorney general of the state.

Go to www.ablongman.com/criminaljustice for audio and activities relating law enforcement procedures to the U.S. Constitution.

This chapter discusses the difficult problem of protecting the rights of those accused of violating the criminal law. The police often are the first to initiate charges against those accused of breaking the law, so oversight of police practices has a prominent role in protecting the rights of the accused. This chapter examines how police procedures such as gathering evidence, performing search and seizures, interrogating suspects and witnesses, and arresting suspects must be carried out within strict guidelines. Also, the chapter discusses oversight of the police to ensure that not only do the police perform their duties within the guidelines, but that the police carry out these duties in a professional and legal manner. It explains how other criminal justice, government, and private agencies play an important role in oversight of police practices and procedures.

procedural law Body of laws for how things should be done at each stage of the criminal justice process.

Rules of Evidence

the main idea 5.1 Police procedure is guided by rules defining what is legal evidence admissible in a court of law.

The police have the primary responsibility for detecting crime, investigating crime, gathering evidence to present in court, and arresting suspects. However, they do not have unrestricted powers in fulfilling these responsibilities and they must perform these duties within proscribed limits set by legislation, judicial oversight, and the Constitution. One of the most influential criminal justice agencies regulating police behavior is the U.S. Supreme Court. The Supreme Court has the power to review cases to determine if the constitutional rights of the accused have been preserved. The Court has the power to establish the rules by which lower courts operate. Each court is governed by rules concerning everyday practices, such as how judges will be assigned cases, the qualification of attorneys to practice before the court, the order of presentation of the case, and the rules regarding proper conduct of attorneys and observers in the courtroom. Rules that relate to the presentation of evidence in a trial are called the rules of evidence.

Rules of evidence stipulate the requirements for introducing evidence and define the qualifications of an expert witness and the nature of the testimony he or she may give. According to the rules of evidence, for example, the prosecutor must show the defense the evidence he or she has gathered against the defendant. Rules define when evidence is relevant to the case and material (relevant to a particular issue in the case). Through its power to decide what evidence can be introduced at a trial, the Supreme Court influences police practices.

Rules of evidence affect police officers' conduct, because collecting evidence is part of their job. If evidence is not collected properly, it can be declared inadmissible, in which case it cannot be used against a defendant. For example, if a defendant is on trial for the illegal possession of drugs and the drugs he or she is accused of possessing are declared inadmissible as evidence, the prosecutor cannot present this evidence to the jury. Thus, the prosecutor has no case. He or she cannot tell the jury that the defendant is accused of possessing something if the object cannot be presented in court. The rules also state that evidence gathered through immoral, illegal, or unconstitutional means should not be used as evidence in a trial. Evidence gathered by such means is not admissible in court, and to avoid this, it is assumed, police officers will follow the rules of evidence.

The Exclusionary Rule

Evidence is declared inadmissible under the **exclusionary rule,** which prohibits the use of evidence or testimony obtained in violation of the U.S. Constitution. The Constitution protects civil liberties and civil rights, which may not be violated by agents of the criminal justice system.

The origins of the exclusionary rule can be traced back to a case heard by the Supreme Court in 1914, ***Weeks* v. *United States.***[2] In the *Weeks* case, the U.S. Supreme Court ruled that evidence against Weeks had been obtained in violation of his protections under the Constitution. Evidence was obtained through a search without a warrant in violation of the Fourth Amendment.

Initially, the exclusion rule applied only to federal courts. The rights guaranteed by the First Amendment (freedom of speech and freedom of association), Fourth Amendment (privacy and search and seizure), Fifth Amendment (self-incrimination and double jeopardy), and Sixth Amendment (the right to confront witnesses) did not apply to the actions of local police or state courts. Until 1949, state courts were free to write their own rules of evidence.[3]

rules of evidence Requirements for introducing evidence and testimony in court.

exclusionary rule Prohibits the use of evidence or testimony obtained in violation of the Fourth and Fifth Amendments of the U.S. Constitution, established in *Weeks* v. *United States* (1914) and extended to the states in *Mapp* v. *Ohio* (1961).

Fruit of the Poisoned Tree Doctrine

At first, the exclusionary rule established in the *Weeks* case applied only to primary (directly obtained) evidence, but not to secondary evidence. For example, if federal agents obtained the business books of a company by unconstitutional means, those books could not be used as evidence to incriminate the defendant, but a copy of the information could. Also, inadmissible evidence could lead to other evidence, which then could be introduced in court. Thus, if an unconstitutional search produced a map indicating where the defendant had buried the body of the person he or she was accused of murdering, the map could not be introduced as evidence. However, using the knowledge obtained from the map, the police officers could go to the gravesite, uncover the body, and introduce it as evidence.

Four years after the *Weeks* decision, the Supreme Court reconsidered the exclusionary rule and added another rule of evidence, known as the **Fruit of the Poisoned Tree Doctrine**. The name of the doctrine comes from the analogy that if the tree is "poisoned," then the "fruit" of the tree also will be poisoned. In ***Silverthorne Lumber Co.* v. *United States*** (1918), the Supreme Court declared that the rules of evidence applied not only to evidence directly obtained by illegal means but also to any other evidence obtained indirectly.[4] Under this rule, the copy of the business books and the body found through the aid of the map are not admissible as evidence.

The U.S. Supreme Court required the federal courts to follow this rule but still did not interfere in the procedures of state courts. Only 17 states chose to adopt similar rules of evidence. However, in ***Wolf* v. *Colorado*** (1949), the U.S. Supreme Court declared that state courts had to enact procedures to protect the rights of citizens against police abuses of search and seizure.[5] *Wolf* v. *Colorado* gave the states wide latitude in developing rules of evidence such as the exclusionary rule and the Fruit of the Poisoned Tree Doctrine to discourage such abuses. Twelve years later, in 1961, the Supreme Court decided that the states had failed to act to protect the constitutional rights of the defendant.

Application to State Courts: *Mapp* v. *Ohio*

Go to http://lp.findlaw.com, the homepage of FindLaw, to access the Supreme Court's ruling in *Mapp* v. *Ohio.*

Generally, the Supreme Court did not interfere with state courts, but with the adoption of the Fourteenth Amendment and the incorporation of the Bill of Rights, this practice started to change. The incorporation of the exclusionary rule illustrates this change. Without any "punishment" for gathering evidence and obtaining confessions contrary to constitutional protections, local and state law enforcement officers paid little attention to the federal constitutional rights of citizens. They knew that any evidence they obtained would be admissible at trial in state court. It was common practice for police to search without a warrant or probable cause, obtain confessions by the use of force, and in general ignore the constitutional rights of suspects. Then, in 1961 in ***Mapp* v. *Ohio*,** the U.S. Supreme Court reversed itself and required state courts to use the exclusionary rule.[6]

The facts of *Mapp* v. *Ohio* are that Cleveland, Ohio, police officers received a tip from an informant that a bombing suspect was at the home of Dolree Mapp and that there was evidence at her house to connect her to the numbers racket. When police officers went to the home of Dolree Mapp and asked permission to search her house, she refused. The police officers returned and announced that they had obtained a search warrant. When she asked to see the search warrant, they showed her a piece of paper, which she grabbed and stuffed into her dress. The police officers forcibly retrieved their "search warrant," which actually was a blank piece of paper.

Fruit of the Poisoned Tree Doctrine Extends the exclusionary rule to secondary evidence obtained indirectly in an unconstitutional search, established in *Silverthorne Lumber Co.* v. *United States* (1918) and in *Wolf* v. *Colorado* (1949).

At that point, the police proceeded to search Mapp's house without the benefit of search warrant, probable cause, or consent. They did not find the bombing suspect or the numbers evidence, but they did find a bag of obscene books and arrested her for possession of obscene materials. Mapp was convicted in state court for possession of obscene materials. Mapp felt that her Fourth Amendment rights had been violated, but when she appealed, the Ohio Supreme Court upheld the conviction. Mapp appealed to the U.S. Supreme Court, which ruled that local police officers were accountable to the same standard as in *Weeks* v. *United States*. Therefore, the evidence obtained illegally was inadmissible. Mapp's conviction was reversed.

Mapp v. *Ohio* was the first case in which the U.S. Supreme Court applied the exclusionary rule to state courts. All state courts were required to adopt rules of evidence, which declared that evidence would be inadmissible in criminal court if it was gathered without benefit of warrant, probable cause, or consent. Other decisions affecting the admissibility of evidence in state courts followed quickly and had sweeping effects on state criminal court procedures.

Today, the rules of evidence in state and federal criminal courts are shaped by numerous U.S. Supreme Court decisions. Furthermore, these rules continue to change as the Court modifies and sometimes even reverses the standard of what is admissible evidence. Police officers in all jurisdictions must adhere to these standards in gathering evidence and obtaining confessions or they will find that the evidence and confessions that they have gathered will be declared inadmissible at trial. The major actions regulated by the exclusionary rule include searches, confessions, and arrests.

▲ check your understanding **5.1 What are the rules of evidence? What landmark cases were involved in establishing the exclusionary rule at both the federal and state levels? How does the exclusionary rule influence police conduct? What three basic standards must be met for evidence to be admissible in court?**

Search and Seizure

▼ the main idea **5.2 The rules of evidence define legal search and seizure of places, automobiles, and persons and also define exceptions to the exclusionary rule.**

The rights of the accused are based on rights guaranteed by the U.S. Constitution, state constitutions, and legislation. Often, the court is called on to interpret the application

Why do these officers have to be mindful of the exclusionary rule? Are they conducting a legal search and seizure? What constitutional rights does the exclusionary rule protect? What is the difference between reasonable suspicion and probable cause as standards of proof in police action? Why does the exclusionary rule have the power to influence police conduct? What are some major exceptions to the exclusionary rule, and why were these exceptions made?

of these rights to specific actions of the police. Numerous changes in law, society, and technology and science have occurred since the drafting of the Constitution. Thus, the Court must often interpret the intent of the Constitution as it is applied to modern society. Inventions such as the telephone, automobile, and the Internet emerged over 100 years after the writing of the Constitution so there is no specific reference in the Constitution as to how these modern technologies affect the constitutional rights envisioned by the authors of the Constitution.

The courts establish guidelines to the police through case law that provides rulings declaring what actions violate constitutional rights. Evidence gathered in a manner that violates the constitutional rights of the accused cannot be used in court to prove the guilt of the defendant. Important Supreme Court rulings that provide such guidance to the police are called *landmark cases.* These landmark cases most commonly concern rights guaranteed by the First, Fourth, Fifth, and Sixth Amendments.

The **Fourth Amendment** states, "The right of the people to be secure in their persons, houses, papers, and effects, against unreasonable searches and seizures, shall not be violated, and no warrants shall issue, but upon probable cause. . . ." The Fourth Amendment does not guarantee absolute privacy in one's person, house, papers, and effects. Actually, the "right to privacy" is not guaranteed in the Constitution but is a right that is "inferred" from rights guaranteed by the various amendments. As such, there are numerous exceptions based on the right of government to regulate behavior and provide for the public good that allow government and criminal justice agencies to obtain what some may consider personal or private information.

For example, when Keith Emerich of Pennsylvania reported to his doctors who were treating him for an irregular heartbeat that he regularly drank over a six-pack of beer a day, his doctors reported this information to the Pennsylvania Department of Transportation as required by a state law. The law required doctors to report any physical or mental impairments that could compromise a patient's ability to drive safely. Emerich had no traffic convictions for over 20 years, but based on the information provided by his doctors, Emerich's driver's license was suspended. Emerich objected that the data he provided his medical doctor were private and confidential and should not have been reported to the commonwealth. However, the court, after considering the balance of medical privacy versus public safety, ruled that in this case, as in other similar cases, the concern for public safety outweighed the individual's right to privacy.

However, in 2004, when the Justice Department wanted Northwestern Memorial Hospital in Chicago to disclose records on abortions performed at the hospital, a federal appeals court rejected the demand. The Justice Department claimed that the abortion records were needed in an upcoming lawsuit to test the claims of doctors who maintained the Partial-Birth Abortion Ban Act would prevent them from performing medically necessary procedures. The federal appeals court rejected the Justice Department's claim, saying that access to such records would violate the privacy rights of women.

In some cases, the courts are required to decide what is a reasonable expectation of privacy. For example, when Lonnie Maurice Hill was arrested in 2003 for drug charges, he challenged the constitutionality of his arrest. Hill and a woman entered a convenience store's one-person unisex restroom. The store clerk called the police and reported this activity as suspicious behavior. When the police arrived, Hill and the woman refused to respond to the officer's request for them to open the bathroom door. When police opened the door they found marijuana and cocaine inside the restroom and charged Hill with drug-related charges. Hill appealed that he had an expectation of privacy in the restroom. At his defense, his lawyer raised the question whether a married couple or a parent and child or a disabled person and an assistant occupying a single-person bathroom would be suspicious behavior. Despite these arguments, the Eighth U.S. Circuit Court of Appeals rejected Hill's claim that his expectation of privacy in the public restroom made the drugs seized by the officer inadmissible as evidence.

At times, the Court must decide how new technology affects constitutionally protected rights, as in the case concerning event data recorders (EDRs). These devices are electronic monitoring systems in cars and trucks that track and record data, such as whether airbags deployed, if passengers wore seatbelts, and the speed of the vehicle. Event data recorders are installed in about 65 to 90 percent of 2004 and later vehicles and the National Highway Transportation Administration has proposed that it be mandatory for EDRs to be installed in all vehicles in 2007.

Typically, EDRs store the last five seconds of data. However, they can easily be programmed to store up to months of data. The data can be retrieved—much like the "black box" of an airplane—in the event of a crash to determine, among other things, the speed of the vehicle at the time of the crash. Also, the data are transmitted to such services as On-Star. Many drivers are not aware that their car is recording such data. Most states have no laws requiring that drivers be advised of this device. Data from EDRs have been used by law enforcement to obtain a number of convictions for vehicular homicide as police can prove the speed of the vehicle and whether the vehicle was accelerating or braking at the time of the accident. Concerned that the collection of such data violates the privacy rights of drivers, North Dakota has proposed legislation that would require that drivers be informed if their vehicles have EDRs installed and that would restrict access of police, insurance companies, and car manufacturers to such data. No doubt the courts will have to decide whether such technology violates the privacy of motorists and whether evidence gathered by EDRs can be used in obtaining criminal convictions.

Search Incident to Lawful Arrest

The Fourth Amendment requires that evidence must be obtained by police with the use of a valid **search warrant** issued by a judge or searches may be based on **probable cause.** Probable cause is the likelihood that there is a direct link between a suspect and a crime. Despite this seemingly limited authority to gather evidence by searches outlined in the Constitution, the courts have authorized a number of other circumstances under which the police can gather evidence without a warrant or probable cause.

The Supreme Court has granted that when the police make a lawful arrest, they are entitled to make a search of the person arrested without a search warrant. This is called **search incident to lawful arrest.** The question that arose was how extensive a search police can make under this justification. The police cannot extend their search to rooms not occupied by the person arrested and to areas beyond the person's reach, as a search incident to a lawful arrest is limited to the area within the immediate control of the person.[7] Otherwise, the evidence obtained is not admissible in criminal court. Evidence obtained from a search incident to lawful arrest can include containers found within the reach of the arrestee, firearms within reaching distance, or evidence under the car seat or couch cushion on which the person is sitting.

In 2004, the U.S. Supreme Court expanded the authority of police to make searches incident to lawful arrest when they ruled that police do not need a warrant to search a car when the person they have arrested was recently in the car. The Supreme Court's ruling permitted warrantless searches whenever the arrestee was a recent occupant and still in the vicinity of the car. The ruling will most likely result in further appeals, as the Court's ruling did not define "how recent is recent, or how close is close." Thus, it will be left up to future cases to determine the limits authorized by this decision.

Plain-View Searches

Evidence in the plain view of the police officer is admissible in criminal court (***Harris v. United States***).[8] This assumes that the police officer had the legal right to be where he or she was. If a police officer is invited into someone's home and that person was thoughtless enough to leave a pile of marijuana on the table that he or she was in the

search warrant Legal permission to conduct a search, signed by a judge.

probable cause Strong likelihood of a direct link between a suspect and a crime.

search incident to lawful arrest Right to search an arrestee without a warrant, established in *Chimel* v. *California* (1969).

process of cleaning and sorting, the Supreme Court has ruled that such evidence obtained in a plain-view search is admissible. However, the police officer cannot move objects to get a view of the evidence.[9] For example, if the marijuana on the table had been completely covered with a cloth, the police officer could not remove the cloth (without permission, a search warrant, or probable cause) to see what was there. Likewise, if a police officer were to enter a room and move electronic equipment to see the serial numbers to check against a list of stolen merchandise and found a match, such evidence would be inadmissible without permission, a search warrant, or probable cause.[10] However, the police do not have to act blind or stupid. In the language of the Court, "inadvertence is not necessary."[11] That is, the police are not required to be heedless or inattentive to their environment. A police officer who sees a cloth covering something on the table and smells marijuana may have probable cause to look under the cloth.

Whether evidence from a **plain-view search** is admissible can depend on even minor variations. For example, if a 6-foot-tall police officer is walking by a 5-foot-high fence and sees a marijuana plant growing on the other side on private property, the evidence is in plain view. If a 5′ 8″ police officer is walking by a 6-foot-high fence and stands on a ladder and sees a marijuana plant growing on the other side, the evidence is not in plain view. Similarly, if a police officer uses a flashlight to look into an automobile at night, the Supreme Court has ruled that the use of a flashlight does not violate the plain-view doctrine. However, if a police officer uses binoculars to view evidence, that may violate the plain-view doctrine.

Consent to Search

If a person gives permission for a search, any evidence discovered is admissible (***Florida* v. *Jimeno,*** 1973).[12] The person who gives the permission must have the authority to do so. For example, a landlord cannot give valid permission to search an apartment currently occupied by a tenant but can give permission once the tenant vacates the apartment. A motel owner cannot give permission to search a motel room rented to a guest but can give permission to search the room after the guest checks out. A parent can give permission to search the room of a legal dependent living in the same house but cannot give permission to search the room of a boarder living in a room rented in the house. The complexity of society has resulted in numerous rulings by the courts defining who has the authority to grant permission to search.

Search of Automobiles

As early as 1925, the Supreme Court addressed the question of the constitutionality of searches of automobiles without a search warrant. Recognizing that the mobility of automobiles adds a new dimension to searches, the Court established the Carroll Doctrine, based on ***Carroll* v. *United States*** (1925).[13] In the **Carroll Doctrine**, evidence obtained in the search of an automobile without a warrant is admissible in criminal court if (1) the police officer has probable cause to believe that a crime has occurred and (2) the circumstances are such that delay in searching the automobile would result in loss of the evidence. This rule requires that an officer must have probable cause to stop the car in the first place.[14] If an officer does not have the authority to stop the car in the first place, any evidence obtained in a search is not admissible.

In ***Illinois* v. *Caballes*** (2005, No. 03923) the Supreme Court extended the powers of the police to search vehicles by permitting a trained dog to sniff a car for drugs without the need for any particular reason to suspect the driver of a narcotics violation. Justice Stevens, arguing for the majority opinion of the Court, said, "A dog sniff conducted during a concededly lawful traffic stop that reveals no information other than the location of a substance that no individual has any right to possess does not violate the Fourth

plain-view search Right to gather evidence in plain sight without a warrant, established in *Harris* v. *United States* (1968) and redefined in *United States* v. *Irizarry* (1982), *Arizona* v. *Hicks* (1987), and *Horton* v. *California* (1990).

Carroll Doctrine Terms defining the admissibility of evidence obtained in a warrantless search of an automobile, established in *Carroll* v. *United States* (1925).

Amendment." The Court's opinion was that so long as the "search" by the dog does not unreasonably prolong the traffic stop and the police had the legal right to stop the vehicle, the police do not need "specific and articulable facts" suggesting drug activity to justify the use of the dog.

Closely related to the Carroll Doctrine is the search of a vehicle that has been lawfully impounded by the police. Any evidence obtained during an inventory of the contents of a lawfully impounded vehicle is admissible in criminal court.[15] For example, if the police arrest a driver for DUI (driving while under the influence of alcohol) and impound the vehicle, they can perform a thorough search of the vehicle, including any locked glove compartments or trunks. They also can remove any boxes, suitcases, or other items and search those items. The police may even force locks for the purpose of inventorying the contents of an automobile. The philosophy is that the police assume liability for the loss of anything of value in the vehicle when they impound it and, therefore, are authorized to inventory the entire vehicle and its contents to establish the presence and value of any contents. Also, locked containers in a vehicle might hide things that pose a danger to police or the public, such as a bomb hidden in a suitcase in the vehicle, in which case the police have a right and duty to determine such danger.

Search of Persons: The Pat-Down

The U.S. Supreme Court has appreciated the fact that the police operate in an environment that can be life threatening. Thus, the police are allowed to take certain reasonable precautions in dealing with the public. In the course of taking reasonable precautions, such as frisking or patting-down a detainee suspected of carrying a weapon, if the police find incriminating evidence, such evidence is admissible in criminal court. The doctrine governing the search of persons without probable cause but with reasonable suspicion is called the pat-down doctrine and has its origins in ***Terry* v. *Ohio*.**[16]

Police officers frequently approach or are approached by citizens to interact. At close range, a citizen's possession of a weapon could be deadly to the officer. In some contexts, the police may be able to determine by simple visual inspection if a citizen is carrying a concealed weapon, but outer clothing often makes it impossible to tell. In such cases, officers are authorized to conduct a limited pat-down search of outer clothing when they have a reasonable concern that the citizen is armed. Probable cause is not required under these circumstances.

The **pat-down search** may be conducted solely to ensure the safety of the officer.[17] If in the course of a pat-down, the police officer feels an object that may be a weapon, the officer legally can reach into the pocket or clothing to further explore the nature of the object. If the officer still believes that the object may be a weapon, he or she may remove the object and examine it. If it is a weapon, and the person is not authorized to carry it, the weapon is admissible as evidence. However, if the officer feels an object that clearly is not a weapon but may be illegal, such as a bag of narcotics, the officer may not reach into the pocket to explore the nature of the object or remove it for inspection. An object acquired in an illegal pat-down search is not admissible as evidence in a court of law, unless it is immediately apparent by touching the object that it is contraband.

In 2004, the Supreme Court significantly altered the scope of the search that the police may conduct justified by the 1968 *Terry* v. *Ohio* case. The Supreme Court upheld the conviction of Larry D. Hiibel of Nevada (*Hiibel* v. *Sixth Judicial District Court*, No. 03-5554) for refusing to give a deputy sheriff his name. Although the offense was a misdemeanor, the court's ruling upheld the concept that in a routine stop of a citizen, the police have the authority to demand that the citizen answer their questions. Previously, it was understood that the police had the power to stop citizens under the authority of *Terry* v. *Ohio* but that the citizens were under no obligation to answer the police officer's

pat-down search Right to search a person for a concealed weapon on the basis of reasonable suspicion, established in *Terry* v. *Ohio* (1968).

diversity in the system

Racial Profiling

Racial profiling is the term used to describe the stopping of persons of color when the stop is based primarily on the fact that they are persons of color rather than reasonable suspicion or probable cause. For example, in 1992, an elderly woman visiting Oneonta, New York, told the police that she had been attacked by a burglar she could only vaguely describe as a black man. The police responded with a vast dragnet that lasted several days and caught up almost all the black men in Oneonta, an overwhelmingly white college town. They got a list of all black men enrolled at the State University of New York College at Oneonta and questioned many of them.[18] However, minority citizens of Oneonta claimed that the police approached black men solely because of their race and that black men were targets of the investigation until they were eliminated as suspects rather than questioning black suspects based on reasonable suspicion or probable cause.

The police may have felt they were justified in stopping and questioning black males based on the victim's description, but critics claim that the true bases of the stops—racial profiling—was revealed in that the police did not limit their stops to black males but also stopped and interrogated black females. In 2005, the New York state court, in response to a 13-year-old lawsuit filed by the black female stopped, ruled that the police violated her civil rights during the sweep in Oneonta.

Racial profiling has become more of a concern regarding police stops of minority motorists. The practice is also known as DWB—"driving while black" or, in the case of Hispanics, "driving while brown." Racial profiling of motorists captured national attention in 1998 when New Jersey state troopers became the focus of an intense investigation into abusive traffic stops based on racial profiling. Two state troopers pulled over three black men and one Hispanic and opened fire on the unarmed men. It is alleged that the troopers singled out the men simply because of their race. However, the troopers claimed that the vehicle was speeding and that they began shooting at the occupants of the van when the driver tried to back up over them with the vehicle. The minority community was angered when a judge dismissed criminal charges against the two troopers.

Despite denials that New Jersey state troopers practiced racial profiling, a federal investigation revealed that not only was racial profiling tolerated, but troopers were instructed "to look for Colombian males, Hispanic males, Hispanic and black males together, and a Hispanic male and female posing as a couple." Troopers also were instructed "to focus on minorities when scanning the roadways as possible drug traffickers."

figure 5.1

Racial Differences in Police Searches

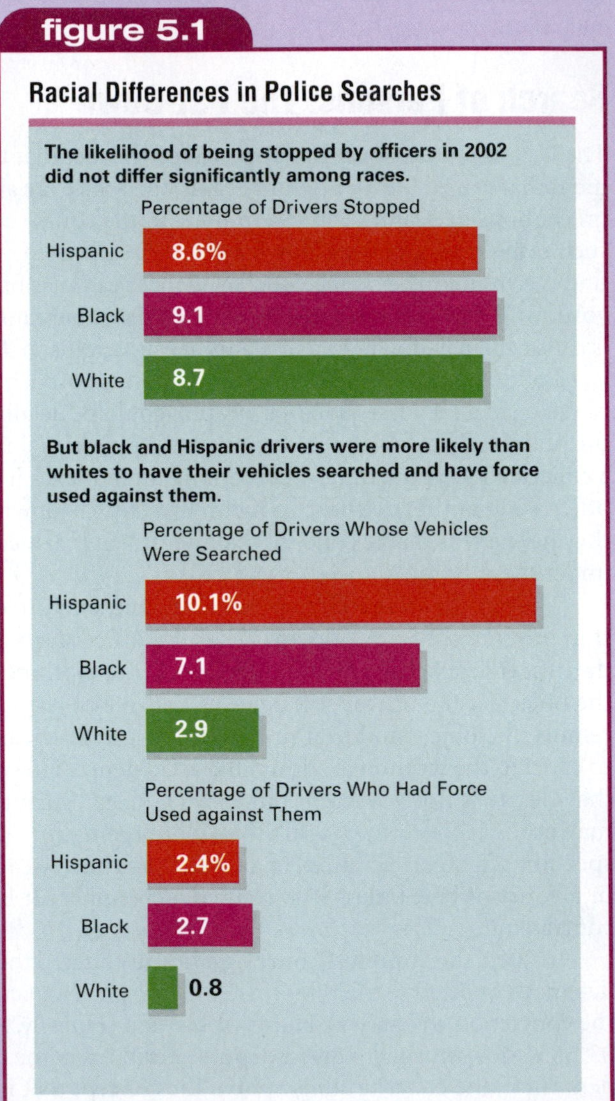
The likelihood of being stopped by officers in 2002 did not differ significantly among races.
Percentage of Drivers Stopped
Hispanic 8.6%
Black 9.1
White 8.7
But black and Hispanic drivers were more likely than whites to have their vehicles searched and have force used against them.
Percentage of Drivers Whose Vehicles Were Searched
Hispanic 10.1%
Black 7.1
White 2.9
Percentage of Drivers Who Had Force Used against Them
Hispanic 2.4%
Black 2.7
White 0.8

Source: Justice Department.

The firestorm caused by the bitter charges and countercharges of racial profiling affected the criminal justice system. In April 1999, North Carolina passed a law requiring the police to record the race, age, and gender of every motorist stopped. Similar laws were passed by other states. In June 1999, President Clinton ordered federal police agencies to gather racial statistics on people they target for traffic stops, border inspections, and other routine searches. In 1999, the American Civil Liberties Union established a national DWB hotline to gather complaints on police racism. In 2000, nearly every state undertook a study to determine the extent of racial profiling by police.

A 2002–2003 Texas survey examined several million traffic stops by 1,060 police and sheriff's departments across Texas and found that about two of every three agencies searched blacks and Hispanics at higher rates than those for non-Hispanic whites. Furthermore, blacks and Hispanics were disproportionately subjected to consent searches without warrants or probable cause more often than non-Hispanic whites. The study found that the higher rates of searches for blacks and Hispanics did not translate into a higher rate of seizing drugs or other contraband.

In 2005, the Bureau of Justice Statistics published a Department of Justice report based on interviews with 80,000 people in 2002. As illustrated in Figure 6.1 the study found that white, black, and Hispanic drivers nationwide were stopped by the police that year at about the same rate, about 9 percent. However, Hispanic and black drivers were subjected to vehicle searches and the use of force or the threat of force more often than whites. Also, Hispanics were more likely to receive a ticket as opposed to a warning.

Following September 11, 2001, persons who appear to be of Middle-Eastern descent have complained that they have been targeted by police based on their ethnicity. Young Middle-Eastern–looking men report that they are subjected to be stopped and questioned by the police in nearly every aspect of their lives, including while driving, at airports, at public sporting events, at border crossings, and other events.

Do you think racial profiling is a significant problem in policing? If so, do you think it is widespread or a concern only to a small number of law enforcement agencies? Do you think there is a trend by law enforcement to stop Middle-Eastern–looking males based on racial profiling? What policies, laws, and practices would discourage racial profiling?

questions. The Court ruled that that there was no violation of the Fifth Amendment for citizens to answer a request to disclose their name and such information does not incriminate the citizen in violation of the Fifth Amendment. The ruling may have been influenced by the concern that if the Supreme Court did not uphold this authority, a ruling the other way would have protected terrorists and encouraged people to refuse to cooperate with police.

Read about the history, current news, and debate on the issue of racial profiling at www.aclu.org/profiling/.

Drug smuggling and other drug laws have resulted in the interesting situation in which people swallow drugs wrapped in some type of protective covering or conceal drugs in personal body cavities in an effort to prevent their detection by the police. Even if the police have probable cause to believe that someone has swallowed illegal drugs in an effort to conceal them, the Court has been fairly consistent in requiring a search warrant to retrieve drugs by medical procedures such as pumping the stomach or conducting invasive searches of the body.[19]

check your understanding 5.2 What does the Fourth Amendment to the Constitution say about search and seizure? In what circumstances can a legal search be conducted, and in what ways are those circumstances open to interpretation? When do searches violate civil rights?

Other Exceptions to the Warrant Requirement

the main idea 5.3 Search and seizure without probable cause, a warrant, or consent is permitted in some circumstances, especially when there is clear and present danger or when public safety is at stake.

Since the 1960s, the U.S. Supreme Court has restricted the situations in which the police may conduct a search without a warrant. However, the Court has continued to recognize that there are certain circumstances that may justify a warrantless search. The two most common exceptions to the requirements for a search warrant are public safety and good faith.

The Public Safety Exception

Certain situations require immediate action by the police. If the police are chasing a person who has just committed a crime using a firearm and catch the person but fail to find the firearm on him or her, the Court has ruled that the police have the right to perform a search without a warrant in places where the person may have discarded the firearm. The justification for this exception is the argument that if the search is not performed immediately, the presence of the weapon in the community may pose a serious threat to public safety.[20] For example, if a person committed armed robbery and fled from the police into a mall, but did not have the firearm when caught, the police would be justified in immediately searching the stores in the mall for the weapon. There is the danger that a citizen, especially a juvenile, might find the weapon and accidentally harm someone by discharging it. The firearm, if found by police in a warrantless search, would be admissible as evidence.

Another example of the **public safety exception** is the acceptance of searches without probable cause or warrant requirement of airline passengers for the public good. The justification for this kind of search is that it is necessary for public safety and that passengers implicitly consent to be searched in exchange for the right to board an airplane. Law enforcement officers extended this philosophy to bus passengers. In an effort to detect drug smugglers who use public transportation to move illegal drugs from Florida to the Northeast, law enforcement officers obtained permission from bus companies to search the possessions and baggage of bus passengers. Arguing that they had the permission of the operating company, similar to permission given by the airline industry to search air passengers, officers began routine searches of bus passengers, a practice known as "working the buses." Evidence seized in these searches could legally justify an arrest and be used as evidence in court.[21]

In 2005, the police extended the public safety exception to justify random searches of subway passengers for explosives in response to perceived terrorist threats against America's mass transit system following terrorist attacks on London's bus and subway system. The American Civil Liberties Union protested the random searches as a violation of the Fourth Amendment. The ACLU expressed concern that if random searches of subway passengers was permitted under the public safety exception, police could extend the scope of the searches to include virtually any public space. The court did not uphold the ACLU's protests.

Also, U.S. Customs officials have been granted greater leeway by the Supreme Court under the public safety exception to conduct warrantless searches. Customs and border agents can conduct extensive searches of persons and property at border checkpoints and crossings without a warrant or probable cause. In fact, customs agents do not even need to justify their search based on reasonable suspicion. The courts have granted ex-

public safety exception Right to search without probable cause for the public good.

criminal justice in the media

Stun Guns

Concern over lawsuits related to the use of deadly force has resulted in the police seeking nonlethal weapons. The most popular nonlethal weapon of choice of police is the so-called stun gun. The device fires a dart connected to a thin wire and delivers an electric shock of 50,000 volts to the victim. The electric shock causes the person to collapse and become temporarily immobilized. The stun gun has become popular with police, as over 5,000 police departments have authorized police officers to carry the weapon. It is estimated that over 100,000 police officers carry these weapons.

The most popular manufacturer of electric stun guns is Taser International. The company claims that test data indicate that the weapon is safe when used as directed. However, public and police concerns have been raised by the fact that since 2000, over 100 people have died after being shocked. Most of these deaths have been blamed on other causes, such as drug overdose, rather than the shock administered by the Taser stun gun. Although few of these deaths have been directly attributed to the electric shock administered by the stun gun, the public and the police have called for further testing and for review of the training and practices related to this weapon.

However, there is public opposition to the use of stun guns. Opposition to the use of stun guns can be attributed to some degree to media coverage of sensational cases in which the person dies or the stun gun is used on juveniles. There are few nationwide standards related to training, policy, and use of the Taser stun gun. Thus, in some police departments, Tasers can be used in situations where the officer would not be authorized to use deadly force, and Tasers can be used against juveniles. Juveniles as young as 6 years old have been shocked with stun guns. Some juveniles have died following such use. Again, these deaths have been attributed to other causes.

Many have expressed concern over the use of Tasers. The Justice Department has called for the study of the risks of Tasers, human rights groups have criticized the use of Tasers, scientists have challenged the data related to the safety of their use (most of the data have come from studies sponsored by Taser International), and school boards have protested the use of Tasers on children. Despite these challenges, Tasers remain popular alternatives to firearms. Their use has been upheld by the courts as an alternative to lethal or deadly force.

Under what circumstances should police be allowed to use Tasers? Should Tasers be restricted to use only when the use of deadly force would be authorized? Should it be prohibited to use Tasers against juveniles? If so, at what age and under what circumstances would the use of Tasers be prohibited? Do you think there is a need for greater oversight and training in the use of Tasers?

tensive search powers that allow agents to conduct searches of persons, to use sophisticated machines to scan for contraband, and to search any luggage or vehicle of the person. Agents have extensive latitude in conducting searches of vehicles without a warrant or probable cause at border checkpoints and crossings, including the authority to disassemble the vehicle to search for hidden contraband. New search procedures aimed at preventing terrorist attacks even allow agents to x-ray vehicles. Such searches do not require reasonable suspicion, probable cause, or a search warrant. Yet, evidence found of illegal activity or contraband such as drugs is admissible in criminal court.[22]

good faith exception Admissibility of evidence obtained in an illegal search when the police are found to have acted in good faith on the belief that their search was legal, established in *United States* v. *Leon* (1984) and *Massachusetts* v. *Sheppard* (1984) in contradiction to an earlier ruling in *Illinois* v. *Gates* (1982).

The Good Faith Exception

Another common exception to the requirement of having a warrant or probable cause to conduct a legal search is when the police act in good faith. In most cases, the **good faith exception** applies when there is some type of clerical error resulting in the police executing what they think is a valid search warrant but in reality it is not. A common example would be when the police have probable cause to obtain a valid search warrant but there is clerical error and the address of the premises to be searched is entered incorrectly in the search warrant document. Acting in good faith that they have a valid warrant, the police search the location described in the search warrant. What happens, if in the course of this mistaken search the police find evidence of criminal activity such as illegal drugs? Since the search was not authorized by the warrant and the police had no probable cause to perform the search of the "innocent" party, is the evidence discovered at the wrong premise admissible in criminal court? Initially, the court did not support the good faith exception, taking the position that good faith by the police does not override the violation of the valid search warrant requirement.[23] However, the court later reversed itself and allowed evidence obtained in good faith but without a valid search warrant to be admitted in evidence.[24] This principle may be expressed as the exclusionary rule applying only in cases in which there is police misconduct involved.

Wiretaps and the Issue of Privacy

Another area affected by the Fourth Amendment in which the Supreme Court has reversed itself is the issue of obtaining evidence by **wiretapping**. At the time the U.S. Constitution was drafted and the rights of citizens were enumerated in the Bill of Rights, there obviously was no mention of the right of privacy of one's telephone communications or messages sent by computer or e-mail. A hundred years after the drafting of the Constitution, the telephone was invented and law enforcement officers begin listening in on private telephone conversations between bootleggers. Using the information obtained by listening to these conversations, the police were able to make arrests and win convictions. In one case, the bootleggers appealed their conviction, and in 1928, the Supreme Court heard its first case in the area of electronic communications (***Olmstead* v. *United States,*** 1928).[25]

Initially, the Court ruled that the telephone lines and public telephone booths were not an extension of the defendant's home and were therefore not protected by the constitutional guarantee of privacy. Thirty-nine years later, the ruling in *Olmstead* was reversed, and it was declared that electronic communication was indeed private communication and protected as a constitutional right (***Katz* v. *United States,*** 1967).[26] Violating this privacy without consent, probable cause, or a warrant constituted illegal search and seizure.

The issue of privacy in relation to electronic communications has gone beyond court-mandated rules of evidence, requiring new legislation. Major pieces of legislation addressing electronic communications privacy are the **Electronic Communications Privacy Act of 1986,** the **Communications Assistance for Law Enforcement Act of 1994,** the **Telecommunications Act of 1996,** and the **USA Patriot Act.** These laws provide specific details governing the collection of evidence by wiretaps and other means and the definition of what electronically transmitted information is protected by the expectation of privacy.

Except in cases of suspected terrorism, law enforcement officers generally must satisfy stringent requirements before they can obtain information transmitted electronically or stored in computer databanks, such as stored e-mail messages. If law enforcement officers fail to follow the provision of the law, not only is the evidence not admissible in court, but for some violations, the officer may be subject to fines or incarceration.

Legislation passed after September 11, 2001, has had a major impact on the powers of the police to conduct searches, especially electronic searches. Post-September 11 legislation has made it easier for federal law enforcement to monitor e-mails and Internet-based phone calls. New Federal Communications Commission rules aimed at making it easier for police to monitor Internet communications have given police greater access to such communications with less and less court oversight.

Concern over the use of cell phones by terrorists to plan and to coordinate attacks has resulted in new rules being applied to cell phone surveillance. Permission to wiretap multiple communication devices, such as one's home phone and cellular phone, may now be given with a single wiretap authorization.

wiretapping A form of search and seizure in which citizens' rights to privacy on the telephone are protected by the Fourth Amendment, first established in *Olmstead* v. *United States* (1928) and extended to e-mail in *Katz* v. *United States* (1967).

The USA Patriot Act modified existing legislation giving greater powers to police and FBI to conduct electronic surveillance. What is the danger, if any, in granting too much power to law enforcement or too little oversight regarding electronic surveillance?

Although concerns about terrorism have resulted in legislation giving the police more power to monitor electronic communications, such concerns have not given police unlimited powers. For example, depending on a wireless phone's capabilities, carriers can determine either precise or rough locations of users when they make or receive calls. Emergency operators can use this feature to locate 9-1-1 calls placed by cell phone users much the same way the 9-1-1 system identifies the location of calls made by non-cell phones. In 2005, when the Federal Bureau of Investigation wanted wireless carriers to continuously reveal the location of a suspect's cell phone as a part of an ongoing investigation, federal judges in Texas and New York denied the FBI's request. Legislation provided that the FBI could, however, request information from wireless carriers such as logs of numbers a cell phone user called and received. To request such information, the FBI only had to show that the information was relevant to an ongoing investigation.

But, when the FBI tried to obtain tracking information using the same standard of proof, they were denied this right. In 2003, the court established that police cannot use a Global Positioning System (GPS) tracker to track a suspect's vehicle without a warrant. Thus, when the FBI requested information that was similar to using the cell phone as a GPS device, the question that arose was, Would such use require a warrant similar to that required for GPS devices? Although federal courts in New York and Texas have denied FBI requests for tracking by wireless carriers, other courts have permitted such tracking. Until a case involving this issue is heard by the U.S. Supreme Court or until legislation is passed that clearly prohibits or denies such tracking without a warrant, the question as to whether probable cause or a warrant is required will be disputed.

Another search power that has been expanded by post-September 11 legislation is the use of national security letters by the Federal Bureau of Investigation. National security letters are a form of administrative subpoena used by the FBI to obtain normally private records such as phone and bank transactions as well as Internet subscriber data. National security letters do not require approval by the courts and there is a low standard of proof and oversight by the Justice Department regarding their use. Legislation provides that those who provide information obtained by a national security letter cannot reveal this fact to the person whose information they provided to the FBI or to the public. As a result of this secrecy, some are concerned that the FBI could or may have abused national security letters as a way to avoid judicial oversight of the public's right to privacy and Fifth Amendment rights. Investigations by the *Washington Post* revealed that since September 11, 2001, the FBI has issued about 30,000 national security letters a year.[27] The investigation by the *Washington Post* indicated that between 2002 and 2004 there were at least 13 cases of violations of the use of national security letters serious enough that the FBI itself determined that they must be reported to an executive branch agency called the Intelligence Oversight Board.[28] The revelation of the extensive use of national security letters has resulted in congressional examination of the use of national security letters and the legislation authorizing their use.

Fleeing Felon and Deadly Force

Public safety is also at the crux of rulings on deadly force used at the discretion of police. Have you seen old movies in which the police shout to a fleeing criminal, "Stop or I'll shoot!"? When the criminal fails to stop, the police either fire warning shots or take aim at the felon. Prior to 1985, shooting at fleeing suspects who refused to stop as commanded was a common and legal police practice involving the use of **deadly force**.

Many police departments had standard operating procedures detailing the circumstances under which an officer was justified in firing warning shots or using deadly force. Some departments allowed officers to use deadly force against fleeing people who were only "suspected" of committing crimes, and some jurisdictions did not differentiate between misdemeanors or felonies when using deadly force against a fleeing suspect. This practice was known as the fleeing suspect or **fleeing felon doctrine**. The police justified this practice on the basis of public safety. They argued that a suspect allowed to escape could be a potential danger to the community. If the person were suspected of having committed murder, they reasoned, a failure to apprehend might create an undue risk for the public—a justification for use of deadly force.

Read an article advising law enforcement officers on how to conduct effective search and seizure at www.fsu.edu/~crimdo/fagin.html.

In ***Tennessee* v. *Garner*** (1985), the Supreme Court disagreed with that reasoning.[29] Attorneys representing Garner, who had been slain by a police officer in pursuit when Garner refused to stop, made the argument that the officer's use of deadly force was a form of search and seizure for which the officer lacked probable cause or a warrant. The Court accepted the validity of the argument and ruled that the search and seizure by deadly force against a fleeing suspect was a violation of the person's constitutional rights. The ruling in *Tennessee* v. *Garner* immediately superceded the rules of all police departments and the laws of the states that had permitted the practice. All law enforcement officers (local, state, and federal) were immediately prohibited from using deadly force as a means to stop a fleeing suspect. If the ruling was ignored, the officer and department could be held liable in a lawsuit for violation of the person's constitutional rights.

This ruling caused great confusion for a period of time as law enforcement officials and state legislators tried to determine the limits of the prohibition.[30] For example, if a person committed murders in the presence of a police officer and then threw down his or her weapon and fled from the scene, and if there were no other way to stop the person from escaping, could the officer use deadly force? The argument for the use of deadly force would be based on the potential threat an escaped murderer poses to a community. The argument against the use of deadly force would be based on the fact that after the person threw down his or her weapon, that person was no longer an immediate threat to the officer or the public, such that the use of deadly force was an unreasonable violation of his or her constitutional rights. If deadly force were used and the person died, he or she would be deprived the right to a trial by jury for the alleged criminal conduct.

Although there are legitimate arguments to support both the prohibition and sanction of the use of deadly force in this case, the present legal position is that when there is a **clear and present danger** to the public posed by the escape of the person, deadly force may be justifiable.[31] In the lack of a clear and present danger, the use of deadly force to apprehend a fleeing suspect or criminal is a violation of the person's constitutional rights.

deadly force Police power to incapacitate or kill in the line of duty.

fleeing felon doctrine Police practice of using deadly force against a fleeing suspect, made illegal in *Tennessee* v. *Garner* (1985), except when there is clear and present danger to the public.

clear and present danger Condition relating to public safety that may justify police use of deadly force against a fleeing suspect.

High-speed vehicular pursuits of fleeing persons have posed a difficult question as to the right of police to engage in such pursuits. A number of such high-speed pursuits have resulted in death or bodily harm to the person being pursued or to innocent parties. Lawsuits have been filed asking the courts to prohibit or at least restrict high-speed vehicle pursuits by the police, but in general the courts have upheld the right of the police to pursue fleeing persons even when there is no reasonable suspicion or probable cause that the person has committed a crime other than a traffic violation. However, police departments have adopted rules and guidelines aimed at reducing deaths and injuries caused by such pursuits by regulating when officers can engage in such pursuits and when high-speed pursuits should be discontinued.

▲ check your understanding **5.3 In what specific circumstances can the exclusionary rule be ignored? How do exceptions to the exclusionary rule impact police pursuits and wiretapping? How do these exceptions highlight conflicts between privacy and security in law enforcement?**

Interrogations and Confessions

▼ the main idea **5.4 In defining admissible testimony, rules of evidence also reflect case law relating to the Fifth Amendment.**

In addition to obtaining evidence through search and seizure, procedural laws affecting police conduct also govern obtaining testimony through interrogations and confessions. The confession is an effective method of convincing a jury that the defendant has committed the crime of which he or she has been accused. In medieval England, confessions were routinely obtained by torture. The **Star Chamber** was an English court interrogation room where confessions were forced through the use of pain. Contemporary British and American courts do not allow the use of torture or pain to obtain a confession. In the United States, the **Fifth Amendment** in the Bill of Rights guarantees citizens the right to avoid **self-incrimination.** (The complete wording of the Fifth Amendment can be found in Figure 5.2.)

Use of Physical Punishment and Pain

Law enforcement practices traditionally have not been conducive to protecting citizens' Fifth Amendment rights. The U.S. Supreme Court first addressed the admissibility of confessions obtained by the use of force in ***Brown* v. *Mississippi*** (1936).[32] The case illustrates the need for court intervention in that the deputy sheriff's officer accused of obtaining a confession from Brown by whipping him did not deny the charge. His defense was that the whipping was "not too much for a Negro; not as much as I would have done it if it were left to me."[33] In *Brown* v. *Mississippi,* the court ruled that confessions obtained by force were tainted.

The court has addressed various other abuses of the Fifth Amendment in landmark cases. In ***Ashcraft* v. *Tennessee,*** it was ruled that confessions obtained by the use of around-the-clock interrogation were inadmissible.[34] Although Ashcraft was not physically beaten, he was interrogated for 36 hours by police officers, an ordeal known as receiving "the third degree." The court ruled that under the circumstances, the confession given by Ashcraft was not voluntary and violated his Fifth Amendment rights.

self-incrimination Involuntary confession or forced testimony of the accused, prohibited by the Fifth Amendment, as in the inadmissibility of evidence obtained by force in *Brown* v. *Mississippi* (1936) and extended in *Ashcraft* v. *Tennessee* (1944) and *Leyra* v. *Denno* (1954).

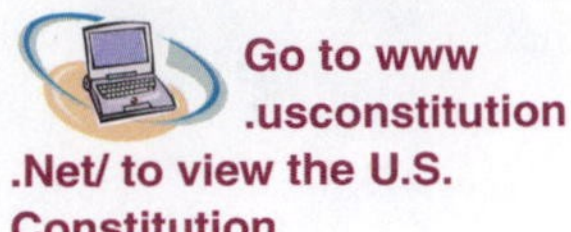

Go to www.usconstitution.Net/ to view the U.S. Constitution.

figure 5.2

The Fourth and Fifth Amendments

Amendment IV
The right of the people to be secure in their persons, houses, papers, and effects, against unreasonable searches and seizures, shall not be violated, and no warrants shall issue, but upon probable cause, supported by Oath of affirmation, and particularly describing the place to be searched, and the persons or things to be seized.

Amendment V
No person shall be held to answer for a capital, or otherwise infamous crime, unless on a presentment or indictment of a Grand Jury, except in cases arising in the land or naval forces, or in the Militia, when in actual service in time of War or public danger; nor shall any person be subject for the same offence to be twice put in jeopardy of life or limb; nor shall be compelled in any criminal case to be a witness against himself, nor be deprived of life, liberty, or property, without due process of law; nor shall private property be taken for public use, without just compensation.

Recent concerns over alleged abuse of terrorist suspects to obtain confessions have been raised in U.S. courts. One of the more common situations is when accused terrorists being tried in U.S. courts claim that their confession was obtained by the use of torture when they were captured outside the United States or that they were transported by the government outside the United States for interrogation using torture to obtain a confession. For example, Ahmed Omar Abu Ali was tried in a Virginia federal court on charges that he was a member of al Qaeda and was plotting to assassinate President Bush. Abu Ali's lawyers wanted their client's confession ruled inadmissible, as Abu Ali claimed that the confession was obtained by the use of torture. He claimed he was arrested in Medina in June 2003 and gave a false confession to stop the torture. Also, he later gave a confession to the FBI, but that confession was ruled invalid because the FBI disregarded Abu Ali's request for an attorney. Therefore, when he was tried in a U.S. federal court, the prosecution relied on the confession he gave in Medina, which Abu Ali claims was obtained by torture. In this particular case the judge ruled that there was insufficient evidence to establish that the confession was obtained through torture and allowed it as evidence. However, most likely there will be more allegations similar to this as more persons are tried for terrorism under similar circumstances and the courts will have to give consideration to what evidence is necessary to establish that a confession was obtained by the use of torture and whether such a confession is admissible.

Lying to the Suspect

Court rulings have not clearly prohibited police from obtaining a confession by lying to the suspect.[35] For example, confessions have been admitted even when obtained by police falsely telling one suspect that his partner in crime had confessed and named him as the "trigger man." Also, confessions have been admitted when obtained by placing a police officer dressed in prisoner clothing in the same cell as the suspect. On the other hand, a confession was prohibited as evidence when the police knowingly lied to a suspect by telling him that an attorney was not available when the suspect attempted to exercise his right to talk with an attorney. Confessions also have been prohibited when obtained through the use of psychiatrists pretending to be medical doctors supposedly helping the accused. In ***Leyra* v. *Denno*** in 1954, the police used a psychiatrist to obtain a confession from the suspect, who thought he was receiving treatment for a medical condition. The psychiatrist persuaded the suspect that he would feel better if he confessed to his crime. The court ruled that such deception was beyond the acceptable limits of professional police conduct and that the confession obtained was inadmissible.[36]

If, in obtaining a confession, the court rules that police conduct is outside the acceptable limits, even if the police are successful in obtaining a confession, the confession will not be allowed to be used in court. If it is used and the defendant is convicted on the evidence of the confession, the conviction can be overturned. For example, in April 2005, a federal judge threw out the prison sentence imposed on Vincent "The Animal" Ferrara, a Mafia captain who pleaded guilty to a 1985 murder. The judge concluded that in order to force a confession, prosecutors withheld key evidence that would have helped exonerate Ferrara of the murder. Ferrara claimed that although he was innocent of ordering the killing, he pleaded guilty in order to secure a lighter sentence for fear that he would receive a life sentence if found guilty by a jury.

Thus, although the government may engage in certain deceptions to obtain a confession, there are limits as to how much information law enforcement can withhold or the type of deceptions prosecutors may attempt in order to obtain a confession. Figure 5.3 lists the standards for an admissible confession. Basically, to be admissible, a confession must be given knowingly, must be voluntary, and cannot be obtained as a result of threat or pain, and the suspect must be informed of his or her rights.

For example, an embarrassing moment for the Federal Bureau of Investigation clearly illustrates the concept that a confession must be given knowingly. During the 1996 Olympic Games in Atlanta, Georgia, the FBI attempted to obtain a confession by deception from Centennial Park bombing suspect, Richard Jewell. Agents contacted Jewell and asked him to participate in a training video they were making in which Jewell was to play the part of the suspect. The agent would play the part of the interrogating officer and would advise him of his rights, which Jewell would waive. On the training video he would consent to the questioning.

The intent of the FBI was to use this consent obtained in the training video as a real waiver and interrogate Jewell on camera. Although it could be argued that Jewell voluntarily waived his right against self-incrimination, and although he was indeed informed of his rights, because of the trickery any confession he gave could not be said to have been given knowingly. The suspect thought he was only pretending to waive his

figure 5.3

Standards for an Admissible Confession

- The confession must be given knowingly and not as a consequence of lies or deception.
- The suspect must be informed of his or her rights.
- The confession must be voluntary.
- Confessions may not be obtained through threats, such as
    - threatening to turn an illegal foreign alien over to immigration authorities for deportation;
    - threatening to report a mother to child protective services for child abuse to have her children taken away from her;
    - threatening to report suspects to a welfare agency for the purpose of having their welfare benefits suspended.
- Confessions may not be obtained through use of pain or through constructive force, such as beating up one suspect in front of another and telling the second suspect that he or she is next if a confession is not forthcoming.

rights for the purpose of making a training video. Furthermore, an embarrassed FBI eventually publicly admitted there was a lack of evidence that Jewell had anything to do with the bombing.[37]

In 1996, the FBI attempted to trick Richard Jewell into falsely confessing to a crime he did not commit. Because the rules for lawful interrogation had not been observed, Jewell's confession would not have been admissible. Why are there rules governing police procedures in interrogations and confessions? What constitutional rights do these rules protect?

Police Lineups

A question related to the Fifth Amendment rights of suspects concerns **police lineups**, in which a victim is given an opportunity to identify a criminal from among a number of suspects. What are a suspect's rights in a lineup? Landmark cases have addressed the following questions:

- Can the police compel a suspect to appear in a lineup?
- Can the police compel a suspect to submit handwriting samples or voice samples?
- What constitutes a "fair" lineup?
- At the scene of a crime, can the police drive a witness by a suspect to see if the witness can identify the person as someone who participated in the crime?
- Does the suspect have the right to have his or her attorney present during a lineup?

Rulings have suggested that suspects' guarantees against self-incrimination apply in police lineups, but not to the degree that they apply in police interrogations. Law enforcement officers need to perform certain investigative tasks essential to gathering information about a crime. So long as the police act in a professional and fair manner, they have greater latitude than in interrogations.[38] For example, police officers can drive a witness by a suspect to see if the witness can identify the person as someone who participated in the crime, and this can be done without informing the suspect or obtaining the suspect's consent. Suspects can be required to participate in a lineup without their consent and can be required to give a handwriting or voice sample.[39]

Lineups must be fair, however, and suspects have the right to have an attorney present. A fair lineup is defined as one that contains suspects who are similar and match the description given by the witness. Fair lineups contain actual suspects and not police personnel masquerading as suspects.[40]

The Right to an Attorney

Read an essay on interrogations and confessions from the perspective of law enforcement at www.courttv.com/confessions/bratton_essay.html.

Because of concern that the rights of the suspect are protected against self-incrimination, the court has required that a suspect is entitled to have an attorney present when he or she is interrogated by the police, as well as in court. The right to have the benefit of an attorney when accused of criminal charges was established in the landmark case of ***Gideon* v. *Wainwright*** (1963).[41] The details of the case are striking, as they illustrate the influence that a single case concerning a relatively obscure defendant can have on the entire criminal justice system.

Gideon was convicted of burglary and sentenced to an extended prison term under the habitual offender act. Gideon did not have the funds to hire an attorney to represent him in court, and the state refused to grant him one free of charge. Left to defend himself, Gideon apparently did not do very well against the trained and experienced state prosecutors, and he was convicted of the crime. While in prison, Gideon sent a handwritten letter to the Supreme Count in which he protested the unfairness of his conviction. He argued it was unfair for him to have to defend himself, without the benefit of counsel, in a court of law against the resources of the state.

After due consideration, the Court agreed with Gideon's position and issued an opinion that he was entitled to a new trial and that at this trial he was entitled to be represented by an attorney. If he could not afford an attorney, the state would have to provide him one free of charge. Gideon was found not guilty in his retrial. Gideon's case established the practice of **indigent defense**. If a person cannot afford an attorney, it is the duty of the state to provide legal counsel.

police lineups Opportunities for victims to identify a criminal from among a number of suspects.

indigent defense Right to have an attorney provided free of charge by the state if a defendant cannot afford one, established in *Gideon* v. *Wainwright* (1963) and extended in *Argersinger* v. *Hamlin* (1972), *In re Gault* (1967), and *Escobedo* v. *Illinois* (1964).

Once this right was established, it was extended beyond the courtroom. In ***Argersinger* v. *Hamlin*** (1972), the right to an attorney was extended to include anyone facing a potential sentence of imprisonment, not just felony charges.[42] It was extended to juveniles accused of crimes in ***In re Gault*** (1967).[43] In ***Escobedo* v. *Illinois*** (1964), the right to an attorney was extended to include the right to have an attorney present during police interrogation.[44]

Interrogations and the War on Terrorism

Civil rights advocates argue that fear of terrorism may endanger constitutional rights granted under the Fourth Amendment concerning search and seizure protections. The American Civil Liberties Union argues that fear of terrorism has resulted in changes in the fundamental constitutional rules governing searches by the police.[45] The ACLU expresses the concern that actions taken to protect the public from terrorism may do so but may also violate constitutional rights. For example, following the July 2005 London subway bombings, police in U.S. cities began random inspections of bags, backpacks, and packages of subway riders. Citizens who refuse to allow the warrantless inspection of their belongings are not permitted to enter the subway system. The director of New York Civil Liberties Union protested, "We all have an interest in protecting our safety and security as we ride the trains. However, searches without suspicion of wrongdoing are fundamentally at odds with our constitutional guarantee of privacy, and placing unfettered discretion in the hands of the police invites racial, religious and ethnic profiling."[46]

The American Civil Liberties Union officials argue that privacy rights have been abandoned as law enforcement agents attempt to assure the public that the transit system is safe from terrorist attacks. Others express concern that such searches could be expanded to include buses, ferries, and public places. Police officials argue that the searches are legal in that they are similar to security searches conducted at airports and that many citizens support the searches. However, civil rights critics argue that even if the searches are legal, they question the loss of privacy rights for what they call "political ploys, false hope, and security Band-Aids."[47]

▲ check your understanding **5.4** **What does the Fifth Amendment to the Constitution say about interrogations and confessions? What are the standards for an admissible confession and a fair lineup? What landmark case established the right to an attorney?**

Arrest

▼ the main idea **5.5** **Procedural laws also govern arrests made by police and define false arrest.**

Limitations on police powers of **arrest** stem from abuses by the English government during the colonial period in the American colonies and in England. As a result of historical suspicion against the government's power to incarcerate citizens on questionable charges or without due process, the powers of the police to make an arrest are limited. Law enforcement officers can initiate an arrest only (1) with an arrest warrant issued by the court, (2) when they observe a violation of the law, (3) under exigent circumstances, or (4) when they have probable cause to believe that someone has committed a crime. In many states, the police are limited to arresting people justified by probable cause that someone has committed a crime only when the crime is a felony.

arrest Restricting the freedom of persons by taking them into police custody.

figure 5.4

The Miranda Rights

- You have the right to remain silent.
- Anything you say can be used against you in a court of law.
- You have the right to talk to a lawyer and to have a lawyer present when you are being questioned.
- If you want a lawyer before or during questioning but cannot afford to hire a lawyer, one will be appointed to represent you at no cost before any questioning.
- If you answer questions now without a lawyer here, you still have the right to stop answering questions at any time.

✔ Do you understand each of these rights I have explained to you?
✔ Having these rights in mind, do you now wish to answer questions?
✔ Do you now wish to answer questions without a lawyer present?

Miranda

In the famous case of ***Miranda* v. *Arizona*** (1966), the court issued an opinion in which it summarized all of the rights of a citizen during police arrest and interrogation.[48] Initially, the court was very strict in requiring that these rights, known as the ***Miranda* rights**, were read word-for-word to all suspects during arrests and interrogations (see Figure 5.4). Gradually, however, the *Miranda* protections have been weakened by exceptions. Courts decided that it was not necessary unequivocally to advise persons of all *Miranda* rights or that they did not have to be advised of their rights at the beginning of questioning. Controversies surrounding *Miranda* have included concerns of law enforcement that the requirement to advise people of their rights impedes efficient police work.

Concerned about the affect of advising suspects of their *Miranda* rights prior to interrogating them, and as the court became more flexible in how police must advise suspects of their *Miranda* rights, some police officers pushed the limits as to acceptable professional behavior. One practice that was rejected by the U.S. Supreme Court in June 2004 (*Missouri* v. *Seibert,* No. 02-1371) was the strategy of interrogating suspects twice—once before reading them their rights and then again after reading them their rights. This practice is known as "interrogating outside *Miranda.*" The interrogation practice is based on the theory that if the police officer can obtain a confession from suspects prior to advising them of their *Miranda* rights, it will make it easier to obtain a second confession after they are advised of their rights since they have already confessed to the crime. The first confession is discarded and the second confession, the one in which the suspect was advised of his or her rights, is used in court. The court ruled that this tactic was a police strategy "adapted to undermine the *Miranda* warnings.

However, not all confessions require that the suspect is advised of his or her *Miranda* rights. Confessions given freely prior to an opportunity for police to advise a suspect of his or her rights are admissible and confessions given to third parties are admissible. An example of this would be spontaneous confessions given by suspects immediately after the arrival of the police, such as the case where a husband who has murdered his wife exclaims, "I murdered her" to the police when they arrive. Another example would be when Cheo Ash, a patient in a Texas state mental hospital, called a nationally syndicated radio talk show and confessed to a 1994 homicide. Since Ash was not being interrogated by the police, it was not necessary for him to be advised of his *Miranda* rights for the confession to be admissible.

***Miranda* rights** Five rights protecting, for example, the right to avoid self-incrimination and the right to an attorney, of which citizens are informed during police arrest and interrogation, established in *Miranda* v. *Arizona* (1966).

Miranda rights are based on the rights against self-incrimination guaranteed in the Fifth Amendment. Not only does the Fifth Amendment protect suspects against self-incrimination during police interrogation but it also protects against self-incrimination during a trial. Thus, defendants have the well-known "right to remain silent" or "Fifth Amendment" right during their trials and cannot be compelled to provide testimony that may incriminate them. Furthermore, the law provides that the prosecution cannot tell or infer to the jury that a defendant's silence implies guilt. Thus, in 2004, the Kentucky Supreme Court overturned a 2002 murder conviction and ordered a new trial for Shane Ragland. The Kentucky Supreme Court ruled that the prosecutor's remarks during his closing statement that Ragland did not testify and, therefore, investigators could not determine exactly where the fatal shot had been fired because the defendant "hadn't seen fit to tell us" was a violation of the defendant's rights. The court ruled that this reference to the defendant's silence was an "intentional and flagrant" violation of the defendant's Fifth Amendment rights.

Entrapment and Police Intelligence Activities

The U.S. Supreme Court has required that arrest cannot be contingent on **entrapment**, in which the police provide the motivation and means for committing the crime (***Jacobsen* v. *United States,*** 1992).[49] Entrapment is a defense against criminal charges in court.

Police intelligence activities in the past have sometimes involved entrapment. During the 1950s, 1960s, and early 1970s, many police departments, especially large departments, engaged in active intelligence gathering. Intelligence gathering occurs when the police gather information about people who are not currently under suspicion or investigation for any specific crime. The primary targets for police intelligence units during these decades were (1) suspected members of the Communist Party, defined as a danger to the United States; (2) people engaged in or suspected of engaging in protest against the United States involvement in the Vietnam War; and (3) people engaged in civil rights protests. The federal law enforcement agency most actively engaged in the gathering of intelligence information was the FBI under the directorship of J. Edgar Hoover.

The justification for intelligence gathering was that if a crime occurred, law enforcement already would have sufficient information about citizens to quickly identify suspects and make arrests, thereby protecting the public from subversives and terrorists. However, abuses by the FBI and state and municipal police departments led to public concern, legislative initiatives prohibiting intelligence-gathering activities, and Supreme Court cases condemning the targeting of citizens for intelligence operations who were not under suspicion of committing a crime. The full extent of FBI abuses finally became known through the Freedom of Information Act, and police intelligence activities came to be seen as an unjustifiable intrusion on the constitutionally protected privacy of citizens. However, attitudes toward police intelligence changed again dramatically on September 11, 2001. Horrifying terrorist attacks on the World Trade Center in New York City and the Pentagon in Washington, DC, changed the balance between privacy and security, with far-reaching consequences.[50] New legislation has enhanced the intelligence-gathering capacity of the FBI.

Terrorism and Arrest without Charges

Critics accuse the Justice Department of denying due process to many persons accused of or suspected of terrorism in the War on Terrorism. For example, a report by Human Rights Watch accuses the federal government of indiscriminate and arbitrary arrests of males from predominately Muslim countries without sufficient probable cause or even reasonable suspicion.[51]

Also, Human Rights Watch and the American Civil Liberties Union accuse the Justice Department of abusing the material witness law to detain terror suspects. The

entrapment Illegal arrest based on criminal behavior for which the police provided both the motivation and the means, tested in *Jacobsen* v. *United States* (1992). Also legal defense in criminal court.

material witness law, enacted in 1984, allows federal authorities to hold a person indefinitely without charging him or her with a crime if they suspect that the person has information about a crime and might flee or be unwilling to cooperate with law enforcement officials.[52] Human Rights Watch and the ACLU charge that the Justice Department has used the material witness law to detain 70 persons, about one-third of them U.S. citizens, on suspicion of terrorism where questionable evidence exists for such detentions. The Justice Department has apologized to at least 13 persons for wrongly detaining them under the material witness law.[53] One of the more publicized abuses of the material witness law was the detention of Portland, Oregon, lawyer Brandon Mayfield, whom the FBI wrongly accused of being connected to the Madrid train bombings of 2004.

Of great concern to those who fear that the War on Terrorism is eroding due process rights is the Justice Department's denial of access to the civilian courts for those accused or suspected of terrorism. The use of the Enemy Combatant Executive Order to detain alleged terrorists and al Qaeda members has seriously alarmed proponents of constitutional rights. The use of this executive order, combined with the use of military tribunals instead of civilian court trials, denies accused enemy combatants access to the civilian courts. This process of determining guilt denies them the due process rights to an attorney, to confront the witnesses against them, to know of the evidence the government has against them, and the right to a public trial by their peers.

material witness law Law that allows for the detention of a person who has not committed a crime but is alleged to have information about a crime that has been committed.

▲ check your understanding 5.5 **In what circumstances can an arrest legally be made? What issues surround the "mirandizing" of arrestees and arrests based on police intelligence work and entrapment?**

conclusion:

Not without Limits

Police officers are given immense powers to fulfill their duties of enforcing the law and preserving public order. However, this power is not without limits. There are limits placed on the power of the police to search, to interrogate, and to restrict the freedom and privacy of citizens and suspects. Policing is an incredibly complex business involving many different and diverse situations and persons, and the limits on police powers reflect this complexity.

The limits on police powers are affected by diverse factors such as social values, technology, legal philosophy, Supreme Court rulings, legislation, and public opinion. Much of the training of the new police officer is devoted to educating him or her as to the limits of his or her authority, as a mistake by the officer can result in the offender escaping justice due to the police officer's error. In the chapter opener, the 95 persons arrested for gambling-related charges during the raid on the Owl's Club were all released without charges due to an error by the police. Regardless of the offense—whether it is murder, rape, or robbery—police error can result in the offender being released. Thus, it is extremely important for police officers to be very knowledgeable concerning the limits of their powers.

Limits on search and seizure and interrogation are not static. Technology has been an important factor in defining the limits of police powers. The automobile, telephone, cell phone, and Internet are examples of technology that required the courts, public, and police to examine the due process rights of suspects and offenders. The War on Terrorism is the most recent phenomenon that has affected due process rights. Concern over the potential threat to public safety has resulted in the demand for new powers concerning the interrogation and arrest of accused terrorists. Fears of attacks by terrorists with weapons of mass destruction have resulted in different standards being applied to interrogation and detention of suspected terrorists. These actions have not gone undisputed, as numerous critics have challenged the constitutionality of denying accused terrorists of due process rights, such as the right to an attorney, the right to know the charges against them, and the right to challenge the legality of their detention in court. In the end, the desire to have an effective and efficient police force must be balanced with the need to protect due process rights and uphold the constitutionally guaranteed rights of citizens.

chapter **summary**

- Rules of evidence influence police procedures in conducting searches and seizures, gathering evidence, making arrests, and conducting interrogations.
- The exclusionary rule, which defines legal versus tainted evidence, was extended to state as well as federal jurisdictions in the landmark case of *Mapp* v. *Ohio.*
- The Fourth Amendment protects Americans from unreasonable search and seizure.
- Exceptions to the warrant requirement include search incident to lawful arrest, plain-view searches, consent to search, and the search of automobiles. The right to conduct a pat-down search of a person without probable cause was established through *Terry* v. *Ohio.*
- Other exceptions to the warrant requirement concern public safety, fleeing felons, good faith mistakes, and some intelligence activities, such as wiretaps.
- The Fifth Amendment protects Americans from self-incrimination, such that confessions may not be obtained through torture, lies, deceptions, unfair lineups, or denial of civil rights.
- Rules of evidence also define lawful arrest, which may not involve entrapment. The landmark case of *Miranda* v. *Arizona* has had a significant impact on police practice during arrests and interrogations.
- Factors influencing police professionalism and accountability are checks and balances in the criminal justice system, criminal and civil prosecutions of police who break the law, and government agencies with preventive oversight functions, such as the FBI.
- The legislative branch of government has oversight powers through the ability to pass and amend laws, such as regulation of wiretaps.
- The courts, especially the U.S. Supreme Court, have indirect oversight power through rulings relating to the exclusionary rule and search and seizure, interrogation, and arrest.
- Prosecuting attorneys or district attorneys can refuse to prosecute cases if they suspect the police have acted improperly.

vocabulary review

arrest, 211
Carroll Doctrine, 198
clear and present danger, 206
deadly force, 206
entrapment, 213
exclusionary rule, 193
fleeing felon doctrine, 206
Fruit of the Poisoned Tree Doctrine, 194
good faith exception, 203
indigent defense, 210
material witness law, 214
Miranda rights, 212
pat-down search, 219
plain-view search, 198
police lineups, 210
probable cause, 197
procedural law, 192
public safety exception, 202
rules of evidence, 193
search incident to lawful arrest, 197
search warrant, 197
self-incrimination, 207
wiretapping, 204

do you remember?

Argersinger v. *Hamlin*, 211
Ashcraft v. *Tennessee*, 207
Brown v. *Mississippi*, 207
Carroll v. *United States*, 198
Communications Assistance for Law Enforcement Act of 1994, 204
Electronic Communications Privacy Act of 1986, 204
Escobedo v. *Illinois*, 211
Fifth Amendment, 207
Florida v. *Jimeno*, 198
Fourth Amendment, 196
Gideon v. *Wainwright*, 210
Harris v. *United States*, 197
Illinois v. *Caballes*, 198
In re Gault, 211
Jacobsen v. *United States*, 213
Katz v. *United States*, 204
Leyra v. *Denno*, 209
Mapp v. *Ohio*, 194
Miranda v. *Arizona*, 212
Olmstead v. *United States*, 204
Silverthorne Lumber Co. v. *United States*, 194
Star Chamber, 207
Telecommunications Act of 1996, 204
Tennessee v. *Garner*, 206
Terry v. *Ohio*, 199
USA Patriot Act, 204
Weeks v. *United States*, 193
Wolf v. *Colorado*, 194

think about this

1. Assume that Mr. Green is a drug dealer who has been convicted twice for sales of drugs to minors. A police officer who knows of Mr. Green's past criminal record sees Mr. Green driving down the street. Mr. Green is not violating any traffic laws and his vehicle is properly registered, insured, and licensed. The police officer pulls Mr. Green over on a "hunch" that he may get "lucky." When the officer pulls Mr. Green over, Mr. Green behaves in a "suspicious" manner. The police officer asks for permission to search Mr. Green's car and Mr. Green refuses. The police officer takes the keys to the car and opens the trunk. The police officer finds over $1 million in heroin. From this example, it is obvious that Mr. Green was engaged in illegal behavior. Should the police officer be punished? Should the drugs be allowed as evidence in a trial? Why or why not?
2. Where would you draw the line between public safety and personal privacy? Do you think existing case laws surrounding the Fourth and Fifth Amendments to the Constitution sufficiently protect citizens' rights to privacy and due process? What, if any, exceptions to these rights do you think are justifiable for protecting public safety? What criteria should law enforcement officers use when abridging citizens' civil liberties?

research navigator

Visit the Research Navigator website (www.researchnavigator.com), login and select the criminal justice data base in ContentSelect. Type in the key words "Internal Affairs Issues for Small Police." Select the article "Internal Affairs Issues for Small Police Departments" by Sean F. Kelly. Large police departments have the budget and personnel to institute Internal Affairs Units to promote professionalism and investigate the behavior of police officers. However, small police departments may be challenged in implementing internal affairs processes which are thought to contribute to professional police behavior.Sample the article and answer the following questions:

1. What are the challenges facing small police departments in developing and administering internal affairs units?
2. What dies Lieutenant Kelly suggest to promote professional behavior in small police departments?
3. Why is it important that small police departments have a clearly stated mission, a values statement, and ethical training for all officers?
4. Once a small police department receives a complaint regarding an officer, what should the department do?

chapter 6

Policing: Issues and Challenges

CHAPTER OUTLINE

LEARNING OBJECTIVES

After reading this chapter, you will know

- Why some people question whether local and state law enforcement have the infrastructure, resources, training, and ability to respond to attacks by international terrorists.
- The definition of terrorism and why it is difficult to come to consensus on who is a terrorist.
- The role of the Department of Homeland Security in the War on Terrorism.
- How the War on Terrorism has made significant changes in intelligence gathering and sharing, urban security, and the power of federal law enforcement agencies.
- Why closing the borders to terrorists is a major goal of the federal government.
- What critics say about the threat to liberties caused by the War on Terrorism.

3 Held Overseas in Plan to Bomb New York Target

New York—Authorities overseas have arrested one man and have taken two others into custody on suspicion of planning suicide bombings in train tunnels beneath the Hudson River between Manhattan and New Jersey. . . . The F.B.I. and New York City police officials have been aware of the group and its discussions for about a year, said Mark J. Mershon, the special agent in charge of the agency's New York office. Police presence at the tunnels in Manhattan that could have been targets has been increased in recent weeks in response to the investigation. "The planning or the plotting for this attack had matured to the point where it appeared the individuals were about to move forward," Mr. Mershon said.

Federal and local law enforcement authorities identified the main subject of the investigation as Assem Hammoud, 31, a Lebanese man who was arrested on April 27 in Beirut. . . . Monitoring of Internet chat rooms used by Islamic extremists led to the arrest of Mr. Hammoud. . . .

Mr. Mershon said an attack was to have been carried out in October or November [2006]. . . . The arrest and the bombing plan were first reported in *The Daily News*. It reported that the would-be suicide bombers had intended to blow a hole in the wall of the Holland Tunnel, allowing the Hudson River to flood the tunnel and Lower Manhattan. But authorities said yesterday that the focus appeared to have been on two PATH railroad tunnels between Manhattan and New Jersey. . . . Mr. Hammoud told his interrogators that one of the plans discussed was to put suicide bombers with explosives in backpacks on a PATH train to destroy the tunnel. . . .

Six foreign governments are assisting in the investigation.

Adapted from "3 Held Overseas in Plan to Bomb Hudson Tunnels." The New York Times Online, www.nytimes.com, July 8, 2006 by Jere Longman and William K. Rashbaum.

introduction:

Evolving Developments and Influences on Policing

Ever since the September 11, 2001, terrorist attacks on the World Trade Center and the Pentagon there have been extraordinary influences shaping the criminal justice system. The result is a criminal justice system that has significantly changed since 9/11 and that is still in the process of changing.

The plot by terrorists to bomb the PATH train tunnels between New Jersey and New York illustrates the nature of these influences. The plot was planned by persons overseas and in Canada who used the Internet to conspire; they never met face to face, never visited the United States, and were never in New York City. Six foreign governments assisted in the investigation. In New York City it was necessary for the FBI, the mayor, the police department, and the Port Authority to cooperate with government agencies and Homeland Security to protect the city and expose the alleged plot. The lead agencies in the investigation were federal agencies. Local and state law enforcement have never had to respond on such a global scale. Interagency cooperation, intelligence capacity to detect plots in advance, new training, and new missions have presented issues and challenges to contemporary policing like they have never faced before 9/11.

This chapter will examine the issues and challenges impacting law enforcement. Many of these issues are directly related to the War on Terrorism; other issues are indirectly related. Discussion will focus on the challenge of responding to international terrorism and its effect on immigration, crime, technology, and constitutional rights.

The War on Terrorism and the Criminal Justice System

the main idea 6.1 Terrorism involves random attacks on noncombatants. Terrorism is a political and value label that makes it difficult for opposing sides to come to agreement regarding the condemnation of the violence.

Although the United States has long endured domestic terrorism, it has not impacted the criminal justice system in the same way as the threat of international terrorism since September 11, 2001. For the most part, the criminal justice system effectively responded to the threats of domestic terrorism. However, effective counterterrorism against international terrorism requires resources that far exceed local police budgets, and international intelligence-gathering powers that are possessed only by federal and military agencies. Although local and state police have a vital role as first responders in the **War on Terrorism,** their traditional relationship with federal and military agencies has been significantly changed. Thus, it is important to examine the distinction between domestic and international terrorism and the unique challenges of international terrorism.

War on Terrorism Declaration by President Bush supported by congressional legislation that defines international terrorists as a threat to national security and provides for greater executive and federal law enforcement powers in ensuring national security.

Generally, terrorists use tactics such as random attacks on noncombatants, symbolic buildings and landmarks, and the infrastructure of a society to achieve their goal of causing general disruption and widespread fear. They typically do not expect this destructiveness to topple the legitimate government, however. On the contrary, terrorists achieve their goals through the *response* of the government to their acts. They count on overreaction of the government and the media. The ability to create widespread fear does not depend on military strength but on the ability of the mass media to magnify

The 9/11 attacks on the World Trade Center and the Pentagon by international terrorists caused widespread fear that other attacks may be possible. This fear of another attack resulted in the public's acceptance of significant changes in federal law enforcement agencies and new powers being granted to these agencies. Do you think the fear of another terrorist attack has diminished?

terrorist actions and to broadcast this image internationally. Terrorists can count on the media to make their actions widely known. As early as 1976, the National Advisory Commission on Criminal Justice Standards and Goals' *Report of the Task Force on Disorder and Terrorism* concluded, "The spectacular nature of terrorist activities assures comprehensive news coverage; modern communications make each incident an international event."[1]

Criminal Justice and Social Justice

Terrorism emphasizes the **social injustice** of government. Ideally, criminal justice and social justice are the same, and what is legal is right. However, this is not always the case. The police, the courts, and the prisons operate in the name of justice but are sometimes found wanting. Terrorist groups take advantage of the social injustice that exists within a society or between societies to justify their violence.

One of the factors that has suppressed widespread terrorism in the United States is the fact that the criminal justice system reflects changing social values. During the course of U.S. history, laws and the criminal justice system have from time to time discriminated against classes of people, have been unjust in their protection of civil and constitutional rights for all people, or have turned a blind eye toward justice for some. However, often these offenses are corrected without violence or overthrow of the government. Such corrections can be seen in U.S. Supreme Court rulings that have offered greater protections to citizens, such as requiring states to provide indigent defendants with free legal counsel, rulings that have restricted the power of the police in interrogating suspects, and civil rights decisions requiring equality for all citizens.

Terrorism and Relativism

Terrorism did not first emerge with the September 11, 2001, attacks. The concept of political terrorism is rooted in the **Reign of Terror** of the French Revolution (1793–1794) during which time the citizens of France rebelled against the tyranny of the ruling class of nobles and clergy. Generally, **terrorism** can be defined as the use of violence to promote political or social change. It is characterized by the ruthlessness and desperate dedication of its advocates and the brutality or destructiveness of their actions.[2] In the United States, the most commonly used definition of terrorism by the government and criminal justice system is contained in Title 22 of the United Sates Code, Section 2656f(d). According to this federal code, "the term *terrorism* means premeditated, politically motivated violence perpetrated against noncombatant targets by subnational groups or clandestine agents, usually intended to influence an audience. The term **international terrorism** means terrorism involving citizens or the territory of more than one country. The term **terrorist group** means any group practicing, or that has significant subgroups that practice, international terrorism."[3] For the purposes of this definition, the term *noncombatant* in addition to civilians includes military personnel who at the time of the incident are unarmed and/or not on duty. It also includes acts of terrorism attacks on military installations or on armed military personnel when a state of military hostilities does not exist at the site.[4]

It is said that "one man's terrorist is another man's freedom fighter." Whether one is viewed as a terrorist or freedom fighter depends to a great degree on whether one agrees or disagrees with the political ideology and goals of those engaged in violence. The American Revolution against England, the Russian Revolution against the Czar, the Hungarian revolt against the Soviet Union, Castro's overthrow of the government of Cuba, the Iranian revolution against the Shah, the Solidarity union movement of Poland, the Irish Republican Army's rejection of British rule, and the Palestine struggle for a homeland are examples of situations in which political leaders used violence to achieve the political and social change they desired.

Terrorism is a political and value-laden label. Those engaged in political violence seldom call themselves terrorists or refer to their actions as terrorism. Rather than *terrorist* and *terrorism,* those engaged in the use of violence to achieve political change use such terms as *freedom fighter, People's Struggle,* or *war of liberation.* As early as 1974, Yassir Arafat, former head of the Palestinian Liberation Organization (PLO), addressed the United Nations Assembly in New York and proclaimed that the efforts of the PLO to liberate Palestinian Arabs from the Israelis was just like the efforts of American colonists to liberate themselves from the British. Arab leaders such as Muammar Qaddafi of Libya and Osama bin Laden have even accused the United States of being the greatest terrorist threat in the world.

▲ check your understanding **6.1** **Why is there disagreement in deciding who is a terrorist?**

Reign of Terror Phase of the nineteenth-century French Revolution in which the revolutionary ruling party used arrests and executions to retain power and suppress opposition.

terrorism Premediated, politically motivated violence perpetrated against noncombatant targets by subnational groups or clandestine agents, usually intended to influence an audience.

international terrorism Terrorism perpetrated by state-sponsored groups, international terrorist organizations, and loosely affiliated international extremists' groups.

The use of violence and terrorism is not new and is worldwide. In this photograph a British soldier drags a Catholic protester during the "Bloody Sunday" killings January 30, 1972. Shortly after, the Irish Republican Army (IRA) declared that their immediate policy was "to kill as many British soldiers as possible." The IRA has been actively fighting for a complete withdrawal of British troops from Northern Ireland since the partition of Ireland in 1921. Can you think of other conflicts in which terrorism is a central strategy of one of the parties to the conflict?

Domestic and International Terrorism

▼ the main idea **6.2 Terrorist groups can be divided into domestic terrorists and international terrorists. Militias, extremist groups, and ecoterrorists are the primary domestic terrorist groups, but they have not caused the widespread fear and disruption attributed to international groups.**

To a large degree, U.S. criminal justice agencies abstain from the political and ethical debates regarding the justification for the use of political violence. The criminal justice system focuses on the criminal nature of terrorism, regardless of the motivation or political ideology, and pursues the goals of protecting the public, apprehending perpetrators of such violence, and determining the guilt and punishment of those accused of terrorism.

However, law enforcement agencies do distinguish between terrorist acts committed by domestic perpetrators of terrorism and foreign perpetrators of terrorism, and the federal government has chosen to respond to international terrorism by characterizing it as a War on Terrorism. According to the Federal Bureau of Investigation's Office of Domestic Terrorism and Counterterrorism Planning, perpetrators of **domestic terrorism** include lone offenders and extremist elements of right-wing groups. Lone offenders often are seeking revenge for individual grievances, carrying out vendettas against other citizens, or protesting against government policies or laws. Many are mentally unstable or belong to countercultures that believe in the violent overthrow of government. Some acts of domestic terrorism are pranks or frauds designed to spread panic or force the government into an emergency response. Such actions also include false bomb threats and mailing threatening letters containing substances that the person claims to be or appear to be biological agents.

domestic terrorism Acts of terrorism committed in the United States by individuals or groups that do not have ties with or sponsorship from foreign states or organizations.

diversity in the system

Freedom Fighters or Terrorists?

An example of how debated the definition of terrorism is can be seen in President William Clinton's 1999 offer of clemency to 12 jailed members of a Puerto Rican nationalist group known as FALN, the Spanish-language initials for Armed Forces of National Liberation. The Puerto Rican nationalists were serving sentences for offenses related to 130 bombings in the United States in the 1970s and 1980s that killed six people and maimed dozens of others. Nearly all U.S. law enforcement agencies opposed the president's offer of clemency. The terrorist attacks had targeted New York City, and the offer of clemency was strongly opposed by New York Mayor Rudolph Giuliani and Senator Daniel Patrick Moynihan. Mayor Giuliani said that Clinton had undercut his own government's efforts to combat terrorism.[5]

On the other hand, Jan Susler, the lawyer who represented the 12 members of the group, said she was "elated by the prisoners' release" and that "it was a tremendous victory and accomplishment for the Puerto Rican people and people who love justice."[6] One member of the group, Edwin Cortes, told the Associated Press before he boarded a plane to San Juan, Puerto Rico, "I'm sure that we'll be received as patriots in our country, not the criminals we've been labeled as in the United States."[7] He was correct. On September 11, 1999, when the members of the group arrived in San Juan, they were greeted by crowds of people waving flags and chanting nationalist hymns. One bystander remarked, "These people are not terrorists. They are heroes, and we support them 100 percent." Another said, "I'm very happy for these guys. They are a symbol of Puerto Rico."[8]

Two disputes between Cuba and the United States regarding alleged terrorists provide further examples of how governments have different views as to who is a terrorist. The United States refuses to deport Cuban-born Luis Posada Carriles to Venezuela to stand trial for the 1976 mid-air explosion of a Cuban aircraft with 73 passengers. The United States claims that Carriles would be tortured if returned to Venezuela. The Cuban government calls Carriles an international terrorist. On the other hand, Cuba demands that the United States release five Cubans imprisoned in America. The Cuban government has mounted an international campaign for the release of the five imprisoned men, claiming that they were in Miami gathering information about terrorist organizations opposed to Castro and are being illegally incarcerated by the United States. The Cuban government has gathered over 3,000 letters from prominent persons throughout the world supporting their demand for their release.

When there is disagreement over whether a person is a terrorist or a freedom fighter, how does one decide between the two?

Domestic Terrorism

The three most common acts of domestic terrorism are (1) acts of violence committed by militias and extremist groups or individuals in protest against government policies, laws, or authority; (2) violence by single-issue extremist groups such as antiabortion groups; and (3) ecoterrorism.

Militias and Extremist Groups Numerous militia and extremist groups have adopted violence as a tactic. The Ku Klux Klan is one of the oldest domestic groups that endorses the use of violence to achieve its goals. Other extremist groups are committed to racial and ethnic segregation, such as the skinheads, neo-Nazis, the John Birch Society, and the Order of Thule. Militia movements that advocate the use of violence include right-wing patriot groups, such as Family Farm Preservation, Posse Comitatus, and the Constitutional Party, which disagree with various laws and policies of the U.S. govern-

In 2003, the Earth Liberation Front (ELF) protested the building of new homes in "conservation areas" by setting fires at different new home construction sites and burning a $50 million apartment complex under construction. Despite the fact ELF has been responsible for extensive property damage, why do you think their actions have not triggered a crisis of confidence in security?

ment. Some militia movements and extremist groups, for example, argue that the U.S. government does not have the power to collect individual income taxes or advocate extreme points of view regarding private property rights, even to the point that the group may argue that it can form its own "government." The FBI estimates that there are nearly 200 militia and extreme right-wing groups. **Timothy McVeigh,** who was responsible for the bombing of the Alfred P. Murrah Federal Building in Oklahoma City, is the most well known individual in this category of domestic terrorism.

Single-Issue Extremist Groups Single-issue extremist groups hold strong opinions on a single issue to the point that members engage in violent acts to impose their beliefs on others. Examples of such groups include antigay groups and antiabortion groups. Extremist antiabortion individuals or groups have engaged in violent acts against abortion clinics, medical personnel, and even clients. These violent acts include harassment, arson, bombing, and murder. Persons who commit such acts are frequently lone individuals rather than an organized group of domestic terrorists. **Eric Robert Rudolph,** responsible for the 1996 Atlanta Olympics bombing and the 1998 bombing of an Alabama abortion clinic, is an example of a domestic terrorist in this category.

Ecoterrorism **Ecoterrorism** is vandalism, destruction of property, and violence with the intent to influence the public with regard to conduct considered harmful to the environment or that violates animal rights. Ecoterrorist groups use tactics such as arson, mail bombs, and destructive raids on animal research facilities to advance their political agenda.

The two most active ecoterrorist groups are the **Earth Liberation Front** (**ELF**) and the **Animal Liberation Front (ALF).** The Federal Bureau of Investigation has labeled ELF as the most serious domestic terrorism threat in the United States. The Earth Liberation Front is credited with committing more than 1,200 attacks causing millions of dollars in damages. Many of the attacks have been against university labs that conduct animal research.[9] The group claims to have destroyed property worth more than $37 million in its attacks.[10] For example, ELF claimed credit for a fire at the University of Washington Horticultural Center that caused more than $2 million of damage, destroying more than 20 years of work and records,[11] and also claimed credit for destroying genetically altered crops at the University of Minnesota.[12] The most expensive single act of ELF's terrorism was the 1998 arson of several buildings and ski lifts in Vail, Colorado, resulting in an estimated $12 million in damage.[13]

ecoterrorism Domestic terrorism that uses violence to influence public policy with regard to conduct considered harmful to the environment or that violates animal rights.

The Hate Directory, www.bcpl.net/~rfrankli/hatedir.htm, is regularly updated and includes a directory of hate groups on the Internet, racist games on the Internet, as well as racist-friendly web-hosting services.

The Animal Liberation Front focuses its actions on "liberating" animals used in scientific experiments. Often these liberation raids are accompanied by destruction of laboratory equipment and research data. For example, ALF broke into the University of Iowa's psychology department's laboratories and "liberated" 88 mice and 313 rats. They destroyed computers and poured acid on papers and equipment, causing about $450,000 worth of damage. In an anonymous message sent after the attacks, the perpetrators wrote: "Let this message be clear to all who victimize the innocent: We're watching. And by ax, drill, or crowbar—we're coming through your door."[14] Some of the animals liberated by ALF in these raids have little chance of living outside of the laboratory they were taken from or may actually pose a risk to the public.[15]

More recently, ecoterrorists have focused on lifestyle terrorism, attacking Sport Utility Vehicles (SUVs), Hummer dealerships, cosmetic companies, and other targets in the name of defending the environment from harmful lifestyle practices of the public. Ecoterrorists are examples of perpetrators who justify their acts of violence by arguing that they are struggling against social injustice. A spokesperson for the ALF said of ALF activists, "History will be written about them. They will be defamed now, but they will be taught to children later. They will write storybooks about these people, like Harriet Tubman."[16]

The U.S. Department of State website, www.state.gov, contains information about travel warnings, crisis awareness, and preparedness, as well as information about countries and regions. There are links to State Department publications on terrorism such as *Patterns of Global Terrorism.*

International Terrorism

International terrorism is perpetrated by state-sponsored groups, international terrorist organizations, and loosely affiliated international extremist groups. States that have been accused at one time or another of sponsoring international terrorist groups are South Korea, Syria, Saudi Arabia, Iran, Yemen, Afghanistan, Libya, and Iraq. **Al Qaeda** is the most well known nonstate terror group. Other international terrorist groups include Aum Supreme Truth (AUM), known for its 1995 sarin nerve gas attack on the Tokyo subway; Basque Fatherland and Liberty (ETA), known for its bombings and assassinations of Spanish government officials; Hamas (Islamic Resistance Movement), known for its suicide bombings against Israeli civilian targets; and Hizballah (Party of God), known for its suicide truck bombing of the U.S. Embassy and U.S. Marine barracks in Beirut.

Militant groups, antiabortion extremists, and ecoterrorists have caused extensive property damage and some deaths, but they have had little impact on public confidence in the criminal justice system and they have not created a crisis resulting in widespread public fear or disrupted the day-to-day activities of the public. However, the new wave of international terrorism following the September 11, 2001, attacks has caused an extensive examination of the role and capacity of the criminal justice system and the government to provide for public safety.

Early attacks by international terrorists did not provoke a nationwide call to arms. For example, neither the bombings of the Puerto Rican liberation group nor the February 26, 1993, attempt to blow up the World Trade Center (WTC) using a 1,500-pound truck bomb resulted in an extensive examination of the vulnerability of the United States to international terrorist attacks. Also, despite damaging attacks by international terrorists against U.S. citizens and military targets overseas that followed the 1993 WTC attack, citizens did not feel particularly vulnerable to attack by international terrorists on U.S. soil. However, the assessment of the ability of international terrorists to successfully attack targets within the United States significantly changed with the September 11, 2001, attacks. The extent of public fear resulting from the 9/11 attacks by international terrorists is evident by the Threat Advisory Level instituted by the **Department of Homeland Security,** wherein the daily color-coded threat level provides recommended actions to defend against the threat of an attack by international terrorists for citizens and law enforcement agencies.

Department of Homeland Security (DHS) Newly created federal agency responsible for a wide range of security measures to protect against terrorist attacks.

check your understanding 6.2 **What are the different types of domestic terrorists? Which have been more disruptive: domestic terrorists or international terrorists?**

The Department of Homeland Security

the main idea 6.3 The federal government has created new federal agencies and reorganized existing federal agencies and has given them the primary responsibility of responding to terrorism.

As early as 1998, some authorities questioned whether the United States was facing a new upsurge of terrorism,[17] and whether the U.S. law enforcement system, with its thousands of semiautonomous local law enforcement agencies, would prove effective in fighting international terrorism.[18]

The tipping point whereby there was a significant shift to reliance on the federal government was the September 11, 2001, attacks on the World Trade Center and the Pentagon. On September 12, 2001, in response to these attacks, President Bush declared war on terrorism and began pursuing a two-prong strategy of (1) aggressive use of military force overseas and (2) greater reliance on federal agencies in responding to terrorism on U.S. soil.

Following the September 11, 2001, attacks, the Federal Bureau of Investigation made counterterrorism its highest priority, but the Bush administration claimed that this was not sufficient in fighting terrorism. The criminal justice system as it existed was considered inadequate in its ability to prevent terrorism by foreign perpetrators. Thus, the Bush administration requested new powers for federal agencies, the formation of new federal agencies, and the suspension of certain civil rights of accused terrorists considered by some to be fundamental to democratic government.

Others concurred with the assessment that the criminal justice system as structured prior to 2001 had inherent organizational and legal obstacles that precluded it from preventing future attacks by international terrorists.[19] The report of the *Strategies for Local Law Enforcement Series* concluded that one of the critical obstacles in responding to terrorism in the United States was that law enforcement does not have the necessary infrastructure and powers to respond to international terrorism. The report declared that September 11, 2001, was a turning point for U.S. law enforcement as immediately following the attacks, local, state, and federal law enforcement agencies faced service demands, problems, and issues that they had never seen before. The report concluded that in examining the collective response and capacity of the various government agencies prior to the September 11 attacks, U.S. law enforcement simply was not prepared for major attacks by international terrorists. Furthermore, the report concluded that there was no simple fix, no quick solution to equipping law enforcement agencies with the ability to prevent and respond to terrorism.

Building a Better Defense

The overlapping system of federal, state, and local governance in the United States results in more than 87,000 different jurisdictions. Prior to the September 11, 2001, terrorist attacks, lack of coordination of the mission, resources, and programs of these thousands of agencies to create a unified defense against and response to terrorism was a key weakness in the War on Terrorism. In an effort to increase homeland security following the September 11 terrorist attacks on the United States, President Bush sought to organize for a secure homeland by issuing the *National Strategy for Homeland Security* in July 2002 and signing legislation creating the Department of Homeland Security (DHS) in November 2002; the cabinet-level Department of Homeland Security was implemented in March 2003.[20] *Homeland security* is defined as "a concerted national effort to prevent terrorist attacks within the United Sates, reduce America's vulnerability to terrorism, and minimize the damage and recover from attacks that do occur."[21] Many other federal, state, and local agencies are involved in homeland security but the Department of Homeland Security has the dominant role as it is the lead federal agency in

The Department of Homeland Security was created with the specific mission of preventing another terrorist attack on the United States. Michael Chertoff, shown here, is the second Secretary of the DHS (Tom Ridge was the first). Despite the relatively short existence of the DHS, extensive reorganizations have been necessary. Do you think the DHS has made the United States more secure against terrorist attacks?

most homeland security initiatives and it has the dominant share of homeland security funding.[22]

Creating the Department of Homeland Security The Department of Homeland Security is described as "a historic moment of almost unprecedented action by the federal government to fundamentally transform how the nation protects itself from terrorism."[23] The creation of the Department of Homeland Security is the most significant reorganization of the United States government since 1947. The DHS consolidates 22 federal agencies and 180,000 employees to create a single agency whose primary mission is to protect the homeland of the United States[24] (see Figure 6.1). In all, the DHS has responsibility for homeland security responsibilities that were dispersed among more than 100 different government organizations.[25] The changes brought about by the creation of the Department of Homeland Security, enabling legislation and changing political ideology, have had a significant impact on the criminal justice system.

One of the important new missions of the DHS is to increase the domestic intelligence capacity of federal and local agencies. The DHS works with the CIA, the FBI, the Defense Intelligence Agency (DIA), and the National Security Agency (NSA) to analyze intelligence and information and to disseminate that intelligence to agencies that need it to counter terrorism. It should be noted that despite the many responsibilities of the DHS for homeland security, the Federal Bureau of Investigation is the primary federal law enforcement agency responsible for the investigation of crimes of terrorism and the apprehension of suspected terrorists.

See www.dhs.gov for more information about the Department of Homeland Security.

Mission and Organization of the Department of Homeland Security In general, the broad mission of the Department of Homeland Security is reflected by its six-point agenda:

1. Increase overall preparedness, particularly for catastrophic events.
2. Create better transportation security systems to move people and cargo more securely and efficiently.
3. Strengthen border security and interior enforcement and reform immigration processes.
4. Enhance information sharing with our partners.
5. Improve DHS financial management, human resource development, procurement, and information technology.
6. Realign the DHS organization to maximize mission performance.

In July 2005, Homeland Security Department Secretary Michael Chertoff announced his plans to reorganize the two-year-old DHS to ensure that the DHS's policies, operations, and structures are aligned in the best way to address the potential threats of terrorism. In part, the timing of the reorganization was motivated by the London subway bombing of the same month. Also, when Hurricane Katrina caused the near complete destruction of New Orleans and the surrounding area, there were severe criticisms of the emergency response measures of the DHS. Many expressed concern that in light of the federal government's poor response to Hurricane Katrina, there was se-

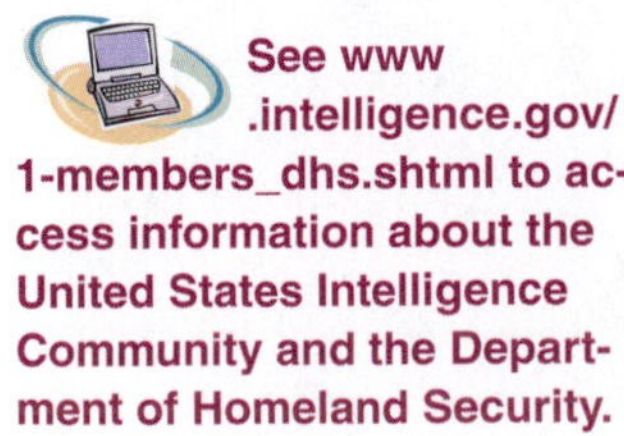

See www.intelligence.gov/1-members_dhs.shtml to access information about the United States Intelligence Community and the Department of Homeland Security.

figure 6.1

Agencies under DHS

The 22 federal agencies that became part of the Department of Homeland Security include such diverse agencies as:

- U.S. Department of Treasury (U.S. Customs Service and Federal Law Enforcement Training Center)
- Department of Justice (some functions of Immigration and Naturalization Service, Office for Domestic Preparedness, and Domestic Emergency Support Teams)
- Department of Defense (National BW Defense Analysis Center and National Communications System)
- Federal Bureau of Investigation (National Domestic Preparedness Office and National Infrastructure Protection Center)
- Department of Energy (Nuclear Incident Response Team, CBRN Countermeasures Programs, and Energy Security and Assurance Program)
- Federal Emergency Management Agency
- Federal Protective Service
- Department of Agriculture (some functions of the Animal and Plant Health Inspection Service and Plum Island Animal Disease Center)
- Department of Health and Human Services (Strategic National Stockpile and the National Disaster Medical System)
- In addition to those government agencies that are under the management of the Department of Homeland Security, the DHS has responsibility for coordinating responsibilities for homeland security that are dispersed among numerous different agencies such as the U.S. Coast Guard and the U.S. Secret Service. Also, the DHS works with public service volunteer organizations such as the Citizen Corps, the Freedom Corps, and the Coast Guard Auxiliary to prepare local communities to effectively prevent and respond to terrorism and to strengthen a culture of service.

rious question as to the ability of the DHS to respond to a nuclear, chemical, or biological attack by terrorists.

The reorganization of the DHS will emphasize (1) increased preparedness, especially for catastrophic events; (2) strengthening border security and interior enforcement, and reforming immigration processes; and (3) hardening transportation security without sacrificing mobility.[26] One of the factors in reorganizing the mission of the DHS is the realization that given the finite resources of the DHS, it will be necessary to narrow the department's counterterrorism focus. Chertoff said that the DHS does not have the resources to protect against every threat and that the DHS must reorganize and "identify the most catastrophic possible terrorist attacks and do what it can to prevent them."[27] The goal of the DHS will be to prevent the most nightmarish attacks and the most consequential threats.[28] For example, Chertoff indicated that the DHS will continue to focus on aviation security despite the public concerns over other forms of public transit raised by the London subway bombings. Chertoff justified DHS's focus on aviation, saying, "A plane used as a missile could kill 3,000 people, while a subway bomb may kill 30 people."[29] Thus, despite the creation of the DHS, it is apparent that local law enforcement agencies will continue to play an important role both as first responders and in prevention and security in counterterrorism. Figure 6.2 shows the final end state proposed by the DHS.

U.S. Government Interagency Domestic Terrorism Concept of Operations Plan (CONPLAN) Federal guidelines that designate which federal agency is the lead agency that is responsible for command and control in the event of a terrorist incident involving multiple federal agencies.

▲ check your understanding 6.3 Why was the criminal justice system not adequate for fighting terrorism? What is the mission of the Department of Homeland Security? Why is the creation of the DHS considered a major reorganization of the federal government?

Criminal Justice Agencies and the War on Terrorism

▼ the main idea 6.4 The United States Government Interagency Domestic Terrorism Concept of Operations Plan promotes cooperation and leadership for federal agencies in responding to a terrorist attack.

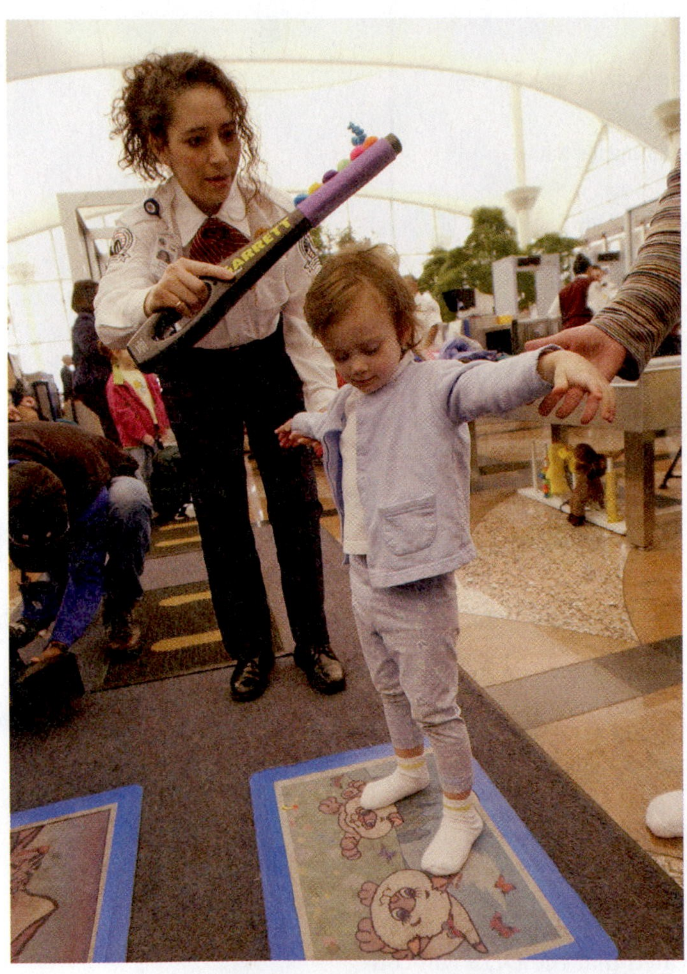

New security regulations require the searching of all airline passengers. The TSA has been criticized for ineffective use of their resources and poor performance in screening passengers. Do you think that TSA security screening is more secure than when security was performed by the airlines and the FAA?

One of the premises underlying the prevention of and response to terrorist attacks, especially attacks involving weapons of mass destruction, is that no single agency has the capacity to prevent and to respond to a terrorist attack. Prevention of catastrophic terrorism is dependent on a unity of effort not only by federal agencies but also between federal and local agencies and among the various local and state agencies at both the operational and tactical levels.[30] Although the DHS provides overall guidance and coordination for the 22 agencies under its control, there is still the need to provide guidance and coordination for numerous other federal, state, and local agencies.

United States Government Interagency Domestic Terrorism Concept of Operations Plan

To promote a coordinated response by federal agencies, the federal government developed the **United States Government Interagency Domestic Terrorism Concept of Operations Plan (CONPLAN)**. The CONPLAN was developed through the efforts of the primary departments and agencies with responsibilities for prevention and responding to terrorist attacks.[31] The purpose of the CONPLAN is to outline

> an organized and unified capability for a timely, coordinated response by Federal agencies to a terrorist threat or act. It establishes conceptual guidance for assessing and monitoring a developing threat, notifying appropriate Federal, State, and local agencies of the nature of the threat, and deploying the requisite advisory and technical resources to assist the Lead Federal Agency (LFA) in facilitating interdepartmental coordination of crisis and consequence management activities.[32]

figure 6.2

Department of Homeland Security Organization Chart (Proposed end state)

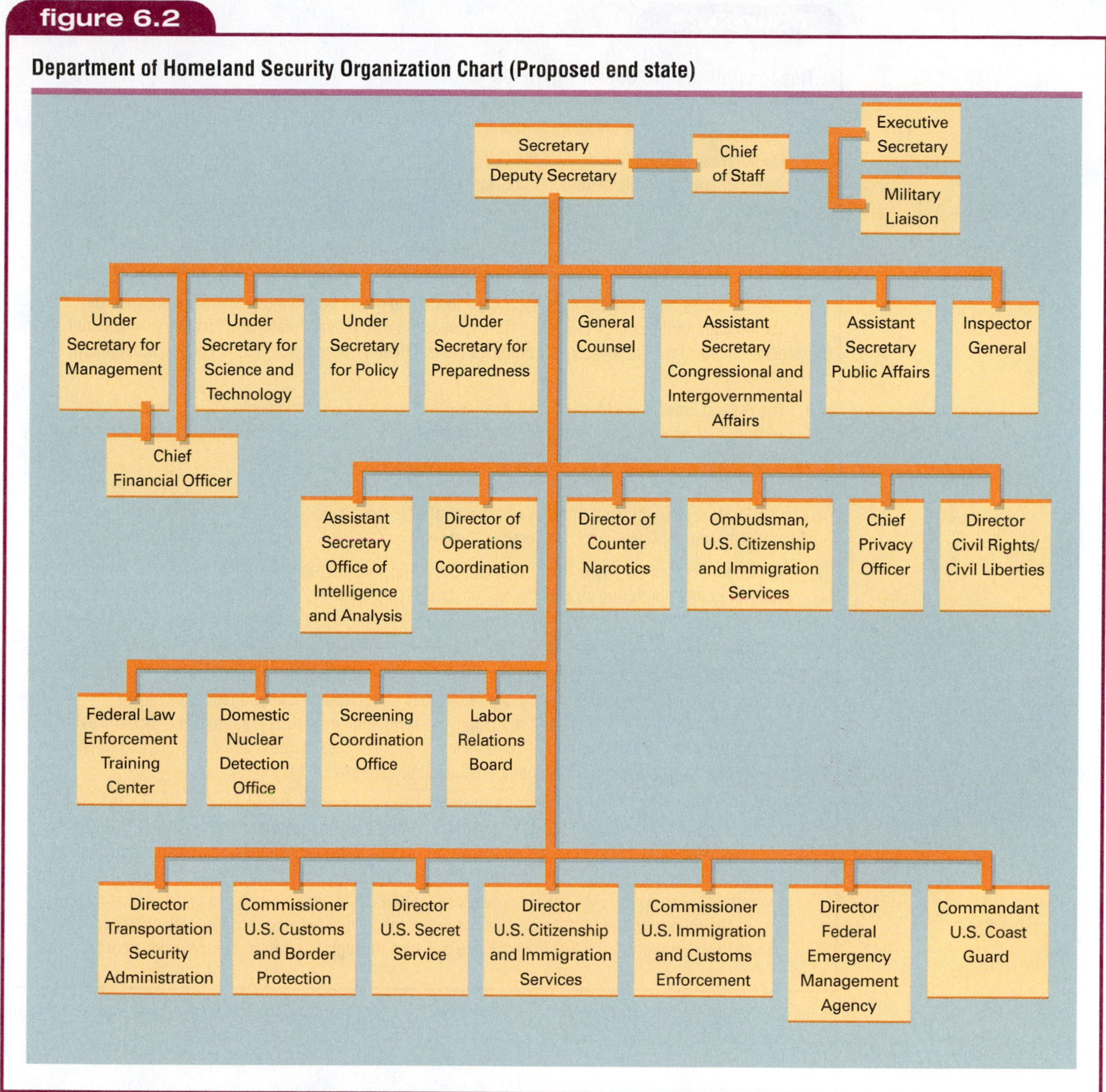

Source: Department of Homeland Security, September 2005.

lead federal agency The agency that is designated as the agency that is primarily in charge of an incident. This agency has the power to direct the actions of other agencies and to call for the use of their resources even though the lead agency may not have direct authority over these other agencies.

The CONPLAN establishes what are known as **lead federal agencies (LFA)**. The LFA is responsible for providing leadership, crisis management, and consequence management actions in the event of a catastrophic terrorist attack. The CONPLAN identifies the LFA that has been established by policy and legislation for various aspects related to a terrorist attack. (See Figure 6.3 for list of lead federal agencies and their responsibilities.) The purpose of the CONPLAN is to ensure the implementation of a coordinated response by federal agencies.

figure 6.3

Responsiblities of Federal Agencies

The CONPLAN defines the following lead federal agencies and their responsibilities:

- The Attorney General, the head of the U.S. Justice Department, is responsible for ensuring the development and implementation of policies directed at preventing terrorist attacks domestically, and will undertake the criminal prosecution of acts of terrorism that violate U.S. law. The Department of Justice has charged the Federal Bureau of Investigation with execution of its lead federal agencies (LFA) responsibilities for the management of a federal response to terrorist incidents. As the lead agency for crisis management, the FBI will implement a federal crisis management response. As an LFA, the FBI is responsible for designating a federal on-scene commander to ensure appropriate coordination of the overall U.S. government response with federal, state, and local authorities until such time as the Attorney General transfers the lead federal agency role to the Federal Emergency Management Agency.
- The Federal Emergency Management Agency (FEMA) is the LFA responsible for implementing the Federal Response Plan to manage and coordinate the federal consequence management response in support of state and local authorities.
- The Department of Defense is responsible for providing military assistance to the LFA and/or the CONPLAN primary agencies during all aspects of a terrorist incident upon request by the appropriate authority and approval by the Secretary of Defense.
- The Department of Energy is responsible for providing scientific-technical personnel and equipment in support of the LFA during all aspects of a terrorist attack involving a nuclear or radiological weapon of mass destruction.
- The Environmental Protection Agency (EPA) is responsible for providing technical personnel and supporting equipment to the LFA during all aspects of a terrorist incident involving a weapon of mass destruction. The EPA assistance and advice includes threat assessment; consultation; agent identification; hazard detection and reduction; environmental monitoring; sample and forensic evidence collection/analysis; identification of contaminants; feasibility assessment and clean-up; and on-site safety, protection, prevention, decontamination, and restorative activities.
- The Department of Health and Human Services (HHS) serves as a support agency to the FBI for technical operations and a support agency to FEMA for consequence management. The HHS provides technical personnel and supporting equipment to the LFA during all aspects of a terrorist incident. Technical assistance to the FBI may include identification of agents and medical management planning. Operational support to FEMA may include mass immunization, mass prophylaxis, mass fatality management, pharmaceutical support operations, contingency medical records, patient tracking, and patient evaluation and definitive medical care provided through the National Disaster Medical System.

Source: CONPLAN: United States Government Interagency Domestic Terrorism Concept of Operations Plan (Washington, DC: Government Printing Office, 2001), pp. 6–7.

First Responders

In responding to terrorist attacks, it is essential that there is cooperation between the federal government and local or state agencies known as **first responder** agencies and among the various first responder agencies themselves.[33] The most important first responders at the operational/tactical level are police departments, fire departments, and local and state health providers. However, historically, the semiautonomous status of the thousands of first responder agencies has not promoted cooperation between federal agencies and first responders or interagency cooperation among first responders. Instead of cooperation, the various agencies have sought to control each other and "to be in charge" at the scene of the crisis.

first responders Law enforcement, firefighters, and medical personnel who are the first to respond to a crisis and incident.

The negative impact of this lack of interagency cooperation was clearly demonstrated during the response to the attacks on the World Trade Center Twin Towers. Lacking a

Are fire personnel or the police in charge at the scene of a possible terrorist incident? This question has resulted in heated debates between fire and police personnel, as each thinks they should be in charge. Who do you think should be in charge of the scene of a possible terrorist incident? Why?

culture of cooperation among the first responder agencies, police, fire, and health agencies "neglected to perform the critical task of information sharing."[34] Even if the police and the fire departments had wanted to share critical information during the crisis, it would not have been possible because the two departments did not have compatible emergency communications equipment. Further, the lack of compatible emergency communications capabilities and interoperable systems is not unique to New York City's police and fire departments. It is more common than not that state and local government first responders lack interoperable communications systems.[35]

The cost of addressing these problems is often more than state and local governments can afford. Upgrading the training, weapons, and equipment of police departments can be such an expense that it will take states and cities years to make the changes. One of the strategies to solve this financial obstacle is for first responders to form mutual aid agreements. Federal, state, and local governments have entered into interstate and intrastate mutual aid agreements. Mutual aid agreements provide for neighboring jurisdictions to assist in providing personnel and resources to their impacted counterparts. There are three types of mutual aid agreements: (1) mutual aid agreements with adjacent jurisdictions, (2) mutual aid agreements between states or between agencies of different states, and (3) mutual aid agreements between local and/or state government and the federal government. Mutual aid agreements allow states and local governments to leverage existing and new assets to the maximum extent possible. Typically, they address such things as the mutual sharing of personnel resources and equipment, communications interoperability, and training.

Conflict between Police and Fire Departments Police departments and fire departments are considered the most important first responders in responding to a terrorist attack but the autonomous relationship between the two departments has created serious debates regarding crisis management command and control. Fire departments and police departments often have conflict when responding to an incident as to who is in charge. In some extreme incidents, police officers have even arrested firefighters on obstruction charges as police and fire personnel disagree over who has the final authority to give orders and make decisions at the scene.

Those who believe that the police should have control of crisis management at scenes involving hazardous materials argue that the police would react better in the event that it is a terrorist attack.[36] They believe the police should have command at hazardous materials incidents until it is determined if the incident is a crime or a terrorist act. They argue that if it is a crime or terrorist act, the police would be better able to gather evidence and engage in crisis management actions that may prevent other coordinated attacks.

Most cities have favored placing the fire department in charge of hazardous materials incidents. Some cities have devised compromise plans to provide for public safety and coordinate the efforts of the fire department and police department. However, for some cities the question has generated significant debate.

The bureaucratic obstacles to multiagency response are difficult to overcome but it can be done. Often the solution requires first responders to work with several agencies and to persuade legislators that new laws are necessary to solve the problem. For example, New York Police Department personnel were concerned about their legal authority to enforce a quarantine and isolation in the event of a terrorist attack using biological agents. Working with city officials, health officials, and federal agencies, New York City's health code was changed to allow the city to detain anyone who health officials suspect of having being exposed to a deadly infectious pathogen.[37]

Police and Their Role in Domestic Intelligence Gathering

Since September 11, 2001, local, state, and federal law enforcement agencies have made great progress in coordinating services, sharing resources, and participating in joint training exercises. One of the most difficult challenges has been the sharing of intelligence data. In a large city there are an infinite number of targets that terrorists could choose to attack: buildings, bridges, tunnels, the electrical grid, the water supply, shopping malls, subways, buses, and more. No police department has the resources to provide security for every potential target. Thus, it is necessary to pick and choose which targets are to be protected. Accurate and timely intelligence that provides advance warning of possible terrorist attacks is critical if local and state police are to engage in preventive actions to minimize the threat of a terrorist attack.

Prior to September 11, 2001, few local and state law enforcement agencies had intelligence units. Those that did were very restricted in the information they could gather. Generally, none of the agencies were engaged in gathering data that would help counter terrorism, as most local and state law enforcement intelligence units focused on organized crime and drug crime. This is because local and state law enforcement agencies were forced by law, court rulings, and regulations to disband their intelligence units in the 1960s and 1970s due to civil rights and privacy abuses.[38] Thus, in the post-9/11 era, where intelligence is considered to be a key strategy in preventing future terror attacks, local and state law enforcement agencies find themselves dependent on federal agencies for intelligence information.

See www.cia.gov for information about the Central Intelligence Agency.

The Federal Bureau of Investigation is responsible for domestic intelligence and the **Central Intelligence Agency** is responsible for foreign intelligence. Prior to September 11, 2001, the FBI and CIA did not share intelligence. Intelligence gathered by the CIA was fed primarily to the president, various federal government agencies, and the Pentagon and various military units. Local and state law enforcement agencies were critical of their dependency on the FBI for intelligence and they complained that the information flow between federal and local agencies is one-way: Local agencies give more to the federal agencies than they get in return.[39]

The 9/11 Commission criticized the lack of intelligence sharing among agencies as one of the reasons that the United States failed to "connect the dots" and piece together the intelligence information that would have enabled action to prevent the September 11 terrorist attacks. For example, there are claims that a secret military intelligence unit called "Able Danger" identified Mohammed Atta and three other of the 9/11 hijackers as likely members of a cell of al Qaeda operating in the United States but did not share this information with the FBI.[40] Other criticisms include charges of the failure of the FBI to integrate intelligence gathered from its own field offices to be able to connect the dots that could have alerted them to the fact that international terror suspects were taking flight training lessons.

Post-September 11, 2001, Intelligence Reforms

Following the September 11, 2001, attacks, intelligence gathering and sharing has been reengineered and a greater emphasis has been placed on intelligence sharing between federal and local law enforcement. New legislation, including the Patriot Act, allows the FBI and CIA to share terror-related intelligence. The FBI and the Department of Homeland Security have been charged with gathering and disseminating intelligence to local and state law enforcement agencies. The Bush administration has adopted a new counterintelligence strategy that calls for coordination among the different agencies responsible for terror-related intelligence and the ability to take preemptive action before a terrorist attack occurs.

One of the reforms was to remove "the wall" established by the Foreign Intelligence Surveillance Act that prevented criminal investigators from using intelligence gathered in national security cases in criminal cases such as terrorist attacks. Prior to the Patriot Act, the Justice Department did not use intelligence gathered in national security cases to obtain search warrants when subjects were suspected of criminal activity. Under the provisions of the Foreign Intelligence Surveillance Act, search warrants and wiretaps could be obtained by showing that "there was probable cause that the subject was the agent of a foreign power." However, under the Fourth Amendment, search warrants require that the law enforcement agency establish that there is probable cause to believe a crime has occurred. In the post-9/11 environment, the Justice Department promised to knock down the wall between agencies that many top officials have said hinders the sharing of intelligence data that would assist in stopping terrorist attacks.[41]

The Bush administration has made several reorganizations of the intelligence community in an attempt to promote coordination and cooperation among the CIA, the FBI, and the DHS.[42] The DHS has its own intelligence directive agency, the Information Analysis and Infrastructure Protection (IAIP) directorate. The responsibilities of the IAIP are to coordinate the gathering of intelligence from all possible sources, both public and covert; to assess the scope of terrorist threats to the homeland from the intelligence gathered; and to respond appropriately by disseminating this information to those agencies that are responsible for providing security against terrorist attacks. In addition to the IAIP, another newly created agency to promote sharing of intelligence is the **Terrorist Threat Integration Center (TTIC).** The mission of the TTIC is to "merge and analyze terrorist-related information collected domestically and abroad in order to form the most comprehensive possible threat picture."[43] The TTIC will have "unfettered access to all terrorist threat intelligence information, from raw reports to finished analytic assessment, available to the U.S. government."[44]

Joint Local–Federal Counterterrorism Task Forces

Some large police departments have turned to joint local–federal counterterrorism task forces to counter the threat of terrorist attacks. **Joint local–federal counterterrorism task forces (JTTFs)** are used to provide additional personnel to focus on counterterrorism activities and as a way to funnel intelligence from federal agencies to local agencies. The first joint terrorism task force began in 1980, in New York City, with 11 New York Police Department officers and 11 FBI special agents. By September 11, 2001, there were 35 JTTFs in operation. By 2003, the number rose to 66 and continues to rise.[45] However, many local departments are critical of JTTFs and do not believe JTTFs are a viable long-term solution.[46] The primary argument is that federal agencies often "do not

joint local–federal counterterrorism task force
Working group of FBI and state and or local law enforcement officers that focuses on preventing terrorism by their joint cooperation and intelligence sharing.

Police executives have complained that joint operations between federal and state/local law enforcement often are ineffective because the federal agencies do not share intelligence in a timely fashion. Police executives have complained that they have had to rely on news broadcasts to obtain current information in a crisis. Do you think local and state police should be given more power to gather intelligence data?

draw on the full capabilities" of local law enforcement, and local law enforcement agencies "often get little back from their investment" in the JTTF.[47]

Informal Intelligence Networks

Frustrated by the "slow and sometimes grudging way that federal officials share information about terrorist incidents," police chiefs are creating their own informal network for the exchange of intelligence.[48] Local law enforcement officials say they are still not getting all the information they need from the federal government and what they are getting does not come in a timely fashion.[49] For example, William J. Bratton, the Los Angeles police chief, said joint terrorism task forces and the DHS are not geared "to providing real-time intelligence to local police" and as a result he often has to rely on cable news networks for information rather than the DHS or other federal agencies.[50] Charles H. Ramsey, chief of the Washington Metropolitan Police, said, "Terrorism always starts as a local event. We're the first responders."[51] He emphasized that local police need real-time raw intelligence immediately, as opposed to the threat advisories and terror analysis issued by the DHS and the FBI. Local police executives stress that they must often make decisions immediately as to how to respond to a possible terrorist attack and that even waiting a day for information passed through federal intelligence networks could be too late.[52] The biggest obstacles to local law enforcement intelligence networks are lack of personnel and resources.

▲ check your understanding **6.4** **What is the importance of a lead federal agency? Why is interagency cooperation important in responding to a terrorist attack? Why is there conflict between police departments and fire departments in responding to terrorist attacks? Why is intelligence critical to responding to potential terrorist attacks and why are police lacking in this ability?**

Influences on Budget and Crime

the main idea 6.5 The fear of terrorist attacks is transforming cities into urban fortresses. Providing security against terrorist attacks is straining police resources.

Federal, state, and local law enforcement agencies have been diligent since the September 11, 2001, terrorist attacks to detect perpetrators planning another terrorist attack on the United States. This diligence has not been in vain, for there have been numerous arrests for terror-related crime. For example, in June 2004, a Somali citizen living in Ohio was arrested and charged in an alleged plot by al Qaeda to bomb an unidentified shopping mall in Columbus.[53] A father and son from a small farming town in California were indicted in June 2005 for alleged terrorism-related crime.[54] A Brooklyn man was arrested in Newark in July 2005 and charged with threatening to blow up commuter trains in New Jersey.[55] Since the September 11 attacks there has been constant warning of possible, sometimes imminent, terrorist plots. The Department of Homeland Security threat advisories have warned of terrorist plots to attack the financial district, commuter trains, symbolic landmarks such as the Brooklyn Bridge and the Golden Gate Bridge, and other targets.

Fear of a terrorist attack is transforming cities into **urban fortresses** as citizens and authorities fearing such attacks have reshaped the cityscape, increased security, blocked off streets, established security screening checkpoints, and imposed random searches of baggage and backpacks of subway passengers. Although federal authorities have assumed much of the responsibility for preventing another major 9/11 aviation-type terrorist attack, the responsibility and costs of providing everyday security to the average citizen as he or she goes about his or her business in the city has fallen primarily on local police.

Fear of terrorist attacks on public buildings and other symbolic targets has resulted in extensive and intrusive physical security. Critics call this *fortress urbanism* and complain that it can be counterproductive because of the psychological effect of such barriers in suggesting the possibility of attack. Do extensive antiterrorism physical security measures reassure you or cause you to fear a terrorist attack?

Physical Security: Straining Police Resources

Cities that are considered likely to be targeted by terrorists are being transformed by roadblocks, checkpoints, and barriers. Parking lots near buildings thought to be at risk are being closed. Even sidewalks are being closed or transformed with security precautions. Concrete barriers, called Jersey barriers, are popping up as authorities take security measures to protect buildings and people. In cities such as New York and Washington, DC, public officials and citizens are complaining that physical security measures are becoming intrusive, backing up traffic, and making the city look uninviting for tourists and residents.[56] Washington, DC, officials complain that the proliferation of concrete barricades and checkpoints is making "this place feel like Fortress Washington."[57] One of the primary reasons for this increased security is fear of terrorists exploding a car or truck bomb, as in the 1993 World Trade Center and the bombing of the Murrah Federal Building in Oklahoma City, or a terrorist suicide bomber.

Such threats are difficult to prevent. It is costing police departments millions of dollars in overtime costs, training, and equipment to fulfill this responsibility. During the heightened public transit alert in New York City following the July 2005 London subway bombings, New York police spent nearly $800,000 a day in additional costs to provide for subway security.

When the terrorist alert-level is raised, it is the local police who are expected to provide the increased security. Additional security duties during times of high alert have strained some local resources to the point that during terrorist alerts they can no longer provide routine services. Even large police departments such as New York City can reach this point. For example, during the 2004 Republican National Convention, all hearings and trials were suspended in New York City courts because police officers had to devote their time to convention security.[58]

Also, as first responders, police officers need the training and equipment to respond effectively and to protect themselves against potential hazards such as toxic substances, chemicals, and radioactivity. Few departments have the budget to purchase such equipment or to provide officers with the necessary training to properly respond to a biological, chemical, or nuclear terrorist attack. Further, in the event of a military-style assault by terrorists on a nuclear power plant, electrical generating plant, or chemical manufacturer, local police may not have the tactical skills and weapons to defeat such an attack. Most likely if such an assault was to occur, the terrorists would be armed with full-automatic, military-style weapons. Basically, local police are not trained for such tactical response and do not have the heavy weapons necessary to respond effectively to such a terrorist attack. In the event of such an attack, the pistol and shotgun that are the typical weapons of the police officer would be inadequate to defeat a fairly large group trained in military tactics using full-automatic weapons.

The War on Terrorism is causing a strain on local police departments in that the call-up of military reserve units is causing a serious strain on staffing police departments.[59] Many police officers are members of military reserve units. The War on Terrorism has resulted in the largest call-up of reserve units since World War II. As a result, the Police Executive Research Forum reported that 44 percent of 976 law enforcement agencies it surveyed reported losing personnel to reservist duty.[60] Some departments reported losing 10 percent of their officers. The call-up of reserve units has forced law enforcement departments to make up for missing officers by paying more overtime, transferring officers to ensure essential services are covered, borrowing officers from other agencies, and using more police volunteers on the streets.[61] For some small departments the call-up has wiped out the police department or the department cannot replace those doing specialized duty.[62]

Terrorist Threat Advisories

In the post-9/11 environment the Department of Homeland Security disseminates intelligence information related to possible terrorist attacks by issuing color-coded terrorist

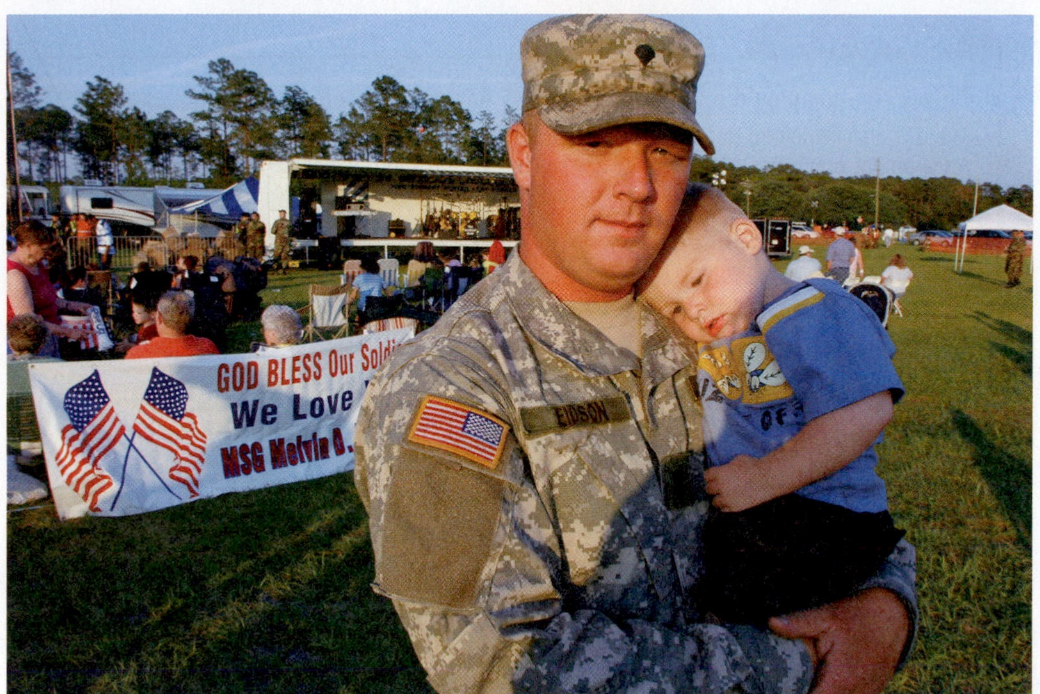

Deployment of the National Guard and reserve forces has negatively impacted local and state law enforcement agencies. Many local and state agencies are suffering personnel shortages due to these deployments, and critics argue that in the event of a domestic crisis, state and local governments would not have the ability to respond. Do you support the policy of using National Guard and reserve forces in Afghanistan and Iraq?

threat advisories to local and state law enforcement agencies known as the **Homeland Security Advisory System (HSAS)**. (These threat alerts are also issued to state, local, and private sector authorities as well as the general public.) The primary purpose of these security threat advisories is to inform and coordinate the antiterrorism efforts of all federal agencies. Threat advisories are binding on all federal agencies (except the military), but advisory for local and state law enforcement. There are five levels of threat level: low (green), guarded (blue), elevated (yellow), high (orange), and severe (red) (see Figure 6.4). The Homeland Security Advisory System can place specific geographic regions or industry sections on a higher alert status than other regions or industries, based on specific threat information.

The value of the threat advisories of the Department of Homeland Security has been questioned. In a survey by the General Accounting Office, agencies reported the warnings were often "vague and inadequate, and had hindered their ability to determine whether they were at risk and what protective measures to take in response."[63] Further, at times the DHS and FBI have issued conflicting advisory warnings.[64] Since law enforcement agencies often encounter millions of dollars in additional costs when the threat advisory level is raised, it is important for the advisories to be meaningful, specific, and accurate. In response to the criticisms concerning the color-coded threat advisory system, the DHS has indicated it will reevaluate its use.[65]

Terror Alerts and Crime One interesting question regarding the HSAS has been the effect of terror alerts on crime. The Kansas City Preventive Patrol experiment suggested that routine preventive patrol did not have an impact on crime rates. That is to say, when routine preventive patrol was increased, crime rates did not decrease and vice versa. However, preliminary statistical studies on the effect of changes in the terror alert level and crime rates has suggested that contrary to previous studies there is a relationship between crime rates and increased police presence. One study indicated that on high-alert days total crimes in Washington, DC, decreased by 6.6 percent and some crimes decreased even more. For example, burglary declined by 15 percent.[66] The study estimated that if there is a 10 percent increase in police presence, crime decreases by about 4 percent.[67] If other studies examining the relationship between high terror alerts yield similar results, conclusions drawn from previous studies such as the Kansas City Preventive Patrol experiment may be revised.

Homeland Security Advisory System (HSAS) Daily color-coded threat advisory to government agencies, police, and the public that recommends appropriate actions in response to the forecasted risk of terrorist attack.

figure 6.4

Citizen Guidance on the Homeland Security Advisory System

The U.S. Department of Homeland Security issues a daily color-coded threat advisory. Government agencies and citizens are advised to respond appropriately when the threat advisory level is elevated. Do you alter your daily activities based on the threat advisory level? If so, how? If not, why not? What can local and state law enforcement agencies do to promote public safety when the threat advisory level is raised?

Recommended Actions for Citizens

GREEN: Low Risk of Attack

- Develop a family emergency plan. Share it with family and friends, and practice the plan. Visit www.Ready.gov for help creating a plan.
- Create an "Emergency Supply Kit" for your household.
- Be informed. Visit www.Ready.gov or obtain a copy of "Preparing Makes Sense, Get Ready Now" by calling 1-800-BE-READY.
- Know how to shelter-in-place and how to turn off utilities (power, gas, and water) to your home.
- Examine volunteer opportunities in your community, such as Citizen Corps, Volunteers in Police Service, Neighborhood Watch, or others, and donate your time.
- Consider completing an American Red Cross first aid or CPR course, or Community Emergency Response Team (CERT) course.

BLUE: Guarded Risk of Attack

- *Complete recommended steps at level green.*
- Review stored disaster supplies and replace items that are outdated.
- Be alert to suspicious activity and report it to proper authorities.

YELLOW: Elevated Risk of Attack

- *Complete recommended steps at levels green and blue.*
- Ensure disaster supply kit is stocked.
- Check telephone numbers in family emergency plan and update as necessary.
- Develop alternate routes to/from work or school and practice them.
- Continue to be alert to suspicious activity and report it to proper authorities.

ORANGE: High Risk of Attack

- *Complete recommended steps at lower levels.*
- Exercise caution when traveling and pay attention to travel advisories.
- Review your family emergency plan and make sure all family members know what to do.
- Be patient. Expect some delays, baggage searches, and restrictions at public buildings.
- Check on neighbors or others that might need assistance in an emergency.

RED: Severe Risk of Attack

- *Complete recommended actions at lower levels.*
- Listen to local emergency management officials.
- Stay tuned to TV or radio for current information/instructions.
- Be prepared to shelter-in-place or evacuate, as instructed.
- Expect traffic delays and restrictions.
- Provide volunteer services only as requested.
- Contact your school/business to determine status of work day.

Source: U.S. Department of Homeland Security with input from the American Red Cross. www.dhs.gov/interweb/assetlibrary/CitizenGuidanceHSAS2.pdf.

▲ check your understanding 6.5 **What changes are occurring in large cities as a result of the fear of terrorist attacks? How has the fear of terrorist attacks affected local police departments?**

The USA Patriot Act

▼ the main idea 6.6 **After September 11, 2001, the USA Patriot Act and the Enemy Combatant Executive Order granted the federal government significant increase in power.**

One of the most significant changes in the criminal justice system has been the shifting balance of power between federal, state, and local law enforcement agencies. The federal government has sought and received new powers to fight terrorism. Today, the cornerstone legislation in the War on Terrorism is the USA Patriot Act.

Following the September 11, 2001, terrorist attacks, Congress quickly enacted legislation to enhance national security. In October 2001, the **USA Patriot Act** (commonly called the Patriot Act) was quickly passed by Congress by an overwhelming majority and signed into law by the president. In the words of then Attorney General John Ashcroft, the Patriot Act provided new powers to federal law enforcement agencies "to close gaping holes in our ability to investigate terrorists."[68]

Despite the broad new powers granted to federal law enforcement by the Patriot Act, there was little consideration and debate by neither the public nor Congress as to the impact of these new powers on basic principles of due process on which the criminal justice system is based. In the post-September 11 environment, while the Justice Department continues to uphold the necessity and effectiveness of the Patriot Act, there is extensive criticism that the Patriot Act infringes on constitutional rights and has given federal law enforcement too much unchecked power. The extent of this opposition is evident by the fact that over 150 local governments and several states have passed resolutions objecting to the legislation.[69]

The Patriot Act provides federal law enforcement greater surveillance powers, it expands federal jurisdiction of terror-related crimes, and it removes some civil liberties protections for those accused or detained under the provisions of the Patriot Act. The Patriot Act provides less judicial review of federal law enforcement agencies in regard to wire taps, intelligence gathering, and search and seizures. Figure 6.5 presents a summary of the provisions of the Patriot Act.

Expanded Search Powers

One of the most significant effects of the criminal justice system is that the authority of federal law enforcement agents to execute searches has been greatly expanded under the Patriot Act. Prior to the Patriot Act, local, state, and federal law enforcement could conduct searches without a search warrant issued by the court only under a number of limited circumstances, such as incident to arrest, plain view searches, and emergency situations. Other than these circumstances, it was necessary for law enforcement agents to present evidence to the court that there was probable cause to conduct the search to obtain permission to perform the search. Further, the court search warrant limited the scope of the search.

USA Patriot Act Legislation that gives federal law enforcement agencies expanded powers to detect, detain, and prosecute terrorists.

The Patriot Act authorized expanded search power, required less judicial oversight of these search powers, and in some cases provided for secrecy concerning the search. A controversial provision of the Patriot Act is Section 213, the so-called sneak-and-peek

figure 6.5

Summary of the Key Provisions of the USA Patriot Act

- Expands the range of crimes traceable by electronic surveillance.
- Allows police to use roving wiretaps to track any phone a terrorist suspect might use.
- Permits law enforcement to conduct searches with delayed notifications—the so-called sneak-and-peak provision.
- Allows FBI agents, with secret court orders, to search personal records (business, medical, library, etc.) without probable cause in a national-security case.
- Lowers legal barriers in information sharing between criminal investigators and intelligence officials.
- Provides new tools for fighting international money laundering.
- Makes it a crime to harbor terrorists.
- Increases penalties for conspiracy, such as plotting arson, killing in federal facilities, attacking communications systems, supporting terrorists, or interfering with flight crews.
- Makes it easier for law enforcement agents to obtain search warrants any place where "terrorist-related" activities occur; allows nationwide search warrants (including the monitoring of Internet use, e-mail, and computer bills) in terrorism investigations.
- Allows the attorney general to detain foreign terrorism suspects—but charges, deportation proceedings, or release must come within a week.
- Sends more federal agents to patrol the United States–Canada border.
- Ends surveillance and wiretap measures in 2005 (renewed).

Source: Excerpted with permission from "Has Post-9/11 Dragnet Gone Too Far?" by Warren Richey and Linda Feldman, from the September 12, 2003 issue of *The Christian Science Monitor* (www.csmonitor.com.)

provision. The sneak-and-peak provision gives federal law enforcement agents the authority to conduct a search with limited judicial review and authorization and provides for delayed notification of the search. Thus, federal agents could enter a house or business and execute a search in secret. If authorities did not find any incriminating evidence, they would not have to inform anyone of the search at that time. If the authorities did find incriminating evidence, they can use the evidence they found to obtain a search warrant by the court. The Patriot Act does not limit the use of this authority only to terrorist-related cases. In addition to the increased power to search under the Patriot Act, federal authorities can use the Foreign Intelligence Surveillance Act to perform similar searches as authorized by Section 213 of the Patriot Act. However, unlike the Patriot Act that provides for delayed notification, the Foreign Intelligence Surveillance Act provides that the subject may never be told about the search at all. The FBI first publicly acknowledged the use of this expanded authority granted by the Patriot Act and the Foreign Intelligence Surveillance Act in the search of the home of Brandon Mayfield, a Portland, Oregon, lawyer who was wrongly arrested and jailed in 2004 in connection with the March 2004 train bombings in Madrid, Spain.[70]

Another controversial section of the Patriot Act is Section 215. Under the authority of Section 215, the Federal Bureau of Investigation has the authority to demand access to certain records without a warrant or demonstrating probable cause to the court. Under this provision any third party—such as a doctor, library, bookstore, university, bank, or Internet service provider—must turn over records requested by the FBI. Furthermore, they are forbidden by law to inform the subject or the public of this release of information.

One of the most controversial debates related to Section 215 is the right of the FBI to use a national security provision to demand records of the reading habits of library patrons. Under this provision the FBI can demand that library personnel provide them with any information they have about a patron and the FBI can request information about documents a patron has checked out of the library. Further, the library personnel cannot tell the patron that they have released this information to the FBI and they cannot make any public comment about the release of the information. The Justice Department argues that if it was revealed that the FBI was seeking information from a certain library or about an individual, the revelation of that information could jeopardize an FBI counterterrorism investigation.[71]

The American Library Association and numerous organizations have strongly opposed the authority of the FBI to demand that libraries must provide secret records of library use by patrons.[72] They claim this law is an invasion of privacy with little chance of providing useful information that would help in the apprehension of terrorists or the prevention of terrorist attacks.[73] The provisions of Section 215 provide that law enforcement officials can request library records for large numbers of people without having to justify any reason to believe they are involved in illegal activity or are involved with terrorism. That is to say, officials could "go on a fishing expedition" and ask for library records of anyone who checked out material about al Qaeda, Osama bin Laden, radioactive-related books, or books that give instructions on making bombs rather than specify the name or names of a specific person.

A study commissioned by the American Library Association reported that law enforcement officials have made at least 200 formal and informal inquiries to libraries for information on reading material and other internal matters. Further information about the extent and use of such search powers cannot be obtained, as library personnel cannot provide any information regarding the extent and nature of these inquiries because the secrecy provisions of the Patriot Act could make it a crime for a librarian to respond to such questions.[74]

Terrorists have increasingly turned to the use of the Internet both as a communication tool and as a propaganda medium. However, prior to the Patriot Act, generally, it was necessary for law enforcement to obtain court-issued search warrants before Internet providers had to release the information regarding websites and customers to law enforcement. The Patriot Act has provided federal law enforcement with greater power to demand electronic information and records.

Criticisms of the Patriot Act Calls by the public and congressional members for repeal of some of the more controversial provisions of the Patriot Act were mounting until the July 2005 terrorist attacks on the London transit system. Following these attacks there was renewed belief by Congress in the necessity for a strong defense against terrorism and so the movement to repeal some of the provisions of the Patriot Act that were set to expire at the end of 2005 lost momentum.[75] However, revelations in December 2005 just prior to the expiration of some of the provisions of the Patriot Act that the Bush administration had engaged in extensive spying on U.S. citizens, secretly searched mosques for radioactive material, and conducted thousands of searches without court authorization resulted in a backlash of opposition against the Patriot Act. In last-minute negotiations the controversial provisions of the Patriot Act were extended and the renewal of the Patriot Act was approved in early 2006.

The Justice Department defends the use of the powers granted by the Patriot Act by pointing to the over 5,000 foreign nationals that have been detained since the September 11, 2001, attacks. However, of these thousands of detentions very few were ever charged with any crime.[76] Also, there have been over one thousand complaints of Patriot Act–related abuse of civil rights or civil liberties.[77]

In some cases, local police have not been in complete agreement regarding the constitutionality of the powers given to federal law enforcement by post-September 11, 2001, legislation. As a result, at times there have been conflicts between local and federal agencies as to the "legality" of certain law enforcement actions. One of the most prominent conflicts was when the Portland (Oregon) Police Department refused to interview foreign students as requested by the FBI. The police department refused to conduct the interviews because it claimed that the FBI did not offer any specific information about any crimes with which the individuals might be involved. Furthermore, the Portland Police Department said it believed that the questions that the FBI wanted the department to ask the students were not appropriate questions, as they asked about noncriminal matters such as religious beliefs and other questions not specifically related to criminal activity or knowledge.[78]

▲ check your understanding **6.6** **What new powers did the federal government obtain to fight terrorism prior to September 11, 2001? What new powers does the Enemy Combatant Executive Order and the USA Patriot Act give the federal government? What are some of the criticisms of the USA Patriot Act? How have accused terrorists been treated differently than accused criminals?**

The Financing of Terrorism

▼ the main idea **6.7** **Terrorist groups must have funds and resources to carry out their attacks. The major sources of funding for terrorism are fund-raising and criminal enterprises. One of the major strategies to defeat terrorism is to cut off the flow of funds to terrorist groups.**

The cost of terrorism is relatively inexpensive, and terrorists seem to have the money they need to engage in a protracted conflict. The September 11 attacks cost al Qaeda an estimated $500,000. However, the al Qaeda network spent less than $50,000 on each of its major attacks.[79] For example, the Madrid (Spain) train bomb attack is estimated to have cost about $10,000 to carry out. The attack on the U.S. destroyer *Cole* in October 2000 is estimated to have cost about $5,000 to $10,000. These cost estimates cover materials as well as gifts to family members of the suicide bombers.

The ability to finance worldwide terrorist attacks is one of the most valuable assets of the al Qaeda network. The wellspring of cash that finances terrorism is a network of illegal enterprises, including unscrupulous charities, drug trafficking, robbery, extortion, kidnapping, credit card fraud, cigarette smuggling, blackmailing, and arms smuggling. American government officials recognize that cutting off terrorists' funding is an important means of disrupting their operations and to that end have engaged in significant efforts to do so.[80] These efforts have affected the financial health of al Qaeda, as it is estimated its annual budget has been reduced from $35 million prior to September 11, 2001, to $5 million to $10 million in 2003, and more than $200 million in terrorists' assets has been frozen worldwide since the 9/11 attacks. Despite significant efforts to cut off funding for terrorism, a United Nations report on the effect of U.N. sanctions against al Qaeda and the Taliban has indicated that terrorists' networks have shown great flexibility and adaptability in keeping the pipeline of money flowing to fund their activities.[81]

Fund-Raising for Terrorism

The United States Treasury Department reports that unwitting or unscrupulous charities are among the biggest financiers of global terrorism. One of the factors that enables unscrupulous charities to raise large amounts of money and to divert the cash to fund terrorism is that observant Muslims consider giving to charity a religious obligation. Generally, Muslims are expected to give 25 percent of their annual income to charity. Taking advantage of this religious tenet, terrorist groups have established a network of charities to funnel money to fund terrorism. This network is worldwide and operates extensively in the United States. Following 9/11 the Bush Administration designated more than 390 groups and individuals as "global terrorists" and froze the assets of these groups and individuals and banned charitable giving to these groups and individuals.[82] Of this number, 27 have been identified as Islamic charities that finance or support terrorism. Most are international relief agencies that for years canvassed the mosques and raised millions.[83] Persons donating to these banned "charities" can be investigated and may be arrested for supporting terrorism.

Charities are important in funding terrorism in two ways. First, charities serve as a direct source of income. One of the biggest Islamic charities funneling money to support terrorism in the United States was the Holy Land Foundation. In July 2004, five former leaders of the Holy Land Foundation were arrested on charges that they funneled $13 million to Palestinian terrorists to support suicide bombers and their families.[84] Former Attorney General John Ashcroft claimed the Holy Land Foundation was the "North American front for Hamas."[85] Many who contribute to these charities that support terrorism do so unwittingly, as the charities claim that they support needy Islamic families and children and hide their support of terrorism from the public. For example, Global Relief Foundation, an Illinois-based charity, sent 90 percent of its donations abroad in 2003 for the support of the al Qaeda, Osama bin Laden, and other known terrorist groups, but most people who contributed to Global Relief Foundation were probably not aware of this fact.[86]

Second, charities are important because they provide a conduit to move money worldwide that has been raised through various illegal enterprises. For example, money that has been raised by various enterprises, including criminal activities, can be "donated" to these charities that support terrorists. Then the charities, under the cover of transferring the money from the United States to overseas, can legally move the money overseas where it will be siphoned off by various terrorist front organizations.

Funding Terrorism through Criminal Enterprises

Of the various criminal enterprises to fund terrorism, drug trafficking is at the top of the list of illegal money-raising activities. The 1992 United Nations International Narcotics Control board report warned of the link between illegal drugs and terrorism. President George W. Bush declared, "It's important for Americans to know that the traffic in drugs finances the work of terror, sustaining terrorists, that terrorists use drug profits to fund their cells to commit acts of murder." The Drug Enforcement Agency (DEA) warns the public that there is a link between drug trafficking and global terrorism, as terrorists use the drug trade to fund attacks.[87] The Islamic terrorists responsible for the Madrid train bombings financed their plot with sales of hashish and Ecstasy.

In the United States there have been a number of specific incidences that demonstrate the link between the funding of terrorism and the illegal drug trade in the United States. For example, a series of DEA drug raids in January 2002 uncovered a methamphetamine drug operation in the Midwest involving men of Middle Eastern descent who were shipping money made from drug sales back to Middle East terrorist groups such as Hezbollah. In January 2004, two Michigan men were charged in connection with a drug ring that authorities alleged provided financial support for Hezbollah.[88] In March 2004, two men pleaded guilty in federal court in San Diego in a scheme to trade hashish and heroin for anti-aircraft missiles that in turn were to be supplied to the Taliban and al Qaeda.[89]

One of the largest sources of income for terrorism from the drug trade is opium from Afghanistan. Despite the U.S. invasion of Afghanistan and the displacing of the

Taliban from power, in 2004, opium from Afghanistan accounted for 87 percent of the world supply, according to data from the United Nations. The opium drug trade accounted for about 50 percent of Afghanistan's 2003 gross domestic product. The opium trade is so ubiquitous in Afghanistan and the link to terror so direct that Antonio Maria Costa, executive director of the Vienna-based United Nations Office on Drugs and Crime, commenting on the illegal drug trade in Afghanistan, said, "The terrorists and traffickers are the same people.[90] The Afghanistan opium drug trade was estimated at about $2.8 billion in 2004. However, little of the profits from the illegal drug trade goes to those who grow the poppies used to produce opium. Most of the profits from the drug trade go to the drug traffickers, warlords, and militia leaders, according to the United Nations.

Cutting Off the Flow of Cash

Overseas the United States is attempting to cut off the cash that terrorists realize from drug trafficking by a two-prong strategy. First, the United States has various in-country programs to reduce drug production. Second, the United States Navy and Coast Guard patrol the high seas to detect and apprehend drug traffickers. Using intelligence and photo imaging data of ship movements, the United States Navy and Coast Guard intercept and inspect ships suspected of transporting illegal drugs.

A new tactic being used in the United States to cut off the flow of illegal cash to terrorists has been the scanning of financial records to persons and organizations suspected to have ties with terrorism to detect "high-risk" financial transactions. In December 2004, the Department of Homeland Security began using various computer databases to allow investigators to match financial transactions against a list of some 250,000 people and firms with suspected ties to terrorist financing, drug trafficking, money laundering, and other financial crimes. Using a network of various private databases, the Department of Homeland Security tries to match financial transactions with people and organizations on the department's terrorist watch list.[91]

Terror-Related Fraud

One of the challenges for the police in the War on Terrorism is the difficult job of fighting terror-related fraud. Millions of dollars of aid money and money that was supposed to go to funding antiterrorism efforts have been siphoned off by terror-related fraud, committed by individuals, by businesses, and by the government. The task of investigating and prosecuting this fraud adds to the responsibilities of the criminal justice system.

Immediately following the 9/11 attacks many unscrupulous individuals engaged in criminal schemes to claim compensation or to establish fraudulent charities to bilk the public for money. For example, an Arkansas woman tried to defraud a fund for victims of the September 11, 2001, attacks, claiming that her dead brother was a firefighter who was killed in the attacks. The scope of the fraud can be appreciated when you consider that the average settlement paid to families of firefighters averaged more than $4 million.[92] In another case, a Michigan man claimed that his brother died in the collapse of the Twin Towers. The man received more than $268,000 before it was discovered that the claim was fraudulent. Insurance companies allege that numerous businesses have filed fraudulent 9/11-related claims.[93] Even state governments have been accused of using antiterrorism funds, claiming it was necessary for responding quickly to possible terror attacks. An audit of the state of Texas indicated that nearly $600 million in federal antiterrorism funds was spent improperly.[94] Despite the potential seriousness of such misappropriation, some of the alleged abuses appear mind-boggling. For example, it is alleged that one jurisdiction purchased a trailer that was used to haul lawn mowers to "lawn mower drag races," claiming the trailer was "emergency equipment."[95]

▲ check your understanding **6.7** **What are some ways that terrorist groups finance their activities? Why is cutting off the source of financial funding important in the War on Terrorism?**

Cyberterrorism

▼ the main idea **6.8** **Some authorities fear that terrorists may be able to cause more harm by a cyberattack than a conventional assault. Terrorist groups are increasingly exploiting the use of the Internet for recruiting, training, planning, and public relations. Some fear that cyberattacks by state-sponsored terrorist groups may rise to the level of warfare.**

Defending cyberspace is a new challenge that emerged with the invention of the Internet. Defending cyberspace from attack by terrorists is a new threat that has become a prominent concern since the 9/11 attacks.

The Federal Bureau of Investigation has defined *cyberterrorism* as "the premeditated, politically motivated attack against information, computer systems, computer programs, and data which result in violence against noncombatant targets by subnational groups or clandestine agents."[96] This definition includes actions by both domestic terrorists and international terrorists operating either in the United States or in a foreign country. There have been no documented cases of a "pure cyberattack" by international terrorists but the National Research Council has warned that "tomorrow's terrorist may be able to do more damage with a keyboard than with a bomb." Former cybersecurity czar Richard Clarke warned Congress in 2003 that there is a "dangerous tendency to dismiss the consequences of an attack on the nation's computer networks because no one has died in a cyberattack and there has never been a smoking ruin for cameras to see."[97]

Even before 9/11 experts warned that cyberterrorism presents a great potential threat to the United States. Since the 9/11 attacks experts have warned of the specter of a "digital Pearl Harbor."[98] Former Central Intelligence Agency Director Robert Gates warned, "Cyberterrorism could be the most devastating weapon of mass destruction yet and could cripple the U.S. economy."[99]

Terrorists could use the strategy of cyberterrorism in the following four ways: (1) use of the Internet to promote terrorism; (2) use of the Internet to gather information for attacks (cyberattacks) and as a tool to attack businesses and websites to disrupt the economy and cause financial loss (cyberintelligence); (3)attacks on critical infrastructures using the Internet to effect physical damage, and (4) cyberwarfare.

Use of the Internet to Promote Terrorism

Military action by the United States has disrupted the terrorist training camps in Afghanistan and Iraq. Also, the United States has increasingly pressured other Middle Eastern nations to take actions against terrorist training camps within their borders. The result is that terrorist groups are turning to the Internet as their new sanctuary.[100] The Internet has become a key tool for both domestic and international terrorist organizations. For international terrorist groups such as al Qaeda the Internet is their new "base." Anonymous Arabic-language Internet websites provide cybersanctuaries for terrorists that are often more difficult to detect and eliminate than physical training camps. Deputy Defense Secretary Paul D. Wolfowitz, in testimony before the House Armed Services Committee, said that terrorists use the Internet as a tool "to conceal their identities, to move money, to encrypt messages, even to plan and conduct operations remotely."[101] It is known that al Qaeda and its affiliates have always used e-mail and the Internet as communication tools. The Internet allows al Qaeda to use a legitimate technology to assist in planning terrorism, recruiting new members, and gathering information that will assist them in their attacks. The Internet has become one of the prime tools of the terrorists.[102]

Federal agencies, including the National Security Agency, the FBI, and the Department of Homeland Security, monitor suspected terror sites on the Internet and sometimes track users. However, the sheer number and anonymity of these jihadist websites makes it virtually impossible to stem the flow of radical Islamic propaganda.[103] Another problem in stopping violent jihadist groups from using the Internet is that censoring Internet websites often raises the constitutional challenge of First Amendment rights.

Cyberintelligence In addition to being an effective method for the distribution of propaganda, the Internet is a strategic tool for terrorists to gather intelligence to assist in planning attacks and a tool to attack businesses and websites to disrupt the economy and cause financial loss.

The Internet has proven to be one of the most valuable sources of intelligence for planning attacks for terrorists. Prior to the 9/11 attacks the amount of information that could be of strategic importance to terrorists that could be accessed by the Internet was overwhelming. Routinely, data about electrical power, gas and oil storage, transportation, banking and finance, water supply, emergency services, and the community of government operations were available from the Internet. Even information that would clearly be of value in the planning of an attack—such as the operational status information of nuclear plants, toxic-release inventory, a listing of all factories and other sources that emit poisonous pollution, information about dangerous pesticides, and detailed maps of power lines, gas lines, and locations of critical emergency supplies used by state Emergency Management Offices—was easily accessible as public documents on the Internet. Even after the 9/11 attacks many sites did not remove information that could equip potential terrorists to carry out an attack, such as the location of fuel storage tanks, maps of electrical grids, information on dams and reservoirs, and building floor plans of state and federal buildings.

Cyberattacks Security experts have warned for several years that cyberterrorism presents a great potential threat to the United States.[104] Even before the 9/11 attacks, the information technology revolution was quietly and quickly changing the way business and government operate. The Internet has become the world's communications network linking banking, businesses, manufacturing, and utilities. In the past, waterways, surface transportation, and air transportation were the vital communication and transportation systems considered to be the engine of commerce. Today, networked computers and the Internet are the lifeline of business and government. Unfortunately, however, the Internet was developed without a great deal of thought about security.[105] This great dependence on information transferred by the Internet and networked computers has created a new vulnerability for society with the potential to bring commerce to a halt and to impact the lives of millions of people worldwide. Intelligence gathered from confiscated computers from al Qaida members, interrogations of captured terrorists, and past actions clearly indicate that terrorist groups are planning attacks to disrupt or disable the Internet and other global communications networks.[106]

Some experts dismiss the threat of cyberterrorism. According to one panel of security experts, "The nation's computer networks face greater threats from non-terrorist hackers, viruses and poorly designed software than from a major cyberterrorism attack."[107] Although the threat of cyberterrorism is minimum according to some, many fear that the *fear* of cyberterrorism is greater than the actual threat that can be documented. In addition, although there have been no catastrophic cyberattacks by terrorists, the same could be said of attacks using airplanes as flying missiles prior to

September 11, 2001. Thus, cyberterrorism is a great concern of both governments and businesses.

Attacks on Critical Infrastructures Using the Internet

Cyberattacks are capable of causing mass disruptions against integrated and heterogeneous defenses. Using complex-coordinated attacks, terrorists have the ability to use the Internet as a direct instrument of bloodshed. These cyberattacks do more than cause damage to computer databases and networks. They have the ability to give terrorists control of the physical structures controlled by computers.[108]

What gives terrorists the ability to use computers to cause damage in the real world are the use of digital control systems (DCS) and supervisory control and data acquisition systems (SCADA). These specialized digital devices are used by the millions as the brains of critical infrastructure in the United States.[109] The report of *The National Strategy to Secure Cyberspace* states that over the last 20 years DCS and SCADA control systems have transformed the way many industries in the United States control and monitor equipment. These two systems do tasks such as collect measurements, throw railway switches, close circuit breakers, and adjust valves in the pipes that carry water, oil, and gas. They can also be designed to control a single device or to monitor and control multiple devices. They can be programmed to make decisions as to what to do and when to do it. The use of DCS and SCADA systems has allowed industry to replace many tasks that were previously performed manually with digital controls. They are used in almost every sector of the economy, including water, transportation, chemicals, energy, and manufacturing.[110] Using the Internet to take control of DCS and SCADA systems, terrorists could use virtual tools to destroy realworld lives and property. Terrorists could combine physical attacks, using explosives with cyberattacks to escalate the damage caused by a physical attack. For example, terrorists could detonate a truck bomb and simultaneously disable the 9-1-1 communications systems to prevent officials from responding to the situation.

When DCS and SCADA systems were designed it was not anticipated that there would be public access to these digital control systems, as they were controlled by local computers without access to the Internet. During the past 20 years many of these systems have been connected to the Internet because this allows companies to reduce personnel and costs. However, connecting these digital control systems to the Internet has created new vulnerabilities. A statement by the Commerce Department's Critical Infrastructure Assurance Office warns that the prevalence of these digital control systems connected by the Internet to run physical assets places the nation at risk. "Digital controls are so pervasive that terrorists might use them to cause damage on a scale that otherwise would not be available except through a very systematic and comprehensive physical attack."[111]

A major concern of government officials is the vulnerability of the North American power grid. Equipment failures not due to cyberattacks by terrorists have demonstrated that it is possible for the grid to go down and that disruption of the power grid causes enormous financial damage, causes fear and disruption of everyday life, and exposes cities to vulnerabilities due to disruption of communications of emergency services such as fire and police. The Commerce Department has conducted mock cyber SCADA attacks against the power grid. These mock attacks have always succeeded in bringing down the power grid.[112]

Cyberwarfare

Cyberattacks by terrorists are a concern, but some government officials, including Richard A. Clarke, former head of the Office of Cyberspace Security under President Bush, consider Cyberattacks by nation-states "the most dangerous threat to this country's computer security."[113] Clarke has indicated that he suspects that about five or six nation-states have attempted cyberattacks on national security computers.[114] The report of *The National Strategy to Secure Cyberspace* stated that in 1998, attackers carried out a sophisticated, tightly orchestrated series of cyberintrusions into the computers of the Department of Defense, the National Aeronautical and Space Administration (NASA), and government research labs. The intrusions were targeted against those organizations that conduct advanced technical research on national security, including atmospheric and oceanographic topics as well as aircraft and cockpit design.[115]

It is easy for the perpetrators of a cyberattack to conceal their identity: thus, cyberattacks have proven attractive strategies for attacking the United States, especially by poorer nations. Nations that would never consider a military assault against the United States may be tempted to launch a cyberattack. Cyberwarfare could be carried out at a fraction of the cost of a conventional war, expose the attacker to much less risk of retaliation, and be initiated anywhere in the world. It is not necessary to physically enter the United States to launch a cyberattack. Mock attacks by the Central Intelligence Agency and the National Security Agency have concluded that cyberterrorism could be the most devastating weapon of mass destruction and could cripple the U.S. economy.

The Internet is a prime target of terrorists because the high-tech economy of the United States is dependent on it. Furthermore, the economy of countries from which most terrorists originate is usually not as dependent on the Internet. Therefore, a disruption of the Internet would have a far greater impact on the United States.[117] Former Central Intelligence Director Robert Gates has warned that as terrorists become more motivated by radical religion, the less the terrorists are concerned about the scale of their violence and the number of innocent lives they are prepared to take.[118] Thus, concerns about both cyberattacks from terrorists and cyberattacks from nations have caused the federal government and military to take actions to develop robust defense capacities against cyberattacks.

▲ check your understanding **6.8** **What are some ways that terrorist groups have used the Internet? How could terrorist groups use the Internet to do physical harm to people and infrastructure targets? Why do some authorities fear that a cyberattack may do more harm than an attack with conventional weapons?**

The Challenge of Illegal Immigration

▼ the main idea **6.9** **The Department of Homeland Security has assumed responsibility for immigration control and enforcement.**

Since 2001, one of the goals of the federal government has been to prevent international terrorists from entering the United States. There are several ways terrorists can enter the country. They can use false immigration papers, they can enter under the pretext of being legal tourists and then not leave when their tourist visas expire, they can enter using student visas, and they can enter illegally and undetected at some point in the 8,000 miles of the Canadian and Mexican borders plus the Atlantic and Pacific coastlines.

Prior to September 11, 2001, immigration control and border security were the responsibility of the Immigration and Naturalization Services (INS). The 9/11 Commission criticized the Immigration and Naturalization Services, claiming that the INS was negligent and failed to prevent terrorists involved in the September 11 attacks from entering the United States. Since 2001, concern over ineffective immigration control and porous border security has led to the dismantling of INS and the transfer of responsibility for immigration control and border security to the Department of Homeland Security. Immigration enforcement functions were placed within the directorate of Border and Transportation Security (BTS), either directly or under Customs and Border Protection (CBP), which includes the Border Patrol and INS inspectors, or **Immigration and Customs Enforcement (ICE)**. The enforcement and investigation components previously performed by INS—such as investigations, intelligence, detention, and removals—were assumed by ICE.[119] The DHS and other federal agencies have taken actions (1) to prevent, detect, and deport those who have entered illegally; (2) to ensure accurate tracking of the entry and exit of foreign nationals to and from the United States; (3) to ensure that those entering the country by using student visas actually enroll and attend the college or program they indicate on their application; and (4) to make it more difficult to obtain false immigration and identification documents.

The power to regulate immigration is an exclusive power given to the federal government; therefore, the DHS is primarily responsible for immigration control and border security. The Department of Homeland Security initiated several programs to seal the borders against terrorists. One of the more controversial programs sought to identify "special interest" immigrants who allegedly had direct or indirect connections to terrorist groups. This program resulted in the arrest of more than 700 people, most from Middle Eastern countries, who were charged with violating immigration laws.[120] Additional security screening for visa applications was required for applications from 26 predominantly Muslim countries. The DHS also initiated the Absconder Apprehension Initiative. The purpose of the program is to identify and expedite the expulsion of immigrants who are facing deportation from countries with an al Qaeda presence.

State and Local Actions to Curtail Illegal Immigration

Although immigration is officially the responsibility of the federal government, many state and city governments are greatly concerned and impacted by illegal immigration. The primary focus of the federal government, especially the DHS, has been on preventing terrorists from entering the United States, but state and local governments have expressed concern over public safety issues caused by illegal immigration. Illegal immigration posed such a threat that in August 2005, the governors of Arizona and New Mexico issued a state of emergency declaration in response to what they described as a public safety concern caused by illegal immigration.[121]

State and local governments cite public safety concerns related to illegal immigrants who commit acts of violence, including murder, drug trafficking, human smuggling, and property damage. New Mexico Governor Bill Richardson declared that as a result of the illegal border crossings, citizens of New Mexico were "devastated by the ravages and terror of human smuggling, drug smuggling, kidnapping, murder, destruction of property and death of livestock."[122] The extent of the problem is illustrated by the fact that at one point on the New Mexico border the Border Patrol estimated there were an average of 175 persons per day caught trying to enter the United States illegally.[123]

The concern for public safety extends beyond border towns, as once in the United States some illegal immigrants engage in violent gang criminality.[124] Violent criminal gangs composed primarily of illegal immigrants can be found in major cities throughout the United States. One of the most serious concerns among law enforcement is the criminal activity of the gang known as MS-13 or Mara Salvatrucha, which has committed numerous violent attacks in major cities throughout the United States. In 2005 and 2006, in a sweep of suspected immigrant gang members called Operation Community Shield, ICE arrested over 1,000 alleged gang members representing 80 gangs in 25 states.[125] Immigration and Customs Enforcement officials said more than 900 of those arrested are eligible for deportation. Antigang ICE officials claim there are thousands of suspected gang members who are in the United States illegally or who have committed serious crimes that make them eligible for deportation. The extent of the criminality of illegal immigrants is seen in that each year ICE deports approximately 80,000 illegal immigrants for criminal activity.[126]

Despite the fact that immigration control is a federal power, many state and local law enforcement agencies feel that they have a public safety responsibility to respond to what they see as a potential threat to their community. Some police departments routinely inform federal immigration authorities whenever they arrest a noncitizen, even a lawful permanent resident.[127] Also, during a check of a person's identity, even if it is for a routine purpose such as a driver's license check, some police departments will notify ICE if the check indicates the person is an immigration violator. In such cases if immigration authorities issue a request for police to hold the person, he or she will be held for 48 hours for pickup by federal officers.[128]

Public safety issues related to illegal immigration have been particularly difficult for rural sheriffs' departments along the Mexican border. These sheriff's departments do not have the personnel and resources to stem the flow of illegal immigrants and drugs that cross the border in their jurisdiction. Sheriffs protest that many of their problems are due to lack of federal law enforcement cooperation and interest in the problems of local law enforcement.

Some local law enforcement agencies are more aggressive in countering the threat they see from illegal immigration. One unique strategy by two New Hampshire towns, New Ipswich and Hudson, was for local police to use state trespass laws to arrest undocumented immigrants.[129] It was short lived, as the New Hampshire District Court declared that the towns' actions could not be upheld because such immigration matters must be left to federal authorities.[130]

Despite the court's ruling other local governments have taken up the fight against illegal immigration. In 2006, Hazleton, Pennsylvania, adopted that city's Illegal Immigration Relief Act, which provides for fines to landlords of $1,000 for every illegal immigrant tenant. Other cities have followed suit and have adopted ordinances aimed at

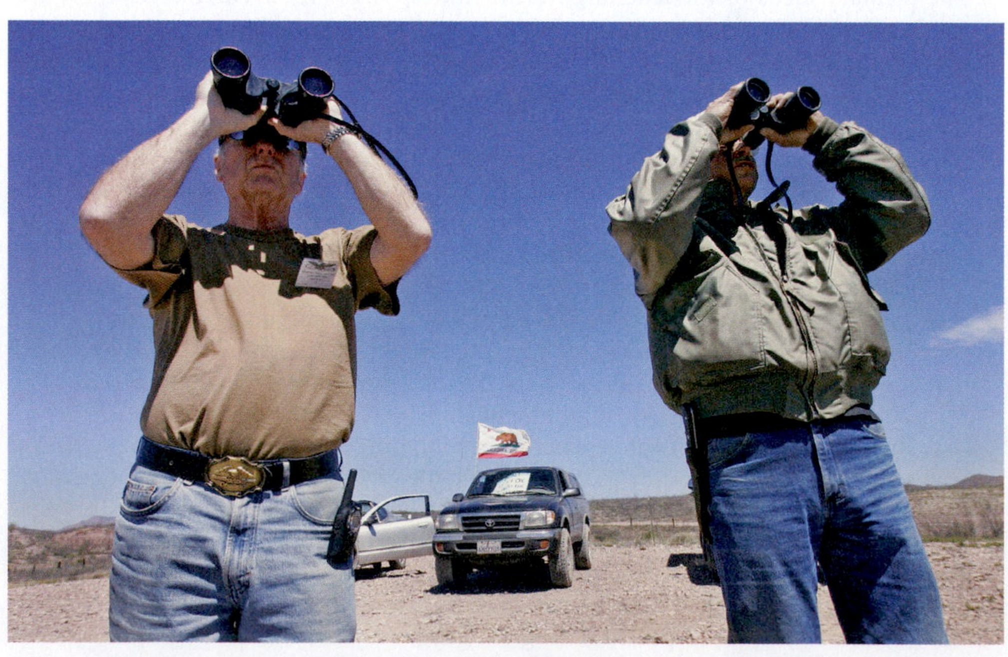

In 2005, volunteers known as Minutemen patrolled the United States–Mexico border in Arizona looking for illegal border crossers. The federal government has discouraged such volunteer movements. Do you believe volunteers such as the Minutemen could make a difference in curbing illegal crossings?

penalizing landlords, companies, and businesses who rent to or hire illegal immigrants. Cities that have adopted such stategies argue that it is the failure of the federal agencies to control illegal immigration that force them to take such actions.

Homeland Security Secretary Michael Chertoff has promised significant strengthening of the DHS's border security efforts. The number of Border Patrol agents has increased from 4,000 prior to September 11, 2001, to over 11,000 in 2005. The DHS spends more than $7.3 billion a year in border-related expenses, a 58 percent increase since September 9/11.[131] Despite these efforts by the DHS to stem the flow of illegal immigrants, some citizens who have become concerned by what they see as the failure of the federal government to secure the borders against illegal immigrants have formed citizen volunteer groups to patrol the U.S.–Mexican border. One citizens' patrol, the Minuteman Project, attracted much public attention in summer 2005 as hundreds of volunteers watched the U.S.–Mexican border for illegal immigrants making their way across the border into the United States. Although there are suggestions that the Department of Homeland Security should use volunteers to assist in patrolling the U.S.–Mexican border, the DHS has indicated that it did not favor the use of such volunteers.[132]

▲ check your understanding **6.9** **Why is closing the borders important in the War on Terrorism? What programs have been adopted to control and enforce immigration? What is the impact of illegal immigration on local law enforcement agencies?**

Constitutional Rights and Homeland Security

▼ the main idea **6.10** **In the 9/11 environment, some liberties have been lost in the pursuit of enhanced national security.**

The U.S. criminal justice system is based on the principle that citizens are entitled to certain inalienable rights provided by the Constitution and Bill of Rights. Citizens are guaranteed such rights as the right of freedom from unreasonable search, the right to confront witnesses, the right to a public trial, the right to know the charges against them, the right to an attorney, and the right of free speech and association. These rights have served as the cornerstone of the U.S. criminal justice system. However, public opinion polls indicate that most Americans believe that some civil rights will have to be sacrificed in the War on Terrorism. The challenge is to balance the loss of civil rights with appropriate national security concerns.

Fewer Liberties, Greater Security?

In the post-September 11, 2001, environment, some acts and behaviors have been prohibited in the effort to promote national security. Congress has provided law enforcement officials with new powers that diminish Fourth Amendment (search and seizure) rights. The justification for the curtailing of these rights is that these new powers and laws promote national security and enhance the ability of law enforcement to detect terrorist cells within the United States and secret plots by terrorists before they can launch a terrorist attack.

You can access the homepage of the American Civil Liberties Union at www.aclu.org. Although not dedicated to the topic of terrorism, the website frequently contains critiques of antiterrorist legislation, policies, and government actions.

Related efforts to promote national security by discovering these terrorist cells have impacted many citizens. For example, in an effort to make it harder for terrorists to avoid detection, policies and practices have been adopted to prevent terrorists from obtaining employment. The purpose of these policies and laws is to make it more difficult for terrorists to remain in the United States or to obtain jobs where they could use their employment to carry out a terrorist attack. However, as a result of such practices, thousands of airline workers who are not terrorists lost their jobs when U.S. citizenship became a job requirement for these jobs. Also, fearing that terrorists may recruit converts from the criminal population, legislation was passed that prohibited persons with felony convictions from obtaining certain employment, such as truck drivers who could transport hazardous materials, or from obtaining jobs on military bases. Since there is no time limit on when one was convicted, some workers with long-past felony convictions have found that they are denied employment or lost their job because of this provision.

In the name of national security, citizens have fewer expectations of privacy rights. Increased domestic intelligence action by the Justice Department has resulted in government access to bank accounts, credit histories, medical records, academic records, travel plans, Internet communications, and cell phone communications. In the effort to ensure national security, the FBI under the Bush administration has engaged in extensive spying on Americans, secret searches of mosques, and scrutiny of hundreds of social action groups such as the American Civil Liberties Union.

Calls for independent bipartisan panels to monitor the possible abuse of civil rights have not overcome the belief by the majority that loss of a certain number of civil rights may be necessary to prevent future terrorist attacks. As a result, there are examples of loss of privacy that prior to the War on Terrorism mostly likely would not have occurred. For example, social security data are normally protected by strict privacy laws. However, the FBI and Social Security Administration have admitted that because of what they deemed were "life-threatening emergency" situations related to possible terrorist attacks, social security data have been shared with the FBI. The Internal Revenue Service also has acknowledged that they have shared income and taxpayer information with the FBI.[133]

Secrecy As citizens' civil rights and privacy have diminished there has been an increase in government secrecy. The United States prides itself on the open nature of its government but in an effort to keep terrorists from gaining information that may prove useful in planning or executing a terrorist attack, the government has become less open. A record 15.6 million government documents, nearly double the number in 2001, were classified in 2004.[134] Even documents that were initially released to the public have been recalled and classified.[135] Also, the DHS and the Justice Department have used other means to keep information from the public, such as designating information that is not classified as "Sensitive Homeland Security Information," "Protected Critical Infrastructure Information," or "Sensitive Security Information."[136]

Free Speech and Protest versus Terrorism

Actions of federal and local law enforcement justified under the pretense of antiterrorism can significantly affect First Amendment rights to free speech, to free association, and to civil protests. There is a difference between terrorism and dissent, civil protest, or expressing disagreement with laws and policies of the government. In a democracy, not every group that claims there is a social injustice or that disagrees with the policies and laws of government or the criminal justice system is a terrorist group. Often, in the name of social justice, people violate the law or protest through civil disobedience, but nonviolent civil disobedience is not terrorism. Drafting laws and policies that distinguish between legitimate civil protests of injustice and the violence of terrorism is one

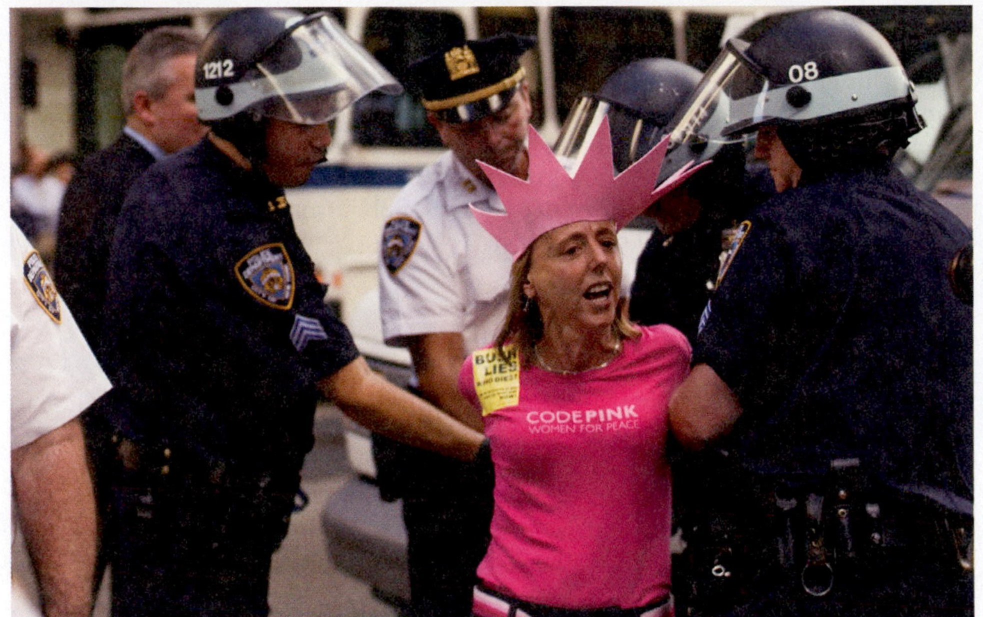

Defenders of civil rights worry that aggressive police actions against legitimate protesters will infringe on civil rights. The American Civil Liberties Union issued a critical report of the actions of the New York Police Department during the 2004 Republican National Convention. Do you think the civil rights of legitimate protesters are being violated by police in the name of antiterrorism?

of the greatest challenges confronting the criminal justice system, as police actions and laws that have been passed to suppress terrorism may also prohibit legitimate expressions of dissenting opinions. As law enforcement agencies, particularly the FBI, have gained new powers to conduct domestic intelligence, critics argue that they again are abusing these powers to monitor the political activities of activist groups, especially those opposed to the Bush administration.

The FBI denies the charges. A statement released by the Justice Department's Office of Legal Counsel said "Any First Amendment impact posed by the FBI's monitoring of the political protests was negligible and constitutional."[137] Protest groups charge that FBI counterterrorism officials have used powers that were supposed to be used to prevent terrorism "to blur the line between legitimate civil disobedience and violent or terrorist activity."[138]

Charges of Unlawful Behavior by the Police Local police departments are also accused of violating First Amendment rights of protesters, with the police claiming that their behavior is motivated by the desire to deter terrorism. For example, during the 2004 Republican National Convention in New York City, the New York Civil Liberties Union accused the police of stifling political protest by abuse of their power and arresting protestors (and innocent bystanders) on trumped-up charges. As evidence of the bad faith of law enforcement in honoring the First Amendment rights of protesters, the New York Civil Liberties Union pointed out that of the 1,670 cases involving the arrest of protesters handled by the Manhattan district attorney, 91 percent ended with the charges dismissed or with a verdict of not guilty after trial.[139] A more serious charge regarding First Amendment violations is the fact that in at least 400 cases, charges were dropped or defendants were acquitted after videotapes or other evidence clearly demonstrated that police officials had given false testimony regarding the alleged actions of the arrested person or the circumstances of the arrest. Videos showed that in a number of incidents the police had actually filed false charges against innocent bystanders.

The New York State Civil Liberties Union accused the police department of overreacting to possible legitimate concerns about terrorist activities and in their effort to prevent such attacks abridged the rights of citizens to protest. They concluded, "In an effort to maintain tight control over protest activity, the NYPD lost sight of the distinction between lawful and unlawful conduct."[140]

Fourth Amendment Rights and Terrorism

Civil rights advocates argue that fear of terrorism may endanger constitutional rights granted under the Fourth Amendment concerning search and seizure protections. The American Civil Liberties Union argues that fear of terrorism has resulted in changes in the fundamental constitutional rules governing searches by the police.[141] The ACLU expresses the concern that actions taken to protect the public from terrorism may do so but may also violate constitutional rights.

Denial of Due Process

Critics accuse the Justice Department of denying due process to many persons accused of or suspected of terrorism in the War on Terrorism. For example, a report by Human Rights Watch accuses the federal government of indiscriminate and arbitrary arrests of males from predominantly Muslim countries without sufficient probable cause or even reasonable suspicion.[142]

Also, Human Rights Watch and the American Civil Liberties Union accuse the Justice Department of abusing the material witness law to detain terror suspects. The **material witness law**, enacted in 1984, allows federal authorities to hold a person indefinitely without charging him or her with a crime if they suspect that the person has information about a crime and might flee or be unwilling to cooperate with law enforcement officials.[143] Human Rights Watch and the ACLU charge that the Justice Department has used the material witness law to detain 70 persons, about one-third of them U.S. citizens, on suspicion of terrorism where questionable evidence exists for such detentions. The Justice Department has apologized to at least 13 persons for wrongly detaining them under the material witness law.[144] One of the more publicized abuses of the material witness law was the detention of Portland, Oregon, lawyer Brandon Mayfield, whom the FBI wrongly accused of being connected to the Madrid train bombings of 2004.

Of great concern to those who fear that the War on Terrorism is eroding due process rights is the Justice Department's denial of access to the civilian courts for those accused or suspected of terrorism. The use of the Enemy Combatant Executive Order to detain alleged terrorists and al Qaeda members has seriously alarmed proponents of constitutional rights. The use of this executive order, combined with the use of military tribunals instead of civilian court trials, denies accused enemy combatants access to the civilian courts. This process of determining guilt denies them the due process rights to an attorney, to confront the witnesses against them, to know of the evidence the government has against them, and the right to a public trial by their peers.

Racial Profiling Over the years much progress has been made in addressing the problem of **racial profiling** by law enforcement. Public opinion polls have indicated that most people disapprove of racial profiling by the police. Prior to 9/11, racial profiling was seen as a problem directed primarily against Blacks and Latinos. However, since September 11, 2001, racial profiling has become a concern particularly for Middle-Eastern–looking males, as public opinion and legislators seem less opposed to racial profiling of Middle-Eastern–looking males, especially at airports and on public transportation.

Since September 11, 2001, some have been so bold as to publicly voice that they favor profiling young Middle Eastern or Islamic men at airports and other high-risk security venues.[145] For example, following the July 2005 London subway and bus bombings, the New York Police Department instituted random searches of passengers' bags on subways and buses. Two New York City officials said, "Police have been wasting time with random checks in efforts to prevent terrorism in the transit system."[146] The two officials argued that random searches were an inappropriate "politically correct" response to possible terrorist attacks and that the NYPD should focus "on those who fit the terrorist profile," whom they identified as young Arab fundamentalists.[147] The two

material witness law Law that allows for the detention of a person who has not committed a crime but is alleged to have information about a crime that has been committed.

racial profiling Allegations that police search and seizures, traffic stops, field interrogations, and arrests are made on nonbehavioral factors related to race and/or ethnicity rather than suspicious behavior or probable cause.

city officials said that they plan to introduce legislation that would allow police to racially profile. The NYPD has publicly stated that it does not seek such power and does not believe racial profiling would be an effective counterterrorism strategy.

The DHS and the Justice Department have denied that any of their policies related to immigration enforcement, screening, or investigation are based on racial profiling. In 2003, the Justice Department issued a policy statement regarding guidelines on racial profiling. The guidelines govern the conduct of 70 federal law enforcement agencies. However, the guidelines do not ban racial profiling. They do bar federal agents from using race or ethnicity in their routine investigations, but the guidelines allow for clear exemptions for investigations involving terrorism and national security matters. The Justice Department claims that a 2003 survey of federal law enforcement agencies concluded that "racial profiling by federal law enforcement agents does not appear to be a systemic problem."[148]

Muslims and Muslim leaders in the United States do not endorse the findings of the Justice Department regarding the absence of racial profiling. They point to the fact that surveys of non-Muslims indicate that those surveyed were more likely to say Islam is more violent than Christianity, Judaism, or Hinduism.[149] They claim non-Muslims in the United States have a negative image of Muslims and perceive them as the primary suspects in suspected terrorism. U.S. Muslims deny any link between Islam and terrorism and point out that Central Intelligence Agency reports show that Latin Americans were responsible for more terrorist incidents than Muslims.[150]

Muslims in the United States point out that hate crimes against Muslims have increased since September 11, 2001, and rose again after the 2005 London transit bombings. They also point out that in some cities with large Muslim populations, the number of Middle Easterners citied for offenses by law enforcement has been significantly higher than all others charged with offenses.[151] Many Muslims report that they fear that "the motives behind some of the post-9/11 security efforts seem aimed at Muslims."[152] As a result, they report that they "keep as low a profile as they can" because they believe that Americans "feel the next terrorist attack will be from a Muslim."[153]

▲ check your understanding 6.10 How has the War on Terrorism affected civil liberties and privacy rights? How has the War on Terrorism affected government secrecy? How have free speech rights been affected by the War on Terrorism? What due process rights have been affected by the War on Terrorism? Why is racial profiling a concern?

conclusion:

Turning the Criminal Justice System Upside Down

The War on Terrorism and the concern for homeland security have had a significant impact on the police and the criminal justice system. Doubtful that the criminal justice system is up to the challenge of responding to terrorism, the federal government has assumed considerable new powers and at the same time has curtailed civil rights that have been considered foundational to the U.S. criminal justice system, such as the right to an attorney, the right of a defendant to know the charges against him or her, the right to remain silent, and the right to a public trial.

The Department of Homeland Security and the FBI have assumed major responsibilities in the War on Terrorism. In their new roles, the traditional relationships between federal and local law enforcement have changed and federal agencies have assumed the lead role in investigating terrorist incidences. The role of police as first responders and the need for coordinated multiagency response to terrorist attacks have exposed critical shortcomings in infrastructure, training, and equipment. The powers of federal agencies have been bolstered by new legislation. However, many of these new powers have been challenged as serious and needless infringements on civil rights.

In summary, the criminal justice system has been turned upside down. Whereas traditionally the focus of the criminal justice system was the local government, the new focus today is the federal government. This new federalism was dramatically illustrated in the government's response to the 2005 relief effort following Hurricane Katrina that hit New Orleans and the Gulf Coast. Hurricane Katrina and the breaching of the levy that surrounded New Orleans resulted in the flooding of nearly 100,000 square miles, tens of thousands of people stranded and homeless, and over one thousand deaths. Traditionally in disaster relief efforts the federal government supplements local and state government relief and rescue efforts. However, the ability of the local and state government to respond was immediately surpassed.

There was widespread criticism when the federal government failed to immediately assume responsibility for rescue and recovery. The public simply assumed that given the extensive federal preparation and focus on catastrophic disaster recovery in preparation for a terrorist attack, that the federal government had the ability to immediately assume command and control of the catastrophic event. When it took days for the federal government to provide rescue relief, the public expressed shock at the slowness of the response and asked, "If the federal government took this long to respond to a natural disaster, what would they have done if this were a terrorist attack with a weapon of mass destruction?"

The War on Terrorism has resulted in a reexamination of some of the most basic practices underlying the criminal justice system. This examination has resulted in law enforcement and government agencies looking at how other nations are responding to similar threats. For example, Israel has fought its own War on Terrorism for decades, and in many respects it is a war that is waged much more fiercely than the one in the United States. As a result, the federal government and the New York City Police Department have examined Israel's response to terrorism to see if there are practices that could be adopted by the United States. Also, close attention is paid to Britain's response to the threat of terrorism, as Britain is considered to have many values similar to the United States.

Finally, the War on Terrorism poses a unique challenge for criminal justice scholars and programs. Criminal justice scholars have spent considerable effort and research during the past half century describing and understanding the U.S. criminal justice system. The War on Terrorism is fundamentally changing the criminal justice system, and scholars will need to examine and explain to what extent the War on Terrorism is altering the criminal justice system. Also, there is the need for research to understand what motivates one to engage in terrorism. As hundreds of years of criminology research has produced extensive knowledge of criminals and victims, now there is the need for research to increase our understanding of terrorism. We need to know the answer to such questions as Why do some people choose terrorism? Why do some choose to be suicide bombers? What is the impact of terrorism on victims? and What are the best practices for responding to terrorism? The more information that scholars can bring to focus on the understanding of terrorism and terrorists, the more likely it is that the government and the criminal justice system will respond with effective actions that diminish terrorism and preserve civil liberties.

chapter summary

- To a large extent the public and the federal government do not believe that local and state law enforcement have the infrastructure, resources, training, and ability to respond to attacks by international terrorists.
- Terrorism is a tactic that involves the use of random attacks on noncombatants and physical targets to cause general disruption and widespread fear.
- There is no international agreement in labeling a group as a "terrorist group" because of the political and social values associated with the use of violence to achieve political and social goals.
- The FBI makes a distinction between international terrorism and domestic terrorism.
- Domestic terrorism includes militias, extremist groups, and ecoterrorists. Ecoterrorists have caused the greatest damage in the United States. The two most active ecoterrorist groups are the Earth Liberation Front and the Animal Liberation Front.
- Al Qaeda is considered the primary terrorist group responsible for attacks on U.S soil.
- Following the September 11, 2001, terrorist attacks, the federal government declared War on Terrorism and has taken a number of actions that have reduced the importance of the role of the state and local criminal justice system in fighting terrorism.
- The FBI and the Department of Homeland Security have assumed the primary responsibility for counterterrorism.
- The Department of Homeland Security was the most significant reorganization of the U.S. government since 1947. The DHS consolidated 22 federal agencies and 180,000 employees to create a single agency whose primary mission is to protect the U.S. homeland.
- Multiple agency coordination is considered essential in order to respond effectively to a terrorist attack.
- Local and state police are considered first responders to a terrorist attack but the federal government still assumes the primary responsibility for responding to a terrorist attack.
- There has been conflict between police and fire departments as to who should be the lead agency as first responder to a terrorist attack.
- Federal authority over terrorist acts has been greatly expanded by new legislation. The most significant source of new federal powers is the USA Patriot Act.
- As a result of the fear of terrorism, U.S. cities are being transformed as new physical security measures are adopted. The increased demand for physical security has caused a great strain on local and state police.
- Local and state police do not have the intelligence data they need in order to respond to terrorism, so they must depend on federal agencies for their intelligence. This fact frustrates many police departments.
- The FBI and the Department of Homeland Security have been given expanded intelligence powers and they are now permitted to share intelligence with the Central Intelligence Agency.
- The DHS Advisory System advises agencies and the public of the potential threat of a terrorist attack.
- Closing the borders to terrorists is a major goal of the federal government and many new initiatives have been adopted to achieve this goal.
- Critics argue that the cost of greater security has been fewer liberties. Of particular concern are losses of First Amendment, Fourth Amendment, and due process rights. Charges of rendition allege that the federal government has engaged in complete denial of due process rights of some terrorist suspects by kidnapping them and transporting them to foreign countries where they are tortured.
- Defending cyberspace from attack by terrorists is a new threat that has become a prominent concern.
- The War on Terrorism has defined a new relationship between the federal government and local and federal criminal justice agencies.

vocabulary review

Department of Homeland Security (DHS), 226
domestic terrorism, 223
ecoterrorism, 225
first responders, 232
Homeland Security Advisory System (HSAS), 239
international terrorism, 222
joint local–federal counterterrorism task force, 235
lead federal agency, 231
material witness law, 257
racial profiling, 257
Reign of Terror, 222
terrorism, 222
U.S. Government Interagency Domestic Terrorism Concept of Operations Plan (CONPLAN), 230
USA Patriot Act, 241
War on Terrorism, 220

do you remember?

al Qaeda, 226
Animal Liberation Front (ALF), 225
Central Intelligence Agency, 234
Earth Liberation Front (ELF), 225
Immigration and Customs Enforcement (ICE), 251
noncombatant, 222
Eric Robert Rudolph, 225
social injustice, 221
terrorist group, 222
Terrorist Threat Integration Center (TTIC), 235
Timothy McVeigh, 225
urban fortresses, 237

think about this

1. Federal government agencies have assumed the major responsibility for counterterrorism, resulting in a significant change in the role between the federal, local, and state governments. Do you agree that it is necessary for federal agencies to assume the role as lead agency in responding to terrorism? Explain your answer.
2. In the War on Terrorism, do you believe that the federal government has overlooked the danger posed by domestic terrorist groups? Explain your answer.
3. The FBI and the Department of Homeland Security have primary responsibility for counterterrorism. How well do you think they are doing in the War on Terrorism? Why?
4. Do you think the fire department or the police department should be the lead agency as first responder in responding to a chemical, biological, or nuclear incident that may be a possible terrorist attack? Why?
5. The Patriot Act has expanded the search and seizure powers of federal law enforcement agencies. Do you think the Patriot Act gives federal agencies too much power, too little power, or just the right amount to prevent another terrorist attack? Explain your answer.
6. Immigration control is a major strategy in preventing another terrorist attack. Do you think the federal government is doing a good job in improving immigration control? Why? If not, what should be done to enhance immigration control?
7. Are federal and local police violating constitutional rights in trying to protect the United States from another terrorist attack? Explain your answer.

research navigator

Visit the Research Navigator website (www.researchnavigator.com), login and select the criminal justice data base in ContentSelect. Type in the key words "Can Citizen Police Academies." Select the article "Can Citizen Police Academies Influence Citizens' Beliefs and Perceptions?" by J. Bret Becton, *et al.* Sample the article and answer the following questions.

1. What is the role of citizen police academies?
2. Why are citizen police academies increasing in popularity?
3. According to the data presented by the authors are citizen police academies promoting positive beliefs, feelings, and perceptions of the police by the citizens?
4. What do the authors suggest to improve the potential for citizen police academies?

chapter 7
The Court System

CHAPTER OUTLINE

LEARNING OBJECTIVES

After reading this chapter, you will know

- The history and dual structure of the court system.
- The difference between criminal and civil law.
- How the federal court system is organized and the responsibilities of each level of the federal courts.
- How the state court system is organized and the responsibilities of each level of the state courts.

In Criminal Cases, A Court Nominee Hews to Rules

If Samuel A. Alito Jr. had been on the Supreme Court back in January [2005], Ronald Rompilla might well be a dead man.

That month the Supreme Court heard an appeal of a decision, written by Judge Alito for a panel of the Third Circuit Court of Appeals, that upheld Mr. Rompilla's sentence for a murder committed in 1988. The Supreme Court, finding that Mr. Rompilla's lawyers had been ineffective representatives at trial, later reversed the ruling in a 5-to-4 vote.

Mr. Rompilla's appeal offers a study of how Judge Alito, President Bush's nominee to the Supreme Court, has handled criminal cases that have appeared before him. Perhaps not surprisingly, the judge, a former federal prosecutor, has often—though far from uniformly—ruled against defendants.

Judge Alito's opinions in criminal cases are meticulously written, with careful deference to the findings of trial court judges and juries and scrupulous determination to fit his decisions into the framework built by past cases. He hews to the rules.

Sometimes the judge's meticulously logical approach and exacting standards worked in favor of a defendant. In a case decided in 2003, for example, Judge Alito wrote a unanimous opinion for a three-judge panel that concluded that Ronald A. Williams, a black man convicted of murder, should be given a chance to show that a juror hearing his case had concealed racist views. In a 2001 case, the judge also sided with a man challenging a murder conviction, this time after finding that the lower court judge had improperly rejected one of the man's arguments.

Again, Judge Alito's reasoning was tight, technical and focused on procedure rather than outcome—as he wrote in the unanimous opinion of a three-judge panel. "Needless to say," he said, "we express no view regarding the merits of the claim."

Adapted from "In Criminal Cases, A Court Nominee Hews to Rules," The New York Times Online, www.nytimes.com, December 25, 2005 by Jonathan D. Glater.

introduction:

The Court as the Hub of the Criminal Justice System

If there is a center to the U.S. criminal justice system, it is the courts. All law enforcement and prosecutorial agencies work to move defendants into the court system, and from the courts defendants are removed from the system if found not guilty or are directed toward the various correctional agencies. Judges are at the center of the court system. The importance of judges rises to national attention when it is time to replace U.S. Supreme Court justices. The character and qualities of nominees are examined and debated. Past decisions are reviewed to determine their legal philosophy. Thus, in 2005, when President Bush nominated Samuel A. Alito Jr. for a vacancy on the Supreme Court, his judicial record was examined to determine what his appointment would do to the conservative–liberal balance of the Supreme Court. This balance is important, as landmark decisions are often decided by a single vote.

The judicial system is rooted in the U.S. Constitution and state constitutions. Unlike the various police and correctional agencies that evolved over a period of time, the federal court system was established by Article 3 of the Constitution. Article 3 established the Supreme Court, authorized Congress to ordain and establish inferior courts as necessary, set an indefinite term of service for federal judges, and provided that the compensation of a judge cannot be reduced during his or her continuance in office. Article 3 also required that the trial of all crimes, except in cases of impeachment, shall be by jury.

From the beginning the nation's founders saw the judiciary, especially the federal courts, as an integral part of the system of checks and balances of power. Thus, unlike police and correctional agencies that are subordinate to various political powers, the federal courts have a degree of independence, even power over the other two branches of government. The U.S. Supreme Court has equality with the executive and legislative branches of government in that it has the power to declare laws and executive orders unconstitutional. At the same time, the federal court system is lacking in political power in that it cannot directly make laws, and the federal court system is completely dependent on the legislative and executive branches for financial resources. The courts, both federal and state, have no "police" to enforce their rulings or to require agencies or personnel to cease and desist practices declared to be unconstitutional. Police and correctional agencies are not seen in the same light as essential to the checks and balances of political power.

From its humble beginning, the United States has crafted a complex judicial system with power to declare an act of Congress unconstitutional,[1] to settle disputes, and to sentence a person to death for violation of the law. The law as interpreted by the judicial system has become the primary arbitrator of right and wrong behavior. The United States is a nation of law, and everyone is assumed to be subject to the law. As Kenneth Starr, independent counsel for the Clinton impeachment trial, declared, "No one—absolutely no one—is above the law."[2]

The judicial system has many characteristics that differentiate it from police and corrections. This chapter examines the roles and characteristics of the court system and as well as the dual federal–state court system.

The Role of the Judicial System

▼the main idea 7.1 The United States has a dual system of courts, federal and state, which adjudicate criminal and civil cases.

Over the centuries, society's ways of dealing with harms against another have changed. At one time, people felt that if another person harmed their reputation, they could challenge the offending party to a duel to the death. In 1804, Aaron Burr, third vice president of the United States, killed Alexander Hamilton, secretary of the treasury, in such a duel. In the western frontier of the late nineteenth century, disputes sometimes were settled by gunfights. Today, however, people are prohibited from seeking private revenge and personal justice through the use of violence. The government requires that all wrongs—whether accidental, negligent, or criminal—be handled by the criminal justice or civil justice system.

The concept of a "court" vested with the power to arbitrate disputes can be traced back to the earliest times. One of the earliest references to *court* refers to the power of kings, rulers, and nobility to resolve disputes. Disputes were brought before the king or ruler, and the parties to the dispute argued their case. The opinion of the monarch frequently was unchallengeable and based primarily on his or her personal power, values, and interpretation of the dispute. As society became more sophisticated, it was necessary to develop a system of **jurisprudence**—a philosophy of law—to settle disputes, to replace the arbitrary authority of kings and rulers. In such a system, there is a body of written law to regulate interactions. These laws or codes provide people with guidelines that regulate behavior.

The Babylonian Code of Hammurabi of the eighteenth century B.C. is one of the earliest legal codes that has been preserved. However, the jurisprudence system of the United States was influenced primarily by the Justinian Code, the Napoleonic Code, and the common law of Great Britain. The Justinian Code, developed under the Roman emperor Justinian I, was influential in shaping the civil law of Europe and of Spanish colonies in Mexico and Latin America. The Napoleonic Code, designed by Napoleon Bonaparte to unify the laws of his empire, became the basis of the legal system of the state of Louisiana, a French colony. English common law was the main foundation on which the American jurisprudence system was built. The earliest colonies in North America were English or became English territories, and jurisprudence in the colonies essentially was the same as in England. After the Revolutionary War, the newly created government of the United States continued to use the English common law model of jurisprudence.

Dual Court System

In the **dual court system,** the court systems of the various states are sovereign governmental jurisdictions, each equal in importance. The federal courts are distinct from the state courts but do have limited jurisdiction over the state courts. This political division of jurisdictions between the federal and state governments is called a dual court system. The term *dual* means that there are two systems of courts. Thus, within both the federal and state systems, there are many further distinctions and divisions of the jurisdiction of the courts. The jurisdiction of the federal courts is defined in **Article 3, Section 2 of the U.S. Constitution** (see Figure 7.1).

The **Eleventh Amendment,** ratified in 1795, restricted the jurisdiction of the federal courts by declaring that a private citizen from one state cannot sue the government of another state in federal court. The **Tenth Amendment** provided that powers not specifically delegated to the federal government were reserved to the states. Under this authority, each state has the responsibility and power to establish its own court system.

jurisprudence The science or philosophy of law.

dual court system The political division of jurisdiction into two systems of courts, federal and state. Under this system, federal courts are separate from but have limited jurisdiction over state courts.

figure 7.1

Article 3, Section 2 of the U.S. Constitution

"The judicial power shall extend to all cases, in law and equity, arising under this Constitution, the laws of the United States, and treaties made or which shall be made, under their authority; to all cases affecting ambassadors, other public ministers and consuls; to all cases of admiralty and maritime jurisdiction; to controversies in which the United States shall be a part; to controversies between two or more states; between citizens of the same state claiming lands under grants of different states, and between a state or the citizens thereof, and foreign states, citizens, or subjects."

Modern American jurisprudence, both federal and state, includes codes of civil, criminal, and public law as well as codes of civil and criminal procedures.

Unlike the thousands of police departments that operate independently of each other, the courts are organized in a hierarchy of authority whereby the decisions of each lower court can be reviewed and reversed by a higher court (see Figure 7.2). Also, unlike the police, wherein federal agencies have no authority over state and local agencies, federal courts do have some authority over state courts. Each state has a final court of appeals, but it is possible to appeal a state decision to the U.S. Supreme Court, which may or may not choose to hear the case. Decisions of lower federal courts also can be appealed to the next higher court and ultimately to the U.S. Supreme Court. When the U.S. Supreme Court makes a ruling regarding the constitutionality of a law, due process right, or rule of evidence, that decision is binding on all federal and state courts.

Civil versus Criminal Law

Individuals are responsible for seeking redress in a civil court when they are harmed by violation of a civil law. **Civil law** is referred to as private law because it addresses the definition, regulation, and enforcement of rights in cases in which both the person who has the right and the person who has the obligation are private individuals. Private law includes (1) redress for harm done to another that is not criminal and (2) contract law regulating the many and varied legal transactions such as inheritance, real and personal property, business organizations, and negotiable instruments.

Harm to another that is noncriminal in nature includes injuries due to the accidental actions of another, the carelessness of another, or the failure of another to act. An example of harm due to carelessness would be a doctor who performs an operation and carelessly leaves foreign objects in the patient. The patient may even die from this mistake, but it may not be a crime. Likewise, a person may be harmed or even killed in an automobile accident, but there may be no criminal intent by the party that caused the injury or death. Civil law also recognizes that a person may be harmed by libel, slander, or fraud.

Torts are private wrongs that cause physical harm to another. If you get angry and strike another, you have committed a tort. Striking another person is also a crime. Thus, some behaviors can be both a tort and a crime. Even serious offenses such as sexual assault can be both a tort and crime. Defendants charged with behaviors that are both a tort and a crime can be (1) prosecuted by the government in criminal court and (2) sued in civil court by the person who was harmed. Even if the governmental prosecution of the defendant for a crime is unsuccessful, the plaintiff can file suit in a civil court and may be successful. One of the major reasons for the different outcomes is the standard of proof required in civil court versus criminal court. The burden of proof in a civil

civil law (private law) Civil law (private law) covers the law concerned with the definition, regulation, and enforcement of rights in cases in which both the person who has the right and the person who has the obligation are private individuals.

torts Private wrongs that cause physical harm to another.

In the early republic of the United States, when the justice system was still a European import, Vice President Aaron Burr killed Alexander Hamilton, Secretary of the Treasury, in a duel to settle a grievance as a matter of honor. In 2005, this historic incident was reenacted by descendants of Burr and Hamilton on the 200th anniversary of the duel. Today's criminal justice system prohibits such actions. How would their grievance toward each other be handled in the American justice system today?

court is a "preponderance of the evidence," whereas the burden of proof in a criminal court is "beyond a reasonable doubt." The O. J. Simpson case for the alleged murder of his ex-wife, Nicole Brown Simpson, and Ron Goldman is an example in which the government was unsuccessful in proving the criminal charges against the defendant, but the victims' families were able to obtain a monetary judgment for damages in civil court.

Private Parties Must Initiate Civil Cases

Redress for civil wrongs, contract violations, and torts must be initiated by the individual and fall within the jurisdiction of the civil court. Civil cases far outnumber criminal cases, and the jurisprudence system is driven primarily by the courts' role as mediator in civil cases.

The criminal justice system is responsible for detecting, prosecuting, and punishing people who violate criminal laws. After a criminal law is passed, it is the responsibility of the police to detect law violators. The responsibility of the court is to determine whether a person violated the law. Finally, the responsibility of corrections is to punish offenders for violation of the law. The criminal justice system exists for the purpose of enforcing obedience to laws that have been created by political bodies such as the city, county, state, or federal government.

The criminal justice system and the civil justice system have certain features in common. They both have courtrooms, judges, and juries, and both use the law as the criterion for settling conflicts between

figure 7.2

Hierarchy in the Judiciary

As this figure suggests, the number of cases appealed up the judicial hierarchy continually decreases. The great majority of cases in both the state and federal court systems are disposed in the lower courts.

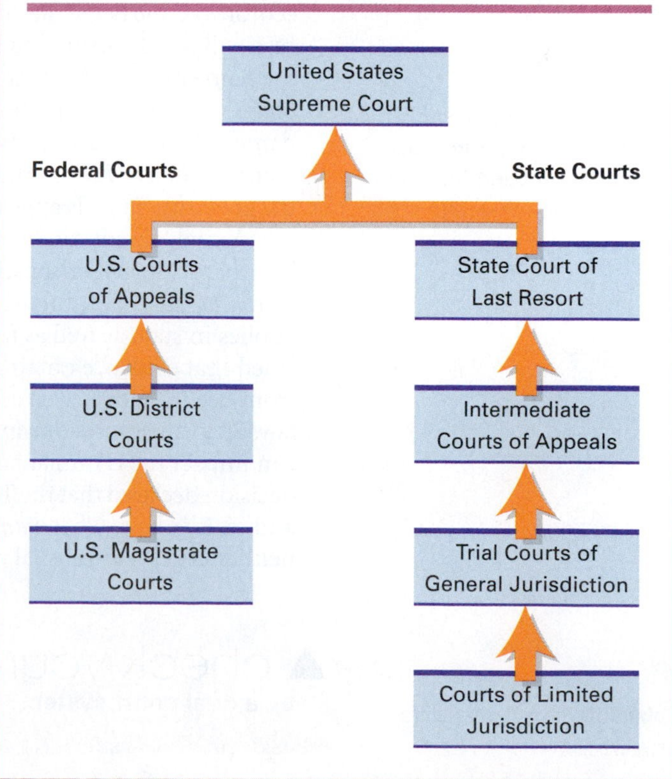

parties. However, there are very significant differences between the criminal justice system and the civil justice system. The civil justice system is for the resolution of private wrongs and injuries. In the civil justice system, both parties to the dispute are private parties (corporations and the government may be treated as private parties in civil cases). Both sides are responsible for their own expenses in pursuing justice. In the civil justice system, one party is said to "sue" the other party. The party that "brings suit," or files the lawsuit, is the **plaintiff**, and the party alleged to have done the harm is the defendant. Civil cases are not heard in criminal court, and civil judges are different from criminal judges. There is a different standard of proof and different rules of evidence.

Punishment in Civil versus Criminal Cases The rules of evidence for civil cases are different from the rules used to conduct criminal cases. In a criminal case, the jury is required to come to a unanimous opinion as to the guilt of the accused. In a civil case, a strong majority vote of the jury is permitted to hold the defendant responsible for the harm he or she is alleged to have caused.

The punishments in a civil case and a criminal case also are different. In a criminal case, the defendant can be fined, sentenced to imprisonment, or even executed. In a civil case, the defendant cannot be sentenced to prison or executed. Most civil cases are settled by fines or orders of the court requiring defendants to do what they promised to do in a contract or agreement or to pay the defendant for injuries or damages.

In a criminal case, the government prosecutes a defendant accused of violating a criminal law. The government bears all expenses related to the prosecution of the defendant. The government may choose to prosecute the defendant even if the person harmed by the defendant does not desire it. In a criminal case, the defendant is alleged to have harmed society.

Naming of Cases A civil case can be distinguished from a criminal case by the way the case is named. Civil cases involve conflict between private parties, so the name of the case will be the last names of the two parties, with the plaintiff listed first, as in *Smith* v. *Jones* or *Hazelwood* v. *Cranberry.* In a criminal case, the government is the prosecutor, and the defendant is the person who is alleged to have committed the crime. The case will first be identified by the government agency prosecuting the case, followed by the name of the defendant, as in *State* v. *Smith, Commonwealth* v. *Hazelwood,* or *United States* v. *Bostick.* When the first name of the case is that of an individual and the second name is that of a government agency or employee, as in *Hurtado* v. *California, Kent* v. *United States,* or *Ruiz* v. *Estelle,* this indicates that an individual has filed a lawsuit against the government or is appealing a lower court verdict.

Go to www.courttv.com for information on current and famous trials, both criminal and civil.

A civil lawsuit can be related to a criminal case, as in cases in which defendants allege that their civil or constitutional rights were violated. For example, in *Klopfer* v. *North Carolina,* the U.S. Supreme Court ruled that the Sixth Amendment right to a speedy trial applies in state as well as federal proceedings, and in *Mapp* v. *Ohio,* the Supreme Court ruled that evidence obtained in violation of the Fourth Amendment must be excluded from use in state as well as federal trials. Also, civil trials in which the defendant files a lawsuit against someone in the criminal justice system, such as a warden or police chief, can impact the criminal justice system. In *Ruiz* v. *Estelle,* for example, the federal court decision declared that the Texas prison system had engaged in unconstitutional practices, and in *Rhodes* v. *Chapman,* the Supreme Court ruled that cell overcrowding is in itself neither cruel nor unusual punishment as prohibited by the Constitution.

▲ check your understanding **7.1** **What is meant by a dual court system? How do civil law and criminal law cases differ?**

plaintiff The party that brings suit in court.

The Federal Court System

the main idea 7.2 The federal court system has a hierarchical structure, including lower courts, courts of appeals, and the Supreme Court.

The authority for establishing a federal court system is in Article 3 of the U.S. Constitution. Congress created the lesser courts referred to in Article 3 on September 24, 1789. Congress passed the federal Judiciary Act that established 13 courts, one for each of the original states. Initially, the federal courts had few cases, as there were few federal laws. The Supreme Court originally consisted of six justices, but today there are nine justices—one chief justice and eight associate justices—on the Supreme Court.

Overview of the Federal Court System

Marbury* v. *Madison For the first three years of its existence, the Supreme Court had virtually nothing to do and did not review any judicial decisions. The landmark decision that established the power and role of the Supreme Court and, by inclusion, its lesser courts was ***Marbury* v. *Madison* (1803).** In *Marbury* v. *Madison,* under the leadership of Chief Justice John Marshall, the Supreme Court claimed the power to review acts of Congress and pronounce whether congressional acts were constitutional. This claim gave the Supreme Court the power to nullify acts of Congress. It also asserted that the Court has the power to review congressional acts without having to wait for a case to be brought before the Supreme Court. This power to declare congressional acts unconstitutional—the power of judicial review—has been the most important power that the Supreme Court exercises. The Supreme Court sees its primary mission as the guardian of the Constitution and accomplishes that goal by exercising its power of judicial review.

The federal court system has undergone significant revisions during its history. Today, instead of 13 courts, the federal judiciary has a unified, four-tier structure of over 100 courts covering the United States and its territories. The federal judiciary is divided into 13 federal judicial circuits that cover various geographical jurisdictions. The geographical jurisdictions of the federal court are much larger than those of the state courts. For example, the Eighth Federal Judicial Circuit includes seven states, the Ninth Federal Judicial Circuit includes nine states, and the Tenth Federal Judicial Circuit includes six states (see Figure 7.3).

The federal court system is responsible for the enforcement of all federal codes in all 50 states, U.S. territories, and the District of Columbia. This includes responsibility for civil, criminal, and administrative trials. The federal court system is also responsible for the trials involving local codes and ordinances in the territories of Guam, the Virgin Islands, and the Northern Mariana Islands. If a person violates a federal law, he or she can be tried at any federal district court within the circuit. Thus, a person accused of mail fraud in Oklahoma could be tried in Oklahoma, Arizona, Colorado, Kansas, New Mexico, Utah, or Wyoming.

See www.uscourts.gov for a wealth of information on the various U.S. federal courts, as well as useful links and employment opportunities.

The federal court system is responsible for both civil and criminal cases. The focus of this book is on the criminal justice system, but there are many more federal district court civil trials than there are criminal trials. Criminal trials, especially trials for violent crimes, are only a small part of the workload of the federal court. In 2004, for example, 71,022 criminal cases commenced in U.S. District Courts and 281,338 civil cases were filed. In 2003, only 397 of the criminal cases were for murder.[3] The majority of defendants (30,668) were charged with felony drug offenses.[4]

As shown in Figure 7.4, the federal court is divided into four tiers of responsibility: the U.S. magistrate courts, the trial courts, the appeals courts, and the U.S. Supreme Court.

figure 7.3

The Thirteen Federal Judicial Circuits

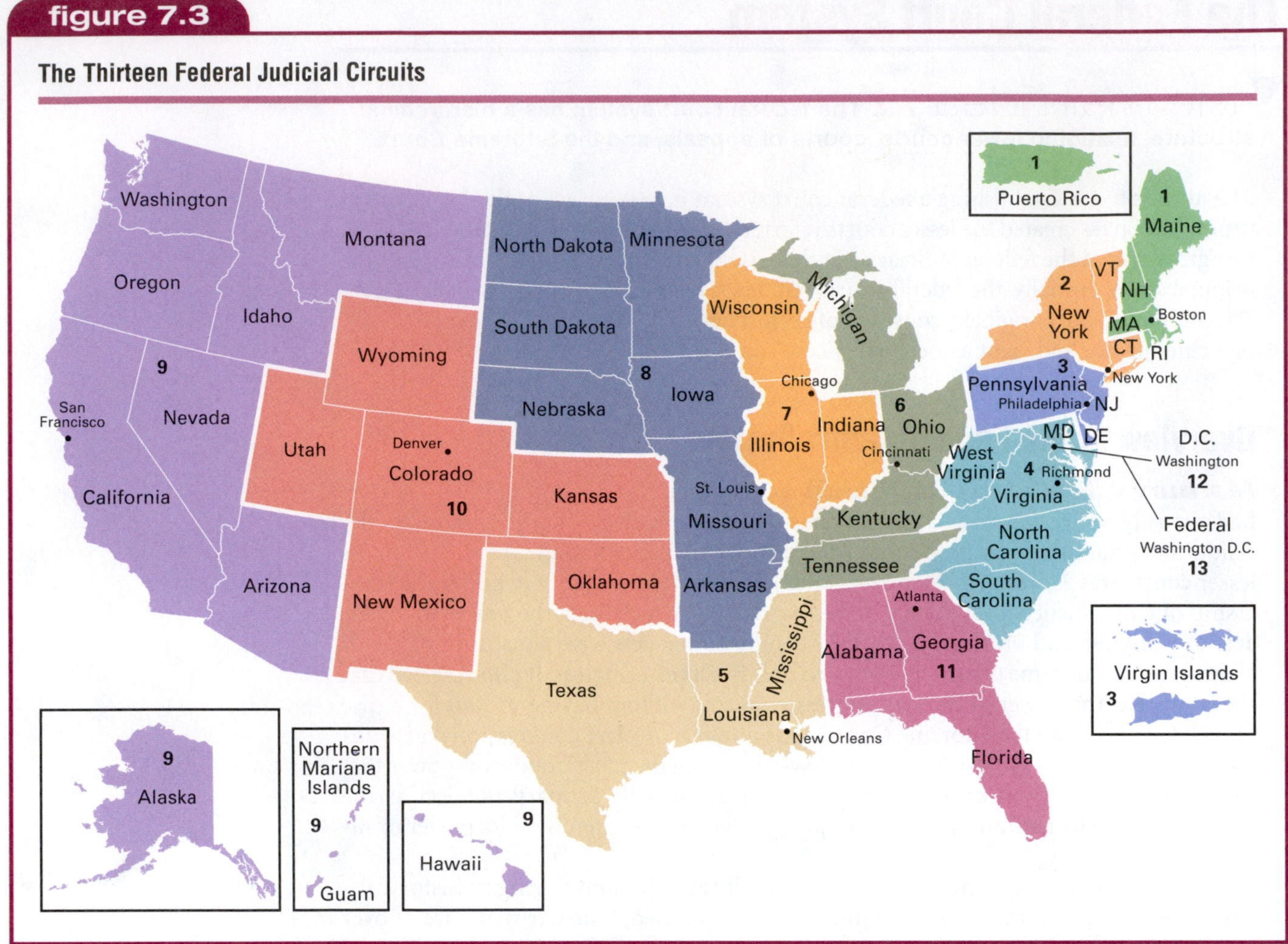

United States Magistrate Courts

U.S. magistrate courts are federal lower courts whose powers are limited to trying lesser misdemeanors, setting bail, and assisting district courts in various legal matters. Federal magistrate courts were created by the **Federal Magistrate's Act of 1968,** which phased out the former ineffective system of part-time U.S. commissioners. U.S. magistrate courts try class A misdemeanors and petty offenses as well as performing such duties as issuing search and arrest warrants, hearing initial appearances, and presiding over preliminary examinations, arraignments, detention hearings, and bail reviews. Magistrate courts are also responsible for hearing pretrial motions and evidentiary hearings. Federal magistrate courts also handle prisoner litigation, such as requests for habeas corpus, civil rights appeals, and evidentiary hearings. Duties of magistrates are summarized in Table 7.1.

U.S. magistrate courts Federal lower courts with powers limited to trying lesser misdemeanors, setting bail, and assisting district courts in various legal matters.

U.S. district courts Trial courts of the federal system.

original jurisdiction The first court to hear and render a verdict regarding the charges against the defendant.

United States District Courts

U.S. district courts are the trial courts of the federal system. They are the courts of original jurisdiction for all federal trials in the 50 states, the District of Columbia, Puerto Rico, and the U.S. territories of Guam, the Virgin Islands, and the Northern Mariana Islands. **Original jurisdiction** means that it is the first court to hear the charges against the defendant and to render a verdict regarding the charges against the defendant. It is the district court that decides if a defendant is guilty. Some federal district courts—such

figure 7.4

The Federal Judiciary

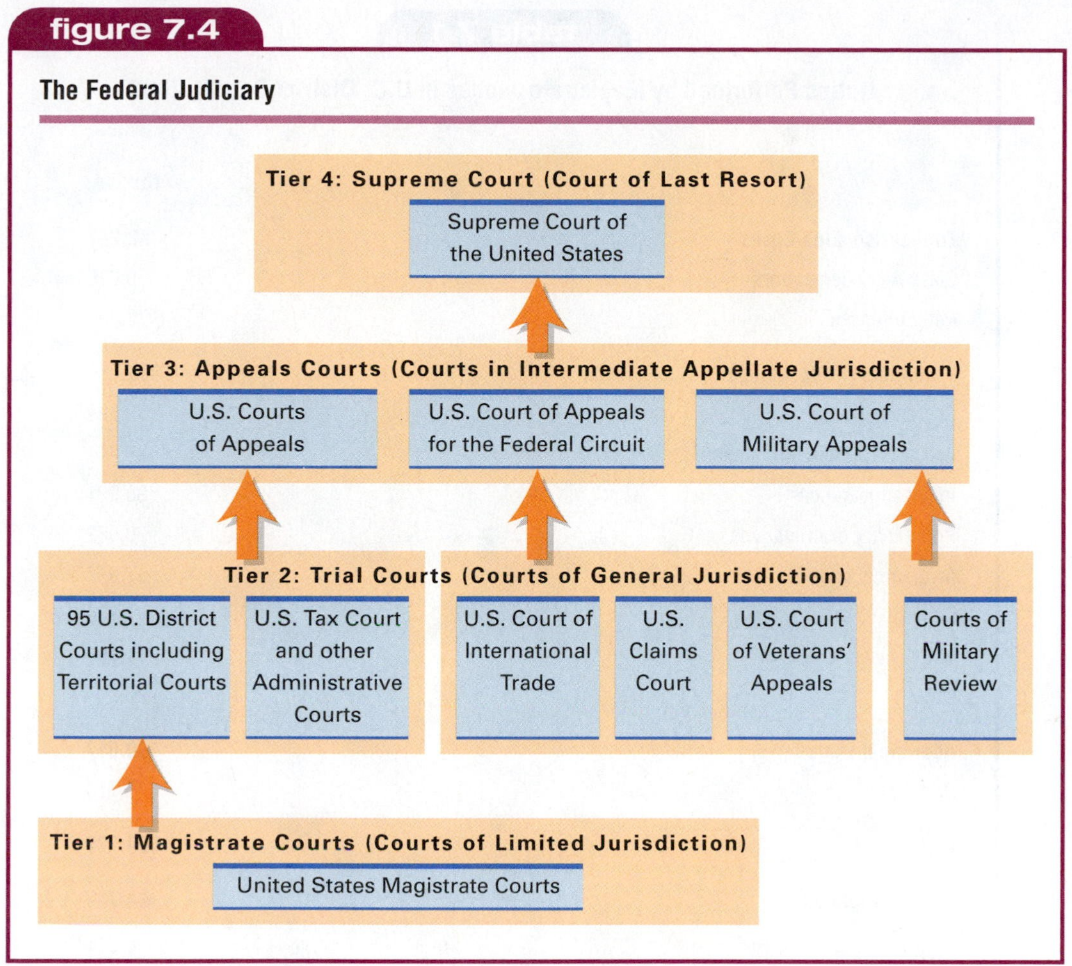

as the United States Tax Court, the United States Court of International Trade, the United States Claims Court, the United States Court of Veteran's Appeals, and the Courts of Military Review—have specific responsibilities.

District courts hear both civil and criminal cases but, as mentioned, the majority of cases are civil cases. Cases brought to district court include a wide variety of topics, including treason, homicide, copyright infringements, traffic offenses on federal reservations, violation of the Securities and Exchange Acts, and violations of federal regulations such as the Endangered Species Acts and the Meat and Poultry Inspection Acts.

There are 95 district courts distributed throughout the United States and the U.S. territories. Each district court has one or more courtrooms with one or more federal district judges. Each courtroom has numerous support personnel attached to it, such as a federal prosecutor, U.S. Marshals Service personnel, and civilian court employees.

United States Courts of Appeals

Appeals are guaranteed by congressional act. Rather than have the Supreme Court handle all appeals, the federal judiciary uses **U.S. courts of appeals** to hear appeals from U.S. district courts. The right of appeal applies to both civil and criminal cases, but the focus of this discussion is on criminal appeals. Criminal appeals to the U.S. Court of Appeals must be based on the claim that the defendant was denied a fair trial or that the law the defendant was convicted of violating was unconstitutional. Defendants cannot appeal on the grounds that they are innocent. The question of guilt is a question of original jurisdiction and is addressed in the U.S. District Court: The judge or the jury heard the

U.S. courts of appeals The panel of federal judges that hears appeals from the U.S. district courts and determines if a judicial error was made that could have substantially affected the court's decision.

table 7.1

Duties Performed by Magistrate Judges in U.S. District Courts, 2002

Activity	Number
Trial Jurisdiction Cases	**82,247**
Class A misdemeanors	9,616
Petty offenses	73,631
Preliminary Proceedings	**315,455**
Search warrants	32,539
Arrest warrants/summonses	31,291
Initial appearances	93,991
Preliminary examinations	20,062
Arraignments	57,977
Detention hearings	47,860
Bail reviews	11,397
Other	20,338
Additional Duties	**490,617**
Criminal	156,115
Civil	**309,720**
Prison Litigation	**24,782**
Civil Consent	**13,811**
Miscellaneous Matters	**45,440**
Total	880,129

Source: Administrative Office of the United States Courts, *Judicial Business of the United States Courts: 2003 Annual Report of the Director* (Washington, DC: USGPO, 2004), pp. 58, 59.

facts of the case and rendered a decision regarding the criminality of the defendant's behavior. Thus, the U.S. appeals court will not conduct another trial to determine the guilt of the defendant.

A fair trial does not mean that the defendant's trial was without error, but it does mean that there was no substantial judicial error that could have affected the outcome of the court's decision. During the defendant's trial in district court, it is the responsibility of the defendant's attorney to object to any procedure or court ruling that is thought to be unfair or unconstitutional. The district judge makes a ruling on the objection raised by the attorney, and the trial proceeds based on the judge's ruling. The objection of the defense counsel is entered into the transcript of the trial. After the trial, if the defense council believes that the ruling of the district judge was not correct, the judge's ruling can be appealed. If at the time of the trial the defense attorney fails to object to an unfair practice, the absence of such an objection can be considered a reason to deny the appeal.

The trial of confessed terrorist Zacarias Moussaoui challenged the court system as it raised many issues regarding the rights of the accused and the government's obligation to make evidence and witnesses available to the defense. President Bush has argued that special military tribunals are more appropriate for trying terrorists. Do you agree?

The role of the U.S. Court of Appeals is to determine (1) whether the district judge made a judicial error and (2) whether the error could have substantially affected the court's decision. If the appeals court determines that (1) the judge correctly interpreted the law or rule or (2) a judicial error was made but the error did not substantially affect the trial's outcome, the appeal can be dismissed. If the appeals court determines that a judicial error was made and the error could have substantially affected the trial's outcome, the appeals court will review the appeal and issue a ruling regarding the error. In criminal trials, judicial error includes, for example, the following:

- Admitting evidence that has been improperly obtained
- Allowing prosecutorial evidence and witnesses not relevant to the trial
- Disallowing defense evidence and witnesses
- Improper trial conduct
- Misbehavior by the jury
- Instructions by the judge prohibiting the jury from considering a lesser offense
- Improper instructions by the judge to the jury

One must remember that there is a difference between judicial error and not guilty. The defendant may indeed have committed a criminal act and is, without question, guilty in the eyes of the public. There may be videotape or eyewitnesses that document the defendant's commission of the crime, and the public may be outraged when a conviction is reversed on appeal. However, to convict the defendant in a court of law, rules must be followed and the rights of the defendant must be protected. The difficult balance between protecting the public from criminals and protecting the rights of defendants has been discussed in previous chapters. Often, it is the courts of appeal that decide what balance will be struck.

U.S. courts of appeals are required to hear the cases brought to them on appeal from the federal trial courts within their circuit. The U.S. Court of Appeals does not conduct a jury trial. Rather, a panel of federal appeals judges, usually three, reviews the case. A review does not mean that the defendant appears before the appeals court. The appeals court may decide to review only the written briefs submitted by the attorneys and to make a decision based on the information contained in the briefs. If the appeals court decides to hear oral arguments, the attorneys come before the court and present their reasoning. Often, there are legitimate differences of opinion among legal professionals regarding an interpretation of a law, constitutional right, or court decision. The attorneys attempt to persuade the panel of judges that their interpretation is the correct one. The appeal focuses on a rule of law and not the guilt of the defendant, so no witnesses or evidence is presented during the appeals hearing. If the U.S. Court of Appeals decides that a substantial judicial error has been made, the court reviews the case and determines the appropriate action to be taken to correct the error. The decision of the appeals court may mean that the defendant receives another trial in which the judicial error is corrected, or the sentence of the defendant may be modified.

There are 13 U.S. circuit courts of appeals and over 165 federal courts of appeals judges. Each of the 13 federal judicial circuits has one location that is the principal seat of federal courts of appeal, and there are two courts of appeals located in Washington, DC. (One of the Washington, DC, courts of appeals handles civil cases related to patents, copyrights, tax disputes, and claims against the federal government.) Appeals court circuits were first established in the original Thirteen Colonies and spread westward as the United States expanded. The geographical jurisdiction of the courts of appeals is called a **circuit court** because, originally, federal appeals judges literally traveled a circuit from one federal district court to another to hear appeals. This geographical origin of the various federal appeals circuits resulted in a disproportionate division of circuit courts east and west of the Mississippi River. There are only 4 U.S. circuit courts of appeals west of the Mississippi River.

As a result of the shift of the population centers from the east coast to the west coast, western U.S. circuit courts of appeals have more cases to review and also greater diversity in the values and cultures of the people within a circuit. The Ninth U.S. Circuit Court of Appeals, for instance, includes the western states of Alaska and Hawaii and the U.S. territories of Guam and the Northern Mariana Islands. When there is widespread diversity, judges of the U.S. courts of appeals do not always have the same interpretation of the Constitution, the law, or criminal procedures. Nevertheless, the federal court system requires that decisions of the U.S. Circuit Court of Appeals are binding on all U.S. district courts within that circuit. For example, an opinion regarding the constitutionality of a search without a warrant in the Ninth U.S. Circuit Court of Appeals would be binding on all U.S. district courts in the Ninth Circuit, though not binding on the district courts in the other circuits. Although not binding, decisions from other jurisdictions can be cited as guidelines.

For information on the U.S. Supreme Court, see www.supremecourtus.gov.

The United States Supreme Court

The **U.S. Supreme Court** is the highest court in the American judicial system. This means that there is no higher authority to which the defendant can appeal a decision of the Supreme Court. A decision by the Supreme Court is final and cannot be overruled by Congress. The only way to affect Supreme Court decisions is for Congress to pass a statute or constitutional amendment altering the wording of a law that the Supreme Court has declared unconstitutional. For example, in 1919, Congress passed the Eighteenth Amendment, which prohibited the manufacture, sale, or transportation of intoxicating liquors, and in 1933, repealed the prohibition with the Twenty-First Amendment. As another example, when the Supreme Court ruled that laws to collect federal personal income tax were unconstitutional (because they violated Article 1, Section 9 of the Constitution), Congress passed the Sixteenth Amendment, authorizing the federal government to lay and collect taxes on personal incomes.

circuit court Any court that holds sessions in various locations within its jurisdiction.

U.S. Supreme Court The highest court in the American judiciary system, whose rulings on the constitutionality of a law, due process rights, and rules of evidence are binding on all federal and state courts.

In addition to its role in the criminal justice system, the Supreme Court exercises other important judicial powers. The Supreme Court is the legal mediator for lawsuits between states and between the United States and foreign countries. The Supreme Court also is the final authority for legal opinions binding on the federal government.

Abraham Lincoln obtained his law license without attending law school. Today, lawyers are required to complete two or three years of law school after their bachelor's degree and pass the bar examination. Why do you think such rigorous standards for formal education have been adopted by the legal profession?

For instance, when controversy arose over the legality of ballots cast in the state of Florida in the 2000 presidential election, the Supreme Court provided the final judgment regarding the vote count.

U.S. Supreme Court cases that determine how the Constitution is to be interpreted are called **landmark cases.** A landmark case is important because once the U.S. Supreme Court makes a ruling, the lower courts have to fall in line with that ruling. Landmark cases end diversity in practices and rulings among the various circuit courts of appeals. U.S. Supreme Court rulings on constitutionality also are applicable to the state courts. Landmark cases are important in determining the constitutional rights of the defendant.

Reviewing Cases Unlike the U.S. circuit courts of appeals, the U.S. Supreme Court does not have to hear a criminal case on appeal. The Supreme Court chooses cases that the justices believe address important constitutional issues. Technically, the Court must review cases when (1) a federal court has held an act of Congress to be unconstitutional, (2) a U.S. Court of Appeals has found a state statute to be unconstitutional, (3) a state's highest court of appeals has ruled a federal law to be unconstitutional, and (4) an individual's challenge to a state statute on federal constitutional grounds is upheld by a state's highest court of appeals. In all other cases, the Court can decline to review a case. In reality, if a majority of justices does not want to review a case, the Court simply affirms the lower court's decision. If the Court decides not to review a case, there is no further appeal to the Court's decision.

In its role of judicial review of a case, the Supreme Court does not conduct jury trials and does not determine whether the defendant is guilty. The purpose of the Supreme Court's review is to determine whether a significant judicial error has been made and if so, determine the appropriate remedy. The Supreme Court has the power to review civil

landmark cases U.S. Supreme Court cases that mark significant changes in interpretations of constitutionality.

lawsuits, criminal cases, and juvenile hearings. The Court is very selective in deciding what cases to review and will not hear a case until all other appeals have been exhausted. For a state case, that means that the case must have been reviewed by the state's highest court before the Supreme Court will consider it for review. Furthermore, the case must involve a substantial federal or constitutional question. In the federal fiscal year 2003, 2,400 criminal cases were filed for review, and only 20 cases were selected for review.[5] Criminal cases comprise less than 15 percent of the cases reviewed by the U.S. Supreme Court. In 2003, the U.S. Supreme Court reviewed 61 private civil cases, 23 U.S. civil cases, and 11 administrative appeals.[6]

The process by which the Supreme Court chooses which cases to review begins with a clerk for a Supreme Court justice—an attorney who performs legal research for the justice. Clerks review the numerous cases that petition to the Supreme Court, select those that may merit consideration, and forward them to the Supreme Court judges. Each judge reviews the case and decides whether the case has the potential to raise a significant federal or constitutional question. If four or more members of the Supreme Court feel that the case meets this criterion, it is selected for review. For cases selected for review, the Court issues a writ of certiorari. This authority to select cases for review is known as **certiorari power**. A **writ of certiorari** is an order to the lower court, state or federal, to forward the record of the case to the Supreme Court. Table 7.2 shows the disposition of writs of certiorari for 2000.

When the Supreme Court selects a case for review, this does not mean that the defendant is not guilty, is freed, or is immediately entitled to a new trial. The Court has several options in reviewing a case. The Court can

1. examine the trial record and facts of the case and determine that no further review is necessary;
2. ask the attorneys representing the appellant to submit a written statement, called a **brief,** stating the substantial federal or constitutional issue they think needs to be decided. (The attorney from the other side submits a rebuttal brief, and the Court decides on the basis of information in the briefs); or
3. decide that the case deserves a hearing.

certiorari power If four members of the Supreme Court believe a case meets its criteria for review, a writ of certiorari is issued, ordering the lower court to forward the record of the case to the Supreme Court.

writ of certiorari The power of the U.S. Supreme Court to choose what cases it will hear.

brief A concise statement of the main points of a law case.

table 7.2

Petitions for Review on Writ of Certiorari to the U.S. Supreme Court Filed, Terminated, and Pending, 2003

	Pending Oct. 1, 2002	Filed	Terminated			Pending Sept. 30, 2003
			Granted	*Denied*	*Dismissed*	
Criminal	927	2,454	20	2,487	3	871
U.S. civil	603	1,175	23	1,182	5	568
Private civil	1,645	2,949	61	2,777	20	1,736
Administrative appeals	87	93	11	80	0	89
Total	3,262	6,671	115	6,526	28	3,264

Source: Administrative Office of the United States Courts, *Judicial Business of the United States Courts: 2003 Annual Report of the Director* (Washington, DC: USGPO, 2004), pp. 79–81.

At a hearing, the two sides are invited to present oral arguments before the full Supreme Court, but these oral arguments do not resemble a trial. There are no witnesses and no jury, and no evidence as to the guilt of the defendant is presented. This hearing is not to determine guilt, but to determine whether the case involves a substantial federal or constitutional issue, and the attorneys must confine their arguments to this issue. The parties to the case may be given only one hour to argue their case. The Supreme Court justices will ask questions of the attorneys, but few cases are decided by this method.

After reviewing a case, the Court declares its decision and can issue a written opinion explaining the reasons for its decision. A case that is disposed of by the Court without a full written opinion is said to be a **per curiam opinion.** The Court can affirm the case or reverse the lower court's decision. In affirming a case, the Supreme Court finds that there was no substantial judicial or constitutional error and the original opinion of the lower court stands. In a criminal case, this means that whatever sentence was imposed on the defendant may be carried out or continued. If the Court is hearing an appeal by the government, which lost the case in lower court, then an "affirm" might mean that the lower court's decision stands.

Remedies for Judicial Error Reversing the case means the Court found that a judicial error or unconstitutional issue was central to the lower court's decision. Most cases are not reversed. The Court reversed about 25 percent of all of the cases decided on merit.[7] In a criminal case, reversal does not mean that the defendant is freed, not guilty, or receives a reduced sentence. It means that the Supreme Court found the conviction of the defendant to be flawed and that conviction is "vacated." After the case is reversed, it is remanded. **Remanded** means that the case is returned to the court of original jurisdiction—the court that first convicted the defendant—with the instructions to correct the judicial error, called a "remedy."

If the judicial error involved the introduction of inadmissible evidence, such as an illegal confession or search and seizure or inappropriate testimony, then the remedy requires a new trial in which the inadmissible evidence cannot be used. If a conviction cannot be obtained without this evidence, the prosecution may decide not to ask for a new trial. In that case, the charges are dismissed and the defendant is set free. If the prosecution decides to retry the case, the defendant may or may not be convicted at the new trial.

Not all judicial errors require a new trial. Judicial errors also can involve an incorrect sentence being assessed against a defendant, and the court of original jurisdiction may be instructed to recalculate the sentence. A common criminal appeal for a reduction of sentence is the appeal for a reduction of a death sentence to the lesser sentence of life in prison.

When a long-incarcerated individual appeals on a writ of habeas corpus, an appeal to the Supreme Court can take decades. Long delays are unusual, however, although in some cases defendants have served the length of their sentence by the time the Supreme Court hears their case. Delays often are due to the large caseload of the Supreme Court and its limited ability to review and decide on appeals. Some critics of the judicial system have argued that such a delay in justice is the same as justice denied. There appears to be no immediate solution to this problem, as new issues raised by the War on Terrorism have only increased the number of legal cases involving substantial questions of constitutional rights, due process, human rights, and civil liberties.

per curiam opinion A case that is disposed of by the U.S. Supreme Court that is not accompanied by a full opinion.

remanded The reversal of a decision by a higher court and the return of the case to the court of original jurisdiction with instructions to correct the judicial error.

▲ check your understanding **7.2** **How was the federal court system established? What cases do magistrate courts hear? What cases do district courts hear? What is needed to have an appeal heard? How does the U.S. Supreme Court operate?**

Characteristics of the State Court System

the main idea 7.3 State courts have jurisdiction to settle legal disputes and criminal matters for violation of local or state criminal ordinances.

State courts are authorized and organized autonomously by each state. If there is a legal dispute between states, the federal courts have jurisdiction. The purpose of state courts is to try defendants charged with violations of state laws or the state constitution. A state also contains smaller political jurisdictions, such as cities and counties, and each of these has its own legal codes. Therefore, states must establish court systems that provide for a defendant to be tried for allegedly violating a city or county ordinance. Like the federal court system, the state court system has a number of specialized courts dealing with noncriminal cases. Also as in the federal courts, criminal trials compose only a small percentage of the state court's activities.

State court systems uniquely reflect the history of each state. For example, Pennsylvania's judiciary system began as a disparate collection of courts, some inherited from the reign of the Duke of York and some established by William Penn. They were mostly local, mostly part time, and mostly under control of the governor. All of the state courts were run by nonlawyers, and final appeals had to be taken to England. The Judiciary Act of 1722 was the colony's first judicial bill. It established the Pennsylvania Supreme Court and the Court of Common Pleas. The court system changed again with the Pennsylvania Constitution of 1776 and the Constitution of the United States. After that, the most sweeping changes in Pennsylvania's judiciary came in 1968. The Constitution of 1968 created the Unified Judicial System, consisting of the supreme court, superior courts, and commonwealth courts; common pleas courts; the Philadelphia municipal court; the Pittsburgh magistrate court; Philadelphia traffic court; and district justice courts. Pennsylvania's State Supreme Court is shown in Figure 7.5.

The state and federal court systems are pyramid-shaped in that there are only a small number of judges in the appellate and supreme courts compared to the hundreds of judges at the lower level. The federal Supreme Court has nine justices and some state supreme courts have fewer. This is a photograph of the 2002 Pennsylvania State Supreme Court, which has seven justices. The original Pennsylvania constitution was drafted by William Penn and adopted by Pennsylvania in 1722. It was the first independent Supreme Court empowered as an independent branch of government with the power to declare laws made by the Pennsylvania legislative body unconstitutional.

figure 7.5

Pennsylvania's Judicial System

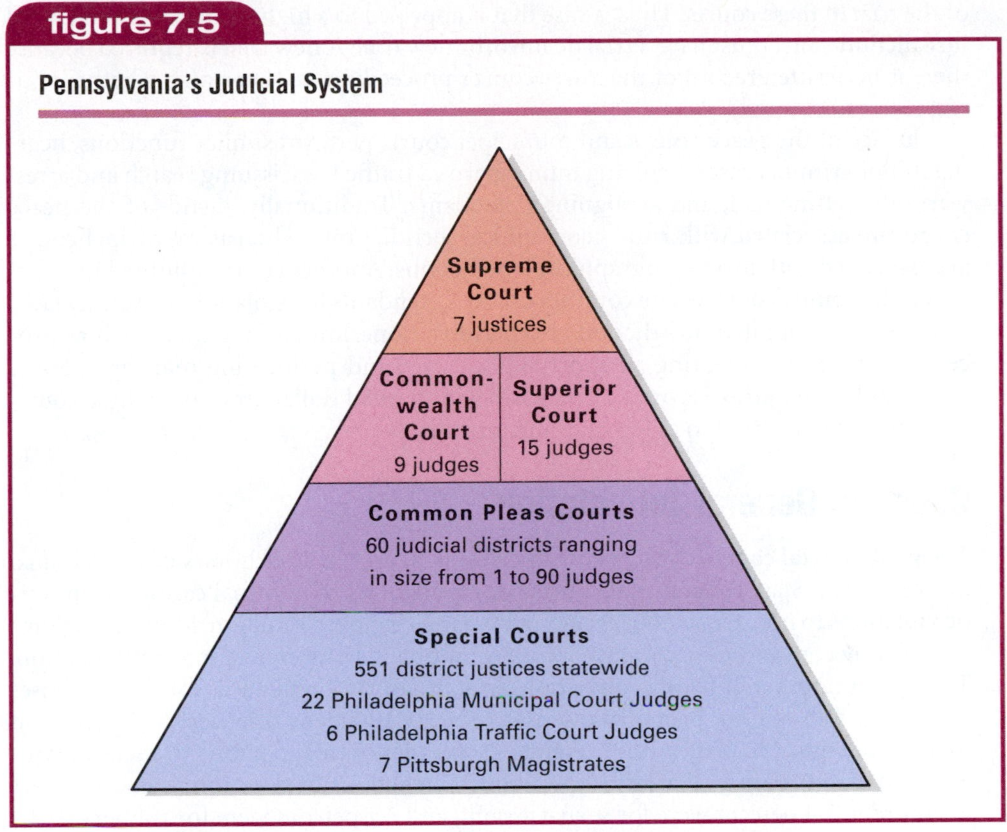

Source: www.courts.state.pa.us/index/ujs/courthistory.asp, "A History of Pennsylvania's Courts."

Each state is a sovereign government and has the authority to establish its own system of state courts. Like Pennsylvania, most states designed their state court system when they were admitted into the Union. Thus, the states consisting of the original Thirteen Colonies have the oldest state courts, and the states of Alaska and Hawaii have the newest. Over time, the philosophy, mission, and values of the citizens of the states change, and many states have found it necessary to redesign their state court system. Most of those states have chosen models that resemble the four-tier federal court system. The four-tier system consists of (1) courts of limited jurisdiction, (2) courts of general jurisdiction, (3) courts of intermediate appellate jurisdiction, and (4) courts of last resort. Each state has unique names for the various courts within its system. Each state has granted different jurisdiction to the various courts within its system based on geography, subject matter, and hierarchy. Each state has a hierarchy of appeals from the lowest court to the court of last resort.

See www.ojp.usdoj.gov/bjs/abstract/sco98.htm, an excellent reference that describes each of the state court systems; it is a publication of the Bureau of Justice Statistics. See *State Court Organization 1998,* by David Rottman et al.

Courts of Limited Jurisdiction

State courts with original jurisdiction—the power to determine if the defendant is guilty—are divided into courts of limited jurisdiction and general trial courts. Courts of limited jurisdiction are known as justice of the peace courts, municipal courts, and magistrate's courts. General trial courts are called circuit courts, superior courts, district courts, courts of common pleas, and court of first instance.

Courts of limited jurisdiction frequently are not **courts of record**—courts in which the trial proceedings are recorded. For example, traffic courts, municipal courts, and county courts frequently are not courts of records because no written record is made

courts of limited jurisdiction State courts of original jurisdiction that are not courts of record (e.g., traffic courts, municipal courts, or county courts).

courts of record Courts in which trial proceedings are transcribed.

of the trial in these courts. Thus, a case that is appealed to a higher court from a limited jurisdiction court must have a trial de novo, or new trial. A new trial is required because there is no written record of the lower court's proceedings to determine whether a judicial error occurred.

Justice of the peace courts and municipal courts perform similar functions, hearing minor criminal cases involving municipal and traffic laws, issuing search and arrest warrants, setting bail, and arraigning defendants. Traditionally, justice of the peace courts are associated with rural geographical jurisdictions, whereas municipal courts are associated with urban geographical jurisdictions. Another court of limited jurisdiction is the county court, where counties can try defendants for violations of county laws. Most courts of limited jurisdiction also perform noncriminal functions, such as processing civil suits, accepting passport applications, and performing marriages. Some courts of limited jurisdiction try civil cases with limited dollar amounts. These courts are commonly referred to as "small claims courts."

Courts of General Jurisdiction

The **general trial courts** of the state judicial system are the workhorses of the criminal justice system. State general trial courts handle all kinds of criminal cases—from traffic violations to murder. In 2002, state courts convicted over 1 million adults of a felony. State felony convictions account for 95 percent of all felony convictions in the nation. The largest number of felony convictions in state courts in 2002 was for drug offenses (340,330), followed by property offenses (325,200), violent offenses (197,030), and weapon offenses (32,470). Although there is a tendency by the public to focus on violent crimes, less than 1 percent of the felony[8] convictions in state courts in 2002 were for murder, 3.4 percent were for sexual assault, and 3.7 percent were for robbery.

General trial courts are courts of record. A full transcription (i.e., a word-for-word recording of the proceeding) is made for every trial in a general trial court. Nearly all appeals for criminal cases originate from state general trial courts.

Appellate Courts

Most states have an intermediate appellate court that acts in a similar capacity as the U.S. Court of Appeals. Some common names for these are Court of Criminal Appeals, Court of Appeals, Appellate Court, Court of Special Appeals, Appellate Division of Superior Court, Superior Court, and Commonwealth Court. These **appellate courts** do not have original jurisdiction and review cases for judicial error and other significant issues concerning due process, civil rights, and federal and state constitutional questions.

Courts of Last Resort

Each state has a court of final appeals. The names given to these various **courts of last resort** are Supreme Court, Supreme Judicial Court, Court of Appeals, and High Court. Oklahoma and Texas have two separate courts of last resort: The Supreme Court of Criminal Appeals handles criminal cases, and the State Supreme Court handles all other cases. Each state determines the number of judges that sit on the court of last resort, typically five to nine justices.

The state court of last resort has appellant jurisdiction and acts much like the U.S. Supreme Court. Its primary purpose in criminal cases is to review a selected number of cases that may have a significant state or federal question. After reviewing the case, the state's court of last resort can decide to affirm the case or to reverse and remand the case. After a criminal defendant has exhausted all appeals in the state court system, he or she can appeal the case to the U.S. Supreme Court.

general trial courts State courts of original jurisdiction; often called circuit courts, superior courts, district courts, courts of common pleas, and courts of first instance.

appellate courts Appellate courts have the authority to review the proceedings and verdicts of general trial courts for judicial errors.

court of last resort A state court that reviews lower court decisions and whose decisions can be appealed to the U.S. Supreme Court.

▲ check your understanding 7.3 **What is the four-tier system of state courts? In which court would you appear for a traffic violation? A misdemeanor charge? A violent felony? A civil rights violation?**

conclusion:

The Judicial System as the Protector of Constitutional Rights

The dual court system of the United States forms a unified judicial system in which a case in the lowest state court ultimately could be reviewed by the U.S. Supreme Court. Likewise, a judicial decision by the U.S. Supreme Court is binding on all federal and state courts. The U.S. Constitution provided the initial authority for a judicial system at both the federal and state levels. Both federal and state courts have undergone extensive revisions since their founding, but the basic principle has remained that the judiciary is an independent, self-regulating, equal power with the legislative and executive branches of the government.

The judiciary not only acts as impartial arbitrator in many matters both civil and criminal but it also serves a very important role in providing checks and balances on the power of the legislative and executive branches. The federal courts, especially the Supreme Court, have assumed the role of defender of the Constitution, and state courts have adopted a similar identity and mission. As defender of the Constitution, the judicial system often is criticized as being more concerned with the rights of the criminals than the guilt or innocence of the defendant and the harm to the victim. In opinion polls in 2004, 58 percent of college freshmen responding say that there is too much concern in the courts for the rights of criminals.[9] Despite these and other criticisms, such as the slowness of processing cases through the courts and the issues of choosing judges, the courts are still considered fundamental protectors of constitutional rights.

chapter summary

- The judiciary is the center of the criminal justice system and is the primary and ultimate arbiter of right and wrong.
- The federal judiciary is a branch of government with the power of checks and balances to prevent abuse by the executive and legislative branches of government.
- The U.S. dual court system consists of a four-tier federal court system and a state court system for each state. In the judicial system hierarchy, higher courts have power over lower courts, and the U.S. Supreme Court has power over the state courts.
- The courts are responsible for both civil and criminal judicial oversight. Most of the court's resources and time are taken up by civil cases.
- The federal court system is a four-tier, unified judicial system composed of magistrate courts, district courts, courts of appeals, and the Supreme Court. The federal courts are divided into 13 geographical circuits. Cases are initially tried in magistrate or district courts. Appeals courts review cases for judicial error. Cases cannot be appealed on the basis of a claim of innocence.
- The U.S. Supreme Court is the absolute court of last resort. Appeals to the U.S. Supreme Court do not resemble trials; for example, the Court does not utilize a jury to hear appeals.
- Each state has the power to organize its own judicial system. Most states have four-tier organizational structures like those of the federal judiciary.

vocabulary review

appellate courts, 280
brief, 276
certiorari power, 276
circuit court, 274
civil law, 266
court of last resort, 280
courts of limited jurisdiction, 279
courts of record, 279
dual court system, 265
general trial courts, 280
jurisprudence, 265
landmark cases, 275
original jurisdiction, 270
per curiam opinion, 277
plaintiff, 267
remanded, 277
torts, 266
U.S. courts of appeals, 271
U.S. district courts, 270
U.S. magistrate courts, 270
U.S. Supreme Court, 274
writ of certiorari, 276

do you remember?

Article 3, Section 2 of the U.S. Constitution, 265
Eleventh Amendment, 265
Federal Magistrate's Act of 1968, 270
Marbury v. *Madison* (1803), 269
Tenth Amendment, 265

think about this

1. Should all states have uniform laws and courts? Consider whether it is fair that an action that is legal in one state may be illegal in another state. Should individual states be able to set their own laws according to their culture and diverse populations?
2. The U.S. Supreme Court hears few of the cases sent to it for review. Why? Should the Supreme Court be expanded, perhaps into divisions for civil and criminal cases, to handle more cases? Should there be a Supreme Court for each federal court district? What would be some pros and cons of expanding the U.S. Supreme Court?

research navigator

Visit the Research Navigator website (www.researchnavigator.com), login and select the criminal justice data base in ContentSelect. Type in the key words "If I ran the criminal." Select the article "If I Ran the Criminal Justice System" by James Morton. In this short essay James Morton, an English attorney, laments the decline of the English criminal justice system. While there are differences between the U.S. and the English criminal justice system, Morton's criticisms of the English system could just as well apply to the U.S. criminal justice system. Read the essay and answer the following questions:

1. Morton laments that the modern British criminal justice system is a bar to "swift and certain justice. According to Morton, what is his major concern regarding the criminal justice system?
2. What is Morton's criticism of plea bargaining in the British system? Is there a similar complaint in the U.S. criminal justice system?
3. What does Morton advocate to improve the criminal justice system?
4. Morton suggests that even if what he advocates to improve the criminal justice system is done, the criminal justice system would not improve. Why? Do you think there is a similar tendency regarding reform of the criminal justice system in the United States?

chapter 8
Courtroom Participants and the Trial

CHAPTER OUTLINE

LEARNING OBJECTIVES

After reading this chapter, you will know

- How to differentiate among the three types of criminal trials.
- How charges against the defendant are determined.
- The major proceedings before a criminal defendant goes to trial, including bail, competency testing, and plea bargaining.
- The laws regarding the right to a speedy trial and rules of evidence.
- The major pretrial motions.
- The roles of the people who participate in a criminal trial.
- The proceedings in the actual criminal trial.

Mom Says No to Trial in Teacher Sex Case

ASSOCIATED PRESS, OCALA, FLA.—The mother of a 14-year-old middle school student says she believes the case of a former teacher accused of having sex with her son should not go to trial. Circuit Judge Hale Stancil last week turned down a plea agreement that would allow the former teacher, 25-year-old Debra Lafave, to avoid a prison sentence.

The boy's mother told the Ocala Star-Banner that she disagreed with Stancil's decision to reject the agreement and set the case for trial. "I strongly feel it would further victimize my son if he was forced to testify in court," she said.

Lafave was charged in 2004 with two counts of lewd and lascivious battery and one count of lewd and lascivious exhibition after she allegedly had sex with the student in a sport utility vehicle while another teenager drove. Intense media coverage would create a "media circus" that would further humiliate her son, she said. If the case goes to trial, the notoriety would follow him forever, she said.

From Associated Press, "Mom Says No to Trial in Teacher Sex Case," New York Times Online, www.nytimes.com, December 12, 2005.

introduction:

The Adjudication Process

A criminal trial is a complex event involving many participants. Many of these participants do their work behind the scenes. Most trials attract little media attention but sensational trials can command nationwide media coverage. The public's perception of a criminal trial is strongly influenced by the media, as few people outside of the criminal justice system have reliable knowledge of the adjudication process. Many people, however, have watched criminal trials portrayed by the media. Some media presentations of trials are pretty much complete fiction. The guilty party rarely, if ever, bursts forth from the public seating and confesses to the crime in the middle of the trial. Despite the importance and complexity of trials, most trials last only a couple of days. *Court TV* and other public broadcasts of actual criminal trials provide the public with an accurate view of a criminal trial, but few viewers have the interest and patience to observe a criminal trial from start to finish, as trials can be boring events to watch.

Trials seek to establish the guilt of the defendant and, if guilty, to determine appropriate punitive sanctions. Trials are complex because many criminal justice agencies and personnel must interact in the pursuit of justice: police, prosecutors, judges, jurors, victims, offenders, and many more. Often the parties in a trial are in conflict with each other so there is no guarantee that the process will go smoothly. Police officers seek to have the most serious charges possible filed against defendants, whereas prosecutors seek to have charges that can get a guilty plea or verdict. Prosecutors seek to convict defendants, while defendants hope for a verdict of not guilty. Victim and defendant may offer different accounts of events.

The case of Debra Lafave, a 25-year-old former teacher accused of having sex with a 14-year-old student, illustrates how interests can conflict. Desiring a conviction, prosecutors agreed to a plea bargain. Desiring to avoid jail time, Lafave agreed to a guilty plea that would result in house arrest and probation. However, Circuit Judge Hale Stancil rejected the plea bargain and set the case for trial. However, the 14-year-old victim's mother refused to cooperate, fearing that a public trial would be detrimental to her son. Without the testimony of the victim, the prosecutor has a difficult challenge in obtaining a guilty verdict from the jury. It is surprising that, given the potential for conflict, the adjudication process works as well as it does.

This chapter provides a description of the adjudication phase—in other words, the criminal trial. It examines the people involved in this process, the decisions that have to be made to bring a defendant to trial, and the opposing ideologies that play out in the adjudication process. These opposing ideologies are the pursuit for punishment for the guilty and the desire to provide the accused with constitutional rights to protect him or her from abuse by the criminal justice system.

Jurisdiction

▼ the main idea **8.1** **Criminal trials take place in three types of courts, chosen on the basis of the jurisdiction and severity of the crime.**

There are three types of criminal trials: criminal trials in courts of limited jurisdiction, criminal trials in state courts, and criminal trials in federal courts. Criminal trials in state and federal courts tend to be complex and involve many more people than criminal trials in courts of limited jurisdiction. Courts of limited jurisdiction include justice of the peace courts, municipal courts, and county courts. The criminal jurisdiction or authority of these courts is limited to the misdemeanor laws of the municipality and county.

Go to www.uscourts.gov/districtcourts.html, the official website of the federal judiciary, for information about district courts, including many links.

Trials in Courts of Limited Jurisdiction

These cases usually concern crimes such as simple assault, disorderly conduct, trespass, and larceny. In a typical case, the defendant is arrested by a local police officer and appears before the court for a trial within a few weeks. Usually, the defendant is not guaranteed the right to an attorney because the punishment does not exceed the threshold at which the government must provide defendants with an attorney if they cannot afford legal counsel. It is not uncommon in a court of limited jurisdiction for the judge and the prosecutor to be part-time employees of the municipality. Most trials consist of the police officer telling the judge what law the defendant is alleged to have violated and the evidence supporting his or her assertion, followed by the defendant's rebuttal. For the most part, these trials are fairly simple affairs. Few witnesses are called to testify, and only a minimum of evidence is introduced. The entire trial may last only minutes.

Courts of limited jurisdiction are not courts of record, and no transcript is made of the proceedings. Scheduling of trials is simple in that many defendants are given the same trial date and time. The court starts the day with the first case and proceeds through the others as time permits. These are not jury trials, and the judge renders an immediate decision following the conclusion of the arguments. The defendant has the right to appeal the decision to a court of general trial jurisdiction.

Each local or municipal court has its own distinctive procedures, depending on factors such as the legal training of the judge, the judicial resources of the municipality or county, and the number of cases that the court hears. In rural areas, the justice of the peace court may be held only once a week, whereas in large urban cities, the municipal court may hear cases daily. Because of the diverse and variable nature of trials in courts of limited jurisdiction, the focus of this chapter is on trials in state courts of general jurisdiction and federal district courts.

Trials in Courts of General Jurisdiction and Federal District Courts

Most felony criminal trials occur in state courts of general jurisdiction or United States district courts. Because there are more felony crimes committed in violation of state laws than federal laws, the number of state felony criminal trials is much higher than the number of federal felony trials. Trial procedures for state and federal courts of general jurisdiction are similar. This chapter discusses the general procedures that apply to both state and federal courts and highlights when there is a difference between the two.

One of the first decisions that must be made when a person is arrested for a felony crime is which court has jurisdiction. The general guidelines for determining jurisdiction have to do with which laws were violated and the geographical location of the crime. If the crime was a violation of both federal and state laws, the defendant may be tried in either or both courts. Violation of federal and state laws are considered different offenses and do not constitute trying the person twice for the same offense, which is prohibited by the Fifth Amendment of the Constitution. Thus, if the crime is in violation of both federal and state laws, it is not considered **double jeopardy** to try the defendant in both federal court and state court. As a practical matter, however, most defendants are not tried in both federal and state courts. Usually, the federal or state prosecutor with the strongest case takes the lead in bringing the case to trial. Bank robbery, both a federal crime and a state felony, is one crime in which this question fre-

double jeopardy The defendant can be charged only once and punished only once for a crime. If tried and found innocent, the defendant cannot be retried if new evidence of his or her guilt is discovered.

quently arises. Federal and state prosecutors could both choose to try the defendant for bank robbery, but usually only one prosecutor files charges. Often, the arresting agency is a factor in determining who files charges. If the bank robber is arrested by the Federal Bureau of Investigation, federal charges are filed, and if the defendant is arrested by the state or local police, state charges are filed.

Federal courts claim jurisdiction for crimes committed in the United States; its territories; maritime jurisdictional limits; federal, Native American, and military reservations; and U.S. registered ships at sea. For a state court to have jurisdiction of a case, all or part of the crime must have been committed within the state. If part of the crime is committed in a state, the state may claim jurisdiction over other parts of the crime, even crimes committed in another state. It is not considered double jeopardy to try a defendant in two or more states for what would appear to a layperson to be the same crime. States are sovereign political entities; thus, violation of the laws of several states is not considered the "same crime," and each state retains jurisdiction.

For example, if a person is abducted in one state and transported across the state line, where he or she is murdered, both states can claim jurisdiction over the crime. Both states could try the defendant for kidnapping and murder, even though the kidnapping happened in one state and the murder happened in another. If two (or more) states claim jurisdiction over a crime, the state officials must negotiate to determine who will first prosecute the defendant. The states also will have to negotiate whether the defendant will be tried in both states if he or she is convicted by the first state. If the defendant is convicted and is to be tried in the second state, the states must negotiate whether the trial will occur before or after the convicted defendant has served his or her sentence for the crime. If the crime is first-degree murder and one state has the death penalty but the other state does not, the decision concerning in which state to try the defendant becomes even more important.

▲ check your understanding **8.1 What cases are brought before the courts of limited jurisdiction? What types of courts hear felony trials? What role does the arresting agency have in determining where a felony case will come to trial? How is jurisdiction determined?**

Charges and Proceedings before Trial

▼ the main idea **8.2 The police and prosecutor work together to determine the charges to be brought against the defendant. After the arrest but before the trial, decisions also must be made about setting bail, determining the defendant's competency to stand trial, and plea bargaining.**

The Constitution requires that citizens must be informed of the charges against them before being tried in a court of law. The first step toward bringing a person to trial is the arrest and booking of the person, which formally charges him or her with having committed a crime. The process of bringing a person to trial involves the joint activity of the police and the prosecutor. One of the first questions to answer is whether the defendant will be arraigned before a state court or in the U.S. magistrate court. The defendant must be arraigned before the court, federal or state, that will exercise jurisdiction over the case. Usually, federal agents take the accused to a U.S. magistrate court for arraignment, whereas local and state law enforcement officers take the accused before the appropriate state court. Because both courts may have jurisdiction in the case, a defendant who is first arraigned before one court may later be arraigned before another.

Determining the Charges: The Police and the Prosecutor

When the accused is first arrested, the law enforcement officer files a report charging the person with a crime. After the person is booked, a magistrate reviews the charges filed against the accused and determines that the police have filed constitutional charges against the person and have provided the person with his or her constitutionally protected rights. The police and the prosecutor then work together to bring the case to trial and secure a conviction, without violating due process.

Historically, the British Crown abused its authority both in England and in the colonies. One common abuse of authority was to charge a person with a crime where no evidence existed to support the charge. After separation from England and to prevent this abuse by the new government, the framers of the Constitution of the United States included the provision that due process must be used in bringing a person to trial for a criminal offense. You will recall that due process has been interpreted to mean that the government needs to present evidence to an impartial judicial body that a crime has been committed and that there is reasonable belief that the person accused committed the crime. The prosecutor, not the arresting officer, is responsible for presenting this evidence.

After reviewing the police reports and in some cases talking to the arresting officers, the prosecuting attorney must decide if he or she wants to proceed with the case or drop it. The fact that the police have arrested and booked a suspect is no guarantee that the prosecutor will see the same merit in the case that the police did. The prosecutor may decide that the police do not have sufficient evidence to prove the charges beyond a reasonable doubt and may refuse to move the case forward. Table 8.1 gives you an idea of the number of federal offenses declined for prosecution in the period between 2002 and

table 8.1

Disposition of Suspects in Matters Concluded by U.S. Attorneys, by Offense, October 1, 2002–September 30, 2003

		Suspects in Criminal Matters Concluded					
		Prosecuted before U.S. District Court Judge[b]		*Concluded by U.S. Magistrate*[c]		*Declined Prosecution*[d]	
Most Serious Offense Investigated[a]	*Total Number of Suspects*	*Number*	*Percent*	*Number*	*Percent*	*Number*	*Percent*
All Offenses[e]	128,518	80,106	62.3%	14,810	11.5%	33,602	26.1%
Violent Offenses[f]	5,765	3,218	55.8	316	5.5	2,231	38.7
Property Offenses	28,270	15,046	53.2	1,917	6.8	11,307	40.0
Drug Offenses	38,537	29,259	75.9	2,426	6.3	6,852	17.8
Public Order Offenses	22,023	6,640	30.2	7,077	32.1	8,306	37.7
Weapons	12,954	9,202	71.0	214	1.7	3,538	27.3
Immigration	20,378	16,529	81.1	2,712	13.3	1,137	5.6

[a]Based on the decision of the assistant U.S. attorney responsible for the matter.

[b]Includes suspects whose cases were filed in U.S. district court before a district court judge.

[c]Includes defendants in misdemeanor cases that were terminated in U.S. district court before a U.S. magistrate.

[d]Includes suspects whose matters were declined for prosecution by U.S. attorneys upon review.

[e]Includes suspects whose offense category could not be determined.

[f]In this table, "Violent offenses" may include nonnegligent manslaughter.

Source: Compendium of Federal Justice Statistics, 2003 (Washington, DC: Bureau of Justice Statistics), p. 32.

2003. About 25 percent of cases presented to federal prosecutors are not accepted for further action.

It is also very common for the prosecutor to modify the charges alleged by the police before moving the case forward. The prosecutor has the option of dropping charges, adding additional charges, or reducing the charges. The police may have arrested the person for first-degree murder, but the prosecutor may believe that the evidence only warrants charges of second-degree murder. This power of prosecuting attorneys is called **prosecutorial discretion.** The prosecutor also exercises power in the preliminary hearing, information, indictment, and arraignment.

Law enforcement and the prosecution are each autonomous criminal justice agencies, but without cooperation between them it is difficult to achieve a successful prosecution. When the police arrest a suspect, the prosecutor has a very short time to decide if the charges are appropriate and if the evidence, even though incomplete at this stage, is sufficient to bring the case to trial. The relationship between the prosecutor and the arresting officer(s) is an important factor in this decision. Serious felony crime is most likely to be handled by veteran detectives who have an ongoing relationship with the prosecutor. The prosecutor depends on the professionalism and competence of these detectives in making the decision to take the case.

In some major cases, the police and the prosecutor work together prior to the arrest of the suspect. In important cases, taking months or years to investigate and compile the necessary evidence, the prosecutor may be an active partner with the police. Some prosecutors even have their own investigative staff that can gather additional evidence to help support the charges. In major felony cases in which the prosecutor and law enforcement officers work together, the prosecutor may want to use the grand jury to obtain an arrest warrant rather than have the police arrest the suspect on probable cause.

Checks and balances against police and prosecutorial power are provided by the initial screening of the first appearance and preliminary hearing. In addition, the prosecutor must present evidence to the court at the arraignment that the defendant should be tried for the offense. At the arraignment hearing, the prosecutor has the dilemma of how much evidence he or she should present to convince the court. The arraignment is the final stage before the trial, and the charges filed at this time are the charges on which the defendant will be tried. The prosecutor needs to present enough evidence to convince the court that the defendant should be held over for trial. However, the more evidence that the prosecutor presents, the more information the defense has to prepare for the trial. Thus, the prosecutor wants to present enough evidence to secure a trial date but not so much that the defense will be able to determine the entire prosecution strategy. Three other important decisions that are made before the trial are (1) setting bail, (2) determining the competency of the defendant to stand trial, and (3) plea bargaining.

Bail

One of the hallmarks of the American criminal justice system is the assumption that the criminal justice system will treat defendants as if they are innocent until they are proven guilty. Essential to the fulfillment of that principle is the premise that the defendant will not be incarcerated prior to conviction unless absolutely necessary for public safety. The mechanism to provide for the pretrial release of the defendant is bail.

Bail has its roots in English history and has been used since before the Norman Conquest in 1066. In an era before prisons were used to detain people prior to trial, the English magistrate would place prisoners with private parties who would guarantee that they would be delivered to the court when it was time for trial. To ensure that these custodians would perform their duties properly, they were required to sign a bond, known as a private surety, promising that if they failed to produce the prisoners on the trial date, they would forfeit a specified sum of money or property. The new American government

prosecutorial discretion The power of prosecutors to decide whether or not to charge the defendant and what the charge will be and to gather the evidence necessary to prosecute the defendant in a court of law.

adopted a variation of this pretrial procedure. Rather than entrust the accused to a custodian, the **Eighth Amendment of the Constitution** recognized the concept of bail and also specified that excessive bail should not be required of the accused. In the U.S. criminal justice system, bail is a system of pretrial release of the accused in a criminal proceeding based on a guarantee by the accused—not a custodian—that the accused will appear in court as required. The most common method of guaranteeing the appearance of the defendant is to require a cash bond or some property of value.[1]

In posting bail, this defendant is legally bound to return to the court for trial. How did the bail system originate, and what is the reason for it? What standards and criteria did the judge use to determine whether or not to allow release on bail in this case? How was the amount of bail determined? In what circumstances might the defendant have used a bail bondsperson? What are some alternatives to the cash bond system? What can happen if the defendant does not show up for the trial?

The Eighth Amendment does not specifically state that a defendant is guaranteed bail. It states only that excessive bail should not be required. The U.S. Supreme Court has interpreted the wording of the Eighth Amendment to mean that the defendant does indeed have a right to bail.[2] Initially, the constitutional guarantee of bail was not a state requirement but applied only to the federal courts.[3] However, the question of whether a state defendant has a guarantee of bail has never been a significant constitutional issue, as state constitutions and judiciary practices have provided defendants with this right. Both the federal and state courts have recognized that the right to bail is not an unrestricted right. The controversy over bail has centered on (1) what is excessive bail, (2) when can bail be denied, and (3) does the bail system discriminate against the poor?

Excessive Bail The Supreme Court has declared that excessive bail must be based on standards relevant to guaranteeing that the defendant will not take advantage of his or her freedom and flee prior to the trial.[4] Thus, there are no standard limits of excessive bail that apply to all cases. The court has the power to consider each case individually, based on the totality of the circumstances. The court can consider factors such as the seriousness of the crime, the defendant's prior criminal record, the strength of the state's case, and the defendant's financial status. In some cases, the court has set bail at millions of dollars and this has not been considered excessive. Table 8.2 gives you an idea of the variability in setting bail.

Denial of Bail Bail is not an absolute guarantee, and defendants, under some circumstances, can be denied bail (*U.S.* v. *Salerno*).[5] Initially, the Supreme Court narrowly defined the purpose of bail as ensuring that the defendant would appear for trial. Both the federal judiciary and the state judiciaries recognized cases in which the defendant's pretrial release could pose a potential danger to society and bail should be denied. Starting in the 1970s, state judiciaries enacted danger laws that allowed the court to deny bail for certain offenses in which public safety could be a concern. The most common use of this denial of bail was for allegations of murder and drug offenses. The 1984 federal Bail Reform Act provided the same authority to federal judges.[6] The **1984 Bail Reform Act** allowed the court to make the assumption that the defendant may pose a danger to others or to the community. Once the court makes this determination, it is the burden of the defendant to demonstrate that he or she is not a flight risk and is not a danger to persons or the community.[7] California law prohibits the court from releasing a defendant on bail who is charged with multiple murder on the presumption that the defendant would be a danger to the community. The O. J. Simpson trial for murder was an example of bail being denied based on the presumption that the defendant could be a danger to the community. Despite arguments of the defense that Simpson was not a flight risk and was able to post a high bail, the state of California denied bail. Figure 8.1 shows the percentages of felony defendants detained on bail and denied bail in a recent year.

For most misdemeanor offenses, bail is set based on a set fee schedule; that is, for most common offenses, a predetermined bail is set by the judge in advance, committed to written record, and used by booking to know what bail to set without a judge's in-

table 8.2

Bail Amounts for Felony Defendants in the 75 Largest Counties, by Percentage

Excessive bail is prohibited. Bail must be relative to the charges against the defendant. Bail for most defendants charged with public order offenses is less than $5,000, whereas bail for most defendants charged with murder is in excess of $25,000.

Most Serious Arrest Charge	Number of Defendants	<$5,000	$5,000–$9,999	$10,000–$24,999	$25,000–$49,999	>$50,000
Violent offenses	8,860	19%	17%	22%	14%	31%
Property offenses	8,562	31	20	23	12	14
Drug offenses	11,162	25	19	26	13	17
Public order offenses	2,720	34	20	20	10	16
All offenses	31,304	26	19	22	13	20

Source: Bureau of Justice Statistics, *Felony Defendants in Large Urban Counties, 2000* (Washington, DC: Department of Justice, December 2003), p. 24.

structions. Bail is an integral part of the initial appearance. For more serious felony cases, there is a bail hearing in which the prosecutor and the defense argue before the judge the merits of pretrial release. In the federal judiciary, bail hearings are held before magistrate judges. In most state courts, bail hearings are handled by courts of limited jurisdiction. Bail hearings are not decided by a jury, and following short oral arguments, the judge has wide discretionary powers as to granting bail and setting the amount.

Discrimination against the Poor If bail requires the posting of a cash bond, it seems obvious that low-income defendants are not going to have access to the right of bail because of their lack of available money. Without the ability to post a cash bond, the poor are condemned to remain incarcerated until their trials. Given the fact that even simple felony cases may take months before they come to trial, the possibility arises that the poor may spend more time in jail awaiting their trials than the length of sentences they may receive at the end of their trials. (When this does happen, defendants are credited with time already served and are released.) Accused persons who are not incarcerated have greater opportunities to assist in their defense. Thus, if bail discriminates against the poor, the poor may not receive the same quality of justice as the rich. Recognizing that a cash bail system may discriminate against the poor, the judiciary has established alternatives.

The Bail Bondsperson In actuality, many people cannot afford the bail that may be required for pretrial release. In felony criminal cases, it is not uncommon for bail to be set at tens of thousands of dollars. The court does allow the bail to be secured by lien on property, and family and friends can help contribute to the bail. Most people, however, simply do not have access to the amount of money required for bail. As a result of this situation, the judiciary provides for a bail bond business. The **bail bondsperson** is an agent of a private commercial business that has contracted with the court to act as a guarantor of the defendant's return to court. The bail bondsperson is not a state or federal employee but is a private party operating a for-profit business.

The bail bondsperson acts as an intermediary and posts the bond for the accused. If the defendant shows up for all scheduled court appearances, the court returns the amount of bail posted by the defendant and the defendant pays the bail bond company a nonrefundable fee for its service. This fee is usually 10 percent of the bond but may be higher, as there is no set limit on the bail bond company's fee. At a 10-percent fee, a person whose bail is set at $1,000 would have to pay the bail bond company $100 for its

bail bondsperson An agent of a private commercial business that has contracted with the court to act as a guarantor of a defendant's return to court.

figure 8.1

Pretrial Detention of Felony Defendants (Percentage denied bail)

Bail is not an absolute right of a defendant. While most defendants charged with minor crimes are released on bail, nearly half of murder defendants are denied bail.

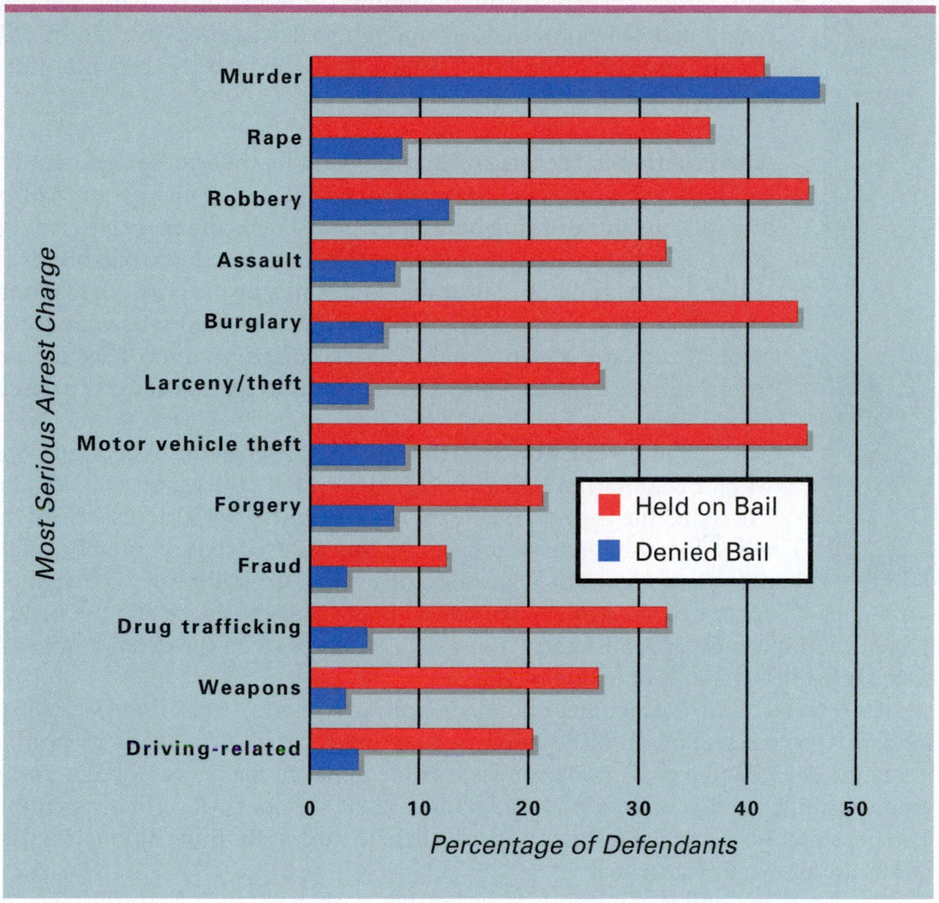

Source: Bureau of Justice Statistics, *Felony Defendants in Large Urban Counties, 2000* (Washington, DC: Department of Justice, December 2003), p. 22.

services. A person whose bond is set at $50,000, a more realistic figure for a serious felony crime, would have to pay $5,000. Bail bond companies can refuse to underwrite the bail of a defendant if they do not believe the defendant is a good risk.

Bond Jumpers and Bounty Hunters A person who fails to show for a court appearance is said to have "jumped bond." When a person jumps bond, the court will allow the bail bondsperson (bondsagent) a certain amount of time to return the defendant to the custody of the court before revoking the posted bond. The bail bond businesses are not criminal justice agencies, but when they post bail for a defendant they are considered to be agents of the court. This power allows the bail bondsagent to require the defendant to sign a legally binding contract, waiving the right of extradition. This means the agent can track down and bring back the bond jumper.

As an agent of the court, the bail bondsagent, who is not a law enforcement officer, does not have to observe the restrictions placed on the police in seeking the return of the person who fails to show for his or her court appearance. Essentially, the bondsagent may use any means necessary to return the person to the jurisdiction of the court. The bondsagent is authorized to carry firearms, can use the threat of force to compel the de-

Go to www.bailacademy.org/index1.html, the site of the Pacific Northwest Bail Enforcement Academy, for a description of the training and duties of bail enforcers, also called "fugitive recovery."

TV celebrity bounty hunter "Dog" is not typical of the average bond jumper agent.

fendant to return, and can kidnap the defendant and forcibly return him or her to the court against his or her will. The bondsagent does not have to have an arrest warrant to enter a private residence where the defendant has sought refuge, and can trespass anywhere the defendant is hiding. The bondsagent is allowed to pay a third party to search for and return a bond jumper. There are no minimum requirements or mandated training for people who track down and return defendants. Commonly called "bounty hunters," bondsagents have greater powers than police officers in the pursuit of bond jumpers.

Alternatives to Cash Bond

Despite the widespread use of the bail bonds system, there are criticisms of it and of the conduct of bail bondsagents in returning bond jumpers. One of the primary criticisms is that even with fees at 10 percent of the total bond, the bail bonds system still discriminates against the poor, and a disproportionate number of the poor who are accused of crimes and have bail set are persons of color. Charges of institutionalized racial discrimination have led both federal and state courts to implement a number of alternatives to the cash bond system.

One of the early experiments in alternatives to the cash bond system was the **Manhattan Bail Project.**[8] In the 1960s, the Manhattan Bail Project tested the use of **release on recognizance (ROR).** This system provides for the pretrial release of the accused based merely on the defendant's unsecured promise that he or she will return for trial. The success of the project has caused many states to adopt the use of ROR. The provision is most appropriate for nonviolent offenses when the defendant has ties to the community and is not a flight risk.

Unsecured bond and signature bond are pretrial release systems that allow the defendant to be released on his or her promise to return for trial. An **unsecured bond** releases the defendant, who signs a promissory note to pay to the court a predetermined amount similar to that set by a cash bail bond if he or she does not fulfill this promise. The percentages of pretrial releases of felony defendants on ROR on different types of bonds are shown in Figure 8.2.

A **signature bond** is commonly used for minor offenses, such as traffic law violations. It is similar to ROR but much simpler. There are no prequalifications for a signature bond, and no one makes an assessment of the defendants' flight risk or danger to the community. A signature bond allows the police officers, acting as agents of the court, to release the accused immediately after they are charged with the offense if they sign a promise to appear in court. When a police officer asks a motorist to sign a traffic citation, the motorist's signature is not a confession of guilt but a promise to appear in court. If the motorist does not sign the citation, he or she forfeits the right to a signature bond and the police officer has the authority to take the motorist into custody. After booking, the motorist will be required to post bond.

Conditional release and third-party custody are interesting alternatives to cash bail. Conditional release and a closely related type of bail, called *supervision release,* require the defendant to agree to a number of court-ordered terms and restrictions. Common terms of conditional release include participation in drug or alcohol treatment programs, attendance of anger-management classes, compliance with a restraining order, and regular employment. Supervision release has the additional stipulation that the defendant, similar to someone on parole or probation, must report to an officer of the court at regular intervals.

Third-party custody allows the court to release a pretrial defendant to the custody of an individual or agency that promises to be responsible for the defendant's behavior and to guarantee his or her participation in the legal process. The two most common conditions are placing a defendant with his or her family or with attorneys who assume

release on recognizance (ROR) Provides for the pretrial release of the accused, based merely on the defendant's unsecured promise of return for trial.

unsecured bond Release based on the defendant's promise to pay the court an amount similar to a cash bail bond if the defendant fails to fulfill a promise to return for trial.

signature bond Release based on the defendant's signature on a promise to return for trial.

conditional release A bail alternative in which the defendant is released from custody if he or she agrees to a number of court-ordered terms and restrictions.

responsibility for their clients. Youthful offenders are the most likely candidates to be placed with their families. An adult member of the family assumes responsibility for a defendant's day-to-day behavior and appearances for scheduled court appointments.

Pros and Cons of Bail Whereas 50 percent of arrested persons are released from jail within 1 day, approximately 28 percent are not released until one week after their arrest and 10 percent remain incarcerated after one month of their arrest. (See Table 8.3 for data on the time from arrest to release on bail or alternative to bail.) For those who will not be prosecuted (remember, about 25 percent of those arrested will not be prosecuted), 1 to 30 days in prison or more can be a significant burden. For those who have been wrongly arrested, spending from 1 to 30 days in jail while waiting for bail can seem unfair and unnecessarily punitive. Thus, there are important reasons for an effective bail system and alternatives to traditional cash bails.

figure 8.2

Pretrial Release of Felony Defendants

The most common form of bail is for the defendant to post a cash bond or to use the services of a bail bondsperson to post a cash bond.

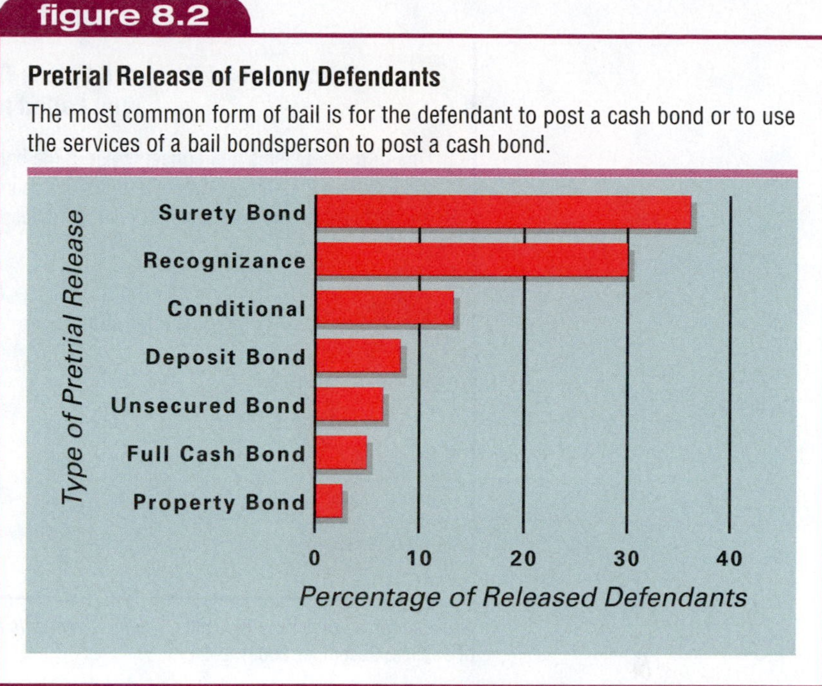

Source: Bureau of Justice Statistics, *Felony Defendants in Large Urban Counties, 1998* (Washington, DC: Department of Justice, November 2001), p. 17.

The advantage of alternatives is that the defendant does not have to pay the necessary money to post the bond, and there is no bail bond fee to pay to a third party. Also, it is to the court's advantage to release as many pretrial defendants as possible. Pretrial defendants who are denied bail are a special category of incarcerated persons. By law,

table 8.3

Time from Arrest to Release for Felony Defendants, 2000

Most defendants are quickly released after being arraigned. About half of all defendants are released within 1 day, and over 90% are released within 30 days.

	Released Felony Defendants in the 75 Largest Counties			
		Percentage Who Were Released Within:		
Most Serious Arrest Charge	***Number of Defendants***	***1 Day***	***1 Week***	***1 Month***
Violent offenses	6,949	42	72	90
Property offenses	9,382	57	82	94
Drug offenses	12,026	47	76	93
Public order offenses	2,849	55	81	93
All offenses	31,206	50	78	93

Source: Bureau of Justice Statistics, *Felony Defendants in Large Urban Counties, 2000* (Washington, DC: Department of Justice, December 2003), p. 19.

Note: Data on time from arrest to release were available for 95% of all cases. Release data were collected for 1 year.

table 8.4

Percentage of Released Felony Defendants in the 75 Largest Counties Who Failed to Appear in Court

One of the criticisms and concerns about the bail system is that some defendants take advantage of their release and flee. Between 11 and 22 percent of defendants fail to return for court appearances, and between 3 and 7 percent of defendants flee and never return, unless rearrested.

Most Serious Arrest Charge	Number of Defendants	Percent Who Failed to Return to Court	Percent Who Remained a Fugitive
Violent offenses	7,246	22	4
Property offenses	9,766	21	6
Drug offenses	12,388	27	7
Public order offenses	2,985	20	4
All offenses	32,386	22	6

Source: Bureau of Justice Statistics, *Felony Defendants in Large Urban Counties, 2000* (Washington, DC: Department of Justice, December 2003), p. 21.

they are not guilty of any crime and cannot be confined as punishment nor placed in a state penitentiary. Most pretrial defendants are incarcerated in county jails, which is costly to the state. Jails are overcrowded, and pretrial defendants take up valuable space that could be better used to house convicted offenders and to relieve overcrowding.

Prosecutors and police often are critical of economic arguments encouraging bail and the pretrial release of defendants in general. Their view is that the defendant will continue to engage in criminal activity. Police argue that some defendants use pretrial release as an opportunity to commit further crimes to pay for their legal fees. For example, Table 8.4 indicates that approximately 22 percent of those released on bail failed to return to court and 4 to 7 percent of those released on bail remained a fugitive. Figure 8.3 indicates that the police are correct to some degree in asserting that those who are released will continue to engage in criminal activity. The figure shows that a significant number of defendants released on bail commit criminal misconduct.

Competency to Stand Trial and the Insanity Defense

Prior to the trial, it is the responsibility of the court to determine that the defendant is competent to stand trial. **Competent to stand trial** means that defendants comprehend the charges against them and are able to assist their attorneys in their defense. Competency to stand trial usually is determined by the ruling of a federal magistrate court judge or similar-level state judge. Health is one of the most common reasons a pretrial defendant may not be competent to stand trial. A defendant who has a serious disease and is undergoing treatment can experience serious side effects that affect his or her judgment. A defendant who is wounded by the police may not be competent to stand trial because of the need for medical treatment. A defendant with a medical condition affecting intellectual capacity may be considered incapable of understanding the charges against him or her. Declaring a pretrial defendant not competent to stand trial is a temporary ruling. When the defendant becomes competent to stand trial, the court will order that the trial proceedings resume or begin.

competent to stand trial
The concept that defendants comprehend the charges against them and are able to assist their attorney in their defense.

The claim that a defendant is not guilty by reason of insanity, is an affirmative defense that must be made prior to the trial. After the insanity defense is declared, the

figure 8.3

Misconduct Prior to Case Disposition by Released Felony Defendants

More serious than the failure to return for a court appearance is a defendant released on bail who commits another crime while on bail. As many as 40 percent of defendants released on bail commit new crimes while on bail.

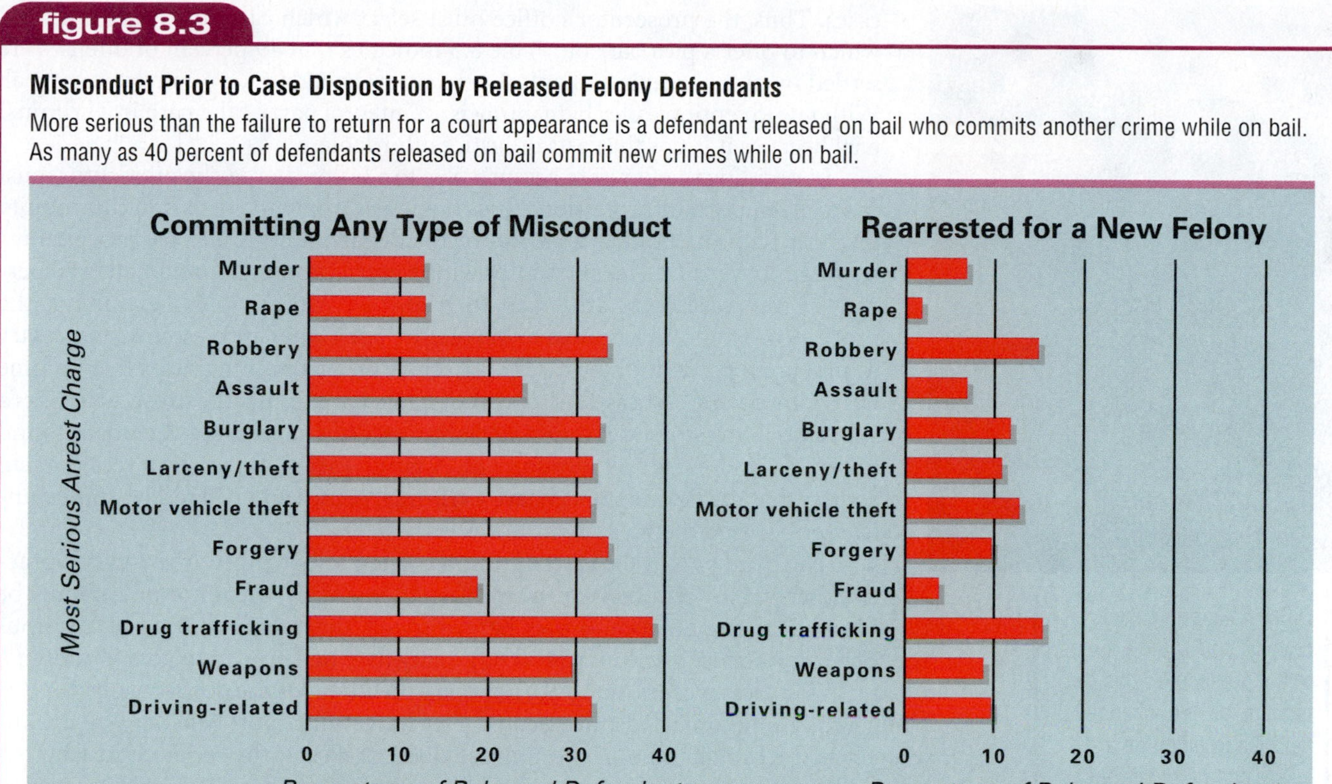

Source: Bureau of Justice Statistics, *Felony Defendants in Large Urban Counties, 2000* (Washington, DC: Department of Justice, December 2003), p. 22.

court orders a series of psychiatric examinations to assess the defendant's mental state. The results of examinations are admissible as evidence during the defendant's trial. A finding of not guilty by reason of insanity is not determined by the medical professionals who examine the defendant, however, but by the jury.

Plea Bargaining

Another pretrial activity is plea bargaining, and a great majority of cases are disposed by this method without ever going to trial. Both the police and the victim often object to the practice of plea bargaining, but the prosecutor must make the best use of the resources of his or her office. The police and the victim object to plea bargaining on the grounds that the offender typically is not punished to the fullest extent of the law. After working to gather the necessary evidence and witnesses to help convict the defendant, law enforcement officers would like to see the defendant prosecuted on the most serious charges. Victims often want the same thing but for revenge or retribution or satisfaction that justice has been provided. Yet the prosecutors decide to offer defendants the opportunity to plead guilty to lesser charges. Why?

One reason is that preparation for trial is a time-consuming and costly endeavor. The prosecutor's office has the actual responsibility for trial preparation and bears the majority of the costs associated with gathering evidence, interviewing witnesses, and other preparations. Most prosecutors have only a limited staff and budget and cannot possibly take every case to trial. Furthermore, the court has only so much time to hear

On advice of defense counsel and at the urging of the prosecutor, this defendant, seated, changed her plea to guilty on a lesser charge of serious bodily injury to a child. Authorities found the defendant's abused 8-year-old daughter living in a closet in the family trailer. As a result of the plea bargain, the case will be disposed without going to trial. What are the advantages and disadvantages of plea bargaining for the defendant? For the prosecutor? For the court? For the criminal justice system?

cases. Thus, the prosecutor's office must select which cases to take to trial and which to offer a plea bargain. Table 8.5 indicates that 49 percent of offenses are settled by plea bargains and only 3 percent of defendants are convicted by trial. With few exceptions, plea bargaining is an integral part of the path in a criminal trial because it keeps the costs of justice affordable.

In deciding to offer or to accept a plea to a lesser charge, the prosecutor must make an important professional judgment as to how to best serve community interests with the limited resources of the department. A plea bargain guarantees a guilty verdict. The prosecutor wins a conviction in approximately 80 percent of the cases that are taken to trial, but without plea bargaining, the prosecutor would not be able to devote the personnel and resources necessary to prepare for trial in these cases. In a sense, plea bargaining helps free up time for the more difficult cases. Also, without plea bargaining, the prosecutor risks a substantial investment in time and resources, only to have the defendant found not guilty and escape all punishment. A guilty plea obtained by a plea bargain assures that the defendant will have a criminal record and will receive some punishment or treatment.

The irony is that the career criminals seem to benefit more from this practice than minor criminals or the innocent. Obviously, the innocent can only be harmed by the practice of plea bargaining. A defendant accused of a serious crime such as capital murder but who is not guilty may be tempted to accept or offer a plea bargain for a lesser crime that does not carry the threat of the death penalty for fear of being wrongfully convicted and executed. Plea bargaining most benefits major criminals such as the burglar who has committed 300 burglaries, the serial rapist who has committed numerous sexual assaults, or the drug dealer who has constantly engaged in the trafficking of drugs.

The prosecutor may not have sufficient evidence to convict a career burglar for all of the burglaries that he or she has committed. The prosecutor may not even know of all of the crimes the defendant has committed. If the prosecutor agrees to charge the defendant with only a single burglary in turn for a confession to 300 burglaries, what does the prosecutor gain? First, the prosecutor and the police get to "clear" the 299 burglaries, even though the defendant is not prosecuted for them. By accepting this offer, the police and the prosecutor can report a higher clearance rate to the public. Second, the prosecutor knows that even if a defendant is convicted of multiple offenses, he or she may end up serving the prison sentences concurrently instead of consecutively. Thus, the extra time and effort required to obtain the multiple convictions may make little difference in the actual outcome.

Finally, the prosecutor may not be completely confident of the evidence or witnesses. Perhaps the prosecutor believes that at the last moment a victim may refuse to testify. Witnesses to crimes committed by gang members or organized crime figures may become concerned about their safety or the safety of their families, for instance, and may refuse to testify or may give weak and inconclusive evidence. A young witness, especially a child, may pose special difficulties for the prosecutor. Or the prosecutor may believe that the reputation of the arresting police officer or reliability of evidence gathered by the police may not stand up to cross-examination. Any of these reasons may make the prosecutor reluctant to take the case to trial.

Plea bargaining can be initiated by the prosecuting or the defending attorney. Plea bargaining can center on the charges or the sentence. At arrest the police and prosecutor typically charge the defendant with as many crimes as possible, beginning with the most serious crime. In return for dropping the more serious charges, the defendant offers his or her guilty plea. Plea bargaining can involve the police, the prosecutor, the judge, and defense counsel but seldom involves the victim. In some cases, the victim is not even informed of the decision to accept a plea bargain. The defendant may provide the police with information regarding other criminals or crimes in return for their help in convincing the prosecutor to accept the defendant's plea bargain. The defendant may

table 8.5

Disposition of Defendants in Large Urban Counties, 2000

Most Serious Arrest Charge	Number of Defendants	Percentage of Felony Defendants in the 75 Largest Counties											
		Convicted							Not Convicted				
			Felony			Misdemeanor							
		Total Convicted	Total	Plea	Trial	Total	Plea	Trial	Total	Dismissed	Acquitted	Other Outcome*	
Violent Offenses	11,288	56%	42%	38%	4%	14%	13%	—%	39%	37%	2%	6%	
Murder	256	66	64	31	33	2	2	0	30	28	2	5	
Rape	675	60	50	47	2	11	10	—	35	33	2	5	
Robbery	2,486	58	50	44	6	8	8	—	38	35	3	4	
Assault	5,635	52	35	32	3	16	16	1	42	40	2	6	
Other	2,237	62	46	43	3	16	16	—	32	31	1	6	
Property Offenses	14,299	66%	50%	48%	2%	15%	15%	—%	25%	24%	—%	10%	
Burglary	3,721	72	59	56	2	13	13	—	23	23	—	5	
Larceny/theft	3,839	66	49	46	3	17	16	1	24	23	—	10	
Motor vehicle theft	1,540	65	56	55	1	9	9	—	29	27	1	6	
Forgery	1,604	68	53	52	2	15	15	—	24	24	—	8	
Fraud	1,797	52	33	33	—	20	19	—	18	18	0	30	
Other	1,798	62	45	43	2	17	17	—	34	33	1	4	
Drug Offenses	17,473	65%	58%	56%	2%	7%	7%	—%	23%	23%	—%	11%	
Trafficking	7,902	74	67	63	4	7	7	—	21	20	—	6	
Other	9,571	58	50	49	1	8	8	—	26	25	—	16	
Public-order Offenses	4,229	72%	56%	53%	2%	17%	17%	—%	22%	21%	1%	5%	
Weapons	1,276	69	56	53	3	13	13	0	27	24	3	4	
Driving-related	1,434	86	70	68	2	16	16	—	10	10	—	4	
Other	1,519	63	42	40	2	21	20	—	30	29	1	7	
All Offenses	47,290	64%	52%	49%	3%	12%	12%	—%	27%	26%	1%	9%	

*Includes diversion and deferred adjudication.

Note: Twelve percent of all cases were still pending adjudication at the end of the 1-year study period, and are excluded from the table. Data on adjudication outcome were available for 99% of those cases that had been adjudicated. Detail may not add to total because of rounding.

—Less than 0.5%

Source: Bureau of Justice Statistics, *Felony Defendants in Large Urban Counties, 2000* (Washington, DC: Department of Justice, December 2003), p. 24.

not have been the principal offender and may offer to testify against other defendants in exchange for a plea bargain. Plea bargains for testimony against fellow partners in crime is risky, however, as the information often is unconvincing to a jury.

In sentence bargaining, the defendant seeks leniency. Sentences can range from probation to life imprisonment. The defendant may offer to plead guilty to the charges in return for the prosecutor's recommendation to the judge for a minimum sentence. Most defendants—especially the guilty—want to avoid jail time, and a sentence of probation, even a long period of probation, is preferable to hard time in prison. Some defendants want to negotiate where they will serve their time or the type of facility or its security level. Because they control the charges to be filed against the defendant, prosecutors can bargain for reduction of the charges directly. However, the judge has control over the sentence, so sentence bargaining frequently involves pretrial negotiation among the prosecutor, defense counsel, and judge. In some cases, a judge may encourage a plea bargain, especially where guilt appears obvious and a trial would only take up the scarce resources of the criminal court. Judges may encourage plea bargaining by making it known that if convicted in a trial, a defendant will receive a more severe sentence than if he or she had pled guilty. Judge participation raises a serious question as to the role of the judge in the adjudication process. The American Bar Association standards recommend that the "trial judge should not participate in plea discussions."[9] The Federal Rules of Criminal Procedure also state that the court should not participate in negotiating guilty pleas.[10] Some states have similar prohibitions. Despite these prohibitions, judge participation in plea bargaining is a characteristic of the criminal justice system.

▲ check your understanding **8.2** **Who determines the charges to be brought against the defendant? What are the prosecutor's powers? How do prosecutors and the police work together to bring charges? How is bail set? Who determines if the defendant is competent to stand trial? What does it mean to be not guilty by reason of insanity? Why do victims and the police often object to plea bargaining? Why do prosecutors and defendants accept plea bargains?**

Preparation for the Criminal Trial

▼ the main idea **8.3** **A criminal case that goes to trial must assure the defendant the right to a speedy trial and legal counsel; must follow specific rules of evidence; and must proceed with the judge, prosecutor, and jury serving specific roles in the trial.**

After adjudication—assuming that the defendant is competent to stand trial, no alternative diversion is offered, and no plea bargain is struck—the case proceeds forward in the criminal justice process. It becomes one of the few arrests that actually results in a criminal trial. For a case to come to trial, it must be placed on the **court docket,** or calendar. Attorneys, defendants, and courtroom personnel must know when the case is scheduled for trial and how long the trial is expected to last, because the demand for judges and courtrooms exceeds the limited resources of the criminal justice system. Defendants released on bail, especially when guilty, may want to postpone their day in court. However, defendants awaiting trial in jail—especially those who are not guilty—want to hasten the day of judgment.

court docket The calendar on which court cases are scheduled for trial.

Once a case is on the docket, the actual time that a defendant must wait for his or her day in court is not left to the defendant or to the government. The **Sixth Amendment of the Constitution** guarantees that defendants will receive a speedy trial, but the Constitution does not define what constitutes *speedy.* The right to a speedy trial is not the same as the statute of limitations. The **statute of limitations** is the length of time between the discovery of the crime and the arrest of the defendant. Various crimes have different acceptable lengths of time between the crime and the arrest. Usually, less serious crimes have a shorter period for arresting the defendant, and more serious crimes have longer periods. Customarily, there is no statute of limitations for the crime of murder. The right to a speedy trial refers to the time between arrest and trial.

The Sixth Amendment Right to a Speedy Trial

Like other amendments in the Bill of Rights, the Sixth Amendment right to a speedy trial originally extended only to federal crimes in federal courts. It was not until 1967 that the Supreme Court made the Sixth Amendment applicable to state and federal courts as well.[11] Prior to then, states did not have to provide a speedy trial unless guaranteed by the state constitution. The definition of *speedy trial* differed substantially among states. Some states required that the trial take place in less than two months' time, and others allowed a case to come to trial years after the defendant was arrested. Initially, the Supreme Court did not provide specific guidelines to help determine what constitutes a speedy trial. The Court took the view that a speedy trial is a relative matter and may vary in length of time from arrest to trial because of the circumstances of the case.[12]

The judicial interpretation of the right to a speedy trial changed dramatically in the late 1960s and early 1970s, beginning with the 1967 case of ***Klopfer* v. *North Carolina.***[13] Peter Klopfer, a professor at Duke University, was arrested for trespassing while engaged in a sit-in at a segregated motel and restaurant. Klopfer initially was tried for trespassing, which resulted in a hung jury. In such cases, the state has the right to retry the defendant. The prosecutor decided not to bring the case to trial, but at the same time refused to dismiss the charges against Klopfer. The laws of North Carolina allowed the prosecutor to postpone a trial indefinitely, even over the defendant's demand for a speedy trial. At the time, the state of North Carolina did not guarantee defendants the right to a speedy trial.

Thus, Klopfer was left in a state of legal limbo. At any time the prosecutor could decide to reactivate the criminal charges against the defendant, and the defendant had no recourse due to lack of a speedy trial. Klopfer's case was appealed to the U.S. Supreme Court on the grounds that North Carolina denied him his constitutional rights. On appeal, the Supreme Court agreed and declared the North Carolina law unconstitutional. The right to a speedy trial was extended to state courts, and spurred by the *Klopfer* case, many states adopted speedy trial legislation. The Sixth Amendment right applies even if a defendant, for whatever reason, does not object to a delay. In 1972, in ***Barker* v. *Wingo,*** the Supreme Court issued a ruling that a defendant's failure to demand a speedy trial does not amount to a waiver of the Sixth Amendment right.[14]

Although guaranteeing the right to a speedy trial, the Sixth Amendment does not specify the remedy if this right is denied. If a defendant is denied a speedy trial, what should the court do? After the *Klopfer* v. *North Carolina* ruling that extended this right to state courts, the Supreme Court found it necessary to review cases in which some state defendants failed to receive a speedy trial. In 1973, the Supreme Court decided that the remedy to be applied when a defendant does not receive a speedy trial is that the charges against the defendant will be permanently dismissed, and the prosecutor subsequently will not be allowed to bring these charges against the defendant. However, the Court also ruled that delays caused by the defendant's actions, such as requests for post-

statute of limitations Legal limits regarding the length of time between the discovery of the crime and the arrest of the defendant.

ponement, claims related to competency to stand trial, and other requests for delays, cannot be considered a denial of the right to a speedy trial.

The Speedy Trial Act of 1974

These Supreme Court rulings caused both federal and state courts to change the way they did business. Previously, the prosecutor could select some cases for prosecution and leave others to a later time without any concern for the delay in bringing a case to trial. After the Supreme Court ruling, the prosecutor had to be mindful of bringing all cases to trial in a timely manner or risk losing the ability to prosecute. The Speedy Trial Act of 1974 turned this concern into a crisis. The **Speedy Trial Act of 1974** required a specific deadline between arrest and trial in federal courts. Fully implemented in 1980, the act required that, except in a few well-defined situations and barring delays created by the defendant, the defendant would be brought to trial within 180 days of his or her arrest or the charges could be dismissed and could not be reinstated. When a federal defendant is charged with a crime, the clock starts, and the prosecutor has 30 days to seek an indictment or information. If the defendant is indicted, the prosecutor has 70 days after the indictment or information to start the trial.[15] The clock is stopped for delays attributable to the defendant, such as postponements or escape to avoid prosecution. The clock does not stop when the delay is attributable to the prosecutor, however, even if the delays are beyond the prosecutor's control. Basically, the Speedy Trial Act requires that federal cases be brought to trial 100 days after the arrest of the defendant (30 days from arrest to indictment plus 70 days from indictment to trial) or the prosecutor runs the risk of having the charges against the defendant dismissed. When this act was passed, many prosecutors were not prepared to bring a defendant to trial so quickly, and many courts were unable to accommodate the demand for speed. Prosecutors were forced to become more efficient and effective in bringing cases to trial, and courts were forced to utilize courtrooms and judges in a more productive manner. Court administrators and the Clerk of the Court came under new pressures to exercise effective management of the court's docket.

See www.law.cornell.edu/rules/fre/overview.html, the Legal Information Institute at Cornell University, for a complete listing of the federal rules of evidence.

Rules of Evidence

Each court is governed by certain rules of evidence. Rules of evidence are laws that shape law enforcement and court practices, defining how the trial will be conducted, how evidence will be introduced, how the parties to the trial will act, and the order of the proceedings. Deviation from rules of evidence constitutes a judicial error, which leads to appeals. If a rule of evidence is violated, the prosecution or the defense can appeal the case. If the appeals court finds that the violation is a serious breach of the rules, the defendant has not received a fair trial.

Each state court and the federal courts have different rules. To represent clients in a particular court, attorneys are required to demonstrate that they have competent knowledge of the rules of evidence for the court hearing the case. To represent a client in a court of appeals or the state or federal supreme court, attorneys may need to pass an examination on the rules of evidence.

Usually, attorneys qualify for practice in state trial courts of limited and general jurisdiction by virtue of their good standing in the state bar association. The federal trial courts have different rules of evidence, requiring that the lawyer demonstrate competency in the federal rules of evidence before he or she can present a case in federal court.

The rules of evidence regulate nearly every aspect of the trial. Rules of evidence can be mundane, such as the rule that only the original of a document can be introduced as evidence. In addition, rules of evidence determine what evidence is relevant, what evidence is permissible, what evidence cannot be introduced, what evidence an expert witness may present to the jury, what questions can be asked of witnesses, and what is required before an item of physical evidence can be introduced into the trial.

careers in the system

Legal Careers

Perhaps the most popular careers in the legal profession are those of lawyer and judge. In the United States, lawyers and judges receive the same legal education. To enter thse professions one must complete two to three years of formal education in law school to obtain a law degree. In addition to formal schooling the prospective attorney must pass a professional examination known as the bar examination in the state in which he or she wants to practice law. This examination assesses the applicant's knowledge of the specific laws and procedures of that state. Most lawyers practice civil law, not criminal law. Those who practice criminal law are divided into defense counsels and those who work for the prosecution.

There are many ways to become a judge. In some states judges are elected, and in others they are appointed. In those states where judges are appointed, candidates are usually required to have a minimum number of years of experience as an attorney to qualify for appointment. Judges are not required to have any special education to qualify for the position. An interesting observation is that there is no requirement that a U.S. Supreme Court justice must be an attorney or judge prior to his or her appointment.

The salary of judges is above the national median salary. For example, the Chief Justice of the U.S. Supreme Court receives an annual salary of $203,000 and the average salary of state judges is $122,418. Despite these high salaries there is a crisis in attracting and retaining highly qualified judges due to the higher salaries that these individuals can make in other occupations.

There are many other occupations in the legal profession. Many of these do not require extensive formal education. The day-to-day management of the cases and paperwork of the court are the responsibility of the court administrator and the Clerk of Court. Court administrators can be judges or nonlawyer professionals hired for their management skills. In larger courts (five or more judges), often a professional position is created to handle the administrative matters of the court.[16] The court administrator works for the judges of the court. A professional court administrator does not perform judicial duties and is not a lawyer. Court administrators perform administrative and clerical duties, do strategic planning to increase court efficiency, manage the trial schedule of the court, and manage the budget. Court administrators also may have responsibility for supervising clerical staff who work for them, making effective use of jurors, and ensuring an adequate supply of jurors for the trials scheduled.

The **Clerk of Court** works directly with the trial judge and is responsible for the court records. Usually, each judge has his or her own Clerk of Court. Large courts may employ assistant clerks of court who help perform routine tasks and paperwork. The Clerk of Court and assistants are responsible for the paperwork generated both before and during the trial. The Clerk of Court issues summonses and subpoenas for witnesses, receives pleas and motions and forwards them to the judge for consideration, and prepares all case files that a judge will need for the day. During the trial, the Clerk of Court records and marks physical evidence introduced in the trial. It is the Clerk of Court who swears in the witnesses. In some jurisdictions, the Clerk of Court has certain signatory powers as an agent of the judge and can issue warrants or perform other judicial powers requiring court oversight.

As a result of the need to bring a case to trial in a timely manner, the job of the court administrator and Clerk of Court are important. Delays due to slow performance of routine tasks necessary to bring the trial to court is not an excuse to deny the defendant a speedy trial. The Clerk of Court and court administrator often are invisible to the public. Much of their work is behind the scenes, but it is essential to the efficient operation of the court.

What roles do court administrators and the Clerk of Court fulfill in the adjudication process? Why is their work important in criminal trials? If you wanted to be a court administrator or Clerk of Court, how could you find out more about these jobs?

If during the trial the prosecutor or defense counsel believes that a rule of evidence has been violated, it is his or her duty to raise objections to the judge. To do this, the attorney says, "I object on the grounds that . . . ." For example, if the prosecution asks a witness a question that the defense feels the witness is not competent to answer, the defense attorney objects on the grounds that the question calls for the

Clerk of Court Government employee who works directly with the trial judge and is responsible for court paperwork and records before and during a trial.

witness to make a conclusion that he or she is not competent to make. Objections include questions that are not relevant to the present case or that call for the witness to comment about the mental state of the defendant (e.g., whether the defendant was angry). If the judge agrees, he or she declares that the objection is sustained, and the witness is instructed not to answer the question or the evidence will not be presented to the jury. If the judge does not agree, he or she overrules the objection. After the trial, the case can be appealed if the prosecution or defense believes the judge made a judicial error.

Pretrial Motions

Rules of evidence include procedures called *motions.* Motions are formal written requests, usually in a specified legal format, requesting that the judge make a ruling regarding some aspect of the trial prior to the start of the trial. The judge makes a decision regarding the motion and informs the parties of the decision. The most common motions are for continuance, discovery, change of venue, suppression, a bill of particulars, severance of charges or defendants, and dismissal.

Motion for Continuance A **motion for continuance** is a request to delay the start of the trial. Either party to the trial can file this motion, but if filed by the prosecutor, the prosecutor will still be required to start the trial within the time limit specified by the Speedy Trial Act applicable to the court. Common reasons for delay include the health of the defendant, lawyer, or prosecutor; delays in obtaining laboratory results about evidence; difficulty in locating witnesses; and the defense's need for more time to prepare for the case.

Motion for Discovery A **motion for discovery** is a motion filed by the defense counsel, requesting that the prosecutor turn over all relevant evidence and a list of witnesses that the prosecution may use at the trial. The prosecutor is required to turn over state's evidence and witnesses, but the defense is not required to provide the prosecutor with similar information. The right of discovery is based on the philosophy that the state is at an advantage. Furthermore, some of the evidence the government has collected may suggest that the defendant is not guilty. Failure to provide the defense with a complete list of witnesses and all physical evidence and evidentiary documents is considered a violation of due process.[17] Due process requires that all witnesses and all kinds of evidence, especially evidence not used by the prosecutor that may suggest the defendant is not guilty, must be delivered to the defense.[18] The defense has a right to see police files and interviews conducted by the police as well as witnesses and evidence developed by the prosecutor's office. This requirement allows the defendant's lawyer to mount a defense against the prosecutor's case.

The right of the defense to see a list of witnesses is related to the Sixth Amendment guarantee of the right to a public trial. A trial is public not only in the sense that the public has knowledge of the trial and may attend the proceedings, but also in that there can be no secret witnesses against the defendant. This right extends to undercover police agents and confidential informants used in the case. While children may be protected to some degree from public view while giving testimony at a trial, their identities must be revealed to the defense.

Motion for Change of Venue A **motion for change of venue** is a request, either by the prosecution or by the defense, to move the trial to another courtroom for a stated reason. The most common reason for a change of venue is the belief that it is not possible to obtain a fair trial due to local knowledge or perception of the crime. Local knowledge or perception of an offensive crime can make it impossible to obtain a jury pool that is not biased against the defendant.

motion for continuance A pretrial request to delay the start of the trial.

motion for discovery A pretrial motion filed by the defense counsel, requesting that the prosecutor turn over all relevant evidence, including the list of witnesses, that the prosecution may use at the trial.

motion for change of venue A pretrial request, either by the prosecutor or the defense, to move the trial to another courtroom.

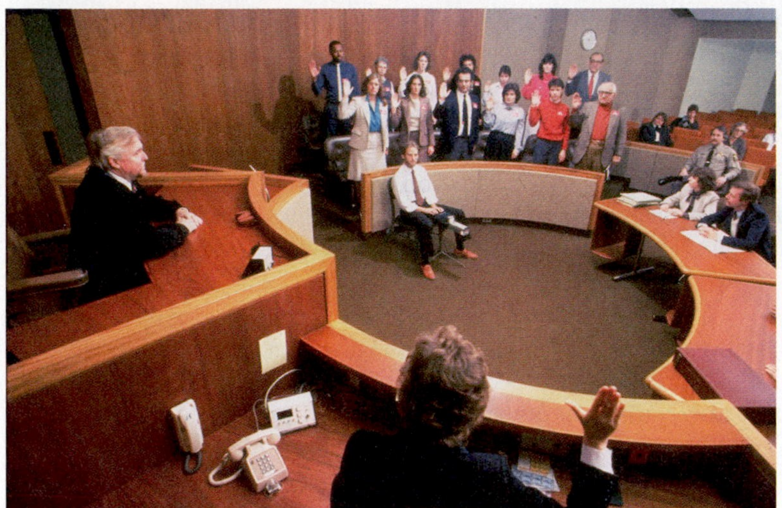

This jury is being sworn in to serve in a criminal trial. The lawyers representing the prosecution and the defense have filed pretrial motions with the judge, which are decided at the start of the trial. What might these pretrial motions have been? Who are all the other trial participants in the courtroom, and what are their roles in the trial process?

Motions for a change of venue can ask only for a change to another court in the same jurisdiction. The jurisdiction of federal trial courts may include several states, however, such that in a federal criminal trial the defendant may ask for a change of venue to a court in another state within the same jurisdiction. Motions for a change of venue do not apply to an appeal, as the appellate court does not use a jury. The judge has the authority to grant or deny the motion and to determine the site of the new trial. A change of venue may involve considerable expense, and the court docket of the new court must be able to accommodate the trial, therefore the judge gives careful consideration to this request.

Motion for Suppression A **motion for suppression** is made by the defense to prevent certain evidence being introduced in the trial. The motion is based on the claim that the evidence was gathered in a manner that violated due process or was unconstitutional.[19] Most motions for suppression are applied to physical evidence or confessions covered by the exclusionary rule. Suppression of evidence can influence the outcome of the trial. The case against the defendant may be seriously weakened if the prosecutor cannot use the defendant's confession or cannot use physical evidence gathered by the police at the scene of a crime. For example, if the defendant's confession is excluded, the jury will not know that the defendant confessed to the crime.

Motion for a Bill of Particulars If a defendant is charged with possession of burglary tools, illegal weapons, drug paraphernalia, or illegal gambling paraphernalia, a **motion for a bill of particulars** allows the defense to receive more details as to exactly what items the prosecution considers illegal. For example, in a case involving a defendant charged with illegal possession of burglary tools, the prosecutor must provide the defense with a list of the tools that will be introduced as evidence of guilt. This list allows the defense attorney to prepare a defense against the charge. If the alleged burglary tools are a screwdriver and a pry bar, the defense has the opportunity to persuade the jury that the defendant had legitimate use for these tools at the time and did not intend to use them to commit a crime.

motion for suppression A pretrial motion made by the defense to exclude certain evidence from being introduced in the trial.

motion for a bill of particulars Allows the defense to receive more details as to exactly what items the prosecution considers illegal if a defendant is charged with possession of burglary tools, illegal weapons, drug paraphernalia, or illegal gambling paraphernalia.

Motions for Severance of Charges or Defendants If Adam and Zelda commit a burglary and are captured by the police, the prosecutor may want to try both defendants at the same trial. If Jake has committed six burglaries, the prosecution may want to try Jake on all six counts of burglary at the same trial. Advantages to the prosecutor in trying multiple defendants or multiple offenses at a single trial are that these trials are cheaper, require less preparation, and provide some advantage in proving the guilt of the defendant.[20] Defendants may believe that being tried for a series of crimes at a single trial or being tried with alleged partners in crime may prejudice their right to a fair trial and therefore request a motion for severance of charges or defendants. A **motion for severance of charges or defendants** requests that the defendant be tried for each charge separately, or that defendants charged with the same crime be tried separately.

Motion for Dismissal The defense attorney claims that the charges against the client should be dismissed on the grounds of lack of evidence, violation of due process, lack of jurisdiction, or any number of other reasons that the case should not proceed to trial. A judge can grant two types of dismissal: with prejudice and without prejudice. A **motion for dismissal** granted with prejudice means that the defendant cannot be recharged with the same crime. A motion for dismissal granted without prejudice means that the case will not proceed to trial, but the prosecutor may correct the defect and arraign the defendant again.

▲ check your understanding **8.3** **Why must the prosecutor ensure that the defendant is brought to trial in a timely manner? How do the rules of evidence affect what the jury gets to hear or see? What tests must evidence meet before it can be presented at the trial? What are seven common pretrial motions and what effect do they have on the trial?**

Participants in the Criminal Trial

▼ the main idea **8.4** **Participants in the criminal trial include representatives of the government and representatives of the defendant, who are part of the courtroom work group, as well as witnesses.**

A typical courtroom is shown in Figure 8.4. Given the many different courts, when the court was constructed, the budget, and many other factors, there are considerable differences among courtrooms. For example, city and county courts of limited jurisdiction might even be temporary court space in a school or public building, whereas the U.S. Supreme Court is very elaborate and reflects the high prestige of the court. Many people work behind the scenes to make a criminal trial possible, but only certain participants are present in the courtroom during the trial. Those present at trial can be divided into three groups: (1) government employees, (2) the defendant and his or her legal counsel, and (3) witnesses and victims. The **courtroom work group** cuts across these distinctions.

motion for severance of charges or defendants A pretrial request that the defendant be tried for each charge separately or that multiple defendants charged with the same crime be tried separately.

motion for dismissal A pretrial defense motion that the charges against the defendant be dismissed.

courtroom work group Adversarial and neutral parties—usually the prosecutor, defense attorney, judge, and other court personnel—who get together and cooperate to settle cases.

On This Side, Representing the State

People at a trial, who are employed by the government, can be divided into four groups: (1) people who work to make the trial possible but do not take any side in the trial; (2) the prosecutor and his or her assistants, who have the responsibility of presenting evidence against the defendant; (3) the judge, who must exercise impartial management of the trial and make decisions regarding proper procedure and due process; and (4) the

figure 8.4

A Typical Courtroom

The typical courtroom is designed for functionality. The three major areas in a courtroom are as follows: (*Bottom*) The public area for the public and the media provides limited seating on a first-come basis; often, for sensational trials, people wait in a line outside the courtroom, hoping to gain entry. The public cannot cross the "bar" that divides the public area from (*Middle*) the courtroom working area, where courtroom personnel conduct the business of the court. Behind the courtroom working area is (*Top*) the private work area, where the judge's office and the jury room are located. Actual courtrooms may differ from this diagram.

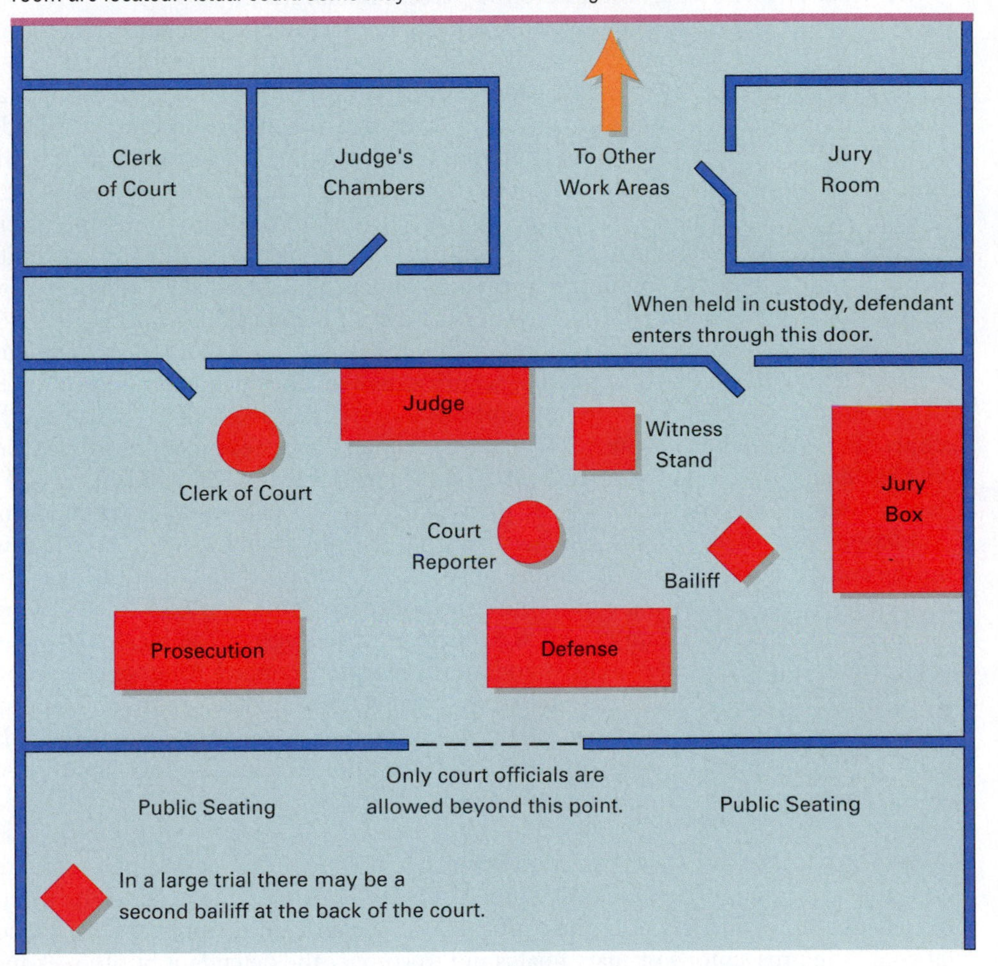

jury, a panel of citizens that has the authority to decide if the defendant is guilty or not guilty.

Taking Care of the Business of the Court The Clerk of Court, court recorder, and bailiff perform important tasks to make the work of the court possible. These people are not part of the prosecution or the defense. Their job is to make it possible for the business of the court to be conducted efficiently and safely. As you have read, the judge's Clerk of Court has important pretrial duties.

The **court recorder,** also called the **court reporter,** transcribes every word spoken by the judge, attorneys, and witnesses during the trial. He or she is responsible for making a permanent written record of the court's proceedings. This written record is required, so if the court recorder is not present or cannot accurately transcribe the proceedings

court recorder (court reporter) Stenographer who transcribes every word spoken by the judge, attorneys, and witnesses during a trial.

for any reason, the trial must be stopped. The court reporter also has the authority to stop a trial at any point if he or she cannot record what is being said. Skill in stenography is the basis on which court reporters are hired. They must be able to record up to 200 words a minute; to achieve this speed, they use a special system of phonetics and computer technology. Most courtroom reporters attend specialty programs that train and certify them for the position. Alternative electronic audio and video technologies have been tried as a means to record the trial proceedings; however, they have not proved as reliable as court recorders. If electronic audio or video technologies fail to capture the trial proceedings, it could very well mean the defendant would be granted a new trial. Thus, the court must have 100 percent reliability.

The **bailiff** is usually a county deputy sheriff or a U.S. deputy marshal. The county sheriff is responsible for providing bailiffs for court security for state courts, and the U.S. marshal is responsible for providing court security for federal courts. The bailiff is an armed law enforcement officer who has the power of arrest and the power to use deadly force if necessary. For most bailiffs, courtroom security consists of escorting the jury in and out of the courtroom and maintaining order in the court at the direction of the judge. However, responding to any breach of security, attempted escape of the defendant, violence, or attack on any person in the courtroom is the bailiff's responsibility. The bailiff may be called on in life-threatening emergencies, as defendants have been known to attack witnesses, judges, attorneys, and even members of the press.

The parties before the court are often emotionally charged, and judges and court personnel often express concerns that security may not be adequate to ensure their safety. Although security checkpoints and metal detectors enhance the security of the court, there is still the ever-present threat to court personnel. Several high-profile security incidents in 2005 emphasized the serious security threats that bailiffs face. In Atlanta, Georgia, on March 11, 2005, Brian Nichols, age 34, on trial for rape and kidnapping, grabbed a gun from a sheriff's deputy during his trial and began shooting in the courtroom. He killed Superior Court Judge Rowland Barnes and his court reporter. He managed to escape from the courthouse and in the process killed another deputy who confronted him as well as a federal customs agent. The incident sparked concern for improved court security and more security personnel. Another courtroom shooting occurred in Tyler, Texas. In June 2005, a Seattle man described as angry about child support rulings was shot to death while brandishing an inert hand grenade in the federal courthouse. These security threats have resulted in demands for enhanced security and better trained and equipped courtroom security personnel.

The Prosecutor The prosecutor is not an employee of the court but does represent the government. The role of the prosecutor is to bring charges against the defendant, gather the evidence necessary to prosecute the defendant, and present the evidence at trial. The prosecutor's primary goal is not to convict the defendant but to seek justice. The American Bar Association's Code of Professional Responsibility states that a prosecutor should not present evidence that he or she knows to be unreliable, nor should the prosecutor hide or withhold from the defense evidence that may suggest the innocence of the defendant. The prosecutor's job is to see that the person who committed the crime is brought to justice and to demonstrate to the court that the evidence supports a conviction beyond a reasonable doubt.

The Judge The judge is a central figure in the trial. The centrality of the judge's role is evident in that, during the trial, the attorneys will address the judge as "the court." The judge is a neutral party. His or her role is similar to that of an umpire or referee at a baseball or basketball game. This role can be complicated in a bench trial when the judge, rather than a jury, determines whether the defendant is guilty. In a bench trial, the judge must act as impartial mediator during the trial and, at the conclusion of the trial, must make a determination of guilt. Bench trials often are prohibited in cases involving serious felonies.

bailiff A county deputy sheriff or U.S. deputy marshal responsible for providing security and maintaining order in a courtroom.

The judge determines what evidence can be presented at the trial, what witnesses can testify and what they can testify to, and when courtroom breaks are permissible. The judge has authority over the courtroom personnel, the attorneys, the jury, members of the media, and the public in the courtroom. The power of the judge lies in his or her absolute and immediate ability to fine or imprison people for **contempt of court.** If the judge believes that an attorney, either defense or prosecution, has violated a professional standard of conduct during the trial, he or she can impose a fine or term of imprisonment. Unprofessional conduct can include being late for court, continuing to argue with the judge when told to stop, or more serious violations regarding witness and evidence integrity. It is difficult to appeal a contempt of court decree. Contempt of court is not a crime and, thus, the person does not have the same rights as a defendant accused of a crime. Contempt of court can bring substantial penalty. For example, witnesses who will not testify may be held in prison for up to two years for contempt of court.[21]

The public, the jury, and the members of the media may be fined or imprisoned for contempt of court. If people in the courtroom are unruly, the judge can impose a fine or hold them in jail for contempt of court. The power of the judge even extends to appropriate dress of persons in the courtroom. Jury members can be fined or imprisoned for violating the orders of the judge not to discuss the case. The media most often run afoul of the judge's authority by violating a **gag order**—an order that the evidence or proceedings of the court may not be published or discussed publicly. If disclosure of evidence or testimony may jeopardize the defendant's receiving a fair trial, the judge has the authority to order all parties to refrain from discussing or publishing this information. Members of the media who violate this order can be held in contempt of court.

The Jury Jurors are citizens required by law to perform jury duty. The court wants jurors who are fair, competent, and able to serve, so citizens can escape jury duty for certain legitimate reasons. Selecting a fair and competent jury and deciding legitimate excuses for jury duty have been major challenges for the court.

The Constitution requires that people be tried by a jury of their peers. The Supreme Court has not interpreted this literally, however. A white, middle-class man does not get a trial by a jury of white, middle-class men. Rather, the jury pool is selected from a broad base of citizens who are representative of the community. Many jurisdictions have used voter registration lists as the pool from which to select jurors. Studies have clearly demonstrated, however, that this pool of candidates is biased, because voter registration lists underrepresent minorities and people with lower income.[22] The current practice in many courts is to select jurors from more representative sources, such as licensed drivers or people listed in the telephone book.

Citizens are paid for jury duty by the government, but the rate of pay is very low, ranging from only a few dollars to $40 per day. Most jurors serve for only short periods of time but may be asked to serve for extended periods; for some jurors, even a few days may impose a severe hardship. Also, some citizens may not be competent to serve as jurors. For these and other reasons, the court may excuse citizens from jury duty. Each jurisdiction determines the rules for excusing citizens from jury service, but the rules must not discriminate against a person because of race, gender, or other characteristics that are considered in violation of the law. For example, until 1975, many states automatically excluded women, especially women with children at home, from jury duty. In ***Taylor* v. *Louisiana*** (1975), the Supreme Court decided that the exclusion of women from jury duty created an imbalance in the jury pool and was not justified.[23] Legitimate reasons for excuse from jury duty include illness, conviction of a felony crime, or not being able to comprehend English. Members of certain professional groups, such as physicians, may be excluded from jury duty, based on the reasoning that jury service would be detrimental to community safety. Other members of professional groups, such as attorneys, police officers, and legislators, may be excluded from jury duty, based on the reasoning that they may not be able to be neutral and make decisions based only

contempt of court A charge against any violator of the judge's courtroom rules, authorizing the judge to impose a fine or term of imprisonment.

gag order A judge's order to participants and observers at a trial that the evidence or proceedings of the court may not be published, aired, or discussed publicly.

on the evidence presented in court. Most jurisdictions require jury service only once a year.

Although essential to ensuring a fair and public trial by his or her peers, jury duty is disdained by some. Thus, it is necessary for the court to ensure that despite the reluctance by some citizens to respond to a summons for jury duty, those called do indeed respond. As a result, there are penalties, including fines and jail time, for those who unlawfully avoid jury duty and for anyone, such as employers, who would interfere with, intimidate, or threaten citizens to prevent them from fulfilling their civic duties.

The Constitution does not require a jury of 12 persons. This number is a tradition but is not a legal requirement, and obtaining 12 people to serve on a jury can be a challenge. All states require 12 jurors for capital cases, and all but six states require 12 jurors for felony trials. Fourteen states allow misdemeanor trials with only 6 jurors. Other states allow criminal trials with a jury of 7 or 8 jurors.[24]

In a criminal trial, the jury is known as the "trier of the facts." The jury has the authority and responsibility to decide which evidence is to be accepted as credible and which is not. If the prosecution introduces witnesses and evidence indicating that the defendant committed the crime, but the defense introduces alibi witnesses who swear the defendant was with them at the time of the crime, the jury decides which evidence is the most credible. If the defendant pleads not guilty by reason of insanity, the jury decides if the defendant was insane. Each side can introduce expert witnesses who testify about the mental health of the defendant, but the jury is the ultimate judge of the defendant's mental state at the time of the crime. It is the jury that decides if the evidence and witnesses prove beyond a reasonable doubt the guilt of the defendant. This is an awesome responsibility, and it is given to 12 laypersons.

On This Side, Representing the Defense

The defendant and his or her attorney are the primary persons on the defense side, and these two sit together at a table at the trial. The defendant may choose to assist in his or her defense or may choose to remain passive and let the defense attorney handle the case.

In any criminal trial in which the maximum punishment exceeds six months in prison, the defendant is entitled to a jury trial and the right to be represented by an attorney.[25] There are two types of defense attorneys: public defenders and private defense attorneys. The defendant hires a private defense attorney and may choose any attor-

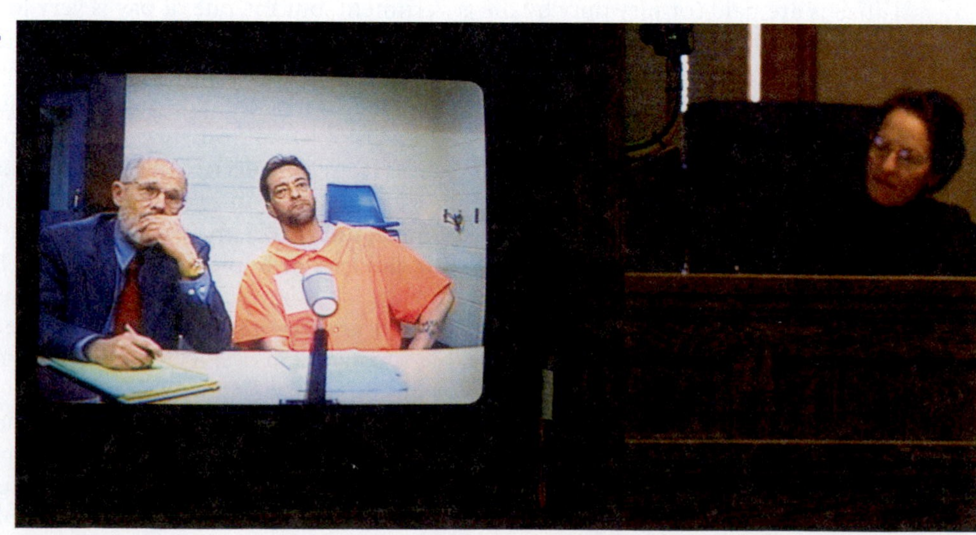

This defendant, Richard Dodd *(center)*, appeared in court before Judge Sylvia Lewis *(right)* with his public defender via closed-circuit television. Dodd was already serving a life sentence for another kidnapping and rape. What difference did it make if Dodd had a public defender? How are public defenders different from private criminal lawyers, court-assigned attorneys, and contract attorneys?

ney registered to practice law before the court. The defendant may hire as many private defense attorneys as he or she can afford. In rare cases, the defendant may choose not to have a defense attorney but to represent himself or herself. The court discourages self-representation but cannot compel a defendant to hire or accept a defense attorney.

The Defense Attorney If the defendant cannot afford to hire a private defense attorney, the court will appoint and pay for an attorney to represent the defendant. A defendant who cannot afford a private attorney is known as an indigent defendant. When a defendant is charged with a crime, a judge inquires as to the defendant's ability to afford an attorney. Defendants indicating they cannot afford an attorney are required to complete a financial statement and submit it to the court. The court examines the defendant's finances and decides on the matter. About half of all criminal defendants accused of a felony crime cannot afford an attorney, and for larger counties this number increases to 80 percent.[26] **Indigent defense** services represent a substantial expense in the criminal justice system. For example, the largest 100 counties handle over 4 million indigent defenses a year at a cost of over one billion dollars.[27]

▲ check your understanding **8.4 What problems arise from having court-appointed attorneys?**

The Criminal Trial

▼ the main idea **8.5 A criminal trial consists of jury selection, presentation of evidence and witnesses, and the closing arguments and verdict.**

The criminal trial is a complex, unpredictable event in the criminal justice process. A defendant has anywhere from less than a 20 percent to nearly an 80 percent chance of being convicted and sentenced to incarceration.[28] The probability of conviction increases as the seriousness of the charge increases. Defendants have nearly an 80 percent chance of being convicted for murder but less than a 20 percent chance of being convicted for fraud. It is difficult to summarize all of the important decisions and strategies of the trial attorneys in a brief explanation. Therefore, this description of the trial process focuses on the sequence of events in an American criminal trial. The trial sequence can be divided into three stages: (1) trial initiation, (2) the presentation of evidence and witnesses, and (3) postargument activities.

Trial Initiation

Once the courtroom work group has determined a case to settle by a trial, several major pretrial activities occur. First, attorneys from each side present pretrial motions (discussed previously) to the court. After the pretrial motions have been disposed of, the next step is to secure a time and judge on the court's docket. Based on past practice and experience, the attorneys attempt to secure a judge who may be favorably disposed to the arguments that they are planning to present in court. In addition, it is extremely important to obtain a jury that is favorably disposed toward one's side.

Jury Selection The jury is supposed to be neutral and unbiased. However, neither the prosecutor nor the defense attorney wants a completely unbiased jury, and both

indigent defense Defense counsel for a defendant who cannot afford a private attorney.

diversity in the system

Defending the Guilty

The defense attorney's job is to represent the defendant's interests. A question often asked is: How can a defense attorney defend a guilty client? However, everything must be done to mount an adequate defense, whether or not the client is guilty. The trial is an adversarial process in which the prosecution and the defense attempt to persuade the members of the jury through evidence and witnesses that their side is the most credible. The question of guilt is more complicated than whether the client committed the crime (e.g., killed the deceased, took the property, or defrauded a victim). Thus, *guilt* is a legal term, not a moral term. A person could rob a bank and kill a police officer responding to the bank alarm, and the state could charge the defendant with first-degree murder and ask for the death penalty. The defense could argue that although there is little dispute that the defendant committed the acts alleged by the state, the defendant did not have the necessary intent (*mens rea*) for first-degree murder—that the defendant did not commit the crime with premeditation or intend to kill the police officer. Lacking the conditions required for first-degree murder, the defense could argue for second-degree murder, a lesser crime that does not carry the death penalty.

The morality of the robbery and death and the sinfulness of the defendant are not the central questions addressed in a trial. The purpose of a trial is to prove beyond a reasonable doubt that the defendant committed the act specified by the charges and with the necessary intent required by the law, and to do this while preserving the rights of the accused. The defense attorney may argue that the client is not guilty because he or she (1) did not commit the crime, (2) is insane, (3) lacked criminal intent (self-defense as opposed to murder), or (4) committed the act under mitigating circumstances (such as duress or necessity), or may use any number of other defenses.

Furthermore, defendants are tried for the crime with which they are charged, and past crimes cannot be considered in determining guilt. Knowledge of a past criminal record may prejudice the jury against the defendant, even if the defendant were not guilty of the particular crime being tried. Yet, it seems logical that a person arrested for possession of burglary tools and who has been arrested over two dozen times for burglary most likely intended to use the tools to burglarize another house. Unless a defendant is accused of multiple crimes simultaneously or of a crime that matches a profile of a serial crime, the jury will not be allowed to hear evidence of the defendant's prior criminal record.

Thus, the criminal justice system does not have the same definition of *guilt* as the religious practitioner, moral philosopher, or average citizen. Furthermore, the criminal justice system cannot always be trusted to properly identify the guilty party. Defense attorneys have seen many defendants falsely accused of crimes. In the final analysis, then, the defense attorney cannot refuse to represent a client because he or she believes the client is guilty. Every client is equal in the eyes of the law and must receive the best defense possible.

What is the role of the defense attorney in a criminal trial? Should defense attorneys knowingly defend criminals who are guilty? Why or why not?

have some influence in shaping the composition of the jury through a process known as **voir dire**. Through the voir dire process, a jury is selected from eligible members of the jury pool. Eligible jury members are called from the jury pool to the courtroom to be interviewed by the attorneys and the judge. During the interview, each side and the judge or attorneys ask the prospective juror questions. Questions usually concern whether the juror has ever been the victim of a crime (especially a crime similar to the one of which the defendant is accused), what the juror knows about the case from the media, whether the juror is related to anyone in the courtroom or the case, and whether the juror already has formed an opinion about the guilt of the defendant.

voir dire The process through which a jury is selected from the members of the jury pool who have been determined eligible for service.

Some people assume incorrectly that if they provide obviously biased answers during voir dire they will be excused from jury duty. If they are excluded from serving on the jury for that trial, however, they must return to the jury pool and wait to be called for another trial. In many courts, a juror is required to serve in the jury pool for an entire week or in a trial lasting only one to three days.

See www.jri-inc.com/, the website of the Jury Research Institute, a trial consulting firm, for descriptions of some strategies used by defense attorneys in jury selection.

In complex criminal trials, especially in which the defendant has retained the services of a private attorney, jurors may be asked to fill out questionnaires in addition to answering oral questions during voir dire. Some attorneys in high-profile cases retain the services of a jury consultant to help analyze the attitudes and characters of the jurors in order to shape a favorable jury through "scientific" jury selection.

Voir Dire and Peremptory Challenge The attorneys shape a jury by exercising their right to challenge a juror's ability to serve on the jury, by asking the juror to be removed for *cause*. The goal of voir dire is to select 12 jurors and a number of alternate jurors, usually no fewer than 2. Alternative jurors are sworn in with the other members of the jury and sit with the jury during the entire trial. If a "regular" juror is unable to complete his or her service—for example, because of illness—an alternate juror replaces the excused juror. An objection to the seating of a juror for cause means that an attorney perceives some bias or characteristic that would prevent a fair trial. For instance, a juror who was recently the victim of a robbery may be excused for cause under the assumption that he or she may be biased against a defendant being tried for robbery. There is no limit to the number challenges for cause that each side may exercise. The judge makes the final decision as to whether or not a juror is excused.

Each side also has a limited number of peremptory challenges it can use to exclude jurors. A **peremptory challenge** is based on a subjective evaluation by the attorney and need not be justified to the court. Until the late 1980s and early 1990s, it was permissible to use peremptory challenges to shape the jury by excluding jurors based on their race or gender.[29] In 1986, the U.S Supreme Court prohibited the exclusion of jurors based solely on race, and in 1994, prohibited the exclusion of a juror based on gender.[30]

Presentation of Evidence and Witnesses

When the jury is seated, the trial is considered to have officially started, and the trial proceeds to the opening arguments and the presentation of evidence and witnesses. Each side is given the opportunity to present evidence and witnesses to persuade the jury for or against the defendant. Usually, the length of the trial is determined in advance, and each side is allotted approximately half the trial time for their arguments.

Opening Statements Before evidence is presented, however, each side has the opportunity to address the court, especially the jury, to explain what the case is about and to provide an overview of what to expect. The attorneys' arguments in the opening statements are not considered evidence. Also, the attorneys are not obligated to do everything they say they will do in their opening statements. The prosecution makes the first opening statement, explaining to the jury the crime of which the defendant is accused, the seriousness of the crime, and the strength of the state's evidence against the defendant. Many defense counselors choose not to present an opening statement or may present only a brief statement contradicting the prosecutor's allegations. The defense may want to hear the evidence of the prosecution and evaluate the strength of that evidence before making a commitment as to what the defense will prove.

The State's Case against the Defendant The state has the burden of proof and must provide evidence and witnesses that convince the jury beyond a reasonable doubt of the defendant's guilt. The state can present four types of evidence: (1)

peremptory challenge The subjective evaluation of the attorney that is used to exclude jurors.

real evidence, (2) testimonial evidence, (3) direct evidence, and (4) circumstantial evidence.

Real evidence is physical evidence such as a gun, a fingerprint, a photograph, or DNA matching. All real evidence is accompanied by an explanation of what the evidence is, how it was gathered, and how it connects the defendant to the crime. For example, the real evidence of an autopsy report on the cause of death is explained by the medical examiner who performed the autopsy. The police officer who found the real evidence of the firearm used to shoot the victim must identify the firearm and explain where it was found and how it was handled.

The explanations of real evidence are examples of **testimonial evidence**—the testimony of a witness. Testimonial evidence may be given by laypersons or experts. Laypersons can testify only to what they heard, saw, felt, smelled, or otherwise directly experienced. Laypersons usually cannot give secondhand or **hearsay evidence**—information about events they only heard from others. An example of hearsay testimony is that of a person who was told by another that the defendant bragged about robbing a convenience store. Expert witnesses, on the other hand, make inferences beyond the facts and give testimony based on their expert knowledge. For example, a medical doctor may testify that the victim was killed by a blow to the head with a blunt instrument and that a hammer found in the possession of the defendant could have been the instrument used to make that fatal wound. The doctor did not see the defendant strike the victim and does not know if the hammer was the murder weapon but is allowed to give expert testimony as to the probable cause of death.

Direct evidence is any real or testimonial evidence that connects the defendant to the crime. An eyewitness who can identify the defendant as the bank robber is an example of direct evidence. **Circumstantial evidence,** on the other hand, can be interpreted in more than one way and does not indisputably link the defendant with the crime. An example of circumstantial evidence is a witness who hears a shot, observes the defendant running from a room, and then enters the room and finds the victim shot. From this testimony, the jury may infer only that the defendant could have been the one who shot the victim. Circumstantial evidence does not prove guilt. In California and other states, the rules of evidence require that if there is more than one interpretation of circumstantial evidence and one of those interpretations is favorable to the defendant, the jury must accept the favorable interpretation as the best explanation.

Not all evidence meets the acceptable **legal standards of evidence** required by the rules of evidence. The evidence and testimony of witnesses must meet three criteria to be used in the trial: (1) The evidence must be competent—legally fit for admission to court. For example, the evidence must be reliable. Polygraph (lie detector) examinations are not accepted as reliable scientific evidence and, thus, are excluded as evidence in criminal trials because they do not constitute *competent evidence.* (2) The evidence has to be material. *Material evidence* has a legitimate bearing on the decision of the case. For example, whether the defendant is a good father and husband is not material to the question of whether he committed arson fraud. (3) The evidence must be relevant. *Relevant evidence* is applicable to the issue in question. For example, evidence that the defendant has a history of domestic violence is not relevant to the question of whether he or she assaulted the victim in the case.

The prosecutor asks a witness to take the stand and give testimony. He or she asks the witness questions to elicit the information about the crime that the witness has. This is called the *direct examination of the witness.* The prosecutor cannot direct or coach the witness to get certain answers, however. For example, the prosecutor cannot ask the witness a "leading question," such as, "Did you see the defendant strike and kill the victim on the night of January 6th at about 8:00 P.M. in the Town Tavern?" Also, the prosecutor cannot ask the witness for information that he or she is not qualified to provide. For example, asking, "Was the defendant happy when he heard about the news of his wife's death?" is inappropriate because the witness cannot know how the defendant was feeling and can testify only to the defendant's actions.

real evidence Physical evidence such as a gun, a fingerprint, a photograph, or DNA matching.

testimonial evidence The testimony of a witness.

hearsay evidence Information about a crime obtained secondhand from another rather than directly observed.

direct evidence Evidence that connects the defendant with the crime.

circumstantial evidence Evidence that *implies* that the defendant is connected to the crime but does not *prove* the defendant is connected to the crime.

legal standards of evidence Evidence and the testimony of witnesses must be competent, material, and relevant.

When the prosecutor is finished, the defense attorney is allowed to question the witness. This is called the *cross-examination.* The defense attempts to show that the witness's testimony is not credible or is contradictory. The defense may attempt to show, for instance, that, with insufficient light, the witness was too far away to recognize the defendant. After the cross-examination, the prosecutor may ask additional questions to repair any damage that the defense may have done to the witness's credibility. This is called the *redirect examination.* Following the redirect, the defense has another opportunity to question the witness, called the *recross-examination.* It is not necessary that the defense cross-examine or recross-examine a witness, however. If the defense chooses not to exercise these options, the prosecution has no further opportunity to question the witness. In the recross-examination and redirect examination, the defense and the prosecution, respectively, cannot introduce new evidence. Their examination is limited in scope to the credibility of evidence presented by the witness in the direct examination. When the prosecution has presented all its evidence and witnesses, the prosecution "rests." The court may offer a short break or may proceed to the first defense witness.

The Defense's Case Before presenting any evidence or witnesses, it is customary for the defense to ask for a motion for directed verdict on the face of the prosecutor's case. The prosecution has the burden of proof in the trial. If the prosecution has not established a *prima facie* case of guilty—that is, clear and convincing evidence of guilt—the judge can direct the jury to return a verdict of not guilty even before the defense presents its case. A request for a directed verdict is rarely granted.

The rules of evidence and the order of examination of the witnesses are the same for the defense as for the prosecution. The defense rests when it has presented all of its evidence and witnesses. The prosecutor may attempt to discredit the defense witnesses and evidence by calling its own witnesses to give testimony. This testimony is limited to refuting the evidence introduced by the defense and cannot introduce new evidence. This is called the *prosecutor's rebuttal* and may be followed by defense counsel's "surrebuttal." Both sides then have exhausted their opportunity to introduce evidence. Very few trials make use of all the opportunities to present and rebut evidence and cross-examine witnesses.

Postargument Activities

After all the evidence and witnesses are presented, each side is given the opportunity to summarize its case to the jury. This is called *closing arguments* or *summation.* Neither side can introduce new evidence or arguments in the closing statements. The closing argument is a persuasive speech to the jury in which the prosecution argues that it has been proved beyond a reasonable doubt that the defendant is guilty, and the defense argues that the prosecution has failed to demonstrate this standard of proof. Closing arguments, especially in capital murder cases, can be emotionally charged speeches to the jury.

Charge to the Jury After the closing arguments, there is usually a short recess while the judge prepares the **charge to the jury**—a written document explaining to the jury how the law is applicable to the case. For example, in a murder case, the judge may instruct the jury about the different degrees of murder and homicide and the conditions necessary for each. The judge also summarizes the evidence and instructs the jury about any point of law concerning the evidence. For instance, the judge may instruct the jury how to treat circumstantial evidence or how to evaluate the truthfulness of contradictory evidence given by prosecution and defense witnesses. The judge also makes clear what evidence can and cannot be considered in arriving at a verdict. For example, the jury cannot perform any independent investigations, discuss the case with anyone other than fellow jurors during deliberation, or seek additional information about the case, especially from the media. The judge's instructions to the jury may be quite lengthy and technical,

charge to the jury Written instructions about the application of the law to a case that the judge gives to the jury to help them achieve a verdict.

and sometimes are grounds for an appeal. If the judge has provided incorrect instructions about the law or the evidence, the defendant can appeal the case on judicial error. Likewise, a prejudicial statement to the jury by the judge can be grounds for appeal.

Jury Deliberations After receiving the judge's instructions, the jury retires to the jury room to deliberate. There is no requirement as to how long or short a time the jury should deliberate before coming to a verdict. In theory, the jury is supposed to withhold judgment until the conclusion of the trial. In practice, however, jurors may have already determined whether or not they believe the defendant is guilty. Jury deliberations can take minutes, hours, or days. The first order of business is for the jury to elect a foreperson who will lead the deliberations.

During deliberation, the jury cannot discuss the case with anyone outside of the deliberation room, nor can the jurors read or listen to any media coverage of the case. Any juror who hears or sees media coverage of the case is required to report this to the judge, who can disqualify the juror and assign an alternate. If the jury cannot come to a verdict by the end of the day, the judge has the authority to sequester the jury to prevent the jury from obtaining outside information. This means that the jurors are required to remain under court supervision rather than return to their homes. Jurors are housed and fed at the expense of the state until they reach a verdict.

When the jurors reach a verdict, they notify the bailiff, who notifies the judge. The judge may ask for the jury's verdict in advance of announcing it to the public if he or she feels that the verdict may cause a strong public reaction that may create a public safety issue. If the jury cannot reach a verdict, the jury is said to be "deadlocked" or a "hung jury," in which case the judge declares a mistrial. Only about 6 percent of juries are unable to reach a verdict. If the judge declares a mistrial, the prosecutor has the option of filing the same charges against the defendant and trying the case again, and there is no limit to the number of times a case can be retried due to a mistrial.

The Verdict The jury renders a verdict on each charge against the defendant. In some cases, as in murder, the jury has the option of finding the defendant guilty or not guilty of various lesser included crimes—such as homicide, involuntary manslaughter, or negligent homicide—instead of the charge filed by the prosecutor. When the defendant is charged with multiple charges, the jury can find the defendant guilty of some of the charges and not guilty of others.

If the jury finds the defendant guilty, but the judge believes that the verdict is contrary to the evidence presented or that the jury did not follow his or her charge in arriving at their verdict, the judge can enter a directed verdict of not guilty. This verdict overturns the jury's verdict. However, the judge cannot overturn a jury's verdict of not guilty, even if the jury violates the judge's instructions and ignores the law pertaining to the case. For example, if the jury refuses to convict the defendant even when the defense does not satisfy the requirements of the law, a situation referred to as *jury nullification,* the judge must accept the jury's verdict.

When the jury reaches a decision, they are brought back into the courtroom to announce the verdict publicly, and the judge asks the foreperson to read the verdict for each charge against the defendant. Each member of the jury is then polled to ensure he or she agrees with the verdict, which must be unanimous. The jury is polled to make sure that no timid juror has been coerced to agree by peer pressure. Once the jury is polled, the verdict is final.

Appeals Defendants found guilty may appeal their verdict to a court of appeals based on the claim of judicial error. The defendant also can ask for a new trial based on the claim that newly found evidence not available at the time of the trial has been discovered and would substantially affect the trial's outcome.

The defendant who is in state custody and is found not guilty is released as soon as possible. If the defendant is found not guilty, the prosecutor cannot ask for a new trial based on either judicial error or newly discovered evidence.

▲ check your understanding 8.5 What is involved in selecting a jury? How does the prosecution's opening statement differ from the defense attorney's opening statement? What are the four types of evidence? What instructions are given to the jury before deliberation begins?

conclusion:

The Trial—Justice Is the Goal

Police charges against the defendant are merely suggestions to the prosecutor. The prosecutor's charges at arraignment are but a hope. The decision of guilt is decided at the trial. Despite a constitutional guarantee of a trial by jury, over 90 percent of those charged with felony crimes choose to forego this procedure and plead guilty. A great number of professionals come together to make a trial possible. In the American judicial system, the trial is a conflict situation between the prosecutor and the defense. At the trial, the playing field is not level, but is tipped in favor of the defendant. The U.S. judicial system recognizes the awesome power of the state compared to the limited resources of the accused and takes a number of opportunities to balance the power between the state and the defendant. Thus, even if the defendant is convicted, he or she has the right to appeal, a right denied to prosecutors if they lose the case. The procedure and rules of the trial are well defined, but the strategy and risk that go into the decision making and presentation of evidence are left to the professional judgment of the participants in the trial. Despite the differences among the various courts, all work toward a common objective—justice.

chapter summary

- Three types of criminal trials are state trials in courts of limited jurisdiction, state trials in courts of general jurisdiction, and federal criminal trials.
- Trials in courts of limited jurisdiction are usually quick, involve misdemeanor crimes, and vary in the degree of professionalism and training of the judge and courtroom personnel.
- Most trials are conducted in state courts of general jurisdiction. State courts and federal courts have different procedures but are more similar than they are different.
- The police and the prosecutor must work together to bring charges against the defendant. This requirement also acts as checks and balances against abuse of power.
- Before the trial, the court decides if the defendant is to be granted bail. Three kinds of bail are cash bond, that provided by bondsagents, and unsecured bond.
- Despite reforms in the bail system, there are still many problems with bail discriminating against the poor.
- Before defendants can stand trial, the court must assess their competence to assist the attorney in their defense and to understand the charges against them. If a defendant is not competent to stand trial, the trial is postponed.
- Plea bargaining is a very important mechanism for disposing of cases, as over 90 percent of defendants plead guilty. Plea bargaining can center on the charges or the sentence.
- Because of the Speedy Trial Act of 1974, most defendants must be brought to trial within 100 days of arrest. This requirement places great stress on the resources of the prosecutor and the court.
- The court administrator and the Clerk of Court play an important role in managing the court docket.
- Prior to the trial, the parties to the case may make a number of pretrial motions, including motions for continuance, discovery, change of venue, suppression, bill of particulars, severance of charges or defendants, and dismissal.
- Many people participate in making a trial possible. The court recorder, also known as the *court reporter*, records every word of the trial. The bailiff is responsible for security. The prosecutor is responsible for presenting the evidence against the defendant.
- The judge is a neutral party to the trial. The judge must ensure that the defendant gets a fair trial. The jury decides whether the defendant is guilty or not guilty.
- Defendants are entitled to court-appointed counsel if they cannot afford a lawyer. The three types of court-appointed counsel are assigned counsel, public defender, and contract attorney.
- The criminal trial starts with the selection of the jury. The state presents its witnesses and evidence first, followed by the defense presentation. After the evidence is presented, the defense summarizes its case, followed by the state's summary.

vocabulary review

bail bondsperson, 292
bailiff, 308
charge to the jury, 315
circumstantial evidence, 314
Clerk of Court, 303
competent to stand trial, 296
conditional release, 294
contempt of court, 309
court docket, 300
court recorder (court reporter), 307
courtroom work group, 306
direct evidence, 314
double jeopardy, 287
gag order, 309
hearsay evidence, 314
indigent defense, 311
legal standards of evidence, 314
motion for a bill of particulars, 305
motion for change of venue, 304
motion for continuance, 304
motion for discovery, 304
motion for dismissal, 306
motion for severance of charges or defendants, 306
motion for suppression, 305
peremptory challenge, 313
prosecutorial discretion, 290

real evidence, 314
release on recognizance (ROR), 294
signature bond, 294
statute of limitations, 301
testimonial evidence, 314
unsecured bond, 294
voir dire, 312

do you remember?

1984 Bail Reform Act, 291
Barker v. *Wingo,* 301
Eighth Amendment of the Constitution, 291
Klopfer v. *North Carolina,* 301
Manhattan Bail Project, 294
Sixth Amendment of the Constitution, 301
Speedy Trial Act of 1974, 302
Taylor v. *Louisiana,* 309

think about this

1. Although the accused is arrested by the police based on probable cause of a crime, the prosecutor ultimately is responsible for bringing charges against the person, plea bargaining, or dropping the case. What kinds of checks and balances could be built into the legal system so that prosecutors do not abuse their power?
2. Some states have prohibited plea bargaining. Do you favor the prohibition of plea bargaining? Why or why not?
3. Do you have any ethical or moral objections to defense attorneys providing aggressive defenses for defendants who appear to be guilty? Explain your answer. If you were charged with a crime you committed, would you simply plead guilty or would you want your attorney to put up an aggressive defense?
4. Some countries use paid professionals as jurors. What would be the advantages and disadvantages of this system compared to the U.S. system? Which do you think is better? Why?
5. Do you think bail discriminates against the poor? Why or why not?
6. There are many criticisms of the system of providing the indigent with defense attorneys. What would you suggest to improve the system?

research navigator

Visit the Research Navigator website (www.researchnavigator.com), login and select the criminal justice data base in ContentSelect. Type in the key words "Doubts about Duke" Select the article "Doubts about Duke" by Thomas Evan and Susannah Meadows. The article reports on the court case against Duke University lacrosse players charged with sexually assaulting an exotic dancer at a party hosted by the team. Court documents indicate that the prosecutor, Mike Nifong, filed charges against the players with very little evidence. Since the article was published the case has been taken over by state prosecutors and Nifong is facing charges of professional misconduct. (There may be further developments in this case as it was pending at the time of this article.) The case brings to the public's attention the great authority exercised by the prosecuting attorney. Sample the article and answer the following questions:

1. The Duke rape case occurred as Nifong was running for re-election as prosecutor. The case became the major focus of the election. What would be the advantages and disadvantages of making the prosecutor an appointed position rather than an elected position?
2. Prosecuting attorneys are charged with executing justice not with convicting those charged. However, the prosecutor is to refrain from public statements condemning the accused before the trial. If the prosecutor strongly believes that the accused is guilty, what is the harm if the prosecutor expresses his or her belief in the guilt of the accused? Why should such behavior be considered a serious ethical violation of the prosecutor's office.
3. What are the consequences if a person is wrongfully accused of a serious crime which receives the public attention that the Duke rape case did? What remedies should be available to a person who is wrongfully accused? Should the prosecutor be punished?

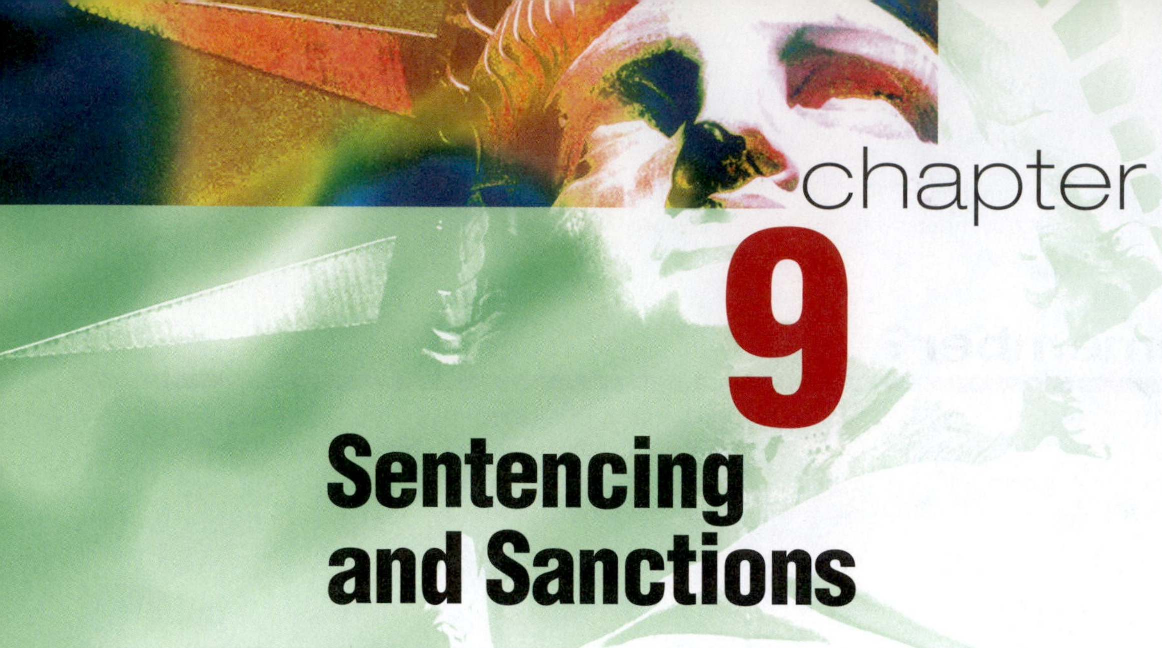
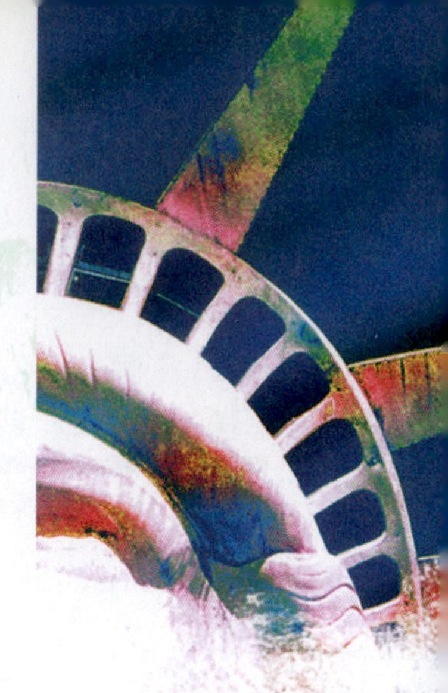

chapter

9 Sentencing and Sanctions

CHAPTER OUTLINE

LEARNING OBJECTIVES

After reading this chapter, you will know

- The five contemporary philosophies regarding the purpose of punishment.
- The types of sentences used for persons convicted of misdemeanors and felonies.
- What takes place during presentencing investigations and sentencing hearings.
- How the "not guilty by reason of insanity" defense is used by defendants and what sanctions are imposed when an offender is pronounced insane.
- The differences between indeterminate and structured forms of sentencing.
- The reasons for controversies surrounding sentencing reform and the death penalty.
- The types of intermediate sanctions, including intensive probation supervision, shock incarceration, shock probation, home confinement, and electronic monitoring.
- The role of programs that prepare inmates for reentry into society, including work release, halfway houses, and day reporting centers.

After 24 Years on Death Row, Clemency Is Killer's Final Appeal

SAN QUENTIN, CALIF.—Stanley Tookie Williams, once a leader of a notorious street gang and now perhaps the nation's most prominent death row inmate, leaned over a small wooden table in a cramped visiting cell here and tried to explain what he used to be and what he has become. "I have a despicable background," Mr. Williams said. "I was a criminal. I was a co-founder of the Crips. I was a nihilist." "But people forget," he added, "that redemption is tailor-made for the wretched." All that stands between Mr. Williams and his execution, set for December 13 [2005], is the possibility that Gov. Arnold Schwarzenegger will commute his sentence to life in prison after a clemency hearing next week.

Such commutations used to be common. Commutations have become rare. No condemned prisoner has been spared in California since 1967. In recent years they have tended to act only to correct errors in the judicial system and, occasionally, to take account of mental illness or retardation.

Adapted from "After 24 Years on Death Row, Clemency Is Killer's Final Appeal," The New York Times Online, www.nytimes.com, December 2, 2005 by Adam Liptak. Copyright © 2005 by The New York Times Co. Reprinted with permission.

introduction:

Convicted—Now What?

Stanley Tookie Williams, co-founder of the Crips gang, was sentenced to death in 1981 for four murders he was found guilty of committing in 1979. Williams denies that he committed the murders but his appeal for clemency to California Governor Arnold Schwarzenegger was based on his claim that after 24 years on death row he has turned his life around. Since his incarceration, Williams has authored children's books, a memoir, and the Tookie Peace Protocol, a set of fill-in-the-blanks forms for rival gangs wishing to declare a truce. He gives antiviolence lectures by phone and he has been nominated for the Nobel Prize for both literature and peace.[1]

Williams's request for clemency received both widespread support and opposition. Steve Cooley, a Los Angeles County district attorney, opposed Williams's request for clemency, saying that Williams's failure to "take any responsibility for the brutal, destructive and murderous acts he committed" means that "there can be no redemption, there can be no atonement, and there should be no mercy."[2] Williams responded, "How can a person express contrition if he's not guilty? They want me executed. Period. I exemplify something they don't want to see happen—a redemptive transformation."[3] Governor Schwarzenegger told reporters, "This is kind of the toughest thing to do when you're governor. And so I dread that situation, but it's something that's part of the job, and I have to do it."[4] Governor Schwarzenegger denied Williams's clemency request and Williams was executed despite much public protest.

This case represents only one of many claims that the criminal justice system is misguided and sometimes just plain wrong in the punishments given to convicted persons. There are over one million felony convictions in state courts and 75,000 felony convictions in federal courts each year. For each conviction there must be a sentence. After the defendant has been found guilty the judge must impose a sanction. Imposing a sentence is a complex interaction of people and philosophies. This chapter discusses the various reasons given to justify criminal sanctions, the process by which a judge determines the appropriate sentence, and the growing public concern that doubts in the infallibility of the court's verdict should result in an examination of the appropriateness of the use of the death penalty. It also examines why prisoner reentry in the criminal justice systems is in crisis and discusses some of the new prevention and community correction programs that are being used to promote successful prisoner reentry.

Purpose of Criminal Sanctions

▼ the main idea 9.1 Some reasons given to justify criminal sanctions are that sanctions prevent crime, incapacitate those who cannot be prevented from committing future crimes, serve as retribution for the harm done by offenders, are a means of rehabilitating the offender, and can be used to restore peace and justice in the community.

With over one million sentences handed down by judges each year there is a great variety in the sentencing of defendants. Some sentences can be pretty unusual. For example, an Olathe, Kansas, high school student convicted of battery for vomiting on his Spanish teacher was sentenced to spend four months cleaning up after people who throw up in police cars.[5] Also, a North Dakota man was sentenced to two days in jail for failing to license his cat.[6] In another case, Family Court Judge Marilyn O'Connor of

Rochester, New York, sentenced a dysfunctional, drug-addicted couple not to procreate again until their children are being raised by a natural parent, or are no longer being cared for at the expense of the public.[7] Sentences can be influenced by a number of factors. For instance, convicted rapist Stephen Terry Bolden was sentenced for multiple crimes, including first-degree rape, by Arizona Circuit Judge George Greene to 99 years plus two consecutive life sentences. When Bolden told Judge Greene that he (Greene) was "real rude during the sentencing hearing," Greene added an additional five days in prison to the sentence.[8]

In some cases sentences can be difficult for judges to determine what is appropriate. In 2005 in Georgia, when Jennifer Wilbanks faked her abduction days before her planned wedding, the court had to determine what was the appropriate sentence for the false police reports she gave in which she alleged she was kidnapped. Judge Ronnie Batchelor of Gwinnett County Superior Court sentenced Wilbanks to 120 hours of community service, ordered her to reimburse law enforcement officials for the money spent in the search for her, ordered her to obtain mental health treatment, and placed her on two years' probation. Was the sentence appropriate? It can be argued on the one hand that the punishment was too lenient, given the nationwide response of law enforcement to these false claims. On the other hand, it can be argued that the punishment was too harsh if one accepts that Wilbanks's actions were triggered by mental dysfunction rather than criminal intent. Thus, Judge Batchelor had the difficult responsibility of determining what sentence to hand down for this highly publicized case that would strike a balance between justice and compassion.

How do judges determine the appropriate punishment for a crime? Judges are guided by the law, as the law must provide the type and range of punishments that may be imposed on conviction. However, these laws are passed by legislators based on public sentiment as to the purpose and effect of various punishments.

The history of punishment in the United States is rooted in economic sanctions, corporal punishment, and death. However, the concept of serving time in a prison or jail as punishment for a crime is a fairly new philosophy of the criminal justice system. Historically, punishments in England and in the American colonies consisted primarily of fines, ordeals, and tortures. Criminals who could not afford to pay the fines imposed on them could be sold into economic servitude, a form of slavery, to pay the fines. **Corporal punishment** included whipping, branding, dunking, the stocks or pillory, and other pain-inflicting rituals.

Five contemporary philosophies regarding the purpose of punishment are (1) deterrence, (2) incapacitation, (3) retribution, (4) rehabilitation, and (5) restorative justice. These are simple categories for classifying punishment, but often the law and circumstances are not so simple. Criminal sanctions may have more than one purpose and may have unstated or contradictory purposes.

Deterrence

Deterrence is based on the principle that punishment should prevent the criminal from reoffending. The problem is to identify what punishment or threat of punishment effectively prevents people from committing crimes or criminals from reoffending. Punishments based on deterrence include economic sanctions, corporal punishment, and threat of bodily harm based on the premise that people seek pleasure and avoid pain. For example, as a means to stop Hartford, Connecticut, high school students from cursing, a joint effort by school and police officials gave citations to students who swear while defying teachers and administrators. Students who swear are fined $103. If the student cannot pay the fine, the student's parents are required to pay the fine. The theory underlying the use of fines is that the painful experience of the fines will discourage students from continuing to swear. In this case the practice seems to support the theory: Although there are critics of the actions of the police and school officials, officials report that the incidents of swearing have dropped to "almost nothing."[9]

corporal punishment The administration of bodily pain, based on the premise that a painful experience suffered as the result of criminal activity will deter future crime.

deterrence Philosophy and practices that emphasize making criminal behavior less appealing.

Corporal Punishment Some people profess that corporal punishment is an effective deterrent to misconduct in raising properly behaved children and ensuring proper conduct in schools. As a result of this deeply rooted belief, attempts to pass laws prohibiting the use of corporal punishment against children and students by parents and teachers have been unpopular and unsuccessful.[10]

Although corporal punishment has been abandoned as an official punishment in the United States, many foreign countries continue to use some form of corporal punishment as an official sentence. In 2000, Nigeria introduced Islamic law, which sanctions the use of corporal punishment. Despite this, Nigeria received international criticism in January 2001 for flogging a 17-year-old Muslim girl 100 times for having premarital sexual relations, and later in August 2001, for sentencing a 20-year-old woman to 100 lashes with a cane for having an extramarital affair.[11] In August 2001, in just 4 days, Iran sentenced 20 people to be lashed. Their crime was drinking alcohol, an offense against Islamic law. Each offender received 80 lashes.[12] In November 2001, Saudi Arabia flogged 55 youths 15 lashes each for harassing women. They were arrested by a special police unit responsible for patrolling large shopping centers and educational institutions. Courts in Saudi Arabia routinely order lashings for minor crimes.[13]

Some people still advocate that the return of corporal punishment would benefit crime control. For example, in 2005, Las Vegas Mayor Oscar Goodman suggested that those who deface freeways with graffiti should have their thumbs cut off on television. He also suggested that whippings or canings should be brought back for children who get into trouble. Goodman said, "I also believe in a little bit of corporal punishment going back to the days of yore. I'm dead serious. Some of these [children] don't learn. You have got to teach them a lesson. They would get a trial first."[14] Despite such vocal advocates for the return of corporal punishment or the adoption of the practice of caning, a common practice for a number of other nations, to the American criminal justice system, there appears to be little support for this movement.

Specific and General Deterrence Two types of deterrence are specific deterrence and general deterrence. **Specific deterrence** is when an individual who has committed a crime is deterred from committing that crime in the future by the nature of the punishment. Punishment with the power of specific deterrence would cause offenders not to drink alcohol again, for example, or not to harass women again, because of the unpleasant experience they suffered for their last offense.

General deterrence is the ability to prevent nonoffenders from committing crimes. General deterrence is based on the logic that people who witness the pain suffered by those who commit crimes will desire to avoid that pain and, hence, will refrain from criminal activity. Based on this belief, corporal punishment is often carried out in public so that others may witness the event. For example, in the Iranian flogging for drinking alcohol, over 1,000 people gathered in Vali-e-Asr Square in Teheran to watch the lashings. In England and the United States, hangings were once a public event, and parents brought their children to witness what happens when one breaks the law. Some advocates of general deterrence today propose that the death penalty would be a greater deterrent to crime if executions were broadcast live on television.

specific deterrence Deterrence based on the premise that an individual is best deterred from committing future crimes by the specific nature of the punishment.

general deterrence Deterrence based on the logic that people who witness the pain suffered by those who commit crimes will desire to avoid that pain and will refrain from criminal activity.

Sterilization and Deterrence The dark side of deterrence is the historical belief, first made popular by Cèsare Lombroso, that crime is hereditary and criminals should be sterilized to prevent future crime. Sterilization of criminals was practiced in the United States during the early twentieth century. In the United States today, a chemical version of castration is legal, but the few cases in which it has been used have drawn criticism and protest. Supreme Court Justice Oliver Wendell Holmes argued for sterilization as an effective means to prevent crime. One criminologist has even argued that the drop in crime in the 1980s and 1990s was due to the increase in abortion in the general population. Other countries have used sterilization to reduce the births of "socially undesirable" persons. Between 1935 and 1975, Sweden sterilized more than 63,000 cit-

What philosophy of criminal sanctioning does corporal punishment reflect? How does making punishment public contribute to that goal? The administration of pain as a sanction against criminal offending has a long history and has been practiced at one time or another in most societies worldwide. What evidence is there that corporal punishment is effective in its goal? What are the other principal types of criminal sanctions?

izens to improve Sweden's genetic stock. In addition, more than 200 mentally ill patients were starved to death between 1941 and 1943, and it is alleged that between 1944 and 1963, approximately 4,500 Swedish citizens were lobotomized, often against their will, as a form of treatment for homosexuality.[15] Until 1996, Japanese law allowed the forced sterilization of people with a broad range of mental or physical handicaps, hereditary diseases, and leprosy. Japanese Health Ministry statistics indicate that nearly 850,000 people were sterilized between 1949 and 1996.[16] The law was changed in 1996 due to a change in public sentiment.

Incapacitation

Another view of punishment is that if criminals cannot be deterred from committing further crimes, they should be prevented from having the opportunity to commit other crimes, a condition referred to as **incapacitation**. The theory of incapacitation assumes that offenders cannot be rehabilitated and it will never be safe to release them back into society. The death penalty is an extreme form of incapacitation in that those offenders executed are guaranteed not to be capable of reoffending. In the absence of the death penalty, incarceration in a correctional institution is the alternative to incapacitate the offender. For example, Australia does not have the death penalty. Thus, when Katherine Mary Knight, age 45 and a slaughterhouse worker, was convicted of stabbing John Price 37 times then decapitating him, skinning his body, and later including his flesh in meals for the son and daughter of the deceased, Judge Barry O'Keefe felt that in absence of the death penalty the only way to ensure public safety was to order that Knight never be released from correctional confinement.[17]

Two of the oldest forms of incapacitation are banishment and transportation. Banishment as a criminal sanction may have begun in prehistoric times. **Banishment** removed offenders from society, often under the stipulation that if they returned, they would be put to death. This removal could be for a period of time or forever. In societies in which the protection and support of the group were essential to survival,

incapacitation Deterrence based on the premise that the only way to prevent criminals from reoffending is to remove them from society.

banishment Removal of the offender from the community.

banishment was considered a punishment nearly equal to death. Today, Georgia and Kentucky still use banishment. District Attorney Kelly Burke of Houston County, Georgia, favors legalized exile and has been successful in banning over 60 criminals from Houston county.[18] **Transportation** removed offenders from society by literally moving them to another place. England made extensive use of transportation as a criminal sanction. Until the American Revolutionary War, prisoners were transported to the American colonies. After the American Revolution, English convicts were transported to Australia until the mid-nineteenth century.[19] Transportation to penal colonies is not practiced today.

Modern means of incapacitation include confiscating the cars of accused drunk drivers and the property and valuables of drug dealers and members of organized crime. The argument of those in favor of the law is that without a car, it would be impossible to drive while intoxicated, and without wealth, it would be impossible to engage in illegal businesses like drug dealing. The most common form of incapacitation, however, is imprisonment. The public belief underlying this practice is that behind bars a criminal is effectively prevented from having the opportunity to commit more crimes. This belief underlies proposals for long prison sentences, especially for repeat offenders. Such a philosophy is sometimes referred to as "warehousing" or "lock and feed." These terms emphasize that the primary purpose of sentencing is to separate the offender from the public for as long as possible.

Those opposed to incapacitation as the primary purpose of sentencing point out that most prisoners are released back into society. They also state that although incarceration may appear to protect the public from the offenders' crimes, it does little to protect fellow inmates and correctional officers from victimization.

Retribution

Retribution, or "just-desserts," argues that criminals should be punished because they deserve it. Retribution is associated with "get-tough" sentencing and the philosophy of an eye for an eye, which advocates that those who do wrong should pay for their crimes in equal measure. Traditionally, retribution was the victim's revenge. The victim was entitled to inflict punishment or to see that punishment was inflicted on the offender. Many who favor the death penalty argue that it is the most appropriate punishment for convicted murderers.

Retribution relates to people's emotional response to a crime. For example, Kim Davis, 34, stole a car in Independence, Missouri. When he discovered that a 6-year-old child had been left in the vehicle, he tried to shove the boy outside. The boy became tangled in the seat belt, but Davis refused to stop. Horrified motorists who witnessed the awful scene pursued him for 5 miles before he was stopped. The boy did not survive the ordeal. Davis was charged with second-degree murder, robbery, child abuse, and kidnapping. A witness to the crime suggested that Davis should be "dragged himself, just like he dragged that kid."[20] In retribution, the criminal suffers—perhaps in a like manner—for the crime. An example of this philosophy of retribution was the 2001 execution of a murderer by a 10-year-old boy under the Taliban's interpretation of Islamic law. Under this interpretation, relatives of a victim carry out the death sentence. Under the supervision of the Islamic court, the 10-year-old boy, the oldest male relative of the murdered man, shot the convicted man as thousands watched in southern Kandahar.[21]

Those who believe the purpose of sentencing is retribution are often disappointed that the offender does not suffer enough as a result of the sentence imposed. Because the U.S. criminal justice system does not allow relatives to carry out the execution of offenders or the offender to be brutalized by corporal punishment, often retribution emphasizes long prison terms. The belief in retribution is reflected in the statement of Malissa Wilkins. Wilkins's two young children were killed when Jennifer Porter, a former elementary school dance teacher, hit the children with her car and killed them. Porter fled the accident. After her arrest and conviction, Florida Circuit Judge Emmett

transportation Eighteenth-century practice by Great Britain of sending offenders to the American colonies and later Australia.

retribution Deterrence based on the premise that criminals should be punished because they deserve it.

In Los Angeles, juvenile offenders work with severely disabled children at El Camino School as part of their jail time and rehabilitation program. Community service is a form of general restitution, which may be appropriate when it is not possible for an offender to remove the specific impacts of his or her crime on the victims. What are some other forms of restorative justice? How might restorative justice programs go hand in hand with rehabilitation programs? Goals of criminal sanctioning in the United States today tend not to focus on rehabilitating offenders and addressing the needs of victims. Why?

Battles could have sentenced Porter to 15 years in prison. However, the judge took into account Porter's clean past record and other factors and sentenced her to 3 years probation and 500 hours of community service. At the sentencing Wilkins sobbed and urged the judge to sentence Porter to prison. Wilkins said, "I want her to be punished. I want her to go to prison. I want her to see what it's like to lose someone."[22] Wilkins's sentiments reflect the underlying philosophy of retribution.

During the nineteenth and twentieth centuries, many prison officials and the public favored the idea that punishment was retribution. As a result, prison conditions often were deliberately harsh and cruel, and physical punishment was administered liberally to inmates. The public expected that prisoners would be punished while incarcerated.

See www.curenational.org, the website of CURE (Citizens United for Rehabilitation of Errants), a nonprofit national organization dedicated to reducing crime through rehabilitation programs and reforms of the criminal justice system.

Rehabilitation

Rehabilitation and restoration are more contemporary philosophies defining the purpose of criminal sanctions. **Rehabilitation** calls for criminal sanctions to "cure" the offender of criminality. The rehabilitation model often is referred to as the medical model in that it views criminality as a disease to be cured. Some believe rehabilitation of offenders is impossible. Advocates of rehabilitation favor approaches involving psychology, medical treatment, drug treatment, self-esteem counseling, education, and programs aimed at developing ethical values and work skills. Most rehabilitation efforts focus on juvenile delinquents and youthful offenders. The juvenile justice system is based on the principle that the primary purpose of the juvenile justice system is to rehabilitate. The criminal justice system and the public may accept that the purpose of criminal sanctions is to rehabilitate children and first-time offenders but often totally reject this premise for repeat and career offenders. Thus, the public may be willing to give the 14-year-old burglar the chance to turn his or her life around, but they would just as soon see the 45-year-old sexual offender spend the rest of his or her life in prison rather than give the system a chance to rehabilitate him or her.

rehabilitation Deterrence based on the premise that criminals can be "cured" of their problems and criminality and returned to society.

restorative justice Model of deterrence that uses restitution programs, community work programs, victim-offender mediation, and other strategies to not only rehabilitate the offender but also address the damage done to the community and the victim.

Restorative Justice

Restorative justice focuses on rehabilitating the victims rather than the offenders. Rehabilitation often is criticized for forgetting the victim. The focus in rehabilitation is on the offender and what needs to be done to make him or her a productive, normal member of society. The restorative justice model does not argue against the rehabilitation of the offender, but it does advocate that the needs of the victim also must be central. Crime

In 1982, John Hinckley was found not guilty by reason of insanity in the attempted murder of President Reagan. Many believed that Hinckley "got away with murder," and in response to public outrage over the outcome of the trial, many states enacted a new type of verdict, "guilty but mentally ill." With this verdict, a defendant is sentenced to prison but is supposed to be given psychological treatment in that setting, whereas with the "not guilty by reason of insanity" verdict, a defendant is acquitted and civil commitment proceedings are undertaken to have the person confined to a mental institution. John Hinckley remains indefinitely confined at St. Elizabeth's Hospital in Washington, DC, but has been allowed short periods of unsupervised release.

has a harmful effect on the victim and society, and justice requires that this harm be removed as much as possible. Restorative justice programs use restitution, community work programs, victim-offender mediation, and other strategies both to rehabilitate the offender and to address the damage done to the community and the victim. South Africa used this model to help heal the division between blacks and whites. South Africa's Truth and Reconciliation Commission allows those who committed hate crimes during apartheid, who confessed and repented of their crimes, to escape criminal sanctions.

One of the characteristics of restorative justice is the concept that the offender should be made to provide some contribution to the community. In the American criminal justice system this concept is translated into practice by sentencing the offender to additional penalties other than or in addition to incarceration. The most common penalties related to restorative justice include sentences requiring restitution to the victim and community service. Table 9.1 shows that in 14 percent of sentences offenders are required to make restitution to the victim. This sanction is most used in property offenses (26 percent) and least used in drug and weapon offenses (6 percent for each). Community service is included as a penalty in 5 percent of all offenses. Community service is based on the philosophy that the offender should provide services that help the community as a way to make up for the harm he or she did to the community.

State Courts and the Insanity Plea

guilty but mentally ill An alternative verdict in capital cases based on the standard that the defendant was mentally ill but also was sufficiently aware (had sufficient *mens rea*) to be held "morally blameworthy" for the crime.

State courts have adopted diverse standards for a successful insanity defense. Some still use the right-wrong test, others have adopted the *Model Penal Code* substantial capacity test (see Chapter 5), and a few have adopted standards combining elements of both of these tests of insanity. A number of states have adopted a new verdict—**guilty but mentally ill.** Michigan was the first state to adopt this verdict in 1975. The verdict provides the jury the option of finding that the defendant was indeed mentally ill, perhaps suffering from a serious mental illness, but that the defendant was "sufficiently in possession of his faculties to be morally blameworthy for his acts."[23]

table 9.1

Felons Sentenced to an Additional Penalty in State Courts, by Offense, 2002

Most Serious Conviction Offense	Percent of Felons with an Additional Penalty of–				
	Fine	*Restitution*	*Treatment*[a]	*Community Service*	*Other*
All Offenses	25%	12%	3%	4%	7%
Violent Offenses	23%	11%	3%	3%	6%
Murder[b]	17	7	1	2	2
Sexual assault[c]	22	10	4	2	7
Rape	21	10	4	1	6
Other sexual assault	23	10	3	2	8
Robbery	13	10	1	2	4
Aggravated assault	27	11	3	3	7
Other violent[d]	26	12	2	4	9
Property Offenses	24%	21%	2%	4%	6%
Burglary	23	20	2	4	5
Larceny[e]	21	19	1	5	7
Motor vehicle theft	22	19	2	3	11
Fraud[f]	28	24	2	5	8
Drug Offenses	27%	6%	6%	4%	7%
Possession	25	3	11	5	11
Trafficking	27	8	2	3	5
Weapon Offenses	18%	4%	2%	4%	6%
Other Offenses[g]	29%	10%	3%	4%	8%

Note: Where the data indicated affirmatively that a particular additional penalty was imposed, the case was coded accordingly. Where the data did not indicate affirmatively or negatively, the case was treated as not having an additional penalty. These procedures provide a conservative estimate of the prevalence of additional penalties. A felon receiving more than one kind of additional penalty appears under more than one table heading. This table is based on an estimated 1,051,002 cases.

[a]Includes any type of counseling, rehabilitation, treatment, or mental hospital confinement.

[b]Includes nonnegligent manslaughter.

[c]Includes rape.

[d]Includes offenses such as negligent manslaughter and kidnapping.

[e]Includes motor vehicle theft.

[f]Includes forgery and embezzlement.

[g]Composed of nonviolent offenses such as receiving stolen property and vandalism.

Source: Matthew R. Durose and Patrick A. Langan, *State Court Sentencing of Convicted Felons, 2002 Statistical Tables* (Washington, DC: Bureau of Justice Statistics, 2005), Table 1.9.

In states that have adopted it, the guilty but mentally ill verdict is an alternative to the not guilty by reason of insanity verdict. Thus, the jury has the option of finding defendants mentally ill but morally responsible for their acts, or insane and lacking the *mens rea* to be held criminally liable. In the latter case, the defendant is involuntarily confined to a civil mental health facility, but if found guilty but mentally ill, the defendant is sentenced to incarceration in a state prison following psychiatric treatment. During confinement at a mental institution, if doctors determine that the defendant is no longer suffering from mental illness, he or she is not released but is transferred to the state prison to serve his or her sentence. The time that the offender spent in the mental institution counts toward the sentence to be served. Once returned to the regular prison population, offenders may still be considered mentally ill to some degree, but their medical and psychiatric problems will not excuse them from incarceration for the crime.

Public Fear of the Insanity Plea

The public fear that the successful use of the insanity defense poses a grave danger because it allows defendants to escape incarceration does not appear to be justified. A very small number of defendants choose to plead not guilty by reason of insanity.[24] Offenders found to be not guilty by reason of insanity rarely obtain their freedom following the verdict.[25] Media coverage has sensationalized unusual cases, such as that of Lorena Bobbitt, who successfully pleaded insanity to a charge of cutting off her husband's penis and was freed completely within two months of the verdict, and John Hinckley, who escaped possible lifetime incarceration by use of the insanity plea. However, these cases are not typical of defendants found guilty by reason of insanity.

What happens in sentencing when a defendant is not successful in his or her insanity plea? The judge may require that after conviction the offender undergo another mental competency examination. If the offender is found mentally unfit for incarceration in the state or federal prison, he or she is placed in a maximum-security mental health facility that can provide appropriate psychiatric treatment. Some states have special correctional facilities for such patients. Medical authorities determine if or when the offender can be returned to the prison population. The time spent in the medical institution counts toward the sentence to be served.

▲ check your understanding **9.1** **What are the five main philosophies regarding the purpose of punishment? How do specific and general deterrence differ? What are the forms of incapacitation and retribution? How do rehabilitation and restorative justice differ? How are cases based on the insanity defense processed and disposed? What are the provisions of the Insanity Defense Reform Act of 1984?**

Sentencing Models

▼ the main idea **9.2** **Two models that govern the practice of sentencing in courts of general trial jurisdiction are indeterminate sentencing and structured sentencing.**

sentencing The punishment for a crime as determined by a judge.

The jury (except in a bench trial) determines the guilt of the defendant, but the judge is responsible for determining the sentence the defendant receives. In **sentencing**, the judge evaluates the circumstances of the cases of everyone who pleads guilty or is convicted of an offense. The judge must also evaluate the possible sentences allowed by law and then select the sentence that best fits the case. All criminal laws passed by the state legislature or the U.S. Congress must specify the punishment or range of punishments that a judge can impose if a defendant is found guilty of violating that law. The only constitutional guideline for sentencing is the Eighth Amendment prohibition against cruel and unusual punishment. The U.S. Supreme Court has allowed a broad interpretation of this amendment and, thus, few punishments have been found to be cruel and unusual.

Go to www.ncjrs.org/txtfiles1/nij/184253.txt. Read a research paper on issues of determinate sentencing—for example, Joan Petersilia, *When Prisoners Return to the Community: Political, Economic, and Social Consequences* (National Institute of Justice, November 2000).

The traditional criminal sanctions that a judge may impose are fines, imprisonment, probation, or some combination of these. Federal judges in U.S. District Court, military judges, and state judges in courts of general trial jurisdiction in states with the death penalty also may sentence a defendant to death. Judges are guided by the law as to the minimum and maximum sentence that a convicted defendant can receive. However, especially for state judges, the difference between the minimum and maximum punishment may vary greatly. Thus, each sentence requires the judge to give careful consideration to the individual circumstances of the case. Seldom is sentencing an automatic or routine function in which the outcome is always predictable.

At one time, state and federal judges had nearly complete discretion in sentencing an offender, because most states and the federal courts used the indeterminate model of sentencing. The **indeterminate sentencing** model gives the judge the most power and flexibility in setting the sentence of the offender. In the late nineteenth century, as incarceration became a common punishment for serious crimes, the predominant correctional philosophy was that offenders should demonstrate that they had changed their criminal attitudes and lifestyles as a condition of release. Thus, judges were given wide latitude in the sentences they could impose for crimes. Because no one could predict exactly when offenders would demonstrate that they were rehabilitated, offenders were given sentences of indeterminate length. For example, an offender might receive a sentence of a minimum of 1 year and a maximum of 20 years in prison. The exact number of years to be served would be determined by the prisoner's behavior and progress toward rehabilitation.

Indeterminate sentencing came under criticism in the late twentieth century. In addition to giving the judge wide latitude in sentencing, indeterminate sentencing also gave extensive power to prison authorities. In reality, it was prison authorities, not the judge, who determined the term of sentence to be served. Prison officials could arbitrarily exercise this power with little or no oversight. To cure the ills of indeterminate sentencing, state and federal legislation adopted **structured sentencing** models, including (1) determinate sentencing, (2) mandatory sentencing and habitual offender sentencing laws, (3) sentencing guidelines, and (4) presumptive sentencing.

indeterminate sentencing A model of sentencing in which judges have nearly complete discretion in sentencing an offender.

structured sentencing A sentencing model—including determinate sentencing, sentencing guidelines, and presumptive sentencing—that defines punishments rather than allowing indeterminate sentencing.

Determinate versus Indeterminate Sentencing

In **determinate sentencing,** the offender is sentenced to a fixed term of incarceration. This term may be reduced by parole or good behavior, but other than that, the inmate knows when he or she is scheduled for release from prison. Determinate sentencing is also known as *flat sentences* or *fixed sentences.* Determinate sentencing was a sentencing reform that emerged in the 1970s to provide more equity and proportionality in sentencing. Proponents claimed that it would eliminate racial discrimination.[26]

Determinate sentencing reform did not become popular, however. Only Arizona adopted a determinate sentencing model. A few other states (California, Illinois, Indiana, and Maine) adopted sentencing models based on determinate sentencing but still provided for discretion in sentencing.[27]

determinate sentencing A sentencing model in which the offender is sentenced to a fixed term of incarceration.

Mandatory Sentencing and Habitual Offender Laws

A controversial sentencing model is **mandatory sentencing**—the strict application of full sentences, adopted because of public perception that offenders were "getting off too light." Concerned that judges were too lenient in sentencing, many states adopted

mandatory sentencing The strict application of full sentences in the determinate sentencing model.

legislation mandating that offenders convicted of crimes serve the sentence for that crime as specified by law. Thus, sentencing was not left to the discretion of the judge. Mandatory sentences have been applied mostly to crimes involving drugs or the use of firearms. For crimes with mandatory sentences, if the defendant is convicted, the sentence for the crime is specified by the law, and the judge has no authority to change the sentence based on mitigating circumstances. For example, if the law states that the prison term for committing a crime with a firearm is two years, then the judge must sentence the defendant to two years. Critics of mandatory sentencing argue that there may be unique circumstances in a case that make mandatory sentences inappropriate. Judges are critical of mandatory sentences, as they greatly reduce the authority of the judge in determining the sentence. Concerned that the criminal justice system was ignoring domestic violence or not taking domestic violence cases seriously, several states adopted mandatory sentencing for conviction of domestic violence. Sometimes, these sentences are for short periods of time, such as 48 hours, or involve only probation. Nevertheless, the convicted offender finds that he or she can no longer escape punishment for domestic violence.[28]

Mandatory sentencing also has been applied to repeat offenders through **habitual offender laws.** California has received much press concerning its **three strikes law,** in which repeat offenders receive longer mandatory sentences. Proponents argue that "getting tough on crime" reduces crime by taking repeat offenders off the streets. Opponents argue that the three strikes law creates situations in which offenders are receiving disproportionately long prison terms for minor crimes, such as possession of drugs. A case in 1998 illustrated this argument when a man who stole four chocolate chip cookies from a restaurant was sentenced to serve 26 years to life in prison under the state's three strikes law.[29] California Judge Jean Rheinheimer sentenced the offender, who had previously been convicted of burglary and assault with a firearm, to this long prison term. The theft carried a maximum 3-year sentence, but Judge Rheinheimer sentenced the offender under the three strikes law. To the defense's request for leniency, Judge Rheinheimer commented, "I just see no reason to say Mr. Weber is anything other than the three-strikes defendant the people and the Legislature had in mind when they enacted this law."[30]

As a result of the "get-tough" sentencing policies, especially the three strikes sentencing policy, the number of convicted felons serving some kind of life sentence has increased 83 percent since 1992.[31] Supporters of these new sentencing policies defend long sentences by citing the significant decline in crime since their adoption, but opponents criticize the long sentences, pointing out that it will cost about $1 million to keep an inmate locked up for life. With over 125,000 inmates sentenced to life terms, the costs, which fall primarily on state taxpayers, of getting tough on criminals is extremely high. As a result of these costs and claims that factors other than long prison terms may account for the significant drop in crime, many states are reconsidering mandatory sentencing and three strikes laws.[32] The American Bar Association (ABA) has recommended an end to mandatory minimum sentences and overly harsh prison terms for nonviolent offenders.[33] A 2004 report by the American Bar Association said that long prison terms should be reserved for criminals who pose the greatest danger to society and who commit the most serious crimes. Ennis Archer, ABA president in 2004, critiques overly harsh and mandatory sentences, saying, "For more than 20 years, we have gotten tougher on crime. Now we need to get smarter."[34] Even Supreme Court Justice Anthony M. Kennedy has criticized overly harsh prison terms for nonviolent drug offenders, saying, "Our resources are misspent, our punishments too severe, our sentences too long."[35]

habitual offender laws Tough sentencing laws, such as "three strikes" laws, to punish repeat offenders more harshly.

three strikes law The application of mandatory sentencing to give repeat offenders longer prison terms.

sentencing guidelines A sentencing model in which crimes are classified according to their seriousness, and a range of time to be served is mandated for crimes within each category.

Sentencing Guidelines

Sentencing guidelines have been adopted by most states. In **sentencing guidelines,** crimes are classified according to seriousness, and a range of time is mandated for crimes within each category. Each state has its own classification for the seriousness of a crime and the corresponding length of sentence that can be imposed for that crime. Federal crimes are defined by Section 3559, U.S. Code, Title 18 into felonies and misdemeanors and are representative of the scheme used by most states in setting sentencing guidelines. The federal court distinguishes five classifications for felony crimes and three classifications for misdemeanors:

- **Title 18 Felonies**

  Class A felony—maximum sentence of life imprisonment or, if authorized, death

  Class B felony—a minimum sentence of 25 years' imprisonment to life imprisonment; the death penalty is not permitted

  Class C felony—a maximum sentence of 25 years but no less than 10 years' imprisonment

  Class D felony—a maximum sentence of 10 years but no less than 5 years' imprisonment

  Class E felony—a maximum sentence of 5 years but more than 1 year of imprisonment

- **Title 18 Misdemeanors**

  Class A misdemeanor—a maximum sentence of 1 year of imprisonment but no less than 1 month of imprisonment

  Class B misdemeanor—a maximum sentence of 6 months' imprisonment but no less than 30 days

  Class C misdemeanor—a maximum sentence of 30 days' imprisonment but no less than 5 days

The sentencing schedule of many states reflects this same graduated sentencing pattern but may have different cut-off points for classifying the sentence. In the sentencing guideline model, the judge must select a sentence corresponding to the seriousness of the crime as defined by the sentencing guidelines.

Presumptive Sentencing

Presumptive sentencing is a structured sentencing model that attempts to balance indeterminate sentencing with determinate sentencing. Presumptive sentencing gives discretionary powers to the judge within certain limits. The best-known presumptive sentencing model is used by the federal court according to the Sentencing Reform Act of 1984. The **Sentencing Reform Act of 1984** set minimum and maximum terms of imprisonment for the various federal offenses. It then provided an adjustment for the offender's criminal history and for aggravating or mitigating circumstances. After conviction, the judge must sentence the offender using the ***Federal Sentencing Guidelines Manual.***[36] Based on the offense and the offender's history, a base sentence is determined in months (e.g., 135–180 months). The offender's sentence can be increased by adding months for aggravating factors such as the use of a firearm, failing to cooperate with arresting authorities, lack of remorse, failure to recover stolen property, and so forth. The offender's sentence also can be shortened by months for mitigating factors, such as cooperating with arresting authorities, making restitution, providing information to authorities leading to the arrest of others involved in the crime, and so forth. The judge literally calculates a sentence using the base sentence in months listed in the *Federal Sentencing Guidelines Manual* and the addition and subtraction of months to this base sentence based on mitigating and aggravating factors. If the judge departs significantly from the *Federal Sentencing Guidelines,* he or she must provide written reasons for this deviation at the sentencing hearing. The prosecution or defense can appeal the sentence.

Federal judges protested the imposition of the federal sentencing guidelines, arguing that they violated the separation of powers clause. The argument was that the legislative

presumptive sentencing A structured sentencing model that attempts to balance sentencing guidelines with mandatory sentencing and at the same time provide discretion to the judge.

branch of the government did not have the authority to dictate sentencing guidelines to the judicial branch of the government. Ironically, the U.S. Supreme Court was the final arbiter of the dispute and ruled that Congress is within its powers to legislate sentencing guidelines.[37]

The Sentencing Reform Act of 1984 restricted, but did not abolish, plea bargaining. First, sentence-reduction plea bargaining cannot permit the offender to receive less than the minimum mandatory sentence for the offense.[38] Second, if plea bargaining results in reduced charges, the court record and plea bargaining agreement must fully disclose the details of the actual crime. Thus, if the crime of sexual assault is reduced to burglary, the court record will still contain the details of the crime of sexual assault. This record is public information. Thus, offenders cannot hide their crimes from the public and the media by plea bargaining to a lesser included crime.

One consideration in the use of presumptive sentencing is that it abolishes parole, or early release from prison. This is a stumbling block for states that want to adopt a presumptive sentencing model similar to the federal court model. Parole provides for the possibility that an offender sentenced to serve nine years in prison may only serve one-third of that time. Many states depend on parole to move offenders through the correctional system, as there are not enough prison beds to accommodate the number of sentenced offenders. Thus, before these states could adopt a presumptive sentencing model, they would have to build more prisons. The federal correctional system has the ability to move inmates throughout the United States, which allows the federal government to manage prison overcrowding by moving prisoners to less-crowded facilities. State corrections do not have this option, however.

Presumptive sentencing, specifically the *Federal Sentencing Guidelines,* was struck down as unconstitutional by the U.S. Supreme Court in January 2005. The Court first ruled in June 2004 that Washington state's sentencing law that was modeled on the federal sentencing guidelines was unconstitutional because it violated the right to a trial by jury. The reasoning was that under the state's sentencing guidelines, similar to the federal guidelines, judges could take into account actions and circumstances related to the case not introduced during the trial in determining the sentence of the offender. The review of state sentencing guidelines was sparked by the review of the financial fraud case of Jamie Olis, who was sentenced to 24 years in prison. In the Washington state sentencing guidelines there were many factors that allowed a judge to increase or decrease the length of the prison term. One of the factors that lengthened the prison term was the financial losses of the fraud. The U.S. Supreme Court ruled that any factor that increases a criminal's sentence, except for prior convictions, must be proved to a jury beyond a reasonable doubt before it could be considered as a factor to increase sentence length.

The Washington state decision affected other states with similar sentencing guidelines. In January 2005, the U.S. Supreme Court ruled that the same reasoning made federal sentencing guidelines invalid (*United States* v. *Booker,* No. 04-104 and *United States* v. *Fanfan,* No. 04-105). The Court ruled that the federal sentencing guidelines violated defendants' rights to trial by jury by giving the judges the power to make factual findings that increased sentences beyond the maximum that the jury's finding alone would support. For example, in 2002, Mohamad Hammoud was convicted of smuggling cigarettes to raise money for the Lebanese terrorist group Hezbollah. He faced a 57-month sentence for that crime, but because of the terrorism connection and other findings by the judge, he was sentenced to 155 years.[39] The Court ruled that such increases are not constitutional.

The U.S. Supreme Court ruled that federal sentencing guidelines are "merely advisory." Justice Breyer, writing for the majority decision, said, "Judges must consult the guidelines and take them into account in imposing sentences. But at the end of the day the guidelines will be advisory only, with sentences to be reviewed on appeal for reasonableness."[40]

As a result of the Court's rulings in the Washington state case in *United States* v. *Booker* and *United States* v. *Fanfan,* state and federal courts will have to review those cases in which defendants were sentenced under state or federal sentencing guidelines. Also, the Supreme Court's ruling has renewed the struggle between Congress and the judiciary for control over setting criminal punishment.[41] In June 2005, Attorney General Albert Gonzales cited the "drift toward lesser sentences" in federal criminal cases and urged Congress to enact a new sentencing system that would incorporate a new system of mandatory minimum sentencing rules.

Truth in Sentencing

Because they cannot eliminate parole, some states have taken another approach, called truth in sentencing. **Truth in sentencing** legislation requires the court to disclose the actual prison time that the offender is likely to serve. Some states (Arizona, California, and Illinois) have gone one step further and adopted what is known as the *85 percent requirement rule,* which states that the offender must serve at least 85 percent of the sentence before becoming eligible for release. Thus, an offender sentenced to 10 years in prison would have to serve 8.5 years before being eligible for early release. Because offenders in many states routinely serve only one-third to one-half of their sentences, the 85 percent requirement significantly increases the actual time in prison.

▲ check your understanding **9.2** **What criticisms were leveled against indeterminate sentencing? What are the three major types of structured sentencing? What are the benefits, drawbacks, and potential abuses of each? How did the Sentencing Reform Act of 1984 change methods of structured sentencing?**

Sentencing and the Death Penalty

▼ the main idea **9.3** **Capital punishment is an ongoing issue in American justice. Imposition of the death penalty requires special procedures in the courts.**

Capital punishment—the death penalty—can be traced back to the earliest records of human history. In English common law, the roots of the American system of justice, even minor thefts could be punished by death, and the prisoner could be tortured in the process. The punishment for treason under English common law in 1776 was to be hanged but taken down while still alive, so bowels could be removed and burned before the prisoners, their heads cut off and their bodies quartered.[42] The American colonists did not shun the use of the death penalty. The criminal codes of 1642 and 1650 of the New Haven colony mandated the use of the death penalty not only for crimes of murder and treason, but also for crimes such as denying the true God and His attributes, bestiality, theft, horse theft, and children above the age of 16 striking their natural father or mother.[43]

Many Western countries, including England, France, Germany, and Italy, have banned the death penalty. Some nations have retained the death penalty in forms that are alien to U.S. values, such as execution by Sharia law, law based on Islamic religious values. For example, in March 2000, Judge Allah Baksh Ranja of Pakistan sentenced to death a man convicted of strangling and dismembering 100 children. The judge ordered Javed Iqbal, age 42, executed in a Lahore park in front of his victims' parents. He told the prisoner, "You will be strangled in front of the parents whose children you killed.

truth in sentencing In the application of presumptive sentencing in states that cannot eliminate parole, the legal requirement that courts disclose the actual prison time the offender is likely to serve.

capital punishment The sentence of death.

Go to www .derechos.org. Derechos Human Rights is the first Internet-based human rights organization. This website offers a plethora of links to sites with information on the death penalty.

Your body will then be cut into a hundred pieces and put in acid, the same way you killed the children."[44] Also, Sharia law allows execution by beheading.

In the United States, lethal injection is the predominant method of execution (37 of the 38 states with a death penalty). Nine states authorize electrocution; 4 states, lethal gas; 3 states, hanging; and 3 states, firing squad. Seventeen states authorize more than one method—lethal injection and an alternative method—usually decided by the condemned prisoner. The federal government uses lethal injection for offenses prosecuted under 28 CFR, Part 26. Federal cases prosecuted under the Violent Crime Control Act of 1994 (18 U.S.C. 3596) call for the method used in the state in which the conviction took place.[45]

The Death Penalty and Abolitionists

On December 1, 2005, Kenneth Lee Boyd was executed by the state of North Carolina. He was the 1,000th person to be executed by the United States since the Supreme Court upheld states' rights to order the death penalty in 1976. Although there were protests against the execution of Boyd, public opinion supports the use of the death penalty. However, an October 2005 Gallup poll showed that public support of the death penalty is dropping. In October 2005, 64 percent of Americans supported use of the death penalty, but that is the lowest level in 27 years, down from a high of 80 percent in 1994.[46] Some people are opposed to the death penalty in specific cases for specific reasons, such as their belief that the person is innocent, the person did not receive a fair trial, or there is reasonable doubt that justifies an alternative sentence other than death. However, some people oppose the death penalty under all circumstances and for all reasons. They do not believe that the government has the right to execute citizens. Those universally opposed to the use of capital punishment are called *abolitionists.*

The debate between abolitionists and those who favor capital punishment is very old. One of the earliest debates about the death penalty was recorded by the Greek philosopher Plato regarding Socrates, who was convicted by the Athenians of corrupting the morals of the youth and was sentenced to death. A friend tried to convince Socrates that he should escape because he was wrongfully convicted, and said that other cities would welcome him as a citizen because they would recognize that the sentence was unjust. Socrates refused, however, arguing, "But whether in battle or in a court of law, or in any other place, he must do what his city and his country order him; or he must change their view of what is just. . . . He who has experience of the manner in which we order justice and administer the State, and still remains, has entered into an implied contract that he will do as we command him."[47] This argument—that there is an implicit contract between the individual and the state—is the crux of one of the most controversial debates in sentencing—the role of capital punishment.

Abolitionists claim that capital punishment is ineffective in preventing crime, is unfairly administered, and is sometimes administered in error, but the central premise of their arguments is that government does not have the right to take a person's life.[48] For example, the **Southern Center for Human Rights** argues against the death penalty, quoting freed slave Frederick Douglass, who became a champion of civil rights: "Life is the great primary and most precious and comprehensive of all human rights . . . whether it be coupled with virtue, honor, and happiness, or with sin, disgrace, and misery, the continued possession of it is rightfully not a matter of volition; . . . [It is not] to be deliberately or voluntarily destroyed, either by individuals separately, or combined in what is called Government."[49] Both abolitionists and proponents of the death penalty also argue for their views on the basis of religious values. Until 1968, abolitionists could be excluded from capital murder juries simply because they opposed the death penalty. Abolitionists opposed being barred from capital murder juries and appealed to the U.S. Supreme Court.

abolitionists People opposed to the use of capital punishment.

In ***Witherspoon* v. *Illinois***[50] (1968) the U.S. Supreme Court declared unconstitutional the common practice of prosecutors of excluding abolitionists from capital murder juries. After the *Witherspoon* decision the composition of juries in capital murder cases changed in that persons opposed in principle to the death penalty could not be excluded from the jury. Obviously, the inclusion of abolitionists on capital murder cases makes it harder, or impossible, for prosecutors to obtain a unanimous verdict for the death penalty.

The Death Penalty and Civil Rights

In the United States, the death penalty sentence can be imposed by the state, the federal court, military courts, and military tribunals. The use of the death penalty by federal courts, military courts, and military tribunals is governed by federal laws, executive orders, and the U.S. Supreme Court. Each state has the option of adopting the death penalty as a legal punishment for crime, and 38 states have done so. States that use the death penalty as a sanction must preserve the civil rights of the condemned prisoner as defined by the state and federal constitutions. Appeal to the U.S. Supreme Court has been a common strategy of abolitionists. Most appeals are based primarily on the Eighth Amendment, prohibiting cruel and unusual punishment, and the Fourteenth Amendment, providing for equality in justice. An early appeal to the U.S. Supreme Court based on the Eighth Amendment was ***Wilkerson* v. *Utah*** (1878).[51] Wilkerson appealed to the U.S. Supreme Court that his sentence of death by firing squad was cruel and unusual, but the Court upheld the constitutionality of the sentence.

The first execution by electrocution took place at Auburn Prison (New York) on August 6, 1890. William Kemmler was sentenced to be executed for murder by use of the newly invented electric chair. Kemmler appealed to the Court that electrocution was cruel and unusual punishment. The Court disagreed, however, and execution by electrocution was added as another method of carrying out the death sentence.[52] In 1947, the Court was asked to take up another gruesome debate concerning electrocution: What if the person survives the first attempt at electrocution? Willie Francis, a 15-year-old black male, was convicted of killing Andrew Thomas by shooting him five times. The apparent motive was robbery; Francis took the victim's watch and four dollars. When the state of Louisiana attempted to execute Francis, the electric chair failed to provide a fatal surge of electricity and Francis survived. He appealed a second attempt as cruel and unusual punishment, but the Court disagreed and he was electrocuted in the second attempt.[53]

The U.S. Supreme Court has also addressed other civil rights issues and the death penalty. For example, the Supreme Court has ruled that persons cannot be excluded from capital murder case juries because of their race. This situation most often arose when the defendant was black and the prosecutor excluded blacks from the jury by use of peremptory challenges. The Court ruled that exclusion of blacks from the jury when the defendant was black was racial discrimination. In 2002, the Supreme Court ruled that only juries, not judges, could decide sentences in capital cases. This ruling overturned state sentencing polices wherein the jury decided the guilt of the defendant but the judge decided whether the defendant would receive life in prison or the death penalty. The Court ruled that only the jury had the right to decide if the defendant should be executed. Also, in 2002, the Supreme Court barred the execution of the mentally retarded, and in 2005, barred the execution of juveniles.

Challenges to the Death Penalty

In 1972, the U.S. Supreme Court effectively banned the use of the death penalty. In ***Furman* v. *Georgia***[54] (1972), the Court issued its most significant ruling regarding the death penalty. Rather than focus on the physical and emotional pain of the prisoner as the grounds for regarding capital punishment as cruel and unusual, Furman's defense argued that the death penalty, as applied, was arbitrary and capricious. This argument presented evidence that a person convicted of a capital offense may or may not

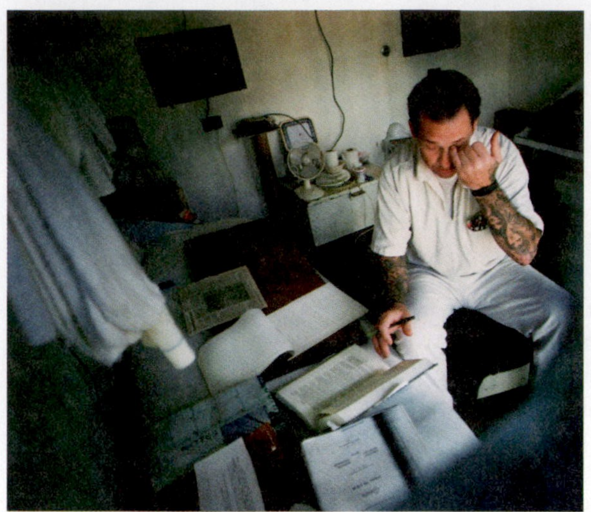

This death row inmate is awaiting execution by the state for a heinous crime. Why has capital punishment had such a long and troubled history in the United States? What legal issues relating to the U.S. Constitution have affected the use of the death penalty? What civil rights issues do abolitionists emphasize in their opposition to the death sentence? How have instances of official misconduct and error caused states to reexamine sentencing in capital cases?

be executed, because the law and the state courts did not systematically apply the death penalty. Who was executed and who was not appeared to be determined randomly. The only common element in executions was not the crime but the socioeconomic and racial characteristics of the offenders—poor and black.

The Supreme Court agreed and declared that all death penalty sentences were suspended until the state could prove that the death penalty was applied fairly. Despite this temporary ban and the Supreme Court's examination of the death penalty laws and practices of each state before the state could reinstitute the death penalty, emphasis on eliminating racial bias and providing uniformity to death penalty sentences continues to be a challenge. Table 9.2 provides demographic characteristics of prisoners under sentence of death in 2004. Note that nearly 42 percent of those under sentence of death at year end 2004 were black, 12 percent were Hispanic, and 2.2 percent were other races. Over 56 percent of those under sentence of death are nonwhite despite the fact that they are a minority of the population. Also, most prisoners who are under sentence of death have less than average education. The median education for those under sentence of death is eleventh grade. Over 52 percent of prisoners under sentence of death did not graduate from high school nor have a graduate equivalency degree (GED).

There are two important points to note about the *Furman* v. *Georgia* decision. First, it did not declare that the death penalty was unconstitutional, only that the manner in which it was applied was unconstitutional. Second, all states were required to submit proof to the U.S. Supreme Court that their use of the death sentence was fair, equitable, and proportional to the crime. In effect, this ruling voided all existing death penalties and death penalty laws. Every prisoner in every state under the sentence of death was given a reprieve. However, rather than require new trials for all prisoners sentenced to death, the Court required only that the death sentence be reexamined. As a result of this ruling, each state that wanted to keep the death penalty as a sanction had to submit legislation to the Court for approval prior to resuming the use of the death penalty. Some states attempted to satisfy the criteria by adopting mandatory death penalties for first-degree murder. The Court refused to allow this strategy, however, and required states to be more specific in defining the criteria to be used in applying the death penalty.[55] The Court further defined its criteria for proportionate punishment when it struck down Georgia's statute authorizing the death penalty for rape.[56] The Court ruled that the death penalty was grossly disproportionate to the crime. As a result, nearly all death penalties are for the crime of first-degree murder with aggravating circumstances.

In 1976, the U.S. Supreme Court issued another landmark decision in ***Gregg* v. *Georgia***[57] (1976), which required a **bifurcated trial** structure in which trials for capital offenses had to be conducted in two separate parts. In the first part of the trial, the jury determines the guilt of the defendant. In the second part of the trial, after the defendant has been convicted, additional evidence can be introduced relevant to the punishment appropriate for the crime. Prior to 2002, while it was common to allow the jury to exclude the death penalty as an appropriate sanction for the crime, in some states the judge determined if the defendant was sentenced to the death penalty.[58] In *Ring* v. *Arizona* (2002) the Supreme Court ruled that a jury, rather than a judge, must make a finding of "aggravating factors" where those factors underlie a judge's choice to impose the death penalty rather than a lesser punishment.[59] Figure 9.1 shows that the number of persons executed since the death penalty was reinstated peaked in 1999, and has steadily dropped since then. This decline is in large measure attributed to calls for reexamination of the death penalty, as many express doubts that death penalty verdicts are infallible.

bifurcated trial Two-part trial structure in which the jury first determines guilt or innocence and then considers new evidence relating to the appropriate punishment.

table 9.2

Demographic Characteristics of Prisoners under Sentence of Death, 2004

Characteristic	Prisoners under Sentence of Death, 2004		
	Year End	*Admissions*	*Removals*
Total Number under Sentence of Death	3,315	125	188
Gender			
Male	98.4%	96.0%	100%
Female	1.6	4.0	0
Race			
White	55.8%	60.0%	56.9%
Black	41.9	40.0	41.0
All other races*	2.2	0	2.1
Hispanic Origin			
Hispanic	12.6%	15.2%	8.5%
Non-Hispanic	87.4	84.8	91.5
Education			
8th grade or less	15.1%	14.0%	16.6%
9th–11th grade	37.2	44.1	37.3
High school graduate/GED	38.5	33.3	37.3
Any college	9.2	8.6	8.9
Median	11th	11th	11th
Marital Status			
Married	22.1%	15.0%	23.9%
Divorced/separated	20.6	22.0	22.8
Widowed	2.9	6.0	3.9
Never married	54.4	57.0	49.4

Note: Calculations are based on those cases for which data were reported. Detail may not add to total due to rounding. Missing data by category were as follows:

	Year end	Admissions	Removals
Hispanic origin	413	20	24
Education	481	32	19
Marital status	335	25	8

*At year end 2003, other races consisted of 29 American Indians, 35 Asians, and 14 self-identified Hispanics. During 2004, 2 Asians and 1 American Indian were removed; and 1 Asian was executed.

Source: Thomas P. Boncrar and Tracy Snell, *Capital Punishment, 2004* (Washington, DC: Bureau of Justice Statistics, 2005), p. 6.

figure 9.1

Executions by Year, 1976–2005

In 1972, the Supreme Court ruled unconstitutional the death penalty as then administered. In 1976, the Court upheld revised state capital punishment laws and the number of death sentences steadily increased. Since 1977, 1,000 people have been executed. Since 1998, more inmates have been removed from a sentence of death than inmates who have been sentenced to death. In recent years, both the number of sentences of death and the number of inmates executed has declined.

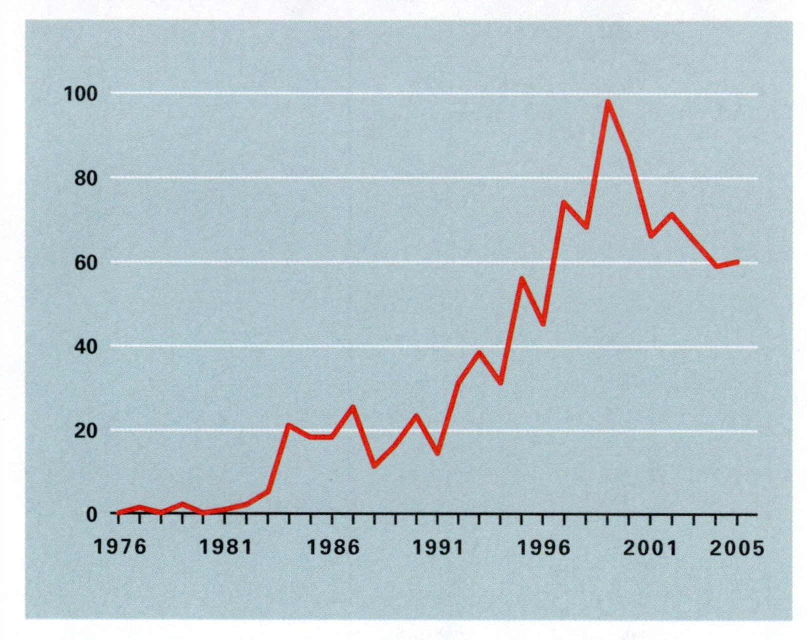

Source: Data from Death Penalty Information Center.

Reconsideration of the Death Penalty

When more death sentences were overturned in Illinois than were carried out, Illinois Governor George Ryan announced in early 2000 that no more prisoners would be executed in Illinois until there was a thorough investigation into the use of the death penalty.[60] The American Bar Association has called for a national moratorium on capital punishment, and 16 other states decided to examine their death penalty laws in 2000.[61] After years of debate, Florida ended the use of the electric chair in 2001.[62] In response to much criticism, Texas joined 15 other states and the federal government in passing a ban on executing mentally retarded murderers.[63] In December 2001, the Kansas Supreme Court ruled that the way the state's death penalty was handed down was unfair and must be changed. The Kansas Supreme Court said, "The provisions of the death penalty violated the federal constitutional provisions against cruel and unusual punishment and the guarantee of due process." This opinion voided the use of the death penalty until the state can rewrite the sentencing language.[64]

Innocent Convicted Perhaps the most significant argument behind the reexamination of the death penalty is the alarming number of persons who have been wrongfully prosecuted and convicted. The death penalty is final and cannot be reversed or corrected. An apology by the criminal justice system for the wrongful execution of a prisoner is insufficient and does not restore the injustice done nor heal the harm to innocent persons. For example, 60 years after Lena Baker, the only woman ever put to death in Georgia's electric chair, was executed, the state of Georgia announced it would posthumously pardon her. Baker, a 40-year-old African American, was put to death in 1945 for killing her employer, a white man named E. B. Knight. At her trial; she contended that he held her as a kind of sex slave and she shot him in self-defense as he was attacking her with a crowbar. An all-male, all-white jury convicted her of capital murder in a one-day trial, and she was executed in Georgia's electric chair less than a year later.[65] However, the Georgia Board of Pardons and Parole made it clear that the board did not find that Baker was not guilty of the crime, but it did find that the decision to deny her clemency in 1945 "was a grievous error, as this case called out for mercy."[66] Furthermore, the wrongful conviction and execution of these prisoners means that the guilty parties escaped the justice that was due them. One study suggests that as many as 23 innocent defendants were executed between 1900 and 1988.[67] The criminal justice system is approaching a near-crisis of credibility regarding the wrongful deaths of persons accused of crime. Partly as a result of DNA evidence, many convicted prisoners are being freed from prison and death row. The impact of DNA evidence combined with recent revelations of official misconduct and corruption by police and prosecutors and with allegations of racial discrimination has led many people to question the continued use of the death penalty as a fair and just punishment.

Official Misconduct and Error A study considering 125 cases published in the *North Carolina Law Review* found that the leading causes of wrongful convictions for murder were false confessions and perjury by co-defendants, informants, police officers, or forensic scientists.[68] The three groups of people most likely to provide false confessions are the mentally retarded, the mentally ill, and juveniles. Malcolm Rent Johnson was convicted of rape and murder in 1982. Johnson claimed he was innocent, but forensic evidence disputed his protests of innocence. Johnson was executed on January 6, 2000. An investigation a year later into the accuracy of the forensic chemist's testimony, which was instrumental in convicting Johnson, strongly suggests that she gave false testimony about the evidence. Also, the evidence suggests that there may be at least two other cases in which the results stated in the lab report and confirmed by the state's forensic chemist contradict independent expert reexamination of the actual physical evidence.[69]

Some prisoners appear to have been wrongfully convicted because they were framed by police and/or prosecutors. Ronald Jones, who said police had beaten a confession out of him, was exonerated of the charges of rape and murder.[70] After Rolando Cruz was convicted of murder and sentenced to death, a reexamination of his case resulted in his release. In addition, charges of conspiracy to obstruct justice and to commit official misconduct were filed against the police and district attorney lawyers who prosecuted Cruz.[71] The investigation into the Los Angeles Police Department Ramparts scandal uncovered evidence that police framed numerous innocent citizens and obtained convictions on the basis of false evidence given by police officers.[72] Walter McMillian was released in 1993 after six years on death row, but the sheriff he claims framed him for the murder that put him there has not been prosecuted.[73] McMillian is one of 30 persons freed from death row who gathered in Chicago in 1998 for the first National Conference on Wrongful Convictions and the Death Penalty.

Some prisoners ended up on death row due to inadequate legal representation at trial. Gary Wayne Drinkard was convicted and spent five years on Alabama's death row. Drinkard was released after it was determined that his defense failed to introduce critical evidence and witnesses that would have proven his innocence. As an example of the need for death penalty reform, Southern Center for Human Rights director Stephen B. Bright presented Gary Drinkard as a witness at hearings on the Innocent Protection Act of 2001. Bright told the committee, "We have been very fortunate that the innocence of some of those condemned to die in our courts has been discovered by sheer happenstance and good luck. . . . The major reason that innocent people are being sentenced to death is because the representation provided to the poor in capital cases is often a scandal." The committee heard testimony that defendants were given lawyers fresh from law school or who had never before tried a death penalty case.[74]

In December 2001, a judge overturned the murder conviction of a man imprisoned for 27 years for murder. The judge ruled that the trial "was plagued by multiple problems which, cumulatively, present the inescapable conclusion that he was denied a fair trial." Even the widow of the murdered victim concurred, saying, "There's so much evidence that it wasn't him, and it doesn't look like there was any that says it was him."[75] Other prisoners who were wrongfully convicted have been released after 13 years,[76] 17 years,[77] and 24 years[78] of wrongful incarceration.

DNA Evidence The advent of DNA testing in the late 1980s has had a tremendous impact on the criminal justice system. By 1997, the FBI crime lab's DNA analysis unit had exonerated about 3,000 suspects. Nearly one in four of the suspects were exonerated but had already been charged with a crime before lab results were returned.[91] There are continuous reports of inmates freed from wrongful incarceration due to DNA evidence demonstrating that they could not have been the offender.[92]

diversity in the system

And Justice for All

A report by the Leadership Conference on Civil Rights, a coalition of 180 civil rights groups, released in May 2000, concluded that blacks and Hispanics are treated more harshly than whites at every level of the criminal justice system, from investigation to sentencing.[79] A racially biased criminal justice system is deep-rooted in American history. In Virginia during the 1830s, there were only 5 capital crimes for whites but at least 70 for blacks.[80] Furthermore, there was a difference in severity of sentencing in which blacks could receive the death penalty for any offense for which a white would receive three or more years' imprisonment.[81]

In 1967, the President's Commission on Law Enforcement and Administration of Justice concluded, "The death penalty is most frequently imposed and carried out on the poor, the Negro, and the members of unpopular groups."[82] A 1973 study of offenders convicted of rape and sentenced to death shows that 13 percent of blacks convicted of rape were sentenced to death, but only 2 percent of whites convicted of rape were sentenced to death.[83] Blacks convicted of raping white women were more likely to be sentenced to death than blacks convicted of raping black women or white men convicted of raping either white women or black women.

Furman v. *Georgia* (1972) explicitly recognized the application of the death penalty as potentially arbitrary and capricious and sought to put an end to sentencing abuses once and for all. The effectiveness of ending racial discrimination in the use of the death penalty is debatable, however. A 1996 Kentucky study of death sentences between 1976 and 1991 found that blacks still had a higher probability of being sentenced to death than did homicide offenders of other races.[84]

The racial bias of the death penalty continues to be controversial. In December 2001, a federal judge overturned the death sentence of Mamia Abu-Jamal. Abu-Jamal had been convicted for the first-degree murder of Philadelphia police officer Daniel Faulkner in 1981. Abu-Jamal claimed he was a political prisoner and victim of racial discrimination.[85] In another case, a federal judge asked prosecutors to explain why they were seeking the death penalty against three alleged Latino drug gang members but not against mob boss Joseph Merlino and three other co-defendants. Lawyers for the defense argued, "No distinction other than the race of the defendants. . .satisfactorily (or rationally) explains the filing of a death notice in the case at hand . . . and the decision not to return it in the Merlino matter."[86]

Despite the decades of statistical data indicating that the death penalty is not color-blind, the U.S. Supreme Court has refused to admit statistical evidence of racial discrimination as a justification for reversing death sanctions against blacks. In ***McCleskey* v. *Kemp*** (1987), the Court said that statistical data alone do not provide the level of proof necessary to claim that a specific death penalty violates the Eighth or Fourteenth Amendment.[87] A convicted person can obtain relief from the death penalty under the claim of racial discrimination only if (1) the decision makers in the case acted with discriminatory intent, or (2) the legislature enacted or maintained the death penalty statute because of an anticipated racially discriminatory effect.[88]

The report of the Leadership Conference on Civil Rights does not blame overt racial bias for the disparities in the criminal justice system. The report, written by lawyers, says that "a self-fulfilling set of assumptions about the criminality of blacks and Hispanics influences the decisions of police, prosecutors and judges in a way that accounts for the gap."[89] The report argues that these assumptions about the criminality of blacks and Hispanics are far-reaching and are a prime cause for such police abuses as false arrest reports, lying under oath, and planting evidence against minority persons.[90]

What is the evidence for racial discrimination in American criminal justice? Should this be accepted as a self-fulfilling prophecy? Would statistics about racial discrimination in sentencing influence a jury to give a lighter sentence? Would a defense attorney use this argument to appeal a death sentence or try to win a stay of execution?

The reliability of DNA evidence and the release of wrongfully convicted prisoners, often after serving years on death row, proves the fallibility of the criminal justice system. Often, the inmates who were released had to fight to get the court to reconsider their cases. Courts have adopted rules limiting the amount of time that may pass before new evidence will be considered[93] or have refused to allow DNA testing of prisoners who have already been executed.[94] In many cases, the criminal justice system has refused to reopen cases where DNA testing could provide new evidence.[95]

A comprehensive study of 328 criminal cases over the last 15 years in which the convicted person was exonerated suggests that there are thousands of innocent people in prison today.[96] The study identified 199 murder exonerations, 73 of them in capital cases. Yet, only two states, Illinois and New York, give inmates the right to use the latest DNA testing. Appeals procedures make it difficult to introduce DNA evidence after conviction. In some cases involving prisoners who have demonstrated through post-trial DNA testing that the trial evidence does not support their guilt, prosecutors still have refused to accept that the convicted defendant may be innocent.[97] The law does not protect the right of convicted inmates to appeal based on DNA evidence, and some states routinely destroy rape kits and other evidence that could be used to establish the prisoners' innocence.[98]

▲ check your understanding **9.3** **What methods of execution are used in the United States? Who are the abolitionists, and what is their cause? Why are trials for capital offenses conducted in two parts? On what grounds has the death penalty been declared unconstitutional, and what are the present rulings? Why are states reconsidering the death penalty today?**

Intermediate Sanctions and Community Corrections

▼ the main idea **9.4** **Intermediate sanctions were developed as a means of transitioning inmates back into society.**

Visit the Vera Institute of Justice at www.vera.org.

Community-based treatment and prevention programs were virtually unknown before the late 1960s. One of the pioneers of community-based programs was the **Vera Institute of Justice** in New York,[99] which in the 1980s spearheaded the use of community-based programs to promote the successful transition of offenders from prison to society. These programs were described as intermediate punishments and later as **intermediate sanctions.**[100] Many early programs addressed pressing concerns of prison overcrowding and skyrocketing costs and were not built on research and experimentation relating to criminological or correctional theory. Instead, early programs grew out of the search for practical and expedient solutions to pressing problems.[101] Thus, there is little surprise that many of the programs have not lived up to expectations. Some have even resulted in substantial harm to the community. According to subsequent research, rehabilitation programs and new forms of supervision in the community have been faulted for not reducing recidivism or providing adequate safeguards for community protection.[102]

intermediate sanctions A term for punishments that restrict offenders' freedom without imprisoning them; community-based prevention and treatment programs to promote the successful transition of the offender from prison to the community.

Returning prisoners who cannot rejoin the community as law-abiding citizens can have a detrimental impact on the community's quality of life. The impact of this influence is made greater by the fact that prisoners tend to return to certain neighborhoods in a city or state rather than being distributed throughout the state. For example, 11 percent of the city blocks in Brooklyn are home to 50 percent of the people in that city who are on parole.[103] Also, approximately 1,800 out of 7,400 adult prisoners released each year in Kansas return to a handful of neighborhoods in Wichita.[104] The failures of the returning prisoners influence what are known as the "tipping points," beyond which communities can no longer favorably influence residents' behavior.[105] Sociologist Elijah Anderson argues that as more and more street-smart young offenders are released back into the community, they exert a strong influence on community disorganization, general demoralization, and higher unemployment. They can weaken the influence of family values and legitimate role models.[106] As the number of offenders in the community increases, their negative influence can reach the point where the community is powerless to exert stable positive influences over them. The structure of the community changes, disorder and incivilities increase, out-migration follows as desirable residents leave, and crime and violence increase.[107] This flood of returning offenders also increases the influence of gang activities in the community.[108]

Community-based intermediate sanctions are strategies aimed at stopping the revolving door of incarceration. The most commonly used programs are:

- Intensive probation supervision programs
- Shock probation and shock incarceration (boot camps)
- Home confinement and electronic monitoring
- Work and education release programs
- Halfway houses and day reporting centers

Intensive Probation Supervision

The three roles of the probation and parole officer include law enforcement officer, caseworker, and community resource broker. However, a factor contributing to the offender's failure is a lack of clarity or agreement about the purpose of probation and parole.[109] There also is a certain amount of conflict among these three roles. The probation and parole officer is faced with conflicting goals and objectives as he or she tries to both enforce obedience to the conditions of supervised release and at the same time act as counselor and encourager. Often, the role mix favors caseworker and community resource broker, and as a result, critics have charged that probation and parole officers have not been very good at ensuring that their clients fulfill the conditions of their treatment.[110] Sometimes, probationers or parolees simply abscond, and probation and parole officers are unable to locate them. In 1999, parole agents in California, for example, lost track of about one-fifth of the parolees they were assigned.[111] Nationwide, about 1 in 11 released offenders abscond.

Go to www.fcc.state.fl.us/fcc/reports/intermed/chz.htm/ to view an evaluation of Florida's intermediate sanctions programs.

In an effort to improve the effectiveness of probation and parole, to ensure community safety, and to promote greater success in reentry, probation and parole officers have adopted a new form of supervision of offenders, called **intensive probation supervision (IPS)**. In IPS, the probation and parole officer has a smaller caseload and more emphasis is placed on offender compliance with the conditions of supervision.[112] The offender may be supervised by a team of probation and parole officers. Instead of meeting briefly twice a month, the offender may be required to report daily as well as submit to on-site visits by the probation and parole officer. Intensive probation supervision can be used with either probationers or parolees. Its use dates back to the early 1950s when California Probation and Parole began to experiment with different-size probation caseloads.[113] Today, IPS programs have been implemented in every state, as well as in the federal system.

intensive probation supervision (IPS) Probation supervised by probation and parole officers with smaller caseloads, placing a greater emphasis on compliance with the conditions of supervision.

On reflection, even some probation and parole administrators admit that traditional programs may have been too lenient in enforcing the conditions of release.[114] Probation and parole officers often believed incorrectly that released offenders would assume responsibility for compliance with the conditions of release. Leniency also stemmed from impossible caseloads and insufficient funding. Despite increases in spending for corrections, few dollars have gone to rehabilitation or probation and parole. Most of the new dollars have gone primarily to building new prisons, maintaining facilities, and paying for the correctional staff to operate institutions.[115] However, only about 5 percent of inmates complete a reentry program prior to release.[116]

Accustomed to being told exactly what to do and how to do it, parolees often expect their supervision officers to relate to them in the same way.[117] They assume that the probation and parole officer will find a job for them, provide them with the guidance they need to find a treatment program, and in general direct their actions to ensure compliance with the conditions of their release.[118] In traditional probation and parole, these expectations are unrealistic, and released offenders often need much more direct supervision than can be given to them.

Intensive probation supervision was designed to provide that direct supervision. As a result, IPS is more punitive and controlling than regular probation and is much more intrusive into the offenders' lives. Probation and parole officers may awaken them during the night with phone calls to verify that they are at home. Supervisors may visit offenders at work sites and at home and routinely conduct searches for possible evidence that they are not in compliance with the conditions of release. Officers search for drugs, child pornography, excessive alcohol, firearms, or expensive possessions that would not be consistent with the offenders' legitimate incomes.

In 1982, Georgia implemented one of the earliest IPS programs. In the Georgia IPS program, probation and parole officers acted more like law enforcement officers than caseworkers.[119] Offenders were held to strict accountability for compliance with the conditions of probation and parole. For example, officers would stake out an offender's home at night to ensure that he or she was not violating curfew. Offenders were required to bring their paycheck stubs to the probation and parole officer to verify their continued employment and hours worked.

New Jersey has one of the most successful and prominent IPS programs, which is designed to handle about 500 offenders at a time. The program provides strict supervision and requires such strict compliance with the terms of release that few offenders have been able to avoid being returned to prison. More than 25 percent of participants have been expelled from the program for violations.[120] However, of offenders who successfully completed the program and have been in the community for 5 years, fewer than 10 percent have committed new, indictable offenses.[121]

Successful IPS programs can save states such as New Jersey millions of dollars over the cost of imprisonment. It is estimated that Georgia's IPS program has saved that state over $20 million.[122] Ohio has had success with its IPS program and has realized substantial savings.[123] Many other communities have adopted similar programs that have achieved goals of accountability, public safety, and cost savings.[124] Still, some probation and parole officers complain that IPS programs substantially change the relationship they have with their clients. Probation and parole officers who view their primary role as counselor and facilitator find that the role of law enforcement officer often runs counter to many of the characteristics that promote effective counseling. In addition, the effective implementation of IPS requires new working conditions and hours, including nights and weekends. As a result, not all probation and parole officers are comfortable with the call for more IPS programs.

Split Sentencing and Shock Probation

When first-time, nonviolent offenders, especially youthful offenders, are convicted of a crime, they assume that they will receive a suspended sentence. Most of the time, they are correct in this assumption. As a result, these offenders often view their first convictions as minor inconveniences, and their encounters with the criminal justice system do little to deter them from further criminal activities. What can a judge do when faced with a first-time offender who is wise to the ways of the system and is anticipating a suspended sentence? To deal with such an offender, judges have adopted the use of split sentencing and shock probation. Both sentences are similar in their goal of impressing on offenders the possible consequences of their behavior by exposing them to a brief period of imprisonment before probation.

In **split sentencing**, after a brief period of imprisonment, usually in a jail for as little as 30 days rather than in a long-term confinement facility, the offender is brought back to court. At that time, the judge then offers the option of probation. In split sentencing, to obtain his or her release from prison the offender does not have to apply for parole, have a parole hearing, or present a parole plan. Split sentencing is effective in two ways. First, the offender was not expecting any prison sentence. Thus, even a brief period of imprisonment comes as a shock. Second, the sentence exposes the offender to the realities of institutional confinement, but the offender is removed before he or she has time to adjust to institutionalization. The belief is that this "shock" will have a deterrent effect on future criminal behavior.

The sentence of shock probation is similar to split sentencing, but in **shock probation**, the offender is transferred to the custody of the state's department of corrections rather than the local jail and must apply for parole. Again, the offender serves only a brief period of incarceration before becoming eligible for parole. The major difference between split sentencing and shock probation is that in the former, the judge has control over the release of the offender, whereas in the latter, the offender's fate is in the hands of the Department of Corrections or the parole board. In shock probation, the offender must convince the paroling authorities that he or she should be released from prison. Technically, this is a form of parole because of the very brief period of incarceration, but it is commonly called shock probation rather than shock parole.

New Jersey's shock probation program is typical.[125] Offenders must serve a minimum of 30 days in prison before they can apply for release. They must submit a personal plan describing what they will do when released. This plan has many of the same requirements as a parole plan. It must detail the problems the inmate has that may jeopardize successful completion of parole, such as alcohol or drug abuse, lack of anger management, or lack of legitimate employment. The plan must detail the community resources the offender can use to help with these problems. The offender also must have a community sponsor and is required to reside with the sponsor on release. If the paroling authority is satisfied with the offender's personal plan, he or she will be granted a 90-day trial release period. If the offender is successful in complying with the conditions of the release plan during this 90-day period, he or she is granted conditional early release, or shock probation.[126]

Go to www.doc.state.ok.us/docs/OCJRC/OCJRC95/950725d.htm to view an evaluation of Oklahoma's shock incarceration program.

split sentencing After a brief period of imprisonment, the judge brings the offender back to court and offers the option of probation.

shock probation Sentence for a first-time, nonviolent offender who was not expecting a sentence, intended to impress on the offender the possible consequences of his or her behavior by exposure to a brief period of imprisonment before probation.

shock incarceration Programs (boot camps) that adapt military-style physical fitness and discipline training to the correctional environment.

Shock Incarceration: Boot Camps

Shock incarceration programs are commonly called "boot camps" because they are modeled after military-style, entry-level training programs. Boot camps are designed to provide alternative sentencing for young, nonviolent offenders. Offenders who participate in boot camps are offered a reduced sentence followed by parole if they successfully complete the program.[127] If they do not complete the program, they are returned to the regular prison population. Although Ohio passed the first shock incarceration law in 1965, the practice did not become common until after 1980.[128] The first shock incarceration programs of nationwide significance began operating in 1983 in Oklahoma and Georgia.[129]

Shock incarceration programs adapt military-style physical fitness and discipline training to the correctional environment, as in basic training in military boot camps. Inmates participate in drill and ceremony, physical training, work (usually hard manual labor), and education. Inmates are organized into platoons of 50 to 60 inmates and may be required to wear military-style clothing. Correctional leaders are called drill sergeants, and inmates are expected to demonstrate unquestioning obedience to their orders. Inmates in boot camps frequently must perform community service work. Inmates of the

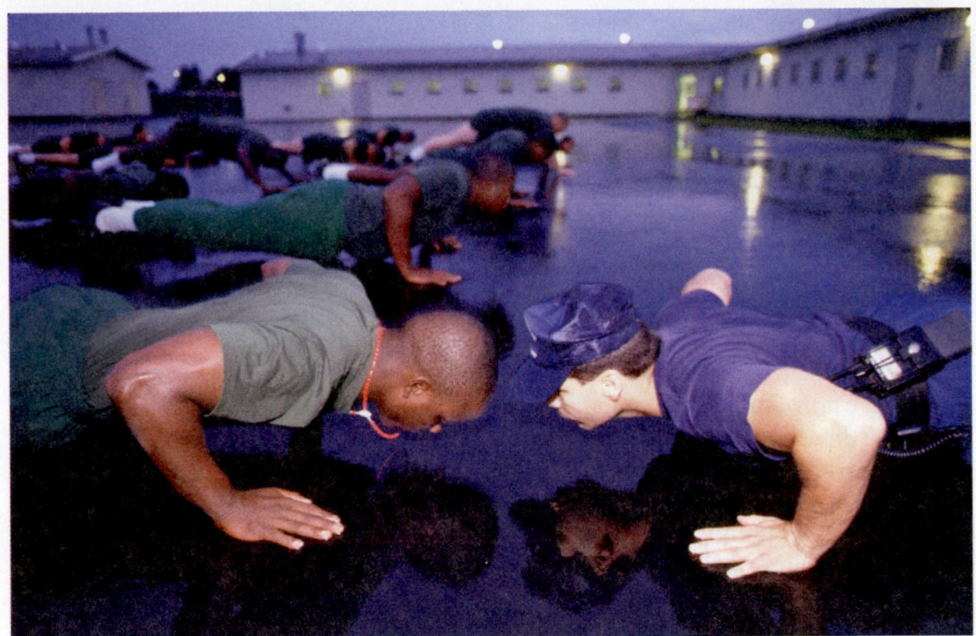

Inmates in a typical military-style boot camp must obey strict rules, work hard, and perform extensive physical exercises. The purpose of this routine is to develop self-confidence and discipline. It is hoped that these traits will keep the offender from reoffending upon release. Do you think military-style boot camps are effective in rehabilitating offenders?

New York shock incarceration programs, for example, help cut firebreaks, maintain public-use areas, help in the aftermath of emergencies such as forest fires and tornadoes, and assist local municipalities and community groups.[130] Shock incarceration programs are rigorous, and a substantial number of inmates do not complete them and are returned to the regular prison population.[131]

Effectiveness of Boot Camps Participation in boot camps is voluntary. The inducement to participate in shock incarceration programs is the opportunity for early parole. Inmates who participate in boot camps serve substantially shorter prison time. A typical boot camp may only be six months in length. One of the main purposes of brief, intensive, shock incarceration programs is to reduce the need for prison bedspace by permitting shorter terms of imprisonment. Although boot camps may be more expensive to operate on a per-day, per-inmate basis, they save money in the long run, because inmates serve less time in a boot camp than they would in a regular prison.[132] The return-to-prison rate for offenders successfully completing adult boot camps is comparable to that of parolees who did not participate in or complete the program.[133] Supporters of the program argue that if the return-to-prison rate for offenders is comparable, boot camps pose no increased risk to the community, cost less than prison, and reduce the need to build more prisons, then they are indeed effective alternatives to prison.[134]

In shock incarceration, the inmate is released to the community well before the normal parole date. The underlying premise is that boot camps promote public safety by building character, instilling responsibility, and promoting a positive self-image so that nonviolent offenders can return to society as law-abiding citizens.[135] There is little direct evidence to support this claim, but boot camps remain popular with the public because they are perceived as being tough on crime.[136] Many state departments of corrections recognize the lack of research underlying the use of boot camps and describe their programs as "experiments."[137]

Home Confinement and Electronic Monitoring

home confinement A court-imposed sentence requiring offenders to remain confined in their own residences.

Home confinement is a sentence imposed by the court in which offenders are legally ordered to remain confined in their own residences.[138] Similar to parents telling their teenager that he or she is "grounded" as punishment for some misdeed, home confinement severely restricts the offender's mobility. Schedules are worked out that allow the offender to leave his or her home for work, medical appointments and services, court-ordered treatment or community service, grocery shopping, and other necessary responsibilities. Offenders cannot leave home for entertainment, to visit friends or family, to take vacations, or for any other purpose not explicitly authorized by the court. Rehabilitation was not one of the goals of early home confinement programs. Early home confinement programs were an intermediate sanction or punishment adopted primarily to reduce prison populations, reduce costs, and increase control of offenders in the community.[139]

The sentence of home confinement is a kind of probation or suspended sentence that carries greater restrictions on the freedom of the offender in the community. Offenders must live in their own home or that of a sponsor (usually a relative) and must pay all of their housing costs. Thus, a prerequisite for home confinement is to have a place to live and a job or other financial resources for self-support. A difficulty of early home confinement programs was ensuring that the offender abided by the restrictions of his or her release and did not leave the home. Probation officers used a combination of phone calls and random home visits or stakeouts to verify that the offender was at home. These practices were labor intensive, however, and ineffective due to the shortage of probation officers to conduct a sufficient number of random home visits to ensure compliance.

The breakthrough in home confinement programs came with the use of electronic monitoring to ensure the offender's compliance. **Electronic monitoring** uses signaling technology to achieve a greater degree of certainty in compliance and at a fraction of the cost of using probation officers for this purpose. The first formal electronic monitoring program was implemented in 1983 in Albuquerque, New Mexico, when district court judge Jack Love, reputedly inspired by a "Spiderman" comic strip, placed a probation violator on electronic monitoring.[140]

Since 1983, the use of electronic monitoring has expanded rapidly. It has been adopted in all 50 states by local, state, and federal correctional agencies.[141] In 1987, only 826 offenders were monitored electronically. This number expanded to 6,500 in 1989, and by 1995, 21,275 offenders were monitored electronically.[142] In 1997, on any given day, about 5,000 adults were on probation under electronic monitoring.[143] Florida's Community Control Program has one of the most ambitious home confinement and electronic monitoring programs in the United States.[144] Spurred in part by an explosive rise in the need for prison bedspace, Florida's Correctional Reform Act of 1983 authorized the use of electronically monitored house arrest as a means to reduce the prison population.

Technological Advances in Electronic Monitoring In the past two decades, there have been significant changes in the technology for monitoring offenders sentenced to home confinement.[145] Early systems were passive-programmed contact systems, which used a computer programmed to make random calls to the offender at times when he or she was supposed to be home. A verification unit was attached to the offender, usually at the ankle or wrist, and when the computer called the home, the offender would have to insert the verification unit in a device attached to the telephone. The verification unit would then send a signal to the computer confirming that the inmate, or at least the inmate's verification unit, was at home. The inmate cannot simply remove the verification unit and leave it with someone else to answer the computer's phone calls. When the inmate reports for face-to-face contacts with his or her probation officer, the unit is examined to ensure it has not been tampered with or removed. A variation on this technology is to use voice identification instead of a verification unit. When the computer calls the offender's home, the offender repeats a phrase for identification. The computer is programmed with the offender's voice print and can match the voice on the phone with the voice print.

electronic monitoring An approach in home confinement programs that assures compliance through electronic means.

Martha Stewart was sentenced to house arrest and had to wear an electronic monitoring device that uses continuous signaling technology. The signaling device can allow her parole officer to verify that she does not leave her home unless authorized. Electronic monitoring of offenders released on probation or parole has become an increasingly popular option.

The next generation of electronic monitoring systems used continuous signaling systems. The advantage of continuous signaling systems is that they monitor the offender's movements 100 percent of the time. The older passive-programmed contact systems have loopholes in that offenders willing to risk it could slip out of the house as long as they did not miss one of the programmed contacts. With continuous signaling technology, in contrast, the offender wore a receiver-transmitter device. Rather than the computer randomly calling the offender's home, a receiver-dialer device attached to the offender's phone constantly sent out a signal when the offender was supposed to be at home. The transmitter-receiver device worn by the offender received this signal and sent a reply verifying his or her presence. The device was programmable and could be adjusted by the probation officer when the offender's schedule changed. Also, the device could be programmed by shaping the signal coverage area to allow the offender to have access to the yard. If there was an interruption in the signal between the receiver-dialer and the inmate's device, the unit was programmed to call the computer and alert the system to a potential violation.

With both the passive-technology-programmed reporting devices and the continuous signaling technology devices, the probation officer needs to confirm that an actual violation has occurred. When the offender fails to answer the telephone or when there is a break in the continuous signal during times when the offender is supposed to be home, a probation officer must contact the offender to confirm the violation.

The third generation of electronic monitoring devices began to emerge in 1997. They incorporated the advantages of global positioning system (GPS) technology, involving the use of satellites, not only to monitor the offender at home, but to have the ability to track every movement of the offender in real time.[146] This technology allows the system to confirm that the offender not only is at home when he or she is supposed to be but also is not violating restraining orders, visiting places where drugs are known to be sold or used, and frequenting off-limits places such as schools or playgrounds. Another advancement in electronic monitoring is the ability to monitor all communications by the offender on the Internet.[147] This ability is especially useful for monitoring sex offenders to ensure that they do not use the Internet for the purposes of contacting and enticing potential victims.

Evaluation and Critique of Electronic Monitoring Counting the number of people on electronic monitoring as potential prison inmates, there is no doubt that home confinement and electronic monitoring have saved the states money, compared with the costs of incarceration. There are significant start-up costs for the equipment purchases required to use home confinement and electronic monitoring, but even after factoring in these costs, most jurisdictions report that the program saves money over prison confinement.[148] Critics claim that this is a false savings, because offenders selected for release subject to home confinement and electronic monitoring are those who probably would have been given a suspended sentence.[149] Another criticism is that the system discriminates against the homeless and the unemployed. These offenders usually are excluded from home confinement programs because of their lack of a place to live, a telephone, and means of support.

A potentially serious criticism of electronic monitoring is that it may interfere with First Amendment and Fourth Amendment rights of offenders and of others with whom offenders come into contact.[150] New GPS tracking technologies combined with other emerging technologies possibly could identify people the offender contacts or could listen in on conversations. At what point will technological advances overintrude on people's privacy and other constitutional rights?

▲ check your understanding **9.4 What are the five most common forms of community-based intermediate sanctions, and how effective is each? What is intensive probation supervision? What are the differences between shock probation and shock incarceration? What issues surround the use of boot camps? How can technology fulfill some of the roles of probation and parole officers?**

Reentry Programs: Preparing Offenders to Take Responsibility

▼ the main idea **9.5 Prison programs in which inmates participate prior to release can help to ease their transition to life in society as law-abiding citizens.**

Go to www.wi-doc.com/wccs.htm for information about Wisconsin's Department of Corrections work release programs.

In addition to the intermediate sanctions of IPS, shock probation, shock incarceration, home confinement, and electronic monitoring, there is a need for treatment programs that focus on preparing inmates for reentry rather than punishing them.[151] Many states and the federal correctional system have implemented programs for preparing returning inmates through treatment and therapeutic programs such as work release, education release, halfway houses, day reporting centers, and drug treatment programs. For example, Ohio has taken initiative to move corrections "toward a new vision of the offender reentry dialogue,"[152] and Michigan has created the Office of Community Corrections with the specific purpose of improving rehabilitative services and strengthening offender accountability.[153]

The federal system has recognized the importance of reentry programs. U.S. Code Title 18, Section 3624 requires that authorities should "to the extent practicable, assure that a prisoner serving a term of imprisonment spends a reasonable part" of the last six months or 10 percent of his or her sentence "under conditions that will afford the prisoner a reasonable opportunity to adjust to and prepare for the prisoner's reentry into the community."[154] The **Reentry Partnership Initiative** is a federal effort to help jurisdictions meet the challenges of offenders returning to the community. The goal is "to improve the risk management of released offenders by enhancing surveillance and monitoring, strengthening individual and community support systems, and repairing the harm done to victims."[155] Other federal legislation recognizes the need for effective community-based reentry programs for adults and juveniles that focus on treatment as well as punishment. Programs organized with the assistance of the **Serious and Violent Offender Reentry Initiative** divide reentry programs into three phases: (1) Protect and Prepare, (2) Control and Restore, and (3) Sustain and Support.[156]

In 2004, the Department of Justice announced that it was committing $6.7 million to the Serious and Violent Offender Reentry Initiative in the effort to improve public safety by addressing the successful reintegration of high-risk, serious offenders returning to their communities from imprisonment. Since 2002, the initiative estimates that more than $120 million has been committed to designing and carrying out adult and juvenile reentry strategies. Other government-sponsored reentry initiatives include the Council of State Governments Reentry and the federal Bureau of Prisons National Institute of Corrections.

A new strategy to promote successful reentry has been the use of **faith-based programs.** In his 2004 State of the Union address, President Bush proposed a $300 million initiative for reentry programs to be conducted by religious-based groups. The faith-based rehabilitation movement extends beyond community services and reaches into the prisons. Many prisons are allowing faith-based groups to provide programs such as vocational classes combined with religious instruction inside the prisons in an effort to prepare the offender for release. The American Civil Liberties Union opposes faith-based groups receiving government money for their programs, claiming it is a violation of the separation of church and state. Others criticize faith-based programs because the programs often require inmates to participate in Bible studies and attend church services. To avoid these criticisms, some faith-based programs operate without receiving government funding. It is too soon to evaluate the effect of faith-based programs on successful reentry. One study of the faith-based rehabilitation group InnerChange suggested that offenders who participated in the program were 50 percent less likely to be arrested and 60 percent less likely to be reincarcerated than those who did not participate.[157]

A significant appeal of reentry programs is that they cost much less than imprisonment. Whereas prison costs can average about $25,000 a year, reentry programs cost about $3,000 annually per inmate. Also, in addition to being cheaper, reentry programs allow states and the federal government to focus on removing the obstacles that keep the recidivism rates high. With two out of three adult offenders returning to prison within three years, there is a lot of room for improvement. Some legislators have championed reentry programs as significant breakthroughs that would break the cycle of offending. In 2004, Senator Sam Brownback (R-KS) expressed his belief that reentry programs could reduce recidivism to 20 percent.[158]

The most often used reentry programs are work release, education release, halfway houses, day reporting centers, and drug treatment programs.

Work Release

How can state and federal programs help to sustain and support inmates in the community? Consider Samson Aguiar, who found his first job in prison working for Oahu's Community Correctional Center for 50 cents an hour plus lunch by grooming and repairing hiking trails along the Manoa Cliff Trail.[159] Unfortunately, despite his desire to work, it may be difficult for Aguiar to find employment once he leaves prison. Former inmates have more difficulty than other people in finding and keeping a job.[160]

Work release programs were first initiated under Wisconsin's Huber Law in 1913 but did not become commonplace until the latter half of the twentieth century.[161] Wisconsin's **Huber Law** permitted county correctional facilities to release misdemeanants for paid work in the community. In 1965, the **Prisoner Rehabilitation Act of 1965** authorized work release for inmates in federal institutions. By 1975, all 50 states and the federal system had some form of work release operating.[162]

Obstacles to Employment

The most serious obstacles facing offenders looking for jobs are (1) public prejudice against hiring ex-offenders, (2) lack of knowledge of how to find jobs, and (3) lack of the kinds of documentation required by employers. Public prejudice against hiring ex-offenders is strong. In a survey, 65 percent of all employers said they would not knowingly hire an ex-offender, regardless of the offense, and 30 to 40 percent said they check for criminal records when they hire employees.[163] Furthermore, ex-offenders are barred from many occupations that require occupational licenses, including law, real estate, medicine, nursing, physical therapy, dentistry, engineering, pharmacy, and education.[164] Often, employers refuse to hire offenders for fear of potential lawsuits through liability for negligent hiring should the offender commit a crime or harm the employers' customers.[165] These fears by employers are not groundless. For example, a family film company that hired inmates as telemarketers was

faith-based programs Programs provided by religious-based and church-affiliated groups. Their role in rehabilitation is controversial because they receive federal money and may combine religious instruction with rehabilitation.

work release Program allowing facilities to release inmates for paid work in the community.

sued by a woman who claimed a prisoner misused company information by sending her 14-year-old daughter a personal letter.[166] A company that hired a woman who, unknown to them, had been convicted of embezzlement found that after six years with the company she allegedly embezzled more than $5 million from the organization.[167]

Ex-offenders often lack the basic knowledge to conduct a successful job search. Many do not know how to fill out employment applications, how to conduct themselves during interviews, how to dress for job interviews, or how to present the attitude of self-confidence that employers want in their employees. Frequently, offenders have had little experience or success in employment prior to prison. Thus, they do not have basic life skills related to job hunting that are often taken for granted by the general population. Furthermore, offenders need to unlearn passive behavior patterns that work well in prison but are a liability in searching for and retaining a job.[168] In prison, offenders become accustomed to being told what to do, when to do it, and how to do it. Obedience to the rules is one of the most important values in prison. When asked to show initiative, demonstrate decision-making skills, and be innovative, inmates often do not have these abilities.[169]

A unique problem that offenders have in getting employment is lack of proper identification (ID). Most people leave prison without a driver's license, passport, social security card, birth certificate, or other photo ID. Many are clueless as to how to obtain the identification they need.[170] Offenders find that even if they are successful in obtaining employment, they may lose their jobs because they cannot supply their employers with proof of identify and citizenship, as required by law.[171]

Work Release Strategies Removing the obstacles to employment requires both community-based and in-prison programs. For example, Texas's Project RIO (Re-Integration of Offenders) provides in-prison vocational training programs to prepare inmates for the workforce and helps them obtain the IDs and documentation needed in the outside world, such as their birth certificate, social security identification, and state photo ID. Authorities hold the documentation for the prisoner and then forward it to the employer or agency as needed after the inmate is released.[172] New York provides inmates with a work release furlough for six weeks up to three months to allow them to find employment.

Recognizing the difficulty that ex-offenders face in finding employment, several states have laws that limit when and to what extent an employer may consider an applicant's criminal record. These laws make it illegal for an employer to discriminate against an ex-offender unless his or her conviction record is related to the duties of the job. Some states allow ex-offenders to seal or expunge their criminal records. Some states offer certificates of rehabilitation to ex-offenders who either have minimal criminal histories or have remained out of the criminal justice system for specified periods of time.[173] Title VII of the Federal Civil Rights Act of 1964 offers some protection against job discrimination against ex-offenders. The Equal Employment Opportunity Commission has determined that policies that exclude individuals from employment on the basis of their arrest and conviction records may violate Title VII, because such policies disproportionately exclude minorities.[174]

Many employers complain, however, that laws banning employers from considering a job applicant's criminal record is not "business-friendly." They claim that such laws "ignore the liability employers face regarding the actions of their workers. Employers get squeezed in the middle. If you don't hire, you get sued, but if you do hire and something happens to customers or other workers, you get sued."[175] To induce employers to hire ex-offenders, the federal government has made tax credits available to employers who do so and has established insurance programs to reduce the employer's exposure to liability for possible misdeeds by inmates.[176]

Some state correctional agencies are becoming more proactive in helping inmates find jobs after release by sponsoring job fairs. Some job fairs are held within the correctional institutions. Prison officials help the inmates prepare résumés and train them in job interview skills. Ohio's Department of Rehabilitation and Correction has sponsored more than 140 job fairs and even holds teleconferences for companies that cannot send representatives.[177] Other correctional agencies have entered into joint ventures with private businesses to offer inmates the chance to work for private companies while in prison and then to transition to civilian employment with the company when they are released from prison.[178] Such partnerships are made possible by changes in federal and state laws that formerly prevented inmates from working in private-sector prison jobs. In 1979, Congress enacted Public Law 96-157 (18 U.S.C. 176(c) and 41 U.S.C. 35), which created the **Private Sector/Prison Industry Enhancement Certification Program.** This program authorizes correctional agencies to engage in the interstate shipment of prison-made goods for private businesses, providing certain conditions are met.[179] The law allows private companies to operate businesses from within the prison and to use inmate labor. The law requires that inmates must be paid at a rate not less than the rate paid for work of a similar nature in the locality in which the work takes place. Prison officials allow the inmates to send some of the money to support their families and to keep a small portion for themselves, and the rest is retained for them until their release. These partnerships help reduce the burden on the state of supporting the inmates' families, provide a source of labor for the businesses, and help the inmates make successful transitions from prison to work after release.

Education Release

Education is recognized as a factor that can make an important difference in the successful transition of offenders from correctional systems back to their communities.[180] Education can make a tremendous difference for offenders, because many are high school dropouts and the work force has few positions for high school dropouts that pay a living wage. It costs an estimated minimum of $22,000 to $60,000 per year to incarcerate an offender, which is much more than the average cost for one year of college or vocational training.[181] Correctional officials have recognized the importance of education, and while in prison it is usually mandatory that inmates without a high school education be given the opportunity to earn a high school equivalency or general education development (GED) degree.

Some correctional institutions bring educational programs into the institution so inmates can further their education while in prison. Others provide education release opportunities for inmates both while in prison and as part of their parole plan. The typical education release program gives inmates the opportunity to attend college or university classes but requires them to return to the institution each day. When educational release is a part of an inmate's parole plan, the inmate is required to attend a vocational training program, community college, or university rather than go to full-time employment. However, inmates must have the means to support themselves and pay for their schooling.

Research has shown that offenders who participate in education programs are less likely to commit new crimes than are inmates who do not participate in such programs.[182] One study tracked 2,305 inmates over three years at the Bedford Hills Correctional Facility, a maximum-security prison for women in New York that has an educational program sponsored by a consortium of private colleges. The study found that only 7.7 percent of the inmates who had taken college courses while incarcerated committed new crimes and were returned to prison after their release, whereas 29.9 percent of the inmates who did not take courses were jailed again.[183]

However, despite the demonstrated benefits of education, similar to employers who are prejudiced against hiring released prisoners, colleges can be prejudiced against admitting ex-offenders—even those who have served their time. For example, in 2005, the University of Alaska refused to admit Michael Purcell to its social work program. Purcell served 20 years for killing a convenience-store clerk when he was 16 years old. He was released on parole in September 2004. Upon his release on parole, he entered a

Organized crime boss John A. Gotti, Jr. was denied the opportunity to participate in early release programs from prisons. Prison officials felt that despite his record of good behavior in prison and meeting the minimum requirements for early release, his release could pose a danger to the community. What type of offenders should be denied early release or community corrections options?

halfway house and took classes at the University of Alaska. However, when he applied for admission to the social work degree program he was denied admission. In rejecting Purcell's application, the social work department cited its policy that they considered persons with criminal records unfit for social work practice.[184] The University of Alaska is not the only university that has such policies discriminating against ex-felons.

Halfway Houses

Halfway houses are transition programs that allow inmates to move from prison to the community in steps rather than all at once by simply opening the prison doors and having them enter the community directly. The first halfway houses in the United States were opened in the mid-1800s, but their use did not become commonplace until the 1950s.[185] The use of halfway houses was encouraged because such a program provided what was considered an essential transition, whereby an inmate could gradually adjust to freedom by a short stay, usually about six months, in a halfway house at the end of his or her sentence.[186]

Today, most halfway houses are nonprofit foundations.[187] The state departments of corrections contract with these nonprofit organizations to provide a gradual transition for the offender from an environment that maintains total control to one that permits partial control before the offender is released into the community. The typical halfway house provides services for 6 to 30 inmates in a minimum-security facility, often a residential home that has been converted into a halfway house. Inmates who do not follow the rules or who "walk away" from the halfway house are returned to prison or charged with the felony offense of escape. The combination of nearing the end of their sentence and risking return to prison with possible added time is an effective deterrent for most participants.

Halfway houses have full-time staff members who provide for the custody and treatment of the offenders. Offenders observe strict curfews, participate in treatment programs conducted by the house staff or community-based agencies, and seek employment or enroll in vocational training or college classes. The program allows a transition period from prison to freedom in that the offender is closely supervised but is given limited freedom within the community and is required to take responsibility for preparing for his or her successful reentry into the community. During the offender's stay in the halfway house, he or she does not have to report to a probation officer, as the house staff perform this function. Usually, the offender is released from the halfway house into the community under the supervision of a parole officer. Halfway houses are excellent opportunities for inmates seeking parole who do not have family or sponsors in the community to help them when they leave prison. Without halfway houses, many of these inmates would not be able to prepare an acceptable parole plan.

The most significant obstacle to halfway houses is the strong community opposition to having such a facility located in one's neighborhood. As mentioned previously, even those who support the concept of halfway houses suffer from NIMBY—Not in My Back Yard. Who wants to live next to a halfway house? Who wants to raise a family, have children play in the yard and neighborhood parks on the same block as a halfway house? Locating communities that are close to employment opportunities and public transportation, essential characteristics for a successful halfway house program, that are willing to allow halfway houses operate in the community is a difficult challenge.

halfway houses Transition programs that allow inmates to move from prison to the community in steps.

day reporting centers An intermediate sanction to provide a gradual adjustment to reentry under closely supervised conditions.

Day Reporting Centers

Day reporting centers are relatively new reentry programs dating to the early 1970s.[188] **Day reporting centers** provide for release from prison that is closely supervised by the state's department of corrections. Inmates live at home rather than being imprisoned or housed in a privately managed halfway house. As the name suggests, inmates report to supervisory centers on a daily basis. Inmates may be sentenced to day reporting cen-

careers in the system

Correctional Case Manager

The author interviewed Jodie Maesaka-Hirata to get her opinion on what it is like to work with inmates to prepare them to reenter society from correctional institutions. Jodie Maesaka-Hirata is a Social Worker V for the Department of Corrections in the state of Hawaii and has worked with inmates and offenders since 1989. She started her career as a Social Worker II, working as a case manager inside Halawa Prison. She says that a big difference between the position of correctional officer and that of case manager is that inmates do not perceive case managers as authority figures. As a case manager, Maesaka-Hirata provides long-term and crisis counseling to inmates, writes evaluations for parole reports, makes housing classifications, and works with the inmates to help them adjust to prison life. During her career, she has worked at many different facilities in many different capacities.

Maesaka-Hirata has worked with both male and female inmates and notes that she has found male inmates to be less verbal, requiring her to be diligent in watching for signs of mood changes, and that they are more likely to exploit kindnesses. She finds that female offenders tend to play on emotions and have more complex social and emotional needs. Women offenders usually are single mothers; financially unstable; victims of physical, sexual, and psychological abuse; ethnic minorities; nonviolent; substance dependent; and homeless. The female offender usually is the primary caretaker for the family, and in Hawaii families usually are multigenerational.

From 1998 to 2000, Maesaka-Hirata worked with female offenders in the SISTERS program. This grant-funded program was a cooperative effort with the Department of Criminology and Criminal Justice at Chaminade University of Honolulu to help prepare female offenders for successful reentry into the community. Maesaka-Hirata teamed with professors from Chaminade to develop and implement a curriculum for female offenders, using volunteers from the university and community. SISTERS focused on teaching basic life skills and daily living skills, such as budgeting, banking, writing checks, planning menus, and buying groceries. Many inmates also were not knowledgeable about basic hygiene, physical health, and family planning. In addition, the program included topics such as self-confidence, interviewing for jobs, résumé writing, how to live with AIDS and HIV, and decision-making skills.

According to Maesaka-Hirata, there is a great need for transition programs, and the most pressing need is for programs that emphasize daily life skills and cognitive changes. The key to successful transition programs is working with the public and preparing the community, because transition programs need community support to be successful. They need the support of neighborhood boards, state politicians, human services agencies, and drug treatment programs.

Correctional case managers typically learn their jobs by shadowing another case manager for a few weeks in on-the-job training. Case managers also receive training on policy and procedures and day-to-day operational skills. New caseworkers may be required to take a medical and psychological examination, have a drug-screening test, and undergo a criminal background check. There is no physical agility testing, but case managers usually must have a minimum of a bachelor's degree, and a master's degree is preferred. Some states require some additional postgraduate coursework to qualify for the position.

Maesaka-Hirata says that working with inmates is not for everyone. There is a certain degree of danger in working with inmates, especially inside the prison and when conducting home visits. Yet, she says that corrections has been a rewarding career: interesting, diverse, and intense. There are good opportunities for upward mobility, and the field gives you the chance to make a positive difference in people's lives.

What risks and rewards are involved in correctional case management? How is the work of a correctional case manager similar to and different from that of a correctional officer or a probation and parole officer?

ters rather than prison or may be released from prison to day reporting centers during the last months of their sentence. Inmates report to and leave from the center during the day to work, to participate in treatment programs, to attend classes or training programs, or to hunt for employment. Day reporting centers maintain daily schedules that must accurately account for inmates' time while in the community. Participants must submit to certain conditions similar to those in a parole plan, such as random drug tests.

correctional case managers Social work caseworkers who specialize in helping offenders adjust to life in prison, release from prison, and successful reentry into the community.

Day reporting centers provide close monitoring of offenders in the community. Inmates must report back to the day reporting center at predetermined times, depending on their schedules, which are tracked by computer. Participants who go to their own homes are required to report to the day reporting center each morning prior to starting their day. Some programs provide residential facilities, in which inmates participate in treatment and counseling programs during the evenings. Inmates usually can earn weekend furloughs, allowing them to leave the facility on a Friday night and return by Sunday evening.

The purpose of the day reporting center is to act as an intermediate sanction for some inmates and to permit a gradual adjustment to reentry for others. Day reporting centers allow departments of corrections to reduce the need for prison bedspace by placing low-security-risk inmates in day reporting centers.[189] For inmates transitioning from prison, day reporting centers allow them the opportunity to reenter the community under closely monitored conditions. Because day reporting centers are not widely used, extensive data are not available to judge their effectiveness. However, data from the Metropolitan Day Reporting Center in Boston, Massachusetts, indicate that inmates who enter the community from the day reporting center rather than directly from jail are less likely to commit new crimes and are more likely to be employed. Furthermore, only about 1 percent of inmates committed a crime while they were in the program.[190]

▲ check your understanding 9.5 **What programs in prisons and in communities are designed to help inmates transition to life in society? What obstacles to employment do ex-offenders face? What benefits do halfway houses offer to offenders?**

conclusion:

A Long Way to Go

What is the purpose of sentencing? Is it to punish the offender, to rehabilitate the offender, or to protect the community? The National Institute of Justice sponsored research that examined the crime-control effects of sentences over a 20-year period, based on 962 felony offenders sentenced in 1976 or 1977 in Essex County, New Jersey.[191] The purpose of this longitudinal study was to examine the effects of the different sanctions on the offenders' subsequent criminal careers. The study concluded that the main sentencing choices available to the judges had little effect on crime-control aims. Specifically, the study concluded that:[192]

- Except for the effect of incapacitation, whether the offender was sentenced to confinement made no difference in the rate of reoffending.
- Where the offender was confined made little difference—except for the unfavorable effect of placement in a youth facility.
- The length of the maximum sentence made no difference.
- The length of time actually confined made a slight difference.
- When jail was imposed along with probation, it made no difference.
- Fines or restitution made no difference.

The overall conclusion of the study was that empirical data suggested that there was little difference in sentences from a crime-control perspective.[193] Such data do not provide a happy ending to the discussion on sentencing. New and innovative sentencing strategies are constantly being tried. Laws defining the punishment for crimes and sentencing guidelines are being revised. People are examining the effect of sentencing and the fallibility of the criminal justice system, and are making new recommendations to improve the criminal justice system.

Sentencing is an important crossroad in the criminal justice system. It is harmful to convict the innocent and to impose sentences that do not deter criminality. It is harmful that there are so many possibilities for error in the use of the death penalty. Sentencing and sentencing reform will continue to be subjects of study and debate.

chapter **summary**

- Five purposes of criminal sanctions are deterrence, incapacitation, retribution, rehabilitation, and restorative justice.
- The jury determines guilt, and the judge determines the sentence the convicted defendant receives.
- Traditional sentences include fines, imprisonment, probation, or some combination. Certain states and the federal courts may impose the death penalty.
- Courts of limited jurisdiction impose short terms of incarceration and relatively small fines for minor offenses.
- Two major sentencing models are indeterminate sentencing and structured sentencing.
- Indeterminate sentencing is based on early release through the parole system.
- Structured sentencing includes determinate guidelines, sentencing guidelines, and presumptive sentencing.
- Mandatory sentencing, three strikes laws, and truth-in-sentencing laws are examples of structured sentencing.
- Research shows that the application of criminal sanctions often has discriminated against black and Hispanic males.
- Thirty-eight states, the federal courts, military courts, and military tribunals can sentence a defendant to death.
- Although the public generally supports the use of the death penalty, there is strong opposition and much controversy.
- Many states are reconsidering the use of the death penalty due to the number of wrongful convictions that have been documented in recent years. DNA evidence has played a major role in freeing the wrongfully convicted.

- Data on the effectiveness of sentencing in reducing crime rates indicate that more study and experimentation are needed.
- New programs include intermediate sanctions and community-based corrections. Intensive probation supervision (IPS) emphasizes strict accountability to the conditions of probation and parole.
- Split sentencing and shock probation require the offender to spend a brief period of time in prison before being granted supervised release in the community. Shock incarceration is accomplished through boot camps for adult and juvenile offenders.
- Home confinement is an intermediate sanction that requires offenders to remain within the home unless specifically authorized to leave. Electronic monitoring effectively and efficiently ensures that offenders remain at home.
- Community-based treatment programs such as work release and education release help offenders obtain work or education so that they will be successful when they reenter their communities.
- Halfway houses are programs designed to help inmates make the transition from prison to community. Halfway houses provide offenders with limited freedom within the community during the last part of their sentences.
- Day reporting centers can be used as intermediate sanctions to keep offenders out of prison.

vocabulary review

abolitionists, 336
banishment, 325
bifurcated trial, 338
capital punishment, 335
corporal punishment, 323
correctional case managers, 355
day reporting centers, 354
determinate sentencing, 331
deterrence, 323
electronic monitoring, 348
faith-based programs, 351
general deterrence, 324
guilty but mentally ill, 328
habitual offender laws, 332
halfway houses, 354
home confinement, 347
incapacitation, 325
indeterminate sentencing, 331
intensive probation supervision (IPS), 344
intermediate sanctions, 343
mandatory sentencing, 331
presumptive sentencing, 333
rehabilitation, 327
restorative justice, 327
retribution, 326
sentencing, 330
sentencing guidelines, 332
shock incarceration, 346
shock probation, 346
specific deterrence, 324
split sentencing, 346
structured sentencing, 331
three strikes law, 332
transportation, 326
truth in sentencing, 335
work release, 351

do you remember?

Federal Sentencing Guidelines Manual, 333
Furman v. *Georgia*, 337
Gregg v. *Georgia*, 338
Huber Law, 351
McClesky v. *Kemp*, 342
Prisoner Rehabilitation Act of 1965, 351
Private Sector/Prison Industry Enhancement Certification Program, 353
Reentry Partnership Initiative, 350
Sentencing Reform Act of 1984, 333
Serious and Violent Offender Reentry Initiative, 350
Southern Center for Human Rights, 336
Vera Institute of Justice, 343
Wilkerson v. *Utah*, 337
Witherspoon v. *Illinois*, 336

think about this

1. In late 2001 and early 2002, several states responded to a widening economic recession by closing jails, reducing sentences for nonviolent crimes, making it easier to win early release, and cutting prison education programs. How will such decisions affect offenders and their communities? To what extent do you think sentencing and parole decisions should be affected by economic considerations?
2. Which of the five purposes of criminal sanctions do you think might work best for a juvenile offender? A drug addict? An armed robber? A domestic abuser? Explain how your punishment fits the crime, yet would not be considered cruel and unusual. Which sentencing model do you prefer overall, and why?
3. Based on what you have learned in this chapter, if you were convicted of a crime, but you were innocent, would you accept the guilty verdict and apologize or show remorse during the presentence investigation in the hope that this attitude would result in a recommendation for a shorter sentence? Why or why not?

research navigator

Visit the Research Navigator website (www.researchnavigator.com), login and select the criminal justice data base in ContentSelect. Type in the key words "I hope someone murders." Select the article "'I hope someone murders your mother!": an exploration of extreme support for the death penalty" by Margaret Vandiver, David J. Giacopassi, and Peter R. Gathje. The article concerns one of the most debated aspects of sentencing in the criminal justice system—the death penalty. The article is an analysis of extreme reactions for the death penalty and against those who publicly oppose capital punishment. Sample the article and answer the following questions:

1. What is the public's opinion toward capital punishment as measured by public opinion polls? (Note: the article was published in 2001 and public opinion as reflected in later polls may differ.)
2. What are the reasons proposed by the authors that explain why some people intensely support capital punishment?
3. In what ways do those who intensely support capital punishment express their support when a scheduled execution is opposed by anti-capital punishment protestors?
4. Do the authors conclude that those who strongly support capital punishment do so based upon rational and utilitarian considerations of the effects and administration of the punishment? Explain your answer.

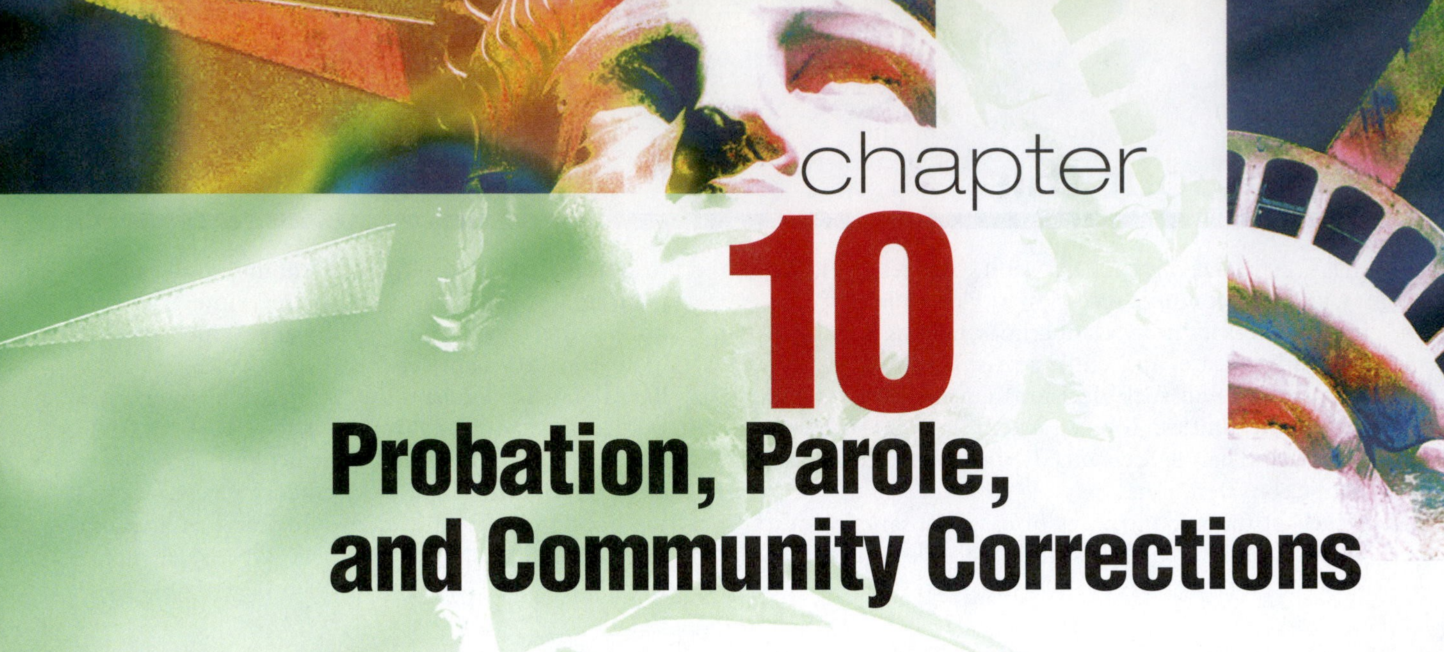

chapter 10

Probation, Parole, and Community Corrections

CHAPTER OUTLINE

LEARNING OBJECTIVES

After reading this chapter, you will know

- The differences between diversion, probation, and parole.
- The definitions and outcomes of mandatory and good-time release.
- The meaning of pardons and commutation of sentence.
- The origins and reasons for probation and parole.
- How a judge decides on granting probation.
- How a parole board decides on granting parole.
- The conditions of probation and parole and when probation and parole can be revoked.
- The advantages and disadvantages of probation and parole for offenders, communities, and the criminal justice system.
- The roles and functions performed by career probation and parole officers.
- New strategies designed to break the addiction-crime cycle, including separate court systems for drug offenders.

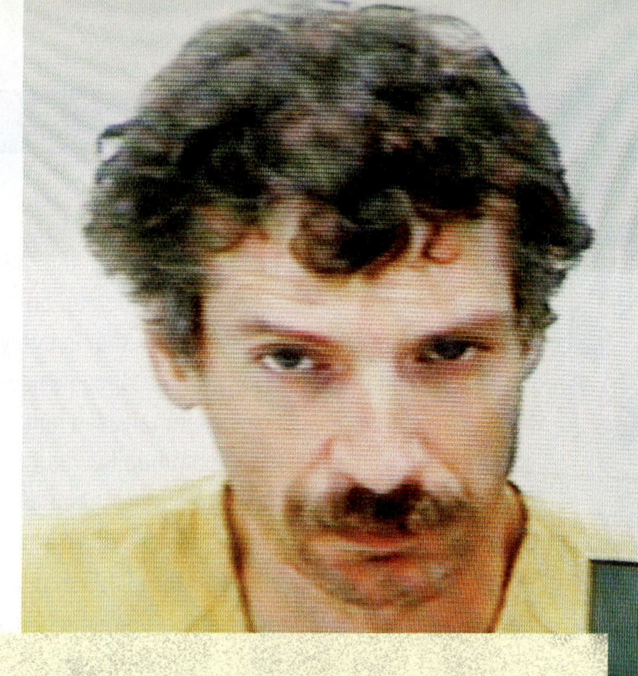

Idaho Girl Found in Denny's; Arrest Made

COEUR D'ALENE, IDAHO (AP)—An 8-year-old girl who disappeared with her brother six weeks ago from a home where family members were bludgeoned to death was spotted early Saturday with a registered sex offender at a Denny's restaurant, officials said.

The girl's 9-year-old brother, Dylan, had not been found, Kootenai County Sheriff's Capt. Ben Wolfinger said. He said the girl was spotted in her hometown by a waitress who apparently recognized her from photographs displayed in the media.

Joseph Edward Duncan III, of Fargo, N.D., was arrested without incident and charged with kidnapping, Wolfinger said. Duncan was being held without bond. Duncan had an outstanding warrant for failing to register as a sex offender and had a history of rape, Wolfinger said. Duncan had been charged with second-degree criminal sexual conduct and attempted criminal sexual conduct in Minnesota for allegedly molesting a 6-year-old boy at a school playground last July.

He had been released by Becker County, Minn., authorities in April on $15,000 bond and ordered to stay in touch with a probation agent. In May, authorities said they were seeking Duncan on a warrant after he failed to do so. Duncan was convicted of raping a 14-year-old boy in Washington state in 1980, when he was 16.

From Associated Press, "Idaho Girl Found in Denny's; Arrest Made," New York Times Online, www.nytimes.com, July 2, 2005.

introduction:

Why Early Release?

Joseph Edward Duncan III could be the poster child for those campaigning for a "get tough on criminals" policy. Those who want to lock up criminals and throw away the key could point to Duncan as the very menace to society that is every citizen's nightmare—a crazed sex-offender who is loose in the community not because he escaped from prison or has not been caught but because the criminal justice system released him. Furthermore, Duncan is not the only example of a prisoner released into the community who has terrorized citizens. Antoinette C. Starks was released from the Maryland Correctional Institute for Women in Jessup about 2:30 P.M. Tuesday, May 24, 2005, after serving 18 months of a 30-month prison sentence. Less than 28 hours after being freed, she was arrested for stabbing a complete stranger at a shopping mall and was prevented from stabbing two other women when she was arrested at gunpoint by an off-duty FBI agent.[1] In another case, David Lee Robinson, age 53, was arrested for 26 bank robberies committed within a year of his release from prison after serving 14 years for nearly 30 other robberies.[2] Such crimes by inmates released from prison have caused many states to pass legislation designed to lengthen prison terms and curtail early release from prison.

The public is concerned that those released early from prison will return to a life of crime. Given the fact that in 2004 nearly 5 million adult men and women were released early from prison on probation or parole, many critics of early release ask how many of the 5 million released early from prison will be like Edward Duncan, David Robinson, or Antoinette Starks?

This chapter examines why the criminal justice system releases prisoners before they have served their full sentence and why convicted defendants are given probation rather than prison time. The chapter discusses the different types of early release, how judges and parole boards make decisions about early release, how probation and parole officers supervise those who are released from prison, and how drug abuse among offenders has led to a separate system of drug courts and drug rehabilitation programs.

Defining Diversion, Probation, and Parole

the main idea 10.1 Alternatives to incarceration include diversion for defendants, probation or suspended sentence for convicted offenders, and parole or early release for prisoners.

An important reason that persons convicted of crimes may not serve the entire length of their sentences is the growing cost of prison. Tough sentencing laws have increased the number of inmates despite a drop in the crime rate. Prisons are expensive, and many states are forced to evaluate whether they can afford to continue locking up criminals for long periods of time. Since the 1970s, the number of state prisoners has increased 500 percent, making prisons the fastest-growing item in state budgets.[3] Many states are finding that prison spending competes with other needs. Taxpayers are reluctant to keep spending money on corrections if that means there is less money to spend on schools.[4] As a result, many states are seeking ways to reduce prison costs, including drastic measures such as closing prisons. California closed five small, privately operated minimum-security prisons in 2002. Ohio, Michigan, and Illinois also have closed prisons. Michigan moved prisoners from jails back to prison to save the $500,000 needed to keep them in local jails. States also are reexamining their ability to pay for long prison terms. Prison terms for nonviolent offenders and habitual offender laws that result in 30+-year prison terms are expensive correctional policies.[5] Also, data on rehabilitation, comparative studies of other countries, and criminal justice scholars maintain that there may be alternatives to prison that provide community safety and better rehabilitation. As a result of these pressures, many states are using new correctional strategies to replace imprisonment.

For comparative information, log on to www.homeoffice.gov.uk/nps to view the website of the National Probation Service for England and Wales.

Before discussing alternative strategies, it is important to define and distinguish diversion, probation, and parole. Some offenders do not serve any of their prison time, whereas others are sentenced to prison but released prior to the end of their term of punishment. Offenders may not serve time because they are diverted from the criminal justice system or because their sentences are suspended.

In **diversion,** the defendant is offered an alternative to a criminal trial, possible conviction, and prison sentence, such as drug court, boot camp, or a treatment program. When a defendant is convicted in a criminal court and sentenced to prison, but the prison term is suspended, the defendant does not have to serve time in prison and is said to be on **suspended sentence**, or probation. Probation, a sentencing option of the trial judge, diverts the offender after conviction but prior to serving prison time.

In parole, the offender has been sentenced to prison, serves a portion of his or her time, and is released before the maximum term of the sentence. The decision to parole a prisoner is made by a parole board. Prisoners released under probation or parole are subject to continued supervision in the community and can be returned to prison if they violate the terms of their release. Other means by which a prisoner can be released from prison other than probation and parole include mandatory release, good-time release, pardon, and commutation of sentence.

Mandatory and Good-Time Release

When prisoners serve the entire length of their maximum sentence, it is required by law that they be released. This is called **mandatory release.** An inmate cannot be held in prison beyond the length of his or her sentence. Even if the prisoner obviously is not rehabilitated or prepared for reentry into society, he or she must be released after serving the time. These prisoners are released without any supervision, without any restrictions on their behavior, and frequently without any support or rehabilitation plan. Mandatory release requires that prison officials release a prisoner who has served the maximum sentence regardless of the danger that the prisoner may pose to the community. Some states have tried to protect the community from offenders who have been identified as sexual predators by prohibiting such mandatory releases until the sexual predator has been declared not a danger to the community upon release. Hence, one of the arguments for early release through probation or parole is that such release, unlike mandatory release, lets probationers and parolees reenter the community with supervision, provides behavioral restrictions, and offers social, mental health, and drug counseling services to the released inmate.

Another form of mandatory release is when prisoners have served less than their full sentences but have earned good-time credit that entitles them to an early release. **Good-time credit** toward early release is a strategy to encourage the prisoner to obey institutional rules, refrain from violence and drug use, and participate in rehabilitation and vocational programs. In place of punishment for disobedience, good-time release gives inmates an incentive to comply with prison authority and rules. When the inmate is processed into the system, a percentage of the inmate's sentence is converted into good-time behavior. For many states, this is 15 percent or more of the time to be served. For example, an inmate with a 10-year sentence could receive a credit of 15 percent of the sentence or 1.5 years as good-time behavior. Good-time computation in the federal system is much less generous than in state prison systems. The **Comprehensive Crime Control Act of 1984,** which includes the Sentencing Reform Act of 1984, reformed the federal good-time provisions such that federal prisoners earn a maximum of 54 days annually after completion of the first year of a sentence.

diversion Sentencing option in which the defendant is diverted from the correctional system through alternatives such as community service, drug courts, boot camps, and treatment programs.

suspended sentence Another term for *probation,* based on the fact that convicted offenders must serve their full sentence if they violate the terms of release.

mandatory release After prisoners serve the entire length of their maximum sentence, it is required by law that they be released.

good-time credit A strategy of crediting inmates with extra days served toward early release, in an effort to encourage the prisoner to obey rules and participate in programs.

This is the entrance to the residence of Marc Rich, the Belgian-born billionaire pardoned by President Clinton who exercised his privilege of executive pardon. Rich was indicted in 1983 on charges of tax evasion, fraud, and participation in illegal oil deals with Iran. Critics suggest the pardon was influenced by large campaign contributions Clinton received either directly or indirectly from Rich. Presidents and governors have unlimited power to grant pardons and there is no oversight over how this power is exercised. Overall, do you think governors and presidents are prone to abuse their unlimited power to grant pardons? Should this power be modified?

Assuming a prisoner had a perfect record and received 15 percent credit for good time on a 10-year sentence, the prisoner's mandatory release date would be in 8.5 years. At that time, the prisoner would be released from prison without serving the entire sentence. However, if the prisoner is caught violating an institutional rule, time is deducted from his or her good time. For example, a prisoner sentenced to serve 2 years with 15 percent credit for good time would be required to serve 730 days (365 × 2) minus 109.5 days (15 percent good-time credit), or a total sentence of 620.5 days. However, if that prisoner gets into a fight, the punishment might be to have 30 days deducted from his or her good-time credit. Now the prison term is 620.5 days plus the 30 days deducted from good time, a sentence of 650.5 days. If the prisoner continues to violate the rules, each violation costs additional good-time days. It is possible that the prisoner could exhaust the supply of good-time credit and find it necessary to serve the entire 2-year prison term. However, prison authorities cannot add to prison time beyond that sentenced originally by the court without a conviction for new crimes.

Prison authorities use the deduction of good-time days to regulate nearly every aspect of the inmate's behavior. Loss of good time can be used as a punishment for both minor and major offenses. An inmate can lose days for not lining up when told to do so, for reporting late to work, for being in a restricted area, for insubordination, for engaging in arguments, for attacks on other inmates or correctional officers, or for possession of contraband. With more serious violations, such as attempted escape or felony crime, the inmate is returned to court for trial and, if convicted, is sentenced to additional time.

Pardon and Commutation of Sentence

Prisoners may not have to serve the entire length of their sentences because they are pardoned or have their sentences commuted. *Pardon* and *commutation* are forms of executive forgiveness, and are not a form of probation or parole. Pardons are sometimes referred to as *clemency.* Pardon and commutation of sentence can be performed only by the governor of the state for state prisoners or by the president of the United States for federal and military prisoners. Pardons and commutations of sentence are acts of mercy and do not indicate that an inmate is not guilty or was wrongfully sentenced.

There are no limitations on the number of pardons that governors and presidents may grant, and there are no guidelines or laws regulating who they may pardon and under what conditions. No one has the authority to revoke a pardon or to overrule the governor or president. They may seek advice in issuing a pardon, but the absolute authority to issue pardons rests entirely within the executive authority. Also, there is no time limit for issuing a pardon. A governor or president can issue a pardon for a crime committed decades ago for which the person has already served the entire length of sentence, or can issue a pardon while an inmate is still serving time. Requests for pardons usually come directly from the inmate or the inmate's supporters.

executive pardon An act by a governor or the president that forgives the prisoner and rescinds the sentence.

commutation of sentence Reduction in the severity or length of an inmate's sentence, issued by a state governor or the president of the United States.

Closely related to **executive pardon** is executive commutation of a prisoner's sentence. In **commutation of sentence**, the governor or president reduces the severity of an inmate's sentence. The most common use of executive commutation is to reduce a prisoner's sentence from death to life in prison and from life without parole to life with parole. For example, in 1997, Hawaii's governor John Waihee reduced the sentences of two inmates convicted of murder from life in prison without parole to life in prison with the possibility of parole.[6]

The powers of pardon and commutation give the executive branch checks and balances on the powers of the courts and legislature. By releasing prisoners, chief executives can intervene to correct or erase perceived abuses or errors in sentencing or corrections. However, there are no checks and balances on the executives' power to issue pardons, creating a potential for abuse. For example, some governors have been accused of accepting bribes for the pardons and commutations they have issued. Even President Clinton was accused by critics of granting presidential pardons in his final days of office to those who had made large political contributions. In 2003, two days before he left office, Illinois Governor George Ryan commuted the sentences of 167 people on death row and pardoned 4 others. Concerned that the inmates had been sentenced to death unfairly, he commuted the sentences of all inmates' sentences to death even if the inmate had not filed a clemency petition. Critics opposed to the unorthodox use of executive power challenged Governor Ryan's actions. However, the Illinois Supreme Court upheld his right to commute the sentence of prisoners, saying, "The governor may grant reprieves, pardons and commutations on his own terms, and the decisions are unreviewable."[7]

The fact that presidents and governors may grant reprieves, pardons, and commutations on their own terms and that these are unreviewable raises some interesting legal questions. For example, could a governor or president pardon himself or herself if convicted of a crime?[8] Another interesting question is can a governor or president issue a pardon before a person is convicted of a crime? President Gerald Ford actually issued such a pardon. On assuming the presidency after the resignation of Richard Nixon for his alleged involvement in the Watergate Scandal, Gerald Ford issued a presidential pardon to ex-President Nixon for any crimes that he may have committed in connection with Watergate prior to any indictment or conviction for such crimes. The "advance" pardon basically put prosecutors on notice that even if they were to successfully pursue criminal charges against Nixon for Watergate-related crimes, it would be useless because he was already pardoned should there be a conviction. Many argued that President Ford exceeded presidential authority by issuing a pardon in advance of conviction, but the pardon was never challenged in court.

▲ check your understanding **10.1** **What are diversion, probation, and parole? At what stage in the criminal justice process does each occur? How is mandatory release different from probation and parole? What are other forms of early release?**

Origins of Probation

▼ the main idea **10.2** **Probation, which has rehabilitation as the goal, allows a convicted defendant to serve time under supervision while living in the community as long as he or she observes the court-ordered conditions of release.**

Probation is a relatively new experiment in American corrections. The roots of probation can be traced to the efforts of **John Augustus** (1785–1859), a wealthy Boston shoemaker who devoted himself to bringing reform to the eighteenth-century criminal justice system. He intervened in Boston's municipal court to divert a number of defendants who were sentenced to serve time in the Boston House of Corrections. Augustus

probation Conditional release of a convicted offender prior to his or her serving any prison time.

was not an officer of the court nor was he connected to the criminal justice system. As a private citizen, he used his personal finances to guarantee bail for defendants selected for diversion from jail. He was critical of the conditions of the jails and prisons of his time and believed that, for many offenders, prison would lead to further harm rather than rehabilitation.

In 1841, Augustus initiated what came to be known as probation. He was in Boston's municipal court when a defendant was convicted of being a common drunk. Augustus asked the judge not to sentence the man to jail but to release him to his custody instead. Augustus assumed responsibility for the man's behavior and provided for his rehabilitation. After 3 weeks, he brought the man back to the court for evaluation. Augustus reported that "the judge expressed himself much pleased with the account we gave of the man, and instead of the usual penalty of imprisonment in the House of Corrections—he fined him one cent and costs, amounting in all to $3.76, which was immediately paid." From that time on, John Augustus monitored court trials and rescued more than 2,000 defendants from incarceration.[9]

Other volunteers continued Augustus's work after his death until Massachusetts passed the first probation statute in 1878. By 1900, four other states had passed similar legislation. By 1920, every state permitted juvenile probation, and 33 states had adopted a system of adult probation. Today, more people are on probation and parole than are sentenced to prison. In 2003, over 4 million adults under federal, state, or local jurisdiction were on probation, and about 775,000 were on parole.[10]

Probation Services

When determining whether to grant probation, local and county court judges typically have little information on which to base that decision. Because most criminals in these courts of limited jurisdiction are convicted of misdemeanors or violations, there is less risk to the community in the event that the judge grants probation. Thus, most local and county courts do not have access to probation services that will provide them with presentence investigation reports. Also, because of the short sentences provided for the offenses (the average sentence is about 4 to 5 months) handled by these courts, probation plans requiring the probationer to participate in long-term treatment, rehabilitation, drug counseling, or anger management is not practical.

Judges in state courts of general trial jurisdiction and federal courts have much more access to probation personnel to provide presentence investigations. Also, because of the length of sentences for felons tried in these courts, probation plans can specify that the probationer participate in long-term programs. Federal probation services are provided to the court by the **Office of Probation and Pretrial Services.** As the name suggests, this office provides assistance to the court both in presentence investigation and in probation services.

State probation offices are organized in different ways and under different authorities. Five common organizational structures for state probation are (1) within the state executive branch, (2) within local (county or municipal) executive departments, (3) under the state judiciary, (4) under local courts, and (5) under various combinations of the first four. Note, however, that probation is not under the authority of law enforcement, the prosecutor, or corrections. In many states, unlike the federal government, probation and parole services are provided by the same agency. In these agencies officers may handle both probation and parole cases.

Both federal probation and state probation services distinguish between probation services for adults and juveniles. Each has separate offices for providing probation to these two populations.

The status of probation officers as law enforcement officers varies state by state. Federal probation officers may be authorized to carry concealed weapons on- and off-duty. Some states grant probation officers the right to carry concealed weapons and some do not. Likewise, states grant juvenile probation officers different privileges with regard to carrying of firearms. Probation officers (both adult and juvenile) do not have the same arrest powers as police officers. The arrest powers of probation officers tend to be limited to probationers. However, with regard to the power of arrest and search and seizure of probationers, probation officers have more extensive authority, as they do not need search warrants to search a probationer, his or her residence, or his or her automobile. Furthermore, probation officers do not have to advise probationers of their Miranda rights when questioning them and probationers do not have the right to remain silent when questioned by probation officers.

Decision to Grant Probation

Probation is a sentencing option of judges. Probation or suspended sentence for both juveniles and adults can be used as a sentence for both minor and serious crimes. In fact, about half of those on probation committed misdemeanors and the other half committed felonies. An important factor in determining whether the defendant receives a suspended sentence is information about potential risks to the community if the offender is released. Judges must decide if the criminal's release poses a serious threat to the community. In many states with indeterminate sentencing, judges have great discretion in the use of probation and can suspend the sentences of those convicted of murder, burglary, theft, or traffic violations. The federal courts and some state courts have limited the judges' discretion through legislation requiring minimum sentences, mandatory sentencing, or structured sentencing. In these jurisdictions, judges may be prohibited from using probation for certain crimes.

Offenders with suspended sentences do not serve time in prison. Thus, the judge must conclude that (1) a sentence of prison time is an inappropriate punishment for the crime; (2) people would not be at serious risk if the offender has extensive freedom of movement in the community; (3) the offender would not benefit from any prison-based rehabilitation program or vocational program offered in prison; (4) the offender can support himself or herself in the community, has a place to live, and is not suffering from serious mental illness; and (5) the offender will not commit another crime. The judge relies to a great extent on the presentence investigation report to make a judgment about the appropriateness of probation. The decision to grant probation as a sentence depends on the quality of information that the judge has about the defendant and his or her past record, social and family interaction, psychological profile, and employment status.

The Office of Probation and Pretrial Services provides federal judges with presentence reports to assist the judge in deciding if probation is appropriate. Federal pretrial sentencing reports have five parts: (1) A narrative of the circumstances of the offense; (2) The defendant's criminal history—that is, previous crimes committed. The defendant's past criminal record is taken into account in determining the appropriateness of probation; (3) A description of the defendant's lifestyle, including employment, family, role in the community, financial obligations, and whether the person if married has provided financial support to his family; (4) The sentencing options that are available to the judge; and (5) A discussion of any factors that may suggest that probation would be an appropriate sentence for the offender. State probation officers provide similar services and reports to state judges.

Fifty-six percent of probationers are sentenced by the courts directly to probation. Most (76 percent) are sentenced to probation without incarceration. Seventy-seven percent of probationers are male and 56 percent are white. Figure 10.1 shows that most of those sentenced to probation were convicted of nonviolent offenses such as larceny/theft (12 percent), drug law violation (26 percent), driving while intoxicated (15 percent), and minor traffic offenses (7 percent).[11]

Most persons under sentence of probation are required to report to their probation officer on a regular basis. About 74 percent of probationers are under active supervision, which requires them to report regularly to a probation authority in person, by

figure 10.1

Characteristics of Adults on Probation, 2004

Gender	
Male	77%
Female	23%
Race	
White	56%
Black	30%
Hispanic	12%
American Indian/Alaska Native	1%
Asian/Pacific Islander	1%
Status of Probation	
Direct imposition	56%
Split sentence	8%
Sentence suspended	24%
Imposition suspended	10%
Other	1%
Type of offense	
Felony	49%
Misdemeanor	50%
Other infractions	1%

Adults Entering Probation	
Without incarceration	76%
With incarceration	14%
Other types	10%
Most Serious Offense	
Sexual assault	3%
Domestic violence	6%
Other assault	10%
Burglary	5%
Larceny/Theft	12%
Fraud	5%
Drug law violations	26%
Driving while intoxicated	15%
Minor traffic offenses	7%
Other	10%

Source: Lauren E. Glaze and Seri Palla, *Probation and Parole in the United States, 2004* (Washington, DC: Bureau of Justice Statistics, 2004), p. 6.

mail, or by telephone.[12] Probation is almost always combined with the requirement for supervision and treatment. Supervision demands that defendants report regularly to their probation officers on a daily, weekly, or monthly basis, depending on a number of factors. In addition, probationers may be required to seek professional treatment or counseling, and one justification for probation is that it allows the court to mandate treatment programs. Often, probationers must pay for treatment programs on their own. About 25 percent of probationers are drug offenders, and the conditions of their release require they complete drug treatment programs and submit to regular and frequent drug testing. Probationers must submit to drug tests whenever probation officers so order. Frequent mandatory drug testing has proved to be an effective strategy in drug rehabilitation.

In 2004, a majority (60 percent) of persons leaving probation successfully completed the terms of their supervision.[13] However as Table 10.1 indicates, not all probationers are able to "remain straight," as 15 percent of those sentenced to probation are returned to incarceration. Of those returned to incarceration, 8 percent are returned for committing a new crime. About 1 in 11, or 9 percent, probationers abscond. That is to say, while on probation, they fail to report to their probation officer and cannot be located. It is the same as if they escaped if they had been sentenced to prison.[14]

Advantages of Probation

The concerns associated with probation are fear of further criminal activity by the defendant and the lack of punishment for the crime committed. However, at a cost of about $1,000 per person per year, probation is much cheaper than prison.[15] If the probationer commits new crimes, however, the cost of the property loss or damage and the intangible costs of pain and suffering of the victims present a different picture. On the other hand, probation promotes rehabilitation through employment, opportunities for normal social relations, and access to community services and resources. Probationers are usually required to be employed or to attend school or vocational training. Employment enables offenders to support themselves and, if married, their families, and to pay taxes. The probationer is therefore not a burden to the taxpayer.

Probationers live in a "normal" environment. By remaining in the community, the probationer avoids the detrimental effects of the prison environment and retains relationships with family and other support groups and services. A number of criminological theories of crime causation suggest that positive attachments to the community are a powerful factor in preventing criminal behavior.

Conditions of probation provide for supervision of the probationer's behavior and lifestyle. Standard conditions require that the probationer maintain employment, have a place to live, refrain from drug and alcohol use, and avoid socializing with known criminals. The probationer is monitored to ensure he or she abides by these conditions. Additional conditions may include successful completion of a drug or alcohol rehabilitation program. Probation sentences can be for as long as 10 years or more, during which time the probationer remains under supervision and must comply with all the terms and conditions of probation. Proponents of probation argue that long-term oversight of offenders at low cost to the community is superior to unsupervised release of prisoners.

Wilbert Rideau spent 44 years in prison in Louisiana for murder. He was repeatedly denied parole despite exemplary behavior, becoming an award-winning journalist, and evidence that he had rehabilitated himself and was no longer a danger to society. Rideau has been called "the most rehabilitated prisoner in America." He never received parole but his case attracted national attention, and in 2000, the U.S. Fifth Circuit Court of Appeals in New Orleans, citing racial prejudice, threw out the 1961 murder conviction. In 2005, Rideau was retried, convicted of the lesser charge of manslaughter, and freed from prison. Why should an offender receive early release from prison?

table 10.1

Adults Leaving Probation

Status	Percent	Percent
Successful completions		60
Returned to incarceration		15
With new sentence	8	
With the same sentence	6	
Unknown	1	
Absconder*		4
Discharge to custody, detainer, or warrant		1
Other unsuccessful*		10
Death		1
Other		9

*In 1995, "absconder" and "other unsuccessful" statuses were reported among "other."

Source: Lauren E. Glaze and Seri Palla, *Probation and Parole in the United States, 2004* (Washington, DC: Bureau of Justice Statistics, 2005), p. 6.

Decisions to Revoke Probation

The decision to grant offenders probation is revocable, because probation is granted under the stipulation that offenders meet all the conditions of their release. Probation status can be revoked at any time if offenders test positive for drugs, are found in possession of a weapon, commit another crime, lose employment, fail to complete a treatment program, or commit any other offense. Offenders whose probation status is revoked are returned to prison to serve their entire sentences. For example, consider an offender sentenced to 5 years in prison with a suspended sentence who is on probation for 4 years but then commits a violation sufficient to have his or her probation revoked. The offender then goes to prison to serve out the 5-year sentence with no credit for any time spent under supervision as a probationer.

Prior to the Warren Court, probation was considered an "act of grace," and the Court did not recognize that the probationer has any due process rights following revocation of probation. In 1967, however, the Court reversed that opinion and ruled that probationers are entitled to due process hearings to establish that they violated their conditions of probation.[16] Today, the Court has ruled that probationers also are entitled to certain due process rights before their probation is revoked.[17]

The decision to revoke probation is initiated by the probation officer. The first step in the revocation process is the probation officer's allegation that the client has violated a condition of probation or has committed a new crime. In most jurisdictions, probation officers have the power of arrest and the authority to remove the probationer from the community immediately. Probation officers can apprehend the probationer and deliver him or her to a jail for detention. In some jurisdictions, the probation and parole officer must notify law enforcement authorities to apprehend the violator.

The probation officer writes a report detailing the alleged violation of probation and submits it to the court; a hearing is held to determine whether there is probable cause to revoke probation. If there is probable cause, the probationer's freedom is revoked and he or she is confined in a correctional institution until a second hearing is held. At the second hearing, the sentencing judge or other impartial judicial authority decides whether the alleged violation warrants revocation of probation and whether the evidence presented is sufficient and trustworthy to justify revocation.

Different rules of evidence apply in the sentencing hearing. For example, probation officers have the right of search and seizure of the probationer and his or her residence without a search warrant, consent, or probable cause.[18] Probation officers do not have to advise probationers of their rights against self-incrimination, and probationers have only limited protection against self-incrimination.[19] Probation officers also can enter and search the probationer's vehicle at any time without permission. Probationers do have the right to counsel at their revocation hearing, and if they cannot afford counsel, they are entitled to a defense counsel paid for by the government.[20]

Imprisonment for violating a condition of probation is called a **technical violation**. Drug use is the most frequent reason that probationers are returned to prison for technical violations. Imprisonment for committing a new crime is not punishment for the new crime but for the crime they committed previously, for which they received probation. Offenders are re-arrested and tried for the new crime. If they are found guilty, their sentence for the new crime is added to the sentence they must serve for their previous crime. Even if the probationer is not convicted in court of committing the new crime, or if charges are reduced through plea bargaining or dismissed, the court still may revoke probation.

Probationers cannot be returned to prison for technical violation for failure to pay a fine or restitution, if it can be proved that the probationer was not responsible for this failure. For example, probationers might lose their jobs through no fault of their own, incur medical bills that prevent them from making payment, or experience some other financial crisis not under their control. These probationers cannot be returned to prison because they lack the money to fulfill their conditions of probation. However, personal

technical violation Grounds for imprisonment of a probationer or parolee based on his or her violation of a condition of release.

bankruptcy ultimately does not excuse the probationer from paying court-ordered fines or restitution.[21]

▲ check your understanding **10.2** **How did probation originate? What are the important factors in deciding whether to grant a suspended sentence? What are the advantages and risks of probation? Under what circumstances can probation be revoked?**

Origins of Parole

▼ the main idea **10.3** **Parole provides for the early conditional release of prisoners, is decided by parole boards, and is supervised in the community by probation and parole officers.**

People often minimize the distinction between probation and parole, but the two are very different practices and have distinct characteristics. While the origins of probation can be directly traced to the early practices of John Augustus, the origins of parole are more diverse. The concept of parole encompasses the practice of conditionally releasing prisoners to the community and the supervision of the released prisoner, or the parolee, in the community. The parolee's early release from prison is conditional, based on compliance with the conditions of release and absence of criminal activity.

The historical roots of parole can be traced to practices of the French, English, and Irish. The term *parole* comes from the French phrase ***parole d'honneur***—the practice of releasing a prisoner for good behavior based on his word of honor that he would obey the law upon release.[22] **Alexander Maconochie** often is credited with developing the **mark system**, a forerunner of the parole system. Maconochie developed this early type of parole system between 1840 and 1844 while he was administrator of Norfolk Island, a prison colony off the coast of Australia. He pioneered the innovative penal strategy of releasing prisoners early on the basis of points, or marks, for good behavior and work performed in prison. The system operated according to a prison token economy in which the prisoner earned marks for good behavior. On imprisonment, each prisoner was assessed a debt in marks to be paid. Additional marks could be assessed against the prisoner for misbehavior or violation of prison rules. At the same time, the prisoner could earn good-credit marks for working, participating in educational programs, and good behavior. Prisoners who earned enough marks to offset the debt of their crime—and any additional debts they incurred while in prison—could buy their freedom. If prisoners had more than enough marks to buy their freedom, the extra marks could be redeemed for cash upon their release.

Maconochie's mark system was based on the premise that prisoners must demonstrate rehabilitation to earn their release from prison. This same basic assumption underlies the use of parole. Parole is based on the idea that prisoners should be released not because they have served a fixed amount of time, but because they have changed their ways. However, unlike modern-day parole, the **ticket of leave** that Maconochie's prisoners purchased with their marks granted them an unconditional release from prison. Released prisoners were not supervised in the community nor subject to any terms of conditional release. Today, on the contrary, parole is always conditional. Parolees can be returned to jail or prison for rule violations or other offenses.

Sir Walter Crofton pioneered the practice of conditional release for inmates prior to completing their sentences based on good behavior. In 1854, Crofton was chairman of the board of directors of Irish prisons. He adopted Maconochie's mark system and

parole d'honneur Origin of parole based on the concept of releasing prisoners "on their honor" after serving a portion of their sentence but before the maximum term.

mark system Early form of parole invented by Alexander Maconochie in which prisoners demonstrated their rehabilitation by earning points for good behavior.

ticket of leave In the mark system, unconditional release from prison, purchased with marks earned for good behavior.

ticket of leave to solve the problem of prison overcrowding. However, Crofton's **Irish system** provided a continuum of conditions of supervision based on the prisoner's behavior. Initially prisoners were placed in solitary confinement but could work their way to greater freedom. In the final stages of the Irish system, prisoners were assigned to work programs outside the prison and could earn a ticket of leave entitling them to early release under supervision. If they disobeyed the terms of their release or committed a new crime, they could be summarily tried and, if convicted, have their ticket of leave revoked. Crofton's Irish system is the model on which the American parole system is based.

Pros and Cons of Parole

Good-time laws were passed as early as 1817 in New York, and they allowed the early release of prisoners with sentences of 5 years or less.[23] However, parole did not emerge as common practice until the end of the 1800s. Even the term *parole* was not used in the United States until 1846.[24] The development of parole came with the use of indeterminate sentencing and efforts to address the correctional needs of youthful offenders. In 1869, Michigan adopted the first indeterminate sentencing law.[25] An **indeterminate sentence** bases release on behavior that demonstrates signs of rehabilitation rather than on a fixed prison term. In indeterminate sentencing, the defendant is given a prison term with a minimum and a maximum number of years to serve. Indeterminate prison terms can have a wide range between the minimum and maximum number of years to serve, ranging from 1 year to life in prison.

The indeterminate sentence was extensively used at the **Elmira Reformatory** for youthful offenders in New York. Prior to the twentieth century and the adoption of the juvenile court system, youthful offenders were not entitled to special treatment in the criminal justice system. Warden **Zebulon Brockway** instituted the practice of early release at Elmira Reformatory in 1876 as a means to promote rehabilitation of youthful offenders, as opposed to punishment. Brockway's use of early conditional release combined with mandatory community supervision was the first significant use of parole in America.[26] As in the origins of probation, the first parole officers were volunteers.[27]

Although it promoted the rehabilitation of offenders in the community, parole did not become an overnight success. By 1900, 20 states had adopted parole statutes, but it was not until after World War II that every state had a parole system. The first federal parole statute was adopted in 1867, providing for the reduction of sentences of federal prisoners for good conduct. However, the federal parole system was not created until 1910. Even during Maconochie's time, the public was opposed to the concept of early release, as indicated by the fact that Maconochie was removed as prison administrator because of opposition to his mark system.

In the United States, public opposition to parole is still widespread.[28] This disdain for parole is reflected in the abandonment of the practice by the federal court system and many states. By the end of 2001, 15 states had abolished parole board authority for releasing all offenders, and another 5 states had abolished parole board authority for releasing certain violent offenders. The public seems to want criminals sentenced to prison "to get the amount of time they deserve."[29] This belief is based in part on the public's fear that prisoners released early will return to a life of crime. For example, in 1994, when Virginia eliminated parole, Governor George Allen predicted that it would prevent 120,000 felonies over 10 years. Allen said, "Virginia is a safer place because we abolished parole."[30] One reason the public feels safer is because indeed probation (and parole) violators commit a significant number of crimes when released from prison. Table 10.2 shows that probation and parole violators committed over 13,000 murders. They committed nearly 13,000 rapes and over 50 percent of the victims were under the age of 12. They committed nearly 50,000 robberies, 19,000 assaults, and 50,000 burglaries. Those opposed to early release, especially parole, say that if these offenders had

Irish system Early form of parole invented by Sir Walter Crofton on the basis of the mark system, in which prisoners were released conditionally on good behavior and were supervised in the community.

indeterminate sentence The defendant is sentenced to a prison term with a minimum and a maximum number of years to serve.

table 10.2

Crimes Committed While on Probation and Parole

On the average, probationers were in the community for 17 months before being returned to prison for the commission of a new crime, and parole violators averaged 13 months on parole. During their time in the community, probation and parole violators committed the following crimes.

Probation Violators	Parole Violators
6,400 murders	6,800 murders
7,400 rapes or sexual assaults (33% of the victims were under the age of 12; 63% under 18)	5,550 rapes or sexual assaults (21% of the victims were under the age of 12; 47% under 18)
17,000 robberies	22,500 robberies
10,400 assaults	8,800 assaults
16,600 burglaries	23,000 burglaries
3,100 motor vehicle thefts	4,800 motor vehicle thefts

Source: Bureau of Justice Statistics, *Probation and Parole Violators in State Prison, 1991* (Washington, DC: U.S. Department of Justice, August 1995), p. 10.

remained in prison, it could be argued that these crimes would not have occurred. They argue that often the cost of the crimes committed by the probation and parole violator is not taken into account when calculating the cost effectiveness of probation and parole.

This fear is not entirely groundless, especially for prisoners released on parole. In 2004, only 46 percent of adults successfully completed the conditions of parole, compared to 60 percent of adults who successfully completed probation (see Figure 10.2). Thirty-nine percent of adults on parole were returned to incarceration, compared to 15 percent of adults on probation. Ten percent of adults on parole absconded.[31] The failure rate for adults on parole is higher despite the fact that 85 percent of adults on parole are under active supervision, which requires them to report regularly to a parole authority, compared to 74 percent of adults on probation.[32]

The public disdain for early release, especially parole, is illustrated by the data in Figure 10.3, which shows that early release of prisoners on parole has dropped significantly from 1980 to 2003, whereas the percent of prisoners who are released due to expiration of sentence (they served the full mandatory length of their sentence) has increased. Early release on mandatory parole has increased. However, unlike discretionary parole, mandatory parole requires the early release of the inmate. That is to say, in states with mandatory parole, early release is required when a prisoner completes a certain percent of his or her time and specific behavioral conditions have been met.

figure 10.2

Percent of Successful Exits, by Type of Supervision, 1995–2004

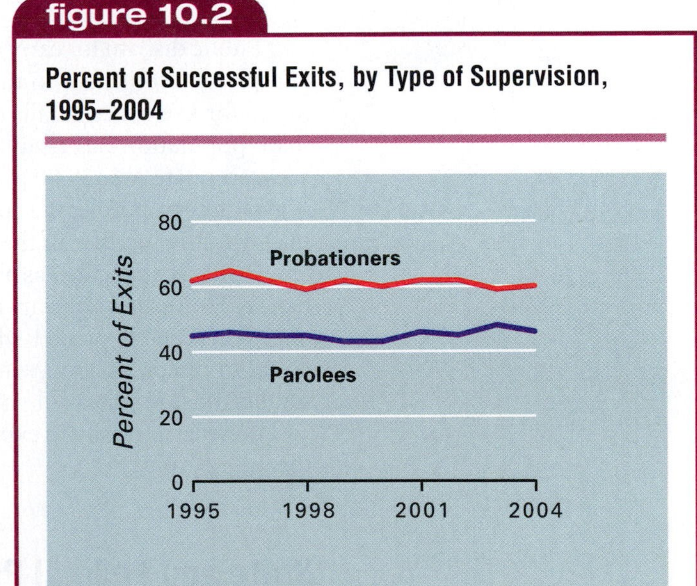

Source: Lauren E. Glaze and Seri Palla, *Probation and Parole in the United States, 2004* (Washington, DC: Bureau of Justice Statistics, 2005), p. 9.

figure 10.3

Releases from State Prison, by Method of Release, 1980–2003

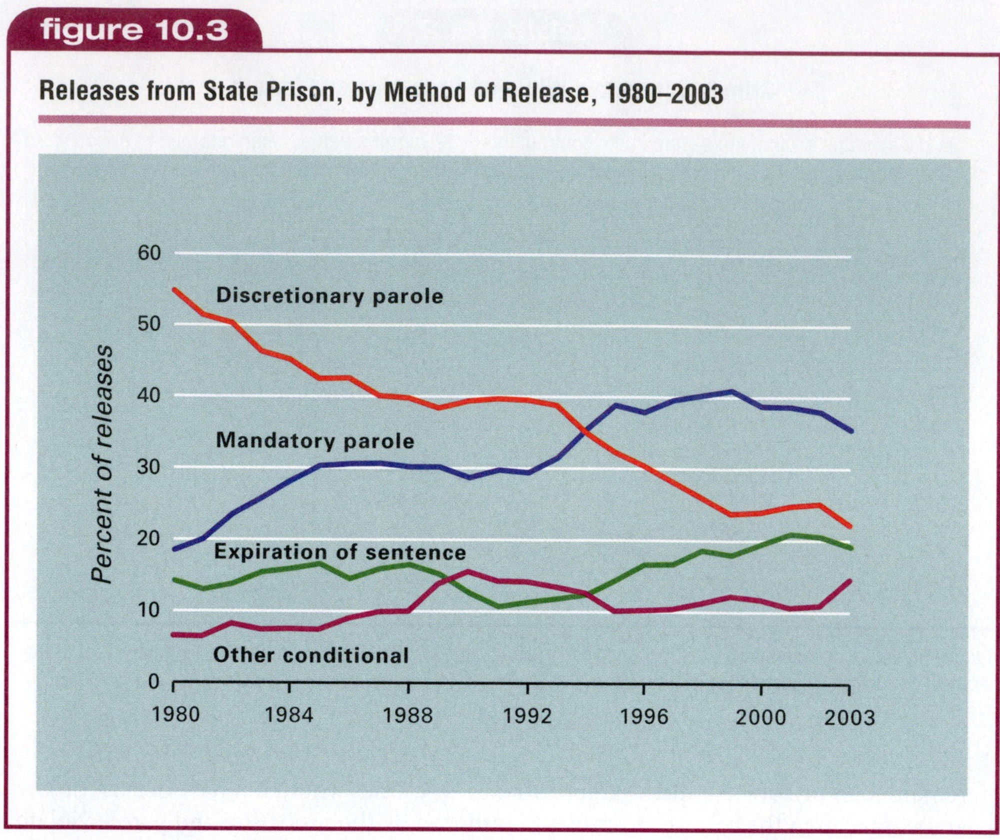

Note: Data are from the National Prisoners Statistics (*NPS-1*) series.

Source: Lauren E. Glaze and Seri Palla, *Probation and Parole in the United States, 2004* (Washington, DC: Bureau of Justice Statistics, 2005), p. 8.

Public disdain for early release has a cost. The number of adults incarcerated in jails and prisons continues to increase, so as fewer inmates are released on parole, the demand for bed space in jails and prison increases. Since abolishing parole, Virginia's inmate population has risen 25 percent and the state has had to build new prisons to accommodate over 3,000 prisoners at a cost of over half a billion dollars.[33] Despite this opposition to parole, the number of adults on parole continues to increase due primarily to the increase in the number of persons sentenced to prison.

Parole is advocated as a correctional strategy for many of the same reasons as probation. However, it appears that the public is wary of the ability of the correctional system to accurately predict which prisoners have been successfully rehabilitated. Before going to prison, nearly two-thirds of inmates have been on probation.[34] Thus, to the public, those inmates did not take advantage of the "act of grace" that was offered them, and there is no reason to expect that they would do any better if offered a second chance through parole.

State and Federal Parole Boards

Parole requires the following elements in order to function: (1) the parole board, (2) an agency to supervise parolees on conditional release in the community, and (3) procedures to revoke parole for those parolees who violate their conditions of parole. The sentencing judge has the authority to grant probation, but parole is not under the au-

The rapid rise in the prison population has resulted in many states scrambling to build new prisons. Prison construction is extremely costly and often prison funding competes directly with funding for health care and education. Should states emphasize alternatives to prison?

thority of the sentencing judge. The **parole board**, not the judge, is responsible for deciding whether an inmate is to receive early release.

Each state establishes its own parole board, and no agency has oversight of all the state parole boards. State parole boards are established by state legislation and administered under the authority of the state's executive branch (i.e., the governor). The legislature retains oversight through their powers of law making and budget approval. The governor appoints the director of the parole board and often the members as well. The state supreme courts and the U.S. Supreme Court have oversight powers in that they can declare certain parole practices unconstitutional.

Two models for administering state parole boards under the authority of the executive branch of government are the independent model and the consolidated model.[35] In the **independent model**, the parole board is an autonomous administrative unit with the power to make parole release decisions and to supervise all conditionally released inmates. In the **consolidated model**, the parole board is under the authority of the state Department of Corrections as a specialty unit within the department that makes decisions about conditional early releases.

State parole boards usually have fewer than a dozen members who may be full-time or part-time appointees. Final decision-making authority for selecting prisoners to release on parole lies with the parole board, but few states have qualifications for who can serve on the board. State parole board members are not required to have a minimum education, do not obtain their appointment by competitive civil service examination, and need not have any background in criminal justice or a related field such as psychology or sociology. A survey by the American Correctional Association revealed that, in the absence of minimum requirements, some state parole board members lack the educational and vocational experience to equip them to make such decisions.[36]

People who serve on state parole boards receive little pay, and there is little opportunity for advancement because of the small size and specialized nature of the job. Service on state parole boards can be a thankless task. Few appreciate the responsibility and hard work of the board, but everyone is quick to criticize the board if a released parolee commits a crime. Because the governor appoints members, the parole board often reflects the political agenda of the governor. State parole board members are neither correctional officers nor law enforcement officers. They do not have the power to carry concealed firearms, or the powers of arrest, search, and seizure. Their duties are mostly

parole board Individuals appointed to a body that meets in prisons to make decisions about granting parole release to inmates.

independent model Decision making about parole is under the authority of an autonomous parole board.

consolidated model Organization of decision making about parole as a function of a state department of corrections.

criminal justice in the media

Who Should Know about Offenders Returning to the Community?

If they could have their own way, offenders released into the community on probation or parole probably would prefer that as few people as possible know of their status. However, the community and the criminal justice system do not see it that way. States have taken steps to make known to the public the presence of offenders on conditional release in the community.

In 1994, 7-year-old **Megan Kanka** was raped and murdered by a convicted sex offender on parole living near the child's New Jersey home. Neighbors were unaware her attacker was a convicted sex offender. Since that time, all 50 states and the federal government have passed some type of law requiring that sexual offenders released from prison must register with local law enforcement authorities. Sexual offenders must register for life, even after they have been completely discharged from the criminal justice system. They must register both in their home state and in states they visit for school or work. States that fail to establish mandatory **sex offender registries** can lose federal assistance money.[37]

In addition, a number of states have placed the names not only of sex offenders, but of all prisoners and parolees in an online database that can be accessed by any citizen. Online lookup sites enable neighbors, employers, victims—virtually anyone—to check to see whether any parolees live in their neighborhoods or have applied for a job. Parolees supported by the Florida Civil Liberties Union in Tallahassee, Florida, have complained that putting their names and criminal status on the Web makes it difficult for them to obtain employment or housing. However, victims' rights groups and the media see the database as essential to public safety. Often the media have taken it upon themselves to publish the names and photographs of released sex offenders or promote access to the sex offender register database.

Should inmates conditionally released back into the community have any rights of privacy? Should their status be public information, available on the Web? Should certain offenders, such as sexual offenders, be required to register with local law enforcement authorities for the rest of their lives?

administrative, with a primary responsibility for making decisions about the early release of prisoners. All states have a parole board, even those that have abolished the practice, as states cannot retroactively revoke an inmate's right to parole. Thus, states that have abolished parole must nevertheless maintain the right to early conditional release for inmates sentenced prior to the abolishment of parole.

Go to www.usdoj.gov/uspc to view the United States Parole Commission's website.

The U.S. Congress created the United States Board of Parole in 1930, creating the first federal parole board. In 1976, the **Parole Commission and Reorganization Act** retitled the agency as the **United States Parole Commission.** The commission consists of a chairperson and commissioners appointed by the president, and regional offices are staffed by hearing examiners, case analysts, and clerical staff. Despite the increasing numbers of federal inmates, the U.S. Parole Commission is in the process of closing down its operations. The Comprehensive Crime Control Act of 1984 abolished eligibility for parole for federal offenders who committed crimes on or after November 1, 1987. Thus, only federal prisoners who committed crimes prior to that date are eligible for parole. The act provided for the abolition of the Parole Commission on November 1, 1992. However, judicial challenges to the elimination of, or reduction in, parole eligibility for those sentenced prior to November 1, 1997, resulted in the Judicial Im-

sex offender registries
Open-access online databases identifying known sex offenders on parole, maintained to protect communities and potential victims.

provements Act of 1990 that extended the life of the Parole Commission until November 1, 1997. The Parole Commission Phaseout Act of 1996 again extended the life of the Parole Commission. This act authorized the continuation of the Parole Commission until November 1, 2002. The National Capital Revitalization and Self-Government Improvement Act of 1997 actually gave the Parole Commission significant additional responsibilities, including responsibility for parole within the District of Columbia. Additional responsibilities have been added by other legislation, such as responsibility for making prison-term decisions in foreign transfer treaty cases for offenses committed on or after November 1, 1987, and jurisdiction over all state defendants who are accepted into the U.S. Marshals Service Witness Protection Program. The Twenty-First Century Department of Justice Appropriations Authorization Act of 2002 again extended the life of the Parole Commission until November 1, 2005. Given the fact that the Federal Parole Commission continues to have authority over certain prisoners, the status of the Parole Commission remains unresolved.

Go to www.cor.state.ky.us to view the Commonwealth of Kentucky's Offender Online Lookup.

The Parole Hearing

Parole boards make decisions through **parole hearings**. State parole boards have tremendous discretion in deciding which inmates to grant early conditional release, and inmates have little power to appeal these decisions. Parole hearings are not at all like trials, and each state and the federal Parole Commission have different procedures for conducting parole hearings.[38] Generally, hearings are brief, private rather than public, and held in the prison where the prisoner is housed. Parole hearings are convened by the parole board or by a hearing examiner who acts as the authorized representative of the parole board. The examiner presides over the hearing and makes a recommendation, which is forwarded to the parole board for formal action.

The board has great control over an inmate's eligibility for parole. When an inmate is processed into prison, his or her file is forwarded to the parole board for review to determine a first hearing date. The parole board reviews the circumstances of the crime and information about the offender and sets a date. For most offenders, the first parole hearing is set after serving one-third of their prison time. The parole board may recommend what they expect inmates to do during this time to increase their chances of obtaining parole. Usually, recommendations relate to participation in educational or treatment programs, vocational training sufficient to allow inmates to support themselves if released, and obedience to prison rules.

The power of the parole board to grant early release and the public expectation that the prisoner will serve out the sentence have created considerable public debate. In states using indeterminate sentencing, the sentence handed down by the judge may be quite different from the time actually served. The judge may sentence a defendant who has committed multiple crimes to two sentences of 10 years for each crime, to be served consecutively. In this case, the inmate is effectively sentenced to 20 years in prison.

However, the parole board has the power to decide that the sentence will be served concurrently—the prisoner serves the time for both sentences simultaneously. The difference between these two interpretations has a great impact on calculating when an inmate is eligible for a first parole hearing. If an inmate is eligible after serving one-third of the sentence, an inmate serving two consecutive 10-year sentences is not eligible for parole until he or she serves one-third of 20 years, or about 6.6 years. If the sentences are served concurrently instead, then the inmate is eligible after serving one-third of the 10 years, or about 3.3 years. Often, the public is critical of parole boards that disregard the judge's instructions and permit concurrent sentences. This lack of truth in sentencing has led many states to adopt new sentencing guidelines that reduce or eliminate parole.

parole hearings Meetings with inmates, attorneys, and others in which the parole board decides whether to grant, deny, or revoke parole.

The parole hearing is conducted in a meeting room, not a courtroom. The board reviews the history of the case and all available information about the prisoner, and then the inmate is brought into the room to state his or her case for parole. All inmates are

The parole hearing is conducted in a meeting room with the parole board or its representatives. Few inmates expect or receive parole at the first hearing. Rather, the parole board sets the date of the next parole hearing. Some states require that all prisoners receive periodic opportunities for parole regardless of the circumstances of their conviction. Thus, a convicted serial killer would receive regular hearings despite the near impossibility that parole would ever be granted.

required to submit a parole plan, which contains detailed plans for employment, education, and living arrangements if released. These parole plans also contain statements explaining why inmates think they are ready for parole, what they have done to prepare for release, what they have done to rehabilitate themselves while in prison, and why they are sorry for the crimes they committed. In some states, inmates may request witnesses to appear at the parole hearing to testify in their behalf, but the parole board may deny this request. Inmates are not entitled to an attorney at their parole hearing. In many states, victims of a crime and law enforcement officers must be notified that an inmate is scheduled to receive a parole hearing, and these parties may appear before the board to testify for or against the release of the inmate. Law enforcement officers typically recommend that parole be denied. The prisoner is not entitled to cross-examine any witnesses that testify for or against his or her parole. The entire hearing lasts only a few minutes. Afterward, the parole board notifies the prisoner of the outcome. If parole is denied, the board is required to give written reasons for its decision.[39]

Standards for Granting Parole The parole board's task is difficult, because predicting which prisoners are ready and able to reintegrate into the community is almost an impossible task. Board members often rely on feelings, common sense, and a sense of what the community would think. Some states and the U.S. Parole Commission have developed decision-making aids to help them make parole decisions. The probability or risk that a parolee will reoffend or be a danger to the community can be ranked on a scale from 1 to 10. However, in those states that use such an instrument, the parole boards are not bound by these devices and have the authority to deny parole even if the prisoner's score indicates a low risk. The American Law Institute has suggested a model protocol for parole boards based on identifying who should *not* be paroled rather than who should.[40]

Prison Overcrowding and Parole One of the most difficult decisions that parole boards have to make is who to release when the prison system is ordered to reduce its population due to overcrowding. If the conditions of imprisonment caused by overcrowding violate the **Eighth Amendment** against cruel and unusual punishment, the state or federal court may order a mandatory reduction in the number of inmates. Overcrowding in itself is not a violation of the Eighth Amendment, but when the overcrowding causes a significant deterioration in the standard of care, prisoners' constitutional rights are violated.

In 2001, for example, inmates of Morgan County Jail in Alabama filed suit on those grounds. The jail was built to hold 96 inmates, but the average prison population was 250. Most of the prisoners were waiting to be transferred to the state prison system, which had no room for them. The state prisoners thus remained crowded into the local jail, awaiting transfer. After a tour of the jail, the judge declared that the "sardine-can appearance of its cells more nearly resemble the holding units of slave ships during the Middle Passage of the 19th century than anything in the 21st century" and that conditions in the jail were "uncivilized, medieval, and barbaric."[41] The judge ordered the immediate reduction of the prison population, which, in the circumstances, constituted an order to release inmates. Many states have found themselves in a similar situation. In these cases, the parole board must meet and decide which inmates can be released immediately, even ahead of their scheduled release dates, to make room for new inmates.

At these "midnight parole hearings," the parole board must meet quickly and release inmates even before they have a parole plan in place. In the late 1990s, the state of Hawaii was under a court order to limit the state prison population to a capped number. To comply with the court order, if the evening prisoner count exceeded the cap, the parole board had to meet during the night to release prisoners before the official morning count. Such parole practices are not sound correctional policy but are political and legal necessities.

Probation and parole officers make home visits to see if offenders are following the conditions of their probation or parole. These visits can include monitoring for alcohol use, as illustrated in this photograph, and random drug testing. What are the advantages of using parole as a transition into society, compared to releasing an inmate directly from prison without any supervision at the end of his or her sentence?

Prison overcrowding also has encouraged states to give inmates liberal good-time credit to speed releases. At the height of overcrowding in the Florida state prison system, some inmates were serving only a small percentage of their original sentences.[42] In 1990, states such as Arkansas, California, Indiana, and Louisiana were granting inmates more than 30 days' good-time credit per month![43] The parole board's task of deciding who to release early is complicated by mandatory sentencing laws. These laws prohibit early release for drug offenders, for example. Thus, parole boards are forced to give early release to violent offenders who are not serving mandatory sentences instead of to nonviolent drug offenders.

Conditions of Parole

Parolees are subject to conditions of release very similar to those for probationers. The conditions of release relate to security (will the parolee abide by the conditions of release?) and to plans for treatment and rehabilitation. Each state has different standard conditions of release, but most are similar to those of the U.S. Parole Commission. Federal parolees are required to abide by 14 **standard conditions of release**[44] (see Figure 10.4). The conditions require the parolee to report to his or her parole advisor within 3 days of release, restrict where the parolee can live and work, require him or her to abide by all laws, and require that all contacts with the police be reported to his or her parole officer. The conditions prohibit consumption of alcoholic beverages to excess, the use of illegal drugs, association with criminals, and possession of firearms. Parolees must cooperate with their probation officer and to submit to drug tests whenever ordered.

In addition to these standard conditions of release, parolees may, and often do, receive other conditions of release that are applicable to the individual's crime and circumstances. For example, sex offenders may be prohibited from living or being near schools, playgrounds, or other areas where children are present. Persons convicted of domestic violence may be prohibited from contact with their victims. Prisoners with a history of drug or alcohol abuse may be required to attend treatment programs.

Revocation of Parole

Similar to probation, parole is revocable. Parole can be revoked for violation of a condition of release, a technical violation, or for commission of a new crime. Revocation of parole is common, as less than 50 percent of parolees are successful in maintaining their freedom after release.[45] Compared to probationers, parolees are more likely to be returned to prison for the commission of a new crime than are people on probation.[46] In 1999, parole violators accounted for more than 50 percent of state prison admissions in California (67 percent), Utah (55 percent), Montana (53 percent), and Louisiana (53 percent).[47] Prisoners released on parole (and probation) are prohibited from possessing firearms, yet 21 percent reported possessing a firearm while under supervision. Of those arrested for committing a new offense, almost 3 of every 4 reported being armed when they committed their offense.[48]

standard conditions of release Federal and state guidelines with rules with which parolees must comply to meet their conditions of release.

figure 10.4

United States Parole Commission

Standard Conditions of Release for U.S. Code Offenders

1. You shall go directly to the district shown on this CERTIFICATE OF RELEASE (unless released to the custody of other authorities). Within three days after your arrival, you shall report to your parole advisor if you have one, and the United States Probation Officer whose name appears on this Certificate. If in any emergency you are unable to contact your parole advisor, or your Probation Officer or the United States Probation Office, you shall communicate with the United States Parole Commission, Department of Justice, Chevy Chase, Maryland 20815.
2. If you are released to the custody of other authorities, and after your release from physical custody of such authorities, you are unable to report to the United States Probation Officer to whom you are assigned within three days, you shall report instead to the nearest United States Probation Officer.
3. You shall not leave the limits fixed by this CERTIFICATE OF RELEASE without written permission from your Probation Officer.
4. You shall notify your Probation Officer within 2 days of any change in your place of residence.
5. You shall make a complete and truthful written report (on a form provided for that purpose) to your Probation Officer between the first and third day of each month, and on the final day of parole. You shall also report to your Probation Officer at other times as your Probation Officer directs, providing complete and truthful information.
6. You shall not violate any law. Nor shall you associate with persons engaged in criminal activity. If you are arrested or questioned by a law-enforcement officer, you shall within 2 days report such contact to your Probation Officer or the United States Probation Office.
7. You shall not enter into any agreement to act as an "informer" or special agent for any law-enforcement agency.
8. You shall work regularly unless excused by your Probation Officer, and support your legal dependents, if any, to the best of your ability. You shall report within 2 days to your Probation Officer any changes in employment.
9. You shall not drink alcoholic beverages to excess. You shall not purchase, possess, use or administer marijuana or narcotic or other habit-forming or dangerous drugs, unless prescribed or advised by a physician. You shall not frequent places where such drugs are illegally sold, dispensed, used or given away.
10. You shall not associate with persons who have a criminal record unless you have permission of your Probation Officer.
11. You shall not possess a firearm/ammunition or other dangerous weapons.
12. You shall permit confiscation by your Probation Officer of any materials which your Probation Officer believes may constitute contraband in your possession and which your Probation Officer observes in plain view in your residence, place of business or occupation, vehicle(s) or on your person.
13. You shall make a diligent effort to satisfy any fine, restitution order, court costs or assessment, and/or court ordered child support or alimony payment that has been, or may be, imposed, and shall provide such financial information as may be requested, by your Probation Officer, relevant to the payment of the obligation. If unable to pay the obligation in one sum, you will cooperate with your Probation Officer in establishing an installment payment schedule.
14. You shall submit to a drug test whenever ordered by your Probation Officer.

Source: www.usdoj.gov/uspc/release.htm

The U.S. Supreme Court has decided that parolees are entitled to certain due process rights, although these rights are substantially less than those of defendants in a trial. Most rights of parolees were established in the 1972 case of ***Morrissey* v. *Brewer*,**[49] which gave parolees some protection against arbitrary and capricious revocation of parole. *Morrissey* v. *Brewer* secured the right to notice and a revocation hearing.

The supervising parole officer initiates proceedings for parole revocation by filing notice of a technical violation or a charge that the parolee has committed a new crime. As noted earlier, the parole officer can file notice of revocation of parole even if charges against the parolee are dropped. A standard of proof that is not sufficient for conviction in court may nevertheless be sufficient to revoke parole.

careers in the system

Probation and Parole Officers

Probation and parole officers enjoy a significant degree of independence in their work. They work directly with offenders, meeting clients in office visits and making scheduled and unscheduled visits to the clients' home and work. Probation officers specialize in supervision of juvenile offenders or adult offenders through separate agencies.

The position is moderately physically demanding, exposes the probation and parole officer to potentially life threatening situations, and is considered stressful. Between 39 and 55 percent of probation and parole officers report that they have been victims of work-related violence or threats. Parole officers who work in a facility or community setting report that they are concerned for their own safety.[50] Federal officers receive hazardous duty pay, for example. Applicants for the position of federal probation and parole officer must be physically capable but may use a hearing aid or glasses. In most instances, the amputation of an arm, hand, leg, or foot will not disqualify an applicant from appointment. Unlike law enforcement officers, probation and parole officers do not attend a training academy, though they may receive brief orientation training. Applicants are expected to already have the necessary counseling and supervision skills required for the position.

Most agencies prefer mature applicants with previous related job experience. Federal probation and parole officers have a mandatory retirement age of 57 after 20 years of service; thus, they must be 37 years of age or younger when first appointed. Maturity is an important characteristic for the job, because probation and parole work requires one-on-one contact with felony offenders in a supervisory capacity. Nearly all successful job applicants have previous experience in counseling, social work, or criminal justice. Caseloads of the probation and parole officer vary significantly. Officers with normal caseload supervise 80 to 150 offenders. The average caseload is 139.

Federal probation and parole officers are considered law enforcement officers and are authorized to carry firearms. The status of state probation officers varies by each state. Some states allow probation and parole officers to carry firearms and some do not.

There are different agencies for adult probation and parole and juvenile probation and parole. Each job has its own requirements, but generally juvenile probation and parole emphasize the need for counseling skills and social work more than adult probation and parole. Some states consider juvenile probation officers law enforcement agents and allow them to carry firearms.

Prior to the increase in the use of community corrections, probation and parole officers generally worked "normal" Monday through Friday hours and spent most of their time in their office. The demands of community-based supervision and intensive supervision has impacted probation and parole in that officers now find they must work evenings, weekends, and sometimes nights. However, unlike police and prisons, generally probation and parole offices generally are not open 24/7.

Unlike law enforcement agencies, probation and parole offices do not use a paramilitary structure or ranks. These officers wear civilian clothing, not uniforms. Frequent travel may be required. In rural areas, officers often must travel many miles to make home visits. Because the job is specialized and has limited duties, opportunities for advancement and horizontal job transfer are limited. Probation and parole officers work for the court, and each court has relatively few officers attached to it. Thus, throughout their careers, probation and parole officers continue to perform similar duties, unless they opt for a position in the administration and supervision of other probation and parole officers.

If you wanted to be a police officer, would you find the position of probation and parole officer just as appealing? What problems do you think a beginning probation and parole officer might face in counseling and supervising older felony offenders? What level of education, skills, and experiences would help a person succeed as a probation and parole officer?

Revocation hearings most often are held in a prison facility and are conducted by the parole board or hearing officers representing the parole board. The parolee has the right to present evidence on his or her behalf and to cross-examine witnesses but may not have the right to representation by an attorney. The U.S. Supreme Court has ruled that states do not have to provide parolees with appointed legal counsel if they cannot afford one. Normally, it is the inmate's responsibility, not the states', to arrange for legal representation at revocation hearings.

Parole violators returned to prison are still entitled to additional parole hearings and may be released on parole again at a later date.[51] Only 16 to 36 percent of rereleased parolees successfully complete parole on their second attempts.[52] For most state and federal parolees, at least a portion of their "street time" will be credited toward their original sentences.[53] Usually, the parole time preceding the violation, noncompliance, or commission of a new crime is counted toward completion of the original sentence. For example, an offender with 5 years left on the original sentence who successfully completes 3 years of parole would have to serve only 2 years on return to prison to complete the sentence.

▲ check your understanding **10.3** **How did parole originate? How does the type of sentencing influence parole? What percentage of parolees successfully completes parole? What are the duties of the parole board? How is a parole hearing conducted? How is parole granted and revoked? What are the federal standard conditions of release?**

Supervision of Probation and Parole

▼ the main idea **10.4** **Probation and parole officers are case workers with law enforcement powers who supervise convicted offenders in the community.**

The actual supervision of defendants released on probation and inmates released on parole is the work of state and federal **probation and parole officers**. As noted earlier, in many states and in the federal system, the same officers supervise both probation and parole and also perform pretrial investigation reports for the court. Probation and parole officers usually are considered law enforcement officers, with the power to carry concealed weapons and the power of arrest. At the same time, probation and parole officers are expected to perform rehabilitation work. This work strongly emphasizes social work and rehabilitation skills as opposed to investigative and police skills. One indicator of the preference for this skill mix is the fact that a federal probation and pretrial services officer must have a bachelor's degree and postgraduate experience in fields such as probation, pretrial services, parole, corrections, criminal investigations, and substance abuse or addiction counseling and treatment. Basic experience as a police officer, a correctional officer, or a security officer does not meet this requirement.[54] Many probation and parole officer applicants have master's degrees.

In the supervision of clients, the probation and parole officer acts as (1) a case worker to help clients succeed in their reintegration into the community and fulfill the conditions of their release; (2) a resource broker to help clients to obtain services, treatment, social benefits, educational opportunities, and employment; and (3) a law enforcement officer and officer of the court empowered to enforce compliance with the court's orders and obedience to the law. The success of a probation and parole officer is judged not by the number of clients he or she returns to prison for violating the conditions of their release but by the number of clients who successfully complete probation and parole. To help the offenders succeed, in addition to providing counseling and guidance, the officer helps them obtain entry into drug treatment programs, vocational training, jobs, housing, medical care, rehabilitation services, and other referrals. The

probation and parole officers
State and federal professional employees who report to the courts and supervise defendants released on probation and offenders released from prison on parole.

Most states and the federal government require that probation and parole officers have a minimum of a bachelor's degree, and many have a master's degree. Because of the strong social work component of the job, many probation and parole officers have degrees in social work, sociology, psychology, education, and public administration. Probation and parole began as volunteer initiatives and still make extensive use of citizen volunteers. The goal is to assist offenders and to help them succeed rather than arresting and punishing them.

probation and parole officer protects the community from any harm that may be done by conditionally released offenders and deters and detects criminal activity on the part of the released offenders. The probation and parole officer also verifies compliance with the terms of release, authenticates the clients' residency and employment, and confirms court-ordered payments of fines or restitution and court-ordered attendance at rehabilitation or treatment sessions. Because of their power to initiate revocation proceedings to return clients to prison, probation and parole officers are more influential than social workers in motivating clients toward rehabilitation and treatment.

Go to www.appa-net.org to view the website of the American Probation and Parole Association.

▲ check your understanding **10.4** **What are the job requirements for a probation and parole officer? What services are performed by the probation and parole officer? How do probation and parole officers help their clients?**

Reentry Programs for Drug Offenders

▼ the main idea **10.5** **The rampant abuse of drugs among offenders has led to a separate system of drug courts and rehabilitation programs.**

Drug use forecasting (DUF) data collected on defendants in 23 cities indicate that 51 to 83 percent of arrested adult men and 41 percent to 84 percent of arrested adult women were under the influence of at least one illicit drug at the time of arrest.[55] In addition, drug use is a significant factor in property offenses, as 16 percent of adult prisoners indicated that they committed their offenses to get money for drugs.[56] Although drug offenders may be nonviolent, during 1999, 12 percent of convicted federal drug defendants received a sentence enhancement for the use or possession of a firearm or other weapon.[57]

Drug crimes have occupied more and more resources of the criminal justice system. Between 1984 and 1999, the number of defendants charged with a drug offense in the federal courts increased from 11,854 to 29,306.[58] The Bureau of Justice Statistics estimates that two-thirds of federal and state prisoners and probationers could be characterized as drug involved.[59] In response to the increased frequency of drug crimes, the criminal justice system has enhanced drug law enforcement efforts and has adopted a get-tough sentencing policy for drug offenders. This tough federal stance has resulted in 62 percent of convicted federal drug defendants receiving statutory minimum sentences of at least five years or more.

However, enhanced enforcement and tough sentencing policies have failed to stem the number of drug offenders. Over 73 percent of state inmates reentering prison have admitted to drug or alcohol involvement while released.[60] Even when sentenced to prison, inmates continue to find ways to obtain drugs. Thus, incarceration in itself does little to break the cycle of illegal drug use and crime. Furthermore, the traditional case disposition process appears to lack the capacity to bring about any significant reduction in drug usage by persons convicted of drug offenses.[61] For a little over a decade, a new strategy to break the cycle of drug use and crime that has led to the revolving door syndrome for drug offenders has been the drug court. The **drug court** approach was started in 1989 as an experiment by the Dade County (Florida) Circuit Court. Today, nearly every state uses some form of drug court program to handle drug offenders. Drug courts have proved effective with adult and juvenile offenders and for use in tribal courts. Figure 10.5 lists the 10 key components of drug court programs.

Adult Drug Courts

In states that have adult drug courts, adult offenders arrested for drug offenses are diverted from traditional case disposition processing as soon as possible. These offenders

figure 10.5

The Ten Key Components of Drug Courts

The operation and components of drug courts vary from jurisdiction to jurisdiction, but the following 10 key components identify state adult drug court programs as proscribed by the Drug Courts Program Office:

- Drug courts integrate alcohol and other drug treatment services with justice system case processing.
- Using a nonadversarial approach, prosecution and defense counsel promote public safety while protecting participants' due process rights.
- Eligible participants are identified early and promptly placed in the drug court program.
- Drug courts provide access to a continuum of alcohol, drug, and other related treatment and rehabilitation services.
- Abstinence is monitored by frequent alcohol and other drug testing.
- A coordinated strategy governs drug court responses to participants' compliance.
- Ongoing judicial interaction with each drug court participant is essential.
- Monitoring and evaluation measure the achievement of program goals and gauge effectiveness.
- Continuing interdisciplinary education promotes effective drug court planning, implementation, and operations.
- Forging partnerships among drug courts, public agencies, and community-based organizations generates local support and enhances drug court effectiveness.

Source: Defining Drug Courts: The Key Components (Washington, DC: Office of Justice Programs, Drug Courts Program Office, January 1997), pp. 1–3.

drug court An approach for dealing with drug offenders that is aimed at breaking the cycle of drug use and crime.

are offered the opportunity to participate in the drug court program rather than traditional case disposition, which results in incarceration. Drug court programs use intermediate sanctions, community-based treatment, and intensive probation supervision to achieve a twofold purpose: (1) to get offenders clean and sober and (2) to compel offenders to participate in a comprehensive treatment program while being monitored under strict conditions for drug use. Almost all drug courts require participants to obtain a GED if they have not finished high school, to maintain or obtain employment, to be current in all financial obligations (including drug court fees and any court-ordered support payments), and to have a sponsor in the community. Some drug programs require offenders to perform community service hours.[62] Figure 10.6 illustrates how offenders are selected for inclusion in the Superior Court Drug Intervention Program.

Go to www.uvm.edu/~vlrs/doc/furloughs.htm for links to articles and statistics about drug courts throughout the United States.

figure 10.6

Case Identification for Superior Court Drug Intervention Program

Drug court programs use a drug test after arrest to identify and divert drug users and drug offenders from traditional case processing as soon as possible. This figure illustrates how drug offenders are identified in the Washington, DC, Superior Court Drug Intervention Program.

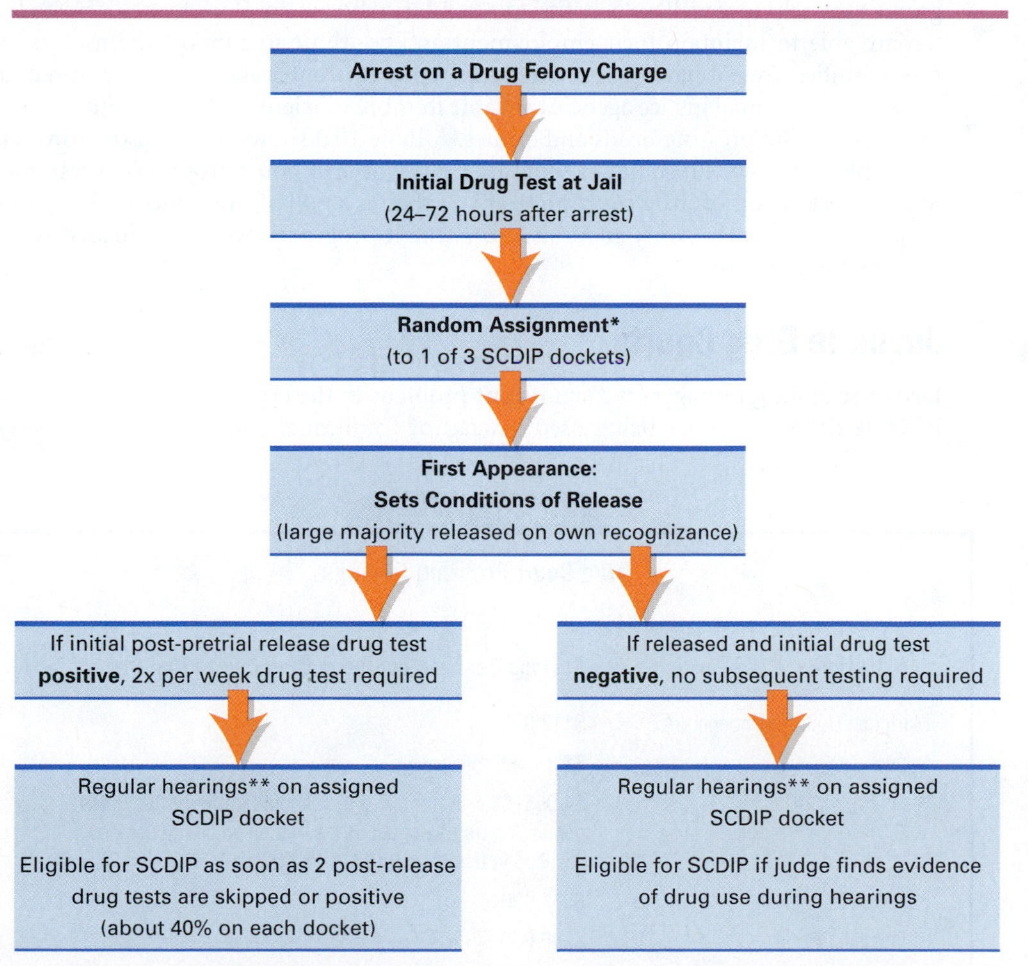

*Defendants were not allowed to transfer to another SCDIP docket.

**Plea offers were made at regular docket hearings and could occur before, after, or at the same time as defendant became eligible for SCDIP, and the program offer was not contingent on acceptance of the plea. However, if the plea were rejected, defendants transferred out of the SCDIP dockets to a trial docket.

Source: Adele Harrell, Shannon Cavanaugh, and John Roman, *Evaluation of the D.C. Superior Court Drug Intervention Programs* (Washington, DC: U.S. Department of Justice, April 2000), p. 3.

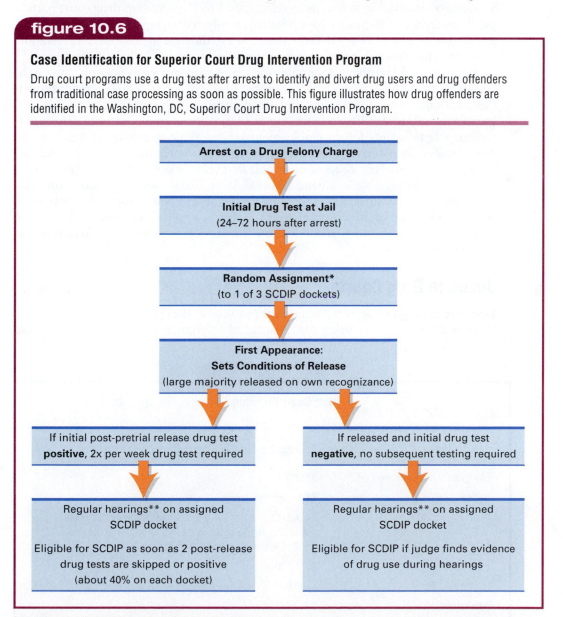

If offenders accept the offer to enter into the drug court program and are accepted, "they are referred immediately to a multi-phased out-patient treatment program entailing multiple weekly (often daily) contacts with the treatment provider for counseling, therapy and education; frequent urinalysis (usually at least weekly); frequent status hearings before the drug court judge (bi-weekly or more often at first); and a rehabilitation program entailing vocational, education, family, medical, and other support services."[63] Figure 10.7 shows the broad variety of treatment programs and support services that are available to participants in drug court programs.

In contrast to the traditional adjudication process in the criminal court, drug court programs are experiencing a significant reduction in recidivism among participants. Whereas about 45 percent of defendants convicted of drug possession will reoffend with a similar offense within two to three years, only 5 to 28 percent of drug court participants reoffend, and 90 percent have negative urinalysis drug reports.[64] Drug court programs also have been shown to save money. By avoiding the high cost of incarceration, some cities have been able to save up to $2.5 million per year in criminal justice costs.[65] By eliminating the revolving door syndrome, drug court programs not only save on the cost of incarcerating repeat offenders but they also save police, prosecutors, and courts the additional costs of processing the offenders through the system. Drug court programs also help save welfare benefits, as offenders who are employed when arrested often are able to maintain their employment and continue to support themselves and their families. By not having drug offenders repeatedly enter and exit the criminal justice system, criminal justice agencies are able to more efficiently allocate their resources to address more pressing needs and crimes.[66] Table 10.3 shows how jurisdictions have been able to achieve substantial savings by the use of drug court programs. A testament to the effectiveness of drug court programs is that in a poll of 318 police chiefs, almost 60 percent advocated court-supervised treatment programs over other justice system options for drug users.

Juvenile Drug Courts

Drug use among teenagers is a significant problem in the criminal justice system, and juvenile drug courts are being used instead of traditional adjudication processes to

table 10.3

Drug Court Program Savings

Jurisdiction	Savings Realized by Use of Drug Court Programs
Maricopa County (Phoenix), AZ	$112,077
Denver, CO	$1.8–$2.5 million
Washington, DC	$4,065–$8,845 per client in jail costs (amount fluctuates, depending on use of jail as a sanction while the defendant is enrolled in the drug court); and $102,000 in prosecution costs
Bartow, FL	$531,900
Gainesville, FL	$200,000
Kalamazoo, MI	$299,754
Klamath Falls, OR	$86,400
Beaumont, TX	$443,520

Source: Drug Court Clearinghouse and Technical Assistance Project, Office of Justice Programs, U.S. Department of Justice, www.ojp.usdoj.gov/dcpo/decade98.htm.

figure 10.7

Treatment and Services Provided by Drug Court Programs

A survey of 212 drug court programs illustrates the broad range of treatment programs and services provided by drug court programs.

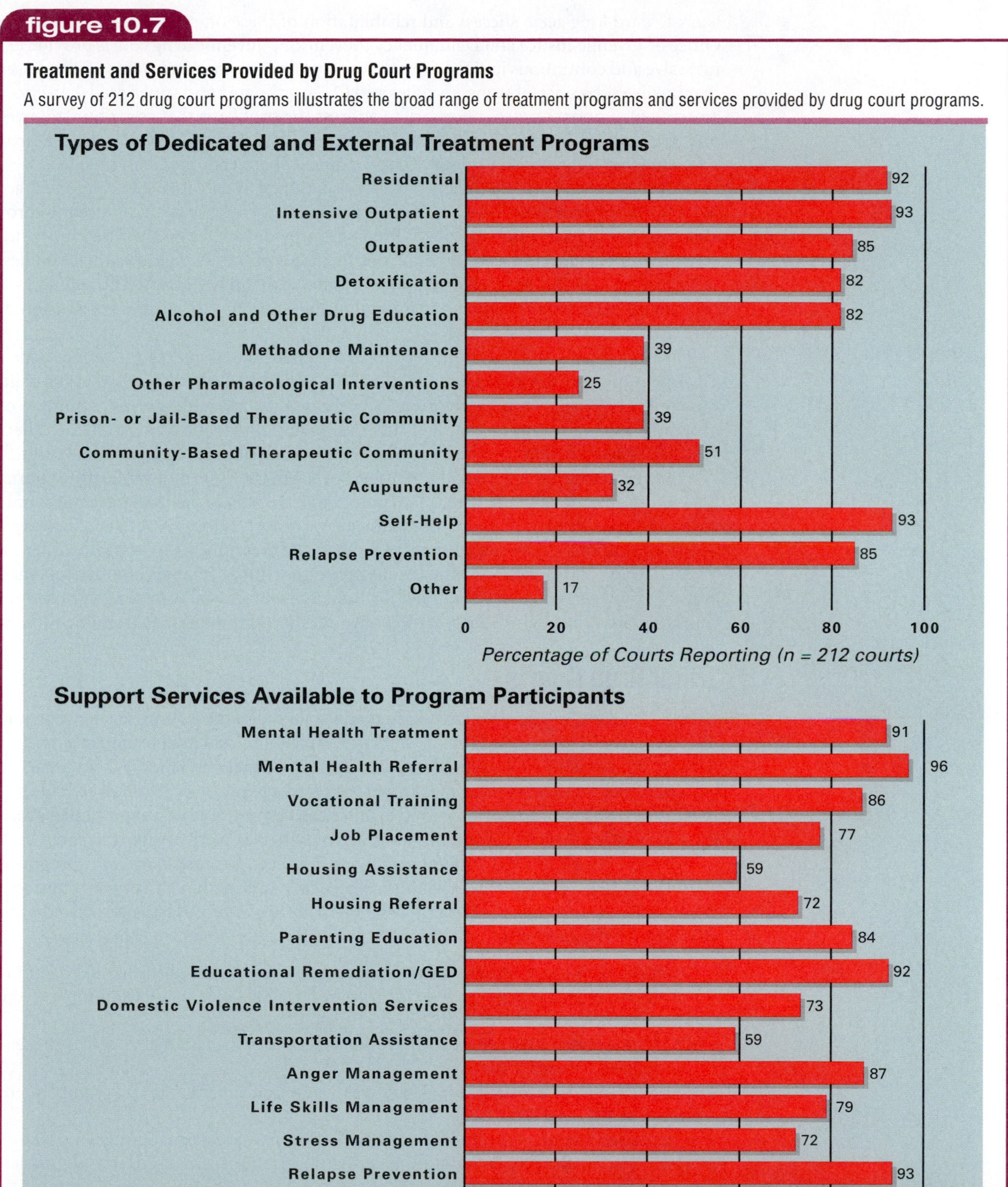

Source: Elizabeth Peyton, *Executive Summary Treatment Services in Adult Drug Courts: Report on the 1999 National Drug Court Treatment Survey* (Washington, DC: U.S. Department of Justice, May 2001), pp. 7–8.

work toward long-term success and rehabilitation of these offenders. According to the Office of Juvenile Justice and Delinquency Prevention, "juvenile drug courts provide (1) intensive and continuous judicial supervision over delinquency and status offense cases that involve substance-abusing juveniles and (2) coordinated and supervised delivery of an array of support services necessary to address the problems that contribute to juvenile involvement in the justice system."[67] Juvenile drug courts, like adult drug courts, have emerged only in the last decade but are quickly being adopted nationwide.

Juvenile drug courts are designed to respond as quickly as possible to delinquent activity so that offenders are held accountable and intrusive intervention can occur to provide treatment and sanction options.[68] Programs provide for court-supervised substance abuse treatment and core services addressing the needs of the juveniles and their families, including educational needs, behavioral problems, and family therapy. The hallmark of juvenile drug courts is the intensive, continuous judicial monitoring and supervision of participants.[69]

Juvenile drug court programs recognize the challenge of addressing family issues. The operating premise is that if family issues are not addressed, it is likely that the child will continue to be involved with drugs and delinquent activity. As a result, a number of programs require parent or guardian supervision and utilize the Multi-Systemic Therapy (MST) approach to provide family-based treatment and to teach parenting skills.[70]

Extensive data are not available to evaluate the effectiveness of juvenile drug courts, but "judges anecdotally report that these programs are able to achieve greater accountability and provide a broader array of treatment and other services to youth and their families than traditional juvenile courts."[71] One-half to three-fourths of youths who enter juvenile drug court programs complete the program.[72] Initial analysis of indicators such as recidivism, drug use, and educational achievement seems to indicate that juvenile drug courts are providing better rehabilitation of youth than are traditional juvenile courts.[73]

Tribal Drug Courts

Unique problems of crime on Indian reservations include a disproportionately high rate of crime compared to general crime statistics. Alcohol and other substance abuse contributes substantially to the crime problem on Native American lands, as more than 90 percent of the criminal cases in most tribal courts involve alcohol or substance abuse.[74] In addition to alcohol abuse, many Native American communities have substantial problems with toxic inhalants. Drug courts were first adopted by Native American and Alaska Native tribal courts in 1997. Interest is growing, however, because drug court programs are more closely aligned with tribal justice concepts and methods than are traditional criminal justice processes.[75] Nevertheless, there are unique problems associated with adapting the drug court concept to meet the specific needs of Native Americans:[76]

- Tribal courts must address the specific cultural needs of their individual communities, including the challenge of incorporating tribal custom and tradition into the tribal drug court.
- The nature and high volume of alcohol abuse cases in most tribal courts present unique adaptation issues.
- Tribal courts face jurisdictional barriers that complicate their ability to implement an effective drug court process.
- Tribes seeking to establish drug court systems often face a broad range of other issues and challenges, including isolated rural locations, small-community issues, lack of resources and services, and lack of funding.

Tribal drug courts generally are called **Tribal Healing to Wellness Courts**. Some programs have developed individual names, using words from their native languages.[77] Healing to Wellness Courts may use traditional treatment processes involving tribal elders, traditional healing ceremonies, talking circles, peacemaking, sweats and sweat lodge, visits with a medicine man or woman, the sun dance, and a vision quest.[78]

Jurisdictional barriers to tribal drug courts include the lack of criminal jurisdiction over non-Native Americans, concurrent state jurisdiction, legal limits in sentencing (to one year or a fine of $5,000, or both), and a historically strained relationship with state courts and state agencies.[79] Also, more than 50 percent of the reservation population is under the age of 18,[80] requiring greater demand for juvenile drug court programs than is the case in the traditional criminal justice system. Data for traditional drug court programs are promising, however, and it is hoped that the drug court concept will prove flexible enough to work with traditional Native justice concepts and methods.[81]

TASC and RSAT

Federal assistance programs such as **Treatment Accountability for Safer Communities (TASC)** and the **Residential Substance Abuse Treatment (RSAT)** for the State Prisoners Formula Grant Program have helped states adopt new comprehensive programs for drug offenders. Federal legislation designed to help states break the addiction-crime cycle of nonviolent, drug-involved offenders include the 1972 Drug Abuse and Treatment Act and the Violent Crime Control and Law Enforcement Act of 1994. Both laws provide federal funds to states to allow them to link the legal sanctions of the criminal justice system with the federally funded therapeutic interventions of drug treatment programs.[82] The major premise of programs funded by the grants is that criminal sanctions can be combined with the reintegration of offenders into the community, and that this can be done through a broad base of support from both the criminal justice system and the treatment community.[83] Combining intermediate sanctions and drug offender treatment programs is both effective and cost efficient. To prevent a return to drug use, these programs provide treatment both in prison and after release through postincarceration supervision. The combination of treatment strategies can reduce recidivism by about 50 percent. In addition to reducing recidivism, drug treatment costs are about $6,500 per year per inmate, whereas imprisonment costs are 4 to 10 times higher.[84]

TASC Treatment Accountability for Safer Communities, a federal assistance program to help states break the addiction-crime cycle.

RSAT Residential Substance Abuse Treatment, a federal assistance program to help states provide for treatment instead of prison for substance abusers.

▲ check your understanding **10.5** **What is the role of alcohol and drugs in criminal offending and crime rates? How do community-based programs address problems of substance abuse through state adult and juvenile drug courts? What special issues and challenges do tribal drug courts face? What are the benefits of federal programs that combine intensive supervision and therapeutic treatment for drug offenders?**

conclusion:

Try, Try Again

The criminal justice system involves a dynamic process that is undergoing constant change, including the corrections component. Many correctional programs, philosophies, and challenges are new and evolving. Jails and prisons used for more than 100 years are being replaced by new structures that are radically different. Probation and parole, which emerged in the early twentieth century, are already being transformed by the new philosophies of intensive probation supervision (IPS) probation and parole and electronic monitoring. In the past 20 to 30 years, new intermediate sanctions have appeared that focus on control and treatment in the community. In the past decade, new programs for addressing the crisis of drug-addicted inmates are winning greater acceptance by the entire criminal justice system and the public.

Ways of looking at corrections are changing as new experiments in control and treatment are being tried. New research indicates that prisoners actually may prefer prison to many of the new intermediate and community-based sanctions. When polled as to their opinion of the harshness of punishments, many offenders say they prefer prison to the intrusiveness and control of IPS and other various community-based programs.[85] Fifteen percent of the participants who apply for early release under the New Jersey IPS program withdraw their application once they understand the restrictions and conditions of the program. When nonviolent offenders in Marion County, Oregon, were offered a choice between a prison term or release under IPS, one-third of the offenders chose prison.[86]

The perfect method to rehabilitate offenders and the perfect method to provide for community safety when offenders are released back into the community have not been found. However, like law enforcement and the judicial system, the correctional system continues to look for new and better ways to protect the community while providing for the successful reentry of offenders into the community.

Why should you be concerned about the success of reentry programs? In 2004, when Oklahoma prisons started a six-part course on maintaining a healthy marriage, many questioned the expense and resources of inaugurating marriage programs in the prison. The response by prison officials to this challenge was simple and direct. "There are 600,000 Americans leaving prison in the next few years. And those guys are all coming to an apartment complex near you."[87] When inmates leave prison and return to the community, it is much better if they are rehabilitated rather than recidivists.

chapter **summary**

- The growing number of offenders and the high cost of prison have resulted in the early release of millions of inmates. Types of early release include mandatory release, good-time release, pardon, commutation of sentence, probation, and parole.
- The practice of probation originated with John Augustus of Boston in the mid-nineteenth century. Probation is a suspended sentence, granted by the trial judge on the basis of information in the presentence investigation report.
- Probation and parole have many advantages, including lower cost, reduction of overcrowding in jails and prisons, and the ability to use community resources to help rehabilitate offenders. Disadvantages include potential dangers to the community and repeat offending.
- Probation can be revoked for a technical violation, noncompliance with court orders, or the commission of a new crime. Probationers and parolees have some due process rights in the revocation of release.
- Parole is conditional early release from prison and is granted by a parole board, which is responsible for deciding which prisoners are released early. Parole hearings do not have to provide the same constitutional rights to inmates that they receive at criminal trials.
- The origins of parole are in Maconochie's mark system, Crofton's Irish system, and early release of youthful offenders at Brockway's Elmira Reformatory in the nineteenth century.
- Inmates who receive parole must abide by certain conditions and comply with laws and terms of release. Parole can be revoked, but the parolee is entitled to notice and a hearing.
- Probation and parole officers perform presentence investigation reports and supervise offenders on conditional release in the community. Probation and parole officers act as case workers, resource brokers, and law enforcement officers.
- Reentry programs for drug offenders emphasize the need to combine the power of the criminal justice system with the effectiveness of treatment programs under strictly supervised conditions. Adult, juvenile, and tribal drug courts are proving to be effective community-based treatment programs.

vocabulary review

commutation of sentence, 364
consolidated model, 375
diversion, 363
drug court, 384
executive pardon, 364
good-time credit, 363
independent model, 375
indeterminate sentence, 372
Irish system, 372
mandatory release, 363
mark system, 371
parole board, 375
parole d'honneur, 371
parole hearings, 377
probation, 365
probation and parole officers, 382
RSAT, 389
sex offender registries, 376
standard conditions of release, 379
suspended sentence, 363
TASC, 389
technical violation, 370
ticket of leave, 371

do you remember?

John Augustus, 365
Zebulon Brockway, 372
Comprehensive Crime Control Act of 1984, 363
Sir Walter Crofton, 371
Eighth Amendment, 378
Elmira Reformatory, 372
Megan Kanka, 376
Alexander Maconochie, 371
Morrissey v. *Brewer,* 380
Office of Probation and Pretrial Services, 366
Parole Commission and Reorganization Act, 376
United States Parole Commission, 376
Tribal Healing to Wellness Courts, 388

think about this

1. Mandatory release after serving a full prison term places a former convict into society with no supervision, no safety net, and no rehabilitation. Consider also that serving a full prison term means that the convict was not able to accumulate good-time credits and was not deemed eligible for parole. This is why some Americans say that to "lock them up and throw away the key" is not an option. What is the solution?
2. In 2002, a Boston-area judge controversially decided to grant probation to several sex offenders. A media storm ensued that raised public fears and protest and jeopardized the safety of the released offenders. Do the mass media act responsibly in covering stories about criminals and the criminal justice system? How can a balance be achieved between the public's "need to know" and the many factors involved in making appropriate probation decisions?
3. Would you hire a convicted criminal to work in your company? Why or why not? Would you pay higher taxes to support government employment of probationers and parolees as community service workers or aid workers abroad? How do problems of finding and keeping employment put released convicts at risk for reoffending, and what is the solution to this vicious cycle?

research navigator

Visit the Research Navigator website (www.researchnavigator.com), login and select the criminal justice data base in ContentSelect. Type in the key words "Getting Serious about corrections" and select the article "Getting Serious About Corrections" by Vincent D. Basile. The article discusses the problem of prisoner re-entry and recidivism. Sample the article and answer the following questions:

1. What is the importance of the quality of service provided to offenders or potential offenders at the point at which they first become involved with the courts or the criminal justice system?
2. What does Basile suggest should be the measure of success of re-entry programs?
3. Why is early identification of those individuals with a predilection for criminal behavior risk important in rehabilitation and breaking the cycle of offending?
4. What suggestions does Basile make to improve the quality of re-entry programs?

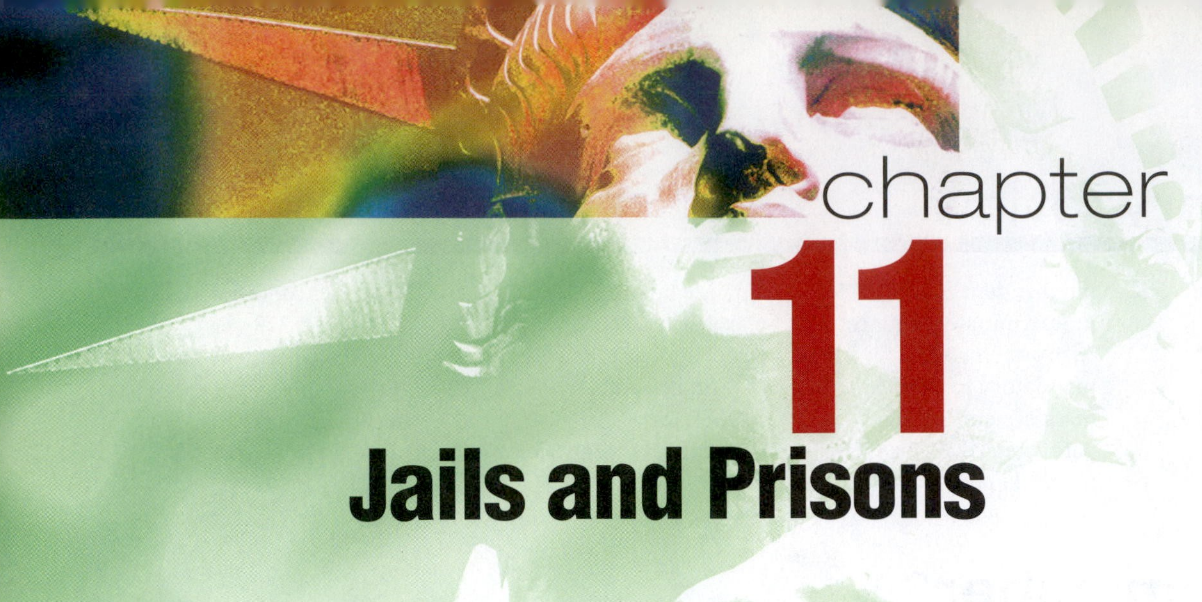

chapter 11
Jails and Prisons

CHAPTER OUTLINE

LEARNING OBJECTIVES

After reading this chapter, you will know

- How jails and prisons developed in the United States.
- The uses of federal, county, and municipal jails.
- How the state prison system is organized and administered.
- Career opportunities in state prison systems.
- The organization and development of the federal prison system.
- The reasons for and pros and cons of private prisons.

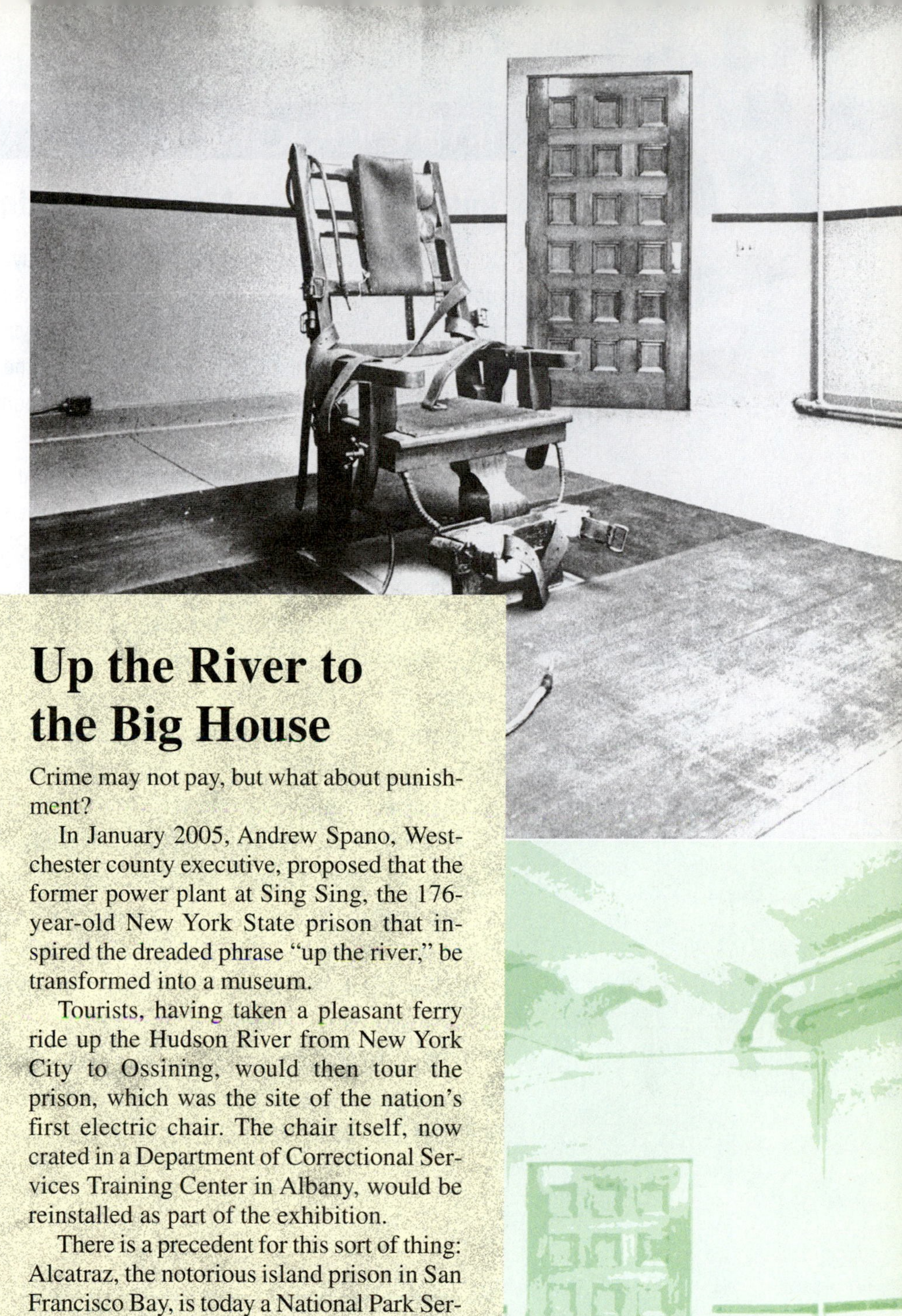

Up the River to the Big House

Crime may not pay, but what about punishment?

In January 2005, Andrew Spano, Westchester county executive, proposed that the former power plant at Sing Sing, the 176-year-old New York State prison that inspired the dreaded phrase "up the river," be transformed into a museum.

Tourists, having taken a pleasant ferry ride up the Hudson River from New York City to Ossining, would then tour the prison, which was the site of the nation's first electric chair. The chair itself, now crated in a Department of Correctional Services Training Center in Albany, would be reinstalled as part of the exhibition.

There is a precedent for this sort of thing: Alcatraz, the notorious island prison in San Francisco Bay, is today a National Park Service site that attracts about 1.3 million visitors a year. The logistics of creating a museum are challenging. For one thing, unlike Alcatraz, Sing Sing is still a state prison, housing more than 1,700 inmates. But Kathleen Hulser, public historian at the New York Historical Society, recalled that the electric chair, which was displayed recently as a part of an exhibit on the Rosenberg atom spy case, was an undeniable attraction.

Adapted from "Up the River to the Big House," New York Times Online, www.nytimes.com, January 9, 2005 by Sam Roberts.

introduction:

Imprisonment—A Modern Invention

As mentioned in earlier chapters, the public displays little interest in the criminal justice system until there is a crisis or some act so repulsive to social values that attention is focused on the offending institution or persons. How far the general public is removed from corrections is illustrated by the interest that the public has not in the actual issues and operations of prisons but in prisons as attractions of interest. Across the country numerous prisons have been converted to tourist attractions.

To a large degree, the modern prison is an American invention. One of the things that the public finds interesting about these prisons is the sheer brutality inherent in the conditions of confinement in these early prisons. Early prisons were purposely designed to appear physically and psychologically intimidating. For example, in 1824, Daniel Rose, the first warden of the Maine State Prison, declared that "state prisons should be so constructed that even their aspect might be terrible, and appear like what they should be, dark and comfortless, abodes of guilt and wretchedness." Not only were prisons designed to look like "terrible, dark and comfortless abodes of guilt and wretchedness," but prison life and treatment of inmates often were abusive and involved extensive use of corporal punishment. At the time, many assumed that such conditions would result in rehabilitation of inmates.

The **incarceration** of accused defendants and convicted offenders has a sordid history. It is a history of violence against inmates, brutal conditions of imprisonment, and theories of rehabilitation based on popular misconceptions and strongly held religious beliefs that emphasized that crime was a moral fault. Governments invested little financial resources into jails and prisons. Often wardens were expected to run state prisons with no state appropriations or resources. The thinking about jails and prisons has changed significantly.

This chapter discusses the development of jails, state prisons, and federal penitentiaries; and how they have been, to a large degree, transformed into new institutions that are significantly different from their historical roots.

Development of American Jails and Prisons

the main idea 11.1 The American prison system has developed from a system that abused and exploited prisoners into one that protects prisoners' rights.

The first institutions for incarceration of prisoners in colonial America and the United States were local jails, which served primarily for detention prior to trial or execution rather than for punishment or rehabilitation of the criminal.[1] In 1681, for example, the community of West Jersey required that condemned persons be kept in safe confinement until the next General Assembly after the governor had reviewed their cases.[2] Prisoners were confined until their punishments could be determined. Prisoners incarcerated in local jails were expected to work for their daily keep or to pay for it. They were not housed at the expense of the community.[3] In colonial America, jails for the most part were operated by private parties, and after the Revolutionary War, they were operated by the sheriff. Early jails were more like secure houses than the fortified structures of today. Apparently, early jails were not all that secure, however, as prisoners often

incarceration The bodily confinement of a person in a jail or prison.

escaped from them. The colony of New Jersey reported 1,830 escapes from jails between 1751 and 1777, an average rate of 67 per year.[4]

Early Jail Conditions

Conditions in early jails were deplorable, and all descriptions of them are difficult to imagine. As jails increasingly were used to incarcerate the mentally ill and the poor, overcrowding became a serious problem. One 1767 description of an early jail in Charlestown (Boston) reported that 16 debtors were housed in a single 12-by-12-foot room. The cell was so crowded that one of the prisoners died of suffocation but could not be removed until all of the other prisoners were first made to lie down to make room to retrieve the dead prisoner.[5]

In early jails, it was the prisoners' responsibility to provide for their basic necessities of life with their own funds or with the help of outside benefactors. Prisoners with the financial resources to provide for themselves could do so, but the state had no obligation to provide food or medical treatment for indigents. The more wealthy prisoners could buy additional cell space, food, and privileges, and even liquor was commonly made available to those who could afford it.[6] Prisoners who could not afford to pay for their accommodations were required to toil on public works projects in exchange for their keep. Those who could not work were allowed to beg passersby for food or money. Records indicate that some prisoners who were unable to provide for their daily needs were allowed to die of starvation.[7]

The portrait of American local jails at the birth of the nation is unpleasant. The jails were filled with all sorts of people—criminals as well as victims of misfortune. Men, women, and children were confined in the same cell, and no attempt was made to protect women and children from aggressive male prisoners. Sick prisoners were not separated from the healthy, so contagious diseases quickly and easily spread in the crowded and unsanitary conditions. Jails were not heated, did not have plumbing, and did not provide adequate per-person sleeping and living space. A primary factor in keeping the local jail population down was the death of many prisoners.[8] In 1777, English reformer **John Howard** traveled extensively in Europe, visiting jails and prisons. As a result, he wrote *State of Prisons,* a critical review of the brutality and inhumane conditions of Europe's penal systems. Howard's book was very influential and contributed to efforts at prison reform on both sides of the Atlantic.

Reform at Last: The Walnut Street Jail

In America, the prison reform movement had its origins with a group of Quakers called the **Philadelphia Society to Alleviate the Miseries of Public Prisons.**[9] In 1787, Benjamin Rush argued for prison reform at a meeting of the Society for Promoting Political Inquiries at the home of Benjamin Franklin. The Philadelphia Society to Alleviate the Miseries of Public Prisons was formed as a result, and this group lobbied the Pennsylvania legislature for humane treatment of prisoners. The group was successful, and in 1790, the Pennsylvania legislature passed a law calling for the renovation of the **Walnut Street Jail** in Philadelphia.[10] In addition to a humane physical facility and adequate food and water supplied at public expense,[11] the reform effort was successful in abolishing the practice of placing men, women, and children in the same cell and allowing prisoners to buy better treatment; prohibiting the consumption of alcohol by the prisoners; and separating the debtors and mentally ill from the criminal population. Children, many confined only because they were orphans, were removed from the jail and housed in a separate building.[12]

Prisoners in the Walnut Street Jail were required to work but were paid for their labor and could earn early release for good behavior. The new jail was a great improvement over previous conditions of imprisonment, and leaders came from other states to investigate the possibility of adopting the Walnut Street Jail model for their states.[13]

Based on principles demonstrated in the Walnut Street Jail, Pennsylvania's Eastern State Penitentiary became the blueprint for American state prisons of the early nineteenth century. The wheel shape of the penitentiary, with separated, large, single cells, reflected solitary, silent penitence, and rehabilitation as the goals of incarceration. How did New York's Auburn system differ from Pennsylvania's penitentiary model?

However, the Walnut Street Jail ultimately failed because of overcrowding, which destroyed its ability to accomplish its mission. As a result of receiving state funding for renovation, the Walnut Street Jail became a temporary state prison, allowing prisoners from other cities in Pennsylvania to be housed there. The jail quickly filled beyond capacity.[14] Conditions deteriorated, and the cost of operating the jail became prohibitive. The goal of making prisons places for rehabilitation was crushed.

Bigger Is Better: Eastern State Penitentiary

By 1820, the hopes that Walnut Street Jail would be the model for prison reform were dashed, and overcrowding of the state's only prison required that a new institution be built. Pennsylvania's **Eastern State Penitentiary,** built in 1829, was an enormous investment of state resources and was based on a new philosophy of rehabilitation. Eastern State Penitentiary was built at the cost of $500,000 to house 250 prisoners. It was the most expensive public building in the New World and the first in the country to have flush toilets and hot-air heating.[15]

Eastern State Penitentiary was not designed as a jail or a prison but as a **penitentiary**. In a penitentiary, it was expected that inmates would reflect on their life of crime and change their ways. To encourage this transformation, Eastern State Penitentiary had an individual cell for each prisoner. Prisoners were required to become proficient at a skill that would support them after their release, such as woodworking or leatherworking. When not working or exercising, prisoners were expected to read the Bible, the only literature allowed in their cells. Prisoners were kept in isolation from one another to avoid corrupting influences, and a "silent system" was enforced. The **silent system** required that prisoners communicate only with guards or prison officials; communication with other prisoners was forbidden. The goal of incarceration was to evoke penitence in the prisoner, with the idea that guilt and remorse or repentence would lead to rehabilitation, and prisoners could be released to lead normal, productive lives. This philosophy was compatible with the classical criminology theories and religious values of the period, emphasizing that crime was a rational choice made by the offender.

penitentiary Correctional institution based on the concept that inmates could change their criminality through reflection and penitence.

silent system Correctional practice of prohibiting inmates from talking to other inmates.

Eastern State Penitentiary was a maximum-security, walled, self-contained institution. It had seven wings like the spokes of a wheel that extended from a hublike center. Inmate cells were located on either side of the wings with outside windows. In the middle of the wing was a central passageway for use by guards and prison officials. Following the model of solitary confinement, the cells were designed so that inmates could not see any part of the prison other than what was directly in front of the cell. Cells were 12 feet long by 7.5 feet wide and had a window. Some inmates had a small outside exercise yard but seldom had a chance to leave their cells. The institution's design called for all activities—working, exercise, eating, and sleeping—to be performed within the individual prisoner's cell.

As with the Walnut Street Jail, many people came to view Eastern State Penitentiary to see if it could be a solution to their penal problems. The single-cell model reduced problems with inmate discipline. Inmates rarely had the chance to violate any rules, as they seldom left their cells or interacted with other inmates. As a result, corporal punishment was practically eliminated. Inmates were motivated to be productive and abide by the rules in exchange for the chance of early release and financial reward for their work.

The Auburn System

During the early history of American prisons, the Walnut Street model of individual cells competed against the Auburn, New York, prison model of the congregate work system for popularity as new prisons were constructed. The single-cell plan was expensive, and as prison populations increased, many states found the cost of single-cell construction was prohibitive and turned to New York's Auburn system as the model for constructing new prisons. Built in 1816, **Auburn Prison** was a walled, maximum-security prison with inmate cells located in the center of a secure building. The cells in Auburn were smaller (7 feet long, 4 feet wide, and 7 feet high), with back-to-back cells stacked five tiers high. This arrangement made it possible to house many more prisoners cheaper and with much less space. Unlike the design of Eastern State Penitentiary, Auburn's design housed inmates in the center of the building without an outside window or exercise area. The cells were poorly lit and lacked access to fresh air. The cells stacked one on top of another created a unique prison architecture, called the **inside cell block**. This architectural model for housing prison inmates became a distinctive feature of the American penal system.

Auburn's cells were too small to be the inmate's "home," as in Eastern State Penitentiary. Auburn's cells were only for sleeping; during the day, inmates were moved to other areas to work and eat. This pattern is known as the **congregate work system**. Because inmates were moved from place to place within the prison, Auburn required a different type of administration. To minimize the opportunity for plotting escapes or uprisings, inmates were not permitted to talk to one another. However, unlike in the Eastern State Penitentiary, the silent system was more difficult to enforce, as inmates worked and ate together and met as they moved from place to place in the prison. To enforce silence, Auburn adopted a system of corporal punishment for violations of the rule. Flogging was administered as punishment, not for the crime but for violating prison rules. The floggings were designed to be painful but not to maim the inmate or require medical attention.[16]

Prisoners being moved from one location to another were required to march in a lockstep formation—marching in unison with one hand on the shoulder of the man ahead and all heads turned in the direction of the guard. When the inmates arrived at their destination, they continued to mark time until commanded to stop. Also, all prisoners had a similar short haircut and were required to wear distinctive clothing with stripes to clearly identify their status as prison inmates. Thus, the prisoners' schedule, movements, and appearance were strictly regulated.[17]

In 1821, the New York legislature passed a law requiring the "worst inmates" held at Auburn to be placed in **solitary confinement**.[18] These inmates were cut off from all contact with other people, including visitors, and were confined to their cells with only a Bible to read. Unlike inmates at Eastern State Penitentiary, however, Auburn inmates in solitary confinement had no work to do, no exercise yard, and a very small cell. Lacking knowledge of the harmful effects of long-term solitary confinement (the sciences of sociology and psychology did not emerge until the 1900s), the legislature had created a

inside cell block Prison construction in which individual cells are stacked back to back in tiers in the center of a secure building.

congregate work system The practice of moving inmates from sleeping cells to other areas of the prison for work and meals.

solitary confinement Practice of confining an inmate such that there is no contact with other people.

prison environment antithetical to rehabilitation. Inmates in solitary confinement had mental breakdowns and committed suicide. The alarming debility and death rates forced the state to abandon this practice.[19]

Because inmates worked together in the Auburn system, the prison could combine their labor in larger and more profitable industries and construction projects. The sale of prison-made goods was so successful, the prison was virtually economically self-sufficient and required few resources from the state budget.[20] While the Eastern State Penitentiary model required more and more state resources to operate as the prison population rose, only 13 years after Auburn opened, the warden announced he no longer needed state funds to run the prison.[21] The Auburn system became the prototype of the American prison. The economic advantages appealed to other states, and between 1825 and 1969, 29 state prisons were built using the Auburn model. Many of these institutions, such as New York's Sing Sing, are still in use today.[22]

Southern Penal Systems

Many northern states used the Auburn system as a prison model. Southern states, however, developed their own unique prison system, based on different historical circumstances. The South retained an agrarian economy rather than building an industry-based factory system. Southern prisons practiced the **convict lease system** to supply the farm labor once provided by slaves. Rather than build large maximum-security prisons to produce prison-labor-made goods, southern states leased prisoners to private contractors. Inmate labor was used for agricultural work, some factory work, and construction work. The private contractor assumed all responsibility for the care and support of inmates and paid the state a fee for the inmates' labor. This prisoner lease system permitted southern states to deal with great increases in the prison population following the Civil War, without requiring the states to finance the construction of prisons. For some states, a significant amount of the state's income was derived from the sale of convict labor.[23]

Visit the website of the Southern Center for Human Rights at www.schr.org.

Following the Civil War, approximately 90 percent of those incarcerated in the South were free blacks. Work and living conditions for inmates were wretched, and convicts worked 12 to 15 hours a day. States did not set minimum standards for living conditions and did not inspect the sites where inmates were housed. Inmates who performed agricultural work often were housed in temporary, portable cages near the work site. Thus, prisoners were no better off than during slavery, and discipline was brutal.[24] To prevent escapes when the prisoners worked in open areas, they were shackled together in what came to be known as the **chain gang**. The prisoner death rate in this system was over twice as high in southern prisons as in northern prisons.[25]

The prisoner lease system was used until the 1930s, when it was replaced by the **prison farm system**, or plantation system. Rather than lease prison labor to private contractors, the state used inmate labor to maintain large prison farm complexes. These prison farms were expected to be self-sufficient and profit-making. Some states expanded the concept and used prison labor to operate other profit-making industries. To reduce the costs of operating prison farms and prison industries, states often used inmates as guards and supervisors of other inmates.

convict lease system In southern penal systems, leasing prisoners to work for private contractors.

chain gang In the southern penal system, convicts chained together during outside labor.

prison farm system In southern penal systems, using inmate labor to maintain large profit-making prison farms or plantations.

Changing social consciousness in the southern states eventually ended for-profit prisons and use of inmate "trusties" to maintain security. Arkansas, however, continued to use the prison farm system, with its many abuses, until the 1960s.[26] A series of U.S. Supreme Court cases then ruled the penal practices in Arkansas unconstitutional.[27] The Court also decided that whipping for disciplinary purposes and the use of electric shock were cruel and unusual punishments. In its decision, the Court declared, "For the ordinary convict a sentence to the Arkansas Penitentiary today amounts to a banishment from civilized society to a dark and evil world completely alien to the free world culture."[28] The state of Texas also practiced the plantation farm system and came under

The chain gang developed in the southern penal system, which reflected the legacy of dependency on cheap or slave labor for the South's agricultural economy. The reemergence of chain gangs in the 1990s led to a storm of protest and questions regarding the constitutionality of this treatment of prisoners. What parts of the U.S. Constitution might relate to the use of chain gangs?

public criticism and the scrutiny of the Court. As in the case of Arkansas, a series of U.S. Supreme Court rulings forced Texas to reform its prison system.

Modernization of Jails and Prisons

Contemporary jails and prisons may appear to the casual observer to be similar to the jails and prisons of the nineteenth century, but on examination, they are very different. Institutional corrections in the twenty-first century are being shaped by many forces of transformation, creating innovative strategies and causing an examination of the reasons for incarceration as a punishment for crime. The use of incarcerations as punishment for crime has resulted in a record incarceration rate for the United States. In 1997, a study of the world's incarceration rate by the Sentencing Project revealed that the United States and Russia had the highest incarceration rates in the world. From a rate of 426 prisoners per 100,000 population in 1991, despite a drop in the crime rate during the 1990s, the incarceration rate in the United States continued to grow every year.[29] The rate of growth slowed in 2000, but the prison population still was at an all-time high and continued to grow, reaching approximately 2 million people in federal, state, and local correctional facilities at year end 2004.[30] With only 5 percent of the world's population, the United States has 25 percent of the world's prisoners.[31] Incarceration must be viewed as a major industry and source of employment in the United States.

Prisons have come a long way from the model of self-sufficient, no-cost-to-the-state prisons of the nineteenth century. Today, prisons are a significant cost to local, state, and federal government, and employment in corrections accounts for 34 percent of the total employees in the criminal justice system.[32] The cost of prisons has increased over 300 percent since 1984. A 2004 study titled "The New Landscape of Imprisonment: Mapping America's Prison Expansion" by the Urban Institute found that some counties in the United States have more than 30 percent of their residents incarcerated. Nationwide, one in every 138 U.S. residents was in prison or jail at year end 2004.[33] In 1923, the United States had only 61 prisons. The number of federal and state prisons grew from 592 in 1974 to 1,023 in 2000. As the number of prisoners and prisons has increased, the cost of corrections to governments has increased. Corrections account for 63 percent of total state justice system expenditures and 29 percent of local criminal justice expenditures (see Table 11.1).

Early prisons often spent no money to house an inmate. In fact, some states even expected that prisons would produce a profit for the state. However, today the average annual cost of housing an inmate in a state prison is approximately $20,000, and the average cost per year of housing a single federal inmate is approximately $23,500. The cost

table 11.1

U.S. Justice System Direct and Intergovernmental Expenditures, by Level of Government and Type of Activity, 2001

	Dollar Amounts (in thousands)				Percent Distribution		
Activity	***Total All Governments***	***Federal Government***	***State Governments***	***Local Governments[a]***	***Federal***	***State***	***Local[a]***
Total Justice System[b]	$167,112,887	$30,443,000	$63,372,304	$83,377,152	X	X	X
Direct expenditure	167,112,887	25,285,000	58,820,452	83,007,435	15.1%	35.2%	49.7%
Intergovernmental expenditure	X	5,158,000	4,551,852	369,717	X	X	X
Police Protection[b]	72,405,970	15,013,811	10,496,730	50,717,839	X	X	X
Direct expenditure	72,405,970	12,470,000	9,219,650	50,716,320	17.2	12.7	70.0
Intergovernmental expenditure	X	2,543,811	1,277,808	1,519	X	X	X
Judicial and Legal[b]	37,751,380	10,230,341	14,443,708	15,938,498	X	X	X
Direct expenditure	37,751,380	8,497,000	13,522,531	15,731,849	22.5	35.8	41.7
Intergovernmental expenditure	X	1,733,341	921,177	206,649	X	X	X
Corrections[b]	56,955,537	5,196,848	38,431,866	16,720,815	X	X	X
Direct expenditure	56,955,537	4,318,000	36,078,271	16,559,266	7.6	63.3	29.1
Intergovernmental expenditure	X	880,848	2,353,595	161,549	X	X	X

[a]Data for local governments are estimates subject to sampling variation.

[b]The total category for each criminal justice activity, and for the total justice system, excludes duplicative intergovernmental expenditure amounts. This was done to avoid the artificial inflation that would result if an intergovernmental expenditure of a government were tabulated and then counted again when the recipient government(s) experienced that amount. The intergovernmental expenditure categories are not totaled for this reason.

Source: U.S. Department of Justice, Bureau of Justice Statistics, *2001 Justice Expenditure and Employment Extracts.* NCJ 202792, Table 1 [Online]. Available: www.ojp.usedof.gowbja/pub/sheets/cjee01.zip.file cjee0101.wk1 [Aug. 6, 2004].

per inmate rises significantly for special prison populations such as the elderly, the mentally ill, inmates with diseases, and maximum-security and death-row inmates. What happened between the nineteenth century and the twenty-first century to cause these changes?

In the late nineteenth century, the classical explanations of criminal behavior were overtaken by biological explanations, such as the criminological theories of Cesare Lombroso, who argued that criminals are naturally inferior persons who cannot control their inborn criminality. If criminality is an inherited trait, it follows that attempting to rehabilitate them is futile, and thus is not a reasonable goal of the criminal justice system. Lombroso's theory influenced corrections in the late 1800s and early 1900s. Penal institutions abandoned a belief in criminals as weak-willed sinners and saw them instead as threats to civilization. American criminologist Earnest Hooton argued that prisoners should be placed on self-contained, self-governing reservations completely isolated from society. Hooton favored the permanent incarceration of what he called "hopeless constitutional inferiors who on no account should be allowed to breed."[34] This philosophy was pervasive throughout the early 1900s. Prisons were operated under the premise that it was best to leave the fate of criminals to correctional authorities. Thus, for the most part, society abandoned the oversight of prisons. Even the courts

diversity in the system

Institutional Racism and Incarceration

If the criminal justice system discriminates against minorities, an indicator of this discrimination is the ratio of minorities to whites in prison. Many other indicators may not show clearly that minorities are treated differently by the system, but incarceration rates clearly demonstrate that there is a disproportionate confinement rate for minorities. If recent incarceration rates remain unchanged, an estimated 1 of every 20 persons (5.1 percent) will serve time in a prison during their lifetime.[35] However, the likelihood of going to state or federal prison is disproportionate when one examines the likelihood of going to prison by race. When the numbers are adjusted for percentage of the general population, the differences by race are enormous. A white male has a 1 in 23 chance of serving time in prison; a Hispanic male has a 1 in 6 chance; and a black male has a greater than 1 in 4 chance.[36]

In the past 10 years, there has been little change in this incarceration rate, as the percentage of prisoners under state or federal jurisdiction by race has changed little.[37] In 1990, 35.6 percent of state or federal prisoners were white, 44.5 percent were black, and 17.4 percent were Hispanic. In 2000, 35.7 percent were white, 46.2 percent were black, and 16.4 percent were Hispanic. Furthermore, when one looks at the statistics for juvenile offenders held as adults, there is an even greater gap between whites and minorities in prison. Twenty-five percent of state prisoners under age 18 are white non-Hispanic, whereas 58 percent are black non-Hispanic, and 15 percent are Hispanic.[38]

Some argue that the criminal justice system does not incarcerate innocent people; thus, all the black males in prison have committed a crime and deserve to be incarcerated. Others argue that the criminal justice system discriminates against minorities from the beginning, especially black males, as they are more likely to be stopped, arrested, charged, convicted, and sentenced to prison than are white males.

One of the effects of the 28.5 percent likelihood of incarceration for black males is their disenfranchisement from the political system. The District of Columbia and 46 states deprive felons of the right to vote while they are in prison. In addition, 32 states bar offenders from voting while they are on probation, and 29 bar voting while on parole. In 14 of these states, felons are barred from voting for life.[39] It is estimated that 13 percent of the nation's black male population cannot vote because they have been convicted of a felony.[40] In some states, such as Alabama and Florida, which have a higher percentage of black male inmates, it is estimated that one in three black men are denied voting rights because of felony convictions.[41]

According to the Sentencing Project, a Washington-based advocacy group for sentencing reform, and Human Rights Watch in New York, as a result of this policy and the disproportionate number of black males in prison and under the supervision of probation or parole, in a dozen states as much as 30 to 40 percent of the next generation of black men will permanently lose the right to vote.[42] The Sentencing Project report suggests that this trend will result in the loss of many of the gains made in the American civil rights movement. People denied the right to vote lack political and economic representation and may no longer see themselves as participants in the democratic process.

How do you explain the disproportionate number of black and Hispanic males in prison? What might be some consequences of the widespread disenfranchisement of large numbers of black and Hispanic males? Should laws depriving convicted felons of the right to vote be repealed?

adopted a hands-off policy. Once a person was incarcerated, he or she was denied access to the courts on any matter concerning his or her treatment or incarceration.[43] It was not until the 1960s that the courts interpreted the constitutional protections as extending to prisoners.

During the Great Depression of the 1930s, many states passed laws prohibiting the sale of convict-made products, which competed with local businesses on the open market. The operating capital that prisons had been able to generate through industries dried up, and prison industries turned to supplying products to the government.[44] During this era, for example, prisons became the exclusive manufacturers of license plates for state governments.

▲ check your understanding 11.1 What were early jails and prisons like? What were the characteristics of the American penal systems developed in the Walnut Street Jail, Eastern State Penitentiary, and Auburn Prison? How and why was the southern penal system different?

Jails

▼ the main idea 11.2 Jails are multipurpose holding facilities and serve as a gateway for the criminal justice system.

The major institutions of modern civilian institutional corrections are the jail, the state prison, and the federal penitentiary. **Jails** are unique, short-term facilities that are used for more purposes than any other type of correctional institution. Jails hold defendants awaiting trial, defendants convicted of misdemeanor crimes, state and federal prisoners, mentally ill persons pending their movement to appropriate health facilities, adults of both genders, and juveniles. Jails hold local, state, federal, and military prisoners; convicted prisoners; absconders; and witnesses. However, the majority of inmates in local jails have not been convicted of a crime. They are waiting to be charged, tried, or transported to another institution. Jails hold everyone from accused murderers to persons detained for littering. Characteristics of jail inmates are summarized in Figure 11.1.

In addition to the fact that they are multipurpose, jails are unique as a gateway into the criminal justice system, and corrections in particular. When a person is detained or arrested for any crime, misdemeanor, or felony, they first are confined in a jail. Only convicted offenders can be confined in state and federal prisons. Thus, all prisoners and most defendants enter the criminal justice system through jails.

Jails are primarily local institutions. There are only 11 federal jails under the supervision of the **Federal Bureau of Prisons (BOP),** and these house less than 1 percent of all inmates.[45] Federal jails do not house the diverse population of prisoners that is characteristic of local jails. The primary purpose of federal jails is to hold federal jail inmates awaiting adjudication or transfer. Federal jails have traditionally used local jails for this purpose, but the serious overcrowding in local jails has often resulted in local jails being unable to accept federal prisoners. Prisoners also are held in military prisons[46] and Native American jails,[47] and some terrorists are held in special military detention centers. These latter correctional institutions are significantly different from civilian correctional institutions and are not discussed in this chapter.

City and County Jails

There are over 3,300 local or county jails, and they vary significantly in size. About 47 percent of these jails have a capacity of fewer than 50 inmates. Less than 3 percent of the jails have a capacity of more than 1,000 inmates.[48] A few jails have very large populations. Three of the largest jails are Rikers Island, Los Angeles County Jail, and the Maricopa County (Arizona) jail. Riker's Island is the city jail for New York City and is one of the largest jails in the United States, both in size and population. Riker's Island is a 415-acre detention facility located on an island in the river. It has an $860 million budget and is

jails Short-term, multipurpose holding facilities that serve as the gateway for the criminal justice system.

figure 11.1

Profiles of Jail Inmates

Number of inmates in jail June 30, 2004: 713,990.

Most jail inmates are never-been-married single males under the age of 34. More than 6 in 10 jail inmates are racial or ethnic minorities. Approximately 28 percent of jail inmates have not been convicted of a crime but are awaiting trial or arraignment. Fifty percent of inmates are expected to serve less than 5 months in jail. The South holds more jail inmates than do other regions.

Gender	
Male	88.4%
Female	11.6%
Offense	
Violent	25.4%
Property	22.4%
Drug	24.7%
Public order	24.9%
Justice Status	
None	46.8%
On probation	33.6%
On parole	12.6%
On bail/bond	6.9%
Race	
White	36.0%
Black	40.1%
Hispanic	18.5%
American Indian/Alaska Native	1.3%
Asian/Pacific Islander	1.1%
More than one race	3.0%

Marital Status	
Married	16.2%
Widowed	1.2%
Divorced	15.7%
Separated	6.7%
Never married	60.1%
Education	
Did not graduate from high school	43.9%
GED	17.1%
High school diploma	25.9%
Some college	10.1%
College graduate	2.9%
U.S. Citizenship	
Citizen	92.2%
Noncitizen	7.8%

Source: Paige M. Harrison and Allen J. Beck, *Prisoners in 2004* (Washington, DC: Bureau of Justice Statistics, 2005).

staffed by 10,000 officers and 1,500 civilians. The inmate population of Riker's Island varies between 15,000 and 20,000 inmates. Los Angeles County Jail and Maricopa County Jail house over 7,000 inmates each.

Local governments must support and staff their jails. Thus, jail facilities vary with the economic prosperity of the city or county. In cities and counties with expanding jail prisoner populations it can be difficult for the city or county to provide quality care and facilities for inmates. Thus, prison life in jails can range from good to bad. When cities and counties are economically challenged and do not have the resources to finance jail operations, conditions in jails can result in lawsuits by inmates and takeover by the courts. For example, in July 2004, Fulton County Jail (Georgia) was sued by inmates, censored by the Southern Center for Human Rights, and the Court threatened to appoint a receiver to oversee the jail. The jail opened in the mid-1980s. While it was under construction, it was determined to be too small, and the number of bunks were doubled, even though the number of showers, toilets, and other utilities remained the same.[49] After it opened, a third bunk was added to many cells to accommodate the increasing population. When that was insufficient, some inmates slept on mattresses in the common area. Court papers described the jail as "windowless, steamy rooms, where the air-conditioning is broken; 59 inmates in one cellblock sharing two showers with backed-up

Despite the immense size of Rikers Island Penitentiary, New York prisoners are still housed in crowded cells due to limited resources. The cost of housing prisoners in city and county jails can be a significant factor in a city or country's budget. What are the alternatives to holding persons in city and county jails?

sewage; inmates without clean underwear and uniforms due to broken laundry service; faulty record-keeping that left inmates locked up although they had served their time; attacks; beatings; escapes. Blocks designed to have 14 guards have only 2."[50]

All states except Connecticut, Delaware, Hawaii, Rhode Island, and Vermont operate local jails, but these five states do have a combined jail–prison system operated by the state. Initially, local jails were operated by the county sheriff, and there was only one jail per county. In many states, this is still true, as about 78 percent of sheriffs' offices operate a jail.[51] Jail operation is still a major responsibility of sheriffs' offices. Fully one-third of all sheriff's office sworn personnel work in jail-related positions, and 56 percent of civilian personnel work in jail-related positions.[52] As Table 11.2 shows, in sheriffs' offices that operate jails, a significant percentage of the jail's personnel perform duties related to jail operations rather than to law enforcement or court security duties. Jails not operated by a sheriff's office are managed by a county department of corrections employing only civilian personnel. Sheriffs' departments and county departments of corrections otherwise perform the same jail functions (see Figure 11.2).

The jail population has more than doubled since 1983. Figure 11.3 shows that the number of persons held in jail continues to rise. The number of persons held in prison in 2004 was 713,990 compared to 507,044 in 1995. In 1999, in an effort to keep pace with the rising jail population, counties were constructing new jail facilities at the rate of about 500 new beds each week.[53] Some jails expanded so rapidly that it was not possible to construct enough new bed space, and prisoners were housed in corridors, outdoor tents, or trailers.

table 11.2

Large Sheriffs' Offices and Officers Performing Jail Operations

In sheriffs' offices that operate jails, a significant percentage of personnel perform jail duties as opposed to law enforcement or court security.

Department	Total Number Full-Time Sworn Officers	Percentage Performing Jail Operations
Los Angeles Co. (CA)	8,107	26
Cook Co. (IL)	5,768	58
Harris Co. (TX)	2,648	55
Broward Co. (FL)	2,419	50
San Diego Co. (CA)	1,999	53
Clark Co. (NV)	1,998	20
Wayne Co. (MI)	1,127	69
Nassau Co. (NY)	1,114	93
Salt Lake Co. (UT)	903	46
Suffolk Co. (MA)	817	98

Source: Bureau of Justice Statistics, *Law Enforcement Management and Administrative Statistics, Sheriffs' Offices, 1999* (Washington, DC: U.S. Department of Justice, May 2001), p. 2.

figure 11.2

Functions of Locally Operated Jails

The following numerous functions performed by local jails make it difficult to operate the jail and manage the inmates. Inmates range from persons waiting to post bail to murderers. Many inmates are in jail for only a brief time. Some inmates are held only until they can be transferred to another institution.

- Receive individuals pending arraignment and hold them awaiting trial, conviction, or sentencing.
- Readmit probation, parole, and bail-bond violators and absconders.
- Temporarily detain juveniles pending transfer to juvenile authorities.
- Hold mentally ill persons pending their movement to appropriate health facilities.
- Hold individuals for the military, for protective custody, for contempt, and for the courts as witnesses.
- Release convicted inmates to the community on completion of sentence.
- Transfer inmates to federal, state, and other authorities.
- House inmates for federal, state, or other authorities because of crowding of their facilities.
- Relinquish custody of temporary detainees to juvenile and medical authorities.
- Operate community-based programs with day reporting, home detention, electronic monitoring, or other types of supervision.
- Hold inmates sentenced to short terms (generally under 1 year).

Source: Doris J. James, *Profile of Jail Inmates, 2002* (Washington, DC: Bureau of Justice Statistics, 2004), p. 2.

figure 11.3

Number of Persons Held in Jail on June 30

Year	Number
1995	507,044
2000	621,149
2001	631,240
2002	665,475
2003	691,301
2004	713,990

Percent change, 2003–2004: 3.3%

Average annual increase, 1995–2004: 3.9%

Source: Paige Harrison and Allen J. Beck, *Prisoners in 2004* (Washington, DC: Bureau of Justice Statistics, 2005), p. 2.

Overcrowding in jails remains a serious problem for many states. State jails typically have occupancy in excess of 100 percent capacity. For example, in 1999, the District of Columbia jail population was occupied at 120 percent of capacity, Virginia at 118 percent, New Jersey at 110 percent, and Massachusetts at 105 percent.[54]

Municipal Jails

Historically, local jails also included local prison facilities maintained by municipal police departments. In some counties, the sheriff maintained the county jail, and the police department maintained a separate municipal jail. These counties had both a municipal court and a county court, with each court housing its prisoners in the appropriate facility. Most municipalities have abandoned the use of the municipal or police jail. Recent state and federal regulations and standards regarding the housing of inmates have made it difficult for cities and towns to support local jails.

Municipal jails should not be confused with police holding cells, booking cells, or lock-up facilities. Nearly all police departments have secure detention facilities that may look like jail cells. The primary purpose of these holding cells is the temporary housing of arrestees until they can be booked and moved to another facility or pay their bail, or until detectives can determine if they are to be charged with a crime. These are not correctional institutions, and prisoners are not sent to these facilities to serve time as their punishment for a crime. Prisoners typically are confined in holding cells only for a period of 48 hours or less.

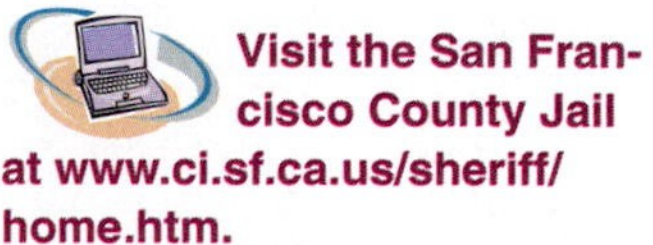

Visit the San Francisco County Jail at www.ci.sf.ca.us/sheriff/home.htm.

▲ check your understanding **11.2** **What are the types and functions of jails? Why are jails considered "gateways" into the criminal justice system?**

State Prisons

the main idea 11.3 **State prisons are correctional facilities with different security levels, prisoner classifications, and administration models for the incarceration of persons convicted of crimes.**

Unlike jails, **state prisons** are correctional institutions containing only convicted offenders, usually felony inmates sentenced to prison as punishment for a crime. Each state operates its own correctional system, and these systems differ significantly from state to state. States also vary in the number of inmates in the correctional system. Inmates in state prisons usually have been sentenced to serve a prison term of a year or more. Thus, different services, procedures, and policies are needed for prisoners than are provided in local jails.

Overall, the number of inmates in state prisons has continued to climb to record incarceration rates. However, the growth in state prison population varies significantly by state (see Table 11.3). Some states are experiencing double-digit growth, whereas other states are actually experiencing a decline in state prisoner population. Overall, state prisons are between 1 percent below capacity and 15 percent above capacity.[55] The majority of prisoners are held in state prisons. Of the approximately 2 million persons incarcerated, about 8 percent are held in federal prisons, 33 percent are held in local jails, and 58 percent are held in state prisons.[56] About 50 percent of state inmates are incarcerated for violent offenses, 20 percent for property offenses, 21 percent for drug offenses, and 7 percent for public-order offenses. Incarceration of female inmates has increased about 6 percent since 1995 but still most state inmates (93 percent) are male.

In the early nineteenth century, most states built one large prison to house all state inmates. It was thought that this economy of scale would provide the best solution to the problem of housing prisoners. There was little effort to separate prisoners on the basis of age, type of offense, length of term, or criminal history. From the beginning, however, early state prisons, unlike early jails, separated prisoners by sex, maintaining separate facilities for female prisoners. Until the late twentieth century, women comprised a very small percentage of felony offenders. Thus, while early prisons for male offenders were built to house thousands of inmates, institutions for female prisoners usually were one-tenth the size. Furthermore, prison architecture reflected the assumption that male prisoners were more aggressive and dangerous, and that female prisoners were more docile and less violent.[57] Based on this assumption, correctional institutions for women often lacked the fortresslike architecture and brutal discipline of prisons for men. Today, states have numerous prisons within their jurisdiction and distribute inmates among them according to a system of prisoner classification.

Prisoner Classification

States have diverse prisons, and inmates can be placed in any prison throughout the state. Each prison is distinguished by its security level and the programs available to inmates at the institution. Before incarceration in a state prison, the inmate undergoes an extensive examination and assessment to determine an assignment to a particular facility. Because inmates remain in state custody for a relatively long period of time, the system attempts to determine the needs of the inmate and any characteristics that might influence placement. The correctional system also evaluates the security risks, staffing impacts, and institutional needs when deciding where inmates go.

This process of **prisoner classification**, performed in a specially designated facility, is commonly known as reception and diagnosis. At the state's reception and diagnosis facility, the classification process includes identification of the inmate, examination of the inmate's criminal record, evaluation of the inmate's mental capacity and psycho-

state prisons Correctional facilities for prisoners convicted of state crimes.

prisoner classification The reception and diagnosis of an inmate to decide the appropriate security level in which to place the prisoner and services of placement.

table 11.3

U.S. Prison Population by State

The nation's prison population rose 1.9% in 2004.

Prison Population	Number of Inmates	Incarceration Rate, 12/31/04	Inmates per 100,000 Residents*	Growth, 12/31/03 to 12/31/04	Percent Change
5 Highest					
Federal	180,328	Louisiana	816	Minnesota	11.4%
Texas	168,105	Texas	694	Idaho	11.1
California	168,556	Mississippi	669	Georgia	8.3
Florida	85,533	Oklahoma	649	Nevada	7.8
New York	63,751	Georgia	574	Kentucky	7.2
5 Lowest					
North Dakota	1,327	Maine	148	Alabama	–7.3%
Vermont	1,968	Minnesota	171	Rhode Island	–2.8
Wyoming	1,980	Rhode Island	175	New York	–2.2
Maine	2,024	New Hampshire	187	Maryland	–2.1
New Hampshire	2,448	North Dakota	195	Kansas	–1.8

*Prisoners with a sentence of more than 1 year.

During 2004—

- Ten states had increases of at least 5%, led by Minnesota (up 11.4%), Idaho (up 11.1%), and Georgia (up 8.3%).
- Eleven states experienced prison population decreases, led by Alabama (down 7.3%), Rhode Island (down 2.8%), New York (down 2.2%), and Maryland (down 2.1%).
- The number of inmates under state jurisdiction increased by 20,759 inmates (1.6%).

On December 31, 2004—

- State prisons were between 1% below capacity and 15% above; federal prisons were operating at 40% above capacity.
- Women were 7.0% of all inmates, up from 6.1% in 1995.
- About half of male state prison inmates were serving time for a violent crime, compared to a third of female inmates. Females were more likely to have a drug offense (31.5%) compared to males (20.7%).
- About 8.4% of black males between ages 25 and 29 were in state or federal prison, compared to 2.5% of Hispanic males and 1.2% of white males in the same age group.

Source: Paige Harrison and Allen Beck, *Prisoners in 2004* (Washington, DC: Bureau of Justice Statistics, 2005), p. 1.

logical stability, and the assessment of other factors that may influence his or her assignment, such as gang membership, age, and educational achievement.

At the classification facility, the inmate is inducted into the state's prison system. Prisoners exchange their clothing for prison clothing, undergo extensive and intrusive searches for weapons or contraband, are photographed and fingerprinted, and are assigned an identification number or prisoner I.D. This process is similar to the booking process that occurs when a person is first arrested for a crime, but it must be repeated, because it is possible that the inmate reporting for prison is not the person who was convicted of the crime. Such a case was discovered in October 2000, when a federal prisoner walked away from a minimum-custody federal correctional facility. When police found and returned the escapee, prison officials found that he was an imposter.[58] The convicted offender had arranged for another person to report to prison and serve time in his place. Officials had failed to detect this switch before the impostor had actually served 18 months of the other man's sentence.[59]

diversity in the system

Women behind Bars

Until the nineteenth century, it was believed that female offenders were "fallen" women and could not be rehabilitated.[60] In the nineteenth century, there were few female offenders, and those few were housed in a section of the men's prison and supervised by male correctional officers. Elizabeth Gurney Fry is credited with establishing the early theoretical and practical bases for women's corrections at Newgate Prison in London in the early nineteenth century. In America, between 1844 and 1848, Eliza W. B. Farnham instituted many of Fry's principles at the women's section of Sing Sing prison in New York. However, public outrage over "soft" treatment of the female offenders resulted in Farnham's dismissal. The first institution expressly for women was the Indiana Reformatory Institution for Women and Girls, built in 1873.

Female offenders have become more common and are routinely housed in separate facilities. Today, men are still nearly 15 times more likely than women to be in a state or federal prison. In 2004, the rate for inmates serving a sentence of 1+ years was 64 female inmates per 100,000 women in the United Sates, compared to 920 male inmates per 100,000 men.[61] However, these figures do not reflect the growing crisis related to incarcerated female offenders. In 1983, there were 15,652 female offenders in local jails, but by 2002, there were 273,224. In 1980, there were 13,400 female offenders serving a sentence of 1+ years in a state or federal correctional institution; by 2004, there were 104,848.

The shift to tougher sentences for drug offenses is a major reason for this dramatic rise in the incarceration rate for female offenders. In many states, the rate of incarceration of female offenders for drug offenses has nearly doubled since 1990.[62] Female offenders accounted for over 15 percent of defendants charged with a drug offense in U.S. district courts in 1999.[63] The number of boys charged with drug offenses in juvenile court from 1989 to 1998 dropped by 2 percent, but the number of girls charged with drug crimes rose by 2 percent.[64] Female offenders comprise 16 percent of the drug cases in juvenile court. In state prisons, 65 to 73 percent of female offenders admitted to regular drug use before incarceration.[65] Furthermore, it is estimated that many female offenders serving time for property and sex crimes were motivated to commit these crimes by the need to obtain money for drugs.

The skyrocketing increase of female offenders has created major problems for the correctional system. Female institutions are becoming overcrowded, and female offenders have less access to vocational, educational, medical, and rehabilitation programs. For example, the percentage of female offenders receiving drug treatment while in prison is declining significantly, despite the high rate of drug use among female offenders. Today, only 15 percent of state prison inmates and 10 percent of federal prison inmates obtain drug treatment while in prison, whereas in 1991, 29 percent of state and 19 percent of federal female offenders reported participation in drug treatment programs.[66]

Martha Stewart's conviction and sentencing to jail time for obstructing a federal securities investigation was a highly controversial white-collar criminal prosecution. Do you think her status as a successful multimillionaire businesswoman influenced either the prosecution of the case or her sentence?

While female offenders suffer many of the same physical and mental health problems in prison as do male prisoners, statistics indicate that the female offenders are more likely to suffer from HIV infection and mental illness than are male inmates. At year end in 2002, about 2.9 percent of female inmates in state prisons were infected with HIV, compared with about 1.9 percent of male inmates. About 24 percent of female inmates in state and federal prisons reported suffering from mental illnesses, compared with 16 percent of male inmates.[67]

Some see female offenders as victims of men.[68] This is the view of feminist criminological theories, which argue that female offenders are victimized by a social and criminal justice system that is biased toward male dominance. Evidence of female offenders as victims of men is seen in the high rate of sexual and physical abuse reported by female offenders. About 57 percent of state female inmates and 40 percent of federal female inmates report that they were sexually or physically abused before admission, whereas only 16 percent of state male inmates and 7 percent of federal male inmates report that they were abused, and the proportions are similar for jail inmates.[69] Abuse of female offenders continues after incarceration, as there are frequent scandals involving correctional officers demanding sex from female inmates. Many former female inmates allege that during their incarceration, sex with male correctional officers in exchange for favors was commonplace. "Sexual favors are part of a hidden prison economy, in exchange for avoiding retribution, getting drugs, or obtaining extra privileges, such as staying up after hours."[70]

More than 1.5 million children in the United States have parents in prison.[71] The burden of incarceration falls heavier on female offenders than on male offenders. Families are more likely to be broken by a woman's confinement in the criminal justice system than by a man's.[72] On average, about 80 percent of female inmates have dependent children.[73] In 1998, 1,400 babies were delivered in prisons, only to be removed from their mothers shortly after birth.

Most mothers plan to return to their families after their release but frequently are poorly prepared for this task. Female offenders have fewer visits with family during their incarceration than do male offenders. One reason for this is that due to a lack of female prisons, female offenders often are incarcerated farther from home than are male offenders. Another reason is that when male offenders are incarcerated, custody of children typically remains with the mother, whereas when females are imprisoned, grandparents frequently become the caregivers of the children. Most data suggest that incarcerated women do not see their children at all.[74] Some innovative programs try to help keep female offenders united with their families. A promising program that is effective, inexpensive, and easy to administer is Girl Scouts Beyond Bars, which provides for regular mother–daughter contact through Girl Scout programs conducted in prisons.[75]

On their return to the community, female offenders are likely to face significant problems, including parental poverty, unemployment, substance abuse, low self-esteem, and ill health. Often, the problems of the parent are visited on the children, as child abuse and neglect are common outcomes. Children of incarcerated parents are five times more likely to offend than are children whose parents have not been incarcerated. This starts a vicious cycle of crime that is difficult to break.

While it is rare for female offenders to be executed, in 2000, there were 54 women under the sentence of death in 18 states.[76] Beginning with the earliest American colonial period, only about 561 women have been executed. Of this number, 137 executions have occurred since 1973.[77] Typically, 5 to 10 female offenders are executed per year. More than likely, the female murderer's victim was a child, spouse, or other family member, or boyfriend.

What are some differences between male and female inmates? Why has female offending and incarceration soared in recent years? What special problems do women in prison face? What are the human costs of female incarceration?

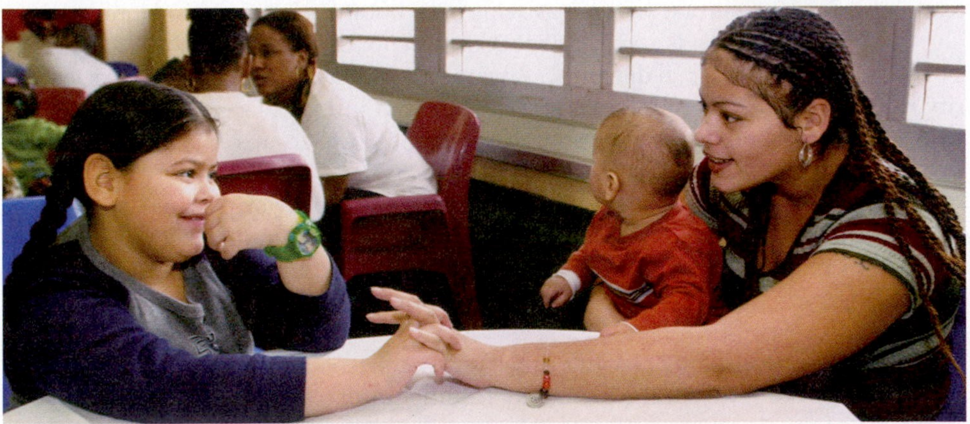

The experience of women in custody can be more troubling than what their male counterparts face. One major difference concerns children. Over half of female inmates have children under age 18, and the majority of the mothers were the primary caregivers at the time of their arrest. At the 1,800-bed detention facility for women at Rikers Island, New York—the nation's largest jail and detention complex—mothers reported that forced separation from their children was the most painful punishment they had to endure.

Security Levels

A primary purpose of classification is to determine what level of security is appropriate for the inmate. The security level of prisons is based on a scale from relatively few or mild security measures in place to prevent escape to many strong or harsh security systems to prevent escape. The levels are minimum security, medium security, and maximum security. Each state has a unique name or number system to identify security levels, but the basic principle is the same from state to state. Some state prisons have the capacity to house inmates with different security level classifications, such as having both medium- and high-security inmates being held in the same institution.

Special Prison Populations

Some prisoners may not be suited to transfer to the general prison population. Because of age, mental illness, depression, other health status, or other characteristic, it may be necessary to keep the inmate out of the general population. During the classification process, the inmate is administered psychological tests to determine his or her mental stability. Incarceration can trigger intense depression, and as a result, some prisoners are high suicide risks. Prison officials attempt to identify such prisoners, provide assistance, and place them under constant observation in what is known as *suicide watch.* Some inmates require psychiatric treatment and would be a danger to others or themselves if placed in the general population. During classification, these inmates are identified and often transferred to appropriate mental health care facilities.

During the classification process, prison officials also try to determine if the inmate's lifestyle or special needs should influence placement. Specific assignments may be based on the inmate's age, sexual orientation, gang affiliation, or physical health. Inmates with significant health problems, such as AIDS or tuberculosis, require extensive health care in prison. Prison officials are responsible for providing appropriate health care and protecting other inmates and staff from infectious diseases.

Young prisoners, usually under 25 or 26 years old, may need to be separated from older, more hardened offenders. Elderly prisoners, an increasing challenge to correctional institutions, also may need to be protected from the general prison population. The "graying of inmates" is becoming more of a problem for prisons because of longer prison sentences and demographic factors such as aging baby boomers in the prison population.

Gang affiliation also is an important consideration in determining where to house a prisoner, and can be a real dilemma. Gang members placed together may post a security risk, as they will conspire together. However, an inmate placed in a housing unit with rival gang members may be assaulted. In some cases, groups of gang rivals forced to live together may engage in gang warfare.

A prisoner's classification may be changed based on behavior, a change in status, or other consideration. For instance, a prisoner assigned to maximum security may be reassigned to medium security based on good behavior and time served. A prisoner assigned to minimum security who tries to escape, on the other hand, may be reassigned to a higher security prison.

A primary reason for classifying and assigning prisoners to various security levels is to enhance the safety of the prison environment both for the inmates and for the staff. One of the measures of the effectiveness of classification and security is the suicide rate and homicide rate in local jails and prisons. Prison homicide rates have dropped 93 percent from 1980 to 2002. Jail homicide rates have remained constant. The jail suicide rate has dropped significantly and prison suicide rates have declined. Jails tend to have 3 times the suicide rate (47 per 100,000 inmates) as in state prisons (14 per 100,000 inmates). Homicide rates were similar in local jails (3 per 100,000) and state prisons (4 per 100,000).

careers in the system

Employment in State Prisons

In most state prison systems, the administrative staff is divided into two major categories: professional staff and correctional or custodial staff. Staffing also may be divided into three categories: administrative, treatment, and supervisory and security.

A large prison, especially a medium- or maximum-security prison, is a self-contained city, and prison officials must provide numerous services to keep the prison functioning. These services relate to prison security and basic operations of providing services to the inmates and staff. Employees who work to maintain supervision and prison security are the correctional or custodial staff employees.[78] In most prisons, these are uniformed employees trained to oversee the safe movement and conduct of the inmate population. **Correctional officers** often have military-type ranks and titles similar to those used in police departments, such as sergeant, lieutenant, and captain. These officers may carry weapons in the performance of their duty and may be authorized to use deadly force to prevent prisoners from escaping. However, they do not have the power of arrest or search and seizure of citizens outside the prison, or the right to carry concealed weapons off-duty.

Entry-level correctional officers usually are required to have a high school diploma and other minimum qualifications, such as good moral character and a level of physical fitness, but the requirements are less stringent than those required for entry-level police officers. Entry-level custodial and security employees receive academy training similar to that provided to police officers, but the training academy for correctional officers normally lasts only about 2 to 6 weeks, followed by on-the-job training. Some states require that entry-level security officers undergo psychological and polygraph examinations, but many do not.

Employees in a prison who provide nonsecurity services, such as treatment staff and administrators, may be medical doctors, dentists, nurses, psychologists, counselors, teachers, recreational specialists, business administrators, secretaries, cooks, librarians, and so forth. If the prison has a prison industry, civilian employees supervise inmates' training and work. If the prison has an educational program, full-time teachers are employed to instruct inmates. The prison may have a hospital or clinic where medical personnel practice. All prisons have counselors who provide drug counseling or mental health services. Unlike the correctional officers, professional staff are civilians and do not wear uniforms. They do not have military-type titles and ranks, do not carry or use firearms, and do not have any police powers or receive academy training, and they are not required to meet physical fitness standards.

Correctional officers and treatment staff generally are civil service employees and obtain their positions by competitive examination and job-related qualifications. They do not serve at the pleasure of the warden or other administrator. In some prisons, the employees are unionized.

How are correctional officers and law enforcement officers alike? How are they different? What other careers can be pursued in the correctional system? What are the key services that prisons, as "self-contained cities," must provide?

▲ check your understanding **11.3** **What is the purpose of state prisons? What jobs are required to run a state prison? What do correctional officers do?**

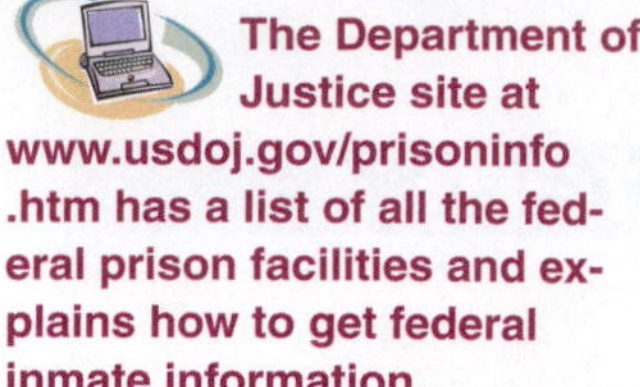

The Department of Justice site at www.usdoj.gov/prisoninfo.htm has a list of all the federal prison facilities and explains how to get federal inmate information.

Federal Prisons

the main idea 11.4 Federal prisons are correctional facilities for inmates convicted of federal crimes.

For over 100 years after the founding of the United States, there were no federal prisons. Federal prisoners were housed in state prisons for a fee. It was not until 1895 that the first federal prison for men was constructed at Leavenworth, Kansas. Using the labor of military prisoners at the nearby United States Disciplinary Barracks at Fort Leavenworth, the first federal prison was built in the architectural style of the times. Leavenworth prison was a walled, maximum-security prison based on the Auburn concept of inside cell blocks and congregate work. As in state prisons and local jails, the number of federal female offenders was only about one-tenth that of male offenders. The first federal prison for women was constructed in 1927. Like state prisons, oversight of federal prisons is balanced among the legislative, executive, and judicial branches of the federal government. The U.S. Congress funds federal prisons, which are under the executive control of the Office of the President. The U.S. Supreme Court has the power of judicial review and can declare that prison conditions are unconstitutional or that inmate rights have been violated.

correctional officer
Uniformed jail or prison employee whose primary job is the security and movement of inmates.

The Federal Bureau of Prisons

Prohibition created many new federal offenses for trafficking in illegal alcoholic beverages, spurring the growth of federal prisons. In 1930, the federal government unified its prisons under the administrative control of the newly formed Federal Bureau of Prisons. After repeal of prohibition, the number of federal prisoners continued to increase due to federal drug prosecutions, firearms violations, and, recently, mandatory sentencing. As the federal prison population exploded, overcrowding became a serious problem, and it was necessary to construct new federal prisons. Because of the nationwide jurisdiction of the federal prison system, new prisons could be built anywhere in the United States. Federal inmates could be housed in any federal prison in the country and could be transferred among the prisons at will. This authority to transfer federal inmates

Military personnel who commit serious offenses are tried in a military court (court marital) and if found guilty serve time in a military correctional institution. The United States Military Barracks (USMB) at Fort Leavenworth, Kansas, is the oldest operating military prison in the United States. Prison labor from the USMB helped build nearby Leavenworth Federal Penitentiary.

anywhere in the United States has been a great advantage of the federal prison system.[79] The ability to transfer inmates from one prison to another, often separated by hundreds or thousands of miles, allows the Federal Bureau of Prisons to move "trouble-makers" and "instigators" from one prison to another. It also allows inmates in overpopulated prisons to be transferred to less populated prisons. Since the Bureau of Prisons was 40 percent over capacity in 2004, this ability to transfer inmates to relieve overcrowding is important.

In 1934, using this power, the newly formed Federal Bureau of Prisons built one of the most infamous prisons in U.S. history—the United States Penitentiary at Alcatraz, California, in San Francisco Bay. The most violent and highest security-risk inmates were then transferred from the various federal prisons to Alcatraz. **Alcatraz** was a maximum-security prison without any rehabilitation, educational, or treatment programs. Its primary goal was the incarceration of high-risk inmates and it gave little, if any, attention to rehabilitation goals, vocational programs, or educational programs. Alcatraz, which at one time housed Al Capone, prided itself on being escape-proof. In 1946, Alcatraz erupted in violence as two correctional officers and three inmates were killed during an escape attempt. Public perception of federal prisons was shaped by this event and by movies about notorious Alcatraz inmates. The prison was closed permanently in 1963 and today remains a popular tourist destination.

Federal Correctional Facilities

Today, the Federal Bureau of Prisons operates over 80 different types of federal correctional facilities throughout the United States, with a total inmate population of over 170,000 in 2004.[80] The Federal Bureau of Prisons central office in Washington, DC, has six regional offices to oversee the operation of federal prison facilities. Federal prisons range from the supermax prison in **Florence,** Colorado, to minimum-security federal prison farms. The federal government even operates "coed" minimum-security correctional facilities, the largest of which is in Lexington, Kentucky. Some federal prison facilities serve primarily as medical centers for federal prisoners, and others as detention centers and prison camps.

Visit the Federal Bureau of Prisons at www.bop.gov/.

Federal prisons use a security and classification system similar to that used by state prisons. New inmates are interviewed and screened to see which facility is most appropriate for them. Based on similar state criteria, the Federal Bureau of Prisons assigns prisoners according to a five-tier classification of its facilities: minimum, low, medium, high, and administrative. In the maximum-security prison, inmates are locked down, have little freedom of movement, and receive no recreational, educational, or vocational programs. At the minimum-security facilities, inmates have great freedom of movement and interaction with other inmates and have access to recreational opportunities and educational and vocational programs.

As in state prisons, the chief executive officer at a federal prison facility is the warden, who has various associates and assistants to help run the administrative units. Employees of the Federal Bureau of Prisons are federal employees, who generally receive better pay and benefits than state prison or local jail employees. Generally, however, the hiring standards are higher. Federal Bureau of Prisons employees may transfer from one federal facility to another, so opportunities for advancement are greater than in state prisons or local jails. As in state prisons, staffing in federal prisons is divided between employees who primarily perform security duties and those who provide treatment services.

▲ check your understanding **11.4 What events spurred the growth of federal prisons? How do federal prisons differ from state prisons in terms of goals, organization, and administration? What career advantages does employment in the federal prison system offer?**

Privatization

the main idea 11.5 Because of overcrowding of correctional facilities and budget constraints in the face of the high costs of prison construction and staffing, state and federal prisoners are being housed in for-profit private jails and prisons.

A trend in corrections has been the **privatization** of jails and prisons. In 2004, 34 states and the federal system reported a total of nearly 100,000 prisoners held in privately operated facilities. Since 2000, about 6.5 percent of state and federal inmates are in privately operated facilities. The Bureau of Justice Statistics reported that in 2004, private facilities held 5.6 percent of all state prisoners and 13.7 percent of federal prisoners.[81] Among states, Texas and Oklahoma reported the largest populations. Six states had at least 25 percent of their prison population housed in private prisons. Since 2000, the number of federal inmates in private facilities has increased 60 percent, whereas the number held in state facilities has decreased 1.3 percent (see Table 11.4).

The primary reason for housing prisoners in private facilities is to reduce costs. As mentioned, federal prisons are operating at 140 percent capacity and state prisons at between 99 and 115 percent capacity. The cost of new prison facilities is extremely expensive. Private prisons allow local jails and state and federal prisons to house prisoners in private facilities and pay a per-diem rate per prisoner rather than build new prisons to accommodate the increasing demand for bed space.

Private prisons look very similar to government prisons. The difference is that private prisons are for-profit businesses that take prisoners from local, state, and federal government and house them for a fee. Charges for housing an inmate in a private facility vary, ranging from about $25 a day per inmate to $100 a day. Thus, in a private prison there might be prisoners from several different counties and states. Also, there may be prisoners from local as well as state and federal prisons. Some prisoners are sent from long distances to be housed in private prisons. For example, Hawaii sends prisoners to private prisons in Texas. These transfers can separate inmates from family, friends, support services, and even their lawyers.

The private prison must pay for all expenses from its revenue to build and operate the prison and still be able to show a profit. Thus, controlling the cost of building and operating a private prison is important to the corporation that wishes to make a profit from its venture. There are several ways that private prisons keep costs down. Companies often receive tax breaks for building private prisons and grants for training employees.

table 11.4

Number of Inmates in Privately Operated Facilities

	Total	State	Federal	Percent of Inmates
2004	98,901	74,133	24,768	6.6%
2003	95,707	73,842	21,865	6.5
2002	93,912	73,638	20,274	6.5
2001	91,953	72,702	19,251	6.5
2000	90,542	75,018	15,524	6.5

Source: Prisoners in 2004 (Washington, DC: Bureau of Justice Statistics, 2005), p. 6.

privatization Trend toward the use of for-profit jails and prisons run by private companies.

Often, private prisons are built in rural areas where land and construction costs are low and wages are below the national average.[82]

Critics of the privatization of corrections argue that given the emphasis on containing costs, private companies provide less training and salary to prison personnel, and have higher inmate-to-correctional officer ratios than do government prisons.[83] Critics express concern that for-profit prisons do not provide the same quality of care and supervision as public prisons and do not provide inmates the same educational, recreational, and rehabilitative services as public prisons.

Proponents of private prisons focus almost entirely on the cost savings. Often, local, state, and federal prisons are under great pressures, including lawsuits, to reduce prison overcrowding. Unable to afford the high cost of constructing new prisons, governments turn to the use of private prisons.

Although private prisons help relieve the burden on overcrowded state and federal prisons, they often are criticized as detrimental to low-income communities, where most private prisons are located. Private companies market their services to the state on promises of providing jobs in low-income communities and providing inmate labor for community projects.[84] With some outstanding exceptions, pay and benefits, however, as well as prison conditions, often are below state standards.[85]

Another concern of critics is the issue of state liability for violation of inmates' constitutional rights and the abuse of inmates while housed in a private prison. Because it placed the inmate in the prison, the state retains liability but little control. Employees of private prisons are not government employees, and they and the companies that operate the prisons do not have immunity from certain lawsuits by inmates that government prisons enjoy.[86] Nevertheless, thousands of lawsuits are filed against state prisons as well as private prisons for violation of inmate rights and substandard prison conditions.[87]

A unique problem for private prisons is the jurisdiction of law enforcement over escaped prisoners. Not all states have enacted legislation that recognizes the potential status of inmates in private prisons as escapees. Thus, a prisoner who escapes from a private prison may not have broken a state law! Also, an assault by an inmate on a correctional officer at a private facility is an assault on a private citizen (a tort), whereas an assault on a state or federal correctional officer is defined as a more serious crime.

▲ check your understanding **11.5 What factors have led to privatization in corrections? How do private and government jails and prisons differ? What are the arguments for and against the use of private correctional facilities?**

The Confinement of Enemy Combatants

▼ the main idea **11.6 Following the terrorist attack on the United States on 9/11, the federal government took a number of actions to increase its role in the fight against terrorism and the treatment of terrorists.**

President George W. Bush authorized a military assault against Afghanistan, citing state-sponsored terrorism by that nation—specifically the September 11, 2001, attacks—as the justification for his action. Following the U.S. invasion of Afghanistan, President Bush issued an executive order concerning how certain prisoners who were captured in Afghanistan would be detained and treated. The executive order, issued November 13, 2001, has been extremely controversial, as it resulted in 680 captured persons being detained in a military prison compound in Guantanamo Bay, Cuba, without charges, access to an attorney, or protection of constitutional rights.

The Geneva Convention

The Geneva Convention of 1864 and its subsequent revisions proscribe the treatment and rights accorded to persons captured on the battlefield during military combat. Normally, prisoners captured in combat would be entitled to the rights and protections of the Third Geneva Convention of 1949, also known as the Prisoner-of-War Pact. The Geneva Convention Prisoner-of-War Pact proscribes that prisoners will not be questioned and do not have to reveal information other than their name, rank, and serial number. It provides for humane treatment with regard to housing and food. It guarantees their fair treatment and protection against criminal charges for the soldiers' battlefield participation except in certain circumstances when the captured solider is charged with war crimes. It also provides that in the event of charges against a prisoner, the prisoner has the right to a civilian attorney of his or her choice and has the right to a trial in a civilian court. The provisions of the Geneva Convention provide for the right of prisoners to communicate and to receive communication. It also provides the right of inspection of the imprisonment of prisoners by international humanitarian organizations such as the Red Cross.

Enemy Combatants Are Not Prisoners of War

President Bush's executive order declared that captured members of al Qaeda are "unlawful" or "enemy combatants." According to President Bush's executive order, unlawful combatants are not entitled to prisoner of war status under the Geneva Convention nor are they accorded the rights and privileges they would have if they were prisoners of war.[88] Bush's executive order provides that as unlawful enemy combatants, the prisoners will be held without access to U.S. civilian courts and without the right of appeal, and are not entitled to the protections of the United States Constitution or the Prisoner of War provisions of the Geneva Convention.

The status of unlawful enemy combatants is usually applied to spies or enemy saboteurs who are behind enemy lines without a uniform.[89] Normally, prisoners of war can be captured and detained but cannot be tried and punished for their participation in combat. However, unlike prisoners of war, unlawful combatants such as spies can be tried and punished by military tribunals for their action.

The United States has not evoked the use of unlawful combatant status since World War II. In 1942, President Franklin D. Roosevelt had six German saboteurs captured in the United States tried by a military court and executed. "The Supreme Court upheld the proceeding, saying that people who entered the United States for the purpose of waging war were combatants who could be tried in a military court."[90] However, many have challenged the rationale that persons captured on the battlefield in Afghanistan are similar to spies or enemy saboteurs without uniform and are therefore unlawful combatants.[91]

The White House's justification for classifying Afghanistan prisoners as unlawful combatants is that the subjects were terrorists, not members of an organized state military, and as such were engaged in unconventional war against the United States. A White House spokesperson, defending the use of enemy combatant status, stated, "We have looked at this war very unconventionally, and the conventional way of bringing people to justice doesn't apply to these times."[92] Furthermore, it was argued by White House officials that tribunals were necessary "to protect potential American jurors from the danger of passing judgment on accused terrorists . . . and the disclosure of government intelligence methods, which normally would be public in civilian courts."[93] Thus, President Bush has declared that terrorists classified as unlawful combatants will be tried by military law.

Criticisms of the Enemy Combatant Executive Order

One reason President Bush's executive order is controversial is because under the order, the president himself—not a court—determines who is an accused terrorist and therefore who is subject to trial by a military tribunal. Furthermore, this decision cannot be appealed to a civilian court, even the United States Supreme Court.[94] Another reason is that critics of Bush's executive order argue that it is a breach of international law guaranteeing fair treatment of prisoners of war. The Geneva Convention provides that no prisoner is to be tried by a court that fails to offer the essential guarantees of independence and impartiality, that prisoners have the right to be represented by an attorney of their choice, and that they have the right of appeal.[95]

Also, the treatment of "enemy combatants" is criticized as it is argued that prisoners of war cannot be interrogated for information under the rights guaranteed by the Geneva Convention, and prisoners held in the civilian court system cannot be interrogated without the protections provided by legal counsel and the Constitution. However, prisoners held as enemy combatants have no protection against interrogation and have no access to legal counsel. It is this ability to interrogate prisoners without restraint, without access to legal counsel, and without the right to remain silent that causes critics to protest. (Some critics have alleged that the military has used torture in interrogating persons held as unlawful combatants.) The justification cited by the Bush Administration for such interrogation is the desire to obtain information about possible plans for terrorist attacks on the United States and/or information that would lead to the capture of other terrorists. The Bush Administration claims that this ability to interrogate the prisoners has produced a wealth of information regarding terrorist plots against the United States and the operation of al Qaeda.

United States Senator John McCain, a naval aviator who spent more than five years as a prisoner of war in North Vietnam, disputes the intelligence value that can be obtained from the prisoners at Guantanamo Bay. Senator McCain argues that most useful operational intelligence information goes stale after about four months. The prisoners have been detained for years and have had no contact with the outside world during that time. McCain argues that the detainees can provide little information of value.[96] Critics

Senator John McCain, who was held as a prisoner of war by the North Vietnamese, is critical of the Bush Administration's interrogation policies of suspected terrorists classified as enemy combatants. McCain led the move to pass legislation that bans the use of torture in interrogating suspected terrorists. Do you believe suspected terrorists should not have the same rights regarding interrogation as suspected criminals?

argue that the elimination of due process for Afghanistan prisoners accused of terrorism and the open-ended indefinite detention of them without charges or access to the courts may provoke other countries to take a similar policy toward U.S. soldiers and/or civilians.[97]

Executive Order Extended to the United States and Citizens

When President Bush issued his executive order declaring that the Afghanistan prisoners captured on the Afghanistan battlefields were enemy combatants, there was the expectation that its use would be limited to non-U.S. citizens and combatants captured on foreign battlefields. In a unique move, the Bush Administration expanded the power of the enemy combatant executive order by declaring "al Qaeda made the battlefield the United States."[98] Based on this argument, the president declared a Qatari student who entered the United States on a student visa an enemy combatant and he declared a U.S. citizen arrested at Chicago's O'Hare International Airport an enemy combatant. The ability of President Bush to extend the jurisdiction of the enemy combatant executive order to noncitizens residing within the United States and citizens in the United States has been described as a "sea change in the constitutional life of this country."[99]

Qatari student Ali Saleh Kahlah al-Marri entered the United States on September 10, 2001, on a student visa. In December 2001, based on intelligence information that he was a "sleeper" operative assigned to help other members of al Qaeda "settle" in the United States, he was picked up by the Federal Bureau of Investigation. He was first held as a material witness in the 9/11 investigation and later charged with lying to the Federal Bureau of Investigation and credit card fraud.[100] On June 23, 2003, less than one month before his civilian trial, President Bush issued a declaration that "Ali Saleh Kahlah al-Marri is, and at the time he entered the United States in September 2001 was, an enemy combatant."[101] The White House claims the classification of Mr. al-Marri was intended to allow officials to interrogate him about al Qaeda.[102] Civil liberties advocates and military law experts criticized the application of the executive order to Mr. al-Marri.

They argue that removing Mr. al-Marri from the civilian court system by declaring him an enemy combatant just weeks before his scheduled trial is a tactic to coerce a plea from Mr. al-Marri and from other terrorists being held on criminal charges. Justice Department officials denied the charge.[103] However, a senior FBI official commented that the "Marri decision held clear implications for other terrorism suspects. If I were in their shoes, I'd take a message from this."[104] Defense Secretary Donald H. Rumsfeld said of the tactic that it "demonstrated the White House's continued commitment to using a range of military and legal weapons to pursue terrorism suspects."[105]

Perhaps the greatest criticism of the Enemy Combatant Executive Order is reserved for the case of Jose Padilla, a U.S. citizen who was taken into custody at Chicago O'Hare Airport in May 2002. He was suspected of being part of a "dirty bomb" plot by al Qaeda.[106] Mr. Padilla was a former Chicago gang member with a long criminal record who converted to Islam. The government arrested him after he returned from a trip to Pakistan. Officials claimed he was "associated" with al Qaeda, met officials of the group in Afghanistan, and received training in explosives in Pakistan. In June 2003, President Bush declared him an enemy combatant and Mr. Padilla was moved from a federal jail in Manhattan to a Navy brig in Charleston, South Carolina.[107]

Jose Padilla is the only U.S. citizen arrested in the United States declared to be an enemy combatant and held indefinitely without charges or without access to an attorney or the civilian courts.[108] In November 2003, lawyers arguing on behalf of Mr. Padilla to a three-judge panel of the United States Court of Appeals for the Second Circuit in Manhattan argued that the government was "distorting principles of American liberty by expanding battlefield concepts to civilian life. . . . The President seeks an unchecked power to substitute military power for the rule of law." The court appeared to be sympathetic to the arguments of the defense. Rosemary S. Pooler, one of the judges hearing the arguments, declared, "As terrible as 9/11 was, it didn't repeal the Constitution."

New Legal Questions The enemy combatant executive order has created new legal questions. As the situation evolves and changes, new challenges emerge. Critics express concern that trials by military tribunal may be used as a tactic to get less important al Qaeda detainees to provide information about senior operational al Qaeda personnel.[109] The prospect of trying foreign citizens, some belonging to countries that are considered allies of the United States, has created foreign policy tensions and concern. For example, a spokesperson for the British Foreign Office has called on the United States "to conduct the tribunals with fairness on issues like access to lawyers, standards of evidence and the right to appeal in the case of a guilty verdict. Clearly, we want the Americans to give us assurances that the international minimum standards of fair trials will be met."[110]

The Bush Administration is feeling the effect of these pressures. Five Pakistanis held at the Guantanamo Bay detention center in Cuba were released in November 2003. As a result of Pakistani government efforts, 21 of the 58 Pakistanis have been released from Guantanamo Bay since November 2002. In March 2004, five British citizens were released, and in January 2005, the United States agreed to release the last four Britons and one Australian who had been held without charge or trial at Guantanamo Bay. Interestingly, the release of detainees often proves to be only the beginning of another problem. One of the Pakistani prisoners released from Guantanamo Bay has filed a lawsuit seeking $10.4 million in damages from the United States for his "illegal detention, torture and humiliation."[111] Often, those returned from Guantanamo Bay back to their native countries have been released without charges being filed against them.[112] This action causes the United States to fear that these combatants will rejoin al Qaeda in its attacks against the United States.

▲ check your understanding **11.6** **What factors led to the greater involvement of the federal government in capturing terrorists? Why is Bush's executive order so controversial?**

Prison Life

▼ the main idea **11.7** **Life in prison poses special problems for inmates, correctional authorities, and the commuity. The criminal justice system is working to reduce sexual violence in prisons, control prison gangs, and improve health and mental health services.**

Sexual Violence in Prisons

Sexual violence in prison has become a national concern. Anecdotal stories, incomplete statistics, and testimonies before legislative bodies and public forums suggest that nonconsensual sexual violence is a serious problem. Inmate lawsuits claim that prison officials turn a "blind eye" toward sexual violence in prison.[113] Some inmates who claim they have been raped in prison state that they were considered the "property" of prison gangs and would be bartered for money or favors.[114] Human Rights Watch issued a report concluding that "rape, by prisoners' accounts, was no aberrational occurrence; instead it was a deeply-rooted, systemic problem. It was also a problem that prison authorities were doing little to address."[115] Spurred by public demands for more accurate information on sexual violence in prisons, President George W. Bush signed into law the Prison Rape Elimination Act of 2003 (P.L. 108-79). The legislation requires the Bureau of Justice Statistics to develop new national data collections on the incidence and prevalence of sexual violence within correctional facilities.

In 2004, the Bureau of Justice Statistics issued its first report. The bureau surveyed 2,700 correctional facilities reporting that there were 8,210 allegations of sexual violence reported and correctional authorities substantiated nearly 2,100 incidents of sexual violence.[116] The most serious forms of sexual violence reported were inmate-on-inmate nonconsensual sexual acts and staff sexual misconduct. Nearly 42 percent of the reported allegations of sexual violence involved staff sexual misconduct, 37 percent involved inmate-on-inmate nonconsensual sexual acts, 11 percent pertained to staff sexual harassment, and 10 percent applied to inmate-on-inmate abusive sexual contact. Juvenile facilities reported the highest rates of alleged sexual violence. The survey data indicated that most allegations of sexual violence could not be substantiated due to a lack of evidence. Males comprised 90 percent of victims and perpetrators of nonconsensual sexual acts in prison and jail.

The study reported that jail and prison authorities had several sanctions for those inmates who were found to have committed sexual violence. The most common sanctions included moving the perpetrator to solitary confinement, changing the inmate to a higher custody level, transferring the inmate to another facility, loss of good-time credit, loss of privileges, and confining the inmate to his or her cell or quarters. Staff members found to have committed sexual violence were discharged, disciplined, or referred for prosecution. Juvenile systems reported the largest numbers of staff referred for prosecution (41 percent).

Go to www.gangsorus.com/ to view the website "Gangs or Us," which provides information on street and prison gangs.

Prison Gangs

Gang activity, a major factor in many prisons, has implications for in-prison and post-prison behavior.[117] The first prison gangs appeared in 1950. Prior to that time, strict control of prisoner movement, limited contact with the outside, absence of work release programs, and a harsh disciplinary code prevented the formation of gangs. Today, prison gangs, known as special threat or **security risk groups**, are a serious problem. For example, Rikers Island in New York has identified 44 security risk groups that operate within the prison.[118] Among the more common gangs operating in prison are the Aryan Brotherhood, the Black Guerilla Family, the Bloods, the Crips, La Nuestra Familia, Latin Kings, Mexican Mafia, Mexikanemi, Neta, and the Texas Syndicate. Most prison gangs are organized along lines of racial and ethnic identity.

Prison gangs pose special security risks and create a higher risk of violence because (1) gang codes of conduct discourage obedience to prison rules and (2) gangs frequently are involved in trafficking of prison contraband and protection. Gang codes require absolute loyalty to the gang. Often, to show one's commitment to the gang, new members must pass initiation tests, rituals that require the new member to make a "hit" on a rival gang member or correctional staff member. The hit usually requires only that the gang member attack the person and draw blood.[119]

Gang membership extends outside the prison. Prison gangs use this characteristic to have fellow gang members smuggle contraband inside the prison during visitations, through staff members who have been bribed, or when the prisoner is outside the prison wall on work details or other forms of release. Prison gangs then use trafficking in **contraband**—such as drugs, cigarettes, money, pornography, and so on—to buy favors, recruit members, pay prison debts, and make a profit. Prisoners who compete with the prison gang business, who inform prison officials about gang activities, or who are unable to pay for gang contraband may become targets of gang violence.

security risk groups Groups that raise special threats, such as prison gangs.

contraband Smuggled goods, such as drugs, cigarettes, money, or pornography.

Many inmates join a gang for protection, so an unintended consequence of longer prison terms has been an increase in gang affiliation. Because prisoners have to stay in prison longer, they feel a greater need to be affiliated with a prison gang to provide them with protection from other gangs, from individual inmates, and from correctional staff members. Gang affiliation guarantees retaliation for any harm caused to a member by others. In extreme cases, such retaliation can lead to a vicious cycle of gang wars, as each gang continues to retaliate for the last attack. Because fear of gang retaliation may be

Prison gangs pose a serious security challenge to jail and prison personnel. Segregation of gang members increases the gang's power and integration of gang members can lead to gang conflict and violence. The gang has power both in and out of the prison. What measures could correctional officials take to deal with gangs in prisons?

much stronger than fear of official prison sanctions, whenever prison rules and gang codes conflict, gang members will obey their gang code.

Health in Prisons

Daniel Tote, age 47, missed his release date from prison. In fact, he remained in prison 10 months beyond the expiration of his sentence. Tote was not released because he was in a persistent vegetative state due to head trauma that he suffered in an attack while in prison. When his sentence expired, there was no place to send him. Nursing homes would not take him, because, as a prisoner, he was not eligible for Medicaid. He had no insurance and no family to care for him. Thus, he remained in the prison infirmary despite the fact that he was a free man. Eventually, the state found a nursing home in which to place him, at a cost to the state of about $40,000 a year.[120] Daniel Tote is an extreme example of a serious problem in the criminal justice system: The physical and mental health of offenders, both incarcerated and released, has become a costly and sometimes deadly public health problem with no end in sight.

Prisoners have significant physical and mental health problems. The health of the average 50-year-old prisoner approximates that of the average 60-year-old person in the free community.[121] In a survey by the Office of Justice Programs, about 40 percent of state inmates and 48 percent of federal inmates age 45 or older said they had had a medical problem since admission to prison.[122] While they are in prison, their health care is the responsibility of the state. When they are released from prison, as most are, these problems do not go away when they reenter the community. Often, the released inmate enters the community with significant physical and mental health problems that can have a serious—even deadly—impact on the public.

The trend toward incarceration of offenders has created an unintended consequence: the creation of long-term health care obligations. As more prisoners are incarcerated and with longer sentences, the cost of prisoners' health care increases dramatically.[123] The impact of this problem can be seen in the fact that the most common Section 1983 lawsuit against jails and prisons involved claims of substandard medical treatment.[124] Many prison facilities now contain geriatric wings due to the high number of elderly inmates. These facilities provide long-term care units staffed by

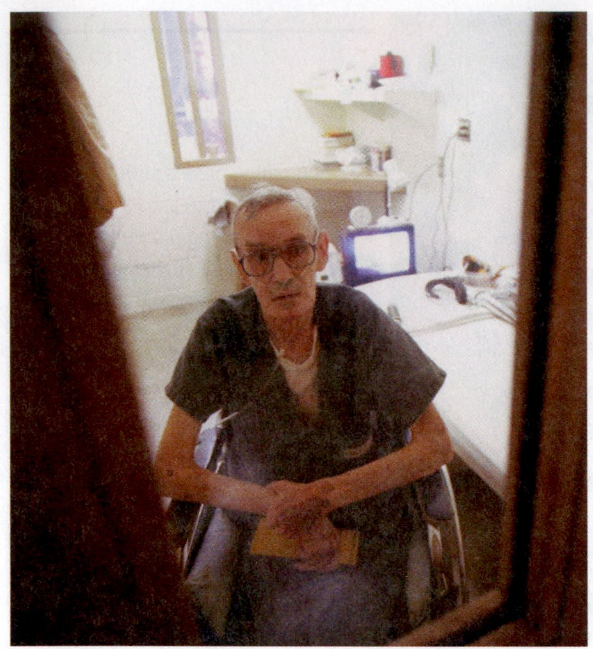

Why might you argue for keeping this prisoner in prison? Why might you argue for his release? In making such a decision, what would be your responsibilities toward the prisoner, the state in which he was imprisoned, and the community to which he would be returned? What if this prisoner had been convicted of a sex crime as a child predator? What if he were a member of a gang? What if he were a victim of prison violence? What if he were mentally ill? What if he were HIV-positive or had AIDS or TB?

nurses instead of correctional officers. Older, ill inmates receive round-the-clock care that costs the state about $65,000 per year.[125]

Studies indicate that, statistically, the risk of recidivism drops significantly with age. However, prisons, especially federal prisons and prisons in states that have abolished parole, often cannot release these inmates. In other cases, elderly offenders cannot be released because they are serving mandatory terms or because there are no community-care facilities to release them to, as in the case of Daniel Tote. As a result, the care of geriatric inmates has become an expensive burden on the criminal justice system. In a system that is constantly competing for public funding of other needs—for example, drug treatment programs, juvenile rehabilitation programs, community policing, and even public schools and highways—it is difficult to justify spending $65,000 a year on care for each elderly prisoner. But can prisoners be released just because they are old and it is expensive to take care of them? About 45 percent of inmates age 50 and older were only recently arrested. Older felons tend to be locked up for more serious crimes, such as rape, murder, and child molestation.[126] These offenders need to be incarcerated for the protection of the public.

HIV/AIDS and Communicable Diseases Sexually transmitted diseases (STDs), including HIV/AIDS and other communicable diseases, pose serious challenges to administrators of both adult and juvenile justice systems.[127] In 2002, the overall rate of confirmed AIDS cases among the nation's prison population was 3½ times the rate of the U.S. general population. Official statistics indicate that about 2 percent of state prison inmates and 1 percent of federal prison inmates are known to be infected with HIV.[128] However, the rate of HIV/AIDS infection is not uniform throughout the criminal justice system. New York, for example, has an HIV-positive prison population of nearly 8 percent, and California has a rate of less than 1 percent.[129] The percentage of HIV-positive inmates has declined since 1998.[130] The problem affects both male and female inmates, but a greater percentage of women (2.9 percent) than men (1.9 percent) are HIV-positive as reported in 2002.[131]

AIDS-related deaths in prison have dropped dramatically, from over 1,000 in 1995 to 283 in 2002.[132] The drop in the death rate is attributed primarily to advances in medical treatments available for HIV-positive patients and better identification and management of HIV-infected inmates by prison administrators.

Prisons are a critical setting for detecting and treating STDs. The testing of inmates for HIV/AIDS varies from state to state. About 19 states test all inmates at admission, whereas other states test inmates only on request or if the inmate belongs to a specific high-risk group. Most HIV-positive inmates were positive when admitted and thus did not become HIV-positive after admission to prison. Inmates contract HIV/AIDS from high-risk behavior, such as intravenous drug use or unprotected sex with partners who are infected. Many female inmates contract HIV/AIDS from prostitution. Because most inmates will be released back into the community, the identification of those with HIV/AIDS is important, as they constitute a significant percentage of the total number of Americans with HIV/AIDS.[133] Unfortunately, only 10 percent of state and federal prisons and 5 percent of city and county jails offer comprehensive HIV-prevention programs for inmates.[134]

Inmates who are HIV-positive pose special problems for correctional administrators. Those inmates cannot be completely isolated from the general prison population. In fact, federal laws regarding inmates' rights of privacy often prohibit prison administrators from making it generally known which inmates are HIV-positive. Thus, prison staff and other inmates may not be aware of which inmates are affected. This lack of knowledge creates concern among the prison staff, as they do not know if they are at risk of HIV infection when they handle inmates. Lacking this knowledge, the prison staff must treat all inmates as if they are potential infection risks. HIV-infected inmates may deliberately attempt to infect prison officials by biting them or by other means.

When inmates who are HIV-positive are released back into the community, they may create a public health hazard without proper care or education. While in prison, inmates receive free medication and treatment, but after release, they may be responsible for their own medical expenses and treatment. Released inmates may pose a serious health hazard if they engage in unprotected sex or share needles from intravenous drug use. Female offenders pose a community health risk, as many return to prostitution to obtain the cash they need.

Prisons and jails also present optimal conditions of the spread of diseases such as hepatitus C, staph infections, and tuberculosis (TB).[135] Tuberculosis can be more difficult to control than HIV because it is more easily spread by contact with active cases. TB-infected inmates released back into the community have the potential to spread the disease further, as TB can remain infectious for a long time. One study reported that in 31 state prison systems, 14 percent of inmates had positive tuberculin skin test results at intake.[136]

Inmates who receive only partial treatment for TB increase the threat of epidemic in the general population, because incomplete treatment raises the risk that the disease will become resistant to medications used to treat it and will not respond to subsequent treatment. Drug-resistant forms of TB could be transmitted to others, and the result could be a widespread public health disaster. Treatment of TB is complicated. A primary TB control measure is the complete isolation of infectious cases to prevent spreading the disease to other inmates. This type of isolation requires negative-pressure isolation rooms with ventilation that does not flow into the general ventilation system. Another complication of TB is that often inmates may be coinfected with both TB and HIV. Because TB can be spread through the ventilation system, prison administrators have to take precautions to keep general prison populations from being exposed. Failure to do so may result in a lawsuit.

Mental Health

Nearly one in five inmates in U.S. prisons reports having a mental illness.[137] A comprehensive Justice Department study of the rapidly growing number of incarcerated, emotionally disturbed people concluded that jails and prisons have become the nation's new mental health care facilities.[138] According to the report, "Jails have become the poor person's mental hospitals."[139]

In the 1960s, legislation was passed that made it difficult to commit mentally ill people who had not committed a crime to civil mental health facilities against their will. As a result, public mental hospitals were forced to release persons committed against their will unless the state could prove that the person was a danger to himself or herself or to the public. The intention of the legislation was that mentally ill people would receive community-based care instead of long-term hospitalization that differed little from incarceration. It was thought that with proper medication, community-based care would be a more humane alternative to long-term hospitalization.[140] Despite the good intentions of legislators, **deinstitutionalization** did not work as planned. There were too few community-based facilities, the mentally ill did not take their medications, and jails and prisons became the dumping ground for the mentally ill.[141] The mentally ill end up in jails and prisons for bizarre public behavior; petty crimes like loitering, public intoxication, and panhandling; as well as serious violent crimes such as murder, sexual assault, and property crime. About half of mentally ill inmates are in prison for a violent offense.[142]

Mentally ill inmates frequently are unable to abide by prison rules and discipline. This is due in part to their mental illness and in part to the overcrowded conditions and

deinstitutionalization Moving mentally ill people from long-term hospitalization to community-based care.

stresses of the correctional institution. Also, because they are unable to have "normal" interpersonal relations—a difficult challenge even for the mentally stable in prison—they are more likely to engage in fights and other violent behaviors. Unable to conform to the rules or to restrain their violent behavior, the mentally ill spend many hours in solitary confinement or segregated housing. Unfortunately, this punishment greatly increases the likelihood of depression and heightened anxiety in the mentally ill inmate.[143] The experience of being incarcerated typically exacerbates the inmate's mental illness.[144] As a result, incarcerated, emotionally disturbed inmates in state prisons spend an average of 15 months longer behind bars than other prisoners. In many cases, the difference is attributed to their delusions, hallucinations, or paranoia, which makes them more likely to get into fights or receive disciplinary reports.[145]

Prison environments contribute to mental health problems. Prisons are **total institutions**, a term sociologist Erving Goffman coined in his study of prisons and mental hospitals.[146] In prison, the inmate has little responsibility, does not have to make decisions, does not have to engage in problem solving, does not have to plan for tomorrow. The institution meets all the inmate's basic needs. The institution dictates the inmate's schedule. Institutional rules are made without any input from the inmate. The environment is rigid, and inmates are expected to conform to the values and expectations of the institution. Individuality is discouraged, dissent is punished, and failure to follow the rules can result in segregation from the prison population. As a consequence, the environment (1) does not promote effective treatment of the mentally ill offender—even people without mental health problems become depressed and mentally ill when exposed to this environment; and (2) encourages the development of **prisonization**—socialization into a distinct prison subculture with its own values, mores, norms, and sanctions.

Prisonization results in a subculture for inmates in which the rules of conduct are distinctly different from the official rules of the institution and from society in general. Prisoners learn to adapt to this prison code and conduct their life in prison by it. However, the mentally ill prisoner, who has difficulty adapting to society in general, often is unable to relate to fellow prisoners and conform to the prison code while, at the same time, maintaining the appearance of obedience to the institutional rules and norms. Often, the result of this failure to adapt to the prison code is dangerous ostracism by both inmates and administrators.

All prisoners are affected by prisonization, which is why most prisoners demonstrate maladaptive behaviors when they are returned to the community. Accustomed to being told what to do, when to do it, and how to do it, released inmates often demonstrate few of the job skills desired by employers. Prisoners who have been incarcerated for long terms may have lost the ability to plan for the future, to take responsibility for their actions, and exhibit proactive behaviors. They have become passive, dependent, and fixated on the rules.

When released back into the community, the mentally ill offender is seldom cured as a result of the treatment received while incarcerated. Even if treatment and medication in prison had made a significant impact on their behavior, it is doubtful that released mentally ill offenders would continue treatment or medication. For example, a Bureau of Justice Statistics survey reported that while an estimated 13 percent of probationers were required to seek mental health treatment as a condition of their sentence, fewer than half fulfilled this requirement.[147]

total institutions Institutions that meet all of the inmate's basic needs, discourage individuality, punish dissent, and segregate those who do not follow the rules.

prisonization Socialization into a distinct prison subculture with its own values, mores, norms, and sanctions.

Neither police nor correctional institutions have been able to make a significant impact on the problem of the mentally ill offender. Providing medications in prison is a temporary approach to a much more serious community problem. In addition to the public-order crimes they commit, mentally ill offenders commit serious offenses. For example, about 13 percent of mentally ill inmates in prisons were convicted of murder, and about 12 percent were convicted of sexual assault. Andrea Yates, for example, was mentally ill when she murdered her five young children by drowning them one by one in the bathtub of her home. Mental health professionals posit that a significant percentage of youths involved in the juvenile justice system have unmet needs for mental health and substance abuse services.[148]

▲ check your understanding **11.7** **What reasons are given for the increasing elderly prison population? In what ways do gangs increase violence in prisons? What problems do privacy laws pose for dealing with inmates with HIV? In what ways do prison environments contribute to mental health problems? What is prisonization, and what are its consequences? Why are problems of prison populations important to the wider society?**

conclusion:

Prisons—The Human Cage

Jails and prisons are designed to hold humans in a secure environment to prevent their escape. Frequently, the concern of the public is not the conditions of the jails or prisons but the perceived risk of escape and fear of harm caused by escaping prisoners. Most citizens strongly object to a jail or prison being built in their neighborhood.[149] Some citizens appear to have little sympathy for incarcerated inmates. For example, in response to a report on four suicides in a municipal jail, one editorial dismissed concerns about the deaths, arguing, "These suspects had been arrested for murder, kidnapping, burglary, drug dealing, assault and drunken driving. I do not consider these deaths as tragic losses. Rather, these four saved the overburdened taxpayers a great deal of money by taking their fates into their own hands."[150]

Jails and prisons represent a substantial financial burden and directly compete with other needed services. Often, people see every dollar that goes into jails and prisons as one less dollar to go to other services, such as schools, hospitals, medical care, public safety, and transportation. For example, when a Pennsylvania jail warden turned in a request for $500,000 for new computers for an educational program for Pittsburgh jail inmates, the county refused to process the invoice.[151] The computers were to be purchased from profits from the jail's commissary, where inmates buy candy, snacks, and toiletries, but the county government argued that the money should be returned to the taxpayers. As one official expressed, "We have taxpayers who can't even afford (computers). Before we give that type of convenience to prisoners, we should balance the budget. It's not our responsibility to educate and entertain the inmates."[152]

Recidivism rates show that jails and prisons have not proved as effective as desired. They have not protected the public from criminal activity in the long run. They have not deterred people from committing crimes through the threat or pain of incarceration, nor have they rehabilitated inmates, whether through penitence, educational training, or harsh discipline. Some have argued that prisons are nothing but warehouses in which inmates are placed because society cannot think of more effective solutions to an age-old problem. The public has become frustrated with the cost and lack of effectiveness of locking criminals in cages and waiting. The trend toward privatization has been one consequence.

chapter summary

- In the United States, Pennsylvania's Walnut Street Jail and Eastern State Penitentiary and New York's Auburn State Prison established uniquely American correctional models.
- Early American jails and prisons had rehabilitation as a goal. Prison labor was exploited, especially in colonies with indentured servitude and in southern penal systems, which operated on a convict lease system. Later, American jails and prisons had retribution as the chief goal.
- Prison reforms following World War II stemmed from the U.S. Supreme Court ruling that inmates have the right to sue the government over prison conditions and civil rights violations.
- Jails are short-term, multipurpose facilities that serve as a gateway to the criminal justice system. Federal jails are operated through the Federal Bureau of Prisons, county jails through sheriffs' departments, and municipal jails through police departments.
- State prisons contain only convicted offenders. States have their own systems, which vary significantly among states. Oversight comes through prison administration, headed by the warden, and through state and federal legislation and state and federal courts.
- State prison employees include correctional officers—civil service employees who perform security services—treatment staff, and other professional personnel. Most state prisons are like small, self-contained cities.
- Federal prisons such as Leavenworth and Alcatraz were built during the prohibition era and are run by the Federal Bureau of Prisons. The federal prison system parallels state prison systems in classification and administration, but federal prisons have higher standards for employment.
- Private jails and prisons developed as a result of overcrowding and the high cost of building and staffing correctional institutions. People disagree about the benefits and costs of privatization to both inmates and communities.

vocabulary review

chain gang, 398
congregate work system, 397
contraband, 420
convict lease system, 398
correctional officers, 411
deinstitutionalization, 423
incarceration, 394
inside cell block, 397
jails, 402
penitentiary, 396
prison farm system, 398
prisoner classification, 406
prisonization, 424
privatization, 414
security risk groups, 420
silent system, 396
solitary confinement, 397
state prisons, 406
total institutions, 424

do you remember?

Alcatraz, 413
Auburn Prison, 397
Eastern State Penitentiary, 396
Federal Bureau of Prisons (BOP), 402
Florence, 413
John Howard (*State of Prisons*), 395
Philadelphia Society to Alleviate the Miseries of Public Prisons, 395
Walnut Street Jail, 395

think about this

1. Two-thirds of inmates become repeat offenders. Is a system that is one-third effective acceptable? What do you think is a reasonable rate of success for prisons, and how would success be measured? After introducing restorative justice programs, countries such as New Zealand and Australia reported significant drops in repeat offending. Why might that be the case? Why haven't restorative justice programs received greater acceptance in the United States?
2. In early 2002, an inmate sentenced to life in prison received a heart transplant, at a cost to taxpayers of nearly one million dollars. Many other prisoners have received liver and kidney transplants. A case was presented before the courts to allow a transsexual inmate (serving a life term for murdering his wife) to receive a sex-change operation. Do you think inmates should have the right to such expensive health care? Why or why not?
3. After reading about the history of punishment and prisons, which goals and method(s) do you think were most effective? How might earlier forms of punishment be updated to fit present-day realities?

research navigator

Visit the Research Navigator website (www.researchnavigator.com), login and select the criminal justice data base in ContentSelect. Type in the key words "Incarceration, Inc." and select the article "Incarceration, Inc." by Sasha Abramsky. The article discusses the role of private jails and prisons in the criminal justice system. Sample the article and answer the following questions:

1. According to Abramsky why is the private prison industry expanding?
2. According to Abramsky what are some of the potential harms of private prisons?
3. Local citizens normally are strongly opposed to the location of a prison or correctional facility in their neighborhood so why are many rural cities aggressively lobbying for a private prison to be built in their area?
4. Do you think private prisons and jails are practical alternatives to the expanding prison population? Explain your answer.

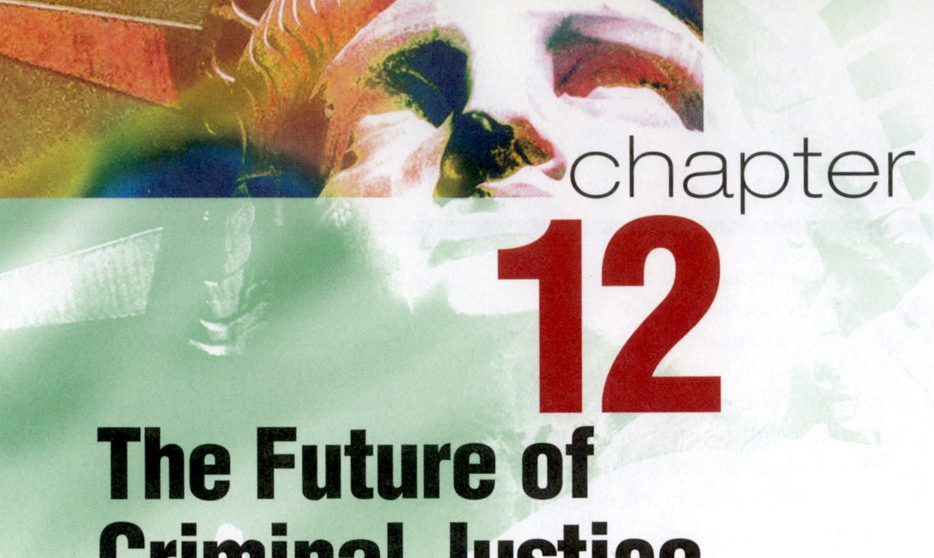

chapter 12

The Future of Criminal Justice

CHAPTER OUTLINE

LEARNING OBJECTIVES

After reading this chapter you will understand

- The challenges facing the criminal justice system in the twenty-first century.
- Why the War on Terrorism and immigration will be prominent influences on the criminal justice system.
- How technology, media, diversity, and isolationism will affect the police.
- The challenge of the courts to create specialized courts and the role of the courts in protecting civil rights.
- The importance of the ability of the criminal justice system to develop models for successful reentry for offenders.

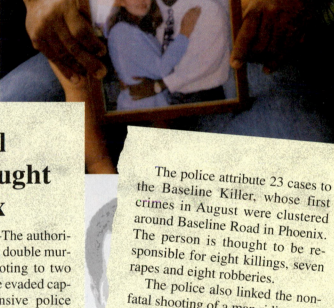

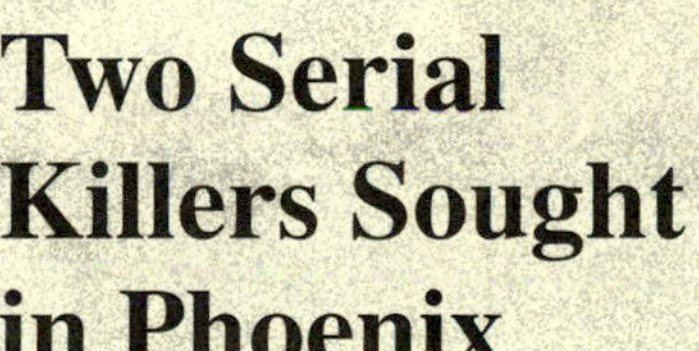

Two Serial Killers Sought in Phoenix

PHOENIX, July 28—The authorities this week linked a double murder and nonfatal shooting to two serial killers who have evaded capture despite an intensive police investigation in Phoenix and its suburbs. The unknown gunmen, who the police believe are acting independently, are thought to be responsible for dozens of killings, rapes, robberies and shootings since last year.

"One of the things we have done investigatively is to go back over cases—and there's a lot of them to go back over," Sergeant Hill said. "In the last year and half, there's been almost 400 homicides and a lot of other violent crimes."

The police attribute 23 cases to the Baseline Killer, whose first crimes in August were clustered around Baseline Road in Phoenix. The person is thought to be responsible for eight killings, seven rapes and eight robberies.

The police also linked the nonfatal shooting of a man riding a bicycle before dawn in the suburb of Mesa on Saturday to the second gunman, who is known as the Serial Shooter. The shooting was a new eastern expansion for the attacker, whose territory has spanned 32 miles from the bedroom cities of Avondale, west of Phoenix, to Mesa, east of Phoenix. The Serial Shooter is believed to be responsible for 5 killings, 17 nonfatal shootings, 12 shootings of animals and one property shooting at a business.

Paul Giblin, "Two Serial Killers Sought in Phoenix," *New York Times*, July 29, 2006. New York Times Online. www.nytimes.com.

introduction:

Broad and Deep

The criminal justice system is enormous in its scope and impact. As Phoenix police were searching for two serial killers in the summer of 2006, the Las Vegas, Nevada, police were searching for ways to enforce a new law prohibiting the feeding of the homeless in the park.[1] Citizens depend on the criminal justice system to protect them from serious criminals such as serial killers and rapists and at the same time to promote quality of life issues by discouraging the homeless to gather in the park for free food. Also, in the twenty-first century the criminal justice system is an integral tool in protecting citizens from terrorist attacks. To respond to this wide range of responsibilities and expectations, the criminal justice system must be flexible, adapted to social values, backed with the resources it needs, and connected to the community, and its personnel must have the skills, knowledge, and abilities to perform its mission with competence and reliability. Few organizations are expected to meet such high standards.

This chapter takes a look at the big picture of criminal justice and discusses the role of the criminal justice system in society, focusing on the future rather than the present or the past. It examines the pushes and pulls of complex social, technological, and legal factors that will influence the direction, responsibilities, and response of the public of the criminal justice system.

Crime in the Twenty-First Century

▼the main idea 12.1 The scope of responsibility of the criminal justice system will expand in the twenty-first century. The War on Terrorism and illegal immigration will be prominent influences upon the criminal justice system.

According to the U.S. Department of Justice, in 2003, the United States spent a record $185 billion for police protection, corrections, and judicial and legal activities. Expenditures for operating the nation's justice system increased from almost $36 billion in 1982 to over $185 billion in 2003, an increase of 418 percent.[2] Why has the cost of the criminal justice system increased so much in such a short time? One might be prompted to ask, "Has there been a 400 percent increase in justice and public safety to match the increase in expenditures?"

In the last 25 years the criminal justice system has undergone significant changes. In the twenty-first century the criminal justice system is facing challenges that were not even anticipated in the 1980s. Crime has become more complex, our understanding of crime more sophisticated, and the resources to prosecute crime more expensive.

In the 1800s, when cities began to adopt the London-style policing of Sir Robert Peel, police departments were concerned primarily with public order and traditional crimes such as murder, robbery, and assault. Today, the definition of crime includes environmental crimes, political corruption, racketeering, international drug and human trafficking, organized crime, white-collar crime, economic crime, and numerous other crimes that differ significantly from "traditional" street crimes and public order crimes. In the last two decades, prosecution of white-collar crimes, organized crime, international drug cartels, economic crime, and environmental crimes has greatly increased.

The city of Las Vegas, Nevada, passed a law making it a crime to feed the homeless in public parks for fear of encouraging the homeless to congregate there and become a nuisance or threat to others. In addition to crime fighting, police are expected to promote quality-of-life issues. Have public expectations of the role of the police become too extensive?

Unlike street crimes, often the perpetrators of these crimes are corporations, international cartels, or criminal networks. Prosecution of corporate crime, such as the Ken Lay and Martha Stewart trials, costs millions of dollars and takes years to investigate and prosecute.

Furthermore, the criminal justice system has recognized the public's demand for accountability in government and business and has undertaken prosecutions of public officials, including investigations into the business transactions of the president and alleged criminal activity of governors, senators, representatives, and lobbyists. Some of these investigations have broken new ground as to the limits of the jurisdiction of the criminal justice system, as when the FBI seized the files of a sitting U.S. congressman from his office. The criminal justice system of the twenty-first century will be responsible for a much broader scope of crimes than ever before.

When the FBI seized evidence from congressional representative William Jefferson's office, many challenged the FBI's actions as a violation of the separation of powers doctrine. The modern criminal justice system has become complex and has entered into new roles. Is there a need for an extensive examination of whether reform is necessary for the criminal justice system?

Municipal governments and states are greatly concerned with the problems of crime and economic impacts caused by illegal immigration. Many state and municipal governments are taking actions of their own to address this problem. What should be the role of local and state police in detouring illegal immigration?

Terrorism and Illegal Immigration

The War on Terrorism and **illegal immigration** are going to be significant factors affecting the criminal justice system in the twenty-first century. The War on Terrorism is producing major changes in the definition of constitutional rights as the executive branch claims far-reaching wartime powers to fight terrorism. The detention of accused terrorists without access to the courts, without the protection of the Fifth Amendment, without access to an attorney, and facing indefinite confinement without charges has resulted in legal challenges by the American Bar Association, the American Civil Liberties Union, and other critics opposed to the usurping of constitutional protections.[3] In the fight against terrorism, the Executive Branch has claimed broad new powers of search and seizure for the U.S. Justice Department and other federal agencies, including the right to secretly monitor e-mails, financial transactions, and telephone conversations, to imprison suspects without charge, and to conduct searches without a search warrant or oversight by the courts.[4]

The detention of hundreds of alleged Afghanistan terrorists at Guantanamo Naval Base has created a legal dispute as never before experienced in the criminal justice system. The legal arguments as to the rights that should be provided to these detainees and the procedure for determining charges, guilt, and punishment will go down in the twenty-first century as one of the great legal debates of the century. The unique nature of this situation is such that new legal arguments are being advanced on both sides as to the proper procedure and rights in dealing with these detainees.[5]

The War on Terrorism is causing a significant financial burden on local law enforcement agencies. Initially, municipal budgets were substantially supplemented with federal grants, but in 2006, the federal government cut federal grants to some cities by as much as 40 percent.[6] As the Department of Homeland Security reveals that the plots to attack New York, Chicago, Los Angeles, and other cities have been foiled and perpetrators arrested, increased diligences and proactive actions against terrorism are expected of municipal police departments.[7] A report released by the Department of Homeland Security in July 2006 listed 8,591 potential terrorist targets in U.S. cities. This list did not include a list of 77,069 commercial sites, governmental sites, health facilities, power plants, and sites with chemical or hazardous materials that the Department of Homeland Security considers at risk of terrorist attack.[8] In the twenty-first century the criminal justice system will need to develop strategies to respond to the threat of terror attacks and will need to fund the resources necessary to implement these strategies.

Although some see illegal immigration as a problem that is related to the War on Terrorism, many U.S. cities see it primarily as a crime and economic impact problem. The problem is not limited to states that share a border with Mexico but even states in the Northeast are beginning to perceive illegal immigration as a major factor in an increasing crime rate and as having a detrimental impact on economic development. Despite the fact that immigration is a federal responsibility, many municipalities are adopting aggressive campaigns aimed at reducing the presence of illegal immigrants in their cities. New municipal ordinances provide steep fines to landlords who rent to illegal immigrants and businesses that knowingly employ illegal immigrants.[9] These actions have been challenged in court as unconstitutional enforcement of immigration laws, but municipalities are aggressively moving forward in adopting new ordinances, claiming that illegal immigration "destroys our neighborhoods and diminishes our overall quality of life."[10] In the twenty-first century, local and state governments will strongly lobby the federal government to stem the flow of illegal immigrants into the United States. If they perceive that the federal government is failing to achieve this goal or is moving too slowly, they will take whatever action they think necessary to fix the problem.

Illegal immigration Entering or remaining in the United States without proper approval by the federal government. Many cities claim that illegal immigration causes a significant public safety and economic problem for their cities and are critical of the federal government's response to illegal immigration.

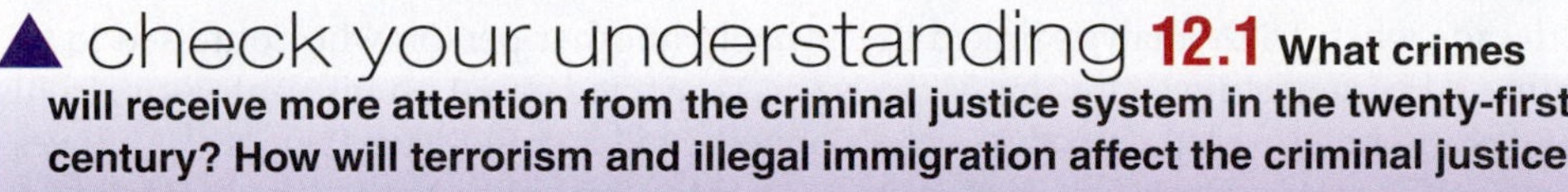

▲ check your understanding 12.1 What crimes will receive more attention from the criminal justice system in the twenty-first century? How will terrorism and illegal immigration affect the criminal justice system?

Police

▼ the main idea 12.2 Factors that will significantly affect policing in the twenty-first century are technology, media, diversity, and the pressure to abandon isolationism.

Local and county police have historically been described as semi-autonomous organizations. In fact, the concept of local police was developed on the premise that these agencies would be controlled by cities and counties as a check against a strong national government. However, the assumptions underlying the roles and responsibilities of local police significantly changed in the late twentieth century and that change is accelerating in the twenty-first century. Some of the more influential factors that will affect policing in the twenty-first century are technology, media, diversity, and the pressure to abandon isolationism.

Technology

Technology has always been an important influence on policing. From the time of the first police departments in the nineteenth century, technology has changed the capacity of both the criminal and the police. Early landmarks in technology included the development of reliable modern firearms, the automobile, the telephone, and the ability to communicate by two-way radio. Each of these had a profound impact on policing. For example, the automobile and two-way radio defined the mode of policing in the post–World War II era, virtually eliminating the former method of foot and horse patrol.

In the twenty-first century, advances in science, communications, and computers are redefining police work. One of the areas most affected by advances in science is in the area of investigations. New scientific investigative tools have enabled police to gather forensic evidence that previously could not even be imagined by the police or the public. At the turn of the twentieth century, the introduction of fingerprints and blood typing revolutionized the identification of suspects and those accused of a crime. As the century continued, new scientific breakthroughs such as ballistic identification continued to expand the investigative prowess of the police. Today, the investigative powers of the police are enormously enhanced by forensic evidence. Microscopic analysis of the smallest of clues left at the scene of a crime can lead to positive identification of the perpetrator or provide information to help the police solve the crime.

DNA analysis has replaced fingerprints as the standard for identifying persons. Furthermore, DNA identification is much more robust than fingerprints, as DNA samples can be collected from numerous sources such as cups, cigarettes, gum, blood, bone, and any body fluid. DNA has been a double-edged sword for the criminal justice system. It has enhanced the investigative abilities of the police, but it has also pointed out blunders and shortcomings of the criminal justice system. Project Innocence at the Benjamin N. Cardozo School of Law has documented over 100 persons who have been wrongly convicted through the use of DNA analysis. Some of these cases of persons wrongly convicted have reflected improper or abusive police practices. For example, Douglas Arthur Warney, a delusional person with an eighth-grade education, was freed from prison after a decade when DNA analysis linked the crime to another person who confessed to the crime. The interesting fact is that Warney was convicted based on his confession. In his confession he provided detectives details only the killer could have known.[11] An investigation into the circumstances of Warney's confession suggests that the mentally impaired Warney was fed critical details of the crime by the homicide detective leading the investigation and Warney repeated these details back to the police in his confession.[12]

The identification powers of DNA technology and the revelation of the number of persons who have been wrongly convicted by use of DNA has resulted in several proposals to improve the criminal justice system. These include proposals that there should be mandatory DNA analysis in all serious crimes where there is DNA evidence. Other proposals extend this mandate to provide DNA testing for persons convicted of serious crimes who proclaim their innocence, if DNA evidence is available. To prevent police misconduct and error during interrogations, other proposals call for the videotaping of all police interrogations so that any misconduct or mistake by the police can be documented.

Can too much of a good thing cause problems? If collecting DNA samples from some persons can enhance police investigative abilities, would collecting DNA samples from everyone provide even greater abilities? One of the most controversial proposals regarding DNA is a call for a universal databank of DNA. A universal **DNA databank** would provide police the ability to match DNA samples found at the scene of a crime with a comprehensive DNA collection to identify whose DNA was at the scene of the crime. This could greatly enhance the ability of the police to solve crimes and to obtain convictions. Nearly all states require that people convicted of a felony submit a DNA sample to a DNA collection system. Would the ability to identify perpetrators be enhanced if the DNA database is expanded? New York state has proposed that all convicted criminals involved in felonies and misdemeanors should submit DNA samples.[13]

Arguments for expansive DNA collections of all criminals are based on the findings that persons who commit serious felonies frequently commit misdemeanors. If a person's DNA was collected when he or she was convicted of a misdemeanor, it would be possible to match a DNA sample from the scene of a felony committed by this person. Arguments against inclusive DNA collections posit that the cost of DNA collection, storage, and analysis could be prohibitive and would yield diminishing returns.[14] Another consideration is the concern over privacy, as the push for inclusive DNA databases could result in the inclusion of noncriminals in the database. During the early years of the FBI, J. Edgar Hoover launched a public campaign to collect the fingerprints of every person in the United States. He promoted such a database, arguing that it would provide police with greater investigative abilities. Similar arguments are being made with regard to the collection of DNA samples.

Civil liberties groups and proponents express concerns that such broad databases may be subject to misuse, and, in the absence of regulation, DNA databases could be used for other than lawful purposes.[15] DNA provides more than just the identity of a person. It also supplies information regarding genetic predisposition to disease, medical health, and other personal information that could be useful to private businesses. For example, health insurers and life insurance companies could use the information obtained from DNA analysis to make decisions regarding insurability or rates.

The use of technology also includes the adoption of computer and Internet technologies by the police. Nearly all police departments employing more than 100 employees use computers. Some police departments have placed computers in police cars and others have adopted the use of PDAs for beat police officers. All major police departments have adopted sophisticated multifunctional computer systems that frequently are integrated with 9-1-1 services. There will continue to be new advances in the use of computers by police departments.

DNA databank Collections of DNA samples much like collections of fingerprints. However, unlike fingerprint collections, DNA samples provide much more information about the subject than just his or her identity.

As a result of the adoption of new technologies, the personnel hired by police departments is changing and will continue to change. Police departments are hiring more technical experts and more civilian employees. During the mid-1900s, most civilians in a police department were secretaries and clerks. Even during the 1970s many police departments used sworn officers for dispatch duties. The adoption of new technologies is creating new nontraditional jobs that are better filled by civilians with specialized training. For example, many police departments are employing civilians to staff crime scene investigation units. These civilian units do not replace the need for detectives but supplement the work of detectives by providing a unit of specialists with technical and scientific training. Also, as police departments adopt more sophisticated computer and communication equipment, the average police officer becomes less and less capable of fulfilling the responsibilities of these positions. As a result of technology use by the police, more police departments will hire a greater number of civilian employees, and often these employees will have specialized training and skills that will enable them to have fulfilling careers with advancement opportunities in the police department.

Media

Advances in media technology, particularly the digital camera, have greatly affected the police both positively and negatively. On the one hand, the digital camera has enabled much greater surveillance capacity of public places and the ability to capture images of crimes in progress and criminals. Many cities are installing more and more cameras to monitor public places. Advances in Internet technology have enabled public and private surveillance systems to link so that the police can access not only images captured by their cameras but also images captured by private businesses, public housing projects, and other government agencies. Some police departments have used the advances in media technology to monitor intersections and automatically issue tickets to persons who run red lights. Other police departments have even used the technology to automatically issue speeding tickets to motorists shown on camera violating the speed limit.

Many police departments have seen the advantages of recording police and citizen interactions and have adopted technology to enable them to do so. For example, many police departments have equipped patrol cars with dashboard-mounted cameras that can capture video and audio of police interactions with citizens. These images have helped in exonerating police officers accused of misconduct, helped convict citizens accused of driving while intoxicated, and helped identify perpetrators who have assaulted or killed police officers during a traffic stop. Also, police departments have installed cameras in police buildings and some departments routinely record all interrogations.

Media images of alleged police brutality have become commonplace. Often the media will show such incidences over and over. Do you think there is an increase in police misconduct or that as a result of greater media coverage police misconduct is just becoming more known to the public?

criminal justice in the media

Science Fiction or Futurology?

The entertainment media provide numerous versions of the future of the criminal justice system. These images include such visions of the criminal justice system as a society policed by robocops, frozen law enforcement officers thawed to fight violent crime because future cops have lost the ability to deal with violence, police officers teaming up with aliens to fight intergalactic crime, timecops who chase bad guys through time warps, where criminal cases are decided entirely by computers, and depicting New York as a lawless penal colony ruled by homicidal criminals. Some shows even suggest an interplanetary council will govern earth and other civilizations. Many of these presentations are pure fantasy.

However, there are serious speculations about the criminal justice system of the future. For example, George Orwell in his novel *1984* described a strong central government that controlled virtually every aspect of society, including thought. Television specials on weapons of the future speculate about nonlethal weapons that may be developed and adopted by police departments. Other documentaries suggest innovative correctional rehabilitation, including biochemical therapies. The criminal justice system has changed tremendously in the last 100 years and has undergone significant change even in the last two decades. Police officers of the 1950s would consider the routine use of computers, digital cameras, the Internet, and modern communications equipment by modern police departments as science fiction.

The future of policing has been depicted in many ways by the media. How would you describe the criminal justice system 20 years from now? Fifty years?

What is your vision of the criminal justice system of 2030? What is your vision of the criminal justice system of 2050 and beyond?

The other side of media technology is that the news media and citizens have been able to record police misconduct. The proliferation of digital cameras and cell phone cameras has enabled the news media and citizens to capture images of police officers assaulting citizens or engaging in illegal or unethical activities. In the recent past the media has aired images of police officers apparently assaulting citizens without justification in New Orleans, Los Angeles, New York, Chicago, Miami, and other cities throughout the United States. Often, the images of these unprovoked brutal assaults are repeatedly broadcast on the news, inflaming the public and, in cases where minority citizens are involved, provoking racial tensions. The actions of the police can come under examination due to images captured by the media and private citizens. For example, during the 2004 Republican National Convention images captured by the media and private citizens documented police misconduct against both protestors and innocent bystanders. As a result of this media evidence hundreds of cases against alleged protestors were dismissed as the media images showed that the police report contained false information regarding the alleged activities of the person arrested.

Diversity

Diversity within U.S. society as well as within police departments will pose significant challenges for the police in the twenty-first century. For the most part, police departments did not open their ranks of employment to minorities and women until the Civil Rights Act of 1967 was amended in 1971 to prohibit discrimination by police departments based on race, gender, ethnicity, and other factors. Since that time, police departments have made advances in achieving diversity but there is still the need for significant efforts to advance diversity employment.

Police departments have been more successful in attracting diverse male employees than they have been in attracting women. Policing is a male-dominated profession. However, police departments, spurred both by the desire to attract qualified females and by lawsuits due to their failure to attract and promote qualified females, have engaged in good faith efforts to hire females. Although numerous studies have indicated that females perform as well as or, in some areas of police work, better than males, discrimination based on standards of physical fitness and maternity continues to be a significant obstacle for police departments. For example, pregnancy is still a prominent problem for female employees in some police departments. Women who become pregnant find that some departments will not provide them with alternative duty assignments, which are commonly referred to as **light duty or desk duty.** Often, the problem with pregnant female officers performing patrol duty is that "bullet-proof" vests and even the officer's duty belt do not properly fit a pregnant officer.[16] Thus, pregnant officers find that they must compromise their safety or forfeit their job.

Diversity in society will prove to be a greater challenge to law enforcement than diversity within the department. In the twenty-first century law enforcement will be challenged by a greater diversity in society than ever before.

Diversity in the twenty-first century goes beyond racial diversity and includes religion and sexual orientation. Society's concern that discrimination should be suppressed is expressed in part in the adoption of legislation defining **hate crimes** and providing

hate crimes Crimes that are considered motivated by hate based on race, religion, ethnicity, sexual preference, or gender. Additional punishment is attached for hate crimes. Concern over the incidences of hate crimes has led to legislation requiring that police departments report the number of hate crimes.

Once a white-male–dominated profession, police work today is done by a much more diverse population. Diversity in the work force has not been without its problems, however, as women and minorities still claim discrimination in hiring and promotion decisions. How might the police attract and keep more diverse persons?

more severe punishment for crimes classified as hate crimes. The War on Terrorism has accented the emphasis on religious diversity, as seen by the number of complaints by Muslims and other persons of Middle Eastern appearance of discrimination and abuse by the police. Furthermore, the War on Terrorism and the Middle East conflict have been blamed for attacks on persons in the United States due to their ethnicity. For example, on July 28, 2006, a man opened fire on the offices of the Jewish Federation of Greater Seattle. Witnesses reported the alleged gunman, a Muslim American, told one of the victims that he was "angry at Israel."[17] Police departments will need to develop new strategies for assessing and responding to hate crimes.

Isolationism

Most police departments in the United States are small. They have less than 100 officers, and many have less than 25. Medium-sized cities of 300,000 may have only 300 to 400 police officers. As a result, most police departments have very limited resources. Police departments are a significant expense for municipalities, especially small cities. Some cities are finding that they cannot afford their police departments. Part of the problem is that historically cities have prided themselves on having independent police departments. Each city has had its own police department, police chief, police officers, fleet of vehicles, and staff to support the police department. The city was responsible for hiring, training, and paying the employees, as well as responsible for the pensions of officers and staff who retired. As the cost of maintaining a police department rose, cities found that there were crimes that their small police departments simply could not handle. Criminals pay no attention to the jurisdiction of cities, counties, and states. Drug trafficking and many other serious crimes are interstate or international crimes. Local police officers with limited resources and jurisdictions that ended with their city, county, or state boundaries were handicapped in fighting crime.

Many metropolitan areas have recognized the obstacles to limited jurisdiction of local police and have formed intercity compacts to create a metro police department with multicity jurisdiction. Also, local police have found that when the challenge of crime exceeds the limited resources they have, it is necessary to form alliances with state and federal police. For example, when Washington, DC, Mayor Anthony A. Williams declared a "crime emergency" in July 2006 due to the surge in homicides and armed robberies, he found it necessary to seek assistance from at least a dozen federal law enforcement agencies to assist the District of Columbia police in combating the crime wave.[18] Smaller cities are finding that local police departments are just too expensive and are moving to consolidated police departments when several cities maintain only one police department, or they are contracting with larger cities, the county, or the state police for police services.

Cities are also discovering that certain crimes require cooperation among cities and federal law enforcement agencies. For example, New York City found that of all the guns used in crimes in the city, 82 percent are brought in illegally from other states. Boston found a similar trend in its gun violence crimes. Thus, New York City and Boston turned to a coalition of 15 cities and the Bureau of Alcohol, Tobacco and Firearms (ATF) to intensify their efforts to combat illegal firearms, as it was evident that it would be impossible to solve the problem on their own.[19]

Police departments in the twenty-first century will be more interdependent both because of financial necessity and because of the changing nature of crime and criminals.

▲ check your understanding **12.2 What are four factors that will affect policing in the twenty-first century? How will these factors affect policing?**

Courts

the main idea 12.3 The courts will face the challenge of developing new courts for special categories of offenders and fulfilling their role of guaranteeing the implementation of constitutionally protected rights.

Significant changes are occurring in the courts. One of the most important of these changes is the adoption of new courts that specialize in certain types of criminal offenses such as **drug courts** and juvenile courts (other than the regular juvenile court). As more information is known about offending and rehabilitation, courts are being used to implement this new knowledge into policy and procedures. Most of these new initiatives have taken place without provisions for evaluation with scientific rigor, so it is difficult to assess the effectiveness of these courts.[20]

In addition to the adoption of new courts, courts, especially the U.S. Supreme Court, will continue to play an important oversight role. This role will include interpreting applications of standing decisions and ruling regarding new situations. For example, in 2006, the U.S. Supreme Court upheld the right of a defendant to hire a lawyer of his or her choice, ruling that forcing a defendant to accept a court-appointed lawyer is grounds for overturning a conviction.[21] Also, in 2006, the U.S. Supreme Court was asked to resolve a conflict between the Justice Department and the U.S. House of Representatives. Federal Bureau of Investigation agents seized the files of Representative **William J. Jefferson** (D-LA) from his congressional office. The Justice Department claimed that such files were not protected by special privilege from search and seizure, whereas the House of Representatives challenged the authority of the FBI to seize such records, claiming a violation of the separation of powers doctrine.[22]

As American society is becoming more diverse through immigration and international interactions the Court will become more involved in interpreting the relationship between international law and the rights of foreign criminal defendants and accused terrorists. As a signatory to several international treaties on human rights there are times when foreign criminal defendants claim special status and rights based on international treaties. In 2006, the Supreme Court had to decide several cases in which foreign criminal defendants claimed special status.[23]

Finally, the U.S. federal courts have become key players in defining the rights of accused terrorists. The Bush Administration and the Justice Department have claimed that persons classified as **enemy combatants** do not have constitutionally protected rights provided to criminal defendants and do not have rights provided by international treaties. In addition to the rights to be afforded to accused terrorists, the courts will also play an important role in ruling on the constitutionality of expanded powers of search and seizure and wiretaps in the War on Terrorism.

In the immediate future the courts will be asked to make critical decisions regarding the use of the death penalty. The U.S. Supreme Court has abolished the use of the death penalty for juveniles and the mentally incompetent. Public opinion supporting the death penalty has declined in recent years due in part to the release of over 100 prisoners on death row for whom DNA evidence showed they were wrongfully convicted. Challenges to the death penalty will continue to be before the courts as opponents of the death penalty seek to abolish its use all together.

drug courts Specialized courts that operate on different principles of law. Often, offenders are given a chance to engage in rehabilitation, avoid prison time, and sometimes even avoid a criminal record. Offenders must meet specific conditions to qualify for diversion to a drug court.

check your understanding 12.3 What important challenges face the courts in the immediate future?

Corrections

the main idea 12.4

Most assessments of corrections call for major changes in correctional services. Reducing violence, public health threats, and recidivism will be major goals of corrections in the twenty-first century.

The United States incarcerates more people and at a higher rate than any other country in the world.[24] At midyear 2005, the nation's prisons and jails held an incarcerated 2,186,230 persons. An additional 1,512,823 prisoners were under the legal authority of a prison system but held outside its facilities.[25] This number translates into an estimated 12 percent of black males, 3.7 percent of Hispanic males, and 1.7 percent of white males in their late twenties are in prison or jail.[26] There are more black males in prison than there are enrolled in institutions of higher education. To incarcerate these persons there are nearly 5,000 adult prisons and jails in the United States.[27] The United States spends $60 billion on correctional services.[28] In the twenty-first century the public and criminal justice system will need to address the failure of American corrections. Three of the most serious problems that need to be addressed are the **culture of violence** in jails and prisons, the threat to public health, and the failure of corrections to prepare inmates for successful reentry into the community.

Jails and prisons have been described as breeding a culture of violence.[29] In the twenty-first century more emphasis will be placed on reducing the violence in jails and prisons, as violence condemns these institutions to failure.[30] Violence makes rehabilitation impossible. Scholars, prison officials, and concerned public groups have examined the problem of violence in prisons and come to the conclusion that the following steps are critical to reducing violence:[31]

- Reduce crowding.
- Promote productivity and rehabilitation.
- Use objective classification and direct supervision.
- Use force, nonlethal weaponry, and restraints only as a last resort.
- Employ surveillance technology.
- Support community and family bonds.

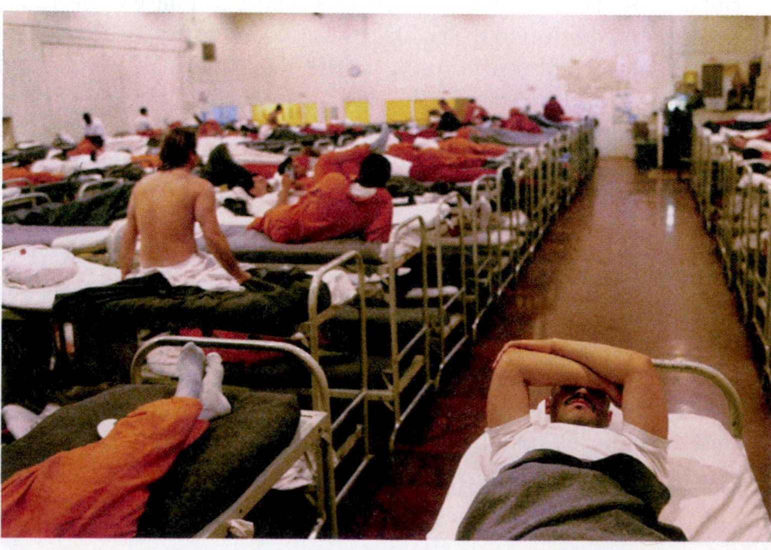

Prison overcrowding is a serious problem. It promotes violence and reduces the ability to supervise and rehabilitate inmates. What are the causes of prison overcrowding? How can overcrowding be reduced while at the same time protecting the public from criminal violence?

The federal government has made grant money available both for research and model projects to reduce violence in prisons. Prison officials, the criminal justice system, and the public have recognized the importance of reducing prison violence and have taken constructive steps toward this goal, such as passing prison rape prevention legislation, establishing programs to counter prison gangs, and improving conditions to reduce violence in prison.

Threats to public health due to poor health care in prison are a concern because what happens in prison does not stay in prison. Some 95 percent of inmates are released; that means that inmates with improperly treated or neglected treatment for communicable diseases, including such deadly threats as AIDS and tuberculosis, reenter the community and become a public health threat. More emphasis is being placed on health care in jails and prisons, as a threat to public health can be just as dangerous or more so than the threat of crime.

If one of the goals of jails and prisons is to promote public safety by removing dangerous persons from the community, they have failed to achieve this goal.[32] Ninety-five percent of persons are eventually released from incarceration and these persons are 30 to 45 times more likely than the general population to commit a crime.[33] It could be argued that the public safety would be better served by not sending convicted persons to prison. Successful rehabilitation and **reentry** is correlated to a good understanding of the causes of criminality. If the causes are not clearly understood, then rehabilitation programs may be completely ineffective because they might focus on the wrong variables. Early theories of criminal behavior often focused on only a few variables that were considered the cause of criminality. One of the primary themes of early criminological theory was the basic premise that crime is a voluntary choice of the offender and this choice can be influenced by the threat of punishment.

Rehabilitate the Young, Imprison the Old

Today there is an understanding that criminality is influenced by numerous variables and that changing these variables can affect the propensity for criminality. However, to a large extent punishment is still the underlying theme of corrections, especially incarceration. However, in the twenty-first century the criminal justice system is investing resources in identifying the most significant influences on juvenile criminality with the goal of lowering the juvenile crime rate. Research has indicated that various social, education, and economic factors affect the criminality rate of juveniles.

One of the surprising facts to emerge from this research is that the age at which young children are affected by these factors is much younger than previously thought. Research suggests that intervention or lack of intervention as early as 4 or 5 years old can influence a young child's development. One of the significant factors that has been identified as influencing juvenile criminality is early onset of drug and alcohol use. In the twenty-first century more resources will be channeled to preventing drug use by juveniles, improving the quality of life of young children, and improving schools.

On the other hand, the public has indicated that they do not believe that theory and research offers any hope in rehabilitating older repeat offenders, especially sex offenders. It appears that society will continue to endorse a "get tough" policy for these offenders and is more willing to put resources into new prisons rather than new rehabilitation programs. The crackdown on sex offenders has become particularly severe, as the public is demanding more disclosure of the identity and location of sex offenders, the lifetime registration of sex offenders with law enforcement, and very restrictive laws as to where sex offenders may live. In some cities, restrictions on where sex offenders may reside are so severe that for all practical purposes there is nowhere they can legally live in the city without being in violation of the law.

Interest and research on reentry policies and programs have become more prominent as the importance of successful reentry has become better understood. The obstacles to successful reentry have been identified. They are mental illness, substance abuse

reentry The process of preparing an offender for release from incarceration back into society.

and dependence, limited employability, extensive criminal histories, and lack of connection with family and community.[34] In the twenty-first century the challenge will be to find programs that can overcome these obstacles. This search will in part be spurred by the high cost of imprisonment and by the failure of traditional incarceration to affect rehabilitation. The correctional system has explored alternatives to incarceration, such as community corrections, boot camps, and intermediate sanctions. In the twenty-first century more longitudinal research is needed to determine the effectiveness of these alternatives. Preliminary research indicates that some alternatives such as boot camps generally had positive effects on the inmates but that significant changes need to be made to the programs to promote successful reentry into the community.[35]

▲ check your understanding 12.4 Why is it necessary to reduce violence in jails and prisons? Why should the public be concerned about prison health care? What is the role of research in correctional research and reentry?

conclusion:

The Grandfather Clause

The term **grandfather clause** refers to a person who is exempt from a new rule, policy, or practice because the new rule, policy, or procedure will apply to all future situations and will not be retroactive for existing situations. In some respects many criminal justice personnel, agencies, and even the public seem to think that they will be exempt from future changes. The U.S. criminal justice and society is undergoing tremendous change, but people, agencies, and communities think or hope that they will not have to change and can continue doing the same thing they have always done.

The criminal justice system has been undergoing continuous and significant changes in the last 75 years and there is no reason to believe that the pace of change will slow down. In fact, there are good reasons to believe, if anything, that the pace of change will accelerate. This change will affect the hiring and training of personnel, the mission of criminal justice agencies, the resources required to perform their mission, the law, social values, and public expectations. Criminal justice personnel will need to be more adept at problem solving, research, and resource management. The public will demand more accountability and expect results. All of these changes will result in a criminal justice system that will continue to evolve, improve, and become more complex and expansive.

chapter summary

- The criminal justice system is undergoing significant changes and spending more money, and more is expected of the criminal justice system than ever before.
- Terrorism and illegal immigration are having significant impacts on the criminal justice system. Although immigration is a federal responsibility, many cities and states are critical of the federal government's response to illegal immigration and are taking measures of their own.

- The courts are experimenting with alternatives to traditional criminal trials but the data from these new courts is not rigorous enough to allow for reliable conclusions as to the effectiveness of these courts.
- The courts will continue to be the protector of civil rights.
- Institutional corrections has been described as creating a culture of violence. There is an urgent need to find alternatives to imprisonment that will promote rehabilitation and successful reentry of offenders into the community.

vocabulary review

DNA databank, 434
drug courts, 439
hate crimes, 437
illegal immigration, 432
reentry, 441

do you remember?

culture of violence, 440
DNA analysis, 433
enemy combatants, 439
grandfather clause, 442
William J. Jefferson, 439
light duty (desk duty), 437

think about this

1. Criminal justice agencies are funded primarily by local and state taxes. Cities and states have significantly different abilities to fund criminal justice agencies, and the quality of justice varies from city to city. Should the federal government assume a greater responsibility for funding local and state criminal justice agencies? Explain your answer.
2. Many cities and states have become very concerned about the affect of illegal immigration on public safety and the economy of the city or state. What should be done to control the flow of illegal immigrants into the United States?
3. Do you favor the collection of DNA samples from as many people as possible for inclusion in a DNA database? Why or why not?
4. Have you noticed any affect of the increasing diversity of the United States on your local or state criminal justice agencies? If so, what are these? If not, why do you think your area has not been affected by this phenomenon?
5. What alternatives to incarceration would you suggest to achieve a greater rehabilitation rate and more successful reentry of offenders into society?

research navigator

Visit the Research Navigator website (www.researchnavigator.com), login and select the criminal justice data base in ContentSelect. Type in the key words "Understanding and Fighting." Select the article "Understanding and Fighting Islamist Terrorism" by Fereydoun Hoveyda. Fighting terrorism is the number one goal of the FBI and billions of dollars are spent in the War on Terrorism. One of the premises is that Islamist fundamentalism promotes anti-democratic governments and oppresses human rights. Thus, in addition to fighting terrorism through law enforcement agencies there must be campaigns to promote democratic values and human rights. Fereydoun Hoveyda is a senior fellow of the National Committee on American Foreign Policy. In this article he offers some short- and long-term prescriptions to promote democracy and human rights in the Middle East. Sample the article and answer the following questions:

1. Why is the culture of violence and death promoted by radical Islam attractive to young Middle Eastern persons?
2. What factors explain the rise of Islam as a major world religion in the some 600 years following its founding in 610 C.E. (Common Era)? Why are these factors important in understanding the philosophy of Muslim fundamentalists today?
3. According to Hoveyda what is the difference between so-called radicals and mainstream Muslims?
4. What short-term and long-term suggestions does Hoveyda recommend to diminish the influence of jihadists?

Endnotes

CHAPTER 1
Criminal Justice

1. Robert E. Pierre and Hamil R. Harris, "A Decade Later, Marchers Look for More," *Washington Post,* October 16, 2005, p. 1.
2. James Q. Wilson, *Thinking about Crime* (New York: Basic Books, 1975), p. 65.
3. Robert Fogelson, "Reform at a Standstill," in Carl Klockars and Stephen Mastrofski (eds.), *Thinking about Police* (New York: McGraw-Hill, 1991), p. 117.
4. American Bar Association, *New Perspectives on Urban Crime* (Washington, DC: ABA Special Committee on Crime Prevention and Control, 1972), p. 1.
5. *The Challenge of Crime in a Free Society: A Report by the President's Commission on Law Enforcement and Administration of Justice* (Washington, DC: U.S. Government Printing Office, 1967), pp. v–xi.
6. Fogelson, "Reform at a Standstill," p. 119.
7. Dae H. Chang and Richard J. Terrill, "An Introduction to the Study of Criminal Justice," in Dae H. Chang and James A. Fagin (eds.), *Introduction to Criminal Justice: Theory and Application,* 2nd ed. (Lake Geneva, WI: Paladin House of the Farley Court of Publishers, 1985), p. 9.
8. Larry Gaines, "Criminal Justice Education Marches On!" in Roslyn Muraskin (ed.), *The Future of Criminal Justice Education* (New York: Criminal Justice Institute, Long Island University, C.W. Post Campus, 1987).
9. Aristotle, *Politics,* translated by Benjamin Jowett (Cambridge, MA: MIT Press, 1994–2000) p. 1118.
10. Ron Fournier, "Americans Face World of Sudden Terror," *Pocono Record,* October 8, 2001, p. A1.
11. Peter McWilliams, *Ain't Nobody's Business If You Do* (Los Angeles: Prelude Press, 1993), p. 43.
12. James Davidson and John Batchelor, *The American Nation* (Englewood Cliffs, NJ: Prentice-Hall, 1991), p. 799.
13. Ibid., p. 815.
14. McWilliams, *Ain't Nobody's Business,* p. 2.
15. Ibid.
16. Wikipedia: The Free Encyclopedia, "Lynching," www.wikipedia.org/wiki/Lynching, October 1, 2005.
17. Mark Gado, "Lynching in America: Carnival of Death," Court TV's Crime Library, www.crimelibrary.com/classics2/carnical/, September 13, 2003.
18. Wikipedia: The Free Encyclopedia, "Jim Crow Law," www.wikipedia.org/wiki/Jim_-Crow_laws, October 1, 2005.
19. Gado, "Lynching in America."
20. Ibid.
21. Ibid.
22. Ibid.
23. Ibid.
24. Ibid.
25. Ibid. The federal legislation was known as the Costigan-Wagner Act.
26. U.S. Department of Justice, Bureau of Justice, Sourcebook of Criminal Justice Statistics. Justice system employment and payroll, March 1997, table 1.15.
27. "Juvenile Delinquency: A Rising Concern: 1861–1916," www.archives.nysed.gov/a/researchroom/rr_ed_reform_intro.shtml.27.
28. *Juvenile Justice: A Century of Change* (Washington, DC: Office of Juvenile Justice and Delinquency Prevention, December 1999), p. 1. NCJ Document No. 178995.
29. Ibid.
30. Howard N. Snyder and Melissa Sickmund, *Juvenile Offenders and Victims: 1999 National Report* (Washington, DC: Office of Juvenile Justice and Delinquency Prevention, September 1999), p. 86. NCJ Document No. 178257.
31. *Juvenile Justice: A Century of Change,* p. 6.
32. Ibid., p. 1.
33. Thomas F. Adams, *Police Field Operations* (Upper Saddle River, NJ: Prentice Hall, 1998), p. 374.
34. Ibid., pp. 373–376.
35. Bureau of Justice Statistics, Federal Criminal Cases Proceedings, 1999 with Trends 1982–1999 (Washington, DC: Department of Justice, February 2001), p. 11.
36. Bureau of Justice Statistics, Federal Criminal Cases Proceedings, p. 12.

CHAPTER 2
Understanding and Measuring Crime

1. Tim Dowley (ed.), *Introduction to the History of Christianity* (Minneapolis: Fortress Press, 1995), p. 142.
2. Richard Trask, *The Devil Hath Been Raised* (Danvers: Yeoman Press, 1972).
3. George Burr (ed.), *Narratives of Witchcraft Cases 1648–1706* (New York: Barnes and Noble, 1959).
4. Cesare Lombroso, *Crime: Its Causes and Remedies* (Montclair, NJ: Patterson Smith, 1968).
5. Edwin Sutherland, *Principles of Criminology* (Philadelphia: Lippincott, 1966).
6. Cesare Bonesana and Marchese Beccaria, *Of Crimes and Punishments* (Philadelphia: Philip H. Nicklin, 1819).
7. Jeremy Bentham, "An Introduction to the Principles of Morals and Legislation," in J. E. Jacoby (ed.), *Classics of Criminology* (Oak Park, IL: Moore, 1979).
8. Richard Louis Dugdale, *The Jukes: A Study in Crime, Pauperism, Disease and Heredity,* 3rd ed. (New York: G. P. Putnam's Sons, 1985).
9. Lombroso, *Crime.*
10. Ibid.
11. Karl Christiansen, "A Preliminary Study of Criminality Among Twins," in Sarnoff Mednick and Karl O. Christiansen (eds.), *Biosocial Bases of Criminal Behavior* (New York: Simon and Schuster, 1985).
12. Patricia Jacobs et al. "Aggressive Behavior, Mental Subnormality, and the XYY Male," *Nature,* 208 (1965): 1351–1352.
13. Robin Marantz Heing, "Dispelling Menstrual Myths," *New York Times Magazine,* March 7, 1982.
14. C. Halwy and R. E. Buckley, "Food Dyes and Hyperkinetic Children," *Academy Therapy,* 10 (1974): 27–32.
15. Sigmund Freud, *A General Introduction to Psychoanalysis* (New York: Boni and Liveright, 1920); Sigmund Freud, *An Outline of Psychoanalysis* (New York: Norton Press, 1963).
16. Adrian Raine, *The Psychopathology of Crime: Criminal Behavior as a Clinical Disorder* (Orlando: Academic Press, 1993).
17. Dean E. Murphy, "Counties Compete to Welcome a Murder Trial," New York Times Online, www.nytimes.com, January 19, 2004.

18. Dean E. Murphy, "Judge Chooses San Mateo County as Site of Murder Trial," New York Times Online, www.nytimes.com, January 21, 2004.
19. Associated Press, "Nurse Admits Murdering Five More Patients," New York Times Online, www.nytimes.com, June 27, 2005.
20. Jodi Wilgoren, "Kansas Suspect Pleads Guilty in 10 Murders," New York Times Online, www.nytimes.com, June 28, 2005.
21. Ibid.
22. Carolyn Marshall, "9 Siblings Dead, Son Says He Hopes Father Isn't Guilty," New York Times Online, www.nytimes.com, March 15, 2004.
23. Samuel Yochelson and Stanton E. Samenow, *The Criminal Personality,* 3 vols. (New York: Jason Aronson, 1976).
24. Robert E. Park and Ernest Burgess, *Introduction to the Science of Sociology,* 2nd ed. (Chicago: University of Chicago Press, 1942).
25. Robert E. Park (ed.), *The City* (Chicago: University of Chicago Press, 1925).
26. Clifford R. Shaw, *Juvenile Delinquency in Urban Areas* (Chicago: University of Chicago Press, 1942).
27. Clifford R. Shaw and Henry D. McKay, "Social Factors in Juvenile Delinquency," in Volume II of the Report of the Causes of Crime, National Commission on Law Observance and Enforcement. Report no. 13 (Washington, DC: U.S. Government Printing Office, 1931).
28. Oscar Neuman, *Defensible Space* (New York: Macmillan, 1972).
29. Mark H. Moore, Robert C. Trojanowicz, and George L. Kelling, *Crime and Policing* (Washington, DC: U.S. Department of Justice, June 1988).
30. Edwin H. Sutherland, *Principles of Criminology,* 6th ed. (Philadelphia: Lippincott, 1966).
31. Robert L. Burgess and Ronald L. Akers, "A Differential Association-Reinforcement Theory of Criminal Behavior," *Social Problems,* 14 (Fall 1996): 128–147.
32. Travis Hirschi, *Causes of Delinquency* (Berkeley: University of California Press, 1969).
33. Francis T. Cullen, *Rethinking Crime and Deviance Theory* (Totowa, NJ: Rowman and Allenheld, 1969).
34. L. Craig Parker, "Rising Crime Rates in the Czech Republic," in Robert Heiner (ed.), *Criminology: A Cross-Cultural Perspective* (Minneapolis: West, 1996), pp. 15–20.
35. Ira J. Silverman and Manuel Vegg, *Corrections: A Comprehensive View* (Minneapolis, MN: West, 1996), pp. 515–518.
36. Bureau of Justice Statistics, *Federal Criminal Cases Proceedings, 1999 with Trends 1982–1999* (Washington, DC: Department of Justice, February 2001), p. 12.
37. Hirschi, *Causes of Delinquency.*
38. Tannenbaum, *Crime and the Community.*
39. Howard Becker, *Outsiders: Studies in the Sociology of Deviance* (New York: Free Press, 1963).
40. Ibid., pp. 8–9.
41. Robert Merton, "Social Structure and Anomie," *American Sociological Review,* 3 (1938): 672–682.
42. Marvin Wolfgang and Franco Ferracuti, *The Subculture of Violence: Toward an Integrated Theory in Criminology* (London: Tavistock, 1967).
43. Albert K. Cohen, *Delinquent Boys: The Culture of the Gang* (Glencoe, IL: Free Press, 1958).
44. Ibid.
45. Walter B. Miller, "Lower Class Culture as a Generating Milieu of Gang Delinquency," *Journal of Social Issues,* 14 (1958): 5–19.
46. Gary Becker, "Crime and Punishment: An Economic Approach," *Journal of Political Economy,* 76 (1968): 169–217.
47. Michael J. Lynch and W. Byron Graves, *A Primer in Radical Criminology,* 2nd ed. (Albany, NY: Harrow and Heston, 1989).
48. Richard Quinney, *The Social Reality of Crime* (Boston: Little, Brown, 1970).
49. Ivan Taylor, Paul Walton, and Jock Young, *The New Criminology* (New York: Harper and Row, 1973).
50. Richard Quinney, *The Crime Problem* (New York: Dodd, Mead, 1970).
51. Freda Adler, *Sisters in Crime: The Rise of the New Female Criminal* (New York: McGraw-Hill, 1975).
52. Daly and Chesney-Lind, *Feminism and Criminology.*
53. Sally S. Simpson, "Feminist Theory, Crime and Justice," *Criminology,* 27 (1989).
54. William J. Chambliss, "Toward a Radical Criminology," in D. Kairys (ed.), *The Politics of Law: A Progressive Critique* (New York: Pantheon Books, 1982).
55. Josiah Stamp, *Some Economic Factors in Modern Life* (London: P. S. King & Sons, 1929), p. 258.
56. Thomas Reppetto, *The Blue Parade* (New York: Free Press, 1978), p. viii.
57. The Cleveland Foundation Survey of the Administration of Justice in Cleveland, Ohio, *Criminal Justice in Cleveland* (Cleveland: Cleveland Foundation, 1922).
58. Illinois Association for Criminal Justice, *The Illinois Crime Survey* (Chicago: Illinois Association for Criminal Justice, 1929).
59. Robert Tannehill, "The History of American Law Enforcement," in Dae Chang and James Fagin (eds.), *Introduction to Criminal Justice: Theory and Application,* 2nd ed. (Lake Geneva, WI: Paladin House of the Farley Court of Publishers, 1985), p. 159.
60. Ibid.
61. The UCR also reports data for "all other offenses" and "suspicion." All other offenses include all violations of state or local laws except those listed in Part I and Part II and traffic offenses. Suspicion includes all offenses in which suspects are released without formal charges being filed against them.
62. C. Kindermann, J. Lynch, and D. Cantor, *Effects of the Redesign on Victimization Estimates* (Washington, DC: Bureau of Justice Statistics, 1997), p. 1.
63. U.S. Department of Justice, Office of Justice Programs, Bureau of Justice Statistics, *NCVS Resource Guide,* October 2004, www.icpsr.umich.edu/NACJD/NCVS/index.html.
64. H.R. 4797, 102nd Cong. 2d Sess. (1992).
65. Jan M. Chaiken and Marcia R. Chaiken, "Drugs and Predatory Crime," in Michael Tonry and James Q. Wilson (eds.), *Drugs and Crime* (Chicago: University of Chicago Press, 1990), pp. 203–204.
66. Elizabeth Shepard, "America's No. 1 Youth Drug Problem . . . Alcohol," *DRIVEN Magazine,* Fall 2000, www.madd.org/news/0,1056,1159,00.html.
67. *The Economic Costs of Drug Abuse in the United States, 1992–2002.* Publication No. 207303 (Washington, DC: Executive Office of the President, December 2004), p. B-17.
68. Ibid., p. V-1.
69. *National Drug Control Strategy* (Washington, DC: The White House, February 2002), p. 1.
70. Rufus King, "It's Time to Open the Doors of Our Prisons," *Newsweek,* April 19, 1999, p. 10.
71. Ellis Cose, "Locked Away and Forgotten," *Newsweek,* February 28, 2000, p. 54; "Race Said to Be Factor in Arrests," *Honolulu Advertiser,* June 8, 2000, p. A3.
72. "CIA Investigation Clears Agency of Ties to Crack Cocaine Dealers," *Honolulu Advertiser,* December 18, 1997, p. A16.
73. Peggy Orenstein, "Staying Clean," New York Times Online, www.nytimes.com, February 10, 2002.
74. Webb v. United States, 249 U.S. 96,
75. Knight Ridder News Service, "War on Drugs Attacked by Lawmaker on Far Right," *Honolulu Advertiser,* October 11, 1999, p. A7.
76. Ibid.
77. *The Economic Costs of Drug Abuse,* p. 34.
78. Ibid., p. 30.
79. Ibid., p. 25.
80. Ibid., p. 82.
81. *National Drug Control Strategy,* p. 95.
82. *The Economic Costs of Drug Abuse,* p. 9.

83. Fox Butterfield, "As Drug Use Drops in Big Cities, Small Towns Confront Upsurge," New York Times Online, www.nytimes.com, February 11, 2002.
84. Alan I. Leshner, "Addiction Is a Brain Disease—And It Matters," *National Institute of Justice Journal,* October 1998, p. 2.
85. Ibid., p. 3.
86. Ibid., pp. 3–5.
87. *National Synthetic Drugs Action Plan: The Federal Government Response to the Production, Trafficking, and Abuse of Synthetic Drugs and Diverted Pharmaceutical Products* (Washington, DC: Office of the National Drug Control Policy, 2004), p. 1.
88. David Jefferson, "America's Most Dangerous Drug," *Newsweek,* August 8, 2005, pp. 42, 46.
89. Fox Butterfield, "Home Drug-Making Laboratories Expose Children to Toxic Fallout," New York Times Online, www.nytimes.com, February 23, 2004.
90. Fox Butterfield, "Across the Rural Midwest, Drug Casts a Grim Shadow," New York Times Online, www.nytimes.com, January 4, 2004.
91. Jefferson, "America's Most Dangerous Drug," p. 46.
92. Ibid.
93. Butterfield, "Across the Rural Midwest."
94. Ibid.
95. Butterfield, "Home Drug-Making Laboratories."
96. Jefferson, "America's Most Dangerous Drug."
97. Aisha Labi, "Duke U. Student Is Free from Jail in Armenia after Conviction on Book-Exploration Charges," *Chronicle of Higher Education* (August 18, 2005).
98. Associated Press, "Sea Marauders Go for Higher Stakes in Violent Game," *Honolulu Advertiser,* May 24, 1998, p. A23.
99. *National Drug Control Strategy,* p. 22.
100. Ibid.
101. Ibid., p. 23.
102. Michael Jonofsky, "Border Agents on Lookout for Terrorists Are Finding Drugs," New York Times Online, www.nytimes.com, March 6, 2002.
103. Thom Shanker, "Pentagon Sees Aggressive Antidrug Effort in Afghanistan," New York Times Online, www.nytimes.com, March 25, 2005.
104. Ibid.
105. James C. McKinley, Jr., "At Mexican Border, Tunnels, Vile River, Rusty Fence," New York Times Online, www.nytimes.com, March 23, 2005.
106. Ginger Thompson, "Sleepy Mexican Border Towns Awake to Drug Violence," New York Times Online, www.nytimes.com, January 23, 2005.
107. Ibid.
108. Associated Press, "Texas Sheriff Says Mexican Military-Issue Items Were Used in Confrontation," New York Times Online, www.nytimes.com, January 28, 2006.
109. Ibid.
110. Matt Richtel, "Investigators Face a Glut of Confiscated Computers," New York Times Online, www.nytimes.com, August 27, 1999.
111. Ibid.
112. Ibid.
113. Carl Kaplan, "A Search Site for School Sites Is Accused of Trespassing," New York Times Online, www.nytimes.com, September 27, 1999.
114. Stephan Lagbaton, "Net Sites Co-Opted by Pornographers," New York Times Online, www.nytimes.com, September 27, 1999.
115. "Storming the Fortress," *Business Week,* February 21, 2000, p. 40.
116. Gannett News Service, "Computers Helping Counterfeiters Cash In," *Honolulu Advertiser,* March 31, 1998, p. 1.
117. Michael White, "Man Ordered to Repay $93,000 for Stock Hoax on Internet," *Honolulu Advertiser,* August 31, 1999, p. C4.
118. Associated Press, "Identity Theft Is Top Consumer Fraud Complaint," *Pocono Record,* January 24, 2004, p. A8.
119. Graeme R. Newman, *Identity Theft* (Washington, DC: U.S. Department of Justice, 2004), p. 4.
120. Ibid., p. 5.
121. Saul Hansell, "Online Swindlers, Called 'Phishers,' Lure Unwary," New York Times Online, www.nytimes.com, March 24, 2004.
122. Ibid.
123. Janis Wolak, David Finkelhor, and Kimberly J. Mitchell, *Child-Pornography Possessors Arrested in Internet-Related Crimes: Findings from the National Juvenile Online Victimization Study* (Washington, DC: National Center for Missing and Exploited Children, 2005), p. ix.
124. Tom Clancy, *Net Force: Point of Impact* (New York: Berkley Books, 2001).
125. "Net Crime Does Pay for Cops," www.cnn.com. March 4, 2000.
126. Vicki Viotti, "High-Tech Crimes and Misdemeanors," *Honolulu Advertiser,* January 22, 1999, p. C1.
127. Doolittle, "Man Pleads Guilty to Selling Porn on Net," p. A3.
128. U.S. Department of Justice, Federal Bureau of Investigation. *White-Collar Crime: A Report to the Public* (Washington, DC: Government Printing Office, 1989), p. 3.
129. Patsy Klaus, *Crimes against Persons Age 65 or Older, 1993–2002* (Washington, DC: U.S. Department of Justice, 2005), p. 1.
130. Ibid.
131. Ibid.
132. Greg S. Weaver, Cathy D. Martin, and Thomas A. Petee, "Culture, Context, and Homicide of the Elderly," *Sociological Inquiry, 74* (2004): 1, 2–19.
133. Kelly Dedel Johnson, *Financial Crimes against the Elderly* (Washington, DC: U.S. Department of Justice, 2004), p. 8.
134. Ibid., p. 9.
135. Ibid., p. 1.
136. Ibid., p. 10.
137. Ibid., p. 6.
138. Craig S. Smith, "Abduction, Often Violent, A Kyrgyz Wedding Rite," New York Times Online, www.nytimes.com, April 30, 2005.
139. Ibid.
140. John Lancaster, "For Pakistani Rape Victim, Battle Carries On," *Washington Post,* March 26, 2005, p. A8.
141. Ibid.
142. Salman Masood, "Pakistani Leader's Comments on Rape Stir Outrage," New York Times Online, www.nytimes.com, September 24, 2005.
143. Glenn Kessler, "Pakistan Lifts Travel Ban on Rape Victim after U.S. Pressure," *Washington Post,* June 16, 2005, p. A22.
144. Owais Tohid, "Pakistan Outlaws 'Honor' Killings," *Christian Science Monitor* (January 20, 2005), p. 6
145. Ibid.
146. Mark Rice-Oxley, "Britain Examines 'Honor Killings,'" *Christian Science Monitor* (July 7, 2004), p. 6.
147. Alasdair Souss, "Women Challenge 'Honor' Killings," *Christian Science Monitor* (March 7, 2005), p. 15.
148. Rice-Oxley, "Britain Examines 'Honor Killings,'" p. 6.
149. Associated Press, "Culture, U.S. Law Clash over Teen Marriage," New York Times Online, www.nytimes.com, January 23, 2005.
150. Craig Perkins, *Weapon Use and Violent Crime* (Washington DC: U.S. Department of Justice, 2003), pp. 1, 2.
151. Ibid., p. 2.
152. Ibid., p. 9.

CHAPTER 3

Criminal Law: Control versus Liberty

1. Robert G. Clouse, "Flowering: The Western Church," in Tim Powley (ed.), *Introduction to the History of Christianity* (Minneapolis: Fortress Press, 1977), p. 264.
2. Joel Samaha, *Criminal Law* (Belmont, CA: West/Wadsworth, 1999), p. 3.

3. Arthur J. Crowns Jr., "The Law," in Dae H. Chang and James A. Fagin, *Introduction to Criminal Justice* (Lake Geneva, WI: Paladin House of the Farley Court of Publishers, 1985), pp. 110–111.
4. Jill Knueger, "With Blue Laws Gone, ABC Rethinks City Limits," *Orlando Business Journal,* May 1, 2000.
5. American Law Institute, *Model Penal Code and Commentaries.* vol. 1 (Philadelphia: American Law Institute, 1985), pp. 1–30.
6. U.S. Constitution, Article X, Section 10. Based on the seventeenth-century philosophy expressed by Lord Edward Coke, "No Crime without Law; No Punishment without Law." Jerome Hall, *General Principle of Criminal Law,* 2nd ed. (Indianapolis: Bobbs-Merril, 1960).
7. People ex rel. Lonschein v. Warden, 43 Misc. 2d 109, 250 N.Y. S. 2d 15 (1964).
8. Lonzetta v. New Jersey, 306 U.S. 451, 453 (1939).
9. State v. Metzger, 319 N.W. 2d 459 (Neb. 1982).
10. Ravin v. State, 537 P. 2d 494 (Alaska 1975).
11. Griswold v. Connecticut, 381 U.S. 479 (1965).
12. Stanley v. Georgia, 394 U.S. 557 (1969).
13. Bowers v. Hardwicke, 478 U.S. 186 (1986).
14. Texas v. Johnson, 491 U.S. 397, 109 S.Ct. 2533, 105 L.Ed. 2d 342 (1989).
15. The court has ruled that begging can be regulated in subways. See Young v. New York City Transit Authority, 903 F. 2d 146 (2d Cir. 1990). However, a general prohibition on all forms of begging may be declared too broad when extended to streets. See Loper v. NYPD, 999 F 2d 699 (2d Circ., 1993).
16. Barnes v. Glen Theatre, Inc., et al. 501 U.S. 560, 111 S.Ct. 2456, 115 L.Ed. 2d 504 (1991).
17. Weems v. United States, 217 U.S. 349, 30 S. Ct. 544, 54 L.Ed. 793 (1910).
18. Ibid.
19. Wilkerson v. Utah, 99 U.S. 130 (1878); in re Kemmler, 136 U.S. 436 (1890); Furman v. Georgia, 408 U.S. 238 (1972); Gregg v. Georgia, 428 U.S. 153 (1976).
20. State v. Kraft, N.W. 2d 840 (Minn. 1982).
21. Harmelin v. Michigan, 50 1 U.S. 957, 111 S.Ct. 2680, 115 L.Ed. 2d 836 (1991); Robinson v. California, 370 U.S. 660, 82 S.Ct. 1417, 8 L.Ed. 2d 758 (1962).
22. People v. Decina, 138 N.E. 2d 799 (N.Y. 1956).
23. George v. State, 681 S.W. 2d 43 (Tex. Crim. App. 1984).
24. People v. Oliver, 258 Cal. Rptr. 138 (1989).
25. Michael v. State, 767 P. 2d 193 (Alaska App. 1988).
26. Commonwealth v. Konz, 498 Pa. 639, 450 A 2d 638 (1982).
27. Samaha, *Criminal Law,* p. 104.
28. However, mere constructive possession of a controlled substance in one's home may be sufficient *actus reus* to constitute criminal intent. State v. Cleppe, 96 Wash. 2d 373, 635 P. 2d 435 (1981).
29. Samaha, *Criminal Law,* p. 111.
30. Ibid.
31. State v. Marks, 92 Idaho 368, 442 P. 2d 778 (1968).
32. People v. Hernandez, 61 Cal. 2d 529, 39 Cal. Rptr. 361, 393 P. 2d 673 (1964); People v. Navarette, 221, Neb. 171, 376 N.W. 2d 8 (1985).
33. State v. Furr, 292 N.C. 711, 235 S.E.2d 193 (1977).
34. People v. Lauria, 251 Cal.App.2d 471, 59 Cal.Rptr. 628 (1967).
35. Nos. 94-0978-CR and 94-1980-Cr, Court of Appeals, Wisconsin, 1995.
36. Young v. State, Md. 298, 493 A. 2d 352 (1985).
37. Le Barron v. State, 32 Wis.2d 294, 145 N.W.2d 79 (1966).
38. "The Roush-Sex Defense," *Time,* May 23, 1988, p. 55.
39. Hampton v. United States, 425 U.S. 484 (1976).
40. Sherman v. United States, 356 U.S. 369 (1958).
41. United States v. Calley, 46 C.M.R. 1131 (1973).
42. Montana v. Egelhoff, 116 S. Ct. 2013 (1996).
43. People v. Alderson and Others, 144 Misc. 2d 133, 540 N.Y. S. 2d 948 (N.Y. 1989).
44. The Crown v. Dudley and Stephens, 14 Q. B.D. 273, 286, 15 Cox C. C. 624, 636 (1884).
45. People v. Goetz, 68 N.Y. 2d 96, 506 N.Y. S. 2d 18, 497 N.E. 2d 41 (1986).
46. Lenore E. Walker, *The Battered Woman* (New York: HarperCollins, 1980).
47. Alan Dershowitz, *The Abuse Excuse and Other Cop-Outs, Sob Stories and Evasions of Responsibility* (Boston: Little, Brown, 1994).
48. State v. Mitcheson, 560 P. 2d 1120 (1977).
49. State v. Valentine, 935 P. 2d 1294 (Wash. 1977).
50. Thomas A. Johnson, *Introduction to the Juvenile Justice System* (St. Paul, MN: West, 1975), pp. 1, 3.
51. Samaha, *Criminal Law,* p. 317.
52. M'Naghten's Case, 8 Eng. Rep. 718 (1843).
53. Samaha, *Criminal Law,* pp. 406–410.
54. Casico v. State, 147 Neb. 1075, 25 N.W. 2d 897, 900 (1947); State v. Ely, 114 Wash. 185 (1921)
55. Commonwealth v. Mlinarich, 345 Pa. Super. 269, 498 A.2d 395, 397 (1985).
56. Frank Schmalleger, *Criminal Law Today* (Upper Saddle River, NJ: Prentice-Hall, 1999), pp. 301–302.
57. American Law Institute, *Model Penal Code and Commentaries,* Section 221.1.
58. Samaha, *Criminal Law,* p. 358.
59. Ibid., pp. 335–337.
60. Thomas J. Lueck, "State Justice Rules against 13 Couples Seeking Same-Sex Marriage," New York Times Online, www.nytimes.com, December 8, 2004.
61. Alan Cooperman, "Foes Confounded by Limited Outcry against Gay Marriage," *Washington Post,* June 20, 2004, p. A3.
62. Ibid.
63. Mary Fitzgerald and Alan Cooperman, "Marriage Protection Act Passes," *Washington Post,* July 23, 2004, p. A4.
64. Adam Liptak, "Bans on Interracial Unions Offer Perspective on Gay Ones," New York Times Online, www.nytimes.com, March 17, 2004.
65. Pam Belluck, "Governor Seeks to Invalidate Some Same-Sex Marriages," New York Times Online, www.nytimes.com, May 21, 2004; Pam Belluck, "Town Set to Defy Governor on Same-Sex Marriage Issue," New York Times Online, www.nytimes.com, May 11, 2004.

CHAPTER 4

Roles and Functions of the Police

1. Thomas A. Reppetto, *The Blue Parade* (New York: Free Press, 1978), p. 17.
2. David Ascoli, *The Queen's Peace: the Origins and Development of the Metropolitan Police 1829–1979* (London: Hamish Hamilton, 1979), pp. 16–17.
3. Ibid., p. 48.
4. Ibid., p. 75.
5. Ibid., p. 93.
6. David Taylor, *The New Police in Nineteenth-century England: Crime, Conflict and Control* (Manchester: Manchester University Press, 1997), pp. 44–55.
7. Dale's law required Jamestown settlers to work or they would not receive food and required strict observance of the rules of the community. Violators could be put to death.
8. The Plymouth Compact, also known as the Mayflower Compact, was a document signed by the Pilgrim settlers, promising to abide by the rules of the community and to work for the common good of the community.
9. Reppetto, *The Blue Parade,* p. 41.
10. Ibid.
11. Ibid., p. 45.
12. Ibid., p. 4.
13. The Chicago School claimed that crime was associated with neighborhoods in which the poor lived. Merton's theory focused on the desire to achieve economic rewards and stated that crime was a way to achieve economic gain.

14. Samuel Walker, *A Critical History of Police Reform* (Lexington, MA: Lexington Books, 1997), p. 9.
15. Larry D. Ball, *The United States Marshals of New Mexico and Arizona Territories, 1846–1912* (Albuquerque: University of New Mexico Press, 1978), pp. 108–118; Herbert A. Johnson, History of Criminal Justice (Cincinnati: Anderson, 1988), p. 92.
16. William C. Cunningham, John J. Strauchs, and Clifford W. Van Meter, *The Hallcrest Report II: Private Security Trends 1970–2000* (McLean, VA: Hallcrest System, 1990).
17. Hubert Williams and Patrick V. Murphy, *The Evolving Strategies of Police: A Minority View* (Washington, DC: National Institute of Justice, January 1990), p. 3.
18. Ibid., p. 5.
19. Ibid., p. 4.
20. Ibid.
21. Ibid., p. 3.
22. Ibid., p. 7.
23. Ibid., p. 5.
24. Williams and Murphy, *The Evolving Strategies of Police,* p. 9.
25. Ibid., p. 7.
26. State laws in southern states prohibiting interracial marriages remained on the books and were enforced by some states well into the twentieth century.
27. Williams and Murphy, *The Evolving Strategies of Police,* p. 2.
28. Ibid.
29. Following the Civil War, southern states sought to limit the right of freed slaves to vote by instituting poll taxes (voters were required to pay a fee each time they voted), literacy tests, grandfather clauses (exempted voters from fees and requirements if their grandfather voted), and Jim Crow laws. Jim Crow laws separated blacks and whites in schools, churches, restaurants, theaters, trains, street cars, hospitals, beaches, and cemeteries. When blacks challenged segregation, the Supreme Court declared in *Plessy* v. *Ferguson* that segregation was permitted as long as separate facilities for blacks and whites were equal. Despite obvious inequalities in facilities, *Plessy* v. *Ferguson* legally sanctioned the practice of segregation.
30. Williams and Murphy, *The Evolving Strategies of Police,* p. 9.
31. Walker, *A Critical History of Police Reform,* pp. 139–166.
32. James Hernandez, Jr., *The Custer Syndrome* (Salem, WI: Sheffield, 1989), p. 33.
33. Ibid.
34. Reppetto, *The Blue Parade,* pp. 55–57.
35. Ibid., p. 243.
36. Ibid., p. 245.
37. Ibid., p. 247.
38. Ibid., pp. 244, 248.
39. Kenneth J. Peak, *Policing America: Methods, Issues, Challenges* (Upper Saddle River, NJ: Prentice-Hall, 1997), pp. 26–27.
40. Bureau of Justice Statistics, *Police Departments, 1999* (Washington, DC: U.S. Department of Justice, May 2001), p. iii.
41. Bureau of Justice Statistics, *Census of State Law Enforcement Agencies, 1996* (Washington, DC: U.S. Department of Justice, June 1998).
42. Bureau of Justice Statistics, *Federal Law Enforcement Officers, 2000* (Washington, DC: U.S. Department of Justice, July 2001).
43. *Report of the Executive Committee for Indian County Law Enforcement Improvements: Final Report to the Attorney General and the Secretary of the Interior* (Washington, DC: U.S. Department of Justice, 1997), pp. 2–3. The primary agencies having jurisdiction on Indian reservations are the Bureau of Indian Affairs Office of Law Enforcement Services and the Federal Bureau of Investigation. The U.S. government has a unique relationship with Indian reservations. Indian reservations were created by treaties, and the U.S. government has a trust responsibility to ensure the sovereignty of each tribal government (25 U.S.C. Section 3601).
44. Ibid., p. v.
45. Bureau of Justice Statistics, *American Indians and Crime* (Washington, DC: U.S. Department of Justice, February 1999), p. v.
46. Ibid., p. 2.
47. "Tribal, Municipal Police Haggle over Arrest Power," *Law Enforcement News* (John Jay College of Criminal Justice, vol. XXV, no. 522), November 30, 1999, p. 6. The authority of the Indian tribal police is defined by 18 U.S.C. Section 1152–1153, 18 U.S.C. Section 1162 (P.L. 280) and the Major Crimes Act of 1994.
48. C. Reith, *A Short History of the Police* (Oxford: Oxford University Press, 1948).
49. See www.usdoj.gov/otj/otjmiss.htm for further information about the Office of Tribal Justice.
50. *Report of the Executive Committee for Indian County Law Enforcement Improvements,* p. 2.
51. Samuel Walker, *Popular Justice: A History of American Criminal Justice* (New York: Oxford University Press, 1980), p. 191.
52. Ibid., p. 192.
53. Ibid.
54. "Cyber Crime," *Business Week,* February 21, 2000, p. 39; "FBI Will Supervise High-Tech Crime Staff," *Honolulu Advertiser,* February 29, 1988, p. A3.
55. Neil A. Lewis, "Ashcroft Permits F.B.I. to Monitor Internet and Public Activities," New York Times Online, www.nytimes.com, June 5, 2002.
56. Don Van Natta Jr. and David Johnson, "Wary of Risk, Slow to Adapt, F.B.I. Stumbles in Terror War," New York Times Online, www.nytimes.com, June 2, 2002.
57. Ibid.
58. Associated Press, "F.B.I. Chief Tells Congress His Agency Needs More Resources," New York Times Online, www.nytimes.com, June 6, 2002.
59. Robert S. Mueller III, "Remarks prepared for delivery by Robert S. Mueller III, Director, Federal Bureau of Investigation at a Press Availability on the FBI's Reorganization May 29, 2002." www.fbi.gov, June 8, 2002.
60. FBI Jobs, www.fbi.gov, June 10, 2002.
61. See www.dea.gov.
62. For a description of campus police and their responsibilities, see Bureau of Justice Statistics, *Campus Law Enforcement Agencies, 1995* (Washington, DC: U.S. Department of Justice, December 1996).
63. Peak, *Policing America,* pp. 64–65.
64. Bureau of Justice Statistics, *Sheriffs' Offices, 1999* (Washington, DC: U.S. Department of Justice, May 2001).
65. James Fagin, "Authority," in Jay M. Shafritz (ed.), *International Encyclopedia of Public Policy and Administration* (Boulder, CO: Westview Press, 1998), p. 163.
66. Bureau of Justice Statistics, *Sheriffs' Offices, 1999.*
67. Bureau of Justice Statistics, *Law Enforcement Management and Administrative Statistics, 1997: Data for Individual State and Local Agencies with 100 or More Officers* (Washington, DC: U.S. Department of Justice, April 1999).
68. Bureau of Justice Statistics, *Local Police Departments, 1999.*
69. Ibid.
70. Charles R. Swanson, Leonard Territo, and Robert W. Taylor, *Police Administration: Structures, Processes, and Behavior* (Upper Saddle River, NJ: Prentice-Hall, 1998), pp. 290–293.
71. Fagin, "Authority," p. 163.
72. Bureau of Justice Statistics, *Law Enforcement Management and Administrative Statistics, 1997,* pp. 91–120.
73. Jack Greene and Carl B. Klockars, "What Police Do," in Carl B. Klockars and Stephen D. Mastrofski (eds.), *Thinking about Police: Contemporary Readings* (New York: McGraw-Hill, 1991), p. 297.
74. Swanson, Territo, and Taylor, *Police Administration,* pp. 160–161.
75. From 1987 to 1997, minority representation among local police officers increased from 14.5% to 21.5%. In sheriffs' offices, minorities accounted for 19% of sworn personnel in 1997 compared with 13.4% 10 years earlier. In 1987, 7.6% of local law enforcement officers were women. In 1997, 15% of sheriff officers, 11% of county officers, and 9% of municipal officers were women. See Brian Reaves, *Profile of State and Local Law Enforcement Agencies,*

1987 (Washington, DC: U.S. Department of Justice, March 1989), and Brian Reaves, *Law Enforcement Management and Administrative Statistics, 1997* (Washington, DC: U.S. Department of Justice, April 1999), p. xiii.

76. Title VII of the Civil Rights Act of 1964 as amended in 1972 required that employment screening be based on bona fide occupational requirements (BFOQ). This requirement was further defined in *Griggs* v. *Duke Power Company* (1971), 401 U.S. 424; *Albemark Paper Company* v. *Moody* (1975), 422 U.S. 405; and *Washington* v. *Davis* (1979), 426 U.S. 299.
77. Brian A. Reaves and Andrew L. Goldberg, *Law Enforcement Management and Administrative Statistics, 1997: Data for Individual State and Local Agencies with 100 or More Officers* (Washington, DC: U.S. Department of Justice, April 1999), pp. 31–40.
78. Herman Goldstein, *Policing a Free Society* (Cambridge, MA: Ballinger, 1977), pp. 283–284.
79. Robert E. Worden, "A Badge and a Baccalaureate: Policies, Hypotheses and Further Evidence," *Justice Quarterly,* 7 (September 1990): 565–592.
80. Reaves and Goldberg, *Law Enforcement Management,* pp. 41–50.
81. National Advisory Commission on Criminal Justice Standards and Goals, Police (Washington, DC: Government Printing Office, 1973), p. 369.
82. As of June 1997, local and state law enforcement agencies required the following minimum level of education to apply for a position as a police agent: 78% require a minimum of a high school diploma, 13% require some college, 7% require a 2-year college degree, and 2% require a 4-year college degree. See Reaves and Goldberg, *Law Enforcement Management,* p. xiv.
83. Peak, *Policing America,* p. 86.
84. Matthew J. Hickman and Brian A. Reaves, *Local Police Departments, 1999* (Washington, DC: U.S. Department of Justice, May 2001), pp. 17–18.
85. Reaves and Goldberg, *Law Enforcement Management,* pp. 61–70.
86. Robert M. Fogelson, "Reform at a Standstill," in Carl B. Klockars and Stephen D. Mastrofski (eds.), *Thinking about Police: Contemporary Reading* (New York: McGraw-Hill, 1991), p. 116.
87. Robert Trojanowicz and T. Nicholson, "A Comparison of Behavioral Styles of College Graduate Police Officers and Non-college Going Police Officers," *The Police Chief,* 43 (August 1976): 56–59; BJS, State and Local Law Enforcement Statistics.
88. Reaves and Goldberg, *Law Enforcement Management,* pp. xiv, 41–50.
89. Ibid.
90. Peak, *Policing America,* pp. 78–84.
91. Reaves and Goldberg, *Law Enforcement Management,* pp. 41–50.
92. Peak, *Policing America,* pp. 84–85.
93. Egon Bittner, "Popular Conceptions about the Character of Police Work," in Carl B. Klockars and Stephen D. Mastrofski (eds.), *Thinking about Police: Contemporary Readings* (New York: McGraw-Hill, 1991), pp. 35–51.
94. James Q. Wilson, *Varieties of Police Behavior: The Management of Law and Order in Eight Communities* (Cambridge, MA: Harvard University Press, 1968).
95. Ibid., p. 5.
96. Fogelson, "Reform at a Standstill," pp. 117–119.
97. Mark H. Moore and Robert C. Trojanowicz, "Corporate Strategies for Policing," *Perspectives on Policing, No. 6* (Washington, DC: National Institute of Justice, November 1988).
98. George Kelling, "Police and Communities: The Quiet Revolution," *Perspectives on Policing, No. 1* (Washington, DC: National Institute of Justice and Harvard University, June 1988).
99. Swanson et al., *Police Administration,* p. 13.
100. Kelling and Moore, "The Evolving Strategy of Policing," p. 14.
101. As of June 1997, 68% of local police agencies reported they had a community policing unit with personnel assigned full time, and 76% reported they had full-time community policing officers. See Reaves and Goldberg, *Law Enforcement Management,* p. 41–50.
102. Herman Goldstein, *The New Policing: Confronting Complexity* (Washington, DC: National Institute of Justice, December 1993), p. 1.
103. Kelling and Moore, "The Evolving Strategy of Policing," p. 1.
104. George L. Kelling and William J. Bratton, "Implementing Community Policing: The Administrative Problem," *Perspectives on Policing, No. 17* (Washington, DC: National Institute of Justice and Harvard University, July 1993), p. 2.
105. Goldstein, *The New Policing,* p. 4.
106. Lee P. Brown, "Community Policing: A Practical Guide for Police Officials," *Perspectives on Policing, No. 12* (Washington, DC: National Institute of Justice and Harvard University, September 1989).
107. Kelling and Bratton, "Implementing Community Policing," p. 2.
108. "Jaywalking Ban," *Honolulu Advertiser,* August 8, 1998, p. E1.
109. Edwin Meese III, "Community Policing and the Police Officer," *Perspectives on Policing, No. 15* (Washington, DC: National Institute of Justice and Harvard University, January 1993).
110. Ibid., p. 2.
111. William Spelman and John E. Eck, *Problem-Oriented Policing* (Washington, DC: National Institute of Justice, January 1987), p. 2.
112. Ibid., p. 3.
113. Ibid., p. 4.
114. Ibid., pp. 6–7.
115. Ibid.
116. William Spelman and John E. Eck, *Newport News Tests Problem-Oriented Policing* (Washington, DC: National Institute of Justice, February 1987).
117. David M. Kennedy, "The Strategic Management of Police Resources," *Perspectives on Policing, No. 14* (Washington, DC: National Institute of Justice and Harvard University, January 1993).
118. Ibid., p. 5.
119. Hernandez, *The Custer Syndrome,* p. 184.
120. Peak, *Policing America,* pp. 402–403.
121. Kennedy, "The Strategic Management of Police Resources."
122. Meese, "Community Policing and the Police Officer," p. 5.
123. A 1995 survey of 2,214 state and local police agencies indicated that 48% of police chiefs and sheriffs agreed that implementation of community policing would require major changes in organizational policies, and 56% anticipated that rank-and-file employees would resist such a change. National Institute of Justice, *Community Policing Strategies* (Washington, DC: National Institute of Justice, November 1995), p. 1.
124. Hernandez, *The Custer Syndrome,* p. 184.
125. Ibid., p. 185.
126. National Institute of Justice, *Community Policing Strategies,* p. 1.
127. Hubert William and Patrick V. Murphy, "The Evolving Strategy of Police: A Minority View," *Perspectives on Policing, No. 13* (Washington, DC: National Institute of Justice and Harvard University, January 1990), pp. 2, 12.
128. Ibid., p. 12.
129. George L. Kelling and James K. Stewart, "Neighborhoods and Police: The Maintenance of Civil Authority," *Perspectives on Policing, No. 10* (Washington, DC: National Institute of Justice and Harvard University, May 1989), p. 7.
130. George L. Kelling, *What Works—Research and the Public* (Washington, DC: National Institute of Justice, 1988), p. 2.

CHAPTER 5

Police Officers and Law

1. Associated Press, "Compromise Proposed to Allow Local Police to Use Radar Guns," *Pocono Record,* September 3, 2001, p. C3.
2. Weeks v. United States, 232 U.S. 383 (1914).
3. Mapp v. Ohio, 367 U.S. 643 (1961).
4. Silverthorne Lumber Co. v. United States, 251 U.S. 385 (1920).

5. Wolf v. Colorado, 338 U.S. 25 (1949).
6. Mapp v. Ohio (1961).
7. Chimel v. California, 395 U.S. 752 (1969).
8. Harris v. United States, 390 U.S. 234 (1968).
9. Horton v. California, 110 S.Ct. 2301 47 CrL. 2135 (1990).
10. Arizona v. Hicks, 107 S.Ct. 1149 (1987).
11. Horten v. California, (1990).
12. Florida v. Jimeno, 111 S.Ct.1801 (1991).
13. Carroll v. United States, 267 U.S. 132 (1925).
14. Ormelas v. United States, 116 S.Ct. 1657 L.Ed. 2d 911 (1996).
15. Colorado v. Bertive, 479 U.S. 367, 107 S.Ct. 741 (1987).
16. Terry v. Ohio, 3129 U.S. 1 (1968).
17. Minnesota v. Dickerson, 113 S.Ct. 2130, 124 L.Ed. 2d 334 (1993).
18. Michael Cooper, "Judge Sides with Woman in Oneonta Profiling Case," New York Times Online, www.nytimes.com, October 29, 2006.
19. Although a search warrant is required to conduct such a search, the court has ruled that a suspect may be x-rayed and detained until the subject passes the swallowed objects. See United States v. Montoya de Hernandez, 473 U.S. 531, 105 S.Ct. 3304 (1985).
20. New York v. Quarles, 104 S.Ct. 2626, 81 L.Ed. 2d 550 (1984).
21. Florida v. Bostick, 111 S.Ct. 2382 (1991).
22. United States v. Martinez-Fuerte, 428 U.S. 543 (1976).
23. Illinois v. Gates, 416 U.S. 318 (1982).
24. United States v. Leon, 468 U.S. 897, 104 S.Ct. 3405, 82 L.Ed. 2d 677, 52 U.S.L.W. 5515 (1984); Massachusetts v. Sheppard, 104 S.Ct. 3424 (1984).
25. Olmstead v. United States, 277 U.S. 438 (1928).
26. Katz v. United States, 389 U.S. 347 (1967).
27. "Checking FBI Spying," *Washington Post,* November 10, 2005, p. A28.
28. Ibid.
29. Tennessee v. Garner, 471 U.S. 1 (1985).
30. Terry R. Sparher and David J. Goacopassi, "Memphis Revisited: A Reexamination of Police Shootings after the Garner Decision," *Justice Quarterly,* 9 (1992): 211–225.
31. Graham v. Connor, 490 U.S. 386, 396–397 (1989).
32. Brown v. Mississippi, 297 U.S. 278 (1936).
33. Kenneth J. Peak, *Policing in America* (Saddle River, NJ: Prentice-Hall, 1993), p. 283.
34. Ashcraft v. Tennessee, 322, U.S. 143 (1944).
35. Donald A. Dripps, "Forward: Against Police Interrogation and the Priviledge against Self-Incrimination," *Journal of Criminal Law and Criminology,* 78 (1988): 701.
36. Leyra v. Denno, 347 U.S. 556 (1954).
37. Kevin Johnson and Gary Fields, "Jewell Investigation Unmasks FBI 'Tricks'," *USA Today,* April 9, 1997, p. 13A.
38. United States v. Karo, 468 U.S. 705 (1984).
39. United States v. Dionisio, 410 U.S. 1 (1973).
40. United States v. Wade, 388 U.S. 218 (1067); Kirby v. Illinois, 406 U.S. 682 (1972); Foster v. California, 394 U.S. 1 (1973).
41. Gideon v. Wainwright, 372 U.S. 335 (1963).
42. Argersinger v. Hamlin, 407 U.S. 25 (1972).
43. In re Gault, 387 U.S. 1 (1967).
44. Escobedo v. Illinois, 378 U.S. 478 (1964).
45. Robert E. Worth, "Privacy Rights Are at Issue in New Policy on Searches," New York Times Online, www.nytimes.com, July 22, 2005.
46. Ibid.
47. Avi Salzman, "Seeking a Safe Journey as Anxiety Rides the Rails," *New York Times Online,* www.nytimes.com, July 24, 2005.
48. Miranda v. Arizona, 384 U.S. 436 (1966).
49. Jacobsen v. United States, 112 S.Ct. 1535 (1992).
50. Michael Kinsley, "When Is Racial Profiling Okay?" *Law Enforcement News,* October 15, 2001, p. 9.
51. Human Rights Watch, *Presumption of Guilt: Human Rights Abuses of Post-September 11 Detainee* (New York: Human Rights Watch, 2002), pp. 3, 6, 46, 55.
52. Eric Lichtblau, "Two Groups Charge Abuse of Witness Law," New York Times Online, www.nytimes.com, June 27, 2005.
53. Human Rights Watch, *Presumption of Guilt,* p. 5.

CHAPTER 6

Policing: Issues and Challenges

1. National Advisory Commission on Criminal Justice Standards and Goals, *Report of the Task Force on Disorder and Terrorism* (Washington, DC: U.S. Government Printing Office, 1976).
2. Samuel T. Francis, "The Terrorist: International and Western Europe," *The Heritage Foundation Backgrounder* (April 1978): 2.
3. United States Department of State, *Patterns of Global Terrorism, 2002* (Washington, DC: U.S. Department of State, April 2003).
4. Ibid.
5. John Broder, "12 Puerto Ricans in Prison Accept Offer of Clemency," New York Times Online, www.nytimes.com, September 8, 1999.
6. Ibid.
7. Dirk Johnson, "Puerto Ricans Clinton Freed Leave Prisons," New York Times Online, www.nytimes.com, September 11, 1999.
8. Associated Press, "Pardoned Militants Return as Heroes," New York Times Online, www.nytimes.com, September 11, 1999.
9. Scott Smallwood, "Speaking for the Animals, or the Terrorists?" *Chronicle of Higher Education* (August 5, 2005).
10. Christine Haughney, "Teenagers' Activism Takes a Violent Turn," *Washington Post,* March 27, 2001, p. A3.
11. Sara Hebel, "Earth Liberation Front Takes Credit for Fire at U. of Washington Horticulture Center," *Chronicle of Higher Education* (February 14, 2001).
12. Robin Wilson, "Extremist Environmental Group Claims Credit for Arson at Michigan State U." *Chronicle of Higher Education* (January 25, 2000); Scott Carlson, "Radical Environmentalists Destroy Genetically Altered Crops at U. of Minnesota," *Chronicle of Higher Education* (February 14, 2000).
13. Associated Press, "Eco-Terrorist Group Takes Credit for Fires at Ski Resort," *Honolulu Advertiser,* October 22, 1998, p. A12.
14. Smallwood, "Speaking for the Animals, or the Terrorists?" p. A9.
15. Alex P. Kellogg, "Animal-Rights Group Takes Hundreds of Ducklings from Cornell University Lab," *Chronicle of Higher Education* (May 2, 2001).
16. Smallwood, "Speaking for the Animals, or the Terrorists?" p. A9.
17. Jonathan S. Landay, "As Radicalism Declines, Terrorism Surges," *The Christian Science Monitor,* August 20, 1998, pp. 1, 10.
18. Peter Grier and James N. Thurman, "Age of Anonymous Terrorism," *The Christian Science Monitor,* August 20, 1998, p. 10; Evan Thomas et al., "The Road to September 11," *Newsweek,* October 1, 2001, p. 40.
19. Gerald R. Murphy and Martha R. Plotkin, *Protecting Your Community from Terrorism: Strategies for Local Law Enforcement, Volume I: Local-Federal Partnerships* (Washington, DC: U.S. Department of Justice, 2003), p. 61.
20. Homeland Security Act of 2002, Pub. L. No. 107–296 (Nov. 25, 2002); Norman J. Rabkin, *Homeland Security: Overview of Department of Homeland Security Management Challenges* (Washington, DC: Government Accountability Office, April 2005), p. 3.
21. *National Strategy for Homeland Security* (Washington, DC: Office of Homeland Security, July 2002), p. 2.
22. Rabkin, *Homeland Security,* p. 3.
23. Ibid., p. 5.
24. George W. Bush, *Department of Homeland Security* (Washington: DC: Government Printing Office, June 2002), p. 1.
25. *National Strategy for Homeland Security,* p. 13.
26. Michael Arnone, "DHS Reshuffles the Deck: Will Chertoff's Reorganization Plan Fix What Needs Fixing?" *Federal Computer Week,* July 18, 2004. www.fcw.com.

27. Eric Lipton, "Homeland Security Chief Announces Overhaul," New York Times Online, www.nytimes.com, July 14, 2005.
28. Eric Lipton, "For New Chief, A New Approach to Homeland Security," New York Times Online, www.nytimes.com, July 18, 2005.
29. Ibid.
30. *National Strategy for Combating Terrorism: February 2003* (Washington, DC: Department of State, Publication 11038, April 2003), p. 27.
31. *CONPLAN: United States Government Interagency Domestic Terrorism Concept of Operations Plan* (Washington, DC: Government Printing Office, 2001).
32. Ibid., p. iii.
33. Dalton, "Effective Intergovernmental Coordination," p. 10.
34. McIntire and O'Donnell, "Fire Chief Challenges New York Emergency Plan."
35. Dalton, "Effective Intergovernmental Coordination," p. 14.
36. Nicholas Confessore, "Mayor Says It's Best."
37. William K. Rashbaum and Judith Miller, "New York Police Take Broad Steps in Facing Terror," New York Times Online, www.nytimes.com, February 15, 2004.
38. Gerald R. Murphy and Martha R. Plotkin, *Protecting Your Community from Terrorism: Strategies for Local Law Enforcement, Volume I: Local-Federal Partnerships.* Washington, D.C.: U.S. Department of Justice, 2003, p. 61.
39. Ibid., p. 9.
40. Douglas Jehl, "Four in 9/11 Plot are Called Tied to Qaeda in '00," New York Times Online, www.nytimes.com, August 9, 2005; Douglas Jehl and Philip Shenon, "9/11 Commission's Staff Rejected Report on Early Identification of Chief Hijacker," New York Times Online, www.nytimes.com, August 11, 2005; Dan Eggen, "Sept. 11 Panel Explores Allegations about Atta," *Washington Post,* August 12, 2005, p. A9.
41. Maria Newman, "Ashcroft Announces New Plan for Sharing Intelligence," New York Times Online, www.nytimes.com, May 14, 2004.
42. Dan Eggen and Walter Pincus, "Bush Approves Spy Agency Changes," *Washington Post,* June 30, 2005, p. A1.
43. George W. Bush, "Fact Sheet: Strengthening Intelligence to Better Protect America." www.whitehouse.gov/news/release/2003/01/print/2003012812.html, January 28, 2003.
44. Associated Press, "Details of Counterterror Center Unveiled." New York Times Online, www.nytimes.com, February 14, 2003.
45. Murphy and Plotkin, *Protecting Your Community from Terrorism,* p. 31.
46. Ibid.
47. Ibid., p. 32.
48. John M. Broder, "Police Chiefs Moving to Share Terror Data," New York Times Online, www.nytimes.com, July 19, 2005.
49. Eric Lichtblau and William K. Rashbaum, "U.S. Steps Down Threat Level for Mass Transit Systems by a Notch," New York Times Online, www.nytimes.com, August 12, 2005.
50. Broder, "Police Chiefs Moving to Share Terror Data."
51. Ibid.
52. Ibid.
53. David Johnston, "Somali Is Accused of Planning a Terror Attack at a Shopping Center in Ohio," New York Times Online, www.nytimes.com, June 15, 2004.
54. Dan Eggen, "Man, Son Indicted in Terrorism Case," *Washington Post,* June 17, 2005, p. A2.
55. Patrick McGeehan, "Brooklyn Man Is Tied to Threat to Blow up New Jersey Trains," New York Times Online, www.nytimes.com, July 16, 2005.
56. David W. Dunlap, "Financial District Security Getting New Look," New York Times Online, www.nytimes.com, November 27, 2003.
57. Rachel L. Swarns, "Is Anti-Terrorist Anti-Tourist?" New York Times Online, www.nytimes.com, October 31, 2004.
58. Thomas J. Lueck, "Convention to Delay Some Cases in City Courts," New York Times Online, www.nytimes.com, July 21, 2004.
59. Sarah Kershaw, "Governors Tell of War's Impact on Local Needs," New York Times Online, www.nytimes.com, July 20, 2004.
60. Associated Press, "War Deployment Drains Police Departments," New York Times Online, www.nytimes.com, February 19, 2003.
61. Ibid.
62. Jennifer Lee, "Thin Work Force of North Dakota Gets Thinner as Residents Go to War," New York Times Online, www.nytimes.com, April 3, 2003.
63. Eric Lichtblau, "Report Questions the Value of Color-Coded Warnings," New York Times Online, www.nytimes.com, July 13, 2004.
64. Eric Lichtblau, "F.B.I. Issues and Retracts Urgent Terrorism Bulletin," New York Times Online, www.nytimes.com, May 29, 2004.
65. Stephen E. Flynn, "Color Me Scared," New York Times Online, www.nytimes.com, May 25, 2005; John Mintz, "DHS Considers Alternatives to Color-Coded Warnings," *Washington Post,* May 10, 2005, p. A6.
66. Jonathan Klick and Alexander Tabarrok, "Using Terror Alert Levels to Estimate the Effect of Police on Crime," *Journal of Law and Economics, 48,* no. 1 (February 16, 2005). http://mason.gmu.edu/~atabarro/TabarrokPublishedPapers.html.
67. Virginia Postrel, "One Possible Cure for the Common Criminal," New York Times Online, www.nytimes.com, June 16, 2005.
68. Dante Chinni, "Ashcroft on Tour and Unplugged," *Christian Science Monitor,* August 26, 2003. www.csmonitor.com.
69. Brian Knowlton, "Ashcroft Pushes Defense of Terror Law," New York Times Online, www.nytimes.com, August 19, 2003.
70. Dan Eggen, "Flawed FBI Probe of Bombing Used a Secret Warrant," *Washington Post,* April 7, 2005, p. A3.
71. Jeffrey R. Young, "FBI Seeks Library Data from Connecticut Institution Under Patriot Act, Court Records Show," *Chronicle of Higher Education,* August 29, 2005.
72. Eric Lichtblau, "Ashcroft Mocks Librarians and Others Who Oppose Parts of Counterterrorism Law," New York Times Online, www.nytimes.com, September 16, 2003.
73. Ralph G. Neas, "Is FBI Spying on Personal Library Records?" *Pocono Record,* February 10, 2003, p. A6; Eric Lichtblau, "Government Says It Has Yet to Use New Power to Check Library Records," New York Times Online, www.nytimes.com, September 19, 2003; Lichtblau, "Ashcroft Mocks Librarians."
74. Eric Lichtblau, "Libraries Say Yes, Officials Do Quiz Them about Users," New York Times Online, www.nytimes.com, June 20, 2005.
75. Dan Eggen, "Renewed Patriot Act Gets Boost in House, Senate Panel," *Washington Post,* July 22, 2005, p. A12.
76. Warren Richey and Linda Feldmann, "Has Post-9/11 Dragnet Gone Too Far?" *Christian Science Monitor,* September 12, 2003, www.csmonitor.com.
77. Philip Shenon, "Report on USA Patriot Act Alleges Civil Rights Violations," New York Times Online, www.nytimes.com, July 21, 2003; Paul von Zielbauer, "Detainees' Abuse Is Detailed," New York Times Online, www.nytimes.com, December 19, 2003.
78. Jennifer Nislow, "Portland Just Says 'No' to FBI," *Law Enforcement News,* November 30, 2001, p. 1,9.
79. Associated Press, "U.N.: Most Terror Attacks Cost Under $50G," New York Times Online, www.nytimes.com, August 27, 2004.
80. "Terrorist Financing," Washington, DC: GAO-01-163, November 2003, p. 1.
81. Associated Press, "U.N.: Most Terror Attacks Cost Under $50G," New York Times Online, www.nytimes.com, August 27, 2004.
82. David B. Ottaway, "Islamic Group Banned by Many Is Not on U.S. Terrorist List," *Washington Post,* Washingtonpost.com, December 27, 2004.
83. Laurie Goodstein, "Since 9/11, Muslims Look Closer to Home," New York Times Online, www.nytimes.com, November 15, 2004.
84. Eric Lichtblau, "Arrests Tie Charity Group to Palestinian Terrorists," New York Times Online, www.nytimes.com, July 28, 2004.
85. "Terrorist Financing," Washington, DC: GAO-01-163, November 2003, p. 14.
86. Ibid., p. 15.

87. Donna Leinwand, "Exhibit Links Terror, Drug Traffic," *USA Today,* September 13, 2004, p. 6D.
88. Associated Press, "Hezbollah Allegedly Linked to Drug Ring," New York Times Online, www.nytimes.com, January 21, 2004.
89. "National Briefing: West," New York Times Online, www.nytimes.com, March 4, 2004.
90. Associated Press, "Drug Profits in the U.S. Linked to Middle East Terrorists," *Pocono Record,* September 2, 2002, p. A5.
91. Thom Shanker, "Navy Seizes Hashish; See Ties to Al Qaeda," New York Times Online, www.nytimes.com, December 20, 2003.
92. Associated Press, "$38.1B Said Paid to Those Affected by 9/11," New York Times Online, www.nytimes.com, November 9, 2004.
93. Michael Slackman, "2 Insurers Say Bank's Suit Tries to Capitalize on 9/11," New York Times Online, nytimes.com, August 26, 2003.
94. Associated Press, "Audit Finds Texas Improperly Spent Terror Funds," New York Times Online, www.nytimes.com, January 8, 2005.
95. Ibid.
96. Ronald L. Dick, "Cyber Terrorism and Critical Infrastructure Protection," www.fbi.gov/congress/congress02/nipc072402.htm, July 24, 2002.
97. Brian Krebs, "Feds Falling Short on Cybersecurity," *Washington Post,* www.washingtonpost.com, April 8, 2003.
98. John Schwartz, "Decoding Computer Intruders," New York Times Online, www.nytimes.com, April 24, 2003.
99. Associated Press, "Ex-CIA Chief Gates Warns on Cyberterror," New York Times Online, www.nytimes.com, December 5, 2004.
100. Tom Regan, "Terrorism and the 'Net," *Christian Science Monitor,* www.csmonitor.com, October 7, 2004.
101. Eric Lipton and Eric Lichtblau, "Even Hear Home, a New Front Is Opening in the Terror Battle," New York Times Online, www.nytimes.com, September 23, 2004.
102. Tom Regan, "Terrorism and the 'Net," *Christian Science Monitor,* www.csmonitor.com, Ocotober 7, 2004.
103. Eric Lipton and Eric Lichtblau, "Even Hear Home, a New Front Is Opening in the Terror Battle," New York Times Online, www.nytimes.com, September 23, 2004.
104. John Schwartz, "Decoding Computer Intruders," New York Times Online, www.nytimes.com, April 24, 2003.
105. *The National Strategy to Secure Cyberspace.* Washington, DC: GPO, February 2003, p. 5.
106. Brian Krebs, "U.S. Government Flunks Computer Security Tests," *Washington Post,* www.washingtonpost.com, November 19, 2002.
107. Patrick Marshall, "Cyberterrorism: A Clear and Present Danger?" *Federal Computer Week,* November 22, 2004.
108. Barton Gellman, "Cyber-Attacks by Al Qaeda Feared," *Washington Post,* June 27, 2002, p. 1A.
109. Ibid.
110. *The National Strategy to Secure Cyberspace.* Washington, DC: GPO, February 2003, p. 32.
111. Barton Gellman, "Cyber-Attacks by Al Qaeda Feared," *Washington Post,* June 27, 2002, p. 1A.
112. Barton Gellman, "Cyber-Attacks by Al Qaeda Feared," *Washington Post,* June 27, 2002, p. 1A.
113. Ariana Eunjung Cha and Jonathan Krim, "White House Officials Debating Rules for Cyberwarfare," *Washington Post,* August 22, 2002, p. A2.
114. Ibid.
115. *The National Strategy to Secure Cyberspace,* Washington, DC: GPO, February 2003, p. 50.
116. Assoicated Press, "Ex-CIA Chief Gates Warns on Cyberterror," New York Times Online, www.nytimes.com, December 5, 2004.
117. Ibid.
118. Ibid.
119. U.S. Citizenship and Immigration Services, "INS into DHS," January 20, 2005, http://uscis.gov/graphics/othergov/roadmap.htm.
120. Michael Janoesky, "9/11 Panel Calls Policies on Immigration Ineffective," New York Times Online, www.nytimes.com, April 17, 2004.
121. Ralph Blumenthal, "Citing Violence, 2 Border States Declare a Crisis," New York Times Online, www.nytimes.com, August 17, 2005.
122. Ralph Blumenthal, "For One Family, Front Row Seats to Border Crisis," New York Times Online, www.nytimes.com, August 23, 2005.
123. Ibid.
124. Timothy Egan, "A Battle against Illegal Workers, With an Unlikely Driving Force." New York Times Online, www.nytimes.com, May 30, 2005.
125. Dan Eggen, "Customs Jails 1,000 Suspected Gang Members," *Washington Post,* August 2, 2005, p. A2.
126. Ibid.
127. Nina Bernstein, "Police Report Noncitizens to U.S., Official Says," New York Times Online, www.nytimes.com, April 23, 2005.
128. Ibid.
129. Associated Press, "Trespass Law Helps Nab Illegal Immigrants," New York Times Online, www.nytimes.com, June 17, 2005; Pam Belluck, "Town Uses Trespass Law to Fight Illegal Immigrants," New York Times Online, www.nytimes.com, July 13, 2005.
130. Pam Belluck, "Towns Lose Tool against Illegal Immigrants," New York Times Online, www.nytimes.com, August 13, 2005.
131. Eric Lipton, "Homeland Security Chief Tells of Plan to Stabilize Border," New York Times Online, www.nytimes.com, August 24, 2005.
132. Associated Press, "Border Patrol Considering Use of Volunteers, Official Says." New York Times Online, www.nytimes.com, July 21, 2005; Associated Press, "U.S. Bars Plan to Let Civilians Patrol Borders," New York Times Online, www.nytimes.com, July 22, 2005.
133. Eric Lichtblau, "Social Security Opened Its Files for 9/11 Inquiry," New York Times Online, www.nytimes.com, June 22, 2005.
134. Scott Shane, "Increase in the Number of Documents Classified by the Government," New York Times Online, www.nytimes.com, July 3, 2005.
135. Eric Lichtblau, "Material Given to Congress in 2002 Is Now Classified," New York Times Online, www.nytimes.com, May 20, 2004.
136. Christopher Drew, "Efforts to Hide Sensitive Data Pit 9/11 Concerns against Safety," New York Times Online, www.nytimes.com, March 5, 2005.
137. Eric Lichtblau, "Large Volume of F.B.I. Files Alarms U.S. Activist Groups," New York Times Online, www.nytimes.com, July 18, 2005.
138. Ibid.
139. Andrew Jacobs, "Banner-Bearing Protester at Convention Is Acquitted," New York Times Online, www.nytimes.com, June 24, 2005.
140. New York Civil Liberties Union, *Rights and Wrongs at the RNC: A Special Report about Police and Protest at the Republican National Convention* (New York: New York Civil Liberties Union, 2005), p. 8.
141. Robert E. Worth, "Privacy Rights Are at Issue in New Policy on Searches," New York Times Online, www.nytimes.com, July 2005.
142. Human Rights Watch, *Presumption of Guilt: Human Rights Abuses of Post-September 11 Detainee* (New York: Human Rights Watch, 2002), pp. 3, 6, 46, 55.
143. Eric Lichtblau, "Two Groups Charge Abuse of Witness Law," New York Times Online, www.nytimes.com, July 27, 2005.
144. Human Rights Watch, *Presumption of Guilt,* p. 5.
145. Tracey Maclin, "'Voluntary' Interviews and Airport Searches of Middle Eastern Men: The Fourth Amendment in a Time of Terror," *Mississippi Law Journal* (January 21, 2005), p. 521.
146. Associated Press, "2 NYC Officials Call for Racial Profiling," New York Times Online, www.nytimes.com, August 3, 2005.
147. Ibid.
148. Eric Lichtblau, "Bush Issues Federal Ban on Racial Profiling," New York Times Online, www.nytimes.com, June 17, 2003.
149. Robin Wright, "Support for Bin Laden, Violence Down among Muslims, Poll Says," *Washington Post,* July 15, 2005, p. A13.
150. Laurie Goodstein, "Muslim Leaders Confront Terror Threat Within Islam," New York Times Online, www.nytimes.com, September 2, 2005.

151. Associated Press, "Dearborn, Mich., Arabs Cited More Often," New York Times Online, www.nytimes.com, November 20, 2003.
152. Laurie Nadel, "For Island's Muslims, a Time to Be Wary," New York Times Online, www.nytimes.com, September 4, 2005.
153. Ibid.

CHAPTER 7
The Court System

1. Marbury v. Madison, 1 Cranch 137 (1803).
2. Law Day speech to the San Antonio Bar Association, May 1, 1998.
3. *Compendium of Federal Justice Statistics, 2003* (Washington, DC: Bureau of Justice Statistics), p. 61.
4. Ibid.
5. Administrative Office of the United States Courts, *Judicial Business of the United States Courts: 2003 Annual Report of the Director* (Washington, DC: USGPO, 2004), pp. 79–81.
6. Ibid.
7. *Sourcebook of Criminal Justice Statistics Online,* www.albany.edu/sourcebook/1995/pdf/t573.pdf, Table 5.76, U.S. Supreme Court Cases Argued and Decided on Merits, 1982–1999.
8. Matthew R. Durose and Patrick A. Langan, *State Court Sentencing of Convicted Felons, 2000—Statistical Tables* (Washington, DC: Bureau of Justice Statistics, 2005), Table 1.1.
9. *Sourcebook of Criminal Justice Statistics Online,* www.albany.edu/sourcebook/1995/pdf/t2103.pdf, Table 2.103, College Freshman Reporting There Is Too Much Concern in the Courts for the Rights of Criminals, 1969–2000.

CHAPTER 8
Courtroom Participants and the Trial

1. Bail is not required in a civil trial, as the court has no jurisdiction to incarcerate either party of a civil suit prior to trial.
2. Hudson v. Parker, 156 U.S. 277 (1895).
3. McKane v. Durston, 153 U.S. 684 (1894).
4. Stack v. Boyle, 342 U.S. 1 (1951).
5. Carlson v. Landon, 342 U.S. 524 (1952); U.S. v. Salerno, 55 U.S.L.W. 4663 (1987).
6. Bail Reform Act of 1984, 18 U.S.C. 4142(e).
7. U.S. v. Hazzard, 35 CrL. 2217 (1984); U.S. v. Motamedi, 37 CrL. 2394, CA 9 (1985).
8. C. Ares, A. Rankin, and H. Sturz, "The Manhattan Bail Project: An Interim Report on the Use of Pre-Trial Parole," *New York University Law Review,* 38 (January 1963): 68–95.
9. Wayne R. LaFave and Jerald H. *Israel, Criminal Procedure* (St. Paul, MN: West, 1984), p. 626.
10. United States v. Werker, 535 F.2d 198 (2d Cir. 1976), certiorari denied 429 U.S. 926.
11. Klopfer v. North Carolina, 386 U.S. 213 (1967).
12. Beavers v. Haubert, 1998 U.S. 77 (1905).
13. Klopfer v. North Carolina, 386 U.S. 213 (1967).
14. Barker v. Wingo, 407 US. 514 (1972).
15. A 30-day extension is granted for indictment if the grand jury is not in session, and a 110-day extension can be granted between indictment and trial in cases in which the delay is due to problems associated with calling witnesses.
16. National Advisory Commission on Criminal Justice Standards and Goals, Courts (Washington, DC: U.S. Government Printing Office, 1973), standard 9.3.
17. Brady v. Maryland, 363 U.S. 83 (1963).
18. Moore v. Illinois, 408 U.S. 786 (1972).
19. Mapp v. Ohio, 367 U.S. 634 (1961); Escobedo v. Illinois, 368 U.S. 478 (1964); Miranda v. Arizona, 384 U.S. 436 (1966).
20. Kenneth S. Bordens and Irwin A. Horowitz, "Joinder or Criminal Offenses," *Law and Human Behavior,* 9 (1985): 339–353.
21. One of the strategies used against organized crime figures is to grant them immunity so that they cannot take the Fifth Amendment, and then ask them questions regarding their organized crime activities and partners. If they refuse to answer, they can be held in prison for contempt of court.
22. Ann Fagan Ginger, *Minimizing Racism in Jury Trials* (Berkeley, CA: National Lawyers Guild, 1969).
23. Taylor v. Louisiana, 419 U.S. 522 (1975).
24. Bureau of Justice Statistics, *Report to the Nation on Crime and Justice* (Washington, DC: U.S. Department of Justice, 1988), p. 86.
25. Baldwin v. New York, 399 U.S. 66 (1970); Gideon v. Wainwright, 372 U.S. 335 (1963).
26. Bureau of Justice Statistics, *Indigent Defendants* (Washington, DC: Bureau of Justice Statistics, February 1996).
27. Bureau of Justice Statistics, *Indigent Defense Services in Large Counties, 1999* (Washington, DC: Bureau of Justice Statistics, November 2000), p. 1.
28. Ibid., p. iv.
29. Swain v. Alabama, 380 U.S. 202 (1965).
30. Batson v. Kentucky, 106 S.Ct. 1712 (1986); J.E.B. v. Alabama ex rel. T.B., 55 CrL. 2003 (1994).

CHAPTER 9
Sentencing and Sanctions

1. Adam Liptak, "After 24 Years on Death Row, Clemency Is Killer's Final Appeal," New York Times Online, www.nytimes.com, December 21, 2005.
2. Ibid.
3. Ibid.
4. Ibid
5. Associated Press, "Teen Who Threw Up on Teacher Sentenced," New York Times Online, www.nytimes.com, July 27, 2005.
6. Associated Press, "Man Jailed for Not Licensing Cat in N.D.," New York Times Online, www.nytimes.com, November 5, 2005.
7. Joyce Purnick, "Can Bench Set Rules for Bedroom?" New York Times Online, www.nytimes.com, May 13, 2004.
8. Associated Press, "Convicted Rapist Tells Judge He's Rude," New York Times Online, www.nytimes.com, November 11, 2005.
9. Associated Press, "Conn. Police Fine Students for Cursing," New York Times Online, www.nytimes.com, December 1, 2005.
10. "Britain Toughens Punishment Laws," *Honolulu Advertiser,* January 19, 2000, p. A3.
11. Associated Press, "Woman Sentenced to 100 Lashes for Extramarital Sex," *Pocono Record,* August 13, 2001, p. A5.
12. Associated Press, "Fourteen Men Lashed in Public in Iran for Drinking," *Pocono Record,* August 15, 2001, p. A5.
13. Associated Press, "Saudi Gov't Flogs 55 Youths, Including 12 Foreigners," *Pocono Record,* November 9, 2001, p. A5.
14. Associated Press, "Mayor: Sever Thumbs of Graffiti Artists," New York Times Online, www.nytimes.com, November 5, 2005.
15. Los Angeles Times, "Sweden Pays 200 Who Were Forcibly Sterilized," *Honolulu Advertiser,* November 14, 1999, p. A17.
16. Associated Press, "Japanese Sterilized in Eugenics Program Demand Apology, Money," *Honolulu Advertiser,* December 21, 1997, p. G12.
17. Associated Press, "Australian Woman Gets Life for Murder, Cooking Body," *Pocono Record,* November 9, 2001, p. A5.
18. Associated Press, "Banishment Now Alternative to Jail," *Pocono Record,* October 24, 2001, p. A6.
19. Ira J. Silverman and Manuel Vega, *Corrections: A Comprehensive View* (Minneapolis: West, 1996), p. 63.
20. Associated Press, "That Man Needs to Be Dragged Himself," *Honolulu Advertiser,* February 24, 2000, p. A6.
21. "Boy, 10, Executes Killer of Father," *Honolulu Advertiser,* February 14, 2000, p. 2A.
22. Associated Press, "Woman Gets House Arrest in Fla. Hit-and-Run," New York Times Online, www.nytimes.com, November 5, 2005.

23. Ira Mickenberg, "A Pleasant Surprise: The Guilty but Mentally Ill Verdict Has Both Succeeded in Its Own Right and Successfully Preserved the Traditional Role of the Insanity Defense," *University of Cincinnati Law Review, 55* (1987): 943, 987–991.
24. Samaha, *Criminal Law,* p. 315.
25. Ibid.
26. G. Kleck, "Racial Discrimination in Criminal Sentencing: A Critical Evaluation of the Evidence with Additional Evidence on the Death Penalty," *American Sociological Review, 46* (1981): 783–805.
27. National Council on Crime and Delinquency, *National Assessment of Structured Sentencing* (Washington, DC: Bureau of Justice Administration, 1996).
28. Associated Press, "Courts Concentrate on Domestic Violence," *Honolulu Advertiser,* November 23, 1997, p. A16.
29. Associated Press, "Judge Says Cookie Thief Must Face Life Sentence," *Honolulu Advertiser,* March 15, 1998, p. 18.
30. Ibid.
31. Alexandra Marks, "Prisons Review Results from 'Get-Tough' Era," *Christian Science Monitor,* May 12, 2004, p. 2.
32. Dean E. Murphy, "California Rethinking '3-Strikes' Sentencing," New York Times Online, www.nytimes.com, October 24, 2004.
33. Associated Press, "ABA: End Mandatory Minimum Prison Terms," New York Times Online, www.nytimes.com, June 23, 2004.
34. Ibid.
35. Ibid.
36. U.S. Sentencing Commission, *Federal Sentencing Guidelines Manual* (Washington, DC: Government Printing Office, 1987).
37. Mistretta v. United States, 488 U.S. 361 (1989).
38. Melendez v. United States, 117 S.Ct. 383, 136 L.Ed. 2d 301 (1996).
39. Charles Lane, "Justices Order Review of 400-Plus Sentences," *Washington Post,* January 25, 2005, p. 7.
40. Linda Greenhouse, "Supreme Court Transforms Use of Sentence Guidelines," New York Times Online, www.nytimes.com, January 13, 2005.
41. Carl Hulse and Adam Liptak, "New Fight over Controlling Punishments Is Widely Seen," New York Times Online, www.nytimes.com, January 13, 2005.
42. George Ryley Scott, *The History of Capital Punishment* (London: Torchstream, 1950), p. 179.
43. Harry Elmer Barnes, *The Repression of Crime* (New York: George H. Doran, 1926), p. 220.
44. "Pakistan Criminal to Be Strangled," *Honolulu Advertiser,* March 17, 2000, p. A2.
45. Bureau of Justice Statistics, *Capital Punishment 2000* (Washington, DC: U.S. Department of Justice, December 2001).
46. Peter Slevin, "More in U.S. Expressing Doubts about Death Penalty," *Washington Post,* December 2, 2005.
47. Plato, "Crito," in Benjamin Jowett, trans., *The Apology, Phædo and Crito of Plato* (New York: P. F. Collier & Son, 1937), p. 40.
48. Richard Cohen, "Despite Data, Politicians Continue to Support Death Penalty," *Pocono Record,* October 1, 2000, p. A7.
49. Southern Center for Human Rights, www/schr.org, January 1, 2002.
50. Witherspoon v. Illinois, 391 U.S. 510 (1968).
51. Wilkerson v. Utah, 99 U.S. 130 (1878).
52. In re Kemmler, 136 U.S. 436 (1890).
53. Louisiana ex. Rel. Francis v. Resweber, 329 U.S. 459 (1947).
54. Furman v. Georgia, 408 U.S. 238 (1972).
55. Woodson v. North Carolina, 428 U.S. 280 (1976).
56. Coker v. Georgia, 433 U.S. 584 (1977).
57. Gregg v. Georgia, 428 U.S. 153 (1976).
58. Used in Arizona, Idaho, Montana, and Nebraska.
59. Used in Alabama, Delaware, Florida, and Indiana.
60. Associated Press, "Several States Reconsider Death Penalty Laws," *Honolulu Advertiser,* February 13, 2000, p. A10.
61. Ibid.
62. "Georgia's Electric Chair Found Cruel and Unusual," Southern Center for Human Rights, www.schr.org, December 28, 2001; Associated Press, "Judge Clears Florida to Use Injection for Execution," *Honolulu Advertiser,* February 13, 2000, p. A10; "Gory Death on Florida Electric Chair Creates Furor," *Honolulu Advertiser,* July 9, 1989, p. A9.
63. "Texas Passes Ban on Executing Mentally Retarded Murderers," *Pocono Record,* May 27, 2001; Charles Lane, "High Court to Review Executing Retarded," *Washington Post,* March 27, 2001, p. 1; Charles Lane, "Court Hears Death Penalty Case: Justices to Rule if Jury Got Proper Instruction on Retardation," *Washington Post,* March 28, 2001, p. A8.
64. Reuters, "Court Finds Death Penalty Is Misused in Kansas," New York Times Online, www.nytimes.com, December 30, 2001.
65. "An Irrevocable Error," *Washington Post,*" August 23, 2005, p. A14.
66. Associated Press, "Executed Woman to Get Pardon in Georgia," New York Times Online, www.nytimes.com, August 16, 2005.
67. Michael L. Radelet and Hugo Adam Bedau, "Fallibility and Finality: Type II Errors and Capital Punishment," in Kenneth C. Hass and James A. Inciardi (eds.), *Challenging Capital Punishment: Legal and Social Science Approaches* (Newbury Park, CA: Sage, 1988), pp. 91–112.
68. Adam Liptak, "Study Suspects Thousands of False Convictions," New York Times Online, www.nytimes.com, April 19, 2004.
69. Deborah Hastings, "Police Say Evidence That Led to Execution Doesn't Actually Exist," *Pocono Record,* August, 30, 2001, p. A5; "Reasonable Doubts: Work under the Microscope," *Law Enforcement News,* May 31, 2001.
70. "Condemned Man Exonerated," *Honolulu Advertiser,* May 19, 1999, p. 3.
71. Associated Press, "Prosecutors on Trial in False Charge of Murder," *Honolulu Advertiser,* March 21, 1999, p. A10.
72. Todd S. Purdum, "Los Angeles Police Officer Sets Off Corruption Scandal," New York Times Online, www.nytimes.com, September 18, 1999.
73. Associated Press, "30 Freed from Death Row Support Reform," *Honolulu Advertiser,* November 8, 1998, p. A10.
74. "Center Director Presents Wrongfully Convicted Client to U.S. Senate Judiciary Committee in Calling for Competent Counsel," Southern Center for Human Rights, www.schr.org, January 2, 2002.
75. Associated Press, "Judge Overturns Murder Conviction," New York Times Online, www.nytimes.com, December 28, 2001.
76. Larry McShane, "62,000 Letters and 13 Years Later, Innocent Man Goes Free," *Pocono Record,* September 23, 2001, p. A4.
77. Associated Press, "Charges Dismissed for 17-Year Death Row Inmate," *Honolulu Advertiser,* March 12, 1999, p. A11.
78. Isidore Zimmerman, *Punishment without Crime* (New York: Manor, 1973).
79. "Justice System Abuses Minorities at All Levels, Study Finds," *Honolulu Advertiser,* May 4, 2000, p. A3.
80. C. Spear, *Essays on the Punishment of Death* (London: John Green, 1844), pp. 227–232.
81. David A. Jones, *The Law of Criminal Procedure* (Boston: Little, Brown, 1981), p. 543.
82. President's Commission on Law Enforcement and Administration of Justice, *The Courts* (Washington, DC: U.S. Government Printing Office, 1967), p. 28.
83. Marvin E. Wolfgang and Marc Riedel, "Race Judicial Discretion, and the Death Penalty," *Annals of the American Academy of Political and Social Science,* 407 (May 1973): 129.
84. Thomas J. Keil and Gennaro F. Vito, "Race and the Death Penalty in Kentucky Murder Trials: 1976–1991, *American Journal of Criminal Justice,* 20 (1995): 17–36.
85. "Judge Overturns Death Sentence for Abu-Jamal," *Pocono Record,* December 19, 2001, p. A8.
86. "Judge Asks Prosecutors to Address Race Question in Death Penalty Case," *Pocono Record,* December 6, 2001, p. A4.
87. McCleskey v. Kemp, 41 CrL 4107 (1987).
88. Ibid.
89. "Justice System Abuses Minorities at All Levels, Study Finds."

90. Ibid.
91. "DNA Tests Clear 3,000 Suspects," *Honolulu Advertiser,* November 30, 1997, p. G2.
92. Associated Press, "Two Inmates Freed after New DNA Tests," *Honolulu Advertiser,* December 7, 1997, p. G10; Associated Press, "DNA Testing Frees Two Inmates Imprisoned 12 Years for Murder," *Honolulu Advertiser,* April 16, 1999, p. A6; Associated Press, "DNA Test Frees 60-Year-Old Inmate," *Honolulu Advertiser,* September 2, 1999, p. 3A; Helen O'Neil, "False Conviction," *Pocono Record,* October 1, 2000, p. A5; Associated Press, "Convicted Killer Freed on New DNA Evidence," *Pocono Record,* March 16, 2001, p. B6; Associated Press, "Convicted Murderer Finally Acquitted," *Pocono Record,* April 5, 2001, p. A4; Associated Press, "DNA Clears Man Jailed for 13 Years for Rape," *Pocono Record,* October 19, 2001, p. C10.
93. R. H. Melton, "Gilmore Sets Limit on DNA Evidence: Window Would Close 3 Years after Trial," *Washington Post,* March 28, 2001, p. 1.
94. Brooke A. Masters, "New DNA Testing Urged in Case of Executed Man," *Washington Post,* March 28, 2001, p. B1.
95. F. Carter Smith and Corbis Sygma, "A Life or Death Gamble," *Newsweek,* May 29, 2000, pp. 22–27.
96. Liptak, "Study Suspects Thousands of False Convictions."
97. Smith and Sygma, "A Life or Death Gamble."
98. Ibid.
99. Mark S. Umbreit, "Community Service Sentencing: Last Alternative or Added Sanction?" *Federal Probation, 45,* 1981, pp. 3–14.
100. Ira J. Silverman and Manuel Vega, *Corrections: A Comprehensive View* (St. Paul, MN: West, 1996), p. 515.
101. Ibid., p. 516.
102. Travis, *But They All Come Back,* p. 3.
103. Analysis by Eric Cadora and Charles Swartz for the Community Justice Project at the Center for Alternative Sentencing and Employment Services (CASE), 1999, cited in Travis, Solomon, and Waul, *From Prison to Home.*
104. "Report of the Re-Entry Policy Council: Report Preview: Charting the Safe and Successful Return of Prisoners to the Community," www.reentrypolicy.org.
105. Petersilia, *When Prisoners Return,* p. 3.
106. Elijah Anderson, *Streetwise: Race, Class, and Change in an Urban Community* (Chicago: University of Chicago Press, 1990), p. 4.
107. Joan Petersilia, "Challenges of Prisoner Reentry and Parole in California," California Policy Research Brief Series, June 2000, www.ucop.educ/cprc/parole.html.
108. Joan Moore, "Bearing the Burden: How Incarceration Weakens Inner-City Communities." Paper read at the Unintended Consequences of Incarceration Conference at the Vera Institute of Justice, New York City, 1996.
109. Office of Justice Programs, *Rethinking Probation: Community Supervision, Community Safety* (Washington, DC: U.S. Department of Justice, December 1998), p. 1.
110. Ibid.
111. Petersilia, *When Prisoners Return,* p. 3.
112. T. Clear and P. Hardyman, "The New Intensive Supervision Movement," *Crime and Delinquency, 35,* 1990, pp. 42–60.
113. R. Carter and L. Wilkins, "Caseloads: Some Conceptual Models," in R. Carter and L. Wilkins (eds.), *Probation, Parole and Community Corrections* (New York: John Wiley and Sons, 1976).
114. Office of Justice Programs, *Rethinking Probation,* p. 2.
115. Petersilia, "Challenges of Prisoner Reentry," p. 2.
116. Ibid.
117. Marta Nelson and Jennifer Trone, *Why Planning for Release Matters* (New York: Vera Institute of Justice, 2000), p. 2.
118. Ibid.
119. James P. Levine et al., *Criminal Justice in America: Law in Action* (New York: John Wiley, 1986), p. 549.
120. Administrative Office of the Courts, "New Jersey Intensive Supervision Program, Progress Report 12, No. 1" (Trenton, NJ: State of New Jersey, 1995), p. 3.
121. Ibid.
122. Joan Petersilia, "Georgia's Intensive Probation: Will the Model Work Elsewhere?" in Belinda McCarthy (ed.), *Intermediate Punishments: Intensive Supervision, Home Confinement and Electronic Surveillance* (Monsey, NY: Criminal Justice Press, 1987), p. 21.
123. Susan B. Noonan and Edward J. Latessa, "Intensive Probation: An Examination of Recidivism and Social Adjustment for an Intensive Supervision Program," *American Journal of Criminal Justice, 12,* 1987, pp. 45–61.
124. "Going Home: Serious and Violent Offender Reentry Initiative." See "Communities in Action," www.ojp.usdoj.gov/reentry/communities.htm, February 16, 2002.
125. Joan Petersilia, *Expanding Options for Criminal Sentencing* (Santa Monica, CA: The Rand Corporation, 1987).
126. Ibid.
127. Cherie L. Clark, David W. Aziz, and Doris L. MacKenzie, *Shock Incarceration in New York: Focus on Treatment* (Washington, DC: U.S. Department of Justice, August 1994), p. 2.
128. Silverman and Vega, *Corrections,* p. 529.
129. Doris Layton MacKenzie and Deanna Bellew Ballow, "Shock Incarceration Programs in State Correctional Jurisdictions—An Update," *NIJ Report: Shock Incarceration* (May/June 1989, pp. 9–10; D. G. Parent, *Shock Incarceration: An Overview of Existing Programs* (Washington, DC: U.S. Department of Justice, 1989).
130. Clark, Aziz, and Mackenzie, *Shock Incarceration in New York,* p. 5.
131. Ibid., p. 4.
132. Ibid., p. 3.
133. Ibid., p. 9.
134. Ibid., p. 10.
135. Ibid., p. 6.
136. Doris MacKenzie and Claire Souryal, *Multisite Evaluation of Shock Incarceration* (Washington, DC: National Institute of Justice, September 1994), p. 1.
137. Clark, Aziz, and Mackenzie, *Shock Incarceration in New York,* p. 4.
138. Joan Petersilia, "House Arrest," *National Institute of Justice, Crime File Study Guide* (Washington, DC: U.S. Department of Justice, 1988), p. 1.
139. Silverman and Vega, *Corrections,* p. 523.
140. Ibid., p. 524.
141. M. Renzema and D. Skelton, *Final Report: The Use of Electronic Monitoring by Criminal Justice Agencies* (Washington, DC: U.S. Department of Justice 1990), pp. 1–3.
142. Bureau of Justice Statistics, *Correctional Populations in the United States, 1995* (Washington, DC: Bureau of Justice Statistics, 1997), pp. 22, 34, 41.
143. Michael Tonry, *Intermediate Sanctions in Sentencing Guidelines* (Washington, DC: U.S. Department of Justice, 1997), p. 10.
144. Petersilia, "House Arrest," p. 1.
145. David C. Anderson, *Sensible Justice: Alternatives to Prison* (New York: The New Press, 1998), p. 44.
146. Ibid.
147. John Schwartz, "Internet Leash Can Monitor Sex Offenders," New York Times Online, www.nytimes.com, December 31, 2001.
148. Christopher Baird and Dennis Wagner, *Evaluation of the Florida Community Control Program* (Madison, WI: National Council on Crime and Delinquency, 1990).
149. J. Muncie, "A Prisoner in My Home: The Politics and Practice of Electronic Monitoring," *Probation Journal,* 37, 1990, pp. 72–77.
150. *Federal Government Information Technology, Electronic Surveillance and Civil Liberties* (Washington, DC: Congress of the United States, Office of Technology Assessment, 1985); R. Ball, R. C. Huff, and J. P. Lilly, *House Arrest and Correctional Policy: Doing Time at Home* (Newbury Park, CA: Sage, 1988).
151. Reginald A. Wilkinson, "Offender Reentry: A Storm Overdue," www.drc.state.oh.us/Articles/article66.htm, January 16, 2002.
152. Ibid.
153. "History of the Office of Community Corrections," www.michigan.gov, February 16, 2002.

154. National Criminal Justice Reference Service, "Prisoner Reentry Resources—Legislation," www.ncjrs.org/reentry/legislation.htm, February 17, 2002.
155. Ibid.
156. Serious and Violent Offender Reentry Initiative, "See Communities in Action," www.ojp.usdoj.gov/reentry/communities.htm, February 18, 2002.
157. Jacqui Goddard, "Florida's New Approach to Inmate Reform: A 'Faith-Based' Prison," *Christian Science Monitor,* December 24, 2003, p. 1.
158. Fox Butterfield, "Repaving the Long Road Out of Prison," New York Times Online, www.nytimes.com, May 4, 2004.
159. Dan Nakaso, "Inmates Pay Debt in Sweat, while Learning Lure of 'Aina,'" *Honolulu Advertiser,* March 11, 1999, pp. A1, A7.
160. Marta Nelson and Jennifer Trone, *Why Planning for Release Matters* (New York: Vera Institute of Justice, 2000), p. 2.
161. Elmer H. Johnson and Kenneth E. Kotch, "Two Factors in Development of Work Release: Size and Location of Prisons," *Journal of Criminal Justice,* 1 (March 1973): 44–45.
162. Silverman and Vega, *Corrections,* p. 520.
163. Harry Holzer, *What Employers Want: Job Prospects for Less-educated Workers* (New York: Russell Sage, 1996).
164. Petersilia, *When Prisoners Return,* p. 4.
165. U.S. Department of Labor, *From Hard Time to Full Time: Strategies to Move Ex-Offenders from Welfare to Work* (Washington, DC: U.S. Department of Labor, June 2001), p. 7.
166. "Woman Files Lawsuit against Company for Using Inmate Telemarketers," *Pocono Record,* November 15, 2001, p. A5.
167. Cheryl Dahle, "What's That Felony on Your Resume," New York Times Online, www.nytimes.com, October 17, 2004.
168. Nelson and Trone, *Why Planning for Release Matters,* pp. 4–5.
169. Ibid.
170. Ibid., p. 3.
171. Rhonda Cook, "State Prison-to-Work Program Falls Short," *Atlanta Journal-Constitution,* June 1, 2000.
172. Nelson and Trone, *Why Planning for Release Matters,* p. 2.
173. U.S. Department of Labor, *From Hard Time to Full Time: Strategies to Help Move Ex-Offenders from Welfare to Work* (U.S. Department of Labor, Washington, DC: June 2001), p. 10.
174. Ibid., p. 11.
175. Susan Kreifels, "New Rules Add Teeth to Convict-Hiring Law," *Honolulu Star-Bulletin,* January 9, 1998, pp. A1, A8.
176. U.S. Department of Labor, *From Hard Time to Full Time,* pp. 9–10.
177. David Koeppel, "Job Fairs Give Ex-Convicts Hope in Down Market," New York Times Online, www.nytimes.com, December 26, 2001.
178. George E. Sexton, *Work in American Prisons: Joint Ventures with the Private Sector* (Washington, DC: U.S. Department of Justice, November 1995), pp. 2, 10.
179. Ibid., p. 3.
180. Ronald D. Stephens and June Lane Arnette, *From the Courthouse to the Schoolhouse: Making Successful Transitions* (Washington, DC: U.S. Department of Justice, February 2000), p. 1.
181. Ibid., p. 3.
182. Thomas Barlett, "Prime Numbers," *Chronicle of Higher Education,* January 19, 2002, p. A7.
183. Ibid.
184. Peter Monaghan, "U. of Alaska Declines to Admit a Killer to Its Social-Work Program, Raising Questions—and a Lawsuit," *Chronicle of Higher Education,* July 13, 2005.
185. O. I. Keller and B. S. Alper, *Halfway Houses: Community-Centered Correction and Treatment* (Lexington, MA: Heath Lexington Books, 1970).
186. Task Force on Corrections, *Task Force Report: Corrections* (Washington, DC: President's Commission on Law Enforcement and the Administration of Justice, U.S. Government Printing Office, 1967); Task Force on Corrections, *Task Force Report: Corrections* (Washington, DC: National Advisory Commission on Criminal Justice Standards and Goals, 1973).
187. Office of Justice Programs, *Rethinking Probation,* pp. 19–21.
188. Dale G. Parent, *Day Reporting Centers for Criminal Offenders: A Descriptive Analysis of Existing Programs* (Washington, DC: U.S. Department of Justice, 1990), p. 1.
189. Dale G. Parent, "Day Reporting Centers," in Michael Tonry and Kate Hamilton (eds.), *Intermediate Sanctions in Overcrowded Times* (Boston: Northeastern University Press, 1995), p. 15.
190. *Criminal Justice Abstracts* (Monsey, NY: Willow Tree Press, 1998), pp. 105–106.
191. National Institute of Justice, *Effects of Judges' Sentencing Decisions on Criminal Careers* (Washington, DC: U.S. Department of Justice, November 1999).
192. Ibid.
193. Ibid.

CHAPTER 10

Probation, Parole, and Community Corrections

1. David Snyder and Jennifer Lenhart, "MD Stabbing Suspect Had Just Left Prison," *Washington Post,* May 27, 2005, p. 1.
2. Associated Press, "Ex-Convict Is Arrested in 26 Bank Robberies," New York Times Online, www.nytimes.com, November 1, 2004.
3. Fox Butterfield, "Tight Budgets Force States to Reconsider Crime and Penalties," New York Times Online, www.nytimes.com, January 21, 2002.
4. Ibid.
5. Ibid.
6. Ken Kobayashi, "Second Chance Starts with Death, New Life," *Honolulu Advertiser,* December 29, 1997, p. A1.
7. Jo Napolitano, "Top Illinois Court Upholds Total Amnesty of Death Row," New York Times Online, www.nytimes.com, January 24, 2004.
8. Associated Press, "Clinton Pardons 33 Convicted Criminals," *Honolulu Advertiser,* December 25, 1998, p. A6.
9. Ira Silverman and Manuel Vega, *Corrections: A Comprehensive View* (Minneapolis/Saint Paul: West, 1996), p. 495.
10. Lauren E. Glaze and Seri Palla, *Probation and Parole in the United States, 2004* (Washington, DC: Bureau of Justice Statistics, 2005), p. 1.
11. Ibid., p. 6.
12. Ibid.
13. Ibid.
14. Ibid.
15. James M. Byrne, *Probation: A National Institute of Justice Crime File Series Study Guide* (Washington, DC: U.S. Department of Justice, 1988), p. 1.
16. In Escoe v. Zerbst, 295 U.S. 490 (135), the Court ruled that probation was an act of grace, and thus the probationer was without due process rights. In Mempa v. Rhay, 389 U.S. 128 (1967), the Court reversed the ruling of Escoe v. Zerbst and ruled that probationers were entitled to due process rights.
17. Gagnon v. Scarpelli, 411 U.S. 778 (1973).
18. Griffin v. Wisconsin, 483 U.S. 868, 107 S.Ct. 3164 (1987).
19. Minnesota v. Murphy, 465 U.S. 420, 104 S.Ct. 1136, 79 L. Ed. 2d 409 (1984).
20. Gagon v. Scarpelli (1973); Mempa v. Rhay (1967).
21. Kelly v. Robinson, 479 U.S. 36, 107 S.Ct. 353, 93 L. Ed. 2d 216 (1986).
22. Silverman and Vega, *Corrections,* p. 501.
23. H. Burns, *Corrections Organization and Administration* (St. Paul, MN: West, 1975).
24. G. I. Giardini, *The Parole Process* (Springfield, IL: Charles C. Thomas, 1959), p. 9.
25. David Dresser, *Practice and Theory of Probation and Parole* (New York: Columbia University Press, 1969), pp. 56–76.
26. Marjorie Bell (ed.), *Parole in Principle and Practice* (New York: National Probation and Parole Association, 1957).

27. A. W. Pisciotta, "Scientific Reform: The 'New Penology' at Elmira, 1876–1900," *Crime and Delinquency*, 29 (1983): 613–630.
28. Bureau of Justice Statistics, *Probation and Parole Statistics.*
29. Chris L. Jenkins, "Ten Years after It Eliminated Parole, VA Considers Costs," *Washington Post,* December 25, 2004, p. B1.
30. Ibid.
31. Glaze and Palla, *Probation and Parole in the United States,* p. 9.
32. Ibid.
33. Jenkins, "Ten Years," p. B1.
34. Bureau of Justice Statistics, *Likelihood of Going to State or Federal Prison* (Washington, DC: U.S. Department of Justice, March 1997). p. 5.
35. Task Force on Corrections, *Task Force Report: Corrections* (Washington, DC: President's Commission on Law Enforcement and the Administration of Justice, U.S. Government Printing Office, 1967).
36. William Parker, *Parole: Origins, Development, Current Practices and Statutes* (College Park, MD: American Correctional Association, 1975).
37. "Federal Funds at Stake for 14 States with Megan's Law Problems," *Law Enforcement News,* November 30, 2001, p. 7.
38. Menechino v. Oswald, 430 F. 2d 403 (2d Cir., 1970); Greenholtz v. Inmates of Nebraska Penal and Correctional Complex, 422 U.S. 1 (1979).
39. Johnson, U.S. ex. Rel. v. Chairman, New York State Board of Parole, 363 F. Supp. 416, aff'd, 500 F. 2d 925 (2d Cir., 1971).
40. Don M. Gottfredson, Peter B. Hoffman, Maurice H. Sigler, and Leslie T. Wilkins, "Making Paroling Policy Explicit," *Crime and Delinquency, 21,* January 1975, p. 36.
41. Southern Center for Human Rights, "Federal Judge Finds Alabama Jail Like a Slave Ship, Orders Immediate Reduction in Population, Other Reforms," www.schr.org/news/news_slaveshipstory.htm, December 28, 2001.
42. James Austin, "The Consequences of Escalating the Use of Imprisonment," *Corrections Compendium,* September 1991, pp. 1, 4–8.
43. Ibid.
44. See www.usdoj.gov/uspc/release.htm, February 4, 2002.
45. Glaze and Palla, *Probation and parole in the United States,* p. 9.
46. Ibid.
47. Bureau of Justice Statistics, *Trends in State Parole, 1990–2000* (Washington, DC: U.S. Department of Justice, October 2001), p. 13.
48. Bureau of Justice Statistics, *Probation and Parole Violators in State Prison, 1991* (Washington, DC: U.S. Department of Justice, August 1995), p. 1.
49. Morrissey v. Brewer, 408 U.S. 471 (1972).
50. *Stress among Probation and Parole Officers and What Can Be Done about It* (Washington, DC: Office of Justice Programs, 2005), p. 1.
51. See www.usdoj.gov/uspc/questions.htm, February 4, 2002.
52. Bureau of Justice Statistics, *Trends in State Parole,* p. 11.
53. See www.usdoj.gov/uspc/questions.htm, February 4, 2002.
54. See www.usdoj.gov/uspc, February 4, 2002.
55. Drug Court Clearinghouse and Technical Assistance Project, "Looking at a Decade of Drug Courts," www.ojp.usdoj.gov/, November 16, 2001.
56. Adele Harrell, Shannon Cavanagh, and John Roman, *Evaluation of the D.C. Superior Court Drug Intervention Programs* (Washington, DC: National Institute of Justice, April 2000), pp. 1–2.
57. John Scalia, *Federal Drug Offenders, 1999 with Trends 1984–1999* (Washington, DC: U.S. Department of Justice, August 2001), p. 10.
58. Ibid., p. 1.
59. Elizabeth A. Peyton and Robert Gossweiler, *Treatment Services in Adult Drug Courts: Report on the 1999 National Drug Court Treatment Survey Executive Summary* (Washington, DC: U.S. Department of Justice, May 2001), p. 5.
60. Allen J. Beck, "State and Federal Prisoners Returning to the Community: Finding from the Bureau of Justice Statistics," Paper presented at the First Reentry Courts Initiative Cluster Meeting, Washington, DC, April 13, 2000.
61. Drug Court Clearinghouse and Technical Assistance Project, "Looking at a Decade."
62. Ibid.
63. Ibid.
64. Ibid.
65. Adele Harrell, Shannon Cavanagh, and John Roman, *Evaluation of the D.C. Superior Court Drug Intervention Programs* (Washington, DC: U.S. Department of Justice, April 2000), p. 2.
66. Ibid.
67. Caroline S. Cooper, *Juvenile Drug Court Programs* (Washington, DC: U.S. Department of Justice, July 1999), p. 14.
68. Ibid., p. 3.
69. Ibid., p. 6.
70. Ibid., p. 9.
71. Ibid., p. 13.
72. Ibid., p. 11.
73. Ibid., p. 13.
74. Tribal Law and Policy Institute, *Healing to Wellness Courts: A Preliminary Overview of Tribal Drug Courts* (Washington DC: U.S. Department of Justice, July 1999), p. 14.
75. Ibid., p. 9.
76. Ibid., p. 2.
77. Ibid., p. 4.
78. Ibid., pp. 9–10.
79. Ibid., p. 12.
80. Ibid., p. 13.
81. Ibid., p. 14.
82. National Institute of Justice, *Reducing Offender Drug Use,* p. 21; Bureau of Justice Assistance, *Treatment Accountability for Safer Communities* (Washington, DC: U.S. Department of Justice, November 1995), pp. 1–2.
83. Bureau of Justice Assistance, *Treatment Accountability for Safer Communities* (Washington, DC: U.S. Department of Justice, November 1995), p. 1.
84. National Institute of Justice, *Reducing Offender Drug Use,* p. 21.
85. Joan Petersilia and Elizabeth Piper Deschenes, "What Punishes? Inmates Rank the Severity of Prison versus Intermediate Sanctions," in Joan Petersilia (ed.), *Community Corrections: Probation, Parole and Intermediate Sanctions* (New York: Oxford University Press, 1998), pp. 149–159.
86. Joan Petersilia, "When Probation Becomes More Dreaded Than Prison," *Federal Probation,* 54, 1990, pp. 23–27.
87. Rick Lyman, "Marriage Programs Try to Instill Bliss and Stability Behind Bars," New York Times Online, www.nytimes.com, April 16, 2005.

CHAPTER 11

Jails and Prisons

1. Law Enforcement Assistance Administration (LEAA), *Two Hundred Years of American Criminal Justice: An LEAA Bicentennial Study* (Washington, DC: U.S. Department of Justice, 1976), p. 46.
2. Harry B. Weiss and Grace M. Weiss, *An Introduction to Crime and Punishment in Colonial New Jersey* (Trenton, NJ: Past Times Press, 1960), pp. 17–18.
3. Ibid., p. 18.
4. Ibid., p. 64.
5. Ibid., p. 10.
6. Ibid., p. 47.
7. Ibid.
8. Norman Johnston, *The Human Cage: a Brief History of Prison Architecture* (New York: Walker and Company, 1973), pp. 13–14.
9. The society still operates under the name of the Philadelphia Prison Society.
10. Joseph M. Hawes, "Prisons in Early Nineteenth-Century America: The Process of Convict Reformation," in Joseph M. Hawes (ed.),

Law and Order in American History (Port Washington, NY: National University Publications, 1979), p. 39.
11. LEAA, *Two Hundred Years*, p. 47.
12. Hawes, "Prisons in Early Nineteenth-Century America."
13. Ibid., p. 40.
14. Ibid., p. 39.
15. LEAA, *Two Hundred Years*, p. 49.
16. O. L. Lewis, *The Development of American Prisons and Prison Customs, 1776–1845* (Montclair, NJ: Patterson Smith, 1996/1922).
17. D. J. Rothman, *The Discovery of the Asylum: Social Order and Disorder in the New Republic* (Boston: Little, Brown, 1971), p. 106.
18. Ira J. Silverman and Manuel Vega, *Corrections: A Comprehensive View* (Minneapolis/St. Paul: West, 1996), p. 78.
19. Ibid.
20. LEAA, *Two Hundred Years*, p. 49.
21. Lewis, *The Development of American Prisons.*
22. John W. Fountain, "Time Winds Down at a Storied Prison," New York Times Online, www.nytimes.com, December 26, 2001.
23. E. Ayers, *Vengeance and Justice: Crime and Punishment in the 19th-Century American South* (New York: Oxford University Press, 1984).
24. M. C. Moos, *State Penal Administration in Alabama* (Tuscaloosa, AL: Bureau of Public Administration, University of Alabama, 1942), p. 18.
25. B. McKelvey, *American Prisons: A History of Good Intentions* (Montclair, NJ: Patterson Smith, 1977).
26. Thomas Murton and J. Hyams, *Accomplices to the Crime: The Arkansas Prison Scandal* (New York: Grove Press, 1969).
27. Holt v. Sarver, 300 F. Supp. 825 (1969); Holt v. Sarver, 309 F. Supp. 362 (E.D. Ark. 1970); Jackson v. Bishop, 404 F. 2d 571 (8th Cir., 1968).
28. Holt v. Sarver, 309 F. Supp. 362 (E.D. Ark. 1970).
29. Sam Vincent Meddis, "U.S. Incarceration Rate Is Highest in the World," *Honolulu Star Bulletin*, January 8, 1991, p. A16.
30. Associated Press, "State Prisons' Growth Rate Slows," *Washington Post*, March 26, 2001, p. A4.
31. Ibid.
32. U.S. Department of Justice, Bureau of Justice Statistics, 1999 Justice Expenditure and Employment, www.ojp.usdoj.gov/bjs/pub/shets/cjee99.zip.
33. Paige M. Harrison and Allen J. Beck, *Prisoners in 2004* (Washington, DC: Bureau of Justice Statistics, 2005), p. 2.
34. David Jones, *History of Criminology: A Philosophical Perspective* (New York: Greenwood Press, 1986), p. 123.
35. Thomas Bonczar and Allen Beck, *Lifetime Likelihood of Going to State or Federal Prison* (Washington, DC: U.S. Department of Justice, March 1997), p. 1.
36. Ibid.
37. Bureau of Justice Statistics, *Prisoners in 2000* (Washington, DC: U.S. Department of Justice, August 2001), pp. 10, 11.
38. Bureau of Justice Statistics, *Profile of State Prisoners under Age 18, 1985–97* (Washington, DC: U.S. Department of Justice, August 2001), p. 1.
39. Gannett News Service, "13% of US. Black Men Barred from Voting," *Honolulu Advertiser*, October 23, 1998, p. A3.
40. Ibid.
41. Ibid.
42. Ibid.
43. American Correctional Association, *The American Prison: From the Beginning* (Lanham, MD: American Correctional Association, 1983), p. 220.
44. Ibid., p. 158.
45. Bureau of Justice Statistics, *Census of Jails, 1999* (Washington, DC: U.S. Department of Justice, August 2001), pp. 1, 7.
46. Military prisoners are primarily military personnel who have been convicted by court martial of violating the Uniform Code of Military Conduct, the body of law that defines crime and punishment for military personnel. In 1997, there were 2,466 military prisoners from all branches of the service (*Sourcebook of Criminal Justice Statistics 2000*, p. 533). The oldest military prison still in operation in the United States is the U.S. Disciplinary Barracks at Fort Leavenworth, Kansas.
47. Thirty-three states contain around 300 Native American areas or reservations. Generally, the local government authority on Native American lands is a tribal government or council. Jurisdiction over crimes in these areas depends on several factors, including the identity of the victim and the offender, the severity of the crime, and where the crime was committed. In 2000, there were 69 facilities operating in tribal lands, holding 1,700 persons in custody. From: Bureau of Justice Statistics, *Jails in Indian Country, 2000* (Washington, DC: U.S. Department of Justice, July 2001), p. 1.
48. Bureau of Justice Statistics, *Census of Jails*, p. 3.
49. Shaila K. Dewan, "Sheriff Accepts Takeover of a Troubled Jail," New York Times Online, www.nytimes.com, July 12, 2004.
50. Ibid.
51. Bureau of Justice Statistics, *Law Enforcement Management and Administrative Statistics, Sheriffs' Offices, 1999* (Washington, DC: U.S. Department of Justice, May 2001), p. 7.
52. Ibid., p. 3.
53. Bureau of Justice Statistics, Census of Jails, p. 4.
54. Ibid., p. 5.
55. Harrison and Beck, *Prisoners in 2004*, p. 1.
56. Ibid., p. 2.
57. American Correctional Association, *The American Prison*, p. 172.
58. Kevin Johnson, "Inmate Swap Worked—Until Impostor Fled," *USA Today*, October 25, 2000, p. 2.
59. Ibid.
60. American Correctional Association, *The American Prison*, p. 172.
61. Harrison and Beck, *Prisoners in 2004*, p. 4.
62. Allen Beck and Jennifer Karberg, *Prison and Jail Inmates at Midyear 2000* (Washington, DC: U.S. Department of Justice, March 2001), p. 5.
63. John Scalia, *Federal Drug Offenders, 1999, with Trends 1984–99* (Washington, DC: U.S. Department of Justice, August 2001), p. 6.
64. Anne L. Stahl, *Drug Offense Cases in Juvenile Courts, 1989–1998* (Washington, DC: U.S. Department of Justice, September 2001), p. 1.
65. Chen, "Number of Women."
66. Ibid.
67. Laura Maruschak, *HIV in Prisons and Jails, 1999* (Washington, DC: U.S. Department of Justice, July 2001), p. 4.
68. Chen, "Number of Women."
69. Caroline Wolf Harlow, *Prior Abuse Reported by Inmates and Probationers* (Washington, DC: U.S. Department of Justice, April 1999), p. 2.
70. Lennie Magida, "Doing Hard Time," *Honolulu Weekly*, July 14, 1993, p. 4.
71. Joan Petersilia, *When Prisoners Return to the Community* (Washington, DC: U.S. Department of Justice, November 2000), p. 4.
72. Marilyn C. Moses, *Keeping Incarcerated Mothers and Their Daughters Together: Girl Scouts beyond Bars* (Washington, DC: U.S. Department of Justice, October 1995), p. 1.
73. Petersilia, *When Prisoners Return.*
74. Chen, "Number of Women."
75. Moses, *Keeping Incarcerated Mothers.*
76. Bureau of Justice Statistics, *Capital Punishment 2000* (Washington, DC: U.S. Department of Justice, December 2001), p. 7.
77. Victor L. Streib, "Death Penalty for Female Offenders January 1, 1973, to December 31, 2000." See www.law.onu.edu/faculty/steib/femdeath.htm, February 14, 2002.
78. Nearly all jails, state prisons, and federal prisons have abandoned the use of the term *guard* to describe security personnel. In the federal prisons, these employees are called *correctional officers*. Correctional institutions do not consider the job title "guard" as appropriately describing the duties of the employee, and use of the term is considered rather derogatory and demeaning of the professionalism required for the position.

79. The actual responsibility for transferring prisoners from one federal facility to another is that of the U.S. Marshal Service. Also, the U.S. Marshal Service is responsible for locating and arresting escaped federal prisoners.
80. Harrison and Beck, *Prisoners in 2000,* p. 2.
81. Ibid., p. 5.
82. Associated Press, "Private Prisons Said to Do Little for Communities," *Pocono Record,* October 22, 2001, p. A5.
83. Ibid.
84. Associated Press, "Private Prisons Said to Do Little for Communities," *Pocono Record,* October 22, 2001, p. A5.
85. Ibid.
86. Richardson et al. v. McKnight, No. 96-318.
87. Bureau of Justice Statistics, *Challenging the Conditions of Prisons and Jails: A Report on Section 1983 Litigation* (Washington, DC: U.S. Department of Justice, December 1994).
88. Deborah Orin, "Bush: Captured Terror Fighters Are Now POWs," *New York Post,* February 8, 2002, p. 12.
89. "Illegal Combatant," Wikipedia: The Free Encyclopedia, www.wikipedia.org, November 17, 2003.
90. Elisabeth Bumiller and David Johnston, "Bush May Subject Terror Suspects to Miliary Trials," *The New York Times,* November 14, 2001, p. B1+.
91. William Glaberson, "Critics' Attack on Tribunals Turns to Law among Nations," New York Times Online, www.nytimes.com, December 26, 2001.
92. Bumiller and Johnston, "Bush May Subject Terror Suspects," p. B8.
93. Ibid., p. B1+.
94. Ibid., p. B1.
95. Glaberson, "Critics' Attack on Tribunals."
96. Neil A. Lewis, "Try Detainees or Free Them, 3 Senators Urge," New York Times Online, www.nytimes.com.
97. John Shattuck, "Human Rights at Home," New York Times Online, www.nytimes.com, December 25, 2001.
98. William Glaberson, "Judges Question Detention of American," New York Times Online, www.nytimes.com, November 18, 2003.
99. Ibid.
100. Eric Lichtblau, "Enemy Combatant Decision Marks Change, Officials Say," New York Times Online, www.nytimes.com, June 25, 2003.
101. FindLaw, www.findlaw.com, June 25, 2003.
102. "Enemy Combatant Charge Marks Policy Change," TalkLeft: The Politics of Crime, www.talkleft.com, June 25, 2003.
103. Ibid.
104. Lichtblau, "Enemy Combatant Decision."
105. Ibid.
106. "Enemy Combatant Sham," New York Times Online, www.nytimes.com, November 19, 2003.
107. Glaberson, "Judges Question Detention of American."
108. Yasser Esam Hamdi is an American citizen who was detained as an enemy combatant but he was captured on the Afghan battlefield.
109. Neil A. Lewis, "Six Detainees Soon May Face Military Trials," New York Times Online, www.nytimes.com, July 4, 2003.
110. Sarah Lyall, "Families of British Terror Suspects Alarmed by Tribunals," New York Times Online, www.nytimes.com, July 4, 2003.
111. Agence France Presse,"5 Pakistanis Freed from Guantanamo," New York Times Online, www.nytimes.com, November 23, 2003.
112. Alan Cowell, "4Britons and an Australian to Be Freed at Guantanamo," New York Times Online, www.nytimes.com, January 12, 2005.
113. Adam Liptak, "Inmate Was Considered 'Property' of Gang, Witness Tells Jury in Prison Rape Lawsuit," New York Times Online, www.nytimes.com, September 25, 2005.
114. Ibid.
115. Human Rights Watch, *No Escape: Male Rape in U.S. Prisons,* www.hrw.org, 2004.
116. Allen J. Beck and Timothy A. Hughes, *Sexual Violence Reported by Correctional Authorities, 2004* (Washington, DC: Bureau of Justice Statistics, 2005), p. 1.
117. Joan Petersilia, *When Prisoners Return to the Community: Political, Economic, and Social Consequences* (Washington, DC: U.S. Department of Justice, November 2000), p. 4.
118. William J. Fraser, "Getting the Drop on Street Gangs and Terrorists," *Law Enforcement News,* November 30, 2001, p. 11.
119. Silverman and Vega, *Corrections,* p. 208.
120. Kevin Dayton, "Release Foreseen for Comatose Halawa Inmate," *Star-Bulletin & Advertiser,* December 8, 1991, p. A3.
121. Petersilia, *When Prisoners Return to the Community,* p. 4.
122. Maruschak and Beck, *Medical Problems of Inmates,* p. 1.
123. "Unintended Consequences of Sentencing Policy: The Creation of Long-Term Healthcare Obligations," in *Research in Review* (Washington, DC: U.S. Department of Justice, November 2001), p. 1.
124. Bureau of Justice Statistics, *Challenging the Conditions of Prisons and Jails: A Report on Section 1983 Litigation* (Washington, DC: U.S. Department of Justice, December 1994, p. 8.
125. Tammerlin Drummond, "Cellblock Seniors," *Time,* June 21, 1999, p. 60.
126. Ibid.
127. Rebecca Widom and Theodore M. Hammett, *HIV/AIDS and STDs in Juvenile Facilities* (Washington, DC: U.S. Department of Justice, April 1996), p. 1.
128. Laura M. Maruschak, *HIV in Prisons and Jails, 1999* (Washington, DC: U.S. Department of Justice, July 2001), p. 1.
129. Ibid.
130. Ibid.
131. Ibid.
132. Ibid.
133. Lawrence K. Altman, "Much More AIDS in Prisons Than in General Populations," New York Times Online, www.nytimes.com, September 2, 1999.
134. Ibid.
135. Karen Wilcock, Theodore M. Hammett, Rebecca Widom, and Joel Epstein, *Tuberculosis in Correctional Facilities, 1994–1995* (Washington, DC: U.S. Department of Justice, July 1996), p. 1.
136. Ibid.
137. Joan Petersilia, *Challenges of Prisoner Reentry and Parole in California,* California Policy Research Center Brief Series, June 2000, www.ucop.edu/cprc/parole.html, February 11, 2002.
138. Fox Butterfield, "Experts Say Study Confirms Prison's New Role as Mental Hospital," New York Times Online, www.nytimes.com, July 12, 1999.
139. Ibid.
140. Ibid.
141. ACLU Newswire, "Jails No Place for the Mentally Ill, ACLU of Mississippi Says," www.aclu.org/news, January 16, 2002.
142. Paula M. Ditton, *Mental Health and Treatment of Inmates and Probationers* (Washington, DC: U.S. Department of Justice, July 1999), p. 1.
143. Petersilia, *When Prisoners Return to the Community,* p. 2.
144. ACLU News Wire, "Jails No Place."
145. Butterfield, "Experts Say Study Confirms."
146. Erving Goffman, *Asylums: Essays on the Social Situation of Mental Patients and Other Inmates* (Garden City, NY: Anchor Books, 1961).
147. Ditton, *Mental Health and Treatment,* p. 9.
148. Linda A. Teplin, *Assessing Alcohol, Drug, and Mental Disorders in Juvenile Detainees* (Washington, DC: U.S. Department of Justice, January 2000), p. 1.
149. David T. Johnson and Meda Chesney-Lind, "Does Hawaii Really Need Another Prison?" *Honolulu Advertiser,* March 29, 1998, p. B1.
150. William D. Nueske, "Four Prisoners Who Killed Themselves Did Us a Favor," *Honolulu Star-Bulletin,* January 13, 1992.
151. Associated Press, "Official Resists Plan of Computers for Jail," *Pocono Record,* January 17, 2002, p. A4.
152. Ibid.

CHAPTER 12

The Future of Criminal Justice

1. Randal C. Archibold, "Las Vegas Makes It Illegal to Feed Homeless in Parks," New York Times Online, www.nytimes.com, July 28, 2006.
2. Kristen A. Hughes, *Justice Expenditure and Employment in the United States, 2003* (Washington, DC: U.S. Department of Justice, 2006), p. 1.
3. Robert Pear, "Legal Group Faults Bush for Ignoring Parts of Bills," New York Times Online, www.nytimes.com, July 24, 2006.
4. Samantha Henig, "Pentagon Surveillance of Student Groups as Security Threats Extended to Monitoring E-Mail, Reports Show," *The Chronicle of Higher Education,* July 6, 2006, p. 1; Eric Lichtblau, "Bush Would Let Secret Court Sift Wiretap Process," New York Times Online, www.nytimes.com, July 14, 2006; Anushka Asthana, "Domestic Detainee From 9/11 Released," *Washington Post,* July 21, 2006, p. A09.
5. Kate Zernike, "Military Lawyers Urge Protections for Detainees," New York Times Online, www.nytimes.com, July 14, 2006; R. Jeffrey Smith, "On Prosecuting Detainees," *The Washington Post,* July 28, 2006, p. A23; R. Jeffrey Smith, "Detainee Abuse Charges Feared," *The Washington Post,* July 29, 2006, p. A01.
6. Sewell Chan and Winnie Hu, "City Will Not Change Its Strategy for Dealing with Terror," New York Times Online, www.nytimes.com, June 7, 2006; Mary Beth Sheridan and Dan Eggen, "D.C. at Low Risk of Attack, Says Federal Agency," *The Washington Post,* June 2, 2006, p. A01.
7. Spencer S. Hsu and Robin Wright, "Plot to Attack N.Y. Foiled," *Washington Post,* July 8, 2006, p. A01; Associated Press, "Arrest of 7 Linked to Plot on Chicago Tower," New York Times Online, www.nytimes.com, June 22, 2006; Associated Press, "More Charges in Georgia Terror Case," New York Times Online, www.nytimes.com, July 20, 2006.
8. Eric Lipton, "U.S. Terror Targets: Petting Zoo and Flea Market?" New York Times Online, www.nytimes.com, July 12, 2006.
9. Julia Preston, "Sheriff Defies Immigrants by Billboard and by Blog," New York Times Online, www.nytimes.com, July 30, 2006; Julia Preston, "State Proposals on Illegal Immigration Largely Falter," New York Times Online, www.nytimes.com, May 9, 2006.
10. Abby Goodnough, "A Florida Mayor Turns to an Immigration Curb to Fix a Fading City," New York Times Online, www.nytimes.com, July 10, 2006.
11. Jim Dwyer, "Inmate to be Freed as DNA Tests Upend Murder Confession," New York Times Online, www.nytimes.com, May 16, 2006.
12. Ibid.
13. Diane Cardwell, "New York State Draws Nearer to Collecting DNA in all Crimes," New York Times Online, www.nytimes.com, May 4, 2006.
14. Thomas K. Duane, "Think Before You Swab," New York Times Online, www.nytimes.com, June 9, 2006.
15. Danny Hakim, "County DNA Lists Include Non-Convicts," New York Times Online, www.nytimes.com, May 16, 2006.
16. Donna Lieberman, "Your Baby or Your Beat," New York Times Online, www.nytimes.com, June 2, 2006.
17. William Yardley and Jodi Rudoren, "Six are Shot at Seattle Jewish Center," New York Times Online, www.nytimes.com, July 29, 2006.
18. Allison Klein, "Feds, Local Police Team Up on D.C. Crime," *Washington Post,* July 22, 2006, P. B01.
19. Sewell Chan, "Seeking a National Voice, 15 Mayors Meet on Gun Violence," New York Times Online, www.nytimes.com, April 26, 2006; Al Baker, "U.S. Will Help New York City Pursue Cases Against Gun Dealers," New York Times Online, www.nytimes.com, May 27, 2006.
20. Glenn R. Schmitt, *Drug Courts: The Second Decade* (Washington, DC: U.S. Department of Justice, 2006), p. 3.
21. Linda Greenhouse, "Justices Uphold Basic Right to Choose Defense Lawyers," New York Times Online, www.nytimes.com, June 27, 2006.
22. Carl Hulse and David Johnston, "To Ease Standoff, Bush Seals Seized Files," New York Times Online, www.nytimes.com, May 26, 2006; Adam Liptak, "Congress and Justice Dept. May Both Be Overreaching," New York Times Online, www.nytimes.com, June 2, 2006.
23. Linda Greenhouse, "Treaty Doesn't Give Foreign Defendants Special Status in U.S. Courts, Justices Rule," New York Times Online, www.nytimes.com, June 29,2006.
24. John J. Gibbons and Nicholas de B. Katzenbach, *Confronting Confinement: A Report of the Commission on Safety and Abuse in America's Prisons* (New York: Vera Institute of Justice, 2006), p. 8.
25. Paige M. Harrison and Allen J. Beck, *Prisons and Jail Inmates at Midyear 2005* (Washington, DC: U.S. Department of Justice, 2006), p. 1.
26. Ibid.
27. Gibbons and de B. Katzenbach, *Confronting Confinement, p. 11.*
28. Nancy G. La Vigne, Amy L. Solomon, Karen A. Beckman, and Kelly Dedel, *Prisoner Reentry and Community Policing: Strategies for Enhancing Public Safety* (Washington, DC: U.S. Department of Justice, 2006), p. 3.
29. Gibbons and de B. Katzenbach, Confronting Confinement.
30. Mary Beth Pfeiffer, "Cruel and Unusual Punishment," New York Times Online, www.nytimes.com, May 7, 2006.
31. Gibbons and de B. Katzenbach, *Confronting Confinement,* p. 37.
32. La Vigne, Solomon, Beckman, and Dedel, *Prisoner Reentry and Community Policing,* pp. 10–12.
33. Ibid., p. 17.
34. Ibid., p. 9; Gibbons and de B. Katzenbach, *Confronting Confinement,* p. 11.
35. Dale G. Parent, *Correctional Boot Camps: Lessons From a Decade of Research* (Washington, DC: U.S. Department of Justice, 2003), p. 1.

Glossary

abolitionists People opposed to the use of capital punishment.

actus reus The actions of the person committing a crime as defined by law, one of the key elements of a crime.

adjudicated A court case is decided without determination of guilt or innocence, especially in juvenile court, when a judge places a juvenile in the custody of the state for treatment or confinement.

alibi A witness or evidence in court establishing that the defendant could not have committed the crime.

anomie Emile Durkheim's concept of normlessness and social isolation as symptoms of a dysfunctional society and causes of deviant behavior.

appellate courts Appellate courts have the authority to review the proceedings and verdicts of general trial courts for judicial errors.

arraignment Short hearing before a judge in which the charges against the defendant are announced and the defendant is asked if he or she is guilty or not guilty.

arrest Restricting the freedom of persons by taking them into police custody.

arson The malicious burning of a structure.

assault The crime of willfully inflicting injury on another.

atavistic stigmata Physical characteristics, representing earlier or prehuman stages of evolution, that were believed to distinguish criminals from others.

attempt An incomplete criminal act, the closest act to the completion of the crime.

bail Release of a defendant from custody on the promise by the accused—not a custodian—often secured with a monetary bond, that the defendant will return to court at the necessary times to address the charges.

bail bondsperson An agent of a private commercial business that has contracted with the court to act as a guarantor of a defendant's return to court.

bailiff A county deputy sheriff or U.S. deputy marshal responsible for providing security and maintaining order in a courtroom.

banishment Removal of the offender from the community.

bench trial Judicial process to determine the guilt or innocence of a defendant in which the determination is made by a judge, not a jury.

bifurcated trial Two-part trial structure in which the jury first determines guilt or innocence and then considers new evidence relating to the appropriate punishment.

biocriminology A new field in criminology encompassing modern biological approaches (such as neurochemistry and neuroendocrinology) to explaining criminal behavior.

Black Codes Laws passed by southern states after the Civil War to disenfranchise freed slaves.

booking Police activity that establishes the identification of an arrested person and formally charges that person with a crime.

brief A concise statement of the main points of a law case.

broken window theory Belief that ignoring public order violations and disruptive behavior leads to community neglect, which fosters further disorder and crime.

burglary A combination of tresspass and the intent to perform a crime.

capital punishment The sentence of death.

Carroll Doctrine Terms defining the admissibility of evidence obtained in a warrantless search of an automobile, established in Carroll v. United States (1925).

causation The legal requirement for a crime that the harm is the result of the union of *actus reus* and *mens rea.*

certiorari power If four members of the Supreme Court believe a case meets its criteria for review, a writ of certiorari is issued, ordering the lower court to forward the record of the case to the Supreme Court.

chain gang In the southern penal system, convicts chained together during outside labor.

charge to the jury Written instructions about the application of the law to a case that the judge gives to the jury to help them achieve a verdict.

chief law enforcement officer Title applied to the sheriff of the county because his or her jurisdiction is greater than that of the local police agencies within the county.

chief of police Title of the chief administrative officer of a municipal police agency. The chief obtains his or her position by appointment of the mayor, city council, or other designated city agency, such as the police commission.

circuit court Any court that holds sessions in various locations within its jurisdiction.

circumstantial evidence Evidence that implies that the defendant is connected to the crime but does not prove the defendant is connected to the crime.

civil law (private law) Civil law (private law) covers the law concerned with the definition, regulation, and enforcement of rights in cases in which both the person who has the right and the person who has the obligation are private individuals.

classical school Theories of crime causation based on Cesare Beccaria's assumption that criminal behavior is a matter of free-will choice.

clear and present danger Condition relating to public safety that may justify police use of deadly force against a fleeing suspect.

clearance rate Percentage of reported crimes determined to be solved.

Clerk of Court Government employee who works directly with the trial judge and is responsible for court paperwork and records before and during a trial.

common law Unwritten, simply stated laws from the English common laws, based on traditions and common understandings in a time when most people were illiterate.

community policing Decentralized policing programs that focus on crime prevention, quality of life in the community, public order, and alternatives to arrest.

commutation of sentence Reduction in the severity or length of an inmate's sentence, issued by a state governor or the president of the United States.

competent to stand trial The concept that defendants comprehend the charges against them and are able to assist their attorney in their defense.

concurrence The legal requirement for a crime that there is a union of *actus reus* and *mens rea.*

conditional release A bail alternative in which the defendant is released from custody if he or she agrees to a number of court-ordered terms and restrictions.

conflict theories Theories of crime causation based on Marxian theory or the assumption that the sources of criminal behavior are class conflict and social inequality.

congregate work system The practice of moving inmates from sleeping cells to other areas of the prison for work and meals.

consent A defense in criminal law in which the defendant claims the action that caused the injury or death occurred during normal, acceptable standards of conduct.

consolidated model Organization of decision making about parole as a function of a state department of corrections.

conspiracy Criminal act requiring no *actus rea* other than communication.

constructive intent When an actor did not intend to harm anyone but should have known that his or her behavior created a high risk of injury.

containment theory Walter Reckless's theory that people are deterred from deviant behavior because of the influence on individuals of both internal and external social control factors.

contempt of court A charge against any violator of the judge's courtroom rules, authorizing the judge to impose a fine or term of imprisonment.

contraband Smuggled goods, such as drugs, cigarettes, money, or pornography.

convict lease system In southern penal systems, leasing prisoners to work for private contractors.

corporal punishment The administration of bodily pain, based on the premise that a painful experience suffered as the result of criminal activity will deter future crime.

correctional case managers Social work caseworkers who specialize in helping offenders adjust to life in prison, release from prison, and successful reentry into the community.

correctional officer Uniformed jail or prison employee whose primary job is the security and movement of inmates.

court docket The calendar on which court cases are scheduled for trial.

court of last resort A state court that reviews lower court decisions and whose decisions can be appealed to the U.S. Supreme Court.

court recorder (court reporter) Stenographer who transcribes every word spoken by the judge, attorneys, and witnesses during a trial.

courtroom work group Adversarial and neutral parties, usually the prosecutor, defense attorney, judge, and other court personnel, who get together and cooperate to settle cases with the least effort and conflict.

courts of limited jurisdiction State courts of original jurisdiction that are not courts of record (e.g., traffic courts, municipal courts, or county courts).

courts of record Courts in which trial proceedings are transcribed.

Crime Clock Data presentation strategy used by the FBI to report crime rates in terms of how often a crime occurs.

crime control model Model of the criminal justice system in which emphasis is placed on fighting crime and protecting potential victims.

crime prevention through environmental design (CPTED) Theory that crime can be prevented through environmental design, particularly urban housing design.

crimes of omission Crimes resulting from the failure to act or the lack of action rather than the commission of illegal acts.

criminal personality Theories from psychology that identify personality traits and habits of mind believed to be associated with criminality.

cruel and unusual punishment Punishment that violates the principle of proportionality and is considered too harsh for the crime committed; prohibited by the Eighth Amendment.

cultural deviance theories Theories of crime causation based on the assumption that criminal behavior is learned through participation in deviant subcultures or countercultures within a society.

cybercrime Crimes against computers, or the use of computers to commit crimes.

day reporting centers An intermediate sanction to provide a gradual adjustment to reentry under closely supervised conditions.

deadly force Police power to incapacitate or kill in the line of duty.

defenses Justifications or excuses defined by law by which a defendant may be released from prosecution or punishment for a crime.

deinstitutionalization Moving mentally ill people from long-term hospitalization to community-based care.

denial of service An attack in which the hacker attempts to crash or clog the targeted Internet site by overloading the website with too many requests for information for the website to respond.

Department of Homeland Security (DHS) Newly created federal agency responsible for a wide range of security measures to protect against terrorist attacks.

deputy chief Title of the second in command of a municipal police agency. This is a position appointed by the chief of police.

deputy sheriffs Law enforcement officers working for the Office of the Sheriff. All law enforcement officers in the sheriff's office, regardless of rank, are deputy sheriffs.

determinate sentencing A sentencing model in which the offender is sentenced to a fixed term of incarceration.

deterrence Philosophy and practices that emphasize making criminal behavior less appealing.

differential association theory Edwin Sutherland's theory that criminal behavior is learned through association with a peer group that engages in criminal behavior.

direct evidence Evidence that connects the defendant with the crime.

diversion Sentencing option in which the defendant is diverted from the correctional system through alternatives such as community service, drug courts, boot camps, and treatment programs.

DNA databank Collections of DNA samples much like collections of fingerprints. However, unlike fingerprint collections, DNA samples provide much more information about the subject than just his or her identity.

domestic terrorism Acts of terrorism committed in the United States by individuals or groups that do not have ties with or sponsorship from foreign states or organizations.

double jeopardy The defendant can be charged only once and punished only once for a crime. If tried and found innocent, the defendant cannot be retried if new evidence of his or her guilt is discovered.

drug courts Specialized courts that operate on different principles of law. Often, offenders are given a chance to engage in rehabilitation, avoid prison time, and sometimes even avoid a criminal record. Offenders must meet specific conditions to qualify for diversion to a drug court.

dual court system The political division of jurisdiction into two systems of courts, federal and state. Under this system, federal courts are separate from but have limited jurisdiction over state courts.

due process Rules and procedures for protecting individuals accused of crimes from arbitrary and excessive abuse of power by the government.

due process model Model of the criminal justice system in which emphasis is placed on protecting the rights of the accused.

duress A legal defense in which the accused acted involuntarily under threat of immediate and serious harm by another person.

ecoterrorism Domestic terrorism that uses violence to influence public policy with regard to conduct considered harmful to the environment or that violates animal rights.

electronic monitoring An approach in home confinement programs that assures compliance through electronic means.

elements of a crime The illegal actions (*actus reus*) and criminal intentions (*mens rea*) of the actor along with the circumstances that link the two, especially causation.

entrapment Illegal arrest based on criminal behavior for which the police provided both the motivation and the means, tested in *Jacobson* v. *United States* (1992). Also a legal defense in criminal court.

exclusionary rule Prohibits the use of evidence or testimony obtained in violation of the Fourth and Fifth Amendments of the U.S. Constitution, established in *Weeks* v. *United States* (1914) and extended to the states in *Mapp* v. *Ohio* (1961).

executive pardon An act by a governor or the president that forgives the prisoner and rescinds the sentence.

ex post facto law A law related to the principle that persons cannot be punished for actions committed before the law prohibiting the behavior was passed.

faith-based programs Programs provided by religious-based and church-affiliated groups. Their role in rehabilitation is controversial because they receive federal money and may combine religious instruction with rehabilitation.

federal law enforcement Law enforcement agency under the control of the executive branch of the federal government.

felicitic calculus In classical and neoclassical theory, such as Jeremy Bentham's, the pain-pleasure principle by which people decide whether or not to commit a crime.

felony Serious criminal conduct punishable by incarceration for more than one year.

feminist criminology Field based on the assumption that gender inequality lies at the heart of crimes in which women are the victims or the perpetrators.

field-training program Probationary period during which police academy graduates train in the community under the direct supervision of experienced officers.

first appearance Judicial hearing before a magistrate, following booking. The magistrate judge reviews the charges, advises defendants of their rights, and sets bail.

first responders Law enforcement, firefighters, and medical personnel who are the first to respond to a crisis and incident.

fleeing felon doctrine Police practice of using deadly force against a fleeing suspect, made illegal in *Tennessee* v. *Garner* (1985), except when there is clear and present danger to the public.

Fruit of the Poisoned Tree Doctrine Extends the exclusionary rule to secondary evidence obtained indirectly in an unconstitutional search, established in *Silverthorne Lumber Co.* v. *United States* (1918) and in *Wolf* v. *Colorado* (1949).

gag order A judge's order to participants and observers at a trial that the evidence or proceedings of the court may not be published, aired, or discussed publicly.

general deterrence Deterrence based on the logic that people who witness the pain suffered by those who commit crimes will desire to avoid that pain and will refrain from criminal activity.

general trial courts State courts of original jurisdiction; often called circuit courts, superior courts, district courts, courts of common pleas, and courts of first instance.

good faith exception Admissibility of evidence obtained in an illegal search when the police are found to have acted in good faith on the belief that their search was legal, established in *United States* v. *Leon* (1984) and *Massachusetts* v. *Sheppard* (1984) in contradiction to an earlier ruling in *Illinois* v. *Gates* (1982).

good-time credit A strategy of crediting inmates with extra days served toward early release, in an effort to encourage the prisoner to obey rules and participate in programs.

grand jury Panel of citizens similar to a trial jury that decides whether there is probable cause to indict a defendant on the charges alleged.

guardianship Social controls of social groups and situations that prevent or decrease opportunities for crime.

guilty but mentally ill An alternative verdict in capital cases based on the standard that the defendant was mentally ill but also was sufficiently aware (had sufficient *mens rea*) to be held "morally blameworthy" for the crime.

Gun Control Act Legislation that banned the mail-order sale of firearms and placed other restrictions on firearms sale.

habitual offender laws Tough sentencing laws, such as "three strikes" laws, to punish repeat offenders more harshly.

halfway houses Transition programs that allow inmates to move from prison to the community in steps.

hate crimes Crimes that are considered motivated by hate based on race, religion, ethnicity, sexual preference, or gender. Additional punishmnent is attached for hate crimes. Concern over the incidences of hate crimes has led to legislation requiring that police departments report the number of hate crimes.

hearsay evidence Information about a crime obtained second-hand from another rather than directly observed.

hierarchy rule Practice in data collection for the FBI's Uniform Crime Reports of counting only the most serious crime in incidents involving multiple crimes or with multiple victims of the same crime.

home confinement A court-imposed sentence requiring offenders to remain confined in their own residences.

Homeland Security Advisory System (HSAS) Daily color-coded threat advisory to government agencies, police, and the public that recommends appropriate actions in response to the forecasted risk of terrorist attack.

homicide Murder and manslaughter.

identity theft Using a name, unique identifying number, or personal information to commit another crime such as fraud or concealment of an offender's true identity.

illegal immigration Entering or remaining in the United States without proper approval by the federal government. Many cities claim that illegal immigration causes a significant public safety and economic problem for their cities and are critical of the federal government's response to illegal immigration.

immunity A legal defense that the accused is exempt from prosecution because of diplomatic immunity, legislative immunity, witness immunity, or professional privilege.

incapacitation Deterrence based on the premise that the only way to prevent criminals from reoffending is to remove them from society.

incarceration The bodily confinement of a person in a jail or prison.

inchoate offenses Incomplete crimes such as solicitation, conspiracy, and attempt.

incomplete crimes Crimes that go beyond thought, but the *actus reus* and mens rea do not coincide because the plans were not carried out for any reason.

independent model Decision making about parole is under the authority of an autonomous parole board.

indeterminate sentence The defendant is sentenced to a prison term with a minimum and a maximum number of years to serve.

indeterminate sentencing A model of sentencing in which judges have nearly complete discretion in sentencing an offender.

Index Crimes The eight crimes in Part I of the Uniform Crime Reports: murder, forcible rape, robbery, aggravated assault, burglary, larceny, motor vehicle theft, and arson.

indictment The formal verdict of the grand jury that there is sufficient evidence to bring a person to trial.

indigent defense (1) Right to have an attorney provided free of charge by the state if a defendant cannot afford one, established in *Gideon* v. *Wainwright* (1963) and extended in *Argersinger* v. *Hamlin* (1972), In re Gault (1967), and *Escobedo* v. *Illinois* (1964). (2) Defense counsel for a defendant who cannot afford a private attorney.

insanity A legal claim by a defendant that he or she did not understand the difference between right and wrong or was suffering from a disease or mental defect that made the defendant unable to appreciate the criminality of his or her action.

inside cell block Prison construction in which individual cells are stacked back to back in tiers in the center of a secure building.

intake The process whereby a juvenile enters the juvenile justice system.

intensive probation supervision (IPS) Probation supervised by probation and parole officers with smaller case loads, placing a greater emphasis on compliance with the conditions of supervision.

intent Criminal intentions or the state of "guilty mind" in *mens rea,* including general, specific, transferred, and constructive intent.

intermediate sanctions A term for punishments that restrict offenders' freedom without imprisoning them; community-based prevention and treatment programs to promote the successful transition of the offender from prison to the community.

international terrorism Terrorism perpetrated by state-sponsored groups, international terrorist organizations, and loosely affiliated international extremists' groups.

Irish system Early form of parole invented by Sir Walter Crofton on the basis of the mark system, in which prisoners were released conditionally on good behavior and were supervised in the community.

jails Short term, multipurpose holding facilities that serve as the gateway for the criminal justice system.

joint local–federal counterterrorism task force Working group of FBI and state and/or local law enforcement officers that focus on preventing terrorism by their joint cooperation and intelligence sharing.

jurisdiction Geographical area of responsibility and legitimate duties of an agency, court, or law enforcement officer.

jurisprudence The science or philosophy of law.

jury trial Judicial process to determine the guilt or innocence of a defendant in which the determination is made by a jury, not a judge.

labeling theory Frank Tannenbaum and Howard Becker's theory that people are strongly influenced by society's expectations of them, such that juveniles labeled as criminals are more likely to become criminals.

landmark cases U.S. Supreme Court cases that mark significant changes in interpretations of constitutionality.

larceny Wrongfully taking and carrying away of another's property with the intent to permanently deprive the property's owner of its possession.

lead federal agency The agency that is designated as the agency that is primarily in charge of an incident. This agency has the power to direct the actions of other agencies and to call for the use of their resources even though the lead agency may not have direct authority over these other agencies.

legal standard of evidence Evidence and the testimony of witnesses must be competent, material, and relevant.

local law enforcement Municipal or county law enforcement; also includes certain special police agencies with limited jurisdiction, such as campus police.

mala in se Acts that are crimes because they are inherently evil or harmful to society.

mala prohibita Acts that are prohibited because they are defined as crimes by law.

mandatory release After prisoners serve the entire length of their maximum sentence, it is required by law that they be released.

mandatory sentencing The strict application of full sentences in the determinate sentencing model.

manslaughter The killing of another without malice, without the specific intent to kill.

mark system Early form of parole invented by Alexander Maconochie in which prisoners demonstrated their rehabilitation by earning points for good behavior.

material witness law Law that allows for the detention of a person who has not committed a crime but is alleged to have information about a crime that has been committed.

mens rea The state of mind and intent of the person committing the *actus reus,* one of the key elements of a crime.

methamphetamine Better known by its street name, *ice, crack,* and *crank,* methamphetamine is a synthetic drug that is inexpensive to make and can be made almost anywhere and by anyone. It is highly addictive and harmful. Meth abuse is spreading rapidly throughout the United States.

metro police Local police agency that spans several geographical jurisdictions, such as cities or city and county.

military police Military personnel with special training and jurisdiction to provide law enforcement services on military installations.

minimal brain dysfunction (MBD) A biological explanation of crime, suggesting that small disruptions of normal brain functioning are responsible for violent behavior.

***Miranda* rights** Five rights protecting, for example, the right to avoid self-incrimination and the right to an attorney, of which citizens are informed during police arrest and interrogation, established in *Miranda* v. *Arizona* (1966).

misdemeanor Less serious criminal conduct punishable by incarceration for less than a year.

mistake or ignorance of fact or law An affirmative legal defense claiming that the defendant made a mistake or acted out of ignorance and therefore did not meet the requirement for *mens rea.*

Model Penal Code Guidelines for U.S. criminal codes published in 1962 by the American Law Institute that define and classify crimes into categories according to victim, including crimes against the state, persons, habitations, property, public order, and public morals.

money laundering Concealment of the source of money.

motion Formal request by the prosecution or defense for the court to rule on any relevant matter in a case, such as the competency of the defendant to stand trial, the location of the trial, the jurisdiction of the court, or objections to evidence gathered by police.

motion for a bill of particulars Allows the defense to receive more details as to exactly what items the prosecution considers illegal if a defendant is charged with possession of burglary tools, illegal weapons, drug paraphernalia, or illegal gambling paraphernalia.

motion for change of venue A pretrial request, either by the prosecutor or the defense, to move the trial to another courtroom.

motion for continuance A pretrial request to delay the start of the trial.

motion for discovery A pretrial motion filed by the defense counsel, requesting that the prosecutor turn over all relevant evidence, including the list of witnesses, that the prosecution may use at the trial.

motion for dismissal A pretrial defense motion that the charges against the defendant be dismissed.

motion for severance of charges or defendants A pretrial request that the defendant be tried for each charge separately or that multiple defendants charged with the same crime be tried separately.

motion for suppression A pretrial motion made by the defense to exclude certain evidence from being introduced in the trial.

murder All intentional killings and deaths that occur in the course of aggrevated felonies.

narco-terrorism The redefinement of drug trafficking as terrorism, used to emphasize its significance.

National Firearms Act Early national legislation that restricted ownership of certain weapons, such as machine guns, by requiring owners to register and pay a tax.

necessity An affirmative legal defense claiming the defendant committed the act as a result of forces of nature and therefore did not meet the requirement for *mens rea.*

neoclassical school A later version of classical theory in which children under the age of seven and offenders suffering mental disease should be exempt from criminal liability because their conditions interfere with the exercise of free will.

neutralization theory Gresham Sykes and David Matza's theory that criminals learn techniques that allow them to rationalize their behavior, deny responsibility for harm, and avoid being guilt ridden.

officer of the court Law enforcement officer that is used by the court to serve papers, provide courtroom security, and transport defendants.

order maintenance (1) A system of maintaining the day-to-day life of ordinary citizens, a primary goal of the criminal justice system. (2) Non-crime-fighting services performed by the police, such as mediation, providing for the welfare of vulnerable persons, and crowd control.

original jurisdiction (1) The first court to hear and render a verdict regarding the charges against the defendant. (2) When the juvenile court is the only court that has authority over juveniles. Juveniles cannot be tried, for any offense, by the criminal court unless the juvenile court grants its permission for the accused juvenile to be waived to criminal court.

page jacking A program that captures a user's computer and directs the computer to a website that the user did not want to go to and cannot exit from except by turning off the computer.

parole Early release from prison before the maximum sentence is served, based on evidence of rehabilitation and the good behavior of the inmate.

parole board Individuals appointed to a body that meets in prisons to make decisions about granting parole release to inmates.

parole d'honneur Origin of parole based on the concept of releasing prisoners "on their honor" after serving a portion of their sentence but before the maximum term.

parole hearings Meetings with inmates, attorneys, and others in which the parole board decides whether to grant, deny, or revoke parole.

pat-down search Right to search a person for a concealed weapon on the basis of reasonable suspicion, established in *Terry* v. *Ohio* (1968).

penitentiary Correctional institution based on the concept that inmates could change their criminality through reflection and penitence.

per curiam opinion A case that is disposed of by the U.S. Supreme Court that is not accompanied by a full opinion.

peremptory challenge The subjective evaluation of the attorney that is used to exclude jurors.

phishing Sending fraud e-mails in an attempt to commit identity theft.

picket fence model Model of the criminal justice system, with the local, state, and federal criminal justice systems depicted as three horizontal levels connected vertically by the roles, functions, and activities of the agencies that comprise them.

piggybacking A form of cybertrespassing.

plaintiff The party that brings suit in court.

plain-view search Right to gather evidence in plain sight without a warrant, established in *Harris* v. *United States* (1968) and redefined in *United States* v. *Irizarry* (1982), *Arizona* v. *Hicks* (1987), and *Horton* v. *California* (1990).

plea Defendant's statement that he or she is guilty, not guilty, or offers "no contest."

plea bargaining Negotiations between the prosecution and the defense for a plea of guilty in exchange for reduced charges or a lighter sentence.

Plessy* v. *Ferguson (1896) U.S. Supreme Court landmark case that established the "separate but equal" doctrine that allowed racial segregation.

police academy Facility or programs for the education and training of police recruits.

police lineups Opportunities for victims to identify a criminal from among a number of suspects.

positive school School of thought that emphasizes the importance of the scientific method to determine the factors that contribute to criminal behavior.

possession Knowingly having, holding, carrying, or knowing the location of an illegal or prohibited item; can constitute the *mens rea* of a crime.

preliminary hearing Hearing before a magistrate judge in which the prosecution presents evidence to convince the judge that there is probable cause to bring the defendant to trial.

presentence investigation report Report on the background of the convicted defendant, the circumstances of the crime, and any other information relevant for determining the most appropriate sentence.

presumption of innocence Most important principle of the due process model, requiring that all accused persons are treated as innocent until proven guilty in a court of law.

presumptive sentencing A structured sentencing model that attempts to balance sentencing guidelines with mandatory sentencing and at the same time provide discretion to the judge.

principle of legality The belief that specific laws defining crimes and penalties for crimes must exist and be made public before the government can punish citizens for violating them.

principle of proportionality The belief that less serious harms should carry lesser punishments than more serious harms.

prisoner classification The reception and diagnosis of an inmate to decide the appropriate security level in which to place the prisoner and services of placement.

prison farm system In southern penal systems, using inmate labor to maintain large profit-making prison farms or plantations.

prisonization Socialization into a distinct prison subculture with its own values, mores, norms, and sanctions.

privatization Trend toward the use of for-profit jails and prisons run by private companies.

probable cause (1) Determination from evidence and arguments that there are valid reasons for believing that the accused has committed a crime. (2) Strong likelihood of a direct link between a suspect and a crime.

probation (1) Disposition in which a convicted defendant is offered an opportunity to avoid serving any time in prison by agreeing to fulfill conditions set forth by the court. (2) Conditional release of a convicted offender prior to his or her serving any prison time.

probation and parole officers State and federal professional employees who report to the courts and supervise defendants released on probation and offenders released from prison on parole.

problem-oriented policing Proactive type of community policing that focuses on solving the underlying problems of delinquency and crime.

procedural due process The requirement that the government must follow established procedures and treat defendants equally.

procedural law Body of laws for how things should be done at each stage of the criminal justice process.

psychoanalytic theory Sigmund Freud's theory that behavior is not a free-will choice but is controlled by subconscious desires.

public safety exception Right to search without probable cause for the public good.

racial profiling Allegations that police search and seizures, traffic stops, field interrogations, and arrests are made on nonbehavioral factors related to race and/or ethnicity rather than suspicious behavior or probable cause.

Racketeer Influenced and Corrupt Organizations Act (RICO) Provides federal prosecutors with the ability to charge a person with racketeering activity, which carries a greater penalty, rather than just the specific crimes committed.

rape (sexual assault) Nonconsensual sexual relations.

reaction formation Albert Cohen's term for his cultural deviance theory in which lower-class youths reject middle-class values that they cannot attain and instead join countercultures that express the opposite values.

reentry The process of preparing an offender for release from incarceration back into society.

rehabilitation Deterrence based on the premise that criminals can be "cured" of their problems and criminality and returned to society.

Reign of Terror Phase of the nineteenth-century French Revolution in which the revolutionary ruling party used arrests and executions to retain power and suppress opposition.

remanded The reversal of a decision by a higher court and the return of the case to the court of original jurisdiction with instructions to correct the judicial error.

restorative justice Model of deterrence that uses restitution programs, community work programs, victim-offender mediation, and other strategies to not only rehabilitate the offender but also address the damage done to the community and the victim.

retribution Deterrence based on the premise that criminals should be punished because they deserve it.

robbery The taking and carrying away of property from a person by force or threat of immediate use of force.

RSAT Residential Substance Abuse Treatment, a federal assistance program to help states provide for treatment instead of prison for substance abusers.

rule of law Principle that standards of behavior and privilege are established by laws and not by monarchs or religious leaders.

rules of evidence Requirements for introducing evidence and testimony in court.

search incident to lawful arrest Right to search an arrestee without a warrant, established in *Chimel* v. *California* (1969).

search warrant Legal permission to conduct a search, signed by a judge.

security risk groups Groups that raise special threats, such as prison gangs.

self-defense An affirmative legal defense in which a defendant claims he or she committed the crime in defense of self and lacked criminal intent.

self-incrimination Involuntary confession or forced testimony of the accused, prohibited by the Fifth Amendment, as in the inadmissibility of evidence obtained by force in *Brown* v. *Mississippi* (1936) and extended in *Ashcraft* v. *Tennessee* (1944) and *Leyra* v. *Denno* (1954).

sentence Disposition of a case by determining the punishment for a defendant convicted of a crime.

sentencing The punishment for a crime as determined by a judge.

sentencing guidelines A sentencing model in which crimes are classified according to their seriousness, and a range of time to be served is mandated for crimes within each category.

sentencing hearing A gathering before a judge that hears appeals, in which the prosecution and the defense argue the accuracy of the presentence report and the appropriateness of the sentence.

sex offender registries Open-access online databases identifying known sex offenders on parole, maintained to protect communities and potential victims.

shock incarceration Programs (boot camps) that adapt military-style physical fitness and discipline training to the correctional environment.

shock probation Sentence for a first-time, nonviolent offender who was not expecting a sentence, intended to impress on the offender the possible consequences of his or her behavior by exposure to a brief period of imprisonment before probation.

silent system Correctional practice of prohibiting inmates from talking to other inmates.

slave patrols Civilian groups in the southern states whose primary role was to protect against rioting and revolts by slaves.

smurfing Buying or stealing of large quantities of cold medicines from stores.

social bond theory Travis Hirschi's theory that strong social and emotional ties to social values and norms lessen the likelihood of deviant behavior.

social control theory Theories of crime causation based on the assumptions that people's belief in and identification with the values of their society and culture influence their behavior.

social determinism The assumption that criminal behavior is caused by social factors and social forces rather than by moral, environmental, psychological, or biological causes.

social disorganization theory Theories of crime causation based on the assumption that social conditions such as poverty, unemployment, poor schools, and substandard housing are significant factors contributing to delinquency and crime.

solicitation The incomplete crime of urging, requesting, or commanding another person to commit a crime.

solitary confinement Practice of confining an inmate such that there is no contact with other people.

somatotype school Theories of crime causation based on the assumption that there is a link between the mind and the body and that this link is expressed in body types, and based on Cesare Lombroso's theory that a criminal can be identified by physical appearance.

special police Police with limited jurisdiction. Special police have very narrowly defined duties and sometimes extremely limited geographical jurisdiction.

specific deterrence Deterrence based on the premise that an individual is best deterred from committing future crimes by the specific nature of the punishment.

split sentencing After a brief period of imprisonment, the judge brings the offender back to court and offers the option of probation.

standard conditions of release Federal and state guidelines with rules with which parolees must comply to meet their conditions of release.

stare decisis The American system of developing and applying case law on the basis of precedents established in previous cases.

state law enforcement Law enforcement agencies under the command of the executive branch of the state government, such as the highway patrol and state police.

state prisons Correctional facilities for prisoners convicted of state crimes.

strain theory Robert Merton's theory that people are naturally law abiding but resort to crime when frustrated in finding legitimate means to economic success.

strict liability crimes Actions that do not require criminal intent to be defined as crimes, such as parking violations.

structured sentencing A sentencing model—including determinate sentencing, sentencing guidelines, and presumptive sentencing—that defines punishments rather than allowing indeterminate sentencing.

substantive due process Limits on the power of governments to create crimes unless there is compelling, substantial public interest in regulating or prohibiting the conduct.

suspended sentence Another term for probation, based on the fact that convicted offenders must serve their full sentence if they violate the terms of release.

TASC Treatment Accountability for Safer Communities, a federal assistance program to help states break the addiction-crime cycle.

team policing Decentralizing development during the 1960s and 1970s in which small units of police personnel took responsibility for a particular geographical area.

technical violation Grounds for imprisonment of a probationer or parolee based on his or her violation of a condition of release.

Tenth Amendment Amendment of the United States Constitution that proscribes that all powers not explicitly granted to the federal government are reserved as state powers.

terrorism Premeditated, politically motivated violence perpetrated against noncombatant targets by subnational groups or clandestine agents, usually intended to influence an audience.

theories Statements of relationship or of cause and effect that attempt to explain or predict behavior or events; theories are macro, middle range, or micro depending on the number of cases and level of generalization.

three strikes law The application of mandatory sentencing to give repeat offenders longer prison terms.

ticket of leave In the mark system, unconditional release from prison purchased with marks earned for good behavior.

torts Private wrongs that cause physical harm to another.

total institutions Institutions that meet all of the inmate's basic needs, discourage individuality, punish dissent, and segregate those who do not follow the rules.

trafficking Movement of illegal drugs across borders.

transportation Eighteenth century practice by Great Britain of sending offenders to the American colonies and later Australia.

tribal police Police agency that provides police services on Indian reservations. Tribal police operate independently of local, state, and federal police due to a special relationship between the United States and Native Americans living on reservations.

truth in sentencing In the application of presumptive sentencing in states that cannot eliminate parole, the legal requirement that courts disclose the actual prison time the offender is likely to serve.

U.S. courts of appeals The panel of federal judges that hears appeals from the U.S. district courts and determines if a judicial error was made that could have substantially affected the court's decision.

U.S. district courts Trial courts of the federal system.

U.S. Government Interagency Domestic Terrorism Concept of Operations Plan (CONPLAN) Federal guidelines that designate which federal agency is the lead agency, that is responsible for command and control, in the event of a terrorist incident involving multiple federal agencies.

U.S. magistrate courts Federal lower courts with powers limited to trying lesser misdemeanors, setting bail, and assisting district courts in various legal matters.

U.S. Supreme Court The highest court in the American judiciary system, whose rulings on the constitutionality of a law, due process rights, and rules of evidence are binding on all federal and state courts.

USA Patriot Act Legislation upon which the government's War on Terrorism is being waged and which provides federal law enforcement agencies with many new powers.

vigilantism The system by which citizens assume the role and responsibility of official law enforcement agencies and act independently, often without observation of due process and rights, to take justice into their own hands.

violation An illegal action that is less serious than a misdemeanor and may carry the punishment of only a fine or suspension of privilege.

void for overbreadth Laws that are illegal because they are stated so broadly as to prohibit legal activities as well as illegal activities.

void for vagueness Laws that are illegal because they do not provide clear and reasonable definitions of the specific behaviors that are prohibited.

voir dire The process through a jury is selected from the members of the jury pool who have been determined eligible for service.

War on Terrorism Declaration by President Bush supported by congressional legislation that defines international terrorists as a threat to national security and provides for greater executive and federal law enforcement powers in ensuring national security.

wiretapping A form of search and seizure in which citizens' rights to privacy on the telephone are protected by the Fourth Amendment, first established in *Olmstead* v. *United States* (1928) and extended to e-mail in Katz v. United States (1967).

work release Program allowing facilities to release inmates for paid work in the community.

writ of certiorari The power of the U.S. Supreme Court to choose what cases it will hear.

XYY chromosome theory Biological theory of crime causation that an extra Y chromosome may lead to criminal behavior in males.

zero tolerance Strict enforcement of the laws, even for minor violations.

zone theory Environmental theory of crime causation based on the belief that structural elements of society such as poverty, illiteracy, lack of schooling, unemployment, and illegitimacy are powerful forces that influenced human interaction.

Name Index

Subject Index

Photo Credits:
Continued from the copyright page.

Page 3, 4, AP/Wide World Photos; 6, Library of Congress.; 10, AP/Wide World Photos; 16, © 2001 Dennis Brack/Stockphoto.com; 18, AP/Wide World Photos; 29, © David Young-Wolff/PhotoEdit; 36, © A. Ramey/ PhotoEdit; 43, © Michael Nagle/Redux Pictures; 45, North Wind Picture Archives; 49, The Granger Collection, New York; 50, University College London Library; 53 left, Library of Congress; 53 middle, Brown Brothers; 53 right, National Library of Medicine; 57, © Vince Bucci/Getty Images; 60, © Underwood & Underwood/CORBIS; 62, © A Ramey/PhotoEdit; 77, © Jeff Greenberg/PhotoEdit; 78, © 2000 Joseph Rodrigues/ Stockphoto.com; 80, AP/Wide World Photos; 81 both, Photos courtesy of the Multnomah County Sheriff's Office; 96, © HBO/Courtesy Everett Collection; 105, © Bob Daemmrich/The Image Works; 109, © Jim L. Shaffer; 114, © B. W. Hoffmann/Unicorn Stock Photos; 115, The Granger Collection, New York; 127, AP/Wide World Photos; 130, © Richard T. Nowitz/CORBIS; 132, © Douglas McFadd/Getty Images; 139, © Marko Georgiev/Getty Images; 141, Hulton Archive/Getty Images; 143, Culver Pictures; 148, © SuperStock, Inc./SuperStock; 157 top both, © Bob Daemmrich/The Image Works; 157 bottom left, © A. Ramey/ PhotoEdit; 158 bottom right, © Richard Lord/The Image Works; 163, © Darren McCollester/Newsmakers/Getty Images; 166, © Michael Newman /PhotoEdit; 170, AP/Wide World Photos; 173, © Bettmann/CORBIS; 175, © Jim L. Shaffer; 177, © Michael Heller/911 Pictures; 180 top, © Robert Voets/CBS Photo Archive via Getty Images; 180 bottom, © Syracuse Newspapers/Dick Blume/The Image Works; 191, © Jefferson Jackson Steele; 195, AP/Wide World Photos; 205, © Mark Wilson/Getty Images; 210, © John Kuntz/Reuters/CORBIS; 219, 221 top, AP/Wide World Photos; 221 bottom, © Reuters/CORBIS; 223, © Thopson/AFP/Getty Images; 225, © Sandy Huffaker/Getty Images; 228, 230, AP/Wide World Photos; 233, © Reuters/CORBIS; 236, © Jeff Greenberg/PhotoEdit; 237, © Bettmann/CORBIS; 239, © Peter Turnley/ CORBIS; 252, © Fred Greaves/ Reuters/CORBIS; 255, © Benjamin Lowy/CORBIS; 263, AP/Wide World Photos; 267, © Mario Tama/Getty Images; 273, AP/Wide World Photos; 275, The Granger Collection, New York; 278, 285, 291, AP/Wide World Photos; 294, © A&E/Courtesy Everett Collection; 298, AP/Wide World Photos; 305, © Jim Pickerell/Stock Boston; 310, AP/Wide World Photos; 321, © Robyn Beck/AFP/Getty Images; 325, © Reuters/CORBIS; 327, © Tony Savino/The Image Works; 328, AP/Wide World Photos; 338, © David Leeson/Dallas Morning News/The Image Works; 347, © Joel Stettenheim/ CORBIS; 349, © Todd Plitt/Getty Images; 354, © Chip East/Reuters/CORBIS; 356, 361, AP/Wide World Photos; 364, © Sean Gallup/Newsmakers/Getty Images; 369, AP/Wide World Photos; 375, © Greg Smith/CORBIS; 378, © Mikael Karlsson/Arresting Images; 379, AP/Wide World Photos; 383, © Mikael Karlsson/Arresting Images; 393, © Evans/ Three Lions/Getty Images; 396, The State Penitentiary for the Eastern District of Pennsylvania, 1855. Lithograph by P. S. Duval and Co., 8 3/4 x 10 7/16. The Library Company of Philadelphia. Engraved by Samuel Cowperthwaite. Courtesy of Eastern State Penitentiary; 399, AP/Wide World Photos; 404, © Michael S. Yamashita/CORBIS; 408, © Stephen Chernin/Getty Images; 409, 412, AP/Wide World Photos; 417, © Andrew Councill/AFP/Getty Images; 421, © A. Ramey/PhotoEdit; 422, © Sean Sayton/The Image Works; 429, AP/Wide World Photos; 431 top, © Monica Almedia/The New York Times; 431 bottom, AP/Wide World Photos; 432, © David McNew/Getty Images; 435, AP/Wide World Photos; 436, © Orion/courtesy Everett Collection; 437, © Skjold Photographs/The Image Works; 440, © Steve Lehman/CORBIS SABA.